THE COWLEY FATHERS

THE COWLEY FATHERS

*A History of the English Congregation of the
Society of St John the Evangelist*

Serenhedd James

CANTERBURY
PRESS
Norwich

First published in 2019 by the Canterbury Press Norwich
Editorial office
3rd Floor, Invicta House
108–114 Golden Lane
London EC1Y 0TG, UK
www.canterburypress.co.uk

Canterbury Press is an imprint of Hymns Ancient & Modern Ltd
(a registered charity)

Hymns Ancient & Modern® is a registered trademark of
Hymns Ancient & Modern Ltd
13A Hellesdon Park Road, Norwich,
Norfolk NR6 5DR, UK

British Library Cataloguing in Publication data

A catalogue record for this book is available
from the British Library

978 1 78622 183 4

Contents

For the Kuttels and the Walkers,
and in loving memory of Bing

Acknowledgements

The Trustees of the Fellowship of St John the Evangelist (UK) Trust Association, invited me to establish the Cowley Project as its Director in 2014 and to write this book as its opening phase. It has been impossible to produce a work of this size and scope without incurring a large debt of gratitude. My parents have been as supportive as ever; and I was fortunate at the outset to have been able to appoint as my research assistant the talented and unflappable Andrew Doll, who cheerfully and competently shouldered a number of tasks – not least the Bibliography – to allow me to undertake more wide-ranging work almost immediately.

The members of the American congregation of the SSJE gave me warm hospitality at their monastery on the banks of the Charles River at Cambridge, MA, and at their country retreat at Emery House, West Newbury. Br Geoffrey Tristram SSJE and Br James Koester SSJE, successive Superiors while the book was being written, were generous with much helpful advice and encouragement; and I was glad to be able to meet the late Br Eldridge Pendleton SSJE shortly before his death. In Boston, the Revd Allan B. Warren III introduced me to the Church of the Advent; and Lynn Smith, the Registrar-Historiographer of the Episcopal Diocese of Massachusetts, welcomed me to the diocesan archives and took me to visit St John's, Bowdoin Street, before its closure.

Long-suffering librarians and archivists have dealt with me patiently and gently: they include Anna James, Librarian of Pusey House; Catherine Hilliard and Marjory Szurko at St Stephen's House; Simon Sheppard and the team at the Church of England Record Centre; and the staff at Gladstone's Library and the Oxfordshire History Centre. Zofia Sulej and Gabriele Mohale at the Library of the University of the Witwatersrand ensured that my visit to the SSJE archives deposited there was as enjoyable as it was fruitful, and I was grateful for the hospitality of the Herzov family during my stay in Johannesburg.

At Cape Town Bing and Flower Walker gave me a home away from home; and thanks are also due to Archbishop Emeritus Desmond Tutu, the Very Revd Michael Weeder, the Revd Richard Cogill, Patricia Ellis, the Revd Richard Girdwood, Walter and Hilary Loening, John Ramsdale, William de Villiers, and the late Canon Rowan Smith. Writers on similar subjects have helped to crystallise my thoughts on a number of occasions: among them Dr Petà Dunstan, Br Steven Haws CR, the Venerable Luke Miller, Dr John Morgan-Guy, Dr Annie Skinner, and Simon Stubbings.

Others have prospered the work in a number of ways, particularly the Rt Revd Norman Banks; Jon and Kirsten Bickford; the Revd Denis Bovey;

Brendan Brett; the Venerable Michael and Mrs (Daphne) Brotherton; the Revd
Alan Carr; Jane Casey; Judith Curthoys; Christopher Eames; Sr Elizabeth Jane
CSMV; Lady Antonia Fraser; Dr Bernard Gowers; the Venerable David Gunn-
Johnston; Michael Hall; John and Audrey Hamilton; Canon Jeremy Haselock;
Catherine Hudson; Peter, Julienne, Melck and Rorke Kuttel; the Revd Dr Ayla
Lepine; Fr Jacob Lewis; Prebendary Paul Lockett; the Revd Graham Lunn; Allen
and Elizabeth Mills; Giles, Dani, Fergus, Rory and Lachie Neville; Dr Mark
Philpott; Harriet Rix; Graham Sanders; William Smith; the Revd John Stather;
Elizabeth Tucker; Sean, Petra, Blue and Keanan Walker; Canon Robin Ward;
Professor Michael Wheeler; the Revd Gavin Williams; and Fr Mark Woodruff.
Peter Saville, then of University College and now of the Middle Temple, read
the chapters on the First World War; and his swiftly tailored response shook
off some slips of the pen. The Revd Professor Mark Chapman generously
read and commented on the manuscript; and the Revd Christine Smith, Mary
Matthews, and the team at Canterbury Press put up with me uncomplainingly
throughout the publishing process. All errors and omissions are, of course,
my own.

That Bob Jeffery, Geoffrey Rowell, and Bing Walker did not live to see the
book completed is a matter of not a little personal sadness. Bob was one of
its doughtiest champions, having spent decades associated with the SSJE:
I benefitted greatly from his memory and insight; and he was still reading
the early part of the manuscript in the final days of his life. Bishop Geoffrey
also encouraged it from the beginning; and while he lived was unfailingly
supportive of my work as a nineteenth-century ecclesiastical historian. Bing
had never heard of the Cowley Fathers until I arrived on his doorstep on the
other side of the world; but he welcomed me nonetheless with the overwhelming generosity that was his trademark. The same generosity characterises his
family spread across the globe; and, with love and appreciation, it is to them
that I dedicate this book.

Acknowledgement of Sources

Every effort has been made to contact the copyright owners, and the publisher would be grateful for information on any omissions.

John Betjeman, "Anglo-Catholic Congresses", *High & Low* (London: John Murray, 1966), p. 37.

Forrest, S. J., *Parson's Play-pen* (London: A. R. Mowbray, 1968), f. 520.

Mascall, E. L., *Pi in the High* (Faith Press, 1959), f. xviii.

ABBREVIATIONS

ASSP	All Saints Sisters of the Poor
BCP	Book of Common Prayer
BHT	Brotherhood of the Holy Trinity
CC	Central Council
CE	*Cowley Evangelist*
CMS	Church Missionary Society
CNI	Church of North India
CR	Community of the Resurrection
CSI	Church of South India
CSJB	Community of St John the Baptist (Clewer)
CSMV	Community of St Mary the Virgin (Wantage)
CWAS	Cowley, Wantage, and All Saints Missionary Association
ECU	English Church Union
FSJ	Fellowship of St John
FSJTA	Fellowship of St John (UK) Trust Association
GenC	General Chapter
GreC	Greater Chapter
NS	*Society and Fellowship of St John News Sheet*
OMC	Oxford Mission to Calcutta
OSB	Order of St Benedict
PC	Provincial Chapter
PH	Pusey House
PM	*Cowley St John Parish Magazine*
RAMC	Royal Army Medical Corps
SDC	Society of the Divine Compassion
SLG	Sisters of the Love of God
SPCK	Society for Promoting Christian Knowledge
SPG	Society for the Propagation of the Gospel in Foreign Parts
SSC	Society of the Holy Cross
SSF	Society of St Francis
SSH	St Stephen's House
SSJE	Society of St John the Evangelist
SSM	Society of the Sacred Mission
UMCA	Universities' Mission to Central Africa
USPG	United Society for the Propagation of the Gospel

INTRODUCTION

Our community is intended in some sort to realize upon the earth
that vision of our great Patron as to the heavenly hope. O may it be!

—Richard Meux Benson SSJE
Instructions on the Religious Life, 1874

By the time Richard Meux Benson died in 1915 the Oxford Movement was in full swing, and on the cusp of its most flamboyant phase. Benson had become regarded as one of its grandees; but that is an image that needs to be treated with some caution, because it is all too easy to lose sight of the more reserved characters of that period behind the colourful priests who led the charge for the later development of Ritualism. Henry Mackay's observation of 1928 that Benson was "an embodiment of the devotion, reserve, austerity and self-effacement of the Tractarians" is an important one, even if it is not quite complete.[1]

Benson was a second-generation Tractarian and, both figuratively and literally, a Puseyite. Like Edward Bouverie Pusey, "the person to whom he owed most intellectually and spiritually",[2] Benson's gifts to the movement as a whole were intellectual, theological, and spiritual; and he did not advocate advanced Ritualism. The Catholic Literature Association's centenary-pamphlet series of 1933, *Heroes of the Catholic Revival*, gives an idea of the balance of the movement's development: there Benson rubs shoulders with obvious names like John Keble, John Henry Newman, and Pusey; but also with Arthur Tooth, Robert Dolling, and Alexander Mackonochie, who were all leading Ritualists.[3]

In 1955 Peter Anson published his definitive study into the development of Anglican religious orders, *The Call of the Cloister*.[4] Anson charted the work of several dozen religious communities – of men and women – that were at that point active in the Church of England. He also noted those that had become extinct, and those that had been received into the Roman Catholic Church. In 1955 the Anglican religious orders were flourishing, and Anson's work was complemented in 1958 by Donald Allchin's *The Silent Rebellion*. In

---

1 H. F. B. Mackay, "Richard Meux Benson", *Saints and Leaders*, London: Society of SS Peter and Paul (1928).

2 A. M. Allchin, *The Silent Rebellion: Anglican Religious Communities 1845–1900*, London: SCM Press (1958), 191.

3 Catholic Literature Association, *Heroes of the Catholic Revival*, London (1933).

4 Peter Anson, *The Call of the Cloister: Religious Communities and kindred bodies in the Anglican Communion*, London: SPCK (1955).

acknowledging *Call of the Cloister*, Allchin described his work as an attempt "to see the subject [the growth of Anglican religious orders] as a whole". He paid particular attention "to examining the ideals which animated the founders of the first communities, the social and cultural background out of which they developed, and the relations of these societies with the Church in general, and in particular with the Episcopate."[5] Allchin regretted the necessary omission of later communities; but naturally included the Society of St John the Evangelist, a community whose later members he knew well.

Away from the general history of his Society, most of what the world has remembered of Benson himself comes from Mildred Woodgate's *Father Benson: Founder of the Cowley Fathers* of 1953. Born in 1886, the year of Benson's resignation as Superior General, Woodgate's literary output was prodigious. Before the Second World War it included about ten children's novels and crime-thrillers (some were written pseudonymously, which makes an exact tally difficult); but, post-war, her output became almost entirely religious, with an emphasis on the founders of religious orders. Part-history and part-hagiography, her subjects included St Vincent de Paul (1958), St Francis de Sales (1961), and St Dominic (1967). In 1956 she also published a biography of George Congreve.

Woodgate's work is not dispassionate, and nor was it intended to be. She touched only very lightly on Benson's extensive theological work, and, as the then-Superior General of the Society, Francis Dalby, wrote, it was "intended to be no more than a plain, straightforward story, depicting [Benson] against the background of the times in which he lived".[6] It was written when there remained elderly members of the Society of St John the Evangelist who as young men had known Benson when he himself was nearing death, and as such was a retrospect of nearly a hundred years of community life furnished with the memories of some of those who had lived through it – although, as we shall see, some parts of the book were more tactful than accurate.

Despite the passing of more than sixty years – a period in which the English congregation of the Society of St John the Evangelist dramatically reduced its active work – Woodgate's book remains a useful and lively resource. It was fleshed out in 1980 by *Benson of Cowley*, edited by Martin Smith. Allchin contributed the opening chapter, placing Benson in context; and Michael Ramsey wrote on Benson's theology of the Atonement. Robert Jeffery, then Archdeacon of Salop, discussed Benson's teachings on the Church and mission; and Rosemary Kemsley SLG presented some aspects of his teaching on the religious life. Smith, who was then a member of the Society, supplied chapters on Benson's theological vision and spirituality; Mark Gibbard SSJE wrote on Benson and the Bible; and Christopher Bryant SSJE explored Benson's prayer-life. It is probably helpful to see Woodgate's *Father Benson* and Smith's *Benson of Cowley* as two sides of the same coin: the former presenting Benson the monk; the latter Benson the theologian. Together the books present different and separate material that combines to give us a good – if not quite complete –

5 Allchin, *Silent Rebellion*, 9.
6 M. V. Woodgate, *Father Benson: Founder of the Cowley Fathers*, London: Geoffrey Bles (1953), vii.

sense of what Benson was about, both in the house at Cowley and in the wider Church.

In 1995 Rowan Strong's book *Alexander Forbes of Brechin* touched briefly on the foundation of the SSJE, because of Forbes's links with the Oxford Movement, his friendship with Benson, and his frustrated desire to be part of the original community.[7] More recently, however, Strong's article in the 2015 *Journal of Ecclesiastical History*, "Origins of Anglo-Catholic Missions: Fr Richard Benson and the Initial Missions of the Society of St John the Evangelist, 1869–1882", has enlarged on the life of the Cowley Fathers in their early days, and shed light on the distinctive approach taken by the Society's early members in their approach to mission-work.[8]

To this corpus of work we may add a number of contemporary records: most notably the *Cowley St John Parish Magazine*, which ran from 1867 – with a brief period in the 1880s as the *Cowley St John Magazine*, after Benson resigned the living – until it was succeeded in 1891 by the *Cowley Evangelist*. That in turn ran until 1968 and served as a monthly digest of news, prayer requests, and pieces of interest to connect the members of the SSJE dispersed across the world. It was succeeded by a much slimmer *News Sheet*, which ceased in 1997, on which the historian is inevitably forced to rely to trace the significant developments in the Society's life in the 1970s and 1980s.

Apart from Benson himself, a number of early members of the Society had biographies and memoirs written about them: they include Charles Grafton, Oliver Prescott, Godfrey Callaway, George Congreve, Charles Field, and Arthur Hall. Published works on others associated with the community in its various expressions include subjects as diverse as Pusey, the second Viscount Halifax, Nehemiah Goreh, John Betjeman, C. S. Lewis, and Rose Macaulay. Some brethren wrote their own memoirs of the work of which they had been part: Grafton, for example, on his work in the States; and Simeon Wilberforce O'Neill, William Longridge, Edward Elwin, and William Slade on India. Callaway wrote on South Africa, and particularly the Society's work in the Transkei. Others – of whom in their different generations Congreve, Longridge, Bryant, Gibbard, Frederick Puller and Philip Waggett were among the most prodigious – published works on their own interests: mainly theological, but not always. A good deal of secondary material touches on the work of the SSJE to a greater or lesser degree: including general works on the religious history of North America, India, and South Africa; as do the histories of the religious orders with whom the SSJE collaborated at home and abroad.

The crowning resource in the study of the Society is the several thousand letters, papers, and images that that make up the bulk of the SSJE archive. This is now in the care of Lambeth Palace Library; and was catalogued by Simon Sheppard in 2013–14. The numerous footnotes citing "SSJE" refer to material in that collection, which includes correspondence of successive Superiors

---

7 Rowan Strong, *Alexander Forbes of Brechin: the First Tractarian Bishop*, Oxford: Clarendon Press (1995).

8 Rowan Strong, "Origins of Anglo-Catholic Missions: Fr Richard Benson and the Initial Missions of the Society of St John the Evangelist, 1869–1882", *Journal of Ecclesiastical History*, no.66, v. 1 (Jan 2015), 90–115.

General, and some of that of other members – although the latter were only allowed to discuss the general affairs of the Society with their chief, or of provinces with the relevant Superior.[9]

Only scant private correspondence has survived, and much of that by chance. At Cowley it became the custom for letters from brethren who were away from the house to be placed in the Library to be read;[10] and while letters might be addressed to a particular member of the community, all were written in the knowledge that they would be seen by many pairs of eyes. Sheppard notes that only Congreve appears to have written regularly and at length on subjects unrelated to the Society or religion. Congreve's papers survived because his distinction meant that they were collated carefully when he died – as were those of Benson himself, and later those of William O'Brien.

The great bulk of the tens of thousands of letters that must have flowed between the houses of the Society has, regrettably, been lost. When the *Cowley Evangelist* ceased to be published it was remarked that "the at present unwritten history of the community lies largely within its pages, although this is much more true of the work in India and South Africa whence a wealth of letters recaptures the events of all those years". This would suggest that the letters home from the colonial missions had been either lost or discarded by December 1968: as such, correspondence referenced only with the name of the writer and a date indicates a letter that survives in the pages of the *Parish Magazine*, the *Cowley Evangelist*, or the *News Sheet*.

The archives at Lambeth Palace also contain the records of meetings of Chapter – the SSJE's instrument of self-governance – and other documents relating to the life of the Society at home and abroad. It should also be noted that not all the Chapter minutes are paginated: a full reference indicates a specific page within a volume; a truncated entry that notes only the relevant volume is preceded by the type of meeting and its date.

Other archival material – relating to the Society's work in North America and South Africa respectively – is in the care of the SSJE brethren at Cambridge, MA, and the Library at the University of the Witwaterstrand, Johannesburg. Even that material, however, cannot bear full witness to all aspects of the SSJE's influence and activity. Graham Greene, reviewing Evelyn Waugh's *Life of Ronald Knox* in 1959, reflected that "when a man prays he is quite alone. His biographer – except when controversy, persecution, sanctity, or disgrace lend to the story a spurious drama – must write a life of his hero which excludes the hero's chief activity."[11]

While the image of solitary prayer does not generally apply to the corporate life of the Cowley Fathers (although it applied to many of the brethren individually) it does point to the countless hours of spiritual work – "today one has been hearing confessions all day"[12] – that inevitably remains hidden from view. As Congreve observed, "the work of a religious Community can never be assessed by any external measure; the essence of its *work* is its *life in*

---

9 *Rule of Life*, no.21, "Of Correspondence".

10 cf Benson, 14 Dec 1910, SSJE/6/1/2/27/9.

11 Graham Greene, *Collected Essays*, London: Vintage (2014), 282.

12 Nicholson, 5 Aug 1910.

God."[13] Of the huge number of spiritual letters that individual members of the Society must have written to penitents and others, we only have a handful of carefully-selected published examples.

References to Luke Miller's work on Congreve, and that of Steven Haws CR on the SSJE's early days in the United States, cite – necessarily loosely – their as-yet-unpublished manuscripts; while the rich veins of the archive of the *Church Times*, now available in digital form, have only been lightly tapped. In its own Anglo-Catholic heyday it was such a doughty supporter of the SSJE that, as one veteran member of its editorial desk has remarked, it seemed to run a story "every time a Cowley Father sneezed".

The book begins with a certain amount of necessary groundwork. The opening chapters place Benson in his own context in Oxford in the 1840s as the influence of the ecclesiastical movement that bore its name was growing in the wider Church of England. They also deal with the place of monasticism in the general Victorian imagination and in literature, and treat some of the small-scale post-Reformation expressions of community that may be claimed to have been influenced – whether deliberately or coincidentally – by monastic ideals; and continue with a consideration of contemporary concerns relating to celibacy and sexuality, unsuccessful attempts by others to found communities for men, and the circumstances surrounding the successful establishment of the Society of St John the Evangelist.

The work goes on to chart the SSJE's work as a parish-based community, and its steady growth at home, in America, and in India in the 1870s and 1880s; its enormous and rapid expansion in the 1890s and 1900s, with the addition of South Africa to its sphere of activity, and the raising of its major buildings at Oxford; its growing identity as a champion of Anglo-Catholic principles, its place in the Anglo-Catholic Congress Movement, and its influence in both the Church of England and the Anglican Communion; its role in two world wars; and its engagement with a changed world and church in the years that followed 1945.

A brief spike in vocations in the 1930s and 1940s was not sustained: attempts to make the Society more attractive to potential postulants had only limited success; and its final decline was rapid, as demonstrated in Appendix 2, which lays out the density of lasting professions against deaths of members. Withdrawal from India and South Africa – but not before stands had been made in the latter over the National Government's policy of racial segregation – was followed by major changes to the SSJE's liturgy, the reordering of its buildings, the embracement of Eastern forms of prayer, and the giving up of the mother house at Cowley in favour of smaller, scattered houses. Ultimately, the members of the Society retreated to its London house, where they continued to offer a ministry of prayer and spiritual direction until its closure and sale in 2012.

Given the far-reaching scope and deep influence of the SSJE in its heyday – to say nothing of the affection in which "the Cowley Dads" were held by ecclesiastical humourists and others – it is remarkable that to date no attempt has been made to collate the piecemeal and scattered material that constitutes

---

13 *CE* Jan 1911.

its archival legacy into a comprehensive history of the whole; particularly after the publication of Alan Wilkinson's *The Community of the Resurrection* (1992);[14] Alistair Mason's *History of the Society of the Sacred Mission* (1993);[15] Petà Dunstan's work on the Society of St Francis, *This Poor Sort* (1997),[16] and the Anglican Benedictines, *The Labour of Obedience* (2009);[17] and Hugh Allen's recent work on Joseph Leycester Lyne's community, *New Llanthony Abbey* (2016).[18] It goes without saying that this book can only really scratch the surface of a work spread over 150 years and four continents; but it is to be hoped that it will to some extent make up for a notable absence in the history of the monastic life for men in the Church of England and the Anglican Communion, and perhaps inspire others to deeper study and reflection on the subject.

Two further observations need to be made. The first is that the concluding chapters of the book are deliberately and necessarily less detailed than the rest of the work, as they relate either to people who are still alive; or to those who have only died within the last thirty years, and who were well-known to many who are still living. The second involves the present highly-charged climate into which a work linked with any part of the history of the British Empire must be launched. I refute the notion that because certain terms – including "Kaffir", "negro", and "coloured" – were used by individual members of the SSJE over a century ago, crude racism played a defining part in the Cowley Fathers' overseas agenda. Instances of their use are reproduced in this book: all in quotation marks, and all in their proper context – out of which they should not be taken.

14 Alan Wilkinson, *The Community of the Resurrection: A Centenary History*, London: SCM Press (1992).

15 Alistair Mason, *SSM: History of the Society of the Sacred Mission*, Norwich: Canterbury Press (1993).

16 Petà Dunstan, *This Poor Sort: A History of the European Province of the Society of St Francis*, London: Darton, Longman & Todd (1997).

17 Petà Dunstan, *The Labour of Obedience: The Benedictines of Pershore, Nashdom and Elmore – A History*, Norwich: Canterbury Press (2009).

18 Hugh Allen, *New Llanthony Abbey: Father Ignatius's Monastery at Capel-y-ffin*, Peterscourt Press (2016).

I WANT TO GO AND BE A COWLEY FATHER

A mother was watching her infant,
   A curly-haired youngster of four.
He had set out his new clockwork railway
   All over the nursery floor.
'Now tell me, my darling,' she murmured,
   'When you're big and your daddy is dead,
Shall we make you a real engine-driver, my pet?'
   Then he looked up and tenderly said:

   'I want to go and be a Cowley Father,
      I do not want to run away to sea.
   I won't be a policeman or a fireman,
      And an actor's life is not the life for me.
   I will not be a gangster in Chicago,
      For the Vicar says such men are very bad.
   So order me a cassock and a girdle,
      For I want to go and be a Cowley Dad.'

A bishop was sitting at dinner
   One night in his palace so fair.
The butler stood close by the sideboard,
   To pour out the wine that was there.
He folded his violet napkin,
   Then said, as he turned to his wife,
'To-morrow, my dear, I must leave you, I fear,
   For I've found my vocation in life.

   'I want to go and be a Cowley Father,
      I won't sit on committees any more.
   Stop pulling wires to get me sent to Lambeth;
      That's no longer my ambition as of yore.
   I'm sorry I must leave you without warning,
      And I know the Dean will think I've been a cad,
   But I'm going back to Oxford in the morning,
      For I want to go and be a Cowley Dad.'

—E. L. Mascall, *Pi in the High* (1959)

1

In the Beginning

Every plant must have its seed.

—Godfrey Callaway SSJE[1]

Richard Meux Benson was born on 6 July 1824, and baptised a month later in the parish church of his family's London home, St George's, Bloomsbury; where the successors of Nicholas Hawksmoor's heraldic beasts gambol at the base of his ziggurat to the glory of the house of Hanover. Benson's childhood seems to have been one of happy, pious affluence, and both his parents were wealthy in their own right: Thomas Starling Benson had business interests in the City, and Elizabeth Meux was the heiress to the Meux brewing fortune. "They were so rich", observed Mildred Woodgate, "that complete security surrounded them at all times".[2]

Benson's young mother was the third wife of his much older father; and, while the Clapham Sect had influenced the entire family, she was a member of Holy Trinity, Clapham, where John Venn had been Rector.[3] Elizabeth Benson was particularly religious,[4] and her spirituality was a formative influence in the family. Geoffrey Curtis CR called her "a devout Christian woman", and she imparted similar qualities to her infant boy.[5] The Bible was at the fore of his childhood reading, and Woodgate considered that his early years were spent "in an atmosphere of love and almost unsullied happiness". He was particularly close to his mother, and, rather than follow his elder brother to Harrow, was educated at home by a tutor.

Woodgate's analysis of the Bensons' domestic affairs may well have been padded with a mixture of legend and speculation, but she pointed to an important consideration when she reminded her readers that Benson was born over a decade before the death of William IV, and that in his late childhood "the wildest stories were abroad" relating about the originators of the new ecclesiastical thinking coming out of Oxford, and their best-selling *Tracts for the Times.*

---

1 E. D. Sedding SSJE (ed), *Godfrey Callaway: Missionary in Kaffraria 1892–1942*, London: SPCK (1945), 19.

2 Woodgate, *Benson*, 1. "Meux" pronounced "mews".

3 Eldridge H. Pendleton SSJE, *Press On, The Kingdom: The Life of Charles Chapman Grafton*, Cambridge, MA: Society of St John the Evangelist (2014), 39.

4 Woodgate, *Benson*, 5.

5 *CE* April 1951.

In 1841 the young Benson sat for a scholarship at Balliol, which he failed to win. But while in Oxford he wandered into the University Church on Sunday morning, and happened to hear John Henry Newman preach. Woodgate did not, perhaps, quite have the measure of the man and his co-workers with her assessment that Benson, "with his Evangelical background, and brought up on the teachings of the Clapham Sect, would have been quite out of sympathy with all that Newman and his followers were fighting for"; but he was deeply moved by the experience and convinced that, whatever the prevailing mood, Newman was sincere and "no charlatan". The young Benson became aware of the affairs of men at a time when much of literate England's attention was focussed on the nascent Oxford Movement.

After a second unsuccessful attempt at the Balliol scholarship, it was agreed that Benson would go up to Christ Church at Michaelmas 1843; but an extended trip to Italy delayed his arrival. In the late summer of 1843 Benson and his sister Sarah took a house in Rome. There they became acquainted with much of Roman society, including Cardinal Acton, discussed theology at length with Jesuits, and were received in audience by Pope Gregory XVI. Benson was nevertheless fastidious about his attendance at the English Church, and any who looked for his conversion to Roman Catholicism were disappointed. On his way back to England, however, he called at the great Benedictine monastery at Monte Cassino.[6]

Meanwhile, in Oxford, controversy dragged on. Arguments continued to rage over the issues raised by the *Tracts* – which had come to an abrupt end in 1841 – and at least some part of the discourse involved the place of monasticism in the life of the Church.[7] For his part, Newman insisted that although not everyone was called to the monastic life, "there are certain individuals raised up from time to time to a still more self-denying life".[8] In 1842 he retired to Littlemore, and in 1843 he resigned from the University Church. Benson matriculated at Christ Church a year later.

The Oxford in which Benson arrived as an undergraduate in 1844 was still in a period of religious upheaval that had begun in the early 1820s when the Regius Professor of Divinity, Charles Lloyd,[9] had set about reforming the way in which theology was taught in the University. Lloyd revitalised the system by providing a series of lectures and tutorials that would be recognisable to today's undergraduates; and among the young college fellows to benefit from this overhaul were the founding fathers of the movement of which Benson would later become a leader, including John Keble, Edward Bouverie Pusey, and Newman himself.

By the time of Benson's matriculation, the *Tracts for the Times* were over, and W. G. Ward had just brought out his infamous *Ideal of A Christian Church*. Keble had retired to Hursley; Newman was on his "Anglican death-bed"; and Pusey

---

6 Woodgate, *Benson*, 6ff.

7 See Greg Peters, *Reforming the Monastery: Protestant Theologies of the Religious Life*, Eugene, OR: Cascade Books (2014), 76ff.

8 John Henry Newman, "Indulgence in Religious Privileges", *Sermons Bearing on Subjects of the Day*, London: Longmans Green (1902), 124.

9 Charles Lloyd (1784–1829) held the Regius Chair from 1822, and was also Bishop of Oxford from 1827 until his early death in 1829.

was still banned from preaching in the University after the controversy over his sermon of May 1843, *The Holy Eucharist A Comfort to the Penitent*. However much he tried to avoid the limelight, Pusey's influence was enormous – not only in Christ Church and in Oxford, but also in the wider Church – and the ban did little more than raise his profile further and make the sermon a bestseller.[10]

At Christ Church Benson gathered around himself a remarkable group of luminaries who went on to eminence and distinction in one way or another. Charles Dodgson was his contemporary, and later achieved fame – and, still later, notoriety – as Lewis Carroll. Frederick Ouseley had inherited his father's baronetcy and went on to become Professor of Music in the University; and Henry Parry Liddon became Professor of Exegesis and a Canon of St Paul's. One of Benson's nearest neighbours and closest associates was Frank Buckland – perhaps one of the most bizarre and talented figures of his age – who was at least as eccentric as his remarkable parents and kept a menagerie in his rooms opposite Benson's own in Fell's Buildings.[11] His father, by then Dean of Westminster, had been a Canon of Christ Church; and as a boy, Buckland junior had ridden a turtle in Mercury, the deep pond in the middle of Tom Quad: a turtle, it seems, destined for the soup course at the dinner to celebrate the Duke of Wellington's installation as Chancellor in 1834.[12] Perhaps it was this familial association that induced the college authorities to tolerate, to a greater or lesser degree, the presence of "marmots, guinea pigs, several snakes, a monkey, a chameleon, while in the courtyard outside were an eagle, a jackal, a pariah dog and even a bear".[13] After a series of unfortunate incidents, however, the bear had to go.[14] Tiglath Pileser, or "Tig", as the bear was known for short, was in the end exiled to Dean Buckland's country living at Islip to join the eagle and the monkey, which had also disgraced themselves.[15]

There was, then, plenty of frivolity in Benson's student life; despite the Earl of Wicklow's view, based on his later rigour, that "he might indeed have been the better for a little seasoning".[16] In the evenings the young men dined in Christ Church hall – now one of the most famous dining rooms in the world, thanks to the *Harry Potter* franchise – and Woodgate pointed to the parties, and the long walks in the surrounding countryside, and Buckland's various interesting visitors, including Florence Nightingale. But there was another

---

10 Pusey had preached on Matthew 26.28, "This is My Blood of the New Testament, which is shed for many for the remission of sins". In the sermon, Pusey restated a number of eucharistic doctrines that, although familiar to ecclesiastical scholarship, had generally passed from view. In the preface to the published text he wrote that "it is impossible not to see, that a controversy has been awakened, which, from the very sacredness of the subject, and the vagueness of the views of many, and the irreverence of the age, one should, of all others, most have deprecated".

11 See G. H. O. Burgess, *The Curious World of Frank Buckland*, London: John Baker (1967).

12 Timothy Collins, "From Anatomy to Zoophagy: A Biographical Note on Frank Buckland", *Journal of the Galway Archaeological and Historical Society*, v.55 (2003), 94.

13 Woodgate, *Benson*, 27.

14 Collins, "Anatomy to Zoophagy", 95.

15 George C. Bompas, *Life of Frank Buckland*, London: Nelson & Sons (1909), 50ff.

16 The Earl of Wicklow, "The Monastic Revival in the Anglican Communion", *Studies: An Irish Quarterly Review*, 42:168 (Winter 1953), 428.

element of the daily round of the Oxford undergraduate in those days, and it was the routine of compulsory prayer. At Christ Church there was a daily service at eight o'clock in the morning, before college breakfast. On Sundays students attended the choral services at the Cathedral, wearing their surplices. The Holy Communion was celebrated once a month.[17]

In this latter routine Benson became thoroughly immersed; and although it seems he had always intended to seek Holy Orders, two events may well have crystallised his thoughts. The first was Newman's reception in October 1845, which was sensational outside Oxford but "almost anticlimactic" within because it had been long expected;[18] and the second was Pusey's resumption of the Cathedral pulpit in February 1846. Pusey's reputation was very great indeed, both in Oxford and much further afield; he was the eponymous – if reluctant – leader of the movement that Newman had now abandoned, and his influence on Benson was profound.

Owen Chadwick described Pusey as a man who had "none of the arts which capture the many [...] of rare and conscientious learning and accuracy, but withal a simple, unworldly, otherworldy soul".[19] But – even without fiery oratory, or expansive gesture, or polemic prose – he captured the many anyway; and when he died "from every corner of the country came creeping the old men still left to whose his name had been a watchword and an inspiration",[20] to stand "four or five abreast" around Tom Quad as he was carried to his grave.[21]

Benson was one of those he inspired: he owed Pusey a great deal, and not least his nomination to a Studentship of Christ Church. Along with Liddon – and, as it happened, George Ward Hunt, who was later (and only briefly) Chancellor of the Exchequer in 1868 – he was elected on Christmas Eve 1846.[22] The conditions of retaining the Studentship were that those elected must take Holy Orders and remain unmarried: Benson was made deacon by Samuel Wilberforce on Trinity Sunday 1848, and ordained to the priesthood in 1849. At one point his mother had hoped that her cousin Lord Brougham, the former Lord Chancellor, would be able to secure him a good living with a decent income;[23] but after a brief spell as an assistant curate in Surbiton he accepted the college living of St James's, Cowley, in 1850. He remained a Student of Christ Church for the rest of his life.

St James's Church now sits just within the Oxford ring road, in a densely populated suburban area: its parish is smaller than it was in Benson's day, but much more populous. In 1850 there was an almost clear sweep of countryside down to Magdalen Bridge; and, although this would begin to change within a

---

17 Woodgate, *Benson*, 28ff.

18 Marvin J. O'Connell, *The Oxford Conspirators: A History of the Oxford Movement 1833–45*, London: Macmillan (1969), 414.

19 Owen Chadwick, *The Mind of the Oxford Movement*, London: Adam & Charles Black (1960), 46–7.

20 Henry Scott Holland, *A Bundle of Memories*, London: Wells Gardner, Darton & Co. (1915), 99.

21 Keith Feiling, *In Christ Church Hall*, London: Macmillan & Co. (1960), 130–1.

22 J. O. Johnston, *The Life and Letters of Henry Parry Liddon DD*, London: Longmans, Green & Co. (1904), 8; Christ Church Archives, Dean & Chapter i.b.10, f.96v.

23 Henry Roxby Benson to Elizabeth Meux Benson, 20 May 1849, in Dorothy M. Bayliffe & Joan N. Harding, *Starling Benson of Swansea*, Cowbridge: D. Brown & Sons Ltd (1996), 107.

decade, when Benson arrived he was the parson of a country parish with only six hundred parishioners. He broke with the tradition of his predecessors and chose to live among his people, rather than riding out from Christ Church; while his widowed mother moved to Oxford to be closer to her youngest son. Benson seems to have thrown himself into his parochial work, but he also maintained strong links with the University and many of its members. Some of these were social – Dodgson once photographed two of his nieces, who were staying with their grandmother, and Benson was delighted when Liddon was appointed Principal of Cuddesdon in 1854 – but by far the most significant was to do with his already fastidious prayer life.[24]

THE BROTHERHOOD OF THE HOLY TRINITY

The Brotherhood of the Holy Trinity began its life at Oxford as the Brotherhood of St Mary in 1844. It was in its origin more antiquarian than devotional; and it underwent a transformation in 1852, when it adopted its new name. At its outset, it was open to non-members of the University; and, after increasing inactivity, it was finally dissolved in 1932.[25] The names of a number of leading second-generation Tractarians appear on its membership roll after 1852, including Benson, Liddon, Alexander Forbes, Edward King, and Arthur Stanton. Charles Lowder was also a member, and Anthony Howe has demonstrated that the BHT played a significant part in the foundation and early life of Lowder's own Society of the Holy Cross.[26] Other notable clergy and laity on the roll include Ouseley and his pupil John Stainer; Robert Bridges, later Poet Laureate; and the architect George Frederick Bodley,[27] who would go on to build the Society of St John the Evangelist's great church on the Iffley Road. Gerard Manley Hopkins considered joining, and was certainly proposed in 1863, but does not seem to have been elected.[28]

Benson was one of the early members of the newly reconstituted society, and his name appears in the minutes with those of the members elected in August 1852.[29] They sought advice for a set of rules that might bind them together, and one of the original members of the Brotherhood of St Mary, Frederick Meyrick, approached Pusey. Meyrick later recalled that "the members [...] who were specially interested in architecture withdrew, and the others set out on their new quest. There was some difficulty in organizing the new plan, and I was requested to ask Dr Pusey for his advice".

Meyrick did not, however, find Pusey's counsel entirely helpful: "Dr Pusey was at this time engaged in the institution and establishment of sisterhoods, and he grasped at this application, which he thought might be utilized for

---

24 Woodgate, *Benson*, 39ff.

25 Archives of the Brotherhood of the Holy Trinity kept at Pusey House, Oxford: letters of various brethren to Darwell Stone.

26 Anthony Howe, "The Rules of the SSC and the Brotherhood of the Holy Trinity", in William Davage (ed), *In This Sign Conquer*, London: Continuum (2006).

27 Bodley was elected on 23 February 1859.

28 BHT Minute Book 7, 4, PH.

29 BHT Minute Book 1, 17, PH

the institution of brotherhoods also. But that was not our purpose." His suggestions were simply too severe: "Full of the notion that he had taken up, Dr Pusey first proposed that the members of the new body should make a rule of walking with their eyes turned to the ground, to avoid temptations and as an act of humility." He also suggested that the members wore a girdle as "a token of self-restraint".[30]

Owen Chadwick thought that in terms of rules of life for religious societies Pusey was "backward-looking, a man of hair-shirt and of such exalted standards that unwittingly he promoted excessive severity of rule",[31] and the BHT adopted neither practice. Meyrick felt that they were "not natural for young men, nor good for them". However, Pusey's suggestion that the society adopt the patronage of the Holy Trinity was approved, as well as "some simple suggestions which might help us towards a good life".[32] The society resolved that:

> [...] those who enter the brotherhood are supposed to adopt (so far as in them lies) the following Resolutions, *viz*:
> I. To rise early.
> II. To be moderate in food.
> III. To devote some time in each day to serious reading.
> IV. To speak evil of no man.
> V. To avoid dissipation.
> VI. To commemorate the Holy Trinity by saying the "Gloria Patri" on first rising in the morning and last thing at night.
> VII. To pray for (1) the Unity of the Church (2) the conversion of sinners (3) the advancement of the faithful, and (4) for the members of the brotherhood generally.
> A more detailed Rule of Life has been drawn up by an experienced clergyman [Pusey] as a standard "to be aimed at, and as a guide to such as are able and willing to practise a stricter Rule, but is not binding on the conscience of any".[33]

Nevertheless, members of the Brotherhood were free to adopt the Rule formally, and in February 1859 the Master, James Millard, "announced that he should be ready to receive the names of those Brethren who wished to take 'the Rules to be aimed at' as binding [during Lent]".[34]

The BHT met formally every couple of months for prayer, fellowship, and almsgiving. The destination of the collection would usually be discussed at the start of each meeting, and regularly went either to supply for local needs, or for worthy causes further afield. The work of various sisterhoods often received donations. As the early members left Oxford the Brotherhood became scattered, and on 1 March 1856 Benson was present at a meeting that

30 Frederick Meyrick, *Memories of Life at Oxford and Elsewhere*, London: John Murray (1905), 174.

31 Owen Chadwick, *The Victorian Church*, London: SCM Press (1987), i:508.

32 Meyrick, *Memories*, 174. It seems likely, given his suggestion of dedication, that Pusey hoped the Brotherhood of the Holy Trinity might complement his women's society of the same dedication at Ascot Priory.

33 BHT Minute Book 1, 3–4, PH.

34 BHT Minute Book 2, 141, PH.

determined to "ask from the Bishop of Brechin [Alexander Forbes] advice as to the adoption of some plan for the closer connection of absent brethren with those resident in Oxford".[35] Forbes attended the meeting of the BHT on 15 October, from which Benson seems to have been absent, and proposed

> That, with a view to keeping alive a more constant sympathy between the resident and non-resident members of the Brotherhood the latter should endeavour:
>
> i. To meet, if possible, to the number of three or more for devotional purposes once a week;
> ii. To keep, for every such association, a Register in which an account of such meetings and of other matters affecting the Brotherhood should be entered;
> iii. To send annually an account of their proceedings to the Brotherhood in Oxford; and,
> iv. That where a Brother is alone or out of the reach of any other members of the Brotherhood he should endeavour to associate with himself for such devotional purposes one or more neighbours who might afterwards be admitted into the Brotherhood.

The members agreed "that the Amanuensis should communicate the above proposed to the absent Brethren", and also noted – almost as an afterthought – "that the weekly Celebration of the Holy Communion at St Mary's [the University Church] had been re-established, and would now depend mainly on the Brotherhood for its support."[36]

Liddon later suggested that Forbes's first three points had, in essence, been "circulated in 1845 by Pusey, Keble, and [Charles] Marriott for use at three hours of the day". Writing in his *Life of Pusey*, he considered that they had been "in daily use by members of [...] the Brotherhood of the Holy Trinity, and noted that later they had become "better known to churchmen through the Intercessory Manual of the Rev. R. M. Benson of the Cowley Society of St John".[37]

Howe suggests that "by the mid-1840s, Pusey was evidently fired by the thought of a monastic revival and saw [the BHT] as his chance". On the suggestions rejected by Meyrick in 1852 he argues that Pusey had "misunderstood the brief, mistaking the Brotherhood to be pseudo-monastic".[38] But, as time went on, the general mood of the membership changed. Meyrick noted that originally all the suggestions were "purely voluntary; there was no compulsion on any one to do them, nothing wrong if they were not done", but that later "some of the members were not contented with anything so vague; they wanted rules, not suggestions".[39] From the Brotherhood's minute-books distinct themes emerge: a sense of community, whether resident in Oxford or dispersed; the importance of corporate prayer; and the practical work of almsgiving. From June 1857, the members' names appear prefixed with "Brother".

---

35 Ibid, 41.
36 Ibid, 51ff.
37 H. P. Liddon, *Life of E.B. Pusey, DD*, London: Longmans, Green & Co. (1893), ii:135.
38 Davage, *In this Sign Conquer*, 28.
39 Meyrick, *Memories*, 175.

The members of the BHT clearly saw an opportunity to extend their network of prayer far beyond Oxford and England. In the period of the BHT's early consolidation, missionary work in the Empire was a pressing matter in the Church of England at large. India was a major concern, and the Society for the Propagation of the Gospel had funded the establishment of a mission at Delhi in 1854. Its work came into sharp and painful focus during the Indian Mutiny of 1857, when the missionaries and their families were murdered; but while the papers agitated for reprisals others immediately offered themselves for the work.[40] Meanwhile, in other parts of the sub-continent others worked to spread the Gospel, with varying degrees of success.

By 1860 the BHT had established "Branch Brotherhoods" with provincial chapters reporting back to the meetings in Oxford – one as far away as New South Wales – and its numbers were growing steadily. Meanwhile, in London Docks Charles Fuge Lowder had founded the Society of the Holy Cross; and from Oxford Benson had encouraged the development of an "association of prayer", which the clergy members of the BHT had been forming in their parishes and among their friends. "Our desire is to have many such local associations with their own specialities of organism", he wrote in 1860, "all forming one great Association of prayer for the unconverted throughout the kingdom". To "kingdom" Benson might also have added "empire": Robert Reynolds Winter, a member of the Brotherhood, wrote from Delhi to say that he was "heartily glad that such an Association should be started", and that he wished to join, beginning with "5 moments [of prayer], at 3 different times [of day]".[41]

Although it is impossible not to regard the Brotherhood of the Holy Trinity as a nursery for Benson's later monastic ideas, on its own terms it stands within a context of upheaval and uncertainty in the wider Church of England. Its members represented to a great extent – particularly in its leadership – a restrained approach to the principles of the Oxford Movement. The 1840s and 1850s may be said to represent the second phase of that movement, as Tractarian principles were diffused in the parochial system by Oxford men who had been up in the 1830s and 40s, and who since been ordained and were running their own parishes. At a time when clergymen across the whole Church of England were experiencing a "profound shift" in their work, and beginning to see themselves as a "vocational profession",[42] the movement picked up pace and was particularly fruitful in developing a sacramental and pastoral theology that placed an emphasis on the Eucharist and the Incarnation.[43] Alongside this, however, went a developing desire among many of the movement's adherents to fuse the theology that came out of Oxford with the antiquarianism coming from Cambridge in the form of the Camden Society. This led, soon enough, to Ritualism.

Pusey tried to distance himself from this development, insisted that "the unadorned simplicity of the Church was fitting in its penitential plainness,

---

40 *The Story of the Delhi Mission*, London: SPG (1908), 9.

41 Winter, 2 Oct 1860, SSJE/6/1/2/11/2/4a.

42 Nigel Yates, *Anglican Ritualism in Victorian Britain, 1830–1910*, Oxford: OUP (1999), 153.

43 John Shelton Reed, *Glorious Battle: The Cultural Politics of Victorian Anglo-Catholicism*, Nashville: Vanderbilt University Press (1996), 29ff.

representing humble sorrow at the divided and unsaintly condition of Christendom",[44] and later complained that his name was associated with Ritualism only because he had been associated with the *Tracts*;[45] but it must also be observed that the wrangling over the plans for St Saviour's, Leeds,[46] suggests that as early as the 1840s even he had embraced Camden principles in matters of church architecture, and was actually "far from indifferent to the 'externals' of worship".[47] In the event, the derogatory terms of "Ritualist" and "Puseyite" became synonymous.

The 1840s saw "surplice riots" in Exeter, and mob trouble related to ritual would break out sporadically in other parts of the county as the next two decades progressed. In most cases they were the caused by the misinterpreted zeal of new incumbents, or by troublemakers with an axe to grind;[48] but the members of the BHT could hardly ignore the developments, for at the Christ Church living of St Thomas the Martyr (then still a quiet parish just outside the city, but transformed in 1852 with the extension of the railway and the construction of the new Oxford Station a stone's throw from the church) Thomas Chamberlain – another Christ Church man in a Christ Church living, who had preceded Benson at Cowley[49] and was arguably the first priest in the Church of England to wear a form of chasuble to celebrate the Eucharist[50] – was quietly introducing liturgical innovations himself.

Chamberlain was an example of the living-out of the sacramental and pastoral theology of the immediate post-Tractarian period: he was for a time deeply unpopular in his parish, and people protested when he introduced innovations including a new altar, candles, and the mixed chalice. But after he devotedly nursed his parish through the cholera that hit Oxford in 1848 and 1854, he was able to introduce Eucharistic vestments and even incense unopposed.[51] Away from individual local successes like Chamberlain's, however, there was a great deal of suspicion of Ritualism – even in its most modest expressions – both in the Established Church and in the nation as a whole.

Edward Norman calls the nineteenth century a "religious age" because it was a period of great public debate on religious questions.[52] Catholic Emancipation in 1829, for example, consolidated the position of English Roman Catholics; while the Reform Bill of 1832 further weakened the grip that the Church of England had exercised, at least nominally, over English religious life since the Reformation. A sense developed in the popular mind – borne out in contemporary print – that Ritualists were a fifth-column for the Pope, the bogeyman of the English Protestant imagination; and Tractarians and post-Tractarians were tarred with the same brush, as we have seen. This turned into near-hysteria in 1850 when Pius IX restored the Roman Catholic

44 Ibid, 57.
45 Liddon, *Pusey*, iv:211ff.
46 Ibid, ii:466ff.
47 Reed, *Glorious Battle*, 21.
48 Ibid, 32ff.
49 Strong, *Alexander Forbes*, 35.
50 Reed, *Glorious Battle*, 53.
51 Ibid, 35.
52 E. R. Norman, *Anti-Catholicism in Victorian England*, London: Allen & Unwin (1968), 19.

hierarchy to England, and Lord John Russell wrote his now-notorious and injudicious *Letter to the Bishop of Durham*, with its implicit denunciation of the followers of the Oxford Movement as "unworthy sons of the Church of England".[53] Excess or mistiming would be open to immediate scrutiny and derision, for "any sort of innovation could be tarred as 'Puseyite'".[54]

GONE BUT NOT FORGOTTEN

Four writers in particular provide useful analyses of the background to the post-Reformation growth of religious communities in the Church of England, and to a greater or lesser extent all channel Henry Parry Liddon's monolithic four-volume *Life of Pusey*. We have already encountered Peter Anson and Donald Allchin; but the third is Michael Hill in his 1973 study of what he calls "virtuoso religion" in the nineteenth-century Church of England, *The Religious Order*,[55] and the fourth is Greg Peters, in his chapter on Anglican monasticism in his 2014 book, *Reforming the Monastery: Protestant Theologies of the Religious Life*.[56] Anson and Allchin wrote at a time when Anglican monasticism was diverse and buoyant, and showed every sign of continuing to thrive in the new Elizabethan age; Hill when the tide had begun to turn; and Peters writes in a period when it is difficult to view traditional religious life in the Church of England as being in anything other than terminal decline.

Anson and Allchin both noted the very short-lived re-foundations of religious houses that were allowed by the terms of the 1536 Act of Suppression, the reconciliation with Rome of the Church of England and the revival of some of the former houses under Mary I, and the final exile of those religious who managed to escape to the Continent. They traced the developments of Richard Hooker, Lancelot Andrewes, and William Laud: Anson particularly cited Laud's personal book of devotions that contained offices for each day of the week and the seven monastic hours, and which was published after his execution in 1645; and also the essentially choral framework of the Book of Common Prayer, and – in the absence of monks and nuns to sing the offices in their quires – the development of domestic religion: middling literate folk reciting Matins and Evensong in their homes. John Cosin's *Hours of Prayer* of 1627 – which appeared out of a need for the Anglican ladies at Court to have some answer to the Books of Hours used by Queen Henrietta Maria's French ladies-in-waiting – contained most of the monastic offices, and provoked the ire of "the more violent Puritans" for being, in their view, too "Popish". George Herbert, meanwhile, rang the bell of his church at Bemerton – as bidden by the Prayer Book – "to make sure that the ploughman should pause in his toil and offer his devotion to God while others were praying in church".[57]

---

53 Chadwick, *Victorian Church*, i:297.
54 Reed, *Glorious Battle*, 35.
55 Michael Hill, *The Religious Order: A study of Virtuoso Religion and its Legitimation in the Nineteenth-Century Church of England*, London: Heinemann (1973).
56 Peters, *Reforming the Monastery*, 53–90.
57 Anson, *Call of the Cloister*, 5ff.

The prayer life of the nation had been changed at the Reformation, but it had not been snuffed out entirely. In 1918 Allan T. Cameron declaimed that "the abiding witness of the woeful suppression [of the religious houses] is the work-house and the gaol";[58] but Peters argues with more nuance that from the time of the Dissolution of the Monasteries "monastic sentiments were frequently expounded", because there were those who saw that alongside the devotional life of the old religious houses a number of social benefits had existed. He notes the suggestions of some that convents should be revived "for the express purpose of providing some place for widows, those deemed unable to marry, and 'spinsters' to reside", and holds up Edmund Burke's sentiments of the late-eighteenth century: that "the monasteries were ideal institutions for the distribution of benevolent forms of charity".[59]

Meanwhile, households still gathered for corporate prayer at designated hours, and it was against this backdrop of quiet domestic piety – coupled with the ceremonial revival ushered in by Andrewes and Laud from the end of the sixteenth century – that Nicholas Ferrar brought his family to Little Gidding in 1625. Allchin described it as having been "the only time between the Reformation and the Oxford Movement [when] the tendency towards the religious life passed beyond opinions and schemes into achievement".[60]

At Little Gidding Peters describes the Ferrars as having "founded a monas-tery for overt religious reasons", and – despite Alan Maycock's insistence that "Little Gidding was in no sense monastic"[61] – argues that the community was at least "monastic in spirit", revolving as it did around constant prayer (and in particular the reading of the Psalms), strict routine, and the recitation of the offices, and with Nicholas Ferrar as both its *paterfamilias* and spiritual head.[62] Anson recorded that Ferrar had travelled extensively on the Continent, and thought it inconceivable that he would not have encountered Roman Catholic monks and friars on his journeys and experienced something of their way of life. But he also followed Maycock in arguing that there was nothing monastic about Little Gidding: despite their rigorous prayer-life Anson felt the com-munity "best described as an attempt to revive the communal way of living of the early Christians".[63]

Ferrar was accused of running an "Arminian Nunnery" by the Puritans in 1641, and he defended himself by declaring that to him "the name of Nuns was odious", and, crucially, that no member of the community had taken any kind of vow. Nunnery or not, after Ferrar's death his family was forced to flee during the English Civil War, and Little Gidding was looted by the Roundheads in 1646. So ended the experiment, and Maycock observed that "it inspired no imitators, attracted no postulants, [and] remained to the end a thing unique and self-contained".[64]

---

58 A. T. Cameron, *The Religious Communities of the Church of England*, London: Faith Press (1918), 159.

59 Peters, *Reforming the Monastery*, 54.

60 Allchin, *Silent Rebellion*, 21.

61 A. L. Maycock, *Nicholas Ferrar of Little Gidding*, London: SPCK (1968), 197.

62 Peters, *Reforming the Monastery*, 54ff.

63 Anson, *Call of the Cloister*, 8ff.

64 Maycock, *Nicholas Ferrar*, 226.

Allchin concurred that Little Gidding "had no followers or successors", but perhaps had the best wisdom on the matter. "It would be fruitless to try and define how closely the Ferrar family approximated to a religious community," he argued. "It was certainly not one in the strict sense of the word [...] Nevertheless when we consider it, it is difficult to say that the community at Little Gidding does not approach as closely to the life of a religious house, as it does to that of an ordinary household."[65]

After Little Gidding, or, more particularly, after the Restoration of the House of Stuart in 1660, there was a succession of small endeavours that amounted to groups of people – mainly women – living in prayerful community.[66] William Sancroft – the Dean of St Paul's who oversaw the rebuilding of his cathedral after the Fire of London and who was later, briefly, Archbishop of Canterbury – directed one made up of "twelve ladies who wished to retire from the world and establish a 'Protestant Nunnery'"; but the scheme failed when the putative mother superior went to Flanders to study Benedictine monastic life, and became a Roman Catholic instead.[67]

Sancroft's fellow non-Juror Thomas Ken, having been deprived of the see of Bath & Wells, oversaw the prayer life of two biological sisters near Bristol – "the Ladies of Naish Court" – whom he described as living in "a kind of nunnery".[68] Other ventures were larger and more successful, but they existed in isolation: in almost every case, their members had been known to each other before they decided on their course. As time went on even some bishops were bold enough to speculate about the possibilities of the restoration of some sort of religious life. In 1723 Francis Atterbury, Bishop of Rochester, bewailed the dissolution of the religious houses as "the great Blemish of our Reformation",[69] and in 1734 Gilbert Burnet, Bishop of Salisbury, proposed that "something like monasteries without vows, would be a glorious design".[70] Samuel Wesley, also influenced by the non-Jurors,[71] felt that it would be "a desirable thing that we had among us some places wherein those who are religiously disposed might have the liberty for a time of voluntary retirement; that they might escape the world".[72]

Early-Victorian England was not without "monasteries without vows", however – or at least not without models of prayer-oriented celibate single-sex communities. One obvious example was the colleges of Oxford and Cambridge: bachelor dons – many of whom were clergy, and who were obliged to relinquish their fellowships if they married – and their students lived in cloister-like quadrangles, prayed together in Chapel, and ate together in Hall. This was no coincidence: most of the colleges had in some way grown

---

65 Allchin, *Silent Rebellion*, 21ff.

66 See also Wicklow, "Monastic Revival".

67 Anson, *Call of the Cloister*, 15ff.

68 Edward H. Plumptre, *Life of Thomas Ken DD*, London: William Ibister (1889), 2:168ff.

69 Francis Atterbury, *Maxims, Reflections and Observations, Divine, Moral and Political*, London (1723), 13.

70 Gilbert Burnet, *History of his Own Time*, London (1734), ii:653.

71 Trevor Dearing, *Wesleyan and Tractarian worship: an Ecumenical Study*, London: Epworth Press (1966).

72 Adam Clarke, *Memoirs of the Wesley Family: Collected Principally from Original Documents*, London: J. & T. Clarke (1823), 127.

out of monastic establishments whose members had been displaced at the Reformation. Newman referenced the consonance in "Snapdragon" in 1827: "May it be! Then well might I in College cloister live and die."[73]

Another model – and one that touches on Edmund Burke's sentiments – was the almshouses. Some of these were relatively recent foundations, established up and down the country, to care for the would-be destitute out of the philanthropy of local worthies. Others, however, had grown out of very significant monastic beginnings. Many medieval hospitals confiscated by Henry VIII's Commissioners had been suppressed, with their inhabitants turned onto the streets; but others were allowed to continue their work under non-monastic oversight.[74]

The daily life of many of these almshouses was almost always overtly monastic. Their inhabitants usually had to be widowed or unmarried; attendance at chapel was compulsory, although the frequency of the requirement varied from place to place; meals were generally taken together in a common hall, although this also sometimes differed; and the whole endeavour was overseen by a Master (or one with an equivalent title), who lived in separate quarters much after the manner of a medieval abbot. An obvious example was Henry de Blois's twelfth-century Hospital of St Cross, at Winchester, where the residents had little houses arranged round a central courtyard like a charterhouse, and which was the model for Hiram's Hospital in Anthony Trollope's Barchester; while another was the Royal Foundation of St Katharine, which occupied buildings near Regent's Park in London.[75]

Bare ruin'd Choirs

Donald Allchin warned against overestimating what he called a "Romantic and medieval tendency" when considering the self-perception of the nascent Anglican communities;[76] but it would have been plain to an educated Victorian that religious orders had been active in England. The relics of English monasticism were everywhere, and their use as inspiration for literature was well-established: the end of the first quatrain of Shakespeare's *Sonnet 73* – "Bare ruin'd choirs, where late the sweet birds sang" – is ostensibly about trees in autumn; but it does not take a great leap of imagination to consider that the Bard was also lamenting the roofless churches with which the countryside was littered.

Those ruins played their part as muses, too. William Wordsworth was not the first to be moved by Tintern Abbey, the great and near-complete ruin in Monmouthshire which inspired *Lines Composed a Few Miles Above Tintern Abbey* in the summer of 1798. Wordsworth – who developed the ruined-monastery meme in his *Ecclesiastical Sonnets* of the early 1820s – was one in

---

73 John Henry Newman, *Verses for Various Occasions*, London: Burns, Oates & Co (1880), 17.

74 Brian Bailey, *Almshouses*, London: Robert Hale (1988), 82.

75 Anson, *Call of the Cloister*, 27.

76 Allchin, *Silent Rebellion*, 40.

a line of poets to have admired the ruin, and Turner had already painted it. "Descriptions of Tintern Abbey should be written on ivy leaves, and with a poet's pen," purred Catherine Sinclair in 1838, "for no other could do justice to the air of solemn grandeur and religious melancholy reigning within its delicate cloisters, and inspiring that mysterious sentiment of awe with which we gaze on an inanimate body from which the soul has departed".[77] This was not an original idea: Crystal B. Lake's article of 2011, *The Life of Things at Tintern Abbey*, highlights five other important but little-known poems about Tintern, pre-Wordsworth, in which the writers treated the Abbey as a monument capable of passing on information about the past to the present.[78] Edward Davies's work of 1786 is an example:

Enclosed with woods and hills on every side,
Stands Tintern Abbey, spoiled of all her pride,
Whose mournful ruins fill the soul with awe,
Where once was taught God's holy saving law;
Where mitred abbots fanned the heavenly fire,
And shook, with hymns divine, the heavenly choir.
[...] Her fine old windows, arches, walls, unite
To fill the mind with pity and delight;
For from her splendid ruins may be seen
How beautiful this desecrated place has been.[79]

Deborah Kennedy has noted that, by the end of the eighteenth century, "ruined monasteries were as much the haunt of artists as antiquarians".[80] Tintern was significant but far from unique: the ruins of many of the former great religious houses – Fountains, Rievaulx, Bolton, to name just a few – became widely known by the Victorian public through the medium of pastoral poem and romantic painting.

There were other clues, too, of what had once been. Almost all the cathedrals and many of the larger churches in England had been served by great monasteries, and many of their cloisters and libraries – where no monks now walked or read – were among the architectural and antiquarian jewels of the nation. Many of the public schools that were re-founded in the nineteenth century had been monasteries: but boys now slept in the dormitories, and the monastic farmland was given over to playing fields. The mementos of monasticism were never very far away: much later, Patrick Leigh Fermor observed that

[...] there is no riddle here. We know the function and purpose of every fragment and the exact details of the holy life that should be sheltering there. We know, too, the miserable and wanton story of their destruction and their dereliction, and have only to close our eyes for a second for the imagination to rebuild the

77 Catherine Sinclair, *Hill and Valley, or Hours in England and Wales*, New York: Robert Carter (1838), 251.
78 Crystal B. Lake, "The Life of Things at Tintern Abbey", *Review of English Studies* (2012), vol. 63, no. 260, 444–465.
79 Edward Davies, *Chepstow: A Poem in Six Cantos*, Bristol: (1786), 26.
80 Deborah Kennedy, "Wordsworth, Turner, and the Power of Tintern Abbey", *The Wordsworth Circle*, vol. 33, no. 2 (Spring 2002), 80.

towers and the pinnacles and summon to our ears the quiet rumour of monkish activity and the sound of bells melted long ago.[81]

There was, however, quite another side to this pastoral and historical image of the monasteries in the popular mind. It was far more sensationalist, and fuelled in no small way by the prevailing enthusiasm of the day for writing in the gothic style. It applied mainly to the Roman Catholic orders that had thrived on the Continent, and which were tentatively putting down new roots in England after fleeing from revolutionary France.[82]

A significant religious-themed gothic novel is *The Monk: A Romance*, produced by Matthew Lewis in the mid-1790s: a tale that has almost everything that an easily-titillated reader seeking evidence of the religious life as the path to perdition could require.[83] The downfall and damnation of the young monk Ambrosio includes an intercepted letter, a poisonous serpent, a cross-dressing temptress, a pregnant nun, a wicked prioress, a dungeon, a couple of ghosts, an incident of rape, a spot of witchcraft, and the Inquisition thrown in for good measure. Eventually Ambrosio sells his soul to Satan; for he has become the "archetypal figure of the lustful, malevolent monk".[84] In many ways the content of Lewis's book is not that remarkable – it is very much in the tradition of Horace Walpole's *Castle of Otranto*[85] of thirty years earlier – but its title stands out. Ambrosio is a monk: the mystery of his life is increased, and his fall is made all the more delicious.

Buildings themselves also captivated people's imaginations. In Jane Austen's 1817 posthumous parody, *Northanger Abbey*, the eponymous country estate of the Tilneys is established as having been formerly a monastery; but, like so many houses of its type, by the time Catherine Morland visits it is a comfortable Georgian home. Nevertheless, Henry Tilney is able mischievously to play on Catherine's fondness for the gothic by setting up the house as somewhere where visiting young ladies are "always lodged apart from the rest of the family [...] along many gloomy passages, into an apartment never used since some cousin or kin died in it twenty years before".[86]

In Charlotte Brontë's *Villette* of 1853 the impressionability of the heroine, Lucy Snowe, is plausible enough for Brontë to have her believe that she has been visited in the night by the ghost of a nun done to death in the garden of the school in which she teaches – it having been, of course, formerly a convent.[87] Nor were Walter Scott or Elizabeth Barrett Browning immune. Scott – whose own home, Abbotsford, had its own monastic associations – called the second canto of *Marmion* "The Convent", and talked of the despotic Abbot who "rose/ To speak the Chapter's doom/ On those the wall was to enclose/

---

81 Patrick Leigh Fermor, *A Time To Keep Silence*, London: John Murray (1957), 8.

82 See Maureen Moran, *Catholic Sensationalism and Victorian Literature*, Liverpool University Press (2007).

83 Matthew Lewis, *The Monk*, Waterford: J. Saunders (1796).

84 Victor H. Brombert, *The Romantic Prison: The French Tradition*, Princeton: Princeton University Press (1978), 55.

85 Horace Walpole, *The Castle of Otranto*, London: Thomas Lownds (1764).

86 Jane Austen, *Northanger Abbey*, London: John Murray (1818).

87 Charlotte Brontë, *Villette*, London: Smith, Elder & Co (1853).

Alive within the Tomb";[88] following it with *The Monastery: A Romance* and *The Abbot* in 1820, which he called "Tales from Benedictine Sources".[89] Browning, meanwhile, in the *Lay of the Brown Rosary*, related the horror of an ivy covered abbey where

> A nun in the east wall was buried alive
> Who mocked at the priest when he called her to shrive,
> And shrieked such a curse, as the stone took her breath,
> The old abbess fell backwards and swooned unto death
>   With an Ave half-spoken.[90]

This meme of murderous priest and complicit abbess was to find its apogee in two books that appeared in the 1830s. Far more salacious than the offerings of Austin and Brontë, *The Awful Disclosures of Maria Monk* was full of tales of helpless women being raped and murdered by wicked priests, abetted by evil abbesses. First published in 1836, it was an instant bestseller, and despite being widely discredited, it ran and ran.[91] It built on the success of Rebecca Reed's *Six Months in a Convent* of 1832, which had caused an angry mob to burn down the Ursuline house near Boston, MA, where she was alleged to have been held captive.[92] Denis Paz described this sort of writing as "a convention that the penny dreadful genre had adapted from the gothic tale, historical novel, and theatrical melodrama".[93] It served to depict monastic life as a high road to illicit sex and death, and it sold like hot cakes.[94]

---

88 Walter Scott, *Marmion*, London: John Murray (1808).

89 Walter Scott, *The Monastery: A Romance & The Abbot*, London: Longman (1820).

90 Elizabeth Barrett Browning, *The Lay of the Brown Rosary* (1840).

91 Maria Monk, *Awful Disclosures of Maria Monk, a narrative of her sufferings in the Hotel Dieu nunnery at Montreal*, London (1836).

92 Rebecca Reed, *Narrative of Six Months' Residence in a Convent*, London (1835).

93 Denis Paz, *Popular Anti-Catholicism in Mid-Victorian England*, Stanford University Press (1992), 62.

94 Noel Coward referenced the monastic-murder tradition in *Operette* (1938): *The stately homes of England / Though rather in the lurch / Provide a lot of chances / For psychical research / There's the ghost / Of a crazy younger son / Who murdered in 1351 / An extremely rowdy nun / Who resented it / And people who come to call / Meet her in the hall…*

2

YOUNG VIPERS

The desert's hair-grown hermit sunk
The saner brute below;
The naked Santon, haschish-drunk,
The cloister madness of the monk,
The fakir's torture show!

—"The Brewing of Soma",
John Greenleaf Whittier, 1872

In the popular Victorian mind the life of any religious community was linked, inevitably, with the Roman Catholicism of pre-Reformation English history, and the Continental present. It was therefore doubly suspect as Popish and foreign, and allied itself naturally with the other causes to be reviled under the "no Popery" rallying cry of the mid-nineteenth century. Edward Norman has noted that these were many, and that, further, "most men easily lumped the Ritualists and the Papists together".[1] The Roman Catholic monastery, then, was a "foreign and wicked institution",[2] and in 1855 it was perfectly resonant for Anthony Trollope to have his eminent lawyer of *The Warden*, Sir Abraham Haphazard, heavily involved in legislation known as "the Convent Custody Bill".[3]

Successive legal cases involving religious houses also fuelled the popular imagination – such as the infamous Connelly Case, which dragged on through the 1850s. Despite previous solemn undertakings, the nun Cornelia Connelly's apostate-priest husband sued for the restoration of his conjugal rights: he failed to receive them but gained custody of their children, whom she never saw again.[4] The case of *Saurin vs Star & Kennedy*, which was heard before the Queen's Bench in Westminster Hall in 1869, saw an erstwhile Roman Catholic nun, Mary Saurin – who had been expelled from her convent near Hull – sue her former superiors for libel and slander. Her complaint was upheld, and the press heralded it as a triumph. But that triumph was not entirely of Protestant over Catholic, as might have been expected. Rather, it served to bolster the

---

1 E. R. Norman, *Anti-Catholicism in Victorian England*, London: George Allen and Unwin, 1968, 13–22.

2 Rene Kollar OSB, *A Foreign and Wicked Institution? The Campaign against Convents in Victorian England*, Cambridge: James Clarke & Co. (2011).

3 Anthony Trollope, *The Warden*, London: Longman, Brown, Green & Longmans (1855).

4 See, *inter alia*, Radegunde Flaxman, *A Woman Styled Bold: The Life of Cornelia Connelly 1809–1879*, London: Darton, Longman & Todd (1991).

thought of many mid-Victorians that the idea of self-governance for women was doomed to failure.[5]

Catherine Morland; Lucy Snowe; Maria Monk; Rebecca Reed; Cornelia Connelly; Mary Saurin: two fictional characters, two authors of highly dubious veracity, and two real nuns; but all of them women. Many historians have rejected "the persistent myth of the Victorian woman" – a domestic creature, protected from the realities of the outside world[6] – but no small part of the widely-held Victorian disdain for the religious life was that it subverted what was generally held to be the familial norm. Advice abounded in women's conduct manuals in which the apotheosis of womanhood was clearly held to be marriage and motherhood: and entirely in a literal and non-spiritual sense. The life of an old maid was to be shunned, and those who embraced it were to be pitied or despised.[7]

John Keble, Edward Bouverie Pusey, and John Henry Newman nevertheless all viewed religious communities as a fruitful way of Christian living – although they differed on the form it should take – and their contemporaries and neophytes shared in their approval to a greater or lesser extent. Yngve Brilioth included the development of monasticism as one of his "Forms of Tractarian Piety", and stressed "the importance of asceticism as a practice in holiness and obedience, strongly emphasised".[8] Hurrell Froude – whose ascetic extremes became well known after the posthumous publication of his *Remains* – was all in favour of a strict and pseudo-medieval monastic model in the Church of England; and Barbara Gelpi explores his differences with Keble on this subject in *John Keble and Hurrell Froude in Pastoral Dialogue*, which explores the response of both to a visit to Tintern Abbey.[9] Keble preferred a much more active model in the style of Little Gidding; but as Greg Peters observes "it would be Froude's, as opposed to Keble's, ideas on monasticism that would come to characterize the larger Oxford Movement".[10]

Newman later included monasticism among the discarded treasures from whose use the Church of England might have benefitted. In the *Apologia* he recalled that, among other things, monasteries would serve to "strengthen and beautify" the life of the Church.[11] His move to Littlemore in 1842 was at least partly driven by his desire to live in religious community, and he was supported and encouraged by Pusey[12] – although neither was really as "vocal"

---

5 Walter L. Arnstein, *Protestant versus Catholic in Mid-Victorian England: Mr Newdegate and the Nuns,* University of Missouri Press (1982), 121.

6 Carmen Mangion, *Contested Identities: Catholic Women Religious in Nineteenth-Century England and Wales,* Manchester University Press (2008), 53.

7 Joan Perkin, *Women and Marriage in Nineteenth-Century England,* London: Routledge (1988), 226.

8 Yngve Brilioth, *The Anglican Revival,* London: Longmans, Green & Co. (1933), 247.

9 Barbara Charlesworth Gelpi, "John Keble and Hurrell Froude in Pastoral Dialogue", *Victorian Poetry* 44:1 (2006), 7–24.

10 Peters, *Reforming the Monastery,* 72.

11 John Henry Newman, *Apologia Pro Vita Sua,* London: Collins (1959), 223ff.

12 Charles S. Dessain (ed), *The Letters & Diaries of John Henry Newman,* Oxford: OUP (2016), 7:263; 267.

on the issue as Peters intimates, despite their private enthusiasm for the idea.[13] By this time, however, Newman's course was set; and, as Peters points out, "the closer Newman got to converting to Roman Catholicism, the more he envisioned the need for Anglican monasticism".[14] It would therefore fall to Pusey to bring it about.

Pusey's correspondence – much of it presented by Henry Parry Liddon in his *Life of Pusey*, a book of which Benson did not entirely approve[15] – demonstrates that he was very much in favour of monasticism. Pusey was entirely supportive of Newman's plans at Littlemore; and perhaps his most often quoted letter on the subject is one that includes the lines "it would be a great relief to have a μονὴ in our church [...] and you seem just the person to form one".[16] Pusey was also much taken with the active Roman Catholic women's orders, and by the end of 1839 he felt that if such a model – he anticipated nursing as an obvious starting point – could be set up within the Church of England then "there would be numbers of people who are yearning to be employed in that way".[17]

This was an idea that would gain more general traction after the outbreak of war in the Crimea in 1853, which Michael Hill describes as an appeal to "foreign competition".[18] He quotes a letter to *The Times* in late 1854: "Why do we have no Sisters of Charity? There are numbers of able-bodied and tenderhearted women who would joyfully and with alacrity go out to devote themselves to nursing the sick and wounded, if they could be associated for that purpose." Peter Anson observed that similar appeals had been made even earlier in the century, most notably by Robert Southey;[19] and many of them could almost have been written by Pusey himself.

Active orders or not, it was Pusey who encouraged Marion Hughes – despite successive divines' apathy towards vows – to swear the traditional threefold oaths of poverty, chastity, and obedience before him on 6 June 1841. Hughes was clear that she regarded these as a solemn commitment to consecrated virginity: "enrolled as one of Christ's Virgins, espoused to him and made His handmaid".[20] But there was as yet no community for her to join; and although Pusey's daughter Lucy intended to follow a similar path, she died in 1844. Soon after Lucy's death, however, Pusey received news that the Bishop of London,

---

13 Greg Peters, *The Story of Monasticism: Retrieving an Ancient Tradition for Contemporary Spirituality*, Grand Rapids, MI: Baker (2015), 226.

14 Peters, *Reforming the Monastery*, 76.

15 H. P. Liddon, *Life of Edward Bouverie Pusey*, London: Longmans, Green (1893–97). "The book would have been better without the illustrations. They are not up to the mark, and the portraits give very little idea of his outward appearance. The picture of him preaching the University Sermon gives one much more the idea of a young polemical orator [...] than of a man coming forth from ascetic retirement, bearing the traces of mental and bodily austerity, and speaking the calm power of the Holy Ghost, not as the head of a party, but as the somewhat saddened but irrepressible instrument of the Divine Will." Benson to Page, 30 Oct 1893, *Letters of Richard Meux Benson*, London: A. R. Mowbray & Co. (1916), 72.

16 Newman, *Letters and Diaries*, 7:266.

17 Pusey, Dec 1839, in Liddon, *Life of Pusey*, iii:6.

18 Hill, *Religious Order*, 180.

19 Anson, *Call of the Cloister*, 26ff.

20 R. T. Warner, *Marion Rebecca Hughes*, Oxford: OUP (1933), 10.

Charles Blomfield, was willing "to entertain any mature thoughts regarding the reinstitution of monasticism in the Church of England".[21]

It was too late for Lucy Pusey; but Anson counted nineteen communities of women – including the Society of the Holy and Undivided Trinity, of which Hughes became the foundress in 1851 – that existed before Benson, Charles Grafton, and Simeon Wilberforce O'Neill took their vows in December 1866.[22] The first, the Sisterhood of the Holy Cross at Park Village, was founded in 1845 but failed because it was the creation of a committee – which included William Ewart Gladstone – and had no natural leader. Its members were also confused about whether its goal was to be mainly active or contemplative.[23]

In the end the Sisterhood of the Holy Cross was subsumed – as were a number of other small communities – by the Society of the Most Holy Trinity, which went on to thrive at Ascot Priory under Priscilla Lydia Sellon, whom Owen Chadwick numbered "among the indomitables of Victorian womanhood".[24] Other communities that survived the two decades leading up to the establishment of the Society of St John the Evangelist included the Community of St Mary the Virgin at Wantage and the All Saints Sisters of the Poor, then still at Margaret Street in London. Both were founded firmly in the tradition of the Oxford Movement, embracing varying degrees of Ritualism; and both would work closely with SSJE, both at home and abroad, in the decades to come.

The Anglican women's communities divided opinion sharply. Hill discusses them, pertinently, in the light of the arguments for deaconesses: the only women's institution that low-church leaders felt was sanctioned by apostolic tradition. Susan Mumm, meanwhile, has identified eight arguments that were employed "to discourage or discredit the work and very existence" of the early sisterhoods:

> the 'family argument'; accusations of Romanism; attacks based on presumed female incapacity for self-government; the complaint that sisterhoods gave women a public face; accusations that ladies were doing the work of servants; disapproval of their financial affairs; anger at their refusal to subject themselves to church order; and a fear that sisterhoods were stripping social life of their best women.[25]

But there were supporters, too – although they were usually exceptional themselves. Florence Nightingale, for example, was "fascinated" by women's communities, which she regarded as "opposed to, and invariably challenging, the hegemony of the patriarchal family".[26] For all her approval in principle, however, Nightingale – who "alienated nearly all of the women under her" – was deeply unimpressed with the Devonport sisters who went to the Crimea as

---

21 Peters, *Reforming the Monastery*, 83.

22 Anson, *Call of the Cloister*, 220ff.

23 Susan Mumm, *Stolen Daughters, Virgin Mothers: Anglican Sisterhoods in Victorian Britain*, Leicester University Press (1999) 6; Thomas Jay Williams & Allan Walter Campbell, *The Park Village Sisterhood*, London: SPCK (1965).

24 Chadwick, *Victorian Church*, i:507.

25 Mumm, *Stolen Daughters, Virgin Mothers*, 173.

26 Hill, *Religious Order*, 143; 172ff; 167.

nurses.[27] Nevertheless, Chadwick felt that "the reality and legend of Florence Nightingale changed English attitudes to the social service of women and brought with it, though slowly, respect for sisters of religion."[28]

Much of the opposition to the sisterhoods of the mid-nineteenth century had to do with the idea of the subversion of the "'angel in the house' construct",[29] in which young women were regarded as the chattels of their fathers and expected to perform certain domestic functions within the family unit. Like their Roman Catholic counterparts, the Anglican sisterhoods suggested that their members had followed a higher calling,[30] and so they "appeared as a threat not only to the integrity of the Protestant [view of the] character of Anglicanism, but also to the *status quo* of Victorian society".[31]

UNMANLY, UNENGLISH, & UNNATURAL

"W hy should we not also have unmarried clergy who shall devote themselves to God's service?" asked the Tractarian clergyman William Gresley in his novel *Bernard Leslie* of 1842, the same year in which John Mason Neale brought out his own fictional exposition on the necessity of monasticism, *Ayton Priory*.[32] "Of all instruments to evangelise our great towns, nothing, perhaps, would be so efficacious as the establishment of colleges of priests or laymen."[33] Robert Lee Woolf observed that Gresley had no depth as a novelist – the same has been said of Neale[34] – but that the purpose of his books was to instruct.[35] George Herring argues that *Bernard Leslie* "became a vehicle for showing how effective Tractarianism was in practice, and for praising its achievements".[36]

Anson, meanwhile, noted that Gresley was not alone in his thoughts.[37] Pusey himself had long mulled over the idea of men's monasticism: he considered that it belonged to the early church, and so was "not Romanist but primitive".[38] Hill notes, though, that "one of the most common observations levelled against the religious orders in the Church of England was that they were 'foreign bodies' in the organism of the Church. More precisely, they were viewed as Romish";[39] and the "no Popery" cry that caught the popular

27 Clive Ponting, *The Crimean War*, London: Chatto & Windus (2004), 197.

28 Chadwick, *Victorian Church*, i:509.

29 Mumm, *Stolen Daughters*, 173.

30 Reed, *Glorious Battle*, 204.

31 Kollar, *A Foreign & Wicked Institution*, 221.

32 John Mason Neale, *Ayton Priory: or, The Restored Monastery*, Cambridge (1843).

33 William Gresley, *Bernard Leslie: or, A Tale of the Last Ten Years*, London: James Burns (1842), 209.

34 William Whyte, *Unlocking the Church: The Lost Secrets of Victorian Sacred Space*, Oxford: OUP (2017), 50.

35 Robert Lee Woolf, *Gains And Losses: Novels of Faith and Doubt in Victorian England*, London: John Murray (1977), 112.

36 George Herring, *What was the Oxford Movement?* London: Continuum (2002), 69.

37 Anson, *Call of the Cloister*, 50.

38 Liddon, *Life of Pusey*, ii:271

39 Hill, *Religious Order*, 181.

imagination in 1850 after the restoration of the Roman Catholic hierarchy and Lord John Russell's *Letter to the Bishop of Durham* was slow to dissipate.

Punch picked up the theme in 1850 with *The Convent of the Belgravians* – which in turn echoes Mumm's observation about the social standing of many of the women attracted to the sisterhoods, with its assurance that the Abbess would be "a real Countess, at the least" – and followed it up with *The Monastery of Pimlico*. The author of the latter clearly had the Tractarians in his sights, for it announced that "the Superior of the Monastery will be an eminent clergyman, recommended for the situation by his ingenuity in interpreting the Articles of Religion in a non-natural sense" – a direct allusion to W. G. Ward's infamous defence of Tract 90[40] – and by placing the monastery in Pimlico the piece tied in neatly with William Bennett's advanced and well-known Ritualism at St Barnabas's, where there were "ritual riots" in the same year. It concluded that the members of the community would ride about on mules, and that therefore "as many donkeys will be kept in the monastery as there are Friars in it".[41]

Away from clever puns, in a very serious way the idea of men's communities inevitably offended against the received natural order of marriage and procreation. They therefore opened up in the popular imagination whole new possibilities for vice and moral turpitude. That Newman's congregation at Littlemore and F. W. Faber's community at Elton had followed their founders into the Roman Catholic Church was bad enough, but most of the communities founded in the 1860s – those contemporaneous with the foundation of the SSJE – were all to a greater or lesser extent influenced by Ritualistic ideals.

Ritualism itself was objectionable to many, and much of the prejudice against the growing emergence of post-Tractarianism from the 1850s onwards stemmed from the view of many that it encouraged its neophytes towards

[...] an element of foppery – even in dress and manner; a fastidious, maundering, die-away effeminacy, which is mistaken for purity and refinement; and I confess myself unable to cope with it, so alluring is it to the minds of an effeminate and luxurious aristocracy; neither educated in all that should teach them to distinguish between bad and good taste, healthy and unhealthy philosophy or devotion.[42]

So wrote Charles Kingsley, Newman's great opponent, with what Geoffrey Best described as his "passionate subscription to the protestant belief that the sacerdotal system was unmanly, unEnglish, and unnatural". At the same time, Ritualism was also inextricably associated with another *bête noire*, and Best observed that "the most unnatural point of this extensive unnaturalness was undoubtedly its insistence on celibacy".

To some extent, concerns about a celibate priesthood in the Church of England were a peculiarly Victorian obsession; and Donald Allchin emphasised that devotional celibacy had not been without its champions among the

---

40 See Wilfrid Ward, *W. G. Ward and the Oxford Movement*, London: Macmillan & Co. (1889).

41 *Punch*, 19:163; 189.

42 Francis Kingsley (ed), *Charles Kingsley: His Letters and Memories of his Life*, London: Kegan Paul (1881), i:201.

Caroline Divines.[43] It must also surely be significant that after the death of Matthew Parker in 1575 it was not until 1691 – after the deposition of the non-juring William Sancroft in 1690 – that a married man, John Tillotson, was named Archbishop of Canterbury.

To Kingsley and those of his party, however, celibacy in the nineteenth-century Church of England risked leading men from normal sexual expression within marriage to all sorts of depraved acts. "The Protestant was led to suspect the sexual morals of the priesthood," Best concluded. "Of course priests would sleep with their housekeepers!"[44] Extra-marital heterosexual liaisons, however, were the least of some people's concerns.

Samuel Butler's semi-autobiographical *Ernest Pontifex, or The Way of All Flesh* appeared posthumously between 1873 and 1884. Butler had declined to be ordained because he found himself uncertain of his faith: Ernest Pontifex is a clergyman whose belief is not much more certain, and who careers from disaster to disaster. On his way, however, he meets Pryer, the senior curate of the parish where he is serving his title. Pryer is an Old Etonian: young, tall, good-looking, and urbane; and not long down from Oxford. He is also a Ritualist, and a homosexual.[45]

In his work on nineteenth-century homosexuality, *Strangers*, Graham Robb notes that although holy orders could seem an attractive option, "men who took refuge in the Church, or who mistook their lack of sexual interest in women for a vocation, often found that they had simply turned themselves into hypocrites".[46] Pryer's friendship group is made up of "young clergymen […] the highest of the high church school", and as he gets to know them, Ernest – who himself has wrestled with same-sex yearnings in the past – is horrified to find that

> certain thoughts which he had warred against as fatal to his soul, and which he had imagined he should lose once for all on ordination, were still as troublesome to him as they had been; he saw also plainly enough that the young gentlemen who formed the circle of Mr. Pryer's friends were in much the same unhappy predicament as himself.

Ernest resolves that the only answer is to marry immediately. But "he did not know any woman, in fact, whom he would not rather die than marry".[47]

Similar suspicions were long-lived, and other commentators were deeply insinuating. When John Kensit reported back to his Protestant Truth Society what he had witnessed at St Cuthbert's, Philbeach Gardens, on Good Friday 1898, he described a "priest in petticoats", and the congregation as "very poor

---

43 Allchin, *Silent Rebellion*, 16ff.

44 Geoffrey Best, "Popular Protestantism in Victorian England", in Robert Robson (ed), *Ideas and Institutions of Victorian Britain: Essays in Honour of George Kitson Clark*, London: Bell (1967), 124ff.

45 Yates, *Anglican Ritualism*, 154.

46 Graham Robb, *Strangers: Homosexual Love in the Nineteenth Century*, London: Picador (2003), 238.

47 Samuel Butler, *Ernest Pontifex, or The Way of All Flesh*, London: Methuen & Co. (1965), 202.

specimens of men [...] a peculiar sort of people, very peculiar indeed".[48] In short, they were queer – in both its older and newer senses.

David Hilliard used Geoffrey Best's phrase in the title of his seminal article of 1982 on sexual identity and religious expression, *UnEnglish and Unmanly: Anglo-Catholicism and Homosexuality*. He, too, noted that for many of their contemporaries the most distasteful element of the religious thought that had grown out of the movement of the 1830s – a distaste fuelled by the injudicious publication of Froude's *Remains* in 1838 – was the emphasis that Newman and many of his circle had placed on celibacy and "the consequent development of religious brotherhoods". This in its essence was offensive to those, Kingsley included, whose view of Christian vocation included the necessity of procreation within marriage.

Although he noted that it was inherently possible that "young men who were secretly troubled by homosexual feelings that they could not publicly acknowledge may have been attracted by the prospect of devoting themselves to a life of celibacy, in the company of like-minded male friends, as a religiously-sanctioned alternative to marriage", Hilliard was at pains to point out that it was not a universal motivation. In fact, he made a point of exempting the SSJE, arguing that as it "maintained a close connection with the intellectual life of the universities and followed a strictly disciplined way of life", it could hardly be accused of such motives. He also included Charles Gore's later Community of the Resurrection in the same category.

The opprobrium meted out to some other communities, however, was not always entirely unjustified. Hilliard noted "a succession of short-lived, often clandestine, brotherhoods and guilds whose members delighted in religious ceremonial and the picturesque neo-Gothic externals of monastic life",[49] and mentioned two in particular that caused consternation in the 1860s. The first was that of Joseph Leycester Lyne, better known by his (self-imposed) name in religion: Father Ignatius.

Sabine Baring-Gould later recalled that Lyne was "impulsive, self-willed, and lacking in judgment"; and that although he had "a beautiful face, with a magnificent voice and flowing oratory, he had no gifts as an organizer, and he committed extraordinary acts of folly".[50] Lyne gathered like-minded men around him at Claydon, near Ipswich, in the early 1860s, and founded a small Benedictine-styled community at Elm Hill, Norwich, in 1863. He later moved it to Llanthony, near Abergavenny, where it folded not long after his death in 1908.

Lyne's accomplishments have been analysed by several writers,[51] but he was no stranger to the local press, either. When he and one of his brethren assist-

---

48 The Protestant Alliance, *Verbatim Report of Speeches* [...] *May 3rd 1898*, London: R. J. Haynes (1898), 23.

49 David Hilliard, UnEnglish and Unmanly: Anglo-Catholicism and Homosexuality, *Victorian Studies*, vol. 25, no.2 (Winter 1982), 185ff. Anson enumerates them in the first chapter of *Call of the Cloister*.

50 S. Baring-Gould, *The Church Revival: Thoughts Thereon and Reminiscences*, London: Methuen & Co. (1914), 356.

51 See Donald Attwater, *Father Ignatius of Llanthony: A Victorian*, London: Cassell & Co. (1931); Arthur Calder-Marshall, *The Enthusiast: An Enquiry into the Life, Beliefs and Character of the Rev. Joseph Leycester Lyne alias Fr. Ignatius, O.S.B.*, London: Faber & Faber (1962); and

ed the Rector of Claydon, George Drury, at Easter in 1863, the *Norfolk News* described them as "a couple of mysterious individuals known in the village as Monks, one being distinguished by the name of Father Ignatius".[52] When he gave a lecture on religious orders, alongside Neale, in November that year, the same paper mused that

[m]ost folk laugh at these eccentricities. But we are not sure that contempt is the precise and only thing they are entitled to. We are more inclined to look at these movements as we should at a brood of young vipers warming on our hearthrug.[53]

Meanwhile, when Lyne and his brethren moved to Norwich, the *News* sent a correspondent round to a service. The account of the community's liturgy in early 1864 has a distinct air of veracity about it, although the reporter was clearly nonplussed by what he saw.[54] The same happened in Holy Week, where the brethren seem to have kept the Triduum with some solemnity.[55] However, in September 1864 Lyne's name was dragged through the press when the *Norfolk News* printed a love-letter written by one of the brethren, Augustine, to a boy who sang in the monastery choir. Public opinion, naturally, was horrified. "We tell everybody", fumed the *Norfolk News*, "that the herding together of men in one building [...] and of boys likewise, with soft, sensitive temperaments, cannot fail to produce abominations."[56] However, it did print Lyne's protest in full, in which he presented the facts of the case as he saw them, accepted the scandalous nature of the letter, and sought to reassure the readership.[57] In early 1868 a former member of the community, James Barrett Hughes would appear at a Protestant meeting in London, and "scandalize the respectable"[58] with tales of what he claimed had gone on at Elm Hill.[59]

The second community mentioned by Hilliard was the Order of St Augustine, founded by George Nugée in 1867. John Shelton Reed called Nugée "Lyne's co-worker in the monastic revival [...] less quixotic, but almost as odd";[60] but, to give him his due, he used his considerable personal wealth to establish a sisterhood to run the Diocesan Penitentiary at Highgate, of which he was Warden; the Sisterhood of St Mary at St Matthew's, Finsbury; and St Paul's Mission College, a community to work among the poor in the slums of Soho. So impressive was his work that Nugée received the express approval of

Peter Anson, *Building up the Waste Places: the Revival of Monastic Life on Medieval Lines in the Post-Reformation Church of England*, London: Faith Press (1973). Baroness de Bertouch's 1904 work, *The Life of Father Ignatius, O.S.B.: The Monk of Llanthony* (London, Methuen & Co.) is hagiographical, with many details supplied by Lyne himself. For a full assessment of Lyne's life and work see Hugh Allen, *New Llanthony Abbey: Fr Ignatius' Monastery at Capel-y-ffin*, Peterscourt Press (2016).
52 "Popery in the Church of England", *Norfolk News*, 18 April 1863.
53 "A Mischievous Brood in the Bosom of the Church", *Norfolk News*, 14 Nov 1863.
54 "Monks and a Monastery in Norwich", *Norfolk News*, 13 Feb 1864.
55 "The Monks during Easter [sic] Week", *Norfolk News*, 2 April 1864.
56 "Ignatius and his Singing Boys", *Norfolk News*, 17 Sept 1864.
57 "Father Ignatius", *Norfolk News*, 24 Sept 1864.
58 Hilliard, *UnEnglish and Unmanly*, 193.
59 "Extraordinary Disclosures", *Norfolk News*, 25 Jan 1868.
60 Reed, *Glorious Battle*, 3.

Archibald Campbell Tait, the vehemently anti-Ritualist Bishop of London. The Brotherhood of the Holy Trinity also approved, and elected Nugée to membership on 12 March 1858.[61]

By 1872 Nugée had set up St Austin's Priory – Hugh Allen considers them to have been "part-time Augustinians"[62] – at Walworth in south London, where Hilliard noted "a round of extremely elaborate services".[63] He had done so because of his desire to found a brotherhood; but he was no ascetic, and wanted the community to suit "his passion for the dramatic side of religion".[64] There he surrounded himself with other "rich men who enjoyed a comfortable life",[65] and Anson observed that "no greater contrast could be found to the world in which Fr Benson established his Society of St John the Evangelist". But at Wymering in Hampshire – while living in some style at the Manor House – Nugée restored the church along Ritualist lines, installed his Sisters of St Mary in the vicarage, and built schools and an orphanage to provide for local poor children.[66]

Lyne and Nugée represent just two examples of founders of religious communities – practitioners of "virtuoso religion" – whose motives were easily misrepresented, and Chadwick's judgment on sisterhoods, that "the best of the early superiors were the unromantic", is pertinent when dealing with the later men's communities.[67] The challenge of Benson's fledgling SSJE was to avoid accusations of scandal and worldliness,[68] and to present itself as a serious endeavour for the glory of God and the sanctification of the flesh.

It is important to separate the theology and ecclesiology of Benson and his first followers from the Ritualism of other adherents of the movement whose practices were those that were able to be fanned into infamy, while retaining the sense that, as John Shelton Reed observed, "[...] side by side with the movement's authentic saints walked some of the most colourful eccentrics of the age, and the story is complicated by the fact that some of the eccentrics had their saintly qualities, and some of the saints their eccentricities."[69]

WHITHER AUTHORITY?

Michael Hill argues that the quest for the idea of the legitimation for religious orders in the Church of England involved a series of appeals to the past,[70] a theme previously taken up by Owen Chadwick.

---

61 BHT Minute Book 2, 71, PH.
62 Allen, *New Llanthony Abbey*, 68.
63 Hilliard, *UnEnglish and Unmanly*, 193.
64 Anson, *Call of the Cloister*, 94.
65 Hilliard, *UnEnglish and Unmanly*, 193.
66 Anson, *Call of the Cloister*, 91ff.
67 Chadwick, *Victorian Church*, i:508.
68 The excesses of Aelred Carlyle and his community on Caldey would come a whole generation later. See, *inter alia*, Rene Kollar, "Lord Halifax and Monasticism in the Church of England", *Church History*, Vol. 53, no.2 (June 1984), 218–230.
69 Reed, *Glorious Battle*, 13.
70 Hill, *Religious Order*, 150–67.

[T]hree strands of thought lived incongruously together: devotional, romantic, pastoral. Devotion was content with peace and simplicity, rows of cells
knocked out of stables, hours of retirement which needed filling with modes of
prayer or penitential discipline. Romance yearned to restore ruined arches, and
could hardly imagine a convent except within Gothic windows and castellated
draught. Pastoral care saw urban deserts and believed that only a community
could settle among them if nourished by private oases, pure amid public dust.[71]

An early-Church appeal was influenced by the Oxford Movement's leaders'
engagement with patristic scholarship: no small part of Pusey's enthusiasm
for sisterhoods, for example, was the influence of "the exaltation of virginity"
that he found in the writings of the Church Fathers.[72] Liddon thought that "this
side of their teaching had been lost sight of by that section of Anglican divines
which regarded antiquity not as a guide in faith and morals, but merely as a
storehouse of polemical weapons against the Church of Rome", but that it had
nevertheless not been entirely forgotten by "the nobler minds in the English
Church".[73]

A medieval appeal, meanwhile, was far less influential, and generally
involved only eccentrics and romantics "on the fringe of the movement";[74]
although Anson considered Samuel Fox's *Monks and Monasteries* of 1845 "a
reasonable apologia for the revival of the late medieval monastic system".[75] But
the post-Reformation appeal, as we saw in the previous chapter, was strong.
Hill concludes that it is impossible to find one single source of legitimation for
the early Anglican communities; but notes that a double economy existed in
which their defenders sought on one hand to reassert Reformation principles,
and on the other to reassure "no Popery" opponents.

A factor also noted by Hill was what he calls "the problem of authority".
A religious order can only exist as part of a church, or else it would be little
more than a club for like-minded people: within the Church of England, then,
any community was in some way tied up with historic parish structures –
especially so when the founder of an order was the incumbent of the parish
where the community was based, like William Butler at Wantage and Benson
himself – and in turn it was also bound to have some sort of relationship with
the bishop of the diocese. The response of that bishop could, and did, make or
break any fledgling community within his jurisdiction.

Park Village was founded in London because Charles Blomfield indicated
that he was willing to countenance it; but misunderstanding and recrimin-
ation followed. Pusey adapted the Roman Breviary for the sisters, maintaining
that it was the same source from which the Prayer Book was taken and that
there were no prayers in it that Blomfield could not have used himself; but
Blomfield disapproved. Pusey had sought authority in the general norms of
the Church; but had found himself thwarted by one of its instruments: "if the
norms on which the organization was based were paramount [as for Pusey

---

71 Chadwick, *Victorian Church*, i:505.
72 Brilioth, *Anglican Revival*, 246.
73 Liddon, *Life of Pusey*, iii:2.
74 Hill, *Religious Order*, 154.
75 Anson, *Waste Places*, 26.

they were] then it was without question legitimate to appeal directly to them rather than necessarily making use of hierarchical channels of authority".[76]

It is impossible to overstate the importance of the goodwill of a diocesan bishop for the flourishing of the early communities. Lyne's contention that his monastery was not under episcopal authority, because many medieval monasteries had been exempt from episcopal jurisdiction, was fatuous. In any case, the exemptions had been granted by bishops exercising the very jurisdiction that Lyne sought to reject; and further to that, as his biographer Donald Attwater pointed out, if Lyne wished to appeal to primitive practice – which he did – then he would have to accept that the Council of Chalcedon forbade the establishment of monasteries without the permission of the local bishop – which he did not.[77] Furthermore, Lyne compounded his difficulties through his own intransigence. After a series of disturbances at Claydon – recounted with *éclat* by Anson – the exasperated Bishop of Norwich, John Pelham, summoned Lyne to his palace and "begged him to give up his eccentricities and absurd dress".[78] When he refused, Pelham inhibited him from preaching in his diocese, although even without a licence Lyne was able to continue his doomed quest to restore medieval monasticism to the Church of England.

Lyne's failure was foretold by many; but perhaps no more clearly than by Samuel Wilberforce, whom he approached for advice about the revival of monastic life in mid-1869. Wilberforce was Bishop of Oxford from 1840 until his translation to Winchester in 1870, where he earned the ultimate distinction of being the last bishop of the Church of England to die on horseback. As David Newsome demonstrated, he was a broad-minded man who "favoured no single party and championed no party cause", and was not afraid of supporting zealous innovations.[79] He had no axe to grind with Thomas Chamberlain: as early as 1846 Wilberforce took the view that, relating to St Thomas the Martyr, Oxford, he would give no decision unless he was specifically asked to make one, as he was "very reluctant to trench upon the large liberty of judgement in all things doubtful conceded by the English Church to her Presbyters".[80]

Wilberforce was also broadly sympathetic to the idea of individuals living in community for spiritual ends, and it is no coincidence that several early communities were founded in the diocese of Oxford.[81] His approval, however, was given on a case-by-case basis: he did not approve of unwarranted excesses, and he certainly did not approve of Lyne. When Lyne wrote to him plaintively in June 1865,[82] Wilberforce replied that he thought he had many gifts, but that he was wasting them by resolutely clinging to a form of appearance that was perfectly ludicrous.

---

76 Hill, *Religious Order*, 178; 192ff.
77 Attwater, *Father Ignatius*, 72.
78 Anson, *Waste Places*, 53.
79 David Newsome, *The Parting of Friends*, London: John Murray (1966), 332.
80 *The Letter-Books of Samuel Wilberforce 1843–68*, Oxfordshire Record Society no.57 (1969), 64.
81 Anson, *Call of the Cloister*, 591ff.
82 Lyne, 2 June 1865, Bodleian, MSS Wilberforce, c.15/42–43.

Your adoption of a dress never suited to English habits [the pun was almost certainly unintentional] – and now pre-eminently unsuitable – is a sacrifice of the kernel to the shell such as I have never seen equalled [...] In adopting this startling exterior you are acting in direct opposition to the principle on which the Order you have assumed did act. For they took the dress to help the work. You mar the work to have the dress. In this merely outward thing I am bound to say that I see the key to all your real hindrances. You are sacrificing everywhere the great reality for which you have sacrificed to a puerile imitation of that phase of service which it is just as impossible for you to revive in England as it would be for you to resuscitate an Egyptian mummy and set it upon the throne of the Pharaohs.

Wilberforce ended his letter by making it clear that – although he had no time for Lyne's fripperies – he did think "that colleges of clergymen, living and acting under the parochial clergy, might meet many of our spiritual wants", and that "brotherhoods of unordained men not in Holy Orders might be of most excellent use".[83]

As Anson observed, Wilberforce had a good grasp of the historic Benedictine rule – notwithstanding the fact that in 1851 Lyne had written to him claiming at that point to be a Passionist[84] – and it is highly significant that shortly after Wilberforce wrote to Lyne dismissing his romanticised ideas of monasticism, he also became engaged in a correspondence with Benson.[85] That correspondence would lead, relatively swiftly, to the establishment of the stable religious life for men in the Church of England.

---

83 Anson, *Waste Places*, 66; Bodleian, MSS Wilberforce.c15/44–49; A. R. Ashwell & R. G. Wilberforce, *Life of the Right Reverend Samuel Wilberforce*, London: John Murray (1883), 166.
84 Lyne, 9 May 1851, Bodleian, MSS Wilberforce, c.10/133–4.
85 Anson, *Call of the Cloister*, 59.

3

HOPES DASHED AND RESTORED

Specified prayers at specified hours.
—Frederick Meyrick[1]

T he presence of women's communities in and around Oxford meant that Richard Meux Benson and his contemporaries were exposed to some idea of what the restored religious life looked like; or at least what it looked like for lay communities with experienced clergymen as directors. In early 1855, John Mason Neale asked Benson's advice on the Rule for his putative Sisterhood of St Margaret at Rotherfield.[2] Benson looked over Neale's proposals and declared them "very good", before suggesting a few "trifling alterations"; but he tempered his advice with the caveat that he was writing "with little experience of the matter".[3] This would change, of course, and quickly. Donald Allchin considered that Benson's later approach to the religious life was "stronger and deeper, and yet more practical and less romantic than Neale's".[4]

In 1860 the idea of groups of clergymen withdrawing from the world needed to be tested, and at about the same time as when Neale was forming his sisterhood, Benson – with others, including Thomas Thellusson Carter of Clewer[5] – began organising clergy retreats. William Butler of Wantage had been sure of their necessity for years, and advocated clergy living in seclusion under community rule for weeks at a time.[6] When in 1860 Richard Hooper published a pamphlet on the subject, Benson wrote immediately to say that he was "greatly interested and pleased" to have seen it, as it was a subject in which he took "a very lively interest".

[S]everal of us for some years past have been in the habit of holding annual Retreats. The Bishop of Oxford [Wilberforce] allowed us the use of Cuddesdon College on one occasion, besides, as you probably have heard, suggesting that there should be such a meeting, and himself being present at it [...] The difficulty is to get men together for a sufficient time.

---

1 Meyrick, *Memories*, 175.
2 See Michael Chandler, *The Life and Work of John Mason Neale*, Gracewing (1995).
3 Benson, 1 Feb 1855, Lambeth Palace Library: MS 4778 ff. 77–8.
4 Allchin, *Silent Rebellion*, 197.
5 Reed, *Glorious Battle*, 99.
6 Allchin, *Silent Rebellion*, 185.

He invited Hooper to join one of the forthcoming retreats, sent him a paper written on the subject by Carter, and apologised for "my boldness in thus addressing you". What is clear is that he and others were in the habit of withdrawing from their work to spend time in community; that this venture had his bishop's support;[7] and that Benson hoped that such ventures might be replicated by others, because he felt that small groups were better than large ones.[8]

To this appreciation of periods of withdrawal was added Benson's strong personal sense of missionary zeal for the conversion of the heathen, as demonstrated by his correspondence with Robert Reynolds Winter.[9] When Benson was promoting world-wide prayer associations as part of the work of the Brotherhood, Winter wrote from Delhi that the idea of prayer associations at home and in the colonies was "certainly most truly Evangelical, in the best sense of the word".[10] He was also enthusiastic about the clergy retreats, despite the impracticability of the idea in India because of the small number of clergy spread over a wide area. Winter did, however, enjoy reading the accounts of the retreats together with his wife, who was also heavily involved in the mission's work;[11] and was always glad to receive news of the Brotherhood and its members.[12] He harked back to earliest days of the Oxford Movement when he remarked that "it does appear of the most vital importance that the Clergy should continually stir up the Spiritual life within them, if they would have any influence over their people". He added that "as you say, this wants something more than multiplied offices, or a minute attention to Ritualism, however important both may be in their way".[13]

That Benson had offered himself for work in India is generally well known; and Winter was almost certainly the unnamed friend of Woodgate's book who had "already preceded him to India and was waiting for him there".[14] In 1859, not long after his mother's death, Benson had opened the new "Iron Church" on Stockmore Street; and he had also moved out of the cottage he had occupied at Cowley to live near the new centre of his growing parish. He intended to stay only briefly, and in August 1859 asked Henry Bailey, Warden of St Augustine's Mission College at Canterbury if he might join the Missionary Union – to which he had felt for a long time united "in all but name".

Benson had intended to spend a year in Calcutta, to gain experience of the local conditions, before gathering "some men to join me in a devotional college in the N. W. Provinces, living upon our own funds, as much in poverty as possible, and as much orientally in every habit and mode of life as possible". His ideal of the community prefigured almost exactly the Society of St John the Evangelist.

---

7 Wilberforce himself took advice on the subject of retreats from Henry Edward Manning, his brother-in-law, in 1850. Bodleian, MSS Wilberforce, c.10/37.

8 Benson to Richard Hooper, 4 Sept 1860 (copy), SSJE/6/1/2/7/1.

9 See *The Story of the Delhi Mission*, London: SPG (1908), 16ff.

10 Winter, 2 Oct 1860, SSJE/6/1/2/11/2/1.

11 Winter, 7 Dec 1861 or 1862, SSJE/6/1/2/11/2/24.

12 Wintern, 7 Oct 1864, SSJE/6/1/2/11/2/27.

13 Winter, 2 Oct 1860, SSJE/6/1/2/11/2/1.

14 Woodgate, *Benson*, 51.

If our numbers allow, there would always be a certain number resident, carrying out the offices of the Home, and two and two we should go out on missionary journeys into the country.

I should like to see, then, a body of men gathered together, whose life of what the world would call self-denial and poverty should be cheered with a greater joy than the world can give, by the sympathy of kindred hearts and the spiritual strength of abundant means of grace.[15]

Benson seems to have intended not only to work on an Indian mission, but to use his funds to establish and endow a missionary college: Peter Anson hinted at the foundation; but not the source of the funds.[16] In this he was guided by Winter, who warned Benson to "please remember that you are near getting on to a time of life when it is not always quite safe to come out here to <u>live</u> here", and particularly urged him to avoid arriving in Calcutta during the rainy season.[17] What was really needed, he thought, was a theological college somewhere in upper India: "something on the plan of Bishop's College [Calcutta], only conducted more after the Spirit of Cuddesdon".[18]

There are many Missionary Schools which educate the boys to a certain point, and there necessarily totally stop. Through these schools and by other means there is now a large number of Christian young men drifting about the country, with a great chance of both doctrinally and morally forgetting their Christianity. In addition to this, there is no place <u>whatever</u> of education for native Clergy or Catechists.

"Such a College as this", he continued, "would supplement the work of all the other Missions in Northern India, and might have a wonderful effect in raising the tone of the whole Native Church". There would also be a devotional effect – and here we see Benson's original idea fleshed out in Winter's proposal – which was much "as you intended your Mission College to be".

With three or four Daily Services; and Celebrations [of the Eucharist] at the least weekly and all Festivals. I should wish it to be conducted with considerable dignity of Architecture, and Music, as in our Best Churches at home. We should then I hope be fulfilling your object of setting the Christian Church as a positive Reality in the eyes of India, and also be supplying an actually existing want of this Branch of the Church.

What was needed was money, of course, and plenty of it. "We should want very much for the Endowment", Winter went on, "for I think there should not be less than at least 4 European Priests [...] Would you be willing to devote

---

15 Benson, 8 Aug 1859, *Letters of Richard Meux Benson*, 227; 229.
16 Anson, *Call of the Cloister*, 76.
17 Winter, 2 Oct 1860, SSJE/6/1/2/11/2/2.
18 David Newsome summed up the formation of men at Cuddesdon at the time: "They must study their Bible and the Greek Testament; they must know the great orthodox classics like Hooker, Pearson on the Creed and Wall on Infant Baptism; they must have a good grounding in early Church history, with a sprinkling of Tertullian and St Augustine thrown in; they must receive an informed statement of popish error through Blunt's English Reformation." *Parting of Friends*, 334–5.

to this that money which you had already intended to devote to the Indian Church? And, better than money, yourself too?"[19]

It is worth observing at this point that Benson was not quite as financially well-placed as he might have expected to have been after the death of his parents. He had held a ten per cent share in the Swansea Vale Railway Company – a family interest – and the Benson and Meux estates were each large in their own right; but both his parents died intestate, and it was left to his brothers Starling and Henry to administer their affairs. He had caused the family acute embarrassment in 1857 when he refused to church a woman married in the registry office unless she and her husband were first married in church: he performed the ceremony without banns or licence, as they were already legally married, and soon found himself before the Assizes. He was cleared, but not before the family name had been dragged through the press; and family letters make it clear that his siblings were less than impressed with their youngest brother's carefree use of their father's money to fund what they saw as his "quixotic habits".[20]

A second setback followed. Samuel Wilberforce – who was also a leading member of the SPG[21] – had initially been supportive of his plans to go to India, and had granted Benson two years' absence from the diocese. But in early 1860 – when "his luggage was actually packed" – Wilberforce changed his mind, and asked Benson to stay at his post.[22] Ostensibly this was to oversee the expansion of the parish with the building-over of Cowley Common; but the thought of the end to which he might use Benson in the Diocese of Oxford can hardly have been absent.

Winter continued to hope for Benson's imminent arrival through 1861; but by 1862 seems to have been resigned to the fact that he was not coming. He continued to write – invariably regretting the length of time it had taken him, sending news of his work, and once half-apologising for having got married[23] – about the fertile missionary field in northern India and the challenges still to be met. He even modified his concerns for Benson's age: "The theory that no one can live long here, unless they come out very young, is I think somewhat exploded [...] I do not think that fear need disturb you".[24] But the die was cast, and Wilberforce had made it clear that he wanted Benson to remain at his post. The great plan for a college in north India came to nothing; and Benson stayed at Cowley.

He bore these disappointments patiently, and threw himself into parish work. He preached a series of sermons for Thomas Chamberlain at St Thomas the Martyr, Oxford, in Lent 1860, and they give some idea of how he reconciled himself to the change of plans. Woodgate noted in those sermons "here and there little evidences of the struggle through which he had passed",[25] and

19 Winter, 15 Dec 1860, SSJE/6/1/2/11/2/5.
20 Bayliffe & Harding, *Starling Benson*, 185; 253;135; 255.
21 R. K. Pugh, *The Episcopate of Samuel Wilberforce, Bishop of Oxford*, Bodleian Library, MS.D.Phil.d.1912.
22 Woodgate, *Benson*, 51ff.
23 Winter, 2 Feb 1863, SSJE/6/1/2/11/2/19.
24 Winter, 24 August 1862, SSJE/6/1/2/11/2/13.
25 Woodgate, *Benson*, 53.

emphasised particularly his words in *The Sacrifice of Praise*: "if you once realise the sacrifice of praise due to God as a privilege, you will not think that He asks you to give up much, but you will wonder at yourself that you do not give up more". He went on to develop the themes of sacrifice as an act of thanksgiving, prayer, and propitiation.[26]

MASTER OF THE BROTHERHOOD

Benson's preaching was stirring, and his writings were in demand. As the years progressed he had become well known in the wider Church of England as a preacher and a teacher on prayer. In addition to the poor woman noted by Woodgate who said of him "that gentleman just opens heaven to me and I can look right in", he was well-regarded and often invited to preach in the capital.[27] In Lent 1862 he began running missions in individual parishes: his first mission at Bedminster set the tone for those that followed, with formal worship and preaching to the well-to-do in the morning, and preaching and Bible study for the poor in the evening; and in 1863 he published a manual of prayer, having taken advice from Butler.[28] He had not, however, abandoned his thoughts of the religious life since the confounding of his plans to go to India; and he became increasingly active in the work of the Brotherhood of the Holy Trinity, which would in itself become deeply influential in later developments.

At about the same time the Brotherhood formalised its procedures, and continued to take an interest in foreign missions while keeping up its rounds of prayer and corporate reception of Holy Communion – when all the members were expected to make their communion on a specified day. It particularly distanced itself from ritual excesses, going as far as to threaten with expulsion any member who embarrassed the Brotherhood in that regard.[29] In June 1863 the brethren were forbidden from "attendance at the services of any religious body (in this Country) not in Communion with the Church of England, or any congregational devotions not consistent with its doctrine or discipline", and at the same meeting procedures were discussed for the expulsion of brethren, should it ever be deemed necessary.

By the mid-1860s the Brotherhood of the Holy Trinity was no longer the small devotional society that it had been ten years earlier. Its roll notes that many of its early members died as the decade progressed; but a General Chapter on 25 May 1864 saw 51 brethren – clerical and lay – gather for General Chapter in the Hall of St Edmund Hall. The principal purpose of the meeting was to elect as Master of the Brotherhood a successor to James Elwin Millard. Initially Henry Parry Liddon was elected; but he was absent and, as his consent had not been sought beforehand, it was felt that the election could not stand. The brethren therefore voted again, and their choice was Benson, who, "after much pressure

---

26 R. M. Benson, *Redemption: Some of the Aspects of the Work of Christ*, London: J. T. Hayes (1861).

27 Woodgate, *Benson*, 54.

28 Ibid, 57.

29 BHT Minute Book 6, 15, PH.

from all present, consented to the Election, and was forthwith Invested by the late Master".[30]

The disenchanted Frederick Meyrick seems to have stopped attending meetings in the 1860s, and he eventually resigned from the BHT in 1869.[31] He had been one of the original three members – with Liddon and Millard – of the newly-constituted society in 1852, but had become dissatisfied at its new direction. He complained that

> [i]nstead of engaging to rise early, they had bound themselves to a definite hour, such as half-past six; instead of prayer, they had to say specified prayers at specified hours; instead of moderation in food, they were to drink only one glass of wine and have so many helpings at meals eating nothing at other times.[32]

Perhaps we should not be surprised that Meyrick – who later came to be regarded as "an ardent Evangelical"[33] – recalled that "the chief mover in this direction was R. M. Benson, afterwards of Cowley."[34]

Benson's tenure as Master was not uneventful. Soon after his election he was asked about the character of the obligation of the Brotherhood's rules, to which his reply was clear.

> They were not strict Rules, but Rules strictly to be aimed at – plainly not to be forgotten. The phrase was used to draw a limit between absolute Rules, which might be a snare, and if broken, must be confessed as a Sin, and on the other hand mere lax rules, which might be looked on as only suggestions. The Rules were to be kept prominently before the mind, and resolutely aimed at as far as possibly.

He also pointed out that the rule that suggested brethren "avoid going to Theatres" was not a blanket ban, and that it was "conceivable that some higher duty as for instance respect for a parent or some other superior might make attendance almost necessary".[35]

In June 1865 Benson suggested that the Branch Brotherhoods be made "entirely subject to the approval of the Master of the B.H.T. who may require them to hold chapters at such times as he may deem convenient and if he see reasonable cause may appoint a new Master of the Branch to supersede the one in office",[36] and after his re-election at the General Chapter that year he presided over a discussion about the Society's constitution, where he "thoroughly approved of the idea of a Committee and proposed that it be appointed to consider the question of Branch Brotherhoods and the Constitution". His proposal was carried unanimously, but others were not: he withdrew two minor

---

30 BHT Minute Book 7, 122, PH.

31 BHT *Roll of the Brethren*, PH.

32 Meyrick, *Memories*, 175.

33 Geoffrey Rowell, Kenneth Stevenson, Rowan Williams (eds), *Love's Redeeming Work: The Anglican Quest for Holiness*, Oxford: OUP (2001), 458.

34 Meyrick, *Memories*, 175.

35 BHT Minute Book 7, 181–2, PH.

36 BHT Minute Book 8, 33, PH.

suggestions relating to the reprinting of the Brotherhood's manual because "he found they did not command general adhesion" despite his protests that they "were not intended as alterations, but literally as explanations of our present practice".[37] One of his withdrawn proposals suggests that he was in favour of the compulsory saying of the Penitential Psalms on Fridays and Fast Days, and the Gradual Psalms on Wednesdays. (That appears to have been the practice of most of the brethren for some time, but they were only compelled to say the Penitential Psalms on Fridays in Lent.) The other was an explanation of the phrase "to be aimed at", in relation to the Rules.

An argument followed about which, if any, of the Brotherhood's devotional practices were obligatory. Benson felt that for the moment it was better "left to the conscience of individual brethren" as to their observance of the customs of the society. This was felt to be unsatisfactory by many, but Benson pointed out that the society had existed for twenty-one years, and that in all that time there had been different opinions among the brethren:

> With any other code of Rules, and if we existed for 100 years, there would still be the same difference. Scattered as we are, we cannot make fundamental changes without much correspondence. The Rules were drawn up for us by a Priest very experienced in the Religious Life, with much care, and the subject must be approached by us with the very greatest caution. We must have the caution of time, or else we shall be exposed to a perpetual want of stability.

He felt so strongly on the importance of giving the matter time that he said he would resign if the matter was raised before the next General Chapter, when the Committee – made up of all the former Masters – would make its report.[38]

By the mid-1860s the Brotherhood of the Holy Trinity was taking an active and growing interest in the life of the Church of England far beyond Oxford. Many of its clergy members were also, like Benson himself, members of the Society of the Holy Cross and of the English Church Union: all brethren were urged to join the latter in 1865.[39]

With a membership active in church affairs and spread – if only thinly – across the world, the use of regular prayers at regular times, the title "Brother", the growing desire of a number of members that the rules should become more binding upon the brethren, and the reintroduction of a Plainsong Society – whose value Benson, who could play the organ to some degree,[40] felt "could hardly be over-estimated"[41] – it is impossible not to see in the development of the Brotherhood of the Holy Trinity a move towards the "quasi-monastic" identity that Pusey had overemphasised in 1852 and that the leaders of the society had at that point rejected. John Kent contended in 1978 that the Society of St John the Evangelist grew out of the Society of the Holy Cross;[42] and to some extent, given the overlap of association, that is true – although it became the practice that any member of the SSC who was later professed in the SSJE

---

37 BHT Minute Book 8, 52; 57, PH.
38 BHT Minute Book 8, 5; 73; 81, PH.
39 BHT Minute Book 7, 282, PH.
40 Woodgate, *Benson*, 20; 22.
41 BHT Minute Book 7, 222, PH.
42 John Kent, *Holding the Fort*, London: Epworth Press (1978), 256.

resigned from the former to avoid the clash of rule.[43] There was certainly a symbiotic element to Benson's later dealings with Charles Fuge Lowder; but it was in the ranks of the Brotherhood of the Holy Trinity that both men cut their teeth.

COMMUNITIES OF MEN

The 1862 Church Congress discussed women's communities, as did the Convocations of the Church of England: "the question of possible communities for men inevitably arose, and in the next few years was widely canvassed".[44] It was well known that Pusey was in favour, and in 1863 the elderly Keble added his support. On 22 July, he preached to the community at Wantage, praising the distinctive vocation of the sisters there. The sermon was published as *Women Labouring in the Lord*, by which time Keble had included the following paragraph.

> And symptoms, I trust [of power given to women in community, to be used for good] are not altogether wanting, of something like the same holy zeal in our young Men also. Why should it not be so? Why may we not hope that even within this generation Christian Brotherhoods as well as Sisterhoods of Mercy may be found taking their places in the work of Christ among us? seeing that there is no more palpable fact in all Church history, than that Almighty God has ever been pleased to make use of such communities – devoted men severing themselves more or less from the ordinary ties and affections of earth – when His time was come for converting, not here and there one, but whole nations, to the obedience of His Son.[45]

Sidney Ollard oversimplified the effect of Keble's sermon on Benson in his *Short History of the Oxford Movement*;[46] and Woodgate herself over-romanticised the story when she wrote that it was "extremely likely that Benson heard those words",[47] because Keble did not use them in the pulpit. But he would certainly have read them later, and can hardly have failed to have been encouraged. He had written in his book *The Wisdom of the Son of David* in 1860 that "the Christian can never walk safely alone" and that "in isolated action there is apt to be pride";[48] but now he was surrounded and supported by men who shared to a greater or lesser extent his vision of the potential for living out a stable religious life within the Church of England – and two of them, Pusey and Keble, were giants in the land.

In 1864 Keble's gauntlet was taken up by Simeon Wilberforce O'Neill, in a three-article series published in *The Ecclesiastic*. O'Neill – who was no relation

---

43 cf SSJE/2/5/310ff.

44 Allchin, *Silent Rebellion*, 184.

45 John Keble, *Women Labouring in the Lord*, Oxford & London: John Henry & James Parker (1863).

46 S. L. Ollard, *A Short History of the Oxford Movement*, London: A. R. Mowbray & Co. (1932), 250.

47 Woodgate, *Benson*, 58.

48 R. M. Benson, *The Wisdom of the Son of David*, London: Bell and Daldy (1860).

to Samuel Wilberforce, but had been named for the Clapham Sect Evangelicals Charles Simeon, who was a friend of his father, and William Wilberforce[49] – had been a mathematics beak at Eton; but by then was Butler's curate at Wantage, and had previously served under Carter at Clewer. He would certainly have known Benson personally, and Woodgate's suggestion that his articles were written with Benson's knowledge and guidance is entirely plausible.[50]

The Ecclesiastic was edited by Chamberlain. He directed his own community of women at St Thomas the Martyr, and by the 1860s was well-established as an advanced Ritualist.[51] O'Neill's articles, which he concluded in 1865, were *An Inquiry after the Secondary Causes of Success in Christian Missions.* The primary cause, naturally, was the Holy Spirit; but the question that O'Neill sought to answer was "What is the system which is most effective in converting heathens to Christianity?" He briefly traced the story of conversions from the work of St Paul and his contemporaries, moving through the saints who brought Christianity to the British Isles, and on to those who converted swathes of pagan Europe; and he concluded that there was a distinct theme that attached itself to their work.

> These narratives seem to lead us irresistibly to the conclusion that monastic bodies have always been the most successful agents in the conversion of heathen nations. The missionaries have both had their training in the monasteries before entering upon their work, and also maintained the outward character of their life when engaged in that work. The missions have been commenced with more or less of outward show, ceremonial and demonstration of power, but whether the exterior life of the missionaries has been grand and imposing, or poor and mean, their interior life has ever been self-denying, regular, and holy.[52]

O'Neill's zeal for converting the heathen had its background in the situation in India, as did Benson's. In 1863 *The Ecclesiastic* had carried a review-article that attacked Henry Venn's book of 1862 on St Francis Xavier:

> [O]n the general subject of missions it contains no confession of our failures; and scarcely an acknowledgment of the successes of the Roman Church [...] Mr Venn, like many other pious and charitable men, seems to labour under the idea that while dissent is an evil, there can be such a thing as an orthodox dissenting body. Such a body cannot exist without a formal denial of more than one article of the Apostles' Creed; and for our part, we cannot help seeing in the confederation of the Church with Lutheran and other missioners in India not only an act of most criminal inconsistency and something worse, but a mode of procedure from which nothing but the shameful and disastrous consequences we have been compelled to witness, could have been fairly anticipated.[53]

The "disastrous consequences" referred to the Indian Mutiny of 1857, during which a number of missionaries and their families had been murdered.

49 Pendleton, *Grafton*, 39.
50 Woodgate, *Benson*, 58.
51 Reed, *Glorious Battle*, 35.
52 "An Inquiry after the Secondary Causes of Success in Christian Missons", *The Ecclesiastic*, London: Joseph Masters (1864), 79–85, 203–217; (1865) 123–31.
53 "S. Francis Xavier", *The Ecclesiastic* (1863), 87.

Although O'Neill did not mention India specifically, it is almost certain – given the context and his later work there – that the article was directed towards India, where Roman Catholic and Lutheran missions were stealing a march on the duty of the Established Church despite the best efforts of the SPG.

As O'Neill was turning his thoughts to India, a different young priest was making his way to Oxford from Boston; and the arrival of the American Charles Grafton in Oxford in the spring of 1865 gave the project a new impetus. Grafton had long harboured a desire to enter the religious life; but there were no viable options in the United States and so he had decided to travel to England to see if he might test his vocation there. He "planned to spend some time in England talking with those interested in the religious life".[54] This included Pusey, Carter, and Neale; but he does not seem to have been aware of Benson until Pusey sent him along to Benson's house on Henley Terrace.[55] As it happened, Grafton had already visited the Iron Church unawares, and had concluded that the celebrant of the Eucharist there must be "a very holy man, a man of great humility and sacrifice".[56]

Grafton also visited the "Benedictines" at Norwich; but, like so many others, left unimpressed.[57] This may not have been unconnected with the fact that his visit coincided with Ascension Day 1865, when Lyne – in yet another burst of pious madness – decided to have a noisy procession of the Blessed Sacrament through the streets at 4 a.m., at which Grafton was prevailed upon to help carry the canopy over the Host.[58] Later in the morning Lyne processed into mass in cope and mitre and carrying a crozier, before discarding them to take his place at the organ; and before the end of the day a fight had broken out outside the Priory, with one of the "monks" joining in enthusiastically and giving "as good as he got".[59]

Writing home to his friend and mentor Oliver Prescott, who also shared his enthusiasm for the religious life,[60] Grafton was clear that Lyne was not to be emulated.[61] In Benson, however, he saw a way of proceeding that might work; and from Benson's viewpoint his arrival must have seemed providential. "Imagine the effect upon Fr Benson's mind", Charles Wood wrote later, "when a complete stranger to him walked in with 'I have come from America. Where is the man who longs to form a religious community in England? I want to find him'."[62]

Grafton's immediate impression was that there was a significant amount of support for the formal establishment of some kind of religious life for men in the Church of England, a thought that can only have been strengthened by meeting O'Neill. A number of men were now taking seriously the potential for the restoration of the religious life, and they looked to Benson to lead them. All

54 Pendleton, *Grafton*, 21.
55 Now 107 Iffley Road, identified by Br Steven Haws CR.
56 Charles C. Grafton, *Letters & Addresses*, New York: Longmans, Green & Co. (1914), 31.
57 Charles C. Grafton, *A Journey Godward*, London: Mowbray & Co. (1912), 40.
58 Anson, *Waste Places*, 70.
59 Allen, *New Llanthony Abbey*, 62ff.
60 See Jervis S. Zimmerman, *An Embattled Priest: The Life of Oliver Sherman Prescott 1824–1903*, AuthorHouse (2013).
61 Pendleton, *Grafton*, 22.
62 Wood, undated. In Pendleton, *Grafton*, 25.

were serious about faith; all had standing in society; and many of them were personally wealthy. Grafton was a Harvard man, and the scion of a prominent and prosperous Boston family. Wood was an Old Etonian, the nephew of a former Bishop of Chester, the son of a former Chancellor of the Exchequer and heir to his father's baronetcy and estates, and a Groom of the Bedchamber to the Prince of Wales.[63] George Lane Fox had been Captain of Boats at Eton, was a well-known figure at Christ Church, and "the pink of the fashion of London Society",[64] and corresponded excitedly with Wood about O'Neill's articles in the *Ecclesiastic*.[65] Alexander Forbes hoped tentatively that he would also be able to be involved in any revival that might come about; but in the end he felt unable to take an active part because of his fluctuating health and his duty to his diocese.[66]

Pusey, sensing a quickening of the mood with the appearance of Grafton, convened a meeting at All Saints', Margaret Street. The meeting was unanimous that a religious community was feasible as long as it had the right Superior, and Benson's name was mentioned in his absence. Anson considered that "until then he had taken little no direct part in the negotiations for establishing a brotherhood"; but he had certainly been at least passively involved for some time.[67]

Benson instigated a series of meetings in the summer of 1865, at the end of which a definitive plan was formed: Grafton, O'Neill, and Reginald Tuke, curate of St Mary's, Soho – in whose rooms one of the meetings had taken place – would go to live in Benson's house near the Iron Church, and try their vocations under his direction.[68] Grafton wrote excitedly to Prescott that "Mr Benson is one of the greatest masters of the spiritual life in England [...] The religious houses are praying for the work, and it has been determined to begin."[69] O'Neill brought out the final part of his article in *The Ecclesiastic*, and it makes obvious that the new society intended to take missionary work seriously from its inception.

> Seeing, therefore, that the need of religious houses of men is so great for the perfection of our Church and her success in propagating the Gospel, it has been resolved to form a monastic body of clergy and laymen under the spiritual direction of a most able guide. The rule of life will not be too lax to be efficient, nor yet so severe as to be burdensome. Its spirit must be the same as that which of old inspired the rules of so many great orders, but its form must be adapted to the present time. The aim and object of this society will be mission work at home and abroad, but it will be free to undertake any other Christian work not directly missionary which may present itself, provided by doing so its first object be not interfered with. Any person who feels called by God to give himself to this work may have further particulars by applying to the writer of this paper.[70]

---

63 J. G. Lockhart, *Charles Lindley, Viscount Halifax*, London: Geoffrey Bles (1935), i:47ff.

64 *CE* Feb 1915.

65 Woodgate, *Benson*, 60.

66 Strong, *Forbes*, 237.

67 Anson, *Call of the Cloister*, 76.

68 Woodgate, *Benson*, 62.

69 Grafton, 17 July 1865. Grafton, *Letters and Addresses*, 40ff.

70 "An Inquiry", *The Ecclesiastic* (1865), 131.

Winning over Wilberforce

Master of the spiritual life or not, Benson needed to square the plan with his Bishop. Wilberforce had scorned Lyne's extravagances; but what Benson proposed was exactly the sort of venture that the bishop had intimated to Lyne he might be willing to support. The letter he received from Benson, shortly after his own dismissing Lyne, is so apposite that it is likely that Benson – who was in regular contact with Pusey, Butler, and Carter – already knew his mind on the subject.

Cowley

My Dear Lord Bishop,

Some Clergymen propose to come and spend a considerable part of the year at Cowley for the purposes of study and prayer. Will your Lordship kindly sanction their preaching for me from time to time – in an informal way? or will it be necessary that they should have a regular licence as my Curates if they are to do so? They would be very thankful to feel that they were living here with your Lordship's full sanction. Some Laymen will also be here, who will study under me, and help in the Parish. I do not think that it is right to compromise a person in your Lordship's position by asking for a definite sanction to more than this. But I would ask for your Apostolick Blessing and Prayers upon our future intentions, which whether or no they come to any wider result will, I hope, be conducive to our sanctification. I need not say that we shall also be most thankful for any counsel which your Lordship may think well to give.

Our intention is to form ourselves into a Congregation of Priests and Laymen, giving up the world, living by simple rule and devoting ourselves to prayer, study, and mission work. I have been asked to head the movement, and with a full consciousness all the while of my own incapacity for such a position, I can scarcely regard it otherwise than as a call from God which I ought to accept. It does indeed seem to me as bringing with it an answer to the prayers of very many years which I had never contemplated.

I have laid down as a fundamental principle of our common action that we shall not only be loyal to the Church of England, but also careful to act in harmony with her ecclesiastical system – not intruding ourselves into any Diocese against the will of the Bishop – nor attempting mission work amongst the poor unless by the invitation of their Parish Priest. For this, amongst other reasons, I have felt it best to retain my Incumbency instead of giving myself up to a more unfettered position, in order that it may be evident that the Superior of the Order is fully amenable to the discipline of the Established Church.

By prayer and study we hope to prepare ourselves for better carrying out our work of missions. Under the same we contemplate undertaking everything as God may open the doors for us.

1. Missions for a week or fortnight in any parish in London or the country where the Incumbent may invite us.
2. More settled mission work in London, where we intend to have a House [...]
3. A House in Oxford for scholars who wish to live by rule while getting a University education, for Students in Theology, for Clergy who wish to retire for a time of study.

4. A Chapel in London where we may chiefly address the educated classes upon the dangers of the fashions and scepticism of the present day.

5. Foreign Missions.

6. Retreats.

Of course we do not contemplate all this as possible, but I lay it before your Lordship as the idea which is in our minds to be carried out as God may give us the necessary funds and men with capacity for this or that kind of work. We shall be but a few in our beginning, but there are many who are thinking of joining us.

We have caused the matter to be hinted to the Bishop of London, and he is willing to promise a favourable welcome to any effort which may be made for the good of his Diocese.

Commending the Congregation to your Lordship's prayers,

I am your Lordship's faithful servant in Christ,

R. M. Benson.[71]

The letter was masterful, because it made clear that Benson and his associates wished only to proceed with Wilberforce's full knowledge and approval; but that bound up with the initial request was an implication that they would be taking their common life further, and that part of it involved a quest for greater personal holiness. Meanwhile, "giving up the world, living by simple rule, and devoting ourselves to prayer, study, and mission work" would have been instantly recognisable to Wilberforce as the characteristics of the historic religious life of which he approved; but it was also tempered by Benson's request for advice and direction.

Benson was also at pains to state his loyalty to the Church of England, and his attachment to canonical obedience: and so distanced himself from men like Lyne. He laid out the aims of the proposed congregation, which were all matters in which he was experienced. J. G. Lockhart, Wood's biographer, felt that Pusey had favoured presenting Wilberforce with a *fait accompli* so that he could not refuse individual points;[72] and Allan Cameron ascribed the same sentiment to Forbes.[73] Instead, Benson laid out a number of purposes in which Wilberforce knew he was either expert, or at least likely to succeed. He also was aware that Benson had a good deal of the "necessary funds" personally, and that he himself had prevented him from deploying them in India five years earlier. Benson closed his letter by demonstrating the point that he proposed to work nowhere without episcopal approval; and there was no way, even had he wanted to, that Wilberforce could have dismissed Benson's letter as a passing whim or fleeing fancy.

Wilberforce's reply was encouraging. He would give public preachers' licences to the clergymen, and wanted them to start their mission work in the parish of Headington Quarry, not far from Cowley, whose church he had consecrated in 1848 but which had had a high turnover of clergy since. "I like the idea of your College very much", he wrote: although it was he, and not

---

71 Benson, undated but almost certainly late July 1865, SSJE/6/1/6/1.

72 Lockhart, *Halifax*, i.118.

73 Cameron, *Religious Communities*, 164ff.

Benson, who used "college".[74] He wished to discuss it further, but followed his initial response with a series of conditions that he felt were necessary, because "the great importance of the move makes me most anxious that it should be protected as far as possible from every element of failure".

I. That there should be no distinctive dress or badge attached to membership in the proposed body.

II. That the rules of the body should *in extenso* be submitted to me for my previous sanction and not afterwards altered without my concurrence as Visitor.

III. That the sanction of the Bishop and incumbent of each sphere of labour be obtained before any such new field of labour is occupied.

IV. That if the scheme of the Hall is carried out my position with regard to it should be Visitor with original and not merely appellate jurisdiction.

V. That there should be no vows.

VI. That all questions of ritual should be decided absolutely by the Bishop and no office be introduced without his previous sanction.[75]

Benson replied immediately and briefly – he was in the middle of preparing for a parish fête – to say that he would write more fully soon, but also that although "my personal respect and allegiance to the Bishop from whom I received my Orders, would incline me to accept all [the conditions] at once", he had also to consider the "public as well as the private bearings of the arrangement", and plan for the future of the scheme as well.[76]

A few days later Benson responded to Wilberforce's conditions in numerical order. The dress of the clerical members of the community would only be distinctive in its "poverty of material", and "in no way different from that worn by ordinary clergy" – although he did not mention the fact that, as contemporary photographs show, they would wear it all the time. The lay brothers would "dress alike" in lay clothes, "but not so as to be evidently wearing a uniform"; and would wear a serge cassock in the house.

On the place of the Bishop within the community, Benson presented a number of prudent reasons why Wilberforce might not necessarily wish for as much direct control as he had seemed to require.

[I]t seems undesirable that any Bishop should be required or supposed to give his entire approval. There can be no reason why the private life of Clergy thus living together should be submitted to diocesan sanction more than of one living singly. I would have the *external* work of the Brotherhood entirely controlled by the authority under whom God has placed them, but the *internal* life of the House could not safely be exposed to such practices that would be beneath notice if we observed them of themselves, would be watched, criticised and censured if the Society gained a fictitious importance by being supposed to represent the Bishop's view of ascetic life [...] As soon as we are supposed to be the agent of any Bishop, we should be the object of attack.

---

74 Wilberforce, 1 Aug 1865, SSJE/6/1/2/35/9ff.

75 Wilberforc, 7 Aug 1865, SSJE/6/1/2/35/11.

76 Benson, 8 Aug 1865, SSJE/6/1/6/1.

Benson also felt that a diocesan bishop, not being a member of the community, "would scarcely be the most fit person to decide upon the spiritual requirements of men who have retired from the world". Such a task would be better left with the community superior.

There were practical considerations that ruled out the idea of bishops sanctioning each new piece of work. Benson was clear that if the Society intended to work in a particular diocese for a long period then its bishop would be consulted; but for less permanent work he would be "satisfied with the Incumbent's sanction". He reassured Wilberforce that "there is no reason why we should imagine ourselves to be special objects of alarm to the Episcopal Bench. As ministers of the Church of England we should be in no better, and not in any worse position than any others". Much the same was true of the idea of the Hall and its relation to the University: if Benson had the approval of the Vice-Chancellor, then there could be "no reason why my Hall should be hampered by any other authority".[77]

Benson devoted the largest portion of his response to the matter of vows, fully aware "that my own convictions are somewhat at variance with your Lordship's". They had corresponded on the matter a decade earlier, when Wilberforce had "with real regret" declined to give his blessing to a young woman who wished to make a "public resolution of chastity and devotion to Christ". He had felt then that the intention would be better carried out privately – because any public resolution would in effect be a vow, which he felt would be full of "danger and probable unlawfulness", and therefore could not sanction.[78]

Benson now appealed to scripture and tradition, and presented a thorough analysis of why he thought that vows might now be beneficial.

> I must entreat your Lordship's forbearance while I speak about vows and review the portions of Scripture upon which I would maintain them [...] Holy Scripture evidently attaches so much blessing to a devoted state that I cannot conceive we ought to allow any English prejudices to interfere. I know your Lordship considers vows unsuited to the English character, and dangerous under our circumstances, and I quite agree that there is in some kinds of vows too much danger unless there be strength of community life. But spiritual life is not of nature, nor of time, but of grace [...] The blessedness of a vow consists in the faith that God will give special gifts as a Covenant God to those who thus definitely give up some possible future of earthly enjoyment for him. [...] Of course, if there be not a call of God, there would be self-will in a vow, and the Society must determine during the Novitiate whether there be such a call [...] Our Lord himself [...] speaks without blame of those who make themselves eunuchs for the kingdom of Heaven's sake, and this must be either naturally, which the Church abominates, or spiritually which the Church has always approved.

---

77 The Vice-Chancellor, John Prideaux Lightfoot, did approve: he granted a licence for Benson to open 2 Magdalen Terrace as a Private Hall; although in the end this part of the scheme was not carried through. SSJE/6/1/1/3.

78 R. K. Pugh & J. F. A. Mason (eds), *The Letter-Books of Samuel Wilberforce, 1843–1868*, Oxfordshire Record Society (1970), 310.

His closing plea amply demonstrates the breadth of Benson's intellect and understanding of ecumenical affairs, and his sincere and realistic engagement with three centuries of Anglican ecclesiastical thought:

> S. Paul carries on the tradition of a life under vows from the Temple to the Christian Church, and the traditions of Catholic Christendom East and West are surely too strong for us to set up our insular morality in opposition to them. If we are to ask for the toleration of a married priesthood from other branches of the Church, surely they must see that we are ready to accept in practice what the English Church has never rejected in theory, a celibate Order of Religious Men.

He ended by saying that he believed "that entire openness is more truly respectful than silence or an assent which might savour of equivocation".

Benson also stood firm on the matter of ritual, not because he wanted particular practices but because he wanted the community to have the freedom to worship as it deemed suitable in its own private devotions: "I think it would be ensnaring for us to be hampered by a provision which no ordinary family is restrained by. They have their private prayers as they like, and so should we." He pointed out that for any extra devotions to be subject to the bishop's approval would render the brethren "greatly hindered", and the requirement would be "either a tremendous burden or a nonentity" – neither of which was desirable. Furthermore, the bishop of another diocese might disapprove of things that Wilberforce had allowed, which would lead to chaos.

Benson's conclusion was a neat summary of his position on how the proposed community might relate to episcopal authority, and gives a clear idea of how Wilberforce's response – whatever it might be – would be crucial for the success or failure of the venture.

> My own feeling therefore is that the private life of the Community should be regulated by the Superior, its public action being held in check by the various authorities ecclesiastical and academical which possess a right to interfere – that the Brotherhood should be in strict obedience of outward conduct, not attempting anything when it was lawfully forbidden – but that the Superior should not be the Bishop's mouthpiece or dependent on the Bishop's will except in so far as his sense of ecclesiastical obedience teaches him to submit. Anything more than this I think would destroy the sense of security and the prospect of success which applies to a private endeavour, and however real in its primary intention by reason of personal confidence in the existing Bishop of the Diocese, would become a snare in time. I scarcely know which would be worse – a definite break between the Community and the Bishop, or an evasion of a particular Bishop's wishes while the Community were outwardly pledged to act in entire submission.[79]

This was something of a gambit: for while Benson was not claiming any kind of canonical exemptions, he was making some clear distinctions between the proper authority of a diocesan bishop and that of the superior of a religious

---

79 Benson, 11 Aug 1865, SSJE/6/1/6/1.

community. He was uncompromising; but he was able to reassure Wilberforce on most of the points, and to differ cogently and reasonably on others.

Wilberforce – who must have been relieved that his correspondence with Benson was so markedly different from his almost simultaneous correspondence with Lyne – could hardly have responded more satisfactorily. On 28 August 1865, he wrote Benson a short and historic letter.

My dear Mr Benson,

I have carefully weighed your letter, and I agree with you that it is better that the Bishop should be responsible only for the *external* work of the Institution you contemplate. In this view I shall be glad to give any clergyman commorant with you public preachers' licences, so long as I can approve of your Institution generally without committing myself absolutely to all its details. This, I believe, is what you desire, and I think it is the best course.

I am ever yours most truly,
S. Oxon Oxon:[80]

A RESPECTABLE VENTURE

Benson had effectively presented Wilberforce with a scheme of which he could approve, and he had been happy to accept it. The future Superior General replied by return of post.

I am very much obliged by your Lordship's kind letter received to-day. I hope that there will be nothing in the future history of our little Brotherhood to forfeit the confidence so kindly given to us by one to whom we naturally look up as the Channel of the Divine Blessing to give life to our little endeavour. I am most deeply grateful for your Lordship's sympathy in this matter.[81]

Owen Chadwick observed that in his appointments Wilberforce was in the habit of selecting impressive men in whom "he placed an unceasing confidence".[82] He also appreciated clergy who placed emphasis on "order, episcopal authority, and interior discipline".[83] He clearly trusted Benson, and David Newsome noted that once his views had been expressed, "he allowed his subordinates considerable discretion, supported them when they were impugned, and intervened directly in their affairs as rarely as possible".

Newsome also suggested that Wilberforce's views softened further as the years passed, and that "as the fears of Romanism gradually subsided and the number of secessions decreased, he was more disposed to make concessions".[84] Wilberforce had been named to the see of Oxford in the wake of Newman's

---

80 Wilberforce, 26 Aug 1865, SSJE/6/1/2/35.
81 Benson, 29 Aug 1865, SSJE/6/1/6/1.
82 Owen Chadwick, *The Founding of Cuddesdon*, Oxford: OUP (1954), 51.
83 David Newsome, "The Churchmanship of Samuel Wilberforce", *Studies in Church History III* (1966), 28.
84 Newsome, *Parting of Friends*, 332ff.

secession, and – despite his "genuine admiration" for the Oxford Movement founders[85] – almost immediately had appeared to question Pusey's loyalty to the Church of England because of his perceived influence over many contemporary converts to Roman Catholicism. It was an imputation from which their former warm relations never quite recovered.[86] It is possible, however, that Wilberforce – who would have known of Pusey's influence in the scheme – supported Benson's request partly in order try to stem what he perceived as a stream of converts by agreeing to open up in the Church of England a devotional path that hitherto had only existed in the Church of Rome.

This consideration was in sharp focus because in the same year Pius IX had appointed Henry Edward Manning, another convert, to the Archbishopric of Westminster; and it is certainly relevant in the establishment of Benson's new community, because even as he wrote to thank Wilberforce for his approval, the future was uncertain. Grafton was already living under Benson's roof; but Lane Fox was on his way to Rome, and was received by Manning in January 1866.[87] Tuke felt unable to leave his curacy because of the poor health of his incumbent (in the end he followed Lane Fox in 1868) and O'Neill, who had family ties but was also considering becoming a Roman Catholic, was wavering.[88] Wood had also withdrawn from the scheme; but at Benson's own request for him "to return to the world and serve the Church in the position to which Providence had called him".[89] As Viscount Halifax he maintained an association with the Society for the rest of his life.[90]

Lane Fox's secession was a grave blow; but in later years Wood made the point that he was "one of those who had a great share in the beginnings of the Cowley Community, and no history of the Cowley Fathers would be complete without a due and loving remembrance of his name".[91] His departure was tempered, however, by the welcome return of O'Neill, who had decided to leave the Jesuits with whom he had been staying and join Benson and Grafton in Oxford.

Both O'Neill and Grafton underwent something of a baptism of fire when cholera broke out in the East End of London in the summer of 1866. Urgent help was asked for in Bethnal Green and Shoreditch, and although Benson could not leave his ever-growing parish he gave both his new assistants permission to go.[92] The Devonport sisters had set up a temporary hospital, and Wood – to

---

85 Newsome, "The Churchmanship of Samuel Wilberforce", 28.

86 Liddon, *Life of Pusey*, iii:40ff.

87 Lockhart, *Halifax*, i:121.

88 *CE* Feb 1915.

89 *CE* Feb 1934. Grafton considered that Wilberforce had also had a hand in it: Grafton, *A Journey Godward*, 40.

90 Wood's father was created Viscount Halifax in 1866, whom he succeeded in 1885. The second Viscount Halifax passed his titles and his Anglo-Catholicism on to his son Edward, who served variously as Viceroy of India, Foreign Secretary, Ambassador to Washington, and Chancellor of the University; was made a Knight of the Garter; and advanced to an earldom. See, *inter alia*, The Earl of Birkenhead, *Halifax: The Life of Lord Halifax*, London: Hamilton (1965).

91 *CE* Feb 1915.

92 Charles Grafton, *A Journey Godward*, London: A. R. Mowbray & Co. (1910), 41ff.

the horror of his newly-ennobled parents – had arrived to act as secretary.[93] Pusey, well into his sixties, was also there; and his mastery of Hebrew proved useful in a heavily Jewish area. All three took their share of the work and the danger before the epidemic passed in the autumn.[94]

Benson's correspondence with Wilberforce had continued; and the bishop's letters were kind, gentle, and reasonable.[95] Occasionally he asked for Benson's own judgement on matters unrelated to the foundation of the community, and in the autumn of 1865 he stopped calling him "Mr Benson" in favour of the more affectionate "Benson". He seems to have been genuinely pleased to have been able to support an endeavour that showed none of the excesses associated with men like Lyne and his followers.

Comparison between the two ventures is inevitable and necessary. Although Lyne was an appealing figure to many, he caused commotion almost everywhere he went. Furthermore, the membership of his community was fluid; and the behaviour of some of them was scandalous. Hugh Allen observes astutely that anyone who seriously considered testing his vocation with Lyne's community "was likely to be a misfit, if not in some sense 'on the run'. Ignatius always believed his geese were swans – until they surprised him by turning out to be geese after all, or birds of an even less attractive feather."[96]

Lyne was also a thoroughgoing Ritualist far ahead of his time, and was naïve to the point of silliness: on at least one occasion he signed a letter to Wilberforce with "✠ Ignatius, Monk O.S.B. by virtue of vows of obedience to the Benedictine Rule, Superior."[97] He never found a bishop of the Church of England who was willing to ordain him to the priesthood, partly because he also showed a significant strain of resistance to ecclesial authority in which he almost delighted. That was a trait that Wilberforce particularly detested, and it was fatal.[98] Arthur Calder-Marshall concluded that because of his "sheer pig-headedness" in his dealings with Wilberforce, Lyne lost for ever his chance of success.[99]

By contrast, the men associated with Benson were genteel and "in good standing",[100] so Wilberforce could rely on them to carry out their mission work within his approved parameters. Benson had been regarded as an amiable character as an undergraduate;[101] but there was also a deeply serious side to his nature, and because of his work with the Brotherhood of the Holy Trinity he was highly regarded as a spiritual writer, preacher, and director. He was also a Student of Christ Church, with its associated dignity in the University, and by the mid-1860s he had been in Oxford for two decades: he was established as the incumbent of a Christ Church living, and was well-known to his people and brother clergy.

---

93 Lockhart, *Halifax*, i:129ff.
94 Woodgate, *Benson*, 74.
95 SSJE/6/1/2/35.
96 Allen, *New Llanthony Abbey*, 226.
97 Lyne, 1 Sept 1864, Bodleian, MSS Wilberforce, c.17/43–44.
98 Newsome "The Churchmanship of Samuel Wilberforce", 33.
99 Calder-Marshall, *The Enthusiast*, 102.
100 Allen, *New Llanthony Abbey*, 226.
101 Woodgate, *Benson*, 20.

Benson did not belong alongside John Shelton Reed's "Ritualist all-stars",[102] and nor did Pusey and Keble, for that matter. Like Pusey, however, he understood how certain aspects of Ritualism could be edifying when applied appropriately. The Eucharist was celebrated "for a long time" in a linen chasuble at the Iron Church, and in an embroidered one on feast days from Christmas 1867 onwards.[103] He was happy to preach for Chamberlain at St Thomas's, and even dedicated a published volume of sermons to him; and as early as 1860 he had been heckled in the pulpit while preaching for Bryan King at the height of the ritual controversies at St George's-in-the-East.[104] He was keen to demonstrate that his practice was within the law,[105] and so wrangled over attending Benediction at East Grinstead[106] – but he gladly preached at the opening of the sisters' new buildings on a sweltering day in July 1870: *The Times* joked that it was "closely bordering on cruelty to preach for three quarters of an hour with the thermometer standing at something like ninety degrees [32°C] in the shade".[107]

In the end, all Benson's qualities combined to ensure that also had the confidence of his bishop, which was crucial. Allchin considered that

> It seems impossible that the Bishop should have permitted anyone to proceed with the formation of a community who had expressed, as Fr Benson had done, his firm intention of taking the vows of celibacy, poverty and obedience; and it is a very great indication of the regard and trust which the Bishop had for Fr Benson that he allowed him to go forward. On Fr Benson's side it would have been equally impossible to make a beginning of the society without the Bishop's general approval.[108]

Benson, therefore, was able to present Samuel Wilberforce – who, as Newsome pointed out, had himself resolved to live an ascetic life in the 1830s before he yielded to a dish of turbot with lobster sauce[109] – with a proposed form of religious life of which the bishop inherently approved. He was also able to overcome the qualms that Wilberforce expressed about certain details of the plan, including those relating to vows. And so, with his self-imposed period of probation having passed, on 27 December 1866 – the feast of St John the Evangelist – with the Bishop of Oxford's blessing, and in the house on the Iffley Road which they had shared since the previous summer,[110] Benson, Grafton, and O'Neill each witnessed another's vows "to live in celibacy, poverty and obedience, as one of the Mission Priests of St John the Evangelist unto my life's end".[111] The work of the Cowley Fathers had begun.

---

102 John Shelton Reed, *Glorious Battle*, 215.

103 *Cowley St John Parish Magazine*, Jan 1868.

104 *Morning Post*, London, 14 July 1860.

105 *PM* Jan 1868.

106 *Wilberforce Letter-Books*, 403.

107 *The Times*, 23 July 1870.

108 Allchin, *Silent Rebellion*, 196.

109 Newsome, "The Churchmanship of Samuel Wilberforce", 38.

110 2 Magdalen Terrace: now 45 Iffley Road, enlarged, and part of the Isis Guest House. Thanks, again, to Br Steven Haws CR.

111 The choice of patron is open to interpretation – Michael Wheeler has explored the emphasis placed on both the Gospel and person of St John the Evangelist in Victorian England. Michael Wheeler, *St John and the Victorians*, Cambridge University Press (2012).

4

FLOREAT COWLEY[1]

No one who has not charge of a Parish can tell the anxieties of a Pastor's heart.

—*Cowley St John Parish Magazine*[2]

At the start of the 1866 General Chapter of the Brotherhood of the Holy Trinity, Richard Meux Benson "delivered an unwritten address" to the members, in the course of which he announced his resignation as Master. The Vicar of Cowley had other definitive plans afoot; although he remained a member of the BHT for the rest of his life. The Brotherhood itself also continued to play its part in the development of the life of the SSJE: of the brethren whose names appear under the Constitution later approved by Bishop Mackarness in 1884 Benson had been a member since 1852, Luke Rivington since 1859,[3] and Arthur Hall since 1865.[4] Frederick Puller had been a member of the Cambridge Theological Society, which had been in close connection with the Brotherhood since the late 1850s, and had himself attended General Chapter in June 1865 as an observer.[5]

By December 1866 it had become clear that the ever-increasing population of Cowley could no longer be sustained by one parish. In fact, the area had been transformed beyond recognition: "The Revd R[obert] Charsley said [on 29 April 1867] that it was now 18 years since he first knew Cowley. He spoke of the time when he had shot snipes upon the very spot where his house now stood."[6] Plans were afoot for a new parish, with Benson as its incumbent and the Iron Church on Stockmore Street serving as its church until a more appropriate building could be raised. In anticipation of the erection of the new parish of Cowley St John, Benson began publishing the *Cowley St John Parish Magazine*, which – although it does not deal directly with the monastic nature of the life of the clergy house – brings into focus the work in which Benson and his assistants were involved. Although Cowley St John was a parish run by what we may now regard as vowed religious, at the time it was a typical

---

1 "In the evening [of the School Sports Day on 30 April 1867], the Revd R. M. Benson gave the prizes to the boys in the presence of various friends in the Schoolroom. We shall end [...] by calling upon our readers to join with us in a wish (which it rests with ourselves under God's grace to make sure) – *Floreat Cowley!*" *PM* May 1867.

2 *PM* Jan 1868.

3 BHT Minute Book 2, 149, PH.

4 BHT Minute Book 8, 159, PH.

5 BHT Minute Book 8, 40, PH. The Cambridge Theological Society effectively merged with the BHT in 1867, becoming the Confraternity of the Holy Trinity. Ibid, 288.

6 *PM* May 1867.

mid-Victorian suburban parish; and the parish magazine served as a digest of news, fundraising, and Tractarian piety.

Benson did not mention anything about the new community in the first edition of the magazine in January 1867; although perhaps he hinted at his hopes when he mentioned – after the importance of building a new National School for the parish children, to supplement the St John's Boys' School on the Iffley Road, and the Girls' School on Marston Street – the "still greater work very necessary; I mean the erection of a large and suitable church, in place of our small iron one".[7] This would, however, also have been entirely consonant with the needs of the new parish.

When Samuel Wilberforce came to confirm at St James's on 22 January 1867, he made a note of it in his diary without comment; but that was generally his custom, and is probably unremarkable.[8] Benson, meanwhile, saw to the various pressing needs of his people: he opened a soup kitchen to help mitigate the effects of the winter on his poorest parishioners,[9] and scrupulously published the accounts in March, when it closed until the autumn.[10] The school he had looked for in January was opened in April with a gala concert, at which Charles Grafton – who had clearly become very popular in his brief time in Cowley – was cheered to the rafters when he rose to speak.[11]

Entertainments for the parish children were arranged: in July a low-scoring cricket match between the boys of the choirs of St James's and the Iron Church took place, which the St James's boys won by 26 runs to 25;[12] and in September a School Treat was held at Magdalen Cricket Ground: "the Boys had their Cricket and Athletic Sports, and the Girls amused themselves with other games [...] Tea was provided at 5.30 in the pavilion and two tents. After which Mr Carter set up a fire Balloon which glided steadily over Headington Hill, while the spectators sang *God Save The Queen*." Later that month Benson's curate, Thomas Willis, was ordained to the priesthood at Cuddesdon – another sign of Wilberforce's ongoing approval.[13]

By November Benson had set up Bible Classes at the National School, where he hoped "to be able to give some religious instruction in a more conversational manner than is possible in Church", and had also persuaded various friends to come and contribute to a lecture series (in addition to his own lectures on the Prophet Daniel, which had been running since August) – beginning with the Warden of Radley on "Up the Nile".[14] In December he was at pains to point out that "Mr Buckmaster made his subject, which may have sounded like a dry one" – it had been advertised at "the Application of Science to the Arts" – "to be really full of amusement and interest"; but also that he was setting up a Bible Class for men in Robin Hood Terrace (now part of Magdalen Road), where he also intended to build a Chapel of Ease.

---

7 *PM* Jan 1867.
8 *PM* Feb 1867; Bodleian, MSS Wilberforce, Dep.e.316/69.
9 *PM* Feb 1867.
10 *PM* March 1867.
11 *PM* May 1867.
12 *PM* Aug 1867.
13 *PM* Oct 1867.
14 *PM* Nov 1867.

Benson's priorities soon shifted from the idea of a replacement for the Iron Church to a permanent building for the National School, and a Chapel of Ease on the east side of the new parish.[15] In his "Parochial Review" of 1867 he mused that "it will be a great joy when we get a Chapel of Ease at Robinhood, a fine schoolroom in place of the wooden one in Princes Street, and finally, a spacious Church, suited to the wants of the district". The wants of the district – the proposed parish boundaries were still being disputed, and the new parish was not erected until 30 July 1868[16] – were great.[17] In addition to the activities above, he also cited the existence of a lending library, operating out of the school on Princes Street; an evening school for girls; clothing and coal clubs for the poor; a little school on Robin Hood Terrace, where children who could not attend the National School were taught; and a men's reading room operating out of the same premises in the evening. He did not mention the discreet work of the House of Compassion for unmarried mothers which also existed.[18]

Benson was meticulous in thanking those lay members of the parish who helped in the various endeavours: he urged his better-off people to continue supporting the new National School, and the less-well-off ones to send their children to it regularly, because "without regularity, no teaching, however good, can avail". Most of all, he was keenly aware that "there are many who still go for Holy Communion to the Churches in Oxford, to which they were accustomed before coming to live on this side of the bridge".

> It would be a very good plan if such persons, although habitually going "up street", were to come at the Great Festivals to communicate along with their fellow Parishioners in their own Parish Church. There is, we may be sure, a very special blessing to be obtained by seeking God's grace in the channels which he has specially provided for us. Attendance at our Parish (or District) Church is not – what people are very apt to think – a mere matter of outward arrangement and indifference. The outward accidents of life are a part of God's Providential discipline, and the more fully we recognise His Hand as controlling all such things, the more we shall find His grace working through them. As we have an *early celebration every Sunday* it would be quite possible for persons to come regularly to Holy Communion here, and then go to the 11 o'clock service for Matins and Sermon wherever they may be most accustomed in Oxford. Although our 11 o'clock service, and our evensong, are often overcrowded, yet is there plenty of room at the 7.30 celebration. The Incumbent wishes earnestly to press upon all Parishioners the duty of coming to that early celebration if they possibly can manage it.[19]

Benson's priorities, then, were to encourage his parishioners to come to the Eucharist at the Iron Church – and to regard themselves as bound to it by their

---

15 *PM* Dec 1867.

16 *PM* Jan 1883.

17 See Annie Skinner, "Unearthing the Past: an exploration into the people behind the development of a Victorian suburb", *Family & Community History*, v.12:2 (Nov. 2009).

18 Phyl Surman, *An Oxford Childhood: Pride of the Morning*, Stroud: The History Press (2009).

19 *PM* Jan 1868.

residence in the parish – and also to care for the poor by providing education and other social services to ameliorate their poverty to some degree.[20] This involved meeting essential needs like food, clothing, and fuel; but it also extended to improving activities like reading and lectures, and, later, a Horticultural Society – "President and Treasurer, Rev. R. M. Benson" – with an annual August show and prizes.

HIDDEN IN PLAIN SIGHT

A part from the mention of Grafton at the opening of the school, there is no hint in the parish magazine of the nascent life of the Society of St John the Evangelist. "We keep very quiet as far as name and dress, etc, are concerned", he wrote;[21] and to some extent, the discreet foundation of the SSJE meant that its interior life could develop with little remark being passed. Michael Hill has observed that brotherhoods were less contentious than sisterhoods, because in Victorian England men had more "role freedom"; and that as the brotherhoods were intended to be made up mainly of celibate clergymen, most of their members already enjoyed a position of authority within the Church. Furthermore, the idea of unmarried men living in community was a reflection of life at the universities; and many communities, like the SSJE, were founded with the intention of supporting parish ministry – and so could be seen to be cooperating with official church structures.[22]

If the devotional life of the new community was hidden from public view, however, the people of Cowley St John could hardly have failed to have noticed the building work taking place on Marston Street. By October 1868 the large red-brick Mission House was ready for occupation; and it was only then that Benson formally introduced the SSJE to the parish. The casual manner of the announcement, however, suggests that his plans were generally well-known: "The Mission House or Central Home for the Mission Priests of St John the Evangelist is now ready, and we are hoping to enter at once." The community now also included Oliver Sherman Prescott, Grafton's friend and mentor from the United States,[23] and Benson's description of the five-day retreat with which the house opened introduced to the parish the idea of how religious life would progress at Marston Street: a daily celebration of the Eucharist at which "those who desire it can communicate"; the sevenfold office: "the ancient custom which we know the Apostles themselves observed – as David had done – of praising God seven times a day"; homosocial community identity: "the Chapel will not be open to ladies"; and silent meals during which "some Religious Book is read aloud". George Lane Fox noted that the daily timetable was "something like this":

---

20 Skinner, "Unearthing the Past", 93ff.
21 Grafton, 7 Sept 1866, in Pendleton, *Grafton*, 31.
22 Hill, *Religious Order*, 204.
23 Zimmerman, *Prescott*, 51ff.

Rise at 5.30; Lauds, Prime, followed by meditation 6; Mattins and Celebration in church at 7.45; Terce 9.30: schools etc; Sext 11.45; 12–2 dinner and recreation. At 2 p.m. Nones, then visiting, work etc; 6 Vespers; 7.30 Evensong in church; then night schools etc, and 10 o'clock Compline etc. and bed. Silence to be observed up to Sext and after Vespers.[24]

Benson's use of "Central Home" was also significant: as well as hoping that the Mission House would be used regularly by retreatants as time went on, he was clear that the Society would also function as "a body of men at the disposal of the parochial clergy" to preach and lead missions in parishes at home; and his intention that the Society should also be established in India and the United States was explicit. Noting also that the Mission House would also function as a licensed University Hall, he signed the article "R. M. Benson, Superior".[25] And so the people of Cowley St John found established in their midst the first stable religious community of men in the Church of England; and Benson hoped that whenever the parishioners heard the bell ringing for the offices – which were sung in the eyrie-like chapel perched on the very top of the building – they would "lift up their hearts unto the Lord at such times wherever they may be".[26]

Benson did not, however, intend to retreat into pious introspection: as Annie Skinner has observed, he was "ambitious in his projects";[27] and the life of the parish continued to burgeon. The Iron Church was too small for purpose, and the financial support of the National Schools in the parish continued to be a priority. Two months after the appeal for funds to extend the Iron Church, the money was raised and the work completed: the acknowledgment that the parish was "indebted principally to the efforts of our respected Churchwarden, the Mayor" underlined the ongoing respectability of the parish and its monkish clergy;[28] although when reporting on strictly parochial matters Benson made a point of suffixing "Incumbent" to his name – he seems to have been keen to make the distinction between the administrative life of the parish and the devotional life of his community.[29]

By 1869 Benson was leading a model Tractarian parish, possessed of many of the hallmarks identified by John Shelton Reed.[30] Although Cowley St John could hardly be described as a slum – looking back in 1882 Benson took the view that "when the Iron Church was first erected in 1859 there were literally no actual poor in the district"[31] – it was later inhabited by plenty of people whose needs, both financial and spiritual, were pressing. Perhaps most telling of all was Benson's own position on Ritualism – what P. T. Marsh called "the

---

24 Woodgate, *Benson*, 72.

25 *PM* Oct 1868; *Letters of Richard Meux Benson*, 232.

26 *PM* Oct 1868.

27 Skinner, "Unearthing the Past", 94.

28 *PM* Jan 1869. The Churchwarden and Mayor was Alderman Joseph Castle – when he died in October 1872 he was mourned has having "taken an active part in all that has concerned the well-being of Cowley St John from the very first". *PM* Nov 1872.

29 *PM* Nov 1868.

30 Shelton Reed, *Glorious Battle*, 29ff.

31 *PM* Jan 1883.

tangible poetry of the Oxford Movement"[32] – as a tool of evangelism in and of itself.

Benson's moderate Ritualism is a facet of his character which has been underplayed in the past. His response to the judgment of the Privy Council on the Ritual Question – the original matter had begun in 1867 when Alexander Heriot Mackonochie was prosecuted for his practices at St Alban's, Holborn – saw him nail his colours quietly to the mast. In February 1869, he deplored generally the interference of the State in what was to his mind a strictly ecclesiastical matter, and particularly the Privy Council's reversal of the Court of Arches' decision permitting lighted candles on the altar during worship.

> Lights as symbolical of holy joy and especially of the presence of Christ with his Church, are evidently of scriptural authority. When we read that there were many lights where the disciples were gathered together, it is plain that there were more than were necessary for purposes of light. The mention of them would be absurd if they had not been used in a festive and symbolical manner.
>
> When the decision was given in favour of them I introduced the practice of lighting them at all our Celebrations [...] Having worshipped most of my life without them, I do not feel so wedded to their use as many others may. But I certainly think that they do assist in giving dignity to the Divine Office, and as King Edward's Injunctions say, they set forth Christ as the light of the World [...] The truth which they symbolize is one which all devout Christians must cherish and therefore I regret [...] the decision of the Privy Council.

His solution, however, shows a hint of the maverick streak that marked out so many of the leading Ritualists who were his contemporaries, friends, and acquaintances[33]: "I am by no means sure that the best way of reconciling it with what I myself believe to be the law of the Church of England, and according with ancient custom and the judgement of the other court might not be this, *viz:*– to have the Candles upon a slab separate from the Altar, standing behind it."[34]

Coupled with Benson's use of vestments at the Iron Church, which we encountered in the previous chapter, we may dissent from Nigel Yates' consideration – in which he channels Peter Anson – that services at Cowley were celebrated "without any liturgical enrichments";[35] and from Mildred Woodgate's canard of Benson as having been "one to whom ritual would make no personal appeal".[36] He was no extreme Ritualist himself – as he neared his eighties he numbered himself among the "men of our age, who perhaps do not care for incense";[37] but he was happy to support those who were, and he was so associated with Ritualism in the popular mind that when in later life he went

---

32 P. T. Marsh, *The Victorian Church in Decline*, London: Routledge & Kegan Paul (1969), 112.

33 Reed, *Glorious Battle*, 69.

34 *PM* Feb 1869.

35 Anson, *Call of the Cloister*, 80; Yates, *Anglican Ritualism*, 79.

36 Woodgate, *Benson*, 96.

37 Benson, 17 Feb 1900, Cambridge University Library, MS(Add.7651):Wyon 9/3/34.

to preach at St Michael's, Portsmouth, he was asked to take his MA hood with him, to assuage the concerns of some of the more suspicious members of the congregation.[38]

More significantly, perhaps, Benson presents himself to us as a *beau idéal* of a mid-Victorian Tractarian incumbent: zealous for souls, administratively competent, awake to the social needs of his people, and intellectually engaged in the religious controversies of his day. His parish, too, represents a model of the enactment of the principles that clergy influenced by the Tractarian movement at Oxford in the decades following the 1830s – a movement that sought "to spread its ideas not only through college common rooms but also bishops' palaces, and above all the parsonages of the Church of England"[39] – carried into their own cures all over the country; even if Benson himself had only gone as far as the other side of Magdalen Bridge. By 1874 the *Tourist's Church Guide* noted that the Iron Church served 3,691 souls; that in addition to candles, its clergy used coloured vestments and Gregorian chant in the course of their services, and that there was a daily celebration of the Eucharist.

The High Mass on Sundays, however, developed more slowly. At first it had "no elaborate ritual", and clerical members of the Society simply performed the functions of deacon and sub-deacon at appropriate points. It was not until the 1890s that "the proper Dalmatic and Tunicle" came to be worn; while simultaneously an earlier children's mass was established "with appropriate hymns", and congregational practice beforehand.[40]

It is deeply significant that this was the context in which the early years of the SSJE were lived out: as an integral part of a thriving and busy parish – each issue of the parish magazine contained a list of that month's baptisms, weddings, and funerals – that stood in a tradition that was gradually becoming part of the mainstream expression of the Church of England's devotional life.

MISSIONARY & MONASTIC MODELS

Benson's passion for mission extended well beyond the boundaries of his own parish, and Robert Jeffery analysed it thoroughly in *Benson of Cowley*.[41] He was one of the leaders of the great Mission to London in 1869;[42] and his community was also involved in its planning and preaching: it produced the *Book of the Mission*,[43] and Simon Wilberforce O'Neill led the closing ceremonies.[44] The fledgling SSJE had become quickly known as a provider of competent

---

38 Brian Taylor, *Brother Michael*, Gloucester: The British Publishing Co. (1964), 10.

39 George Herring, *The Oxford Movement in Practice: The Tractarian Parochial World from the 1830s to the 1870s*, Oxford: OUP (2016), 2.

40 Page, 12 March (early 1890s?), Cambridge University Library, MS (Add.7651):Wyon/9/3/98.

41 R. M. C. Jeffery, "'When all are Christians None are': Church and Mission in the Teaching of Father Benson", in Martin Smith SSJE (ed), *Benson of Cowley*, Oxford: OUP (1980), 119ff.

42 Kent, *Holding the Fort*, 258ff.

43 *Book of the Mission*, Holborn: Knott (1869).

44 *Pall Mall Gazette*, 25 Nov 1869.

missioners, to the extent that by 1869 Samuel Walker – "Ecclesiastical Art Photographer to the Bishops and Clergy" – was offering photographs of Benson, Prescott, and Grafton at a shilling each;[45] and the Society, such as it was, advertised its own *Suggestions as to the Conduct of a Mission*[46] and *The Evangelist Library Catechism*.[47] Local newspapers noted missions led up and down the country[48]; while open air services with hymns and sermons were held in the poorest parts of Oxford.[49]

The SSJE's reputation was far-flung: an angry writer in the *Morning Post* after the Mission to London claimed that the Society, in its support of the controversial practice of auricular confession, was attempting "to re-establish priestly tyranny", annihilate Anglicanism, and restore England to the Papacy;[50] while the Guernsey *Star* accused it of "Rampant Puseyism" and "Anglican Popery".[51] The Society's Anglo-Catholic credentials were already impeccable, and the standard low-church accusations of seeking to undo the Reformation continued as the years went by.[52] At one point the SSJE was accused of practising flagellation, after Congreve preached at the Plymouth Church Congress in 1876: a reporter misunderstood his reference to self-mortification, and let his imagination run wild.[53] A few years later it sent priests to provide for the people of St John's, Miles Platting, during the incarceration of its Vicar, Sidney Fairthorn Green, in the wake of his prosecution by the Church Association under the Public Worship Regulation Act of 1874;[54] and it even appeared in *Punch*.[55]

But mission was all. In 1869 the Mission House hosted George Wilkinson's second Anglo-Catholic Mission Conference;[56] and the Cowley St John Missionary Association continued to grow through the 1870s. "We must not let our own wants at home make us apathetic in regard to this work", wrote Benson. "The extension of Christ's Kingdom is our great duty."[57] The parish and the Society duly observed enthusiastically the various Days of Intercession for Mission promoted by the Society for the Propagation of the Gospel and the Church Missionary Society.[58]

Charles Gore later stated that Benson "never laid stress on any particular rule", and that "he made a rule, as the other great founders of religious communities made their rules, as seemed best adapted to the needs and necessities of the time."[59] He certainly consulted Lucas Holstenius' *Codex Regularum*

---

45 *Church Times*, 31 Dec 1869, 522.
46 *Church Times*, 22 Oct 1869, 411.
47 *John Bull*, 3 Sept 1870.
48 cf *Sheffield & Rotherham Independent*, 26 Feb 1872; *Birmingham Daily Post*, 28 Sep 1872.
49 *Birmingham Daily Post*, 13 Feb 1873.
50 *Morning Post*, London, 29 Nov 1869.
51 *Star* (St Peter Port), 4 Jun 1870.
52 cf *The Times*, 3 Nov 1881.
53 *Plymouth & Cornish Advertiser*, 15 Nov 1876.
54 *Manchester Times*, 9 April 1881.
55 *Punch*, 30 Sept 1882.
56 Kent, *Holding the Fort*, 251.
57 *PM* Jan 1872.
58 *PM* Dec 1872.
59 *CE* March 1915.

Monasticarum of 1661;[60] but Eldridge Pendleton considered that he favoured a later model based on that established by St Vincent de Paul in seventeenth-century France, and championed in England by Ignatius Spencer in the early 1840s.[61]

> Vincent de Paul formed an order that attracted young men hungry for committed spiritual life and eager to carry the hope of the Gospel wherever it was needed. His company of mission priests sent teams of men into towns and villages to preach and teach, to reach everyone, from the youngest child, and were held at times of day before and after the agricultural work of the peasantry. Because the ministry was arduous and physically depleting, these missionaries were not on the road all the time. After each mission they returned to the mother house in Paris for rest and spiritual replenishment, in the form of month-long retreats for which all members gathered.[62]

It is a convincing argument, and both Anson and John Kent took a similar view;[63] but the founding members of the Society were also imbued with nineteenth-century Revivalism. Benson's mother was influenced by the Clapham Sect; and so was O'Neill's father – his forenames were no coincidence. It is worth adding, however, that the brand of Revivalism which influenced Benson and O'Neill was, like their foray into monasticism, utterly respectable. Many members of revival movements ended up as Dissenters, and the Establishment was deeply suspicious of the fervour of "Enthusiasm" that such movements often encouraged. Ronald Knox thought that the Oxford Movement's "whole programme was a return from the charismatic to the institutional";[64] while the members of the Clapham Sect remained staunchly within Church of England. On the other side of the Atlantic, however, Dwight Moody's style of evangelism had influenced the young Grafton; and Pendleton thought that the early members of the SSJE most likely borrowed from Moody's methods when carrying out mission work.[65]

Rowan Strong has recently raised another important consideration. Although the Tractarians and their successors laid a good deal of emphasis on mission, for the most part they focussed their efforts on the urban poor at home. "This domestic mission", he writes, "conceived more as recapturing the lapsed rather than evangelising the unChristian" led to the rise of the model of the slum-priest, which would for decades continue to be the Anglo-Catholic model of priesthood *sans pareil*. That model, in its turn, was almost invariably connected with advanced Ritualism. Benson, as we have seen, was neither slum priest nor advanced Ritualist. His approach to mission focussed instead

---

60 PC 1924, SSJE/3/1/146.

61 It is likely that Patrick Leigh Fermor had the Cowley Fathers in mind when he referred to an Anglican monastic community keeping the precepts of St Vincent de Paul in *A Time to Keep Silence*. Leigh Fermor, *A Time to Keep Silence*, 92n.

62 Pendleton, *Grafton*, 38.

63 Anson, *Call of the Cloister*, 77; Kent, *Holding the Fort*, 251.

64 Ronald Knox, *Enthusiasm: A Chapter in the History of Religion*, Oxford: Clarendon Press (1950), 550.

65 Pendleton, *Grafton*, 39.

on the growth of personal holiness, and "an evident sanctification originating in baptism to which the unconverted would be attracted, and upon which basis the lapsed would be revived".[66]

AMERICAN ADVERSITY

It was to the lapsed that the Society first turned its attention; and despite Benson's own zeal for the unconverted of India, it was perhaps inevitable that the SSJE should first go to the United States. At the end of the 1860s the four members of the Society – early growth of numbers was slow – were neatly divided into two Englishmen and two Americans. It had always been understood that Grafton would return to the United States, and he and Benson had agreed that his considerable personal wealth would be kept separate from the Society's finances and used to fund future work in America. Grafton and Prescott had been leaders of the movement to establish the religious life in the Episcopal Church, such as it was, and had themselves dabbled with community life before Grafton's journey to England.

Soon after Prescott took his vows in June 1870 he was sent to St Clement's, Philadelphia, to assist the relatively new Rector, Herman Batterson, in his implementation of Tractarian and Ritualist principles there – and so St Clement's became the first church in the United States to be served by a Cowley Father.[67] Further north, the parish corporation of the Church of the Advent in Boston – where Grafton had been converted from the Congregationalism of his early life[68] – approached Benson during the parish's interregnum and asked the Society "to assist the rector *ad interim* [Moses Stickney] in carrying on the work of the parish".[69] It was anticipated that initially the SSJE would work in the parish from Advent Sunday 1870 until the following Trinitytide.[70]

The request was no coincidence, as links with the Church of the Advent had been long-established: one of its leading laymen, George Shattuck, had been admitted to the Brotherhood of the Holy Trinity in 1857, having given "an account of the work and organisation of the Guild of the Advent".[71] And so, on All Saints' Day 1870, Benson, O'Neill, and Puller sailed on the *Tarifa* to see what might be done. Before he left Benson called a parish meeting, and gave strict instructions to the parishioners on what their duties were while he was away. He followed this up with a letter on 31 October: "be diligent in your attendance at all the means of grace, and in your prayers." In his absence, Grafton was to hold the fort at the Mission House; while Robert Page, a priest testing his vocation to the Society's life, was to run the parish.[72]

---

66 Rowan Strong, "Origins of Anglo-Catholic Missions", 91;99.
67 Zimmerman, *Prescott*, 53.
68 Pendleton, *Grafton*, 35.
69 Robert Cheney Smith SSJE, *The Shrine on Bowdoin Street*, Boston: SSJE (1958), 10.
70 Shattuck *et al*, 7 Oct 1870, Massachusetts Diocesan Archives, Advent: Box 2.
71 Smith, *Bowdoin Street*, 37; 34.
72 *PM* Nov 1870.

The voyage to Boston was not without its trials: despite some smooth days, there were others when the sea was "what *sailors* call smooth" and Benson and his companions were too sick to say mass in their cabin. But they made good time, and arrived at Boston twelve days after leaving Liverpool. They were warmly welcomed by the members of the Church of the Advent, whom Benson thought "a fine hearty set of laymen".[73]

Samuel Wilberforce had been translated to the see of Winchester in 1869; but Benson travelled to America with a letter written in the bishop's own hand, and which Wilberforce had given him the option of amending as he saw fit[74]:

To the Right Rev Fathers, the Bishops of the Protestant Episcopal Church in America, Grace, mercy, and Peace from God our Father and the Lord Jesus Christ.

Whereas Richard Meux Benson, a Priest of Good Standing and well known personally to me in my late Diocese of Oxford is about to journey to your Land seeking to advance the Kingdom of Our Dear Lord, and has sought of me Letters Commendatory to you, I hereby commend him to you in the name of the Lord and pray you to allow and aid him according to your office his Godly Ministrations within your Dioceses and to receive him into them as a brother beloved.

And so I heartily bid you farewell, beseeching the Good Lord to have you in His Holy Keeping.

Given at Winchester
Oct 18 1870
S. Wintonensis:

Despite "the heartiness of the welcome" that the brethren received at the Advent,[75] it was to prove a difficult and inauspicious start. As Robert Cheney Smith noted in his history of St John's, Bowdoin Street – the former Church of the Advent, which would become the centre of SSJE life in the United States for decades – "some Churchmen [...] viewed with alarm the presence of men who had taken monkish vows, who wore strange garbs, who held beliefs which were unpopular in the Episcopal Church, and who, above all, were under the jurisdiction of the Church of England".[76] Bishop Manton Eastburn of Massachusetts was among them: he was a dour Low Churchman whose relationship with the Church of the Advent had been adversarial for years,[77] and he refused to give either Benson or O'Neill licences to minister in his diocese. Benson protested firmly:

As I have preached the Gospel of Christ without let or hindrance in almost every diocese of England, often at the request of the Bishops themselves [...] I hope you will not refuse me the like freedom in this great Continent.

---

73 *PM* Dec 1870.
74 Wilberforce, 21 Oct 1870, SSJE/6/1/2/6/7.
75 *PM* Dec 1870.
76 Smith, *Bowdoin Street*, 10–11.
77 Zimmerman, *Prescott*, 11ff.

I have brought you the Apostolical Benediction of two of our Bishops, commending me to your sympathy, and you think me unfit to be the bearer of such a Message. I am ready to meet any public charge, whether before a tribunal of this Country or my own, but I would respectfully suggest that a silent refusal [...] is indeed refusing to recognise Communion with the Church which I represent.[78]

Eastburn was unyielding, and told Shattuck on the same day that "I do not see my way clear at present to the granting to Mr Benson of the licence which he desires."[79] A further letter of protest from the parish was similarly dismissed.[80]

Eventually, after a lengthy correspondence between the Bishop and the parish officers it was agreed that the English brethren "should hold only such meetings in the Sunday-school room and elsewhere as might be held by any laymen, performing no priestly acts in this diocese so long as the bishop objected".[81] Faced with this prohibition, Benson agreed that Prescott should take charge of the Advent, and accordingly Prescott was summoned to Boston. Benson – one of the preeminent teachers, preachers, and spiritual guides of the Church of England – taught the Sunday School classes with O'Neill.

In February 1871, they both went to carry out mission work in the Bahamas at the invitation of the Bishop of Nassau[82] – establishing a link with that diocese which would reach its zenith in 1942 when Spence Burton SSJE became its bishop – and a month later Benson left for Chicago, where he was to lead a mission at the Cathedral and to preach at Milwaukee. On his way, Bishop Henry Potter welcomed him warmly in New York, and took him to meet the students at the General Theological Seminary; and a short trip to Canada took him to the Niagara Falls.

I found a stone from which I brushed away the snow and made it the Superior's Stall for the occasion. [...] So I sang a choral Matins, Lauds, Prime, and Terce, with the voice of many waters and mighty thunderings for an accompaniment, and felt the Society all round about.[83]

At home, the parish magazine was in different hands; and not least in the sub-editing, which deteriorated, in retrospect, to the point of hilarity. In June 1871, what should have read "Fr Benson after his Mission in Milwaukee, went farther West [and] made a visit to Nashotah [House], a large theological Church College" appeared as "Fr Benson after his Mission in Milwankie, went farther West [and] made a visit to Nasbotch". On a serious note, this must have been because whoever was transcribing Benson's letters home had never heard of the misspelled places, let alone seen them written down. Having been foiled at the Advent, Benson was breaking new ground for the Society elsewhere;

78 Benson, 18 Nov 1870, Massachusetts Diocesan Archives, Advent: Box 2.
79 Eastburn, 18 Nov 1870, Ibid.
80 Shattuck *et al*, 21 Dec 1870, Ibid.
81 Smith, *Bowdoin Street*, 11.
82 *PM* April 1871.
83 Benson, 7 Mar 1871, *Letters of Richard Meux Benson*, 81.

and he returned to Boston by way of Pittsburgh and Baltimore, preaching as he went.[84]

The English "Evangelist Fathers", as the parish magazine had referred to them since they left Cowley, were welcomed by many diocesan bishops in the United States – but not by the Bishop of Massachusetts, where they had been specifically asked to work. Eastburn's restrictions were intolerable, and after more mission work in Canada Benson and O'Neill sailed from Halifax at the end of August:[85] a grand parish tea party welcomed them home a month later.[86] The solution to the American problem was obvious: if the work of English brethren was contentious, then the SSJE in the United States would have to be established by Americans.

Grafton sailed in late November 1871. He was in the first instance to take charge of the Church of the Nativity at Bridgeport, CT, which Benson had identified as a suitable setting for the American novitiate.[87] As Jervis Zimmerman observes, the two centres of the Society were to be Bridgeport under Grafton and Boston under Prescott; but there was much to-ing and fro-ing.[88] Prescott returned to Cowley at the end of June 1872, and his place at the Advent was taken by Grafton, who was soon joined by other brethren from Cowley.[89] Arthur Hall replaced Grafton briefly at Bridgeport; but the house there closed in 1874, with Hall joining Grafton at the Advent.[90] Three Sisters of the Society of St Margaret also travelled to Boston to help in the parish of the Advent – the first of many women religious with whom the SSJE would collaborate closely in their work.[91]

The members of the SSJE wished to be mission priests, and they could hardly have been called to a more fertile part of the vineyard. The Church of the Advent was situated within the largest concentration of black residents in the city: the area was known colloquially as "Nigger Hill". Just over its brow, however, was the golden-domed State House, and Boston Common with its elegant mansions belonging to the leading local families; so the district was very much "a mixture of social classes and economic extremes".

The Advent was remarkable in Boston for "its Tractarian emphasis on personal conversion through sacramental grace, and its commitment to the poor and needy"; but it was also known for the quality of its preaching and the beauty of its services, and had a choir school that supplied boy choristers. With the arrival of the SSJE it became also a centre from which missions were sent to other parishes; and all these aspects, coupled to the fact that it was in a poor part of Boston but supported by some of the city's leading families, combined to make it distinctive. Grafton's evening catechism classes for the poor were well attended, and were followed by refreshments and Compline – what we might today call an approach of teaching, fellowship, and prayer.

---

84 *PM* June 1871.
85 *PM* Aug 1871.
86 *PM* Oct 1871.
87 *PM* Dec 1871.
88 Zimmerman, *Prescott*, 55.
89 *PM* July 1872.
90 Zimmerman, *Prescott*, 55. Bishop Eastburn seems to have relented since 1871.
91 Smith, *Bowdoin Street*, 13.

Hall – "his attractive and eloquent assistant" – gave erudite lectures on theological subjects to audiences of well-to-do members of the congregation. Eldridge Pendleton concluded that the SSJE's early successes in Boston after its initial discouragement was because of "their courageous and unstinting work with the poor, but also because of the spiritual and intellectual vitality of their evangelism".[92] It was a model of mission that would serve the Society well as time drew on.

Prescott returned to St Clement's, Philadelphia, in 1875, to take up the Rectorship; and was joined there the following year by Basil Maturin. Almost immediately – and in the context of the General Convention of the Episcopal Church's censuring of various liturgical practices – both men became embroiled in controversy that centred around issues of episcopal authority and provincial allegiance. It was rumoured in the press that St Clement's was to be taken over by the Society, and Prescott tried to reassure Bishop William Stevens of Pennsylvania that his membership of the SSJE would in no way compromise his canonical obedience to his bishop.

Stevens was not reassured, and his disgruntlement centred on the fact that both Maturin – whom he had inhibited almost as soon as he arrived in his diocese – and Prescott were both licensed to Cowley St John, which Stevens regarded as a contravention of the canons of the Episcopal Church. Once Maturin was licensed in the Episcopal Church his inhibition was lifted;[93] but Prescott – who seems to have thrived on controversy in the manner of many of his contemporary English co-religionists – continued to lock horns with Stevens as the decade progressed; and matters in the United States – both at St Clement's and at the Advent – would soon come to a dangerous head.

INTO INDIA

In the wider Church the Society's reputation continued to grow – and faster than its still-modest size. In June 1871 Bishop Robert Gray of Cape Town – the hero of the Brotherhood of the Holy Trinity in the Colenso affair – asked Benson for help in his diocese. In 1857 the Brotherhood's attention had been called to "the efforts that were being made to establish a Mission in Central Africa, and it was agreed that the B.H.T. should put itself in communication with his Grace the Metropolitan of Cape Town with a view to aiding him in his endeavours".[94] The parish magazine often contained letters from missionaries in Africa, in whose work the early members of the Society took an interest, and Benson had corresponded with Gray in the 1860s about the missionary needs of South Africa.[95] He now responded enthusiastically, even if he had to decline the request: "it was a very great pleasure to me to receive the kind invitation which you have given us. I hope it may some day be possible for our Society to avail itself of it. We are growing in numbers, but we are not yet strong enough

---

92 Pendleton, *Grafton*, 36ff.
93 Zimmerman, *Prescott*, 58; 65.
94 BHT Minute Book 2, 137, PH.
95 Gray, 13 June 1864, SSJE/6/1/2/12/1.

to put out a fresh branch."[96] The Society retained an interest in African affairs, and in time its own work in South Africa would become a major expression of its life.

Like South Africa, India – apart from being in Benson's own sights – had also been a particular concern of the BHT. In November 1857 – in the context of the Mutiny and shortly after the National Day of Humiliation – it had resolved "that it be recommended that throughout Advent the 67th Psalm be said in conjunction with the Prayers now appointed for Sext with a view to the Propagation of the Gospel in India especially in awakening a desire in the hearts of some of the Brotherhood to give themselves up as Missionaries for this work";[97] and among those who heeded the call had been Benson's correspondent Robert Reynolds Winter.[98]

Fourteen years later, in 1872, Bishop Robert Milman asked Benson for help in the diocese of Calcutta – they had discussed the possibility as early as 1867[99] – and was glad to hear that he might "be able at last to carry out [his] old idea".[100] A year earlier, Bishop Henry Douglas of Bombay – who was himself a Tractarian and moderate Ritualist[101] – had made a similar request.[102] In 1868 Indian work had been one of the founding principles of the Society – "we contemplate eventually a Mission work in India whenever our numbers may allow" – and Benson was adamant about how "very important it is that the Mission work of India should be strengthened".[103] Although he had declined Gray's invitation for the Society to go to South Africa, he felt able to respond positively to the Indian requests: numbers at home were increasing gradually; and by then Gray was dead, and so in no position to take offence.

Once more Benson hoped to travel to India – Douglas had deemed his presence "highly desirable".[104] However, he soon received a testimonial presented to him by his parishioners asking him not to go. It did not necessarily impress him. He pointed out that his journey was not for pleasure; that he had held off going for thirteen years for the sake of the parish's needs; and that he would return before too long – Luke Rivington would run the parish in his absence. He was particularly irked that "as I read through the list of those who have signed the Memorial, I cannot but regret that many of them, seldom, if ever go to Church". While he was glad of their affection, "personal friendship carries us on together for a few years only [...] if they did value my ministrations as an ambassador of Christ, I should indeed rejoice even more".[105] Benson had no time for sentimentality when there were souls to be saved; but in the event he

96 Gray, 1 June 1871, in Charles Gray (ed), *Life of Robert Gray, Bishop of Cape Town*, London: Rivingtons (1876), ii:553ff.

97 BHT Minute Book 2, 45, PH.

98 *The Story of the Delhi Mission*, London: SPG (1908), 16.

99 Milman, 31 Aug 1867, SSJE/6/1/2/11/4.

100 Milman, 19 April 1872, ibid.

101 Henry Alexander Douglas, *A Charge Delivered At his Primary Visitation*, Bombay: Education Society (1875).

102 Douglas, 30 Nov 1871, SSJE/6/1/2/11/5/1ff.

103 *PM* July 1868.

104 Douglas, 22 Aug 1873, SSJE/6/1/2/11/5/3ff.

105 *PM* Aug 1873.

stayed once more at his post. "I asked the Bishop to decide," he wrote to Hall in September 1873, "and he thinks best not".[106] In August, Benson had published in the parish magazine a long Litany for the Conversion of India – just after the results of the Cowley St John Horticultural, Pigeon, and Rabbit Show.[107]

Yet again the ever-growing and varied needs of the parish – the Iron Church had to be enlarged in 1873[108] – kept Benson in England; but his dream of enabling mission work in India was nevertheless finally realised, albeit vicariously. When Page and his party sailed for Bombay on the *Muriel* in November 1873 after a bittersweet farewell gathering,[109] they took with them a portable altar and the chalice and paten from the Iron Church – although this was more practical than symbolic, as the plate ordered for the Indian mission had simply not arrived in time.[110] O'Neill followed in January – although the new priest-novice he took with him left after six months[111] – and "an Association for Intercessory Prayer on behalf of Indian Missions" was formed to prosper the work,[112] with even the parish children later corralled into prayer and modest almsgiving.[113]

The Free Church of Scotland Monthly Record reported – not entirely approvingly – that the Anglo-Catholic party in India was "in raptures" at the SSJE's arrival. The annual report of the Bombay Church Union – which provided support toward the initial establishment of the SSJE in India[114] – noted in 1874 the arrival of Page and John Biscoe, and described their companion Thomas Craister as "a Medical Associate".[115] The provision of medical care was reflected in other contemporary colonial missionary endeavours, and would also later play a large part in the Society's work in South Africa. After settling temporarily at Holy Trinity, Sonapur – a slum district in the north-east of the city – the brethren set about learning Marathi, and began to take stock of the wider area.[116]

By early 1875 Rivington had arrived to replace Biscoe, and Douglas – "always ready to forward the work of the Society"[117] – had asked the SSJE to take over St Peter's Church, Mazagon, before he was invalided home to die. Mazagon had long ceased to be a sleepy fishing village, and was now a bustling suburb: crowded, noisy, and hot. Ecclesiastical partisanship extended well into the Empire: a low-church portion of the congregation of St Peter's left in protest in 1876, citing their objection to Ritualism; and when the Peninsular and Oriental Company presented stained glass to St Peter's, *John Bull* noted that it was "to

106 Benson, 28 Sept 1873, in Woodgate, *Benson*, 118.

107 *PM* Aug 1873.

108 *PM* June 1873.

109 *PM* Dec 1873.

110 Fr [Edward Fenton] Elwin SSJE, *Thirty-Nine Years in Bombay City: Being the History of the Mission Work of the Society of St John the Evangelist in that City*, London: Mowbray & Co. (1913), 5.

111 Walter Wyon, notes on Christmas Retreat 1873, Cambridge University Library, MS(Add.7651):Wyon/9/1/1.

112 *PM* Nov 1873.

113 Page to the Children of the Parish, 20 April 1881, *PM* July 1881.

114 Elwin, *Bombay*, 15.

115 SSJE/6/1/2/11/16.

116 Woodgate, *Benson*, 119.

117 *PM* Jan 1876.

the delight of the [Anglo-Catholic] *Church Times,* and the horror of the [low-church] *Record."*[118]

When Douglas's successor Louis Mylne arrived in July 1876 his first act was to go to the nearest church to sing *Te Deum* for his safe passage. As he landed at Mazagon pier, that happened to be St Peter's, so the SSJE was associated with the new Bishop of Bombay from his first moments in the diocese.[119] Mylne was a Keble man, and the parish magazine noted his appointment with approval.[120] Others were less enthusiastic: the *Pall Mall Gazette* reported concerns that Mylne's mind was being poisoned in the SSJE's favour, to the detriment of low-church mission work.[121]

Despite the heat and humidity, Page threw himself into the work; and as time went on letters poured in from Bombay describing the seemingly incessant activity of the Indian mission. The brethren established medical facilities, parish schools for both expatriate and Indian children, and began to minister among destitute orphans. An organ was acquired and choral services established – there was even a little choir school[122] – and lectures were given on religious topics. Rivington "met some very nice young Hindoos" who he felt were, like others, ripe for conversion.[123] St Peter's thrived soon enough, and its infrastructure bore a striking resemblance to Benson's own work at Cowley – even down to the parish teas and the leading of missions in other places. Woodgate described Page as untouched by the heat, and padding the parish "with as much activity as if he was treading the streets of Oxford".[124]

Services began in the Marathi language in 1879, led by Nehemiah Goreh – whose language skills were of immediate and obvious value; and of whom more will be said. O'Neill had arrived in Bombay in 1874; but had gone on to work in Calcutta with Milman. After some time spent visiting and preaching at various mission stations he settled in Indore in 1875 – the British Resident welcomed him cheerfully to "the worst place in India"[125] – where he cultivated an extreme style of asceticism in the face of Benson's view that the brethren had a duty to keep themselves in good health: "We cannot afford to waste lives […] As you would take care of a piano, or any handsome school furniture, or a chasuble, so you must take care of a priest;"[126] which itself channelled Milman's advice of years earlier that "any <u>rule</u> in India must be adapted to the great heat".[127]

Gradually the brethren began travelling further afield; and their constant letters home were filled with news of the sights, smells, and sounds of the strange new country in which they found themselves. They were, however, not without significant supporters; and it is notable that at St Peter's School's

118 *John Bull,* 21 Aug 1875.
119 Elwin, *Bombay,* 28ff.
120 *PM* March 1876.
121 *Pall Mall Gazette,* 7 Nov 1876.
122 H. E. W. Slade SSJE, *A Work Begun: The Story of the Cowley Fathers in India 1874–1967,* London: SPCK (1970), 39.
123 *PM* July 1875.
124 Woodgate, *Benson,* 119.
125 Ibid, 128.
126 Benson, 5 Nov 1874, *Letters of Richard Meux Benson,* 37.
127 Milman, 31 Aug 1867, SSJE/6/1/2/11/4.

first Prize Day in 1879 the guest of honour was the Governor of the Bombay Presidency, Sir Richard Temple, while the Bishop of Calcutta, Ralph Johnson – who was also Metropolitan of India – presented the prizes.[128] It established a custom that continued for years to come.

CONSOLIDATION AT COWLEY

Gifts continued to be sent to Bombay from Cowley,[129] where things also moved on apace. On 6 May 1873 – the Feast of St John before the Latin Gate – Prince Leopold, Duke of Albany, laid the foundation stone for the new St John the Evangelist National Hospital for Incurables.[130] Its original purpose was short-lived; but its establishment brought to Cowley Harriet Brownlow Byron's All Saints Sisters of the Poor – who were already well-established as an experienced nursing order[131] – and the need to find a use for the buildings after it closed provided the Sisters with a new convent just a few minutes' walk from the Mission House.

Benson had provided the land himself; and he had been involved with the community since the end of the 1860s, when he had assisted Upton Richards, Vicar of Margaret Street and Chaplain of the community, as Richards's health declined. When he died in 1873 Benson was his obvious successor as Chaplain, and so in addition to John Mason Neale's Society of St Margaret at East Grinstead and William Butler's Community of St Mary the Virgin at Wantage, the All Saints Sisters now also came to be closely associated with the SSJE[132] – in 1893 the *Cowley Evangelist* described All Saints' Day as "a second patronal festival for those of us who see the work and lives of the All Saints' Sisters in three-quarters of the world".[133] In time they would be joined also by the Sisters of the Love of God, the Sisterhood of the Holy Childhood, and the Community of St John the Baptist at Clewer; and over the following decades all would collaborate in one way or another with the Society's work at home and abroad.

Aside from practical considerations – Peter Mayhew notes that at one point the SSJE's laundry was brought weekly from Marston Street – in the All Saints Sisters Benson had a formidable taskforce to whom his word was law: Mayhew considered that "Mother Foundress and her Sisters seem to have given [him] total obedience"; and when he asked them in 1878 to join Page in Bombay, they obliged.[134] Edward Elwin considered their arrival to be "an event of far-reaching importance as regards the furtherance of religious progress in Bombay";[135] and a year later the All Saints Bombay Mission Association was founded to

---

128 *PM* Feb 1880.

129 *PM* May 1884.

130 *PM* June 1873.

131 Peter Mayhew, *All Saints: Birth and Growth of a Community*, Oxford: Society of All Saints (1987), 108ff.

132 Ibid, 130ff.

133 *CE* Nov 1893.

134 Mayhew, *All Saints*, 134; 53; 161.

135 Elwin, *Bombay*, 36.

support their work.[136] They followed the Wantage Sisters, who had gone out in 1877 to work at Poona – where the governing classes of Bombay spent monsoon season – and where they would themselves soon be joined by members of the SSJE. Next to the hospital Benson intended to raise a new church to ease the overflowing Iron Church on Stockmore Street. The ground was broken in 1875, and the building was conceived as a memorial to Charles Longley, who had been Vicar of Cowley in the 1820s and had died as Archbishop of Canterbury in 1868.

The new parish was growing in all directions, both figuratively and literally. In October 1869, the *Oxford Times* noted that "in the ever-increasing district of Cowley St John there is scarcely a street but what has received some addition during the last twelve months."[137] Devotional Guilds were established; temperance societies set up; prayer associations formed; subscriptions raised for all kinds of work; schools established and maintained; social gatherings for parishioners arranged, and parties laid on for the choir. Within a decade of his momentous correspondence with Wilberforce, Benson had transformed his quiet living into a thriving centre of activity; and from the curious red brick building on Marston Street, with its narrow windows and its rooftop chapel, his Society of Mission Priests had established centres of mission in America and India, and was growing steadily. By the end of the 1870s the three founding members of the SSJE had been joined by eight other men who had also made their life vows: in addition to those named above they included Maturin and George Congreve.[138]

There were plenty of visitors, too. Benson noted that between forty and seventy men attended the annual October retreat between 1870 and 1884, and that there were on average 130 guests a year in the same period. They included a smattering of Americans, a couple of colonial princelings, and a number of men who would later join the Society themselves; but most of the regular visitors were parish priests on retreat: they included Oxford Movement figures like Charles Fuge Lowder, founder of the Society of the Holy Cross and its associated Sisterhood at St Peter's, London Docks; and Robert Suckling, who later succeeded Thomas Thellusson Carter as Superior of the Confraternity of the Blessed Sacrament. Black sheep also came; and the man calling himself "Frank Austin Rolfe", who stayed for five months in 1883, was almost certainly using a combination of two later pen names of the infamous Frederick William Rolfe – Graham Greene's "spoiled priest", and author of *Hadrian the Seventh*.[139]

Ninian Comper first came to the Mission House in 1874 as a ten-year-old boy: writing to his friend Richard Assheton, Congreve – who was a friend of Comper's father – noted that "he reads nearly all day, and helped by being in charge of the door now and then and is very well-behaved and obliging."[140] It was Congreve who first opened the young Comper's eyes to ecclesiastical architecture; and his visit was the start of a lifelong association with the Society. He later lodged in the house in Clerkenwell provided by the Sisters of

136 *PM* Dec 1879.
137 *Oxford Times*, 16 Oct 1869.
138 Profession Book, SSJE/1/4.
139 Greene, *Collected Essays*, 130ff.
140 Miller, *Congreve*.

Bethany for their SSJE chaplain during his indenture with G. F. Bodley, whose work he would enhance at Cowley fifty years later.

Owen Chadwick noted that the SSJE was "widely approved by the end of the seventies";[141] and the same could be said of the movement from which it had grown. In 1868 the Liberal Party had come to power under William Ewart Gladstone, who had matriculated at Christ Church 1828 – the year of Pusey's appointment to the Regius Professorship of Hebrew – and had himself been deeply influenced by Oxford Movement ideals. Gladstone's Crown appointments reflected his confidence in the movement's leaders, and in turn gave confidence to others. William Bright was made Regius Professor of Ecclesiastical History in 1868; Wilberforce – a friend of the movement, at least – was translated from Oxford to Winchester in 1869; and Henry Parry Liddon and Richard Church went to St Paul's as Canon and Dean respectively in 1870 and 1871. Perhaps most significantly of all, Edward King – who was closely associated with the Society – was appointed Regius Professor of Pastoral Theology in 1873.

Wilberforce's translation to Winchester had been, naturally enough, a matter of concern. His support had been crucial in the establishment of the SSJE, and, even with Gladstone as Prime Minister, there was uncertainty over who might replace him at Oxford – both as bishop of the diocese and as Visitor to the Society. Benson's resort, as ever, was to prayer:

> How little do people reflect upon the great duty of constant prayer that we may have Bishops appointed who shall really be diligent in promoting the work of God's Church. We should be especially careful to make this a matter of prayer at all times when we know that any fresh appointments are about to be made. God will give us good Bishops if we are only earnest in asking Him.[142]

His prayers were answered in the appointment of John Fielder Mackarness, in whom the Society found another friend. Benson assured him that "as we had learnt to love our bishop during the last quarter of the century, so we were able to yield that love to himself [Mackarness], not as a formal tribute of empty expression, but as a heartfelt reality of childlike affection, to one who came amongst us as his Lordship did […] in all the kindliness of a heart naturally loving, and the supernatural power of the love which the Holy Ghost inspires".

When Mackarness administered confirmation in the Iron Church in June 1871 – the first confirmation to take place there – he urged the candidates to be faithful in their reading of the Bible, constant in prayer, and frequent in their reception of Holy Communion: these were Oxford Movement principles writ large. The bishop also made the point, in 1872, that he could never come to Oxford from his palace at Cuddesdon without passing through the parish – and so he saw much more of the parish than any other in his diocese.[143] The Society's early growth and achievements, then, quite apart from Benson's own work in the parish, were nurtured within an increasingly sympathetic ecclesiastical context: under two benevolent bishops, and with the support – both

---

141 Chadwick, *Victorian Church*, ii:338.
142 *PM* Sept 1869.
143 *PM* Dec 1872.

spiritual and financial – of many of the people of the parish and others beyond its bounds, as borne out in the lists of subscribers to various good works which appeared from time to time in the parish magazine. By 1878 the chancel of the new church of Ss Mary & John had been completed, and Sunday services were being held there – but Mackarness would only consecrate the building once some of the nave had been built, and so appointed parishioners were sent door-to-door to secure donations.[144] Some of their methods were robust: a formerly lukewarm parishioner later recalled that while he was considering subscribing, his visitor challenged him with "whilst you are thinking, souls are dying". He duly made his contribution; and started going to church.[145]

At the same time the Vicar of Cowley St John never lost sight of his other identity – that of the Superior of a religious community. He continued to encourage, teach, and invigorate the members of the SSJE through letters to individual brethren at home and abroad, and the preached retreats that had been at the heart of the life of the Society from the beginning. Among the subjects on which he chose to address the assembled members in July 1874 was "Hope".

> A religious must essentially be a man of great hope. His whole life is one of hope. He is ever living in the future. Though things should be realized around him beyond all conception, yet he dares not pause to think upon them; he is still looking out. Though things be dark and threatening, he dares not draw backward. He must still be looking on.[146]

It was wise advice that would serve the Society of St John the Evangelist well in the next decade; for the 1880s were years of significant gains, but also of painful losses.

---

144 *PM* Jan 1878.
145 *PM* Feb 1882.
146 R. M. Benson, *Instructions on the Religious Life*, London: Mowbray & Co. (1935), 111.

5

Growing Pains

Avoid sitting on sofas.
—SSJE Rule

The 1880s saw the beginnings of the heyday of the Oxford Movement: Owen Chadwick argued that by the middle of the decade it was "at last attaining the summit of its influence in the Church of England".[1] It was also a period during which the growth of the religious communities became impossible to ignore at an official level, both in the Church Congresses and in Convocation, which Donald Allchin charted in the second part of *The Silent Rebellion*. The Church Congress of 1888 discussed "The Desirableness of Reviving the Common Religious Life for Men", and Benson was invited to speak: the first occasion, Allchin observed, "on which a member of a religious community had spoken of the inner justification of the religious life".[2]

Benson was clear that to approach the subject from a point of view of the useful work that might be carried out by men's orders was to fall at the first hurdle. "There can be but one reason for entering a religious life", he urged, "one adequate reason, one only reason – a call from God to do so". Having established that point, he was insistent on others: the religious life existed to do good work for God's sake rather than to satisfy a contemporary desire for secular philanthropy; to witness to the joy of poverty and to encourage the wealthy to spend their money on godly purposes; and not, above all, to provide cheap labour for the Church. The idea of the last was "a sacrilege, an insult to God".[3]

The life of the Society of St John the Evangelist had grown significantly since its inception in 1866. Charles Grafton's idea that its members might be called the "Johnians" came to nothing;[4] but almost from the beginning the brethren were referred to colloquially either as the "Evangelist Fathers", which did not stick, or as the more homely and affectionate "Cowley Fathers", which did. Fourteen men were professed as the 1880s rolled on, including Edward Osborne, Frederick Puller, and the layman William Maynard Shaw. Shaw was a son of the parsonage and had worked for both Kempe and Bodley; and as Br Maynard his considerable practical skills would come into their own as the Society raised new buildings at home and abroad in the years ahead. The

---

1 Owen Chadwick, *Victorian Church*, ii:338.
2 Allchin, *Silent Rebellion*, 139ff; 152.
3 *Church Congress Report* (1888), 724ff.
4 Grafton, 2 Sept 1866, in Pendleton, *Grafton*, 31.

rest were all experienced clergymen: Puller was very well regarded indeed, and by the time of his death had declined the episcopate thrice.[5] They were each given specific duties, and areas of the parish in which to concentrate their efforts.[6]

Nevertheless, Benson's address to the Church Congress in 1888 came towards the end of a decade that was a period of great upheaval in the Society; and one in which the advances it made were tempered by very grave setbacks. The American work continued to expand, and novices and priest brethren continued to be sent from Cowley to both Boston and Philadelphia. From both houses the members of the Society led missions across the nation, directed women's communities, cared for the needs of the poor, and visited the sick – much as they did at home. As Eldridge Pendleton observed, however, this constant activity came with its own dangers; and the first to succumb was the Provincial Superior, Grafton himself.[7]

Grafton's health had collapsed in 1875, and it had not been unanticipated. As early as 1872 George Shattuck had warned Benson that he was working too hard and refused to rest; and eventually he suffered a total breakdown. He was sent back to Cowley to recuperate; but although he seems to have regarded his bodily sufferings as pain to be borne for the sake of the glory still to come, there were also mental effects which caused him to question his vocation. While he was at the Mission House he and Benson discussed and disagreed about the future of the American work: Grafton wanted the order in the United States to be independent of Cowley, while Benson refused to countenance the idea.

Disappointed, and after a period of travel in Europe, Grafton had returned to Boston in 1877 and reassumed charge of the Church of the Advent, which had outgrown its site on Bowdoin Street – the ground was broken for a new and much larger building in 1879. His quarrels with Benson continued, however: they revolved mainly around the issue of whether the American congregation might be given its independence, and the Society's lack of a written constitution.

To be fair to Benson, Grafton and Prescott had been at the centre of various disagreements with the ecclesiastical authorities in the Episcopal Church from the beginning – and Prescott from even earlier – and he had been obliged to travel to the United States twice in 1880 alone to try and calm the situation at St Clement's. By 1881 Prescott, to whom, apparently, "all questions of ceremonial meant much",[8] had been inhibited again – although the inhibition seems to have come more from the prejudices of the new Bishop of Maryland, William Pinckney, than from any action of Prescott's – and the embarrassment caused Benson to ask him to resign. He made it clear that it was not a matter of obedience; but that if he remained at his post the other members of the Society who assisted him would be withdrawn.

---

5 *CE* March 1938.
6 Congreve, *Reminiscences*, SSJE/6/5/5/2.
7 Pendleton, *Grafton*, 45.
8 Woodgate, *Benson*, 112.

The ultimatum hints at the issues of divided loyalties that seemed to surround the controversies at St Clement's, and to some extent at the Advent as well. Both Grafton and Prescott were incumbents in the Episcopal Church, and members of the SSJE. They owed canonical obedience to the unsympathetic bishops of their diocese; and religious obedience to their Superior. This was a tightrope that all parties trod with difficulty: Prescott complained that Benson did not understand the workings of the Episcopal Church, and Jervis Zimmerman has noted that "as an American Rector, Prescott felt bound to make the Parish his first interest, while Fr Benson thought that the Society should have been Prescott's first consideration".[9] Obedience to one might seem disobedience to the other.

Benson did not help matters by attempting, at a distance, to direct the work of Prescott's SSJE assistants and that of the All Saints Sisters who had arrived to work in the parish in 1880. This was symptomatic of the problem of there being no written constitution that laid out explicitly who was responsible for whom; and of decisions regarding localised overseas work being made at Cowley, four thousand miles away. All in all, Prescott felt that Benson "had little or no knowledge of our national churches – the Constitution and Canons of our Church and the practical working of our ecclesiastical system".[10] It was a pertinent point – and a similar controversy had arisen when Benson had sent Osborne to assist at the Advent without the bishop's knowledge or permission. The Church in India was essentially run as a colonial offshoot of the Church of England; whereas the Episcopal Church in the United States had developed along different and independent lines. In the former the SSJE was part of the Establishment; and in the latter it was a foreign institution. "It is impossible", wrote Prescott a little later, "for our Society to be what it ought to be if the Episcopate is united against it [...] as it is presented to them with a foreign ecclesiastic as its head".[11]

This was a long way from Benson's assertion of 1865 that the Society would "not intrude ourselves into any Diocese against the will of the Bishop"; and Grafton and Prescott were torn. Matters came to a head in 1881, when Benson wrote an indiscreet letter to Arthur Hall, after Grafton had intimated that unless a separation could be agreed then he and others would be forced to consider withdrawing from the Society.[12]

> Much as one must regret losing Father Grafton and Father Prescott – either or both of them – one feels it is only the manifestation of a loss accomplished long ago. They have both of them lost their vocation and perhaps they ought to have been expelled. One does not like to realize such facts, but, of course, as long as they continue with us, although they may keep us from the dust of a smash, they still more keep us back from vital progress.[13]

---

9 Zimmerman, *Prescott*, 84ff.
10 Mayhew, *All Saints*, 14.
11 Prescott, 10 Jan 1882, in Zimmerman, *Prescott*, 94.
12 Pendleton, *Grafton*, 47ff.
13 Benson, 13 Sept 1881, in Pendleton, *Grafton*, 69.

This was a disastrous lapse of judgement; because, although Benson tried to conceal the letter, the Superior of each house customarily opened incoming post. Glancing at the envelope, Grafton – who happened to be in the house when the post arrived – thought that the handwriting was that of a friend in Oxford, and duly opened it himself.

Benson had taken a gamble, and it had failed. Grafton was horrified by the fact that he had tried to convey the message to Hall by means of trickery, and even more so by what he had said about him, a Provincial Superior, to a junior member of his own house. A series of recriminatory exchanges followed; while Prescott asked for a meeting at Cowley between himself and Benson, Grafton, and O'Neill "to consider and arrange the whole matter of the relationship of the English portion of the Society to the American branch and so clear the way for a constitution which shall recognize the fact that the Society is a coalition of priests belonging to two separate and independent Churches".[14]

Benson was unyielding; and in any case thought that Grafton was far from being in his right mind. Shattuck had intimated, after his return to the Advent in 1877, that Grafton was not entirely recovered from his breakdown; and from Cowley his behaviour seemed to be becoming ever more erratic. Writing to Walter Gardner, Benson noted that he had heard "a sad account of Fr Grafton", which reported that

> on the F[east] of the Holy Name after celebrating he burst forth in a long extempore prayer which he screamed out alluding to his own sincerity and the persecution of his enemies – then he gave the congregation Benediction with the Blessed Sacrament and remained prostrate before it until after Nones.[15]

Meanwhile, Prescott declined Benson's request for him return to Cowley unless it was for the quadripartite meeting that he had requested;[16] and by August 1882 there was only one possible outcome: the separation of the American brethren from the Society. Grafton, Prescott, and Gardner, together with Br Benedict, requested and were granted release. There was even confusion over the nature of the parting, however, with at least Grafton and Prescott hoping that they might still form the nucleus of an American congregation of the SSJE.[17]

The division also tore apart the parish of the Advent. Pro-Grafton and pro-Benson parties formed, the members of the Vestry took sides, and the arguments were carried on in the local press and the *Living Church*, the Episcopal Church's weekly newspaper. In addition, a majority of the members of the Society of St Margaret – which had flourished since its arrival in Boston in the early 1870s – refused to live under the Wardenship of a priest who was no longer a member of the SSJE. Eventually it was arranged that Grafton would remain Rector of the Advent and refound the parish in the new building on Brimmer Street, and the sisters who left the Society of St Margaret were con-

---

14 Prescott, 16 Feb 1882, in Zimmerman, *Prescott*, 95.
15 Benson, Aug 1882, SSJE/6/1/2/3/2/20.
16 Prescott, 4 July 1882, in Zimmerman, Prescott, 96ff.
17 Pendleton, *Grafton*, 70; Zimmerman, *Prescott*, 98.

stituted into the Sisterhood of the Holy Nativity. The old building on Bowdoin Street was rededicated to St John the Evangelist and became the Society's mission church in Boston, led by the English brethren assisted by the Society of St Margaret; and Prescott resigned from St Clement's.

Mildred Woodgate's cheery assertion that "no bitterness seems to have been engendered by them, Father Benson and Father Grafton remaining the same friends they had always been" was painfully wide of the mark.[18] In 1884 Benson was clear that "nothing would make it possible for us to receive [Grafton] back into the Community"; but he conceded that nonetheless "our hearts have never lost their hold upon him".[19] It was not until many years later that they achieved anything approaching reconciliation; but in his memoirs Grafton referred his former Superior as "that dear and wise saint",[20] and in 1912 sent him fond greetings from his deathbed.[21] When Prescott died in 1903 the Cowley Evangelist insisted, too, that "though circumstances have for some years past separated Father Prescott from outward action along with the Cowley Fathers, yet the bond of brotherly love was never broken".[22]

The events of 1882 bring us, unavoidably, to a consideration of Benson's actions in the light of his dealings with the American brethren. Looking back on the period in 1958, Robert Cheney Smith considered that "the underlying cause of the trouble seems to have been Father Grafton's unwillingness to accept the decision of his Superior that he was incapable of assuming the leadership of an affiliated branch of the Society of St John the Evangelist in America".[23] Cheney Smith was writing at some distance, however, and from a position of loyalty to his Society and its Founder. Benson can hardly be regarded as having been blameless in the matter. Sixteen years of uncertainty perhaps explain Grafton's impatience; but the Founder's intransigence and inflexibility compounded the matter and made the situation more difficult than it might otherwise have been.

Zimmerman considers that Gardner was responsible for the publication of correspondence between himself and Benson;[24] with a foreword that effectively accused the latter of duplicity and subterfuge. Prescott was more explicit: Benson's character, he thought, was "a grand puzzle".

I never met a man with whom acquaintance, as acquaintance goes in the world, was more edifying. He is full of zeal and devotion and he stirs one's better nature like a breath from heaven. I do not see how he could tell a wilful lie to save his soul. And yet in carrying out his religious ideas, I cannot recognize him as true or honest, but I think that I knew him to be very immoral indeed [...] Time and time again he has told me things were so and so when I had proof that they were not [...] But no, he had said it, and obedience demanded that what he said should be done and obedience was the duty even if truth was nowhere.

---

18 Woodgate, Benson, 114.
19 Benson, 16 Nov 1884, SSJE/6/1/2/3/2/39.
20 Grafton, Journey Godward, 63.
21 Pendleton, Grafton, 172.
22 CE Jan 1904.
23 Cheney Smith, Bowdoin Street, 13.
24 A Reprint of Letters to the Superior of the Society of St John the Evangelist, Oxford (1883).

"He is a saint with a mission," concluded Prescott, "and that mission he thinks must be carried out without regard to things honest or lovely or of good report".[25]

Benson was certainly authoritarian: Woodgate described him as "ruling his Society as the autocrat he was at heart".[26] From the All Saints Sisters of the Poor he demanded – and received – unquestioning obedience. He had particularly insisted upon it in the mid-1870s when he disapproved of several feasts that the sisters wished to include in their new office book, with the exception, incongruously, of St Vincent de Paul – to whom he seems to have had a particular devotion, which in itself supports Pendleton's suggestion that the SSJE was based on a Vincentian model.[27] His ascetic spirituality was extreme, even in his own day, and this would put strain on the community. As Peter Mayhew observed,

> Fr Benson's goodness and his intellectual and spiritual powers were great beyond all dispute [...] Yet a concentration on the being of God and on the Cross of his Son, to the detriment of present circumstances, has its difficulties and dangers. It may indeed be possible for some to be conscious at the same time of the presence of God and of urgent human need. For others it may seem necessary to give completely undivided attention for a time to the remedying of some form of human suffering. In problems of relationships in a Community, it may be vital to concentrate completely upon the achieving of a mutual sensitivity.[28]

THE SOCIETY CONSTITUTED

B enson undoubtedly failed to achieve mutual sensitivity in the American business; but – as upsetting as the separation was – the burgeoning life of the Society meant that other work also needed to be nurtured and sustained. A new house had been built at Mazagon in 1880, O'Neill had begun work at Indore, and in 1882 the Indian mission was further augmented when the Society began its official connection with the Clewer Sisters' mission at Poona at Louis Mylne's request; although individual brethren had been associated with the Poona mission since the Society's arrival in India.[29] The building of the Church of the Holy Name began in 1883, and Mylne himself stayed at the Mission House at the end of the year.[30] Meanwhile, the ongoing viability of the North American work was demonstrated by a new venture in British Columbia, where the Bishop of New Westminster, Acton Sillitoe, had invited the Society to work the previous year.[31]

At home, the construction of the new parish church of Ss Mary & John continued, but although it was consecrated by John Mackarness on 6 November it

---

25 Prescott, 20 Mar 1885, in Zimmerman, *Prescott*, 103.

26 Woodgate, *Benson*, 91.

27 Pendleton, *Grafton*, 37.

28 Ibid, 57.

29 Edward Elwin, SSJE, *Forty-Five Years in Poona City*, London: Mowbray & Co. (1922), 22.

30 *SSJE Chronicles*, SSJE/6/1/1/8/85; 113.

31 *PM* Aug & Sept 1882.

was very much an exercise in economy.[32] Introducing the designs at a parish meeting, the architect, Alfred Mardon Mowbray, explained that "in accordance with the Vicar's wish, the design of the remainder of the building was as simple as was consistent with the dignity due to its sacred character and of the chancel already erected; but although for a time it would have to depend for its beauty principally on its proportion, he had taken care to leave ample opportunity for enrichment in the shape of both carving and other decoration [...] The tower had been designed so as to allow the portion above the belfry floor being added later if necessary."[33] In the end most of Mowbray's potential additions, including the aesthetically much-needed spire, remained unexecuted.[34]

1883 also represents a high-water mark of the English congregation's work, because it saw the SSJE continuing its work in America and India, newly established in Canada, and about to embark on one of the most important and significant steps of its life: its work in South Africa. The strong ties between the Society of St John the Evangelist and the All Saints Sisters of the Poor were described by Mayhew as "a special and blessed relationship";[35] and in 1883 the sending of Puller to Cape Town as chaplain to the Sisters' work there opened a chapter in the Society's history quite distinct from any other.

The departure of the American brethren was distressing; but it was not in the end a disaster. The Society continued to flourish in the United States and elsewhere; but the episode seems to have stirred Benson into action. One of Grafton's complaints had been that there was still no formal SSJE constitution; and it was becoming clear that, faced with ever-growing overseas work, it would be impossible for Benson to continue to run the Society personally. In this context, Woodgate's observation that "with a Society which boasted men of the calibre of Father Congreve, Father Puller and others, it was obvious that power and authority must be shared, and clearly defined rules laid down" is particularly perceptive;[36] and although it was too late to retain Grafton and Prescott, by 1884 Benson was willing to constitute the Society formally.

A ledger was begun, which opened with the words "In the Name of the Father and of the Son and of the Holy Ghost. Amen. Book of the Chapter of the Society of St John the Evangelist." This was the first in a series of Chapter Books that continued in use until 2012, and the first piece of business was the laying down of the Society's Statutes: "On Monday Sept 15th 1884 at the Mission House, Cowley St John, after Terce and the Litany of the Holy Ghost said in Chapel, the Revd the Father Superior General opened a Conference of the Professed Fathers mentioned below, in the Library of the Society, and invited them to consider a draught [sic] of Statutes for the Community which he laid before them."[37]

---

32 *PM* Feb 1882.

33 Ibid.

34 Jennifer Sherwood and Nikolaus Pevsner, *The Buildings of England: Oxfordshire*, London: Penguin Books (1974), 341.

35 Mayhew, *All Saints*, 162.

36 Woodgate, *Benson*, 147,

37 SSJE/2/1/1.

The "Professed Fathers mentioned below" were George Congreve, Robert Page, Arthur Hall, Luke Rivington, Walter Wyon, Basil Maturin, William Black, George Sheppard, Frederick Puller, William Longridge, and Willard Huson (who would become a Roman Catholic only a few weeks later).[38] The influence of the Brotherhood of the Holy Trinity remained strong; and almost every one was also a member of the English Church Union, as was Benson.[39] As early as 1872 the tone had been set with a robust opposition to any attempt to remove the Athanasian Creed from the Book of Common Prayer – "The truth which is set forth in this Creed is necessary to salvation, for if we reject it we reject that knowledge of God which He has been pleased to give us respecting Himself" – and the *Parish Magazine* had embarked on a frenzy of solid Trinitarian teaching in verse: "Whate'er Thou art is of Thyself / In bliss unchanged to be, / Father, and Son, and Holy Ghost, / One God eternally."[40]

After a lengthy discussion agreement was also reached as to the most appropriate form of the Statutes. They opened with an affirmation of the Society's corporate identity:

> The Society of the Mission Priests of St John the Evangelist has been formed for the cultivation of a life dedicated to God according to the principles of poverty, chastity, and obedience, and will occupy itself in works both Missionary and educational, both at home and abroad, for the advancement of the Kingdom of Christ, as God in His good Providence may seem to call.
>
> They will also have Lay Brothers united with them in dedication to the Religious Life who shall assist as far as they can in the works of the Society, but the Government of the Society shall rest with the Professed Fathers only.[41]

The Statutes established a number of important principles that would direct the work of the Society in the decades ahead. The pain of Grafton and Prescott's separation was immediately visible in Statute 1 – "All members of the Society must be careful to observe all canonical obligations belonging to any position which they may occupy in any diocese" – and a good deal of discussion had taken place on the embarrassing and delicate matter of the withdrawal of the American brethren.[42] Benson was also keen to establish in Statute 2 that the brethren were individuals bound voluntarily together, and that their membership of the Society did not release them from "any constitutional claim upon their obedience belonging to the Church or her authorities". Statute 3 specifically anticipated increasing overseas work: no member of the Society would be sent abroad without his consent.

The Superior General – Benson had clearly amended the nomenclature to reflect the overseas work – would be elected every three years, and there was no limit on the number of terms he might serve (Statute 4). This would be by a clear majority in a secret ballot, in which only professed priest-brethren might vote. Statute 10 detailed the process by which any future stalemate might be

38 *SSJE Chronicles*, SSJE/6/1/1/8/50.
39 ECU Archives, PH.
40 *PM* April & May 1872.
41 *Statutes of the Society of St John the Evangelist*, SSJE/1/4.
42 SSJE/2/1/6–42.

broken, and every effort was made for every eligible member of the Society to be able to cast his vote: in the case of brethren not being able to return home to vote in the election of a Superior General, a Provincial Chapter would be held in advance and the votes sent or brought to General Chapter (Statute 8); and, failing that, a member on a distant mission might communicate his own vote through his Provincial Superior (Statute 15). That said, any members of the Society still not able to cast a vote within the various provisions made were bound to "accept the decision of the majority as cheerfully as if they had been able to give their vote" (Statute 14). On matters requiring discussion in General Chapter, the overseas brethren sent in their comments on agenda proposals in advance, which were then read out.

A number of themes emerge from the Statutes, which give an insight into the mind of the members of the Society in the mid-1880s. There was a clear and distinct separation, for example, between the priest-brethren and the lay brothers; with the latter to be formed separately and excluded from the Society's formal channels of self-governance – the Rule was clear that laymen were "subordinate members".[43] This drew on the prevailing contemporary mood in the Catholic movement regarding the involvement of the laity in ecclesiastical affairs: as early as 1868 Rivington had addressed a meeting of the Church Union and maintained that "the laity were there simply to listen not to vote [...] It was not that he undervalued the office of the laity, whose high and noble prerogative it was to listen and obey, but it was for the ministers of the Church with all their responsibilities to magnify their office, if so be that others would intrude upon it."[44] Such an argument reflected the practice of the Roman Catholic Church, and it was aired well enough for Walter Walsh to rebuke Rivington, who was by then himself a Roman Catholic, for it in his *History of the Romeward Movement in the Church of England* over thirty years later;[45] but in any case and at the time of the vote on the Statutes only two lay brothers had been professed: Benedict in 1877, who had since left, and Maynard in 1883.[46] In many of the contemporary women's orders a similar distinction was made in favour of the choir sisters.[47]

Clear forms of governance were laid out, and the management of the Society's finances was explained. Processes by which appointments within the Society would be made were presented, as well as how postulants would be formed and novices elected for profession – or not. The Statutes also included the manner in which even a Superior General might be forced to resign in the event of failure of "government, morals, or doctrine" (Statute 22). But within the clarity of the 84 or so Statutes – some were removed later, and others modified by votes in Chapter – were also a number of sensible caveats. Given the nature of the order's work – and particularly its presence in India and South Africa – each Provincial Superior was to be "careful to see that the rules and customs of

43 *Rule of Life*, no.1, "Of the Objects of the Society".
44 ECU Circular, 1 Feb 1868, 64–5, PH.
45 Walter Walsh, *The History of the Romeward Movement in the Church of England 1833–1864*, London: James Nisbet & Co. (1900), 48–9.
46 SSJE/1/4/11.
47 Mumm, *Stolen Daughters*, 8.

the Society are observed in all the Houses under his jurisdiction, *due allowance being made for any local necessity* [my italics]" (Statute 39).

All correspondence was to pass through the hands of each house Superior; but an exception was made for letters to or from members' "own Superiors in Religion or the immediate members of their own families" (Statute 56). This ensured that the brethren had access to independent spiritual advice when needed, and – although Benson put great emphasis on the element of the detachment from the world in the religious life[48] – regular contact with their loved ones. Although those elected for profession might make a financial contribution to the Society – an appropriate sum would be agreed upon – it was not an obligation (Statute 69); and any income belonging to a particular member of the Society was not required to be paid into the Common Fund, as had been the case with Grafton in 1866 (Statute 70). Those in receipt of a private income were the successors of the "men of independent means" whom Benson had envisaged would join him when he discussed his ideas for work in India with Robert Milman in 1859.[49]

The Superior General's word was law – except when it was not. A good deal of authority, for example, rested with the Provincial Superiors: Statute 18 gave them the authority, acting together, to nullify the Superior General's otherwise absolute veto of business proposed by individual priest-brethren. They also had the authority (Statute 21) "if unanimously presented" to force the Superior General to call a General Chapter at any time. Perhaps this, more than anything, presents us with the Society's vision for the years ahead: by 1884 the Society of St John the Evangelist was a growing religious order with serious international interests; which the Superior General could hardly be expected to govern alone.

The brethren also voted formally to accept the *Rule of Life*, which hitherto had only really existed in verbal addresses by Benson from the 1870s onwards, and the on the necessity of which he had been unequivocal: "we have to act by Rule."[50] Unlike the rules of the Brotherhood of the Holy Trinity – "not strict Rules, but Rules strictly to be aimed at"[51] – the *Rule of Life* of the Society of St John the Evangelist contained the principles by which each member of the Society would live, each day. In 1918 Allan Cameron considered the Rule to be "one of the severest in Christendom"[52]; and although Benson mitigated "avoid sitting on sofas" with "at any rate do not lounge on them" – perhaps that particular exhortation should be seen in the light of his explanation of the apparent ban on theatre-going in the BHT, and his advice given to the young Charles Gore on fasting in other people's houses[53] – it generally points to an austerity and strictness that may well seem baffling to modern sensibilities.

"It is the object of the Society of St John the Evangelist", declared *Of the Objects of the Society*, "to seek that sanctification, to which God in his mercy calls us, and in so doing, to seek, so far as God may permit, to be instrumental

---

48 R. M. Benson, *Instructions on the Religious Life*, London: Mowbray & Co. (1935), 81ff.
49 Benson, 10 June 1859, SSJE/6/1/2/11/1.
50 Benson, *Instructions on the Religious Life*, 50.
51 BHT Minute Book 7, 181ff, PH.
52 Cameron, *Religious Communities*, 66.
53 G. L. Prestige, *The Life of Charles Gore, A Great Englishman*, London: Heinemann (1935), 15.

in bringing others to be partakers of the same sanctification, bearing always in mind that above all things it is necessary for those who carry out the work of Missions to abide in Christ, apart from Whom we can do nothing." Candidates who felt called to the work were not to be "rejected because some one particular gift may be wanting", and nor were they to be discouraged if they were poor: "all, whether contributing money to the funds of the Society, or not, must remember that it is their duty to help the Society forward by the exercise of all *spiritual* energies which they possess [my italics]". Postulants would be "thoroughly instructed" on their obligations, and spend a month on spiritual retreat before receiving the habit; after which as novices they were expected "cheerfully [to] perform whatever duties are assigned to them in the House or Garden, however menial".

The novitiate was designed to be especially rigorous, and its expectations are worth quoting at length:

> They shall learn the Psalter, and other parts of Holy Scripture, by heart, in the English version, and when it is possible in the original tongues.

> They shall be kept apart from the Professed, as much as possible, and shall never speak expect with those who are set over them, unless the special leave of the Superior be granted.

> They must be practised in bearing all kinds of humiliations, and must be trained to live simply with the desire of the glory of God.

> Constantly they must dwell upon the thirty years of the hidden life of the Incarnate Word, that they may learn patiently to wait until the time when they shall be put forward for profession.

> They must understand that the whole success of their future life depends primarily upon the exactness with which they carry out the rule of their novitiate, and the prayerfulness with which it is sanctified.

A man who stayed the course and was professed was left in no doubt of the nature of that action. "Deadness to the world must henceforth be complete. Any conscious violation of such deadness becomes a grievous sin. Earthly hopes and fears are to be entirely put away." His cell was "the grave in which the Religious is buried to the world, and the Paradise in which he finds heaven begin" – notwithstanding the fact that it was intended that the Superior should "from time to time change the articles in the various cells in order to preserve a spirit of detachment". These were particularly hard sayings whose implications would cause deep concern within a few years, as we shall see.

The rest of the Rule contained instructions on the Three Vows, on the living out of Poverty, Chastity, and Obedience, and on the wearing of the habit – "the symbol of our separation from the world and its vanities". It dealt with each member of the Society's devotional life, and even the posture that should be assumed both in and out of worship. *Of Demeanour* reads rather like a lesson on deportment.

The Brethren shall accustom themselves, whether alone or with others, to sit and stand straight, not lounging on tables or chairs, nor cross-legged. The hands should be held quietly before the person and generally joined unless occupied in holding the cloak.

The customary tokens of reverence shall be shown by all those who are their Superiors in the Community, uncovering the head when passing them, or speaking to them, thus, Laymen before Priests, Novices before professed.

All shall rise at the entrance of the Father Superior, or, in his absence, of the Father Assistant, or when he leaves the room.

Recollectedness of demeanour must be carefully cherished when out walking, but there must be no appearance of gloom.

Haste and noise must always be avoided.

In moving about the house and at meals much pain should be taken to be as quiet as possible.

Meanwhile, "in Chapel there should be devotional composure, but any obtrusive exaggeration of voice and gesture is to be avoided. The palms of the hands should be joined together and lifted up when kneeling or standing for praise or prayer, unless they are occupied in holding the book – but they should be held to the breast and not far away from the person". Outside the house, "in speaking to strangers there must always be cheerfulness and courtesy, and all appearance of haste or annoyance must be carefully eschewed". Naturally, the brethren were to "as much as possible avoid speaking with women out of doors", nor "walk alongside women alone unless there be some great necessity, or in country places where they are staying with their family". Perhaps the last point amply demonstrates the social make-up of the professed members of the Society as it stood in 1884.

Other matters were dealt with in turn: *Brotherly Correction*, which was to be given with the "meekness and gentleness of Christ", and received "with thankfulness"; *Private Reading* – emphasis to be laid on Patristic works, and newspapers not to be read until the afternoon, "except it be for momentary enquiry on some occasion of special emergency, or when travelling on the rail-road"; and *Conversation*, which was to be frequently of "Holy Scripture and points of moral theology".

The Rule also dealt with the keeping of *Silence* – "the chief joy of the Religious"; *Correspondence* – all to be sent through the hands of the Superior in each place, "those to relatives sealed – others open"; *Recreation* – walks to be taken on Sundays and one weekday a fortnight "with such companion as may be assigned by the Father in charge"; *Leaving the House* – forbidden without permission; use of the *Library* – all books to be returned before Saturday Compline; and of *The House in General* – "nothing is to be taken from one room to another without leave". The sick were to accept their illness "with penitence and thankfulness", and to be cared for with observance of the Rule: "A sick room should be a chamber of devotion [...] It must never degenerate into a chamber of idle gossip".

Visitors were to be "treated with courtesy", but not used as an excuse for breaking the Rule, particularly in respect of silence. Travel was to be as inexpensive as possible while remaining seemly, and was to be used as an opportunity for intercessory prayer for fellow travellers, and for edifying conversation when appropriate. Rules for missions followed, and then instructions about the reading of the Rule itself: part of it was to be read aloud each day; and each Father was to read it in its entirety once a month, confessing any breaches at a Chapter of Faults.

Last of all, perhaps inevitably, came the regulations relating to the lay members of the Society. They were effectively the successors to the lay brethren of earlier centuries: separated from the choir monks, and under the charge of a Master. Their common room was theirs alone (they were forbidden from using any other), and they would have books provided – "but they must not take books from the Library of the Society". They were allowed to write to their parents once a fortnight; while any other letters were only to be written with permission of the Master, and, of course, to be handed to him unsealed.

The Master was also in charge of their devotional life: he was to give them meditations to carry out, and instruct them when to make their confessions – normally to the Superior. As the instructions continue it is easy to glean what their position and function was within the house. They were to attend Lauds and Compline, and "such other of the offices as their work may allow". There was a truncated version to be said when they could not get to Chapel, and "those who are in the kitchen will say their abbreviated office together". They were to be "loving amongst themselves and respectful to their Superiors, always uncovering the head, or bowing when they pass one of the Fathers, and rising when any Father comes into the room". They were to rise at 5 o'clock every morning, and to put their gaslights out at 10 p.m.

The *Rule of Life*, as adopted, was to a great extent based on ancient monastic principles, but brought into line with British life in the second half of the nineteenth century. It would be tweaked from time to time by General Chapter, but in its general form stood as the touchstone of the Society's life for nearly a century – and it would be appealed to again and again as successive Superiors General attempted to steer the Society through the turmoil of the decades to come. The Statutes, meanwhile, were adopted in Chapter on 15 September 1884, and ratified by Mackarness a week later. Together with the Rule they were printed and bound, pocket size, to be a *vade mecum* for each member of the Society.[54] Benson caused a memorandum to be appended to the discussions of the first proper Chapter Meeting:

> In the afternoon of the Monday following the Chapter Sept 22 1884 The Revd the Father Superior General with all the Members of the Society at that time in England waited upon the Lord Bishop of Oxford at Cuddesdon. His Lordship received them in the Palace Chapel, and after declaring his acceptance of the office of Visitor to which he had been elected by the Chapter, gave his blessing to the Society collectively and individually, laying his hands upon each one present. The book, containing the Statutes and the Spiritual Rule as adopted

---

54 SSJE/1/1/4.

by the Chapter and approved by the Bishop were then signed by each of the Professed Fathers kneeling at the steps of the Altar.[55]

DEAD TO THE WORLD

The official constitution and ratification of the Society was part of what Grafton had felt necessary for its ongoing flourishing, but he was not there to see it; and neither was O'Neill, who had died of cholera at Indore in 1882.[56] The newly-ratified Society, then, included only one of its original members: Benson himself. His stubbornness had played a part in the withdrawal of the Americans; but there are signs of other aspects of his character which, combined with a strict interpretation of the Rule, were also problematic.

Despite its busyness and its successes at home and abroad, life in the Society – or at least at the mother house on Marston Street – was perhaps not as happy as it might have been. Benson's spiritual output in the 1880s was immense: as well as his oversight of the Society he produced the third volume of his *Spiritual Readings* in 1882; two volumes of *The Final Passover* in 1884 and 1885; and *The Magnificat* in 1889. The impression of the writing of these works – as all of his books, to say nothing of his voluminous letters to members of the Society – is one that Woodgate was at pains to present as carried out in "the candle-lit cell in which the Superior sat, his pen driving so rapidly over his paper, [with] little in the way of heat".[57]

As can be seen in the Rule, and as Rosemary Kemsley observed in *Benson of Cowley*, he "very often compared the religious life to entry into the tomb. When the door of the Mission House chapel closed on the community assembled for a profession ceremony the brother or father to be professed was to think of the stone being rolled across the door of the sepulchre".[58] For Benson the living-out of the life was in the context of extreme self-discipline; but it was a form of self-discipline so rigid that almost none of his brethren could come near to it. Perhaps O'Neill came closest, before his early death: his asceticism and devotion made such an impact among the people at Indore that his grave was still garlanded with fresh flowers,[59] and his former house referred to as "the Padre Sahib's Church".[60]

In addition, the idea of the Tractarian "reserve" of earlier decades, of which Pusey had been a model exponent and which Allchin described as having been "a question of the utmost importance", was passing from the scene. True, Benson was the "many-sided person" that Olive Wyon described in 1963;[61] but despite the affectionate tone of many of his letters to individual

55 SSJE/2/1/43.
56 *PM* Sept 1882.
57 Woodgate, *Benson*, 122.
58 R. Kemsley SLG, "The Religious Life: Aspects of Father Benson's Teaching", in Smith, *Benson of Cowley*, 109.
59 Traill, 28 Aug 1905.
60 Samuel Gopal, "Simeon Wilberforce O'Neill", *Nagpur Diocesan Quarterly*, July 1904.
61 Olive Wyon, *Living Springs: New Religious Movements in Western Europe*, London: SCM Press (1963), 45.

brethren, his careful notation of their birthdays in his personal Calendar,[62] and the undoubted succour that his spiritual advice gave to many, Allchin also pointed to a lack of intimacy that was easily perceived as aloofness in his personal dealings with the members of his Society.[63] Benson often felt lonely, and said as much to O'Neill in 1875; but he felt that "loneliness has its trials, but it has great blessings belonging to it. We need loneliness for the purpose of training. How God trained in loneliness the great men of old!"[64] Ten years later, however, his ongoing emphasis on deadness to the world – of which all this was a part – left many of his brethren with the distinct feeling that their Superior, whatever saintly qualities he may have possessed, was cold and detached.

Luke Miller's work on Congreve has thrown up a number of issues that reflect the consequences of this impression; but chief among them is the notion that under Benson's rule "friendship and fellowship were deliberately rejected and the Mission House was a frankly unfriendly place." Looking back on his own time in the novitiate, Congreve recalled that "no affectionate intercourse ever came to life among us", and that during Recreation the brethren "were wont to sit out the half-hour and listen with intellectual respect and expectation to anything that might fall from the Superior, but among ourselves we knew so little of one another, and were so isolated, so dead to one another that we had little enjoyment of recreation and were glad when it was over". Maturin lamented that he found it "so dull and gloomy [...] I don't find much difference between the Silence Day and any others – sometimes in Recreation times nobody comes into the Common Room [...] Then the food is so poor".[65]

Given that the Rule specifically forbade conversation on "any matters engendering controversy or party spirit" and expected that "the exposition and illustration of Holy Scripture and points of moral theology shall frequently form the subject of conversation in the Common Room"[66], it is perhaps not hard to imagine why brethren frequently found reasons to be absent from Recreation. Furthermore, the food certainly was poor. Although guests seem to have been fed well, the brethren ate sparsely. Woodgate recorded a novice with a delicate digestive system, who took up his pen after one Good Friday when the main meal had been "ninepence worth of sprats" divided between the entire community:

I smell a rat – it is a sprat
For our Good Friday dinner.
Please give me one that is well done,
Or else I shall be thinner.[67]

Benson also seemed to make a virtue of secrecy. When he catalogued the Mission House Library, he did so without help and worked through the night;

62 *SSJE Chronicles*, SSJE/6/1/1/8/153ff.
63 Allchin, *Silent Rebellion*, 188ff.
64 Benson, 22 April 1875, in *Further Letters of Richard Meux Benson*, 44.
65 In Miller, *Congreve*.
66 *Rule of Life*, no.22, "Of Conversation".
67 Woodgate, *Benson*, 99ff.

so that no one had an inkling of the project until it was complete.[68] Congreve also remembered that "when he returned to the Mission House after some work or distant journey, we never expected to hear him speak to us of anything that had happened while away, whether of failure or success"; and added that when he died it was remarked that some of the brethren hardly really knew him at all.[69]

There were now other members of the Society who had their own ideas about how the religious life might be best lived out – particularly Congreve, who was Assistant Superior – and the Rule and Constitution did not necessarily allay existing concerns. By the late 1880s there was worry that the various active parts of the work in America and India were becoming detrimental to the monastic element of the Society's life; but that it was inevitable as it was only in the parish work that the far-flung brethren could realistically find congenial company: "we retreated from deadness within into the little comfort of the welcome of the people amongst whom we worked".[70] The Rule, while exhorting missioners to avoid "the lowering effect of living among secular comforts", conceded that there would be occasions when "through courtesy or health it may be necessary to accept some of the proper indulgences".[71] Maturin's observation was that "at the Mission House there was this solitude, gloom, and austerity – at all the branch houses, secularity".[72] Each seems to have been an antidote to the other.

When he resigned the living in 1886 in favour of William Scott – who had been curate of Cowley St John since the year before, after having served at St Mary's, Paddington – Benson knew that the parish was thriving.[73] By then the Iron Church was effectively the monastery church; but members of the Society would continue to minister in the parish of Cowley St John for another century. The Society also retained oversight of the schools that adjoined its property;[74] and in 1894 the Sisterhood of the Holy Childhood would be founded to prosper that work in particular.[75]

Benson "always set great store by parish work," wrote Woodgate. "He, who was a Religious above all else, could never minimize its value. A parish priest himself for many years, he realized the importance of the life, and it was his wish that the members of his Society should take their part in it. They were never to feel, he insisted, that such work might mar their religious vocation."[76] This was inevitable, of course, for a community that had grown out of the life of a parish, with the incumbent – as with so many contemporary women's communities – being the *genius loci* of both institutions; but striking a balance between the active and contemplative aspects of community life would be an ever-present concern as time went on.

---

68 Ibid, 91.
69 Miller, *Congreve*.
70 Ibid.
71 *Rule of Life*, no.32, "Of Missions".
72 Miller, *Congreve*.
73 *PM* Oct 1886. The framed and illuminated testimonial presented to him on his retirement survives at St Stephen's House.
74 Woodgate, *Benson*, 145.
75 *CE* Jan 1895.
76 Woodgate, *Benson*, 144.

Some of the brethren busied themselves with hobbies: in 1886 Br Walter – three years after his appointment as "Bee Master"[77] – advertised honey from the Mission House hives at a shilling a pound;[78] but "Benson's perceived personal coldness," as Miller puts it, "had a deleterious effect on the ability of the Superior to lead. Coupled with his theological insistence on total and unquestioning obedience, the life of the Mission House, physically and emotionally austere, became intolerable to many, and few who came to try the life stayed with it."[79]

Benson's own notes indicate that between 1870 and 1884 over forty priests and laymen were admitted to the Society as postulants, but did not proceed to the novitiate. To attract men to Cowley was one thing; to keep them was another.[80] They came of their own calling – Puller later spoke of Benson's "holy horror of anything like touting for postulants" – but he was perfectly happy to send them away again if he felt that they had "no true vocation for the religious life".[81]

Nehemiah Goreh, who described himself as "a converted Brahman of Benares",[82] was a case in point. Coming from a wealthy high-caste family, he had abandoned his former life to be baptised; and after ordination he was of immense value to the work at Bombay and Poona. It is true that in his case a number of concessions and dispensations were made, and perhaps he did not in the end have a vocation to the religious life;[83] but he was, as his biographer Charles Gardner observed, utterly un-European – he even eschewed the clerical collar because in his view it gave the impression "that a man by becoming a Christian becomes an Englishman"[84] – and when he came to begin his novitiate in 1876 he was horrified at what he found.

> At once I felt miserable. Oh, those cold cells, in which one has no privacy! That horrid English food, and then Fr Benson told me to wash the floor of my cell. I told him at once I could not do it, and to send someone else. Those Fathers do menial work. I have seen Fathers washing the Mission House stairs. Oh, how I hate the life![85]

When Goreh finally abandoned the attempt in 1885 (long after the period of time allowed for the novitiate by the new Constitution) Benson wrote to him fondly that "you must not think that we shall have any the less affection for you because you go elsewhere";[86] but it did not seem to occur to him that any part of the problem had been to do with the utter bleakness of life at the

---

77 *SSJE Chronicles*, SSJE/6/1/1/8/132.

78 *PM* Sept 1886.

79 Miller, *Congreve*.

80 *SSJE Chronicles*, SSJE/6/1/1/8, 86–7; cf Walter Wyon's notes on the Christmastide retreat, 1873: Cambridge University Library, MS(Add.7651):Wyon/9/1/1.

81 *CE* Feb 1915.

82 Nehemiah Goreh, *A Letter to the Brahmos from a Converted Brahman of Benares*, Allahabad: North India Tract Society (1868).

83 Woodgate, *Benson*, 150.

84 C. E. Gardner SSJE, *Life of Father Goreh*, London: Longmans, Green & Co. (1900) 8.

85 Ibid, 211.

86 Benson, 17 Dec 1885, in Gardner, *Goreh*, 317.

Mission House, which must have been nearly unbearable for someone used to a gentler life in a warmer climate. Two years later in his *Proofs of the Divinity of Our Lord*, Goreh was clear that "Providence has certainly prepared us, the Hindus, to receive Christianity, in a way in which, it seems to me, no other nation – excepting the Jews, of course – has been prepared."[87] His departure may well have been a great missed opportunity for the Society's future work in India.

"The deadness in the house never chilled nor narrowed Fr Benson's heartiness and natural affection", recalled Congreve, but "he could never purge us of our disastrous community deadness because he practically lived outside the vault in the open sunshine. He did not need 'comfort of love' in community life because he had another life, into which he could slip two or three times a day, his pastoral and public life which was full of sympathy and the most worthy Christian interests."[88] It was a far cry from what the Rule envisaged in its saying that "the deadness of the Religious is not dull apathy, but triumphant joy in the consciousness of possessing a true eternal life, from which nothing but the lingering life of the world holds us back."[89]

Alistair Mason noted the all-pervading influence, for better or worse, of the personality of the Founder in most of the communities established in the mid-nineteenth century[90] – the Community of St John the Baptist later preserved the memory of Thomas Thellusson Carter with a recumbent life-size alabaster effigy under an oak canopy next to the altar in the chapel at Clewer.[91] Congreve, with the support of Maturin, decided that something had to be done about life at Cowley. Towards the end of 1889 he addressed a letter to his Superior which was as frank as it was brutal:

I have after each Chapter for several years had the thought in my mind, and discussed with myself whether I should mention it to you, what I am going to mention now […] It has several times occurred to me, and now it seems to be settled thought, that just now your best way of helping and directing the community would be to stand apart from the centre for a time. I do not mean merely to resign allowing yourself to be re-elected, but to insist upon the community putting the charge for three years at any rate, in the hands of some member whom you might indicate to them. (I feel fully the responsibility of suggesting this to you; it has never as far as I know been hinted in the Society, nor have I ever hinted it to any until now that I say it to you.) I have a good hope that if you did this, no harm would come of it, but that a certain hope and interest would revive in the members of the Community who are dissatisfied and disappointed with the way things are going among us. I think it would be worth even a great risk (I don't think this need be a risk) to return heart to the community, if it is disheartened and disaffected – I should personally not delight in changes – but I wish to be absolutely indifferent except to what is of Religious Principle, and the

87 Nehemiah Goreh, "Proofs of the Divinity of Our Lord, stated in a Letter to a Friend [Pandita Ramabai]", quoted in Robin Boyd, *An Introduction to Indian Christian Theology*, Delhi: ISPCK (1969), 55.
88 Miller, *Congreve*.
89 *Rule of Life*, no.5, "Of the Professed".
90 Mason, *SSM*, 4ff.
91 Anson, *Call of the Cloister*, 305.

sticking to our Rule and Constitution. I shall always heartily accept whatever you may decide; but my pre-judgement (entirely without consulting anyone) is as I have said.[92]

It was a bold move; but what was perhaps more remarkable was that Benson appeared to take his points on board.

In 1890 Benson was sixty-six years old, and had led the Society of St John the Evangelist for nearly a quarter of a century. In that time the ecclesiastical movement of which he had been a part had grown and developed in ways that had seemed unthinkable five decades earlier. When *Lux Mundi* appeared in 1889 it horrified him; but it was clear that the essays, with their liberal approach to certain aspects of theology and ecclesiology, had struck a chord with a younger generation of leaders – and its editor, Charles Gore, would found the Community of the Resurrection three years later. According to Leonard Prestige, Benson, notwithstanding the fact that Gore was one of his neophytes, referred to the work as *"Lux Mundana"*;[93] and even in his eighties he was railing against the Higher Criticism school of biblical exegesis, which he hated. When he suspected the Wantage Sisters of flirting with it, he was blunt: "if they sanction such teaching one would rather that they should come to an end".[94]

Congreve felt that his resignation "would awaken some life in the Society", and Benson, after a period of reflection, agreed.[95] "I think perhaps we may get a little fresh blood into the Society by a little shaking," he noted later.[96] Miller considers that, in what followed, "this most authoritarian of men demonstrated a new teaching in humility";[97] and at the Chapter meeting on 4 August 1890, Benson resigned as Superior General. An election duly followed, and the lot fell upon Robert Lay Page.[98]

---

92 Congreve, 1889, SSJE/6/5/2/1/111ff.
93 Prestige, *Gore*, 105.
94 Benson, 18 July 1907, SSJE/6/1/2/26/5.
95 Miller, *Congreve*.
96 Benson, 29 Sept 1890, SSJE/6/1/2/25/18a.
97 Miller, *Congreve*.
98 GenC 1890, SSJE/2/1/104.

6

BUILDING FOR SUCCESS

Delightful division of Mankind – Seculars, *people who give money;* Religious, *people who spend it!*

—Richard Meux Benson SSJE[1]

The Society of St John the Evangelist as it stood at the end of the 1880s was not necessarily that which Richard Meux Benson had envisaged a quarter-century earlier. Two years after he addressed the Church Congress in 1888, Benson was unseated in the gentlest of coups and the direction of the life of his Society changed once more. He professed himself quite happy to hand his life's work to Robert Page. "It is no disappointment to see Father Page occupying my old place," he told George Hollings.

> I have held it quite long enough, and I am sure that it is greatly for the benefit of the Society that Father Page should take office now, and hold it while I am still alive to help in many ways [...] The new Superior is a great organiser, and has a thorough grasp of the Religious Life.[2]

The new arrangements were announced immediately:

> The Triennial Chapter of the Society was held at the conclusion of the July Retreat. At this Chapter Father Benson resigned the office of Superior, having held it nearly a quarter of a century.

> F. Page, who has been working in India the last seventeen years, was elected Superior of the Society for the next three years. F. Puller will be coming home from Cape Town in March to act as Master of the Novices.[3]

One of the issues that surrounded Benson's resignation had been the novitiate at Cowley. It was a significant and ongoing concern: "The Master of the Novices shall have the spiritual training of all novices in Holy Orders or preparing for the same."[4] Frederick Puller's return proved less than straightforward, as almost simultaneously – demonstrating amply his impact not only in Cape

---

1 Benson, 19 Jan 1881, SSJE/6/1/2/1/6ff.
2 Benson, 29 Sept 1890, SSJE/6/1/2/25/18ff.
3 *PM* Sept 1890.
4 Statute 30, *SSJE Statutes*, SSJE/1/4.

Town but further afield[5] – he was elected to the see of Zululand. He left the decision in Page's hands; but the general feeling at Cowley was that although the consecration of a member of the Society to the episcopate would be an honour, and would enable the SSJE to lead another missionary enterprise, the nurturing of new members of the Society must come first. George Congreve thought that "unless we have a Master of Novices we cannot have a Novice and without Novices as a Society – we come to an end". Basil Maturin was blunter: "If he is to go, we may as well pack up, and leave Cowley altogether."[6]

The Society had reached what Luke Miller has called "an existential cross-roads": torn between expanding its already considerable overseas and colonial mission work, and consolidating its identity at home. Congreve felt strongly that Page "must ask one of its members to forego preferment for himself and turn down the opportunity for the Society to lead what was clearly a significant piece of mission work".[7] Page decided that, on balance, Puller had better return home to shore up the long-term future of the Society: "it would be simply ruinous to our community for Fr Puller to leave [...] The future of our Society as a Religious Community very largely depends on him."[8]

The decision of the new Superior General was not well received in South Africa;[9] and Bishop William West Jones of Cape Town openly expressed his frustration.[10] If churchgoers in Cape Town felt that they had lost a distinguished clergyman in the person of Puller, however, his successors were equally – if differently – impressive. Page himself, meanwhile, had overseen the Indian work since 1873; and the return of both men from their respective fields left a definite gap. The *Cowley St John Magazine* noted that the Society "should be very glad to hear of two Priests who could offer their services for work in Bombay, Poona or Cape Town for a time"; and volunteers soon presented themselves.[11]

Benson himself embarked on a grand tour – documented by Woodgate[12] – that took him from Oxford to Boston by way of India, Hong Kong, Japan, and Canada. Congreve's first thought had been that the Founder might simply move to London and oversee the establishment of the looked-for house in the metropolis;[13] but the final decision had the double benefit of fulfilling Benson's own twice-thwarted dream of going to India, and of removing the former Superior General from the Mission House for a period of time. He took his leave on All Saints' Day, 1890, with "a few words of affectionate farewell to those who are so closely united with me".[14]

Other farewells were less affectionate. Benson maintained an antipathy towards Roman Catholicism for his whole life – in 1865 he had corresponded

---

5 Peter Hinchliff, *The Anglican Church in South Africa*, London: Darton, Longman & Todd (1963), 228.

6 *Correspondence: Puller/ Zululand*, SSJE/9/2/3/7.

7 Miller, *Congreve*.

8 SSJE/9/2/3/7/12ff.

9 "Cowley and Zululand", *The Southern Cross*, 15 May 1891.

10 West Jones, 22 April 1891, SSJE/9/2/3/7/19ff.

11 *PM* Sept 1890.

12 Woodgate, *Benson*, 153ff.

13 SSJE/6/5/2/1/119ff.

14 *PM* Nov 1890.

with John Henry Newman on the subject of re-baptism and re-ordination[15] – and he could not understand its appeal to those who felt drawn to secede: least of all erstwhile members of his own Society.[16] When Luke Rivington became a Roman Catholic at Easter 1888, he was simultaneously horrified and outraged. "[His family] were quite prepared for him to do to any mad thing, but this step had not occurred to them."

Rivington was something of a celebrity convert: his preaching had attracted the attention of the Queen herself; while the Prince of Wales had been "very much taken with him", to the end that he had declared he should be sent to India as a bishop. He received Holy Communion for the first time as a Roman Catholic at the Pope's own hands, and the press had a field day;[17] but Benson was clear that "one may feel confident that however much damage he may do to us, he will do no good to the Romans".

> In joining Rome one must join not merely the Roman Church of 1888 but the Church of centuries past with all the abominations of the Popes [...] if these illustrate the holiness the list of Antipopes makes the unity of the Church of Rome a farce.[18]

Stuckey Coles later observed that "a thought of disloyalty to the Church of England was to him a thing to be treated like a foul thought". Benson resolved not to speak of the matter in the Mission House; but in his letters he railed against Rivington for weeks.[19]

It would be nearly a decade before Benson returned to Oxford, and his letters home charted his travels in minute detail – with those addressed to Page beginning fastidiously with "My Dear Fr Superior". It is not unreasonable, perhaps, to view the period of the Founder's absence as a time of growth unlike anything that the SSJE had seen before, and which it would never see again. No fewer than twenty-three new members of the Society had made their vows by the time the new decade drew to a close.[20] Many of them were set to work in the various far-flung enterprises that flourished in the United States, Canada, India, and South Africa; and other domestic offshoots were either thought of or established. The Society had no intention of establishing a house at Worksop after the Duke of Newcastle transferred the advowson of Worksop Priory to the Society in 1891, and the Superior General had to correct the *Church Times'* suggestion that that such a course was planned;[21] but in 1896 the Society accepted the invitation of the Bishop of Argyll & the Isles, Alexander Chinnery-Haldane, to take over the running of Bishop's House, a retreat house on the Isle of Iona which had been built by his wife.[22] Chinnery-Haldane's

---

15 Newman, 11 Aug 1865, SSJE/6/1/2/6/1.

16 Woodgate, *Benson*, 149.

17 Benson, 23 March 1888, SSJE/6/1/2/2/115.

18 Benson, 12 April 1888, SSJE/6/1/2/2/120ff.

19 Benson, 16 March 1888, SSJE/6/1/2/2/113ff.

20 *Profession Book*, SSJE/1/4.

21 *Church Times*, 20 Nov 1891; 5 Feb 1892.

22 SSJE/2/1/260. Anne Chinnery-Haldane was the only child of the Revd Sir Nicholas Chinnery, Bt; and Chinnery-Haldane had added his wife's name to his own when they were

thinking was not as obscure as might at first appear: the SSJE was already tangentially linked with his remote diocese through his predecessor, George Mackarness. His brother was the Society's former Visitor, John Mackarness, who had died in 1889 and been succeeded as Bishop of Oxford by the Bishop of Chester, William Stubbs.

FERTILE GROUND

One of Page's first acts as Superior General was to oversee the transition of the *Cowley St John Magazine* into the *Cowley Evangelist*. Described as "a Monthly Paper on Subjects Missionary and Religious", the first edition was introduced as "an old friend under a new name"; but the change amply reflected the developing self-identity of the Society in the early 1890s as an evangelical tool of Empire – or perhaps an Imperial tool of evangelism.

> It is plain that the Church has an overwhelming responsibility towards the peoples of India. The confusion of tongues at Babel was a Divine judgment for the sin of mankind. The English tongue is the solvent of national distinctions, operating not slowly, but very steadily, in all parts of the world. The gathering of so many nations, whether subjects or allies, into a community of language, marks out the English Church as the power to whom God would entrust the future spiritual destinies of the world that she may recall them not merely into a solidarity of political freedom, but the glorious unity of the Divine Life.[23]

To that end, the SSJE's colonial work remained a priority. Perhaps this was to be expected, given that the new Superior General had been Provincial Superior in India and that the Novice Master had held the same office in South Africa. Furthermore, the Society regarded its far-flung work as held in constant prayer by an even more disparate body of Associates, both lay and ordained; and supported in other practical ways by the work of missionary guilds at a more local level.[24] Nor did it become blind to the needs of the work at home: all that went on overseas did so against a backdrop of preaching, retreats, fundraising, management of the schools, and corporate intercessory prayer – even, from 1894, under the oversight of Hollings, the sombre work of prayer for criminals due to be executed. Those who expressed willingness to be involved in the last were informed that

---

married in 1864. She had come into her considerable inheritance four years later, after her parents were killed in the Abergele rail disaster.

23 *CE* Jan 1891.

24 The *Missionary Guild for St Philip's, Capetown*, expected its adult members to contribute a shilling a year and to try and collect money from others also. Women were to produce a garment a quarter to be sent to Cape Town, and men were to provide two books – "except cheap novels and old school books". Children were to give a halfpenny a month, with girls sending two pieces of needlework a year; and both boys and girls were expected to contribute either two picture books or two toys, or one of each. They were also encouraged to collect books and toys from their friends. *CE* Sept 1893.

[...] from time to time names of the condemned will be sent to you on a postcard, thus:

NICOLAS SLOWE, c, June 4: e June 22

c stands for date of condemnation; e of execution.

The usual rule in England is that a capital sentence is executed during the week following the third Sunday after it has been pronounced: and in the county of London always on a Tuesday.

Those sending in their names are under no other obligations than to remember each person named at least once in the Holy Eucharist, and to pray for his conversion daily, using any words that may seem best, together with the Lord's Prayer.[25]

Far away in India, Benson's temporary presence in Bombay from 1890, where the work of SSJE and the All Saints Sisters continued to grow, focussed things to some extent; but the Indian expansion that had begun before he resigned the Superiorship was also coming to fruition. The work of the redoubtable Dr Gertrude Bradley, its medical missioner, enabled the Society to work with women even beyond the reach of the Sisters. The SSJE supported, with the ASSP, the work of Henry Lord and his assistant clergy at St John's Mission, Umarkhadi, a few minutes' walk away from the compound at Mazagon; and also ran missions to homeless lepers, and to the Jews. The last found an indirect vindication years later in Alfred Joseph, a distinguished scientist who had been ordained after his conversion to Christianity "as a man of mature years", and was professed in the Society in 1937.[26]

There was no compromise to be had in the encounter with local religions: a vignette from Poona in June 1883 neatly combines the challenges faced by the Society with both its response and its hopes for the future:

The masonry work of the foundations of the Church was commenced today. The Hindu builders I found had been performing some idolatrous rites over the first stones, painting them red, putting cocoanut and flowers, &c. I heard of this and got some of the boys to bring pails of water and then make the builders wash off every speck of red paint on pain of having to pull up all the stones and put them down again. Our head carpenter has become a catechumen.[27]

The church at Panch Howds, Poona, dedicated to the Holy Name of Jesus, had been opened – although still then unfinished – at Christmas 1885. Contemporary photos show its striking neo-Classical interior, with its magnificent marble altarpiece, and its rows of mats for the worshippers to sit cross-legged on the floor in the local custom. Bishop Louis Mylne of Bombay later said that a visitor would find its services being "entered into with great heartiness, and their highest Eucharistic aspirations would be satisfied, but they would find no ritual, nor teaching, nor music which outran the capabilities of the congregation".[28]

---

25 CE July 1894.
26 CE Nov 1951.
27 Uncertain, possibly Page, 25 June 1883.
28 CE July 1894.

The collaborative work with the Community of St Mary the Virgin had grown to include schools, hostels, and an orphanage. A letter from Benson, written at Christmastide 1890, demonstrates amply the extent to which SSJE was willing to meet the Indian members of its flock on their own terms, both in church and in the day-to-day life of the Missions.

We had the first Evensong of Christmas in the Church of the Holy Name. Several strangers and heathen were at the end of the Church. At midnight, Fr Goreh celebrated chorally in Marathi, and I preached. Cecil Rivington interpreted for me. He does this very well indeed; his manner and fluency are quite equal to those of a native [...] I celebrated for the Wantage Sisters in their Chapel at 6, and then assisted Rivington in Church at 7.

We had [...] dinner at 2, after native fashion, by invitation of the young men in the Students' Home. The table cloth spread upon the floor, with napkins in front of the places where we were to squat on our heels, a party of about 20. Then we began with some very sweet pastry and milk and ghee; then rice and real curry, to be taken up by three fingers and the thumb. It was not dipping with one another in the Jewish custom, for we each had our own plate, and alongside each was a plate with various minor articles, intended to contrast with the sweet cakes, and certainly not failing of that result. They made one very much inclined to take refuge in the cocoanut pastry lying upon the other side of one's plate, which was very nice indeed. After this refection, we went to the Sisters' School, S. Michael's Orphanage, where I distributed prizes.[29]

Other customs – those that were in opposition to Christian principles – were done away with. Chief among them were those relating to caste: and in this the Wantage Sisters led the way. The *Cowley Evangelist* reported in February 1891 that "a very interesting social gathering was lately held at the Sisters' School of the Epiphany."

Some Brahmin gentlemen of the advanced school expressed a wish to be invited that they might partake of food prepared and served by Christians, and so make a public profession of breaking their caste.

It was deemed to have been a triumph: "the event of the evening came off – the open breaking of caste by partaking of the tea and biscuits, which were handed round, by Christians and Hindu alike. Small as the circumstance may seem, it marks quite an era in the history of the Hindu life in Poona, that Hindu gentlemen should have combined together to give a blow in public to the great caste system which for centuries has enthralled their nation". Nehemiah Goreh, who knew better than anyone the significance of the step that his former co-religionists had taken, was astonished.[30]

So far-reaching was the combined Indian work that from 1893 it had its own dedicated association – "The St Mary & St John Missionary Guild" – and its own monthly journal, *The Star in the East*, which was to the Indian missions what the *Cowley Evangelist* was to the Society as a whole. It reflected the credit

---

29 Benson, 26 Dec 1890.
30 *CE* Feb 1891.

that properly belonged to all three communities who made up the SSJE mission work in India, and whose early links each with the other were now transformed into major collaborations several thousand miles away from home.

In Cape Town, the Society's work – which had begun with its connection with the All Saints Sisters of the Poor – was also growing. Unlike India and the United States, South Africa had not been included among the SSJE's early missionary ambitions; but the early brethren were not uninterested in African affairs, and Benson had regretted having to decline Bishop Robert Gray's invitation for the Society to work in his diocese in 1871.[31] Twelve years later, things had changed. Before his secession Rivington spent a good deal of time in South Africa, and his letters home give an idea of how fertile the vineyard seemed to be.

After his arrival in 1883, Puller soon found himself working among the Cape Malays, as Gray had originally intended – but he found a small number of black Africans in the area, to whom he also ministered.[32] He was assisted by an African catechist, John Xaba: sermons were translated into Xhosa, and soon it became the default language for much of the Society's worship in South Africa as the brethren became more proficient.[33] By the 1890s the Society was assisting the All Saints Sisters in their work among fallen women in Cape Town; and Cape Dutch was also being used regularly.[34]

Although Robert Jeffery observed that Benson's own view was that "the faith must be expressed through the culture in which it is placed",[35] it is also worth noting that even Simeon Wilberforce O'Neill, who lived more indigenously than any other member of the Society anywhere, was willing to enlist the help of imperial structures from time to time. Commenting on the SSJE's early Indian work, Rowan Strong has observed that, although the adoption of local customs was by no means unique to the Society – many other missionaries, including the Salvation Army, operated similar strategies – the work took its place in the "hybrid marginality" of life in British India.[36] The same phrase could just as easily be applied to the Society's efforts in the racial melting-pot of Cape Town, or in the more genteel segregation of Boston.

A New Church

By the time of Page's election, the SSJE was a community whose work was constantly growing – particularly overseas – and the Society could reasonably look to the future with confidence. It was this confidence, after the nervous years of the 1880s, which inspired the Society to embark upon the

---

31 Robert Gray, 1 June 1871, in Gray, *Life of Robert Gray*, ii:553ff.

32 Hinchliff, *Anglican Church in South Africa*, 228.

33 See *Petition of the Rev Fr Puller SSJE for the Dedication of S. Philip's School Chapel*, 3 April 1886, Witwatersrand Historical Papers, AB1363/C11.5(1). The foundation stone had been laid on 16 July the previous year. Wood, *West Jones*, 284.

34 *CE* Aug 1892.

35 Smith, *Benson of Cowley*, 119.

36 Strong, "Origins of Anglo-Catholic Missions", 106ff.

boldest and most significant of all its projects – the building of the new Church and Mission House at Oxford.

In January 1891, the Superior General took a sounding, through the first edition of the *Cowley Evangelist*, as to whether there was any appetite in the wider SSJE community – that is, those who received the magazine as Associates and other well-wishers – for a replacement for the Iron Church on Stockmore Street. The idea of a new community church had been in Benson's own mind since the 1870s, when it became clear that the Society's "old iron friend" would not last much longer; and he regretted the fact that it had not been started when he resigned as Vicar in 1886 – the site on the Iffley Road had already been chosen.

Page soon found himself overwhelmed by the response. It was "a disgrace", wrote one correspondent, "that the church of the Cowley Fathers should be in such a condition, or indeed, that they should worship in a 'tin tabernacle' at all". Others wrote with more tongue-in-cheek observations: a former choirman who had emigrated to Canada said that it was frequently 20 degrees below freezing in his adopted land; but that it reminded him of Christmas in the Iron Church. Donations began to arrive, and in February George Frederick Bodley inspected the site.

It is likely that Benson had previously discussed the possibility of Bodley and his partner Thomas Garner taking on the project; and even before he received the formal commission two of Bodley's sisters had donated to the building fund. The choice was no coincidence: Bodley was long acquainted with many members of the Society through the Brotherhood of the Holy Trinity, of which he had been a member since February 1859; and when Robert Reynolds Winter received plans from him for the SPG church in Delhi, he pointedly referred to him as "our Brother Bodley".[37]

Bodley was also well known to Puller, who had seen to it that he received the commission to build St German's Church at Roath just before he resigned the living to enter the Society; and to Congreve through Maynard Shaw, who had been involved in the decoration of his former church at Frankby. Michael Hall considers that it was through this work for Congreve that Shaw, who had been one of Bodley's assistants in the 1870s, came to be professed in the Society. In Br Maynard Bodley had access to a talented lay brother whom he knew well, and could trust to act as Clerk of Works *in situ*.[38]

The *Cowley Evangelist* was at pains to emphasise that the new building would function as a continuation of the Iron Church, with the approval of the Vicar.

[T]he ecclesiastical position of the clergy and congregation will remain un-altered. It will stand on land belonging to the Society, in close contiguity to the Mission House: it will be used for the private services of the Fathers and Brethren, but it will be open to the general body of the faithful, as is the Iron Church [...] The Vicar in a letter to the Father Superior has expressed himself in a very friendly way towards the undertaking.[39]

---

37 Winter, 26 Aug 1861, SSJE/6/1/2/11/2/9.

38 For a full architectural consideration of the building, see Michael Hall, *George Frederick Bodley and the Later Gothic Revival in Britain and America*, Yale University Press (2014), 373ff.

39 *CE* March 1891.

Bodley & Garner estimated that the building proposed could be erected for about £11,000,[40] which far exceeded anything the Society could hope to provide itself. Benson had run through his inheritance; and when his eldest brother Starling died suddenly in 1879 he had not been among the legatees of his considerable estate. However generous and well-intentioned Benson's largesse may have been, Starling Benson's biographers have suggested that he excluded his youngest brother from his will out of exasperation with his apparent "fecklessness in the management of the world's goods". As late as 1891 Benson was still asking his brother Henry for large sums, which he thought could easily be spared: Henry Benson could only throw up his hands, and ask "where is the money to come from?"[41]

In July 1891 Charles Wood – who had been elected President of the English Church Union in 1868, and had succeeded to his father's titles in 1885 – led the charge to raise the sum in the national press.[42]

Sir,

It is proposed to build, as soon as sufficient funds can be collected for the purpose, a new Church behind the site of the present Mission House, as the Church of the Society of St John the Evangelist (the Cowley Fathers) at Oxford. The need of this has been felt for a long time, and has of late become pressing [...] Thirty-one years is a long time for the existence of a temporary Church, and no one will be surprised to hear that many of the corrugated iron plates composing the roof are riddled with holes, and the rain descends freely.

Those who are fully acquainted with the work which the Evangelist Fathers are doing, not only at home, but in India, Africa, and America, will, I am sure, be among the first to wish to have their share in erecting a proper Church for the use of the Community; but I do not think the desire will be confined only to them. There is a widespread feeling that the Community is a wealthy body. This I know, as a matter of fact, to be the reverse of the case. Whatever private property the Founder, Father Benson, may have had has been expended in various good works, and the Society has the privilege of poverty rather than riches, and their small means is scarcely sufficient for carrying on their present works.

A great deal has been said lately in Convocation and elsewhere on the revival of the Religious Life among men, and how much might be done by organised bodies of clergy and laity living together a common life, and free to devote themselves entirely to Missionary and other work at home and abroad. All the more reason it is, therefore, that we should do what lies in our power to further the work of a Brotherhood which can appeal to such manifest tokens of God's blessing resting up on it, as is the case with the Society of St John the Evangelist, and by a generous contribution at the present time to enable the Fathers, to whom many of us owe so deep a debt of gratitude, to conduct the Services of the Church in a place somewhat less unworthy of God's Holy name than the only building they can at present call their own.

I am, &c,
HALIFAX

---

40 CE May 1892.
41 Bayliffe & Harding, Starling Benson, 255; 277.
42 cf Church Times, 17 July 1891.

In the 1890s the SSJE lived to a great extent off its members' distributed patrimony. One of the brethren who had retained control of his income, for example, was Walter Wyon. He had kept his account at his family bank, and his account books show modest but ongoing expenditure on Society business: haircuts; train tickets; new knives for the kitchen; postage stamps; threepence given to a beggar.[43] But even if the Society was not a wealthy body, it could hardly be said to have lacked friends in high places, both at home and overseas.

Apart from Viscount Halifax, the fundraising committee for the new Church included five other peers – the Duke of Newcastle and Lords Nelson, Clinton, Forbes, and Strathmore[44] – churchmen such as Thomas Thellusson Carter; William Lake, Dean of Durham and Gladstone's nephew-in-law; the Warden of Keble, Robert Wilson; the Regius Professor of Ecclesiastical History, William Bright; and a smattering of other distinguished gentlemen.[45] The money already raised was deposited in an account at Coutts.

Alistair Mason, writing in the context of the Society of the Sacred Mission, observed that "a great number of Anglo-Catholics have had links with religious orders, and with individuals within them. The religious orders have a public and talismanic role: religious houses attract visitors, even in great numbers; many people seek out monks as experts in the spiritual life."[46] That was increasingly true of Cowley in the 1890s; but at the same time that he intimated that there was enthusiasm for a new church, Page was also pragmatic about the fact that the Society still needed more vocations. In his first Lent as Superior General he noted that "we have been obliged to decline so many kind invitations for help in Lent and Holy Week. We would ask our friends to pray for the increase of the Society, that we may be the better able to fulfil the work to which God has called us."[47]

The American work was in a period of flux: the Society withdrew from Philadelphia in 1891, and the situation was further complicated by Arthur Hall's election as Bishop of Vermont in 1893.[48] It simultaneously expanded its presence in Boston by increasing its already-established work with the Society of St Margaret among the local black population;[49] which work very publicly associated the SSJE with both the white and black communities. Similar principles were applied in India and South Africa; but the work in both places seemed constantly in need of more manpower: Page noted in June 1892 that the Society was again "urgently in need of two Priests", one for Bombay or Poona and the other for Cape Town.[50] The decision to build a new church in Oxford was taken in the hope and anticipation of further growth to come, rather than as a self-congratulatory reflection of success already achieved.

---

43 Cambridge University Library, MS(Add.7651):Wyon 9/1/3.
44 The maternal great-grandfather of Her Majesty the Queen.
45 *CE* Aug 1891.
46 Mason, *SSM*, 4.
47 *CE* Feb 1891.
48 *CE* Oct & Nov 1893.
49 cf Hall, 25 June 1891.
50 *CE* June 1892.

As donations began to trickle in, Bodley urged the Society to proceed with the contract for the foundations of the new building, on the grounds that "the laying of a corner stone [...] would help to bring in funds". This seemed a reasonable suggestion to Page, and the Bishop of Oxford agreed: Stubbs made it known that he would be willing to lay the foundation stone on 6 May 1893 – the feast of St John before the Latin Gate – if funds were forthcoming.[51] That they were not was a matter of serious concern, and in 1893 the Society almost abandoned Bodley & Garner's plan in favour of a cheaper building. The Committee, however, held its nerve; and by early 1894 enough money had come in from various sources (including the sale of some SSJE property) to press ahead with the first stage of building to the original design.

Bodley supplied the *Cowley Evangelist* with a preliminary sketch, and described the design as "of early-14th century character, and [...] strictly English". As in the case of Ss Mary & John in the previous decade, the design might be added to later – the individual cost of each of the fittings was laid out to entice any would-be donors. The church was to be

> not simply a mission church or chapel of ease, worked by the neighbouring clergy of the community, and only differing from similar churches at Poona or Boston or Capetown in its proximity to the Mother House. It will be [...] in a real though modified sense, the Community Church of the Society of St John the Evangelist. We say, in a modified sense because not all the offices of the day will necessarily be said in the Choir of the Church; the Chapel of the House will still be maintained, at least, for the present. But in the new Choir, and at the new Altar, Mattins and Evensong of course will be said, and the Holy Eucharist celebrated twice daily at least, as heretofore in the Iron Church; and the Church will be so built that at no distant date, if the circumstances of the Society seem to allow the change, it may be possible for the Choir to become in all essentials the Chapel – the religious home of the community, so that the voice of praise may be once more, as of old all over England, heard at frequent and regular intervals throughout the whole day under the roof of a public church.[52]

The Superior General broke the ground on 14 February, and work began on the foundations. The readers of the *Cowley Evangelist* received the ground-plan in June, and with it the news that the foundation stone had been laid on 10 May – over a year later than had been hoped; but on the Octave day of the Ascension and still within that of St John before the Latin Gate. The foundations were "deep and wide and solid [...] bound with strong concrete, a symbol to the Fathers of the Society". Using a silver trowel presented to him by Page, Stubbs laid the foundation stone in the centre of the east wall, after High Mass in the Iron Church and a procession to the new site. It was placed over some earth brought from the site of St John's trial by oil at Rome, some coins, and a copy of the *Cowley Evangelist*. The inscription read

---

51 *CE* Jan 1893.

52 *CE* March 1894. This apparent willingness to envisage a future in which Benson's chapel at the top of the Mission House ceased to be the location of the regular offices perhaps anticipated the next stage of the project.

AD HONOREM DOMINI JESU CHRISTI
[*To the honour of Our Lord Jesus Christ,*

FUNDAMENTI UNICI
the Chief Cornerstone

ET AD INCREMENTUM SACROSANCTÆ ECCLESIÆ DEI VIVI
and for the increase of the Holy Church of the Living God

SUPER PETRAM FUNDATÆ
founded on the Rock

HUIC LAPIDEM PRIMARIUM POSUIT
this Foundation Stone was laid

SOCIETATIS SANCTI JOHANNIS EVANGELISTÆ ROGATU
at the request of the Society of St John the Evangelist

DIE MAI DECIMO ANNO SALUTIS MDCCCXCIV
on 10 May 1894

INTRA OCTAVAS SANCTI JOHANNIS ANTE PORTAM LATINAM
in the Octave of St John before the Latin Gate

WILLELMUS EPISCOPUS OXONIENSIS
by William, Bishop of Oxford

VISITATOR ET ORDINARIUS
Visitor and Ordinary]

The text of the stone is not so remarkable – and the use of Latin reflects no more than the custom of the University. What is more telling is the text chosen for the stone placed immediately above, from 1 John 1.3: *Quod vidimus et audivimus adnuntiamus vobis* – "that which we have seen and heard declare we unto you".

The sentiment was echoed through the ceremonies. In his sermon, Bright – "one of the oldest friends of the Society" – talked of how the building of the new community church had been an aspiration for the entire body of people associated with the SSJE: "at Capetown, and Bombay and Poonah, in Vermont, and in that steep Street in Boston which was made sacred by the presence and labours of the Father Founder". The laying of the foundation stone of a church was, he said, an act of faith and hope – one that meant that those present believed in "a God of the future as well as the present and the past, and a Christ the same today as yesterday and forever".

Bright went on to enumerate the various difficulties facing the Church – discouragement, division, unbelief, and "the well-meant but sometimes dangerous ventures of social change".[53] Against these difficulties, then – in the manner of their Oxford Movement forebears – the members of the SSJE were to be a bulwark: the new foundation stone was to be their rock, and the completed church their castle. He did not expound his private views on the plans for the anticipated tower, which he told Wyon that he thought to be "simply ugly", despite Bodley's "unique genius" and the excellence of the rest of the building.[54]

---

53 *CE* June 1894.
54 Bright, 15 Nov 1896, Cambridge University Library, MS(Add.7651):Wyon/9/3/36.

After lunch in the schoolroom, Page read out messages from various well-wishers – chief among them Benson himself, who had written from Boston to say that he and the American brethren – represented by a "Stars and Stripes" on the podium – would be "present in spirit" and in the hope that the new church would "last with a life continually developing until time shall be no more".[55] Grafton, by now Bishop of Fond du Lac, wrote to say that he had heard "with great joy" that the new church was to be built, and that he knew of "nothing so needed, nothing that will more strengthen the Church cause".[56] Perhaps most welcome of all the messages of goodwill was that morning's anonymous gift of £500 – which took the total raised well over what was needed for the first stage of work.[57]

By the end of the year over half the funds necessary for the completion of the church had been raised; and the Society's thoughts turned to the fittings. Donors were invited to subscribe to individual pieces; and the list itself reflects the developments in the liturgical life of the Catholic Movement. Items that would have provoked general outrage in the 1860s – among them altar crosses and candlesticks, vases for flowers, three hanging lamps for the sanctuary, a Sanctus bell, a rood on the screen, and a statue of St John – raised little comment by the 1890s.[58]

By April 1895 the chancel and side chapels had been built, together with much of the nave. The downpipes had already been cast, with a Christogram on a shield above "A.D. 1895" – perhaps today the only visible clue of the initial slowness of the work. The *Cowley Evangelist* reported the progress with satisfaction, and included two photographs of the work from east and west. There was a flurry of industry, with the masons producing "finished mullions and trefoils and arch-mouldings faster than they can be set" – and Congreve had had the satisfaction of setting in place the floriated cross on the eastern gable.

A new house was also being considered: the doorway at the east end of the Church, visible in the accompanying photograph, was "left unfinished for the attachment of a cloister which would lead from the Church to the New Mission Building which has been proposed". The statues for the Annunciation either side of the East Window were already donated; Halifax was to give the rood screen; and Lady (Edith) Euan-Smith, wife of the former Consul-General at Zanzibar, would donate the profits from her *Twenty-Four Hymn-Tunes* to the organ fund.[59] The completed instrument was eventually installed – if not fully paid for – in 1897, when Basil Harwood played for its first Evensong on All Saints' Eve.[60]

Even after several other worthy demonstrations of *noblesse oblige* and many smaller donations from humbler folk – a guinea here, a shilling there – more

---

55 Benson, 1 May 1894.
56 Grafton, 25 April 1894.
57 *CE* June 1894.
58 *CE* Nov 1894.
59 Edith Euan-Smith, *Twenty-Four Hymn-Tunes*, London: Laudy & Co. (1895).
60 *CE* Dec 1897. The installation of the organ was bittersweet, as the builder, William Thynne, had dropped dead while fine-tuning the last pipes in his workshop. Ernest Grimes, the community's Precentor, duly appealed for – and received – donations to help support Thynne's "young widow and a little boy of four years, both quite unprovided for".

money was still needed to complete and furnish the building: by July 1895 the cost had risen to £14,000.[61] The purpose of it all was explicit: "There is a special interest in the raising of this first Church in England connected with the revised Monastic Institute. The fabric and design is such that it may be, in larger times, a monument of our new beginnings, and of the faith and hope of English men in a day of small things."[62]

The work continued slowly, but by the end of the year most of the structure (except the westernmost part, which would include the tower) was complete. The choir and nave ceilings had been decorated by Br Maynard with extracts from Psalm 148 set between stylised roses and pomegranates, while the cornices had been painted with quotations from the Revelation of St John[63] – Duncan Convers later suggested that "the visions of S. John in Patmos supply a scheme far higher, nobler and grander than the meaningless forms which do duty so often".[64] Victorian concerns for an efficient heating system were addressed, and Charles Eamer Kempe had been approached regarding the stained glass.[65]

All this was very satisfactory to Stubbs, and a discreet note in the *Cowley Evangelist* in February 1896 announced that he would dedicate the building on 12 May – the Tuesday in the Octave of St John before the Latin Gate, the feast which had by now come to be observed as the Society's major patronal festival. A grander notice appeared in April, announcing the times of masses on the day itself, the time of the dedication service, arrangements for luncheon, the times of trains from Paddington and Reading, and the reminder that "trams run [from] Oxford Station to Marston Street". By the end of the month it was clear that so many people intended to be present that there would need to be six masses in the morning, and that entry to the service of dedication would have to be by ticket.

Fresh Fruit

The Society and the parishioners bade farewell to the Iron Church on Sunday 10 May, and early on the Tuesday morning – after the brethren had sung Lauds and Prime for the first time in the new choir – the Superior General celebrated the first mass in the Church of St John the Evangelist, at the high altar.[66] Its black marble *mensa* was not yet in place; neither were the choir stalls nor the figures of the rood, which had been acquired by Halifax

---

61 *CE* July 1895.

62 *CE* April 1895.

63 The words chosen were the parts of creation exhorted by the Psalmist to sing the praises of the Lord. The easternmost bay of the nave, just before the beginning of the repeated *Alleluia* over the community's stalls, has *senes* – "old men" – but it remains unclear whether or not the pun was deliberate.

64 *CE* Sept 1898.

65 *CE* Oct 1895.

66 The Iron Church's fittings – with the exception of the wooden altar, which was burned – were distributed among various clergy, and some of the vestments sent to mission stations overseas. Most of its reusable structure was turned into a covered walkway connecting the Mission House with the new church. *CE* July 1896.

and were being sent from Oberammergau; and most of the windows were still filled with plain glass.

At 9.15 a.m. Maturin sang High Mass, with "incense used for the first time with us, Brother Maynard being the Thurifer".[67] Puller had opposed its introduction in the Iron Church two years earlier; but Page had thought the worship there "poor and mean for a Society of Priests", and had already commissioned full High Mass sets "made in all the colours".[68] Other members of the Society favoured the development, and the move to the new building set the tone for the SSJE's worship from then on: "the Roman use so far as it can be adapted to our present Prayer Book service".[69]

The vestments and hangings were those designed by Bodley specially for the building, "of an excellent sobriety and beauty"; and the music was led by George Herbert Palmer. He was already established as a leading authority on plainchant, and had designed the organ himself with the Society's worship in mind.[70] The *Cowley Evangelist* mused that "the sweetness and delicacy with which this most devout music was rendered by the boys and men of the choir speaks wonders of the training bestowed".[71] The trebles sang from the rood-loft, in their new cassocks and surplices, and one of the cantors downstairs was Walter Frere – who in 1892 had co-founded the Community of the Resurrection at Pusey House, and would later become Bishop of Truro. Only a year later the Chairman of the Musical Association noted approvingly that he had visited the church and was "much delighted with the capital results which had been obtained by the use of the Solesmes system of plain-song. It is worth a journey to Oxford to hear how well those little parish-boys are trained."[72]

Shortly before noon, the long procession of choir and clergy – including Arthur Headlam, Robert Ottley, Stuckey Coles, as well as a number of priests whose names who would later appear in the Society's Profession Book – left the Mission House singing the Litany of the Holy Ghost and made its way through the gardens to the church, which it entered through the north door.[73] At the west end of the incomplete nave it met the Bishop of Oxford and his attendants, and after the customary liturgical greetings Stubbs assented to Page's request for him to dedicate the building. The *Veni Creator* was sung, and then the entire company processed around the church while the choir sang Psalms 24 and 48.

The dedication itself took place at the high altar, and after the singing of *Angularis fundamentum* the Dean of Christ Church, Francis Paget – who would succeed Stubbs as Bishop of Oxford and Visitor to the Society five years later – preached on Exodus 31. "It is a high and manifold hope", he said, "that the dedication of this church today brings home to us afresh the hope that God is indeed renewing and increasing in the Church of England the special calling

---

67 Incense was already in use in India: see Chapter 7.
68 Page, 12 March (early 1890s), Cambridge University Library, MS(Add.7651):Wyon/9/3/98.
69 Page, 26 Feb 1894, SSJE/6/3/2/3.
70 "George Herbert Palmer", CE July 1926.
71 CE June 1896.
72 *Proceedings of the Musical Association* (24th session), Taylor & Francis Ltd (1897), 90.
73 SSJE/11/2/5/10.

of men to the life of Brotherhoods." It was a neat summary of the importance of the new Church within the life of the Society, and of the importance of the Society within the life of the contemporary Church of England.

After lunch – *maigre*, as it was Rogationtide – various worthies made brief speeches, including Page, Bodley, and Halifax. Although Benson had written warmly from Boston – "how pleasant it is to think of the joy of you all entering into the use of the New Church!"[74] – the last touched upon the elephant in the room when he noted that "there was a pathos in that day's proceedings as well as a joy, for Father Benson was not with them; Father Grafton, though soon to be in England, was now Bishop of Fond du Lac; and Father O'Neill had gone to his reward."

> His Lordship then spoke of the Society of St John the Evangelist with all that warmth of affectionate enthusiasm which is so characteristic of him – of that which had been accomplished in the past, and of what promised for the future, but most emphatically of that which was a cause for the deepest thankfulness to Almighty God – the real revival of the life of the Evangelical Counsels among men by a society of priests and lay brothers.

The day continued with a service for the parish children, Solemn Evensong, the Litany in procession, and ended with Compline. "Our day was really over", recorded the *Cowley Evangelist*, "a peaceful and calm day for all its work and the multitude of friends, and a day in which every capability of thankfulness was helped to the uttermost by all the influences about us – the most perfect sky full of glorious sunshine, the most unfailing kindness, and the upholding power of genuine devotion pouring from many hearts to meet the love of God". It went on seamlessly to remind its readers that the Society still needed about £6,000 to complete the work.[75]

The symbolism of the building as a type for the male religious life in the Church of England reached its apogee a year later, when Kempe installed the great east window above the high altar. The design had been the subject of not a little discussion, as it was felt that Bodley's original suggestion of a crucifixion scene merely doubled the imagery of the figures on the rood screen, which had by then arrived. Furthermore, as Puller explained from the pulpit,

> on the East wall of the Church in the sanctuary, over the altar, it is a mistake to let the culminating idea stop short at the cross of Calvary in its shame and humiliation. The culminating idea ought in some way to suggest the triumph over death, and the production of the ripened fruits of redemption.

Drawing together John 15 and Revelation 22, he noted that the two passages spoke of "the same blessed mystery of the glorified Cross, and of the union of the saints with the Saviour, once crucified, and now living with the life of glory". To that end, the lowest part of the window's middle light depicted St John on Patmos, writing the last chapter of Revelation, accompanied by his eagle and the inscription *Ego Johannes qui audivi et vidi hæc* – "I, John, am the

---

74 Benson, 4 May 1896.
75 *CE* June 1896.

one who heard and saw these things". The rest of the window was filled with part of his vision from Revelation 22.2: "there [was] the Tree of Life, which bare twelve manner of fruits". The tree in this case was a vine, hung with grapes. At its apex was a cross with the image of Christ crucified, and on top of that was a nest occupied by a pelican in her piety. Two angels held the obvious legend *Ego sum Vitis, vos palmites* – "I am the Vine, and you are the branches"; while further down appeared *Lignum Vitæ* – "the Tree of Life".

The choice of the twelve fruits was particularly deliberate. "Of course", continued Puller, "there are in union with Our Lord saints of every condition and of every sex and of every age. But as this Church has been built to provide a place in which the Fathers of our Society may minister, and as we, as members of the Society, are bound by the monastic vows of poverty, chastity, and obedience; therefore the twelve saints depicted in the side lights of the window have been chosen from among the great monastic saints." St Antony of Egypt was included; as was St Basil, vested in the robes of the Eastern Church. St Benedict was there, with St Columba, St Augustine of Canterbury, St Aidan, the Venerable Bede, St Boniface, St Bruno, St Bernard of Clairvaux, St Dominic, and St Francis of Assisi. They all appeared out of large blossoming flowers, and it does not take a great leap of the imagination to regard the pruned branches of the vine as a metaphor for the rigours of the monastic life, and the unopened buds as portents of other great monastic saints to be raised up in the future: either through the SSJE or the other enduring communities that had sprung up in its wake.[76]

In this interpretation also lies the clue to the work on Iona. It was no coincidence that Chinnery-Haldane transferred Bishop's House to the SSJE in 1897 as part of the commemorations of the thirteen-hundredth anniversary of the death of St Columba. He regarded it as the restoration of the religious life to the island, and "one of the great pleasures" of his life; and the Society immediately began to run it as a centre for both private and guided retreats.[77] At about the same time the idea of a similar house in London – which had been part of Benson's plan back in 1865 – was also raised.

To Page and his confrères, the 1890s must have seemed like a great period of growth and blessing, and it is worth pondering the developing charism of the SSJE at that time. Viewed through the lens of an increasingly buoyant and confident Catholic movement within the Church of England, the Society had been transfigured far beyond its humble beginnings at 2 Magdalen Terrace at the end of 1866. Some of the Founder's plans had not grown – the idea of a Permanent Private Hall had come to nothing[78] – but Benson had been kept fully informed of the various developments that had taken place after his resignation of the Superiorship, and had made a particular point of expressing his support for the new church.

For all of what Peter Anson called its "refined austerity",[79] the new conventual church represented far more to the SSJE than just an aesthetically pleasing

---

76 Anson, *Call of the Cloister*, 90ff.

77 *CE* July 1897.

78 *Vice-Chancellor's Licence*, SSJE/6/1/1/3.

79 Peter F. Anson, *Fashions in Church Furnishings 1840–1960*, London: Faith Press (1960), 234.

building. It was raised as a statement of the Society's self-identity, and its confidence in its vocation in the life of the Church of England, at home and abroad. Stubbs's "well-weighed words" were instructive: the church was to be "the central home of the corporate life of the Society, from which the members will go out helped with the prayers of their Brethren, and to which they will return from time to time for rest and refreshment after work done or attempted for God".

Benson reflected on the dedication ceremonies from Boston.

> So we enter upon a new phase of life, and we must go forward joyously and hopefully. God who has led us through the last 36 years will lead us onward. We have not quite reached the 40 years of the wilderness wanderings, but we seem to be entering upon the new stage which crossing the Jordan represents. We must not think that a new Church is our resting place. We have to look forward to many a Jericho that must fall down, and we have to fight our way onward with fasting and prayer, to enter upon cities that we builded not, and claim the promises of God's ever increasing love.[80]

The Church was to be – with the hoped-for new Mission House – the point around which the rest of the life of the Society would revolve: a fixed aspect in the life of a community in almost constant activity, at home and abroad.

That activity needed committed and sustained support. Distinguished visitors came and went – the Orthodox Archbishop of Finland paid an ecumenical courtesy call in July 1897 – but there was a steady stream of humbler folk, clergy and laymen, who came privately and for the regular organised retreats. The community's schools were being enlarged and improved, and the first Sisters of the Holy Childhood – of whom "the Superior of the S.S.J.E. will always be the Warden" – were professed in the Holy Spirit Chapel of the new church in July 1896, to help with the work of educating the local children.[81] The presence of a female community at 9 Marston Street, just a few yards away, enabled the Society to begin small retreats for women also. Further afield, the various appeals for funds as the decade progressed demonstrate amply the heavy emphasis placed by the Society on its colonial work, and its rallying of influential friends to its cause.

Page was never afraid to ask for money; and Benson's insistence in 1888 that the purpose of the religious was not to provide cheap labour for the rest of the Church seems to have rung true. Within the Society there was some concern, however, that the elegance of the "sumptuous" building and its costly fittings amounted to a departure from its vow of poverty. At a meeting of the Society's Council in July 1896, the Superior General abandoned for the time being his plan of moving all the services to the new church. The services there would be those that had taken place formerly in the Iron Church; while the Society's own devotions – for now – would remain in the old chapel under the roof of the Mission House.[82]

---

80 Benson, 10 May 1896.
81 *CE* March 1919.
82 SSJE/6/9/1/2.

Generally speaking, the Society's confidence in its developing identity was not unreasonably enhanced by its growing membership – the change of leadership had had the desired effect – and during the 1890s it had attracted a number of professed brethren who were already distinguished in the wider Church. Although Philip Waggett's profession in 1896 had added another star to the SSJE's scholarly firmament, chief among them was Puller. His learning came into its own in the mid-1890s when he was invited to observe the discussions that eventually led to Leo XIII's promulgation of *Apostolicæ Curæ*; for despite the fact that his *Primitive Saints and the See of Rome*[83] had firmly rejected the papal claims of primacy, his "full and accurate erudition" had won the confidence of Louis Duchesne,[84] and his scholarship was respected in Rome – and particularly by Fernand Portal.

Goreh, although not technically a member of the SSJE when he died in 1895, was so inextricably linked to it that he was deeply mourned by the Society and others beyond it.[85] Sir Monier Monier-Williams – the scholar of India who had controversially bested Max Müller in the election to the Boden Professorship of Sanskrit in 1860, and founded the Oxford Indian Institute in 1883 – wrote that "his death has deprived me of a valued friend, almost a brother [...] I was indebted to him for many useful criticism and suggestions in writing my Manual on Hinduism for the S.P.C.K., and my larger work on Brahminism."[86]

Not everyone who encountered the SSJE, however, was convinced of its mission and purpose. George Santayana was vague about dates, but must have visited the Mission House at some time in the late 1890s, at Waggett's invitation; and his description of lunch on Sunday gives us an insight into the table practice of the day.

> The refectory was imposing: plain high white walls, with only a large crucifix over the Abbot's chair [*sic*], and a long narrow table, with a white table-cloth, running to the right and left of him along three sides of the room. The monks all sat with their backs to the wall, leaving the inside of the square empty.

The rest of his observations are more contentious. Rose Macaulay thought that Santayana was "curiously egotistical"; and that although he was an atheist he still "could like no religion but the R. C. Church". As Macaulay also noted, "he utterly despised the Fathers".

> If I described the poses and movements of those poor monks, especially of the young ones, it would be thought a gross caricature. Even to me now it seems incredible that I actually should have seen the idiotic manners that I saw; may I not have dreamt the whole thing afterwards? Yet there was pathos in these absurdities, because these souls, in need of religion, were groping for expression and for support in an age and in a Church that had subordinated religion to national pride and to worldliness.

---

83 F. W. Puller, *The Primitive Saints and The See of Rome*, London: Longmans, Green & Co. (1893).

84 T. A. Lacey, *A Roman Diary*, London: Longmans, Green & Co. (1910), 8.

85 *CE* Jan 1896.

86 *CE* Dec 1895; cf *Father Nehemiah Goreh and Sir M. Monier-Williams*, Calcutta & London (1880).

None of this had any basis in the facts of the depth of the significant processes of thought and prayer that had gone into framing the house customs at Cowley. Santayana concluded, after one visit, that the community "had to rediscover or to imitate a cultus: but for discovery they had no genius and for imitation no taste and no innocence".

> They therefore seemed fools or hypocrites, when they were sincerely groping after spiritual rebirth. Not all, perhaps; because in the revival of Catholicism in England, both Anglican and Roman, there was also a silly aesthetic sensual side, all vanity and pose and ritualistic pedantry, as in Frederick Rolfe; and this may have contributed something to the affectations of the Cowley monastery.[87]

In citing the deeply-controversial Frederick Rolfe as a type of the Catholic revival, Santayana sinks his own argument – to conflate Rolfe's type of religion with that practised at Cowley in the 1890s is to compare apples with oranges – and his hastily-formed bitter comments may easily be dismissed.

Nevertheless, it is worth remembering that the Cowley Fathers were not without their critics, and some of those were even among their own ranks. Rivington had seceded to Rome in 1888, to be followed by Maturin in 1897[88] – although the latter soon returned to Oxford as Roman Catholic Chaplain to the University. Hall, meanwhile, had withdrawn from the Society when he became Bishop of Vermont in 1893; but remained in close contact with his former brethren, both publicly and privately. Ten years earlier the departure of these members might well have compounded fatally the circumstances of the earlier losses of Grafton and Prescott; but the foundations of the Society of St John the Evangelist were now so well consolidated that the superstructure was left secure.

---

87 George Santayana, *My Host the World*, London: Cresset Press (1953), 114.
88 See Maisie Ward, *Father Maturin: A Memoir*, London: Longmans, Green and Co. (1920).

7

SUBJECTS MISSIONARY
AND RELIGIOUS

So admirable a work deserves the warmest support.
—Winston Churchill[1]

The burgeoning missionary endeavours of the Society of St John the Evangelist continued to grow as the nineteenth century drew to a close; and they did so in the context of general expansion of missionary work across a range of enterprises. Jeffrey Cox dates the beginning of a missionary "Imperial High Noon" to 1870:[2] just after the foundation of the SSJE, and shortly before the first brethren went to India. The American work had its ups and downs; but essentially it existed within the structural stability of a parish system – albeit one that could be significantly compromised by the disapproval of an unsympathetic bishop. Most of the Society's early work in the United States and Canada was tied to daily parish life, and had the additional benefit of being carried out in the context of a common language and a familiar climate. It was in was in India and South Africa, where the bishops were generally sympathetic, that the SSJE came into its own.

When Sir Theodore Hope – who had formerly a been senior member of the Bombay administration – chaired a meeting on behalf of the Ss Mary & John Missionary Guild in June 1894, he was clear that in India the SSJE saw its work as committed to "the building up of the native Christian Church, as they found it there, and to those Europeans and Eurasians they found on the spot".[3] Although the Society's work was enabled to a great extent by the mechanism of the Empire in both India and South Africa, it did not regard its mission as primarily a chaplaincy to sahibs and settlers – although it inevitably performed that function as well – or a ministry of provision to the locals.

By the mid-1890s the carpentry school that had been set up at Poona in the late 1870s to give a number of the mission's young men a skilled trade was inundated with orders: its students had even furnished Bishop Louis Mylne's private chapel at Bombay. Mylne noted approvingly that at Poona the SSJE "had a Mission which was free from that reproach sometimes levelled at native Christians in India – that they were eating the bread of idleness and were

---

1 *CE* June 1902.
2 Jeffrey Cox, *The British Missionary Enterprise since 1700*, New York: Routledge (2008), 171ff.
3 *CE* July 1894.

dependent upon Europeans".[4] "Dear, dirty old Poona" swiftly became another important strand of the SSJE's work in India:[5] in the eighteenth-century it had been the political centre of the Maratha Empire, and the seat of its Peshwas; and that it was the place of the monsoon residence of the Governor of Bombay when the Cowley Fathers arrived was not entirely a coincidence.

The 120-mile journey from Byculla, the nearest station to the Mission House at Mazagon, to Poona took about six hours; and it passed through the striking Bhor Ghat, which had been opened up in the 1860s. The rock formations petered out at the hill station of Matheran, where the All Saints and Wantage Sisters had houses, and where from time to time members of the SSJE went on furlough. From there the line rose sharply to Khandala, another regular retreat spot, where the climate was drier and the air clearer than in the humid stickiness of Bombay. Charles Gardner observed that a Cowley Father alighting at Poona in the 1890s would invariably be recognised by any of the railway officials who had been at school at St Peter's, and so a brief but cheerful reunion would take place "while shaking oneself into comfort" before driving into town.

Unlike the melting pot that was Bombay – but like many other cities in British India – Poona was divided into the City and the Camp. The Camp was the European district, and the City was home to the local population. "The first impression of Poona city", remarked Gardner, "is how wholly it is given to idolatry."

> We pass clusters of small temples at either side. Then, at nearly every street junction is a tombstone-looking shrine. Within it is a vermillion bedaubed hideous idol, or merely a conical stone, the *ling*, the sacred symbol of Shiva, in a niche. At every boundary is the grotesque monkey god, Hanuman's idol, the Hindu Terminalia [...] Here and there, in the middle of the street, quite independent of obstructiveness, is a small temple shrine, a low tower, built on a walled foundation, a sacred tree bending over it, a narrow space in front, occupied by a sleeping devotee or more active worshipper, and within, at the back, a larger idol; or perhaps, another ling with its stone, bull-couch and guardian Nandi. The sacred thing is the stone cone, smeared with oil and red lead, and probably covered in yellow flowers; the more imposing bull is only the sentry on guard.

The SSJE mission was at the edge of the City, near the five large cisterns – "Panch Howds" – that gave the location its name. It was a better address than "Vetal Peit", an older name for the area, which was best translated as "Devil's Quarter". The apposition was certainly not lost on Gardner, who took to his theme with gusto.

> The various houses of the Mission, as they cluster around the lofty Church [of the Holy Name], itself seeming to claim the spot, and spread along the ground, seem to be more and more encroaching upon the territory of the great enemy of our salvation. Already the name of Vetal Peit is becoming lost, and "Panch Hauds" is taking its place as a landmark, and "near the Church" is found to be a

---

4 *CE* July 1894.
5 Elwin, 14 May 1898, SSJE/9/1/4/2.

safer direction, even to the pagan, than the old designation. Salem of the Hittites is rapidly becoming Jerusalem, the City of the Great King, the true Son of David; and Solomon, the Prince of Peace, is building His temple on the threshing floor of Arannah, the old Canaanite Jebusite chief. And, best of all, many are asking their way to Zion.[6]

The image of the Christian conglomeration at Panch Howds as a metaphor for the heavenly Jerusalem was not confined to Gardner's pious prose. For Edward Elwin only a few years later it stood in direct contrast to "the squalor and filth and heathen misery and idolatry of Poona City".[7] Meanwhile, from the Wantage Sisters' convent the Community of St Mary the Virgin supplied nurses to the Sassoon General Hospital, and teachers to St Mary's High School, both in the Camp. On the mission itself they ran St Michael's School for low-caste girls brought up in paganism; and the School of the Epiphany for Indian girls from English-speaking Christian homes. One of the things the Sisters did was teach the girls to eat with implements, a practice of which Gardner thoroughly approved. While the traditional method had been good enough for Benson only four years earlier;[8] at Indore even Simeon Wilberforce O'Neill had eaten with a fork.[9]

Other customs were simply taken over: writing home in early February 1899 Elwin noted that "the Dewali festival is so pretty but so meaningless that it can safely be incorporated into the Church life of our people; and then, held on Candlemas Day, it becomes full of teaching for both Christian and heathen."[10] Hugh Nicholson was more suspicious: he called Diwali "one of the few Hindu festivals that have some beauty about it [...] there is less idolatry about it than others, although it is not altogether free from its taint";[11] but Elwin was always open to similar opportunities: later, at Yerendawana, he welcomed the regular gifts of flowers for the chapel from the local Hindu boys.

> The idea is to make a sweet scent, not to display the flowers. The boys bring merely the flowers without any leaf or stalk, and I put these into a little brass bowl and put it on the altar. The flowers are highly scented, and the chapel is soon filled with perfume. This seems much more like a real offering than the pyramids of flowers put on altars to be seen by the congregation.[12]

The buildings of the SSJE mission proper at Panch Howds, apart from the Mission House itself, included a boarding house for the boys of St John's School, St Pancras's Orphanage, and St Nicholas's School for younger boys. Occasionally orphans turned up with the post: the eleven-year-old Timothy and his much younger brother Paul "had to be signed for as you might sign for a box of candles". They settled in soon enough, despite the fact that Timothy – who instantly endeared himself to everyone on the mission through his total

---

6 Gardner, 24 August 1894.
7 Elwin, 13 Oct 1900.
8 Gardner, 24 Aug 1894; Benson, 26 Dec 1890.
9 Samuel Gopal, "Simeon Wilberforce O'Neill", *Nagpur Diocesan Quarterly*, July 1904.
10 Elwin, 9 Feb 1899.
11 Nicholson, 7 Nov 1912.
12 Elwin, 12 Oct 1905.

devotion to Paul – was "entirely untrained and unsophisticated, so that we never know exactly what he is going to do next".[13]

St Joseph's Industrial School included the carpentry shop – obviously – the drawing school, and accommodation for the apprentices. From the orphanage and the junior school boys progressed to St John's or St Joseph's; and from St John's many went on to Bishop's College, Calcutta, to take degrees. Other cottages housed lay mission workers, on whom the clergy depended for practical support in their regular rounds of preaching and catechising.[14] The carpentry shop was vital, and in October 1897 its "most pressing need" was "a fit man to undertake to superintend and develop our school of Christian carpenters".

> The importance of this school to the native Christian community cannot be exaggerated. A native becoming Christian and losing his caste, loses also his trade and livelihood. The Church is bound to help him and his children to learn to earn their own living honestly. On this account we would appeal to all our friends to consider whether they know of any carpenter with a missionary vocation, who would have the heart to offer himself for this work, for Christ's sake, and ability of character to carry it out, and to let such a man know of our need. It is obvious that for the office of Superintendent a fair knowledge of carpentry is necessary, and some experience in business ways.[15]

It was nearly a year – "just in time to save the workshop from ruin", grumbled Elwin[16] – before the advent of David Gardner, complete with his own bicycle, could be looked for with enthusiasm.[17]

The architectural glory of the mission at Poona was the Church of the Holy Name; and its fanciful neo-Classical style was in stark contrast to Bodley's strict neo-Gothic at Cowley. The altarpiece, which would not have looked out of place in a renaissance basilica at Rome, was made from dozens of different marbles and dominated by an enormous tabernacle. Robert Page's liturgical leaning was always "more towards Roman than Sarum",[18] but it was not to everyone's taste. Mylne disliked the ensemble, and called the tabernacle "prominent and aggressive", but let it pass.[19] The apse was hidden behind, and functioned as the monastic choir – it communicated directly with the house. The pulpit was decked with gold-bordered red hangings, and the lectern was an enormous brass eagle with matching candlesticks. The only other ornaments, except for some modest gilding, were the Stations of the Cross that adorned the walls of the aisles.

Charles Gardner's presence at Dedication Festival in 1894 gives an idea of how colourful the worship at Poona was, even if the church was still relatively bare. He writes of "the varied and bright costume" of the congregation at

---

13 Elwin, 27 Sept 1898.
14 *CE* May 1895.
15 *CE* Oct 1897.
16 Elwin, 18 July 1898.
17 Elwin, 15 Aug 1898.
18 Page, 26 Feb 1894, SSJE/6/3/2/3/3.
19 Mylne, 1 Oct 1888, SSJE/9/1/4/6.

High Mass – celebrated in Marathi – with the "magnificent" gold-and-white vestments of the sacred ministers, and the scarlet cassocks of the servers, including a thurifer, who came from the school and orphanage. At a time when the SSJE in England had yet to introduce incense to its worship, he felt that "no unprejudiced Churchman could be otherwise than gladdened by the whole service, including its ritual".[20]

The SSJE formally took over the mission at Panch Howds in the same year, eight years after first sending brethren to work there. William Relton became local Superior, and the soaring church tower with its ring of eight bells was completed three years later – but not before he had died from complications of an injury sustained in the works yard.[21] The mission had also had to contend with the plague that had swept through the City; but at Christmas 1897 Elwin was optimistic that the boys who were being trained to ring the bells would soon be excellent.[22] He later realised that as the tower had the best view in Poona it could usefully be used to entice non-Christian visitors to the mission, and began conducting tours.[23]

A medical mission was also established, complementing the work in Bombay, which continued to grow,[24] and where Gertrude Bradley – by then fluent in Marathi and known to her patients as "Doctor Madam"[25] – felt that "the whole tone of the mission" was improving.[26] It was the All Saints Sisters of the Poor who undertook most of the nursing work associated with the Society in India – they were stationed in Bombay, where the need was greatest. The Cowley Fathers served as their chaplains while they ran the Sir Jamsetjee Jeejebhoy Hospital – the "J.J." – and St George's Hospital in Bombay itself. They also oversaw the girls' division of the Cathedral School, and naturally they established themselves near the SSJE Mission House at Mazagon. When plague broke out in 1896 they endeared themselves to the local community by caring for the local population without distinction of creed – a well-trodden path to acceptance.[27]

The controversies surrounding the provision of Christian medical facilities and its reception by the indigenous population in India have been explored by David Hardiman; and any consideration of the SSJE's medical work in India and South Africa is inevitably touched by the complex issues surrounding the obvious appeal of a group whose members could heal and bind more effectively than traditional local methods. Suffice to say, what the SSJE presented – quite unlike the rudimentary treatment offered by early missionaries – was a sophisticated arrangement with qualified medical staff and trained nurses.[28]

---

20 Gardner, 24 Aug 1894.
21 *CE* March 1897.
22 *CE* Jan 1898.
23 Elwin, 26 May 1898.
24 *CE* March 1895.
25 "M.I.B." to Page, 6 Sept 1902.
26 *CE* May 1895.
27 H. E. W. Slade SSJE, *A Work Begun: The Story of the Cowley Fathers in India 1874–1967*, London: SPCK (1970), 36ff.
28 David Hardiman, *Missionaries and their medicine: A Christian modernity for tribal India*, Manchester University Press (2008).

CAPE TOWN

The work in South Africa matured after that in India, for the simple reason that it had begun a decade later. The choice of Frederick Puller to found the work was inspired. In 1883 he had only recently been professed in the Society, but he was highly thought of in ecclesiastical circles – he had declined the see of Zanzibar shortly before sailing for the Cape[29] – and on Sunday 8 May, having landed two days earlier, he found himself lunching with the Dean of Cape Town and then preaching at the Cathedral in the evening. "One feels that one is led to make a start here," he told Benson later.[30]

The mission work began in a small cottage on the foothills of Table Mountain, the home of the remarkable Lydia Williams. An emancipated slave who bore the scars of the *sjambok* with which she had been beaten when in bondage, she encouraged Puller to use it as for mission services and a Sunday School. Services continued at the cottage long after the mission's buildings had been erected – it was a useful outpost for ministry to the Cape Dutch population in the upper part of the district, with room enough for forty, and portraits of the Sacred Heart and the Prince of Wales.[31] In later years most of the parish would gather on 2 December for "Lydia's Day", when her little cottage would be decked in flowers for the traditional tea-party, and Lydia would tell her harrowing story from slavery to freedom – which, naturally, reflected her journey from unbelief to faith – to the assembled company before leading them in prayer.[32]

The SSJE was not without friends and supporters in Cape Town – and that was just as well, for there was much work to be done. In 1884 the Society's purview was defined as being concerned with the chaplaincy of the All Saints Sisters; the care of St Philip's district, then part of the Cathedral parish; the evangelisation of the black African men in the area; and the conversion of the Cape Malays. To that the clergy of the mission also added the Cape Dutch population that they found in the shanties on the slopes of Table Mountain: they found "touching survivals of a lost Christianity" in an area where "the Christian ideal is as little felt as the Christian moral law, and [...] Christian doctrine is unknown".[33]

As time went on the Society took over the care of a number of outlying mission stations, as well as the notorious Robben Island, then still a leper colony within sight of St Philip's; built a small monastery on Chapel Street, raised a Mission School; and opened St Columba's Home on Sir Lowry Road to provide accommodation, training, and catechism for black African men who might otherwise be destitute.[34] The choice of patron reflected the difficult task in hand. "He was a missionary saint," Puller wrote bluntly, "working

---

29 *CE* March 1938.
30 Puller, 26 Nov 1884.
31 *St Philip's Mission, Capetown*, SSJE (1901), 13.
32 cf Bull to Page, 4 Dec 1901.
33 *St Philip's Mission*, 4; 14.
34 Ibid, 7.

among a rude and simple people. The great African saints, such as Athanasius, Augustine and Cyril, seemed too much of theologians to be suitable."[35]

Puller was soon joined by George Sheppard; by 1885 they had been given charge of the "Kaffir Mission" at Papendorp,[36] and by 1886 they had built a Mission School on the corner of Chapel Street and what is now Cowley Street, with the original St Philip's as the school chapel.[37] Sheppard succumbed to fever contracted while visiting the sick during the typhoid epidemic of 1888;[38] and in 1889 the Sheppard Memorial Infant School was raised in his memory, with a tablet recalling his work in the district.

Peter Hinchliff particularly noted Puller's full contribution to the life of the Church in South Africa, and some of his surviving correspondence bears out the great extent to which Bishop William West Jones – who personally gave the altar at old St Philip's before consecrating the building in April 1886[39] – relied on him for advice on the canonical structures of the diocese.[40] Although the buildings Puller raised would have looked perfectly ordinary in Oxford, "he attempted to make the rites of Christian initiation as close as possible to those of the early Church",[41] and practised dramatic full-immersion baptism.

> The catechumens are clothed in dark-blue serge garments down to the feet [...] They make the Baptismal vows audibly, turning westward in renouncing Satan, and to the east in pronouncing the Creed. Then as each candidate goes down the steps into his grave, he kneels, so that the water reaches to his shoulders; at the Name of Each Person of the Trinity the head is bent and dipped right under the water by the hand of the officiating Priest. As the baptized man comes out of his grave a white cloak is thrown round him, and he is led away to a room where he dresses. When all are dressed in their new white suits, (linen jacket and trousers,) they return to their places by the font [...] After the service, tea is ready for them at the Mission House, for till now they have fasted. Such is the first page in a new volume of life for the man who came two or three years before in the devil's livery of heathen dirt and rags, to S. Columba's.[42]

"We would not exchange it for affusion on any consideration," he declared later; although he made an exception for "clinical cases".[43] The choice as patron of St Philip the Deacon was no accident,[44] and in 1886 the first group of black

---

35 Puller, 14 July 1886.

36 Michael H. M. Wood, *A Father in God: the Episcopate of William West Jones, DD*, London: Macmillan & Co. (1913), 284.

37 See *Petition of the Rev Fr Puller SSJE for the Dedication of S. Philip's School Chapel*, 3 April 1886, Witwatersrand Historical Papers, AB1363/C11.5(1). The foundation stone had been laid on 16 July the previous year. Wood, *West Jones*, 284.

38 *PM* June 1888.

39 It was not only spiritual: in 1885 he gave a legacy of £3000, with Benson's approval, towards the building of the ASSP's House of Mercy at Liliebloem. Wood, *West Jones*, 131; 284.

40 Witwatersrand Historical Papers, AB1230f.

41 Hinchliff, *Anglican Church in South Africa*, 171.

42 *St Philip's Mission*, 27.

43 *Bloemfontein Quarterly*, Jan 1905.

44 cf Acts 8.26–40.

Africans to be baptised after formation at St Columba's included Bernard Mizeki.[45]

The Society's new house on Chapel Street was completed in 1894, which enabled the community to move to a permanent home "after having been compelled to wander from one unsuitable and leaky house to another".[46] It would look "rather strange", thought Edward Osborne, who was then serving as Provincial Superior, "standing alone on a very barren and desolate piece of ground, but other houses will soon spring up near it, and it will have quite a fatherly look, towering two stories high, while every house is only one".[47] The neighbouring plot of land to the north was earmarked for the new St Philip's Church.[48] By 1896 Osborne was clear that the successes of the mission meant that Old St Philip's was no longer big enough.

> This chapel holds 300 only! We have daily Eucharist, and [public] Evensong on Thursdays and Saturdays. We cannot use it more for daily services as it is a school both day and night all through the week. There are 300 communicants attached to the Mission. Over 1,150 persons have been baptized in the mission, of whom more than 100 are adult Kafirs brought in from heathenism [...] The Mission needs at once a church to hold 750 to 800 people.[49]

West Jones agreed, and pledged his support. Puller, writing from Cowley, observed that since his arrival in Cape Town the district had grown from 1500 to 6000 souls who spoke "fifteen or sixteen different languages", and that as it continued to increase a properly-sized church had become "an absolute necessity" if the Society was going to retain the lead it had gained from the absence of other denominations within the mission's boundaries. "A strong effort made now," he urged, "will, with God's blessing, have an untold result for good."

Osborne was succeeded by Philip Waggett in 1896. Like Puller, Waggett had been a professed member of the Society for under a year when he was sent to Cape Town; but before he entered the novitiate he had exercised a prodigious ministry in the London slums, and was well-regarded as a preacher.[50] It was work that prepared him well for St Philip's, and his first task was to bring the Society's work more fully to the Cape Malays.

The care of the Malay population of the district – Waggett described it as being made up of "every kind of Mohammedan, whatever his race"[51] – had been entrusted to the SSJE since its arrival in Cape Town; but it was felt at Cowley that the mission had had "so much other work to do that it has been impossible to fulfil that department of our obligations". Accordingly, it was decided to establish a medical mission among them – linked to St Philip's –

---

45 Puller, 9 March 1886.

46 *St Philip's Mission*, 4–5.

47 Osborne, 16 May 1894.

48 John Nias, *Flame from an Oxford Cloister: The Life and Writings of Philip Napier Waggett SSJE*, London: Faith Press (1961), 58.

49 *CE* Aug 1896.

50 "St Philip's Mission", *The Cape Church Monthly and Parish Record* (Sept 1896), 141; 188; 25ff.

51 *CE* Aug 1899.

which would be run by Edith Pellatt, a newly-qualified medic who had volunteered for the work.

> Miss Pellatt has passed her final examination at the London Society of Apothecaries, qualifying in medicine, surgery, and midwifery, and she has had a varied hospital experience both in London and elsewhere. She also has the advantage of having studied the Arabic language, the knowledge of which will undoubtedly be of great service among Mohammedans.[52]

Pellatt and Waggett arrived in Cape Town together, on the *Lismore Castle*. Page travelled with them, as he intended to visit St Philip's before travelling on to the Indian missions with Osborne: Waggett recalled the ship dropping anchor in Table Bay, and Osborne coming aboard and falling to his knees to receive the Superior General's blessing.[53]

The dispensary was set up almost immediately, although money was short and the "invaluable"[54] Pellatt had to earn her living by private practice alongside her work for the mission, but was deemed after a while to have won over the people.[55] In addition to her medical services she taught a scripture class on Sundays and "English reading, writing and sums" to street boys – "full of mischief and of the knowledge of the lowest life" – on two evenings each week.[56] Waggett – supported in England by his mother, his sisters, and his surgeon-brother Ernest – appealed for funds, and by August 1897 the work of the dispensary was "well under way, and winning many friends among the Malay community", and a local chemist was supporting its work.[57]

At the same time the continuing influx of black Africans to Cape Town in search of work – a trend noted twenty years earlier by Anthony Trollope[58] – meant that St Columba's Home, which had originally only housed half-a-dozen men[59] – needed to expand considerably. This element of the SSJE's ministry was always challenging, and frequently disheartening. In the mid-1890s Osborne had to mete out stern discipline to drunkards and adulterers, while comforting others whose families in the countryside had been sold to Portuguese slave traders by tribal rivals: "the Portuguese [...] are the curse of Africa, a blight wherever they go, and the fosterers of all evil." He saw "many bright things and much to be thankful for, but Mission Work is often a *via dolorosa*".[60]

52 *CE* Aug 1896.
53 Nias, *Waggett*, 58.
54 Waggett, 15 Feb 1898.
55 Cecil Lewis & G. E. Edwards, *South Africa: The Growth of the Church of the Province*, London: SPCK (1935), 31.
56 *St Philip's Mission*, 19.
57 Nias, *Waggett*, 59.
58 Anthony Trollope, *South Africa*, London: Chapman & Hall (1878), 67ff.
59 *St Philip's Mission*, 25.
60 Osborne, 4 July 1894.

ANCIENT & MODERN

Osborne's comments were brought into sharp focus when, on 18 June 1896, Bernard Mizeki met his death.[61] He had been one of Puller's early converts, and was among the first group of men who had been baptised in the temporary St Philip's Church a decade earlier. Since then he had worked as a "Native Reader" – that is, a catechist of the kind on whom the new arrivals from Cowley depended while they learned the local language – and in 1891 had answered Bishop George Knight-Bruce's request for indigenous volunteers to help him in the establishment of the new diocese of Mashonaland, in what is now Zimbabwe.[62]

Writing in the *Mashonaland Quarterly*, Puller recalled that "remarkably enough, when one thinks that he is in all probability the first, or one of the first, of the Martyrs of South Africa, the day of his baptism [7 March 1886] was the Feast of St Perpetua, one of earliest and most illustrious of the Martyrs of North Africa. That year Quinquagesima Sunday fell on the same day. It also happened to be the very first service ever held in [old] St Philip's."[63]

Puller's influence was immense;[64] and if the blood of the martyrs is the seed of the Church, then Bernard Mizeki shines like a ruby in the crown of the SSJE's spiritual legacy in Southern Africa.[65] His lasting impact was emphasised when the shrine raised on the site of his death was consecrated by the Bishop of Southern Rhodesia in 1938,[66] with the address being given by the Governor, Sir Herbert Stanley.[67] Mizeki's memorial in new St Philip's was dedicated by the Archbishop of Cape Town in 1946, incorporating the head of the *badza* that he used to till his garden.[68]

Mizeki's godmother had been the enigmatic Paula von Blomberg. She had also supported the Society's work in Cape Town from the beginning, and Jean Farrant, when compiling her book on Mizeki, noted that Blomberg "worked with the Cowley Fathers, supervising the nightschools both at Papendorp and St Philip's. She was [...] completely dedicated to saving Africans in employment from the vicious influences of the 'locations'. The Fathers spoke of her with great affection and admiration, but none of them today [the mid-1960s] know who she was, where she came from, how she came to take up this work nor what happened to her [...] She is mentioned frequently in the reports of the Fathers to Cowley, but it is always assumed that Cowley *knew* all about

---

61 See Jean Farrant, *Mashonaland Martyr: Bernard Mizeki and the pioneer Church*, Oxford: OUP (1966). The FSJTA continues to award grants in Bernard Mizeki's name for the training and development of lay ministers.

62 See G. W. H. Knight-Bruce, *Memories of Mashonaland*, London & New York: Edward Arnold (1895); Pamela Welch, *Church and Settler in Colonial Zimbabwe: A Study in the History of the Anglican Diocese of Mashonaland/Southern Rhodesia, 1890–1925*, Boston: Brill (2008).

63 *Mashonaland Quarterly*, November 1896.

64 Hinchliff, *Anglican Church in South Africa*, 228.

65 cf Tertullian, *Apologeticum*, ch. 50.

66 Knight-Bruce's successors were Bishops of Mashonaland until 1915, when they became Bishops of Southern Rhodesia. The see reverted to its original nomenclature in 1952.

67 *Consecration of the Shrine*, Witwatersrand Historical Papers, AB247f(2).

68 See E. H. Roseveare, "Bernard Mizeki: The Story of an African Martyr", *The Cape Times*, 15 June 1946.

her."[69] Farrant, who was herself tied to the SSJE through her membership of the Fellowship of St John,[70] relied to a great extent on Blomberg's own book, *Allerlei aus Süd-Afrika*, which recounts her work there; but even with the benefit of her memoirs she remains an elusive figure.[71]

Waggett was clear that the SSJE's work in Cape Town "all comes back to Fr Puller".[72] He later observed that life there was so diverse that "here the Church might gather news of the faith in every tribe and place, and send forth reporters of the Truth into every quarter."[73] At the end of 1897 the diversity and busyness of the mission work was neatly summed up by the forthcoming "short season of treats".

> S. John's Guild, Monday; Tuesday, the good children at the home – a long and brilliant day of pleasure; today [Dec 29], the mothers; tomorrow, Day School; Friday, the Christians of S. Francis; Saturday, S. Alban's Guild for Boys, and Liliebloem. Next week: Monday, the Moslems of S. Francis; Tuesday, Sunday School, at Rondebosch; Wednesday, S. Columba's dessert (they had the beef and pudding on Christmas Day); Thursday, the Boys' Evening School and the Guild of S. Monica (Mothers) to the country; Sunday, the great stone-laying of S. Columba's; 10th and 11th, our little Retreat; 12th, Clerical Conference; 13th, the Synod. Meanwhile we must contrive to see our Confirmation candidates a great deal, that they may be ready for S. Paul's Day [Jan 25].[74]

He had also acquired a new site for St Columba's Home and begun raising funds for a new building,[75] which he thought might resemble the recent additions to Balliol College.[76] The foundation stone was laid by the Bishop-Coadjutor of Cape Town, Alan Gibson, on 9 January 1898 – the service included "Onward, Christian Soldiers", "The Church's One Foundation", and "O God, Our Help in Ages Past", sung in Xhosa.[77] Nine months later, the completed new Home – with dormitory space for eighty, a Chapel, and a meeting-hall – was blessed by West Jones, who was by then Archbishop,[78] in the presence of the Bishops of St John's, Bloemfontein, Zululand, Mashonaland, and Lebombo, the Sister Superior of the ASSP, and a bevy of local worthies.[79]

Like their Indian counterparts, the African catechumens – Frederic Powell later called them his "black swans"[80] – were customarily given new names at baptism. At Easter 1898 Waggett asked for prayers for Stephen, Thomas, Joseph,

---

69 Witwatersrand Historical Papers, AB799/Eb1.

70 *CE* April 1967.

71 P. D. von Blomberg, *Allerlei aus Süd-Afrika*, Gütersloh: Bertelsmann (1899).

72 Waggett, 5 Jan 1898.

73 P. N. Waggett SSJE, "Church Affairs in South Africa", *Journal of Theological Studies*, v.1, Jan 1900, 212ff.

74 Waggett, 29 Dec 1897.

75 Waggett, 27 July 1897.

76 Waggett, Jan 5 1898.

77 *CE* March 1898.

78 Cape Town had been designated an archbishopric after the Lambeth Conference of 1897 resolved to confer the dignity upon certain metropolitical sees.

79 *CE* Dec 1898.

80 Powell, 29 Nov 1899.

Peter, Elijah, Henry, Philemon, and two Johns.[81] The local Xhosa language, however, with its various types of click and rising and falling intonations, was a regular feature of the mission's worship. Writing home a day after Christmas 1898, George Hodge described the solemn mass of Christmas morning: with Powell "getting along with the service in Kafir [Xhosa] famously, and now and then a 'click' came my way quite audibly".[82] Soon there was a monthly Xhosa mass, and also services for the small number of Afrikaans speakers in the district. The concern for worship in the language of the local people was not confined to the Cowley mission: most of the local clergy, including the Archbishop, became liturgically multilingual.[83] When Charles Turner travelled to Zululand in 1912 he said mass in Zulu, describing it as "not unlike *our* language [Xhosa; my italics], though they use a good many different words, and they use clicks less".[84] Soon afterwards Gerald Maxwell observed, in the course of a visit to India, that it seemed odd to hear "all the old familiar tunes sung to Marathi words, just as I heard them sung to Xhosa translations in South Africa [...] It seems an extraordinary ingenious thing to have reproduced Hymns Ancient & Modern in so many different languages."[85]

In 1898 Waggett entered into discussion with Herbert Baker – who was in the process of raising the new St George's Cathedral, and would go on to become one of South Africa's most distinguished architects – about the new St Philip's Church. Some of the money had already been contributed in small amounts by the congregation of Old St Philip's;[86] some had been sent out from England after urgent appeals and the establishment of the Missionary Guild of St Philip; and Waggett ran himself ragged to raise the rest.[87] The original grand Italianate design – which had appeared in the *Cape Church Monthly* in September 1896 above a tribute to the departing Osborne[88] – was drastically simplified, and the new plans that appeared in the *Cowley Evangelist* at the end of 1899 bore more than a passing resemblance to Arthur Blomfield's work of three decades earlier at St Barnabas's, Jericho. West Jones laid the foundation stone of the much-needed new building on 4 February: "the neighbourhood was *en fête*, gaily decorated with flags, and our people showed their appreciation of this important development of the Mission by attending the ceremony in large numbers."[89] The nearly-completed building was consecrated on 31 December, on the eve of the new century: and Lydia Williams' signature – she was by then the senior member of the congregation – appeared on the petition for consecration alongside those of the clergy and churchwardens.[90]

Waggett was not there to see it. His biographer, John Nias, considered that he had overworked himself in the effort both to raise funds to build the

---

81 Waggett, 12 April 1898.
82 Hodge, 26 Dec 1898.
83 *St Philip's Mission*, 5.
84 Turner, 16 Oct 1912.
85 Maxwell, 26 Dec 1913.
86 *CE* Aug 1896.
87 cf *CE* April 1899.
88 "St Philip's Mission", *Cape Church Monthly*, 141.
89 *CE* March 1899.
90 *CE* Feb 1900.

church, and to establish a "Home for Inebriates" on the Cape Flats.[91] In fact he had suffered a nervous breakdown, and he was recalled to Cowley in August. George Congreve, who was no stranger to the South African mission, was sent to take his place.[92]

Not long after Congreve's arrival the Second Boer War broke out; but, despite the general upheaval in Cape Town – a steady stream of soldiers used their time there before going on to the fighting "to pay us a visit and prepare themselves for whatever God has in store for them"[93] – his presence seems to have been a calming influence in the house. Luke Miller suggests that he brought order in a way that Osborne and Waggett had not, and that he re-emphasised the call to the Religious Life by preaching "hope and happiness" after years of "building and business".[94] Congreve could hardly sit on his hands, and soon found himself attending to "the Parochial work, Guilds for men, women, lads, and school girls, a Temperance Society, Burial and Medical Aid Societies, and a branch of the Girls' Friendly Society".[95]

The general and premature assumption that the war would be won by mid-1900 increased dramatically the potential for the Society's work in South Africa, and Benson himself led the appeal for funds as victory seemed to draw near; before the Boers' lengthy guerrilla-campaign that followed the annexation of the Orange Free State and the Transvaal.

> As we come forth triumphant, let us give to God the praise! Terrible as the enslavement of the Kaffir tribes has been, there is one feature which as Christians appeals to us even more than the brutality by which they were outwardly held in bondage. Under the Boer government every hindrance was placed in the way of the Kaffirs becoming Christians. We must see that as we have effected the external deliverance, we are also giving the native tribes a welcome into the Church of Christ. When we think what God has done for us in this war, we are bound to do our utmost for the extension of the Kingdom of Christ.

He envisaged a situation in which the Society might be called upon to minister in many more places than just Cape Town, and urged his readers to "see that we are rising up to the greatness of our position".

> We have to anticipate a vast and immediate accumulation of responsibilities. Already the necessities of our Mission have quite outgrown the capacities of St Philip's, both financially and personally. It is a matter of absolute necessity that some of the work should be taken off the hands of the Cowley Fathers. Otherwise the Mission will suffocate itself by its very growth. Large funds are wanted for the erection of missionary buildings and the maintenance of regular assistants who may begin fresh work among the white people while the Fathers may be left more free to do the Mission work and superintend the whole.[96]

91 Nias, *Waggett*, 69.
92 Miller, *Congreve*.
93 Grimes, 15 Dec 1899.
94 Miller, *Congreve*.
95 *St Philip's Mission*, 7.
96 *CE* April 1900.

Certainly the war meant more work in Cape Town: the All Saints Sisters were nursing wounded Boer prisoners, and to Congreve's own mission duties was added the chaplaincy of a new police training camp. Most of the material in his book *The Spiritual Order* was composed in Cape Town, and in his dedication to his nephew Walter Congreve – who saw much of his uncle while he recovered from wounds sustained in action at Colenso, for which he was later awarded the Victoria Cross[97] – Congreve gives a sense of the variety of his work in South Africa while apologising for the disparate nature of the material:

> In preparing these papers I was never writing a book, but meeting as I might the need of each anxious day [of the war] as it came. The hearers I addressed were as various as the Sisters of Mercy of All Saints, a Military Congregation at Johannesburg, the Cape Mounted Police, the Cathedral Congregations at Capetown and Grahamstown, the Guild of St Barnabas for Nurses, and our dear sons the Christian Natives at St Columba's and at Ndabeni.[98]

Ndabeni was an outpost of the Cowley mission that had been established after plague hit Cape Town in 1901. Although the outbreak was almost certainly caused by fleas on rats that travelled in imported horse-fodder from South America, it was blamed on the squalid living conditions of the black population. They were soon segregated outside the city – with the exception of the residents of St Columba's Home, whose quarters were relatively hygienic, and who were dispensed by Walter Stanford, the Secretary of State for Native Affairs[99] – and the SSJE followed its people to the infamous "Location" at West Jones's request.[100] Worship began in a tent, but soon an iron church was raised and dedicated to St Cyprian of Carthage, with the brethren sleeping there overnight as directed.[101] Essentials were soon being sent from Cowley, and Lilian Rousby – a member of the Guild of St Philip – sailed to Cape Town to take charge of the school, which she soon declared to be "the best equipped in the Division".[102] The establishment of mission outposts as the need arose would be an ongoing feature of the SSJE in South Africa over the next six decades.

The work at Ndabeni was not the first outcast ministry that the SSJE had undertaken since its arrival in Cape Town. Robben Island had been in Puller's sights from early on, and in 1890 William Watkins – who had arrived in 1887 to help with the Malay work – was given charge of the leper colony there. Successive brethren took the boat regularly to minister among the inmates, and in 1897 the island was reorganised to be part-leper colony, part-lunatic asylum, and part-prison. Waggett had been deeply moved by the lepers' plight.

---

97 Walter Congreve was on Lord Roberts' staff, and went on to serve with distinction in the First World War. He later rose to the rank of General, was knighted, and ended his days as Governor of Malta. Roberts' son and heir, Frederick, won a VC with Congreve at Colenso, but died of his wounds. See Thomas Pakenham, *The Boer War*, London: Weidenfeld & Nicolson (1979), 235ff; L.H. Thornton & Pamela Fraser, *The Congreves*, London: John Murray (1930), 34ff.

98 George Congreve SSJE, *The Spiritual Order*, London: Longmans, Green and Co. (1905), viii.

99 Bull, 16 April 1901.

100 Wood, *West Jones*, 341.

101 Bull, 15 Sept 1903.

102 *CE* Feb 1904; Lilian Rousby, *Under Table Mountain*, London (1906).

It seems very hard to them that when God's Hand is heavy upon them, man should be hard on them next – taking them from their homes, and their wives, cooping them on part of an island, presiding over them with men in uniform, and making them sleep in wards. It is hard for them not to feel as if they are made felons; and it is all the harder because felons are trooping to and from their work on the same island, and the poor lunatics haunt it too [...] A place to pray for.[103]

Congreve recalled that when he visited the leper colony and attended the men's service, he was – apart from the chaplain – "the only person in the church who was not a leper". When he preached at the women's service his words were translated by an inmate, "her head and face hidden by her shawl, [who] came very quietly and modestly and sat on the lower chancel step at the feet of the preacher, and interpreted the address, sentence by sentence, in a gentle voice".[104] A similar arrangement was in place at the cottage services, where Congreve felt that although the devout Cape Dutch layman who acted as interpreter "evidently improves upon the sermon greatly, often leaving the preacher far behind, and travelling into regions of thought which are all his own, returning at last safe to earth again and to the scarcely necessary preacher", his heart was in the right place and his ministry a great boon.[105] At other times preaching was done with a magic-lantern, which always drew a crowd.[106]

It is perhaps through Congreve that we see the aims of the original SSJE mission to South Africa most clearly. When the Duke and Duchess of Cornwall & York – the future George V and Queen Mary – visited in 1901 he instructed the children that as they watched the firework-display on top of Table Mountain they were to "say in their hearts 'God bless the Duke and Duchess, and Lord give us peace'."[107] Certainly he shared the imperial assumptions of the day, and was a great admirer of Cecil Rhodes: another son of the parsonage, and generous in his philanthropy towards the Society's work.[108] Henry Bull was more circumspect: when Rhodes lay dying he noted that they had been praying from him in Church, because of the position he occupied in the Cape – "whatever opinions may be entertained of his public life".[109] Nevertheless, the cross and candlesticks that accompanied Rhodes's coffin on the funeral train from Cape Town to Rhodesia came from the altar of the Mission House.[110]

Congreve's vision for the Society's work at the Cape, in fact, went far beyond superficial imperial tub-thumping. When he preached in Johannesburg in early 1902 on Hebrews 11.10 – "For he looked for a city which hath foundations, whose builder and maker is God" – he looked to a bright future after the

---

103 Nias, *Waggett*, 62.
104 *CE* Jan 1906.
105 *St Philip's Mission*, 13.
106 cf Wallis, 15 April 1914. "We adjourned to the School for a Magic-lantern Service. This was, as always, well attended by others as well as by our own flock. Mrs Rousby very kindly lent her lantern and manipulated it herself."
107 Congreve, 19 Aug 1901.
108 cf Bull, 23 April 1902.
109 Bull, 5 March 1902.
110 Bull, 26 Nov 1902.

Boer conflict was ended: "as we give ourselves to Him, that He may build us one by one into His City, we shall learn the true ideal, and may be allowed to contribute our life to the building up of a new South Africa, according to the pattern of God's building."[111] Ultimately, the task lay not in the civilising of the savage; but in the conversion of the heathen, and the profound eschatological task of the building up of Christ's kingdom on earth.

> The Saints are not all English people, all sons of the British Empire, but of *all* nations and tongues. They are of all races and colours and make up *one* people, God's People, One Empire, Christ's Empire: and whatever their language, Dutch, English, Kaffir, they belong to us, if we belong to Christ.[112]

To this he might also have added "Greek". By the end of 1901 Old St Philip's had been lent to the then-relatively-small Greek community in Cape Town for the celebration of their Divine Liturgy after the arrival of their new priest, Fr Artemios. He spoke little English (his usual interpreter was the Greek Vice-Consul); and his people had to borrow various liturgical items to use until they could acquire their own. Bull noted with pride that "they were very pleased to find a censer available";[113] and Nalbro' Robinson recounted the Easter services in 1902 in great detail, analysing them in comparison to the rites of the Western Church.[114]

Soon afterwards, Bull summarised the Cape Town work in advance of Page's tour of the overseas missions.

> *Services.* In Capetown—at S. Columba's, at the Docks, at the Old Somerset Hospital, and at the convict-station. At the Location—at S. Cyprian's and in heathen huts. In the Neighbourhood—at Simonstown, Somerset West, Newlands, Rondebosch and Mowbray. Four Catechists and some twenty Preachers are engaged.

> *Night Schools.* There are three Native Night Schools, with little short of 200 names on the books, all under Government Inspection—at S. Columba's, S. Cyprian's and the Docks—employing twelve native teachers, with white help also.

> *Native Day School* at S. Cyprian's.[115]

It was not for nothing that when the young Winston Churchill attended a meeting of the Missionary Association for Cape Town at Grosvenor House in 1902 he declared, in the light of the opportunities afforded by the end of the Boer War – in which he had himself played an eventful and well-documented part – that "so admirable a work as that carried on by the St Philip's Mission" deserved the warmest support.[116]

---

111 *The Star* (Johannesburg), 1 Feb 1902.

112 Miller, *Congreve*.

113 Bull, 31 Dec 1901. "The railway company wished to preserve the car in which Mr Rhodes was carried, with all its fittings, as a memorial at Kimberley, and proposed to present us with others as substitutes. I think Mr Masey communicated with Mr Comper, and the result is very satisfactory."

114 *CE* July 1902.

115 Bull, 13 Aug 1902.

116 *CE* June 1902.

8

A New Century

We must consecrate this opening century to God, so that when centuries shall no longer be counted, we may have our part in the Kingdom of the Eternal.

—*Cowley Evangelist*[1]

As 1900 approached the brethren at Cape Town were keeping chameleons, whose party-trick was to delight visitors by changing colour when placed on different shrubs.[2] Perhaps not unsurprisingly, the heady exoticism of the Society's colonial missions from the late 1880s to some extent obscures the work that was being done at the same time by the SSJE in England, the United States, and Canada – what might be described as the English-language portion of the Society's ministry. Almost all the priest-brethren of the Society served in South Africa, India, and North America for varying lengths of time; and the news briefs at the back of the *Cowley Evangelist* recorded departures, returns, and redeployments on a regular basis. Similar announcements noted missions preached in parishes; and retreats led at the Mission House, on Iona, and elsewhere.

The American work was served by its own journal, *The Messenger*, and so it did not receive as much prominence in the pages of the *Cowley Evangelist* as the rest. It was amply supported by a number of wealthy individuals *in situ* – chief among them Isabella Stewart Gardner – and there were very few appeals for its support, whereas the necessity of sending money to India and South Africa was a constant theme. In practice, the life of the American brethren was much like that of their English counterparts – except that the distances travelled were significantly greater and the congregations much more diverse.

As per the Rule, the Founder himself wrote regularly from Boston with news; and his letters always took precedence over any others in the *Cowley Evangelist*. He noted with a combination of bemusement and concern some of the follies of American life, drawing out theological truths when he could. A six-day and six-night bicycle race took place in New York: "many were dropping off their wheels in sleep; others were raving [...] The faces of the men as photographed during the time were frightful with the violence of passion which distorted their features [...] Was this not exactly like the world's round, year after year? O if we could only see the photograph of souls straining year after year to win some object of ambition!"[3] In the Yukon he discovered that

---

1 *CE* Jan 1901.
2 Bignold, 22 Nov 1903.
3 Benson, 14 Dec 1897.

in winter fires were lit to thaw the ground before the gold diggers could start work: "we want fires to thaw this frosty humanity before the soil can be really workable. I suppose really nothing but the fire of persecution can burn deep enough. Unless people have to suffer for the truth's sake they cannot value it."[4] Elsewhere he thundered against divorce;[5] and mourned the death of William Ewart Gladstone: he thought his funeral "one of the great closing events of the century [...] The coming century seems to open with prospects altogether different from those which belonged to his public life."[6]

The Society's work continued to find particular emphasis among the non-white population. In late 1897 Charles Field attended a conference of clergy with similar missionary interests, at which the highlight was "High Mass, sung by a colored Priest, with two white Priests for Deacon and Sub-Deacon [...] I wished our millions of colored people could have been present. A High Mass is the most converting service." The conference was opened by Owen Waller, who was Rector of St Luke's, Washington – "a large colored church" – but who, more significantly, had been at school at Cowley St John. There was impatience at the apparent lethargy of the American bishops:

> a very healthy discontent with the slowness of the progress of the work of evangelization, and no one can wonder at this. The earnest colored men are rightly disgusted at the apathy shown by a large portion of the Episcopal Church as to the conversion of their people. They feel that the Church neglects them or leaves them to the Baptists and Methodists. They want their own Bishops, and it is not possible to deny their claim much longer. I do not believe that white Bishops will ever evangelise the colored people of the South.[7]

Field soon set out on what he called "a series of missionary journeys" to support his non-white colleagues, accepting invitations to preach and lecture in their parishes. Almost immediately he was diverted by William Longridge – who was serving as American Provincial – to Montauk Point, beyond the Hamptons on Long Island, to minister to soldiers returning from the Spanish-American War. Yellow fever had swept through the troops in Cuba, and he went to assist the chaplains, many of whom were also gravely ill, in ministering to over twenty-five thousand men: "a special call came for help, and it was impossible to refuse [...] the Red Cross took me in, and gave me a bed". On his arrival he presented himself to the various commanding officers. "Colonel Roosevelt", he particularly noted, "was very kind. He is likely to be Governor of New York."[8]

Three years later Teddy Roosevelt succeeded William McKinley as President of the United States; and when Field and Edward Osborne attended Prize Giving at Groton School in May 1904 President Roosevelt was the guest of honour. "Fr Field said something about Montauk," wrote Osborne, "and Mr Roosevelt's whole face lighted up, 'Ah, those Montauk days!'" The three men

---

4 Benson, Jan 1898.
5 *CE* Jan 1899.
6 Benson, 31 May 1898.
7 Field, 23 Sept 1897.
8 *CE* Nov 1898.

talked in depth about "the general coloured question"; and the President was enthusiastic and encouraging. "The work you Fathers are doing for them is what is needed", he said. "They must be educated and raised up; they must have a fair chance given to them."[9] That Field's work had won him well-connected friends was well known in the Society: "how often we used to chaff him", reminisced Henry Bull after his death in 1929, "that if there was an inauguration of a President, or the foundation stone of a national memorial to be laid, Father Field had an engagement just then at Washington!"[10]

In the summer of 1898 he opened a children's home at an old farm near Foxborough, thirty miles south of Boston, where "invalid colored children and those without proper homes or care or educational advantages could be taken and benefited both physically and morally, and fitted for the life which was before them", which he also dedicated to St Augustine. In addition to the residents, it later functioned as a summer camp for dozens of non-white children who would come each summer from the city to enjoy the fresh air, the open space, and the numerous animals. "The Revd C. N. Field is a Father of the Society of St John the Evangelist," wrote a local newspaper a few years later, "more frequently referred to as the Cowley Fathers, which has head-quarters at Oxford, Eng., and a branch at Bowdoin Street, Boston. [There] he entered upon what he considers his life work, the amelioration of the condition of colored children."[11]

When the Cowley Fathers in Boston went to preach a mission in Ottawa in the autumn of 1898, Field's letters home again gave an insight into their peripatetic life. "When I last wrote we were holding the Mission in the Cathedral at Ottawa and after that we dispersed, Fr Osborne going South, and Fr Conran, West." He himself was heading to Raleigh, NC, eight hundred miles away (stopping on the way at St Paul's, K Street, Washington, to lead a parish retreat) to visit and preach at St Augustine's School – "[a] School of our Church for training colored teachers", which the American brethren visited regularly. It was a ready witness to the Society's concern for the evangelisation of the non-white population in the United States.

It is hard to find much interest in the Church for the colored people, and yet it ought to be the great missionary work of the Church in America. The governor of the state who lives in Raleigh has been very unfortunate in stirring up the negroes by his hard speeches. Riots have happened lately at Wilmington near here in which several negroes have been shot. It seems such a shame that a people who can be so easily taught, and are naturally so quiet and peaceable, should not have the best training instead of being made the tools and the victims of political demagogues.[12]

Field's work soon took him from Boston to Baltimore, then on to Washington, Richmond, Salisbury, Nashville, Spartansburg, and Atlanta – a round-trip

9 Osborne, 26 May 1904.
10 *CE* Feb 1929.
11 *CE* Feb 1904.
12 Field, 15 Dec 1898.

of over two thousand miles.[13] His earnestness was frequently tinged with humour: "The bishop has been here this evening [...] and we had an O'possum for dinner. This is the great colored dish, but my taste is not colored. I have not seen the animal alive, but when cooked it looks like an ichthyosaurus with an abbreviated tail [...] Please pray for St Augustine's School in the intercessions at Cowley. Black America needs many prayers, and which is the blackest part of it no one can tell."[14]

Benson concurred. Writing just before Christmas he noted that Osborne had preached a course of lectures during Advent on the nature of the Church. The attendance had been good, but the people were sluggish, and "much more quick to take up new fancies than to rise up to the demands of old truths".

It is sad to think that eighteen centuries have passed by, and millions, though calling themselves Christians, have so little knowledge of what the Apostles' Creed really means. The worst of it is that they are not only ignorant, but are content to be so. To accept Christ as Saviour implies accepting Him as a Law of Life, a Pattern to be followed, a Power to be used. That is what people are unwilling to do. The modern notions which fill up the religious atmosphere of the present day serve to gratify curiosity and amuse the mind with fancies, and that is all that is commonly cared for.

He returned to the theme in Holy Week, citing the American separation of Church and State as a stumbling block to conversion of life.

With the public schools non-Christian, and the homes absolutely void of Christian control, the rising generation has no opportunity of coming to any knowledge of such matters. Things which one used to feel were matters of course are simply unknown to the vast majority of people round about us this country. Of course, in such an utter state of ignorance there is no reason why the rising population should take any interest in going to Church. They do not know what to do when they are there. They do not know what it means. In this country we want Christian schools more than churches.

Benson feared that at Easter churchgoers would be more cheerful "because of its music than because of its promise"; and concluded that "we need to cherish a longing for the great day that we may welcome Christ in the glory of the resurrection. The worship can never rise up to much earnestness unless we are hastening the day of the Lord."[15]

In addition to its parish work at Bowdoin Street the SSJE also branched out into mission work at Harvard University;[16] but the interstate travel still seemed relentless. In October 1900 Osborne described a mission-trip from Boston to Cleveland, then Chicago, and, by way of Nashotah House, on to Fond du Lac, where he stayed with Bishop Grafton. It was another journey of about 2,500 miles; and he looked forward to his return to Boston: "I do not expect to be

---

13 Field, 12 Dec 1899.
14 Field, 15 Dec 1898.
15 Benson, 8 April 1899.
16 *CE* Jan 1905.

away again until the end of January – nearly four months of uninterrupted life at home. We have several invitations for Missions, two in Chicago, besides Cleveland and Milwaukee; but these must wait."[17] Meanwhile, Field had undertaken the grim task of acting as emergency chaplain to the Red Cross in the aftermath of the catastrophic Johnstown Flood at the end of May 1899, which had left over two thousand people dead.[18]

By 1900 Benson had left the American work behind. Nine years after he left the Mission House on Marston Street for India, the General Chapter of 1899 had voted to bring him home – Frederick Puller thought it "a great joy";[19] although Benson himself had in fact declined Page's invitation for him to return as early as 1892.[20] Osborne, however, was there to stay. In 1902 he told the Superior General that in his habit on the train from Boston to Kansas City he had been called "Father" as far as New York, "Bishop" until St Louis, and "Cardinal" for the rest of the journey. "You will be amused", he joked, "at my speedy ecclesiastical promotion".[21] Perhaps it was not without prescience: in 1904 he was elected coadjutor Bishop of Springfield. It "cut very deep", he said, to have to "ask [the] brethren of the Society very lovingly for their cordial release and for their sympathetic prayers" so that he could take up his new work.[22] Duly freed, he was consecrated in St John's, Bowdoin Street, on 23 October; and Charles Grafton and Arthur Hall both travelled to Boston to take part in the laying-on of hands.[23] Like them, he never forgot his membership of the SSJE, and photographs of Benson, Page, and "one of all the Brethren at Cowley" hung in his rooms until his death.[24]

Benson's absence from England had only really been figurative: his letters had continued to pour into Cowley; and in the wider Church his literary output was prodigious. By the end of the century he had published an exposition on the first nine chapters of the Book of Proverbs, *The Wisdom of the Son of David* (1860); his *Manual of Intercessory Prayer* (1863); another work on the Discourse at Capernaum at John 6.25ff, *Bible Teachings* (1875); a set of meditations for the Church's year, *Benedictus Dominus* (1876–78); one for Advent, Christmas, and Epiphanytide, *Readings for Every Day* (1879–82); his work on the Magnificat (1889); an *Exposition of the Epistle of St Paul to the Romans* (1892); all four volumes of his meditations on the Passion, *The Final Passover* (1884–95); and *The Way of Holiness*, a commentary on Psalm 119 (1900).

Other members of the Society also contributed to the theological and intellectual life of the Church. Osborne had produced books for children on the Life of Christ, Old Testament typology, and the Apostles' Creed – some of which were translated into Zulu and Xhosa for use in South Africa – and Field had written on the Way of the Cross. Charles Gardner had produced a number of works on the Catechism, and his *Life of Father Goreh*; while in *Marriage and*

---

17 Osborne, 20 Oct 1900.
18 *CE* Feb 1925; David G. McCulloch, *The Johnstown Flood*, London: Hutchinson (1968).
19 Puller, 2 Oct 1899, CUL MS (Add.7651) WYON/9/3/99.
20 Benson to Page, 15 May 1892, SSJE/6/1/2/8/5.
21 Osborne, 3 Feb 1902.
22 Osborne, 5 Aug 1904.
23 Osborne, 11 Aug 1904; *The Living Church*, 29 Oct 1904.
24 *The Death of Bishop Osborne*, CE Sept 1926.

Divorce in the United States Duncan Convers had drawn the robust yet unsurprising conclusion "once married, married 'til death".[25] Puller had written with his customary scholarly erudition on the Eucharistic fast, his magisterial *Primitive Saints and the See of Rome*, and in French on *Des Ordinations Anglicanes et le Sacrifice de la Messe* as part of his contribution to the discussions leading up to *Apostolicæ Curæ*. George Hollings, who after the Founder was at this point perhaps the Society's leading expert on the religious life – alongside George Congreve, soon to publish his own works on the subject – had already produced ten books on spirituality and the interior life. The Society also produced "Tracts for Parochial Distribution", as well as "Occasional Sermons" which could be handed out to individuals seeking particular guidance on a number of subjects. Their titles ranged from the cheerful *Everlasting Punishment* to the rhetorical (and perhaps obviously self-answering) *How shall I spend Good Friday?*

Through the published works of its members the SSJE was able to extend its sphere of influence far beyond Cowley, its daughter houses, and the Society's various missions and retreats. And yet, in a divided Church of England, its Catholic credentials did not always find favour; even at a time by which John Shelton Reed concludes that Anglo-Catholicism had become "increasingly conventional, almost respectable"[26] – a fact borne out within the present work by the genteel names appearing on the SSJE's lists of subscribers as time went on.

After Bishop Edward King of Lincoln had been prosecuted for Ritualism in 1888 the SSJE was drawn into the controversy raised by John Kensit and the Protestant Truth Society in the 1890s, which Owen Chadwick called "the worst of the century after the riots over papal aggression in 1850–2".[27] Benson – his own Ritualist sympathies notwithstanding – felt that some clergy had gone too far, and bemoaned "the wild enthusiasm which one cannot feel to be really promoting God's glory, although it seems to arouse the blasphemy of the Protestant public".[28] To that end, one of the rules for members of the Society visiting Ritualistic churches in London was clear that "it shall not be considered that any one is bound in conscience to follow any practice that he believes to be contrary to the Rubrics."[29]

Subsequent questions raised in Parliament in the course of the debates leading up to the Benefices Act of 1898 centred around, as Chadwick put it, "whether there was indeed a conspiracy to turn the Church of England into a popish church".[30] Chadwick identified three main catalysts to this renewed aggression: the publication of Walter Walsh's *Secret History of the Oxford Movement* in 1897;[31] the ongoing interest of the newspapers in "rare ritual";

---

25 Duncan Convers SSJE, *Marriage and Divorce in the United States: as they are and as they ought to be*, Philadelphia (1889), 245.

26 Reed, *Glorious Battle*, 264.

27 Chadwick, *Victorian Church*, ii, 355.

28 *CE* July 1898.

29 *London*, SSJE/7/1/1/8.

30 Chadwick, *Victorian Church*, ii, 355.

31 Walter Walsh, *The Secret History of the Oxford Movement*, London: Church Association (1897).

and the conversations involving Lord Halifax and the Vatican, which led to Leo XIII's condemnation of Anglican orders in 1896.[32]

The first amounted to "the unveiling of an Anglo-Catholic underworld".[33] It was mainly an attack on the Society of the Holy Cross; but the SSJE was tangentially implicated because a number of brethren, including Benson and Page, had connections with the SSC. The second involved the SSJE inasmuch as its churches were numbered among the many hundreds which, by the end of the 1890s, were Ritualist in their liturgical practice. The *Cowley Evangelist* responded to the renewed turbulence in the same way that the Parish Magazine had responded to the ritual controversies of 1869 – literally. It simply reproduced Benson's own comments at that time under their original headings: *Silentium et Spes* and *On the Personality of Satan*.

The third, however, touched on the Society more pressingly in the person of Puller. He was on good terms with Halifax, with whom he had been at Eton, and Gladstone;[34] and was much involved in ecumenical work on the Continent. His broad historical scholarship and particular expertise on the early Roman Church made him naturally suspect, despite his firm rejection of its claims. Having taken part in the discussions leading up to *Apostolicæ Curæ*, he spent Holy Week 1898 observing the ceremonies at Florence[35]; and almost certainly he was the author of the *Cowley Evangelist*'s lengthy statement regarding *Sæpius Officio*, the reply to Pope Leo of the Archbishops of Canterbury and York.

"It has not been our custom", opened the piece, "to use the pages of the *Cowley Evangelist* for the discussion of controversial subjects." However, it represented a useful opportunity for the Society firmly to nail its Catholic colours to the Anglican mast.

> Over and above the value of the Encyclical as a reply to the Bull, there are other incidental matters connected with this Archiepiscopal pronouncement, which are likely to make it of very great advantage to the Church [...] By implication [the Archbishops] repudiate the old mistake that it is the doctrine of the Church of England that there are two Sacraments only [...] Moreover they dwell on the fact that the Priest "has what is called the power of the keys."

"But perhaps the most important doctrinal passages in the whole document", it continued, "are those which deal with the teaching of the Church of England on the subject of the Eucharistic Sacrifice."

> We all believe that the Sacrifice of the eternal Priest is the Sacrifice of Christ Himself. He is not only the Priest but also the Victim. And the Archbishops tell their brethren, the Bishops of the Universal Church [*Sæpius Officio* was addressed to the entire episcopate, after the primitive practice] that the teaching of the Church of England is that the Sacrifice of the Church, which is offered at the Consecration, is in some way one thing with this Sacrifice of the eternal Priest; in other words – in some way Christ Himself is offered at the Consecration of the Eucharist.

---

32 See also Yates, *Anglican Ritualism*, 314ff.
33 Chadwick, *Victorian Church*, ii, 355.
34 Puller, 27 Aug 1895.
35 Puller, 13 April 1898.

"It is much to be hoped", it concluded, "that our brethren, who belong to other branches of the Catholic Church, may through this Encyclical be led to realise that God is in us of a truth, and that as a result the blessed day of the re-union of the Churches may be hastened."[36] For some, however, *Apostolicæ Curæ* was a death-blow. Benson never quite forgave Basil Maturin for his secession to Rome: when Maturin came to look at the new buildings a few years later, he bumped into Br Maynard in the nearly-finished cloister. "I cannot help thinking", sniped the Founder, "that he was looking under the loose pavement to see if his heart was not buried there."[37]

TOWER OF STRENGTH

Petà Dunstan has observed that by the end of the 1890s there was less hostility towards the religious life in the wider Church of England; and cites particularly the achievements of the nursing and teaching sisterhoods, and "the sheer numbers of vocations". At the same time, new bishops were being consecrated who had been influenced to a greater or lesser extent by the Oxford Movement, and so were more open to the idea of the religious life; and the communities themselves "had come to realize that they needed bishops".[38] In response, the 1897 Lambeth Conference resolved – in Resolution XI – that it viewed "with thankfulness the revival alike of brotherhoods and sisterhoods and of the office of deaconess in our branch of the Church". It further commended "to the attention of the Church the Report of the Committee appointed to consider the Relation of Religious Communities to the Episcopate". The Committee was charged with continuing its work "in view of the importance of the further development and wise direction of such communities".[39]

It may have taken a while for the other communities to realise the importance of cordial relations with their bishops for their flourishing; but the Cowley Fathers had been in the vanguard. Benson had been determined to operate with an episcopal *nihil obstat* from the beginning; and to this the SSJE had added the bitter and simultaneous experience of functioning as best it could under unsympathetic bishops at Boston and Philadelphia.

Dunstan notes that "being linked to rebelliousness and ecclesiastical lawlessness was an image hard for Religious to dispel" – but the SSJE, as we have seen, was very much of the Establishment. The Society was certainly able to be viewed with much less suspicion than that of other contemporary communities: Ignatius Lyne's monks were still at Llanthony, for example; and George Nugée had only recently died, after being drawn into the controversial Order of Corporate Reunion. The SSJE's corporate life was by now Catholic without being Roman; ascetic without being moribund; and Ritualist without being Popish – at least by its own lights.

---

36 *CE* April 1897.

37 Benson, 27 Dec 1900, SSJE/6/1/2/3/4/15.

38 Petà Dunstan, "Bishops and Religious 1897–1914", *Anglican Religious Life Journal*, no. 1 (March 2004).

39 Lambeth Conference 1897, Resolution 11.

That said, the SSJE was also determined to retain its independence as a distinct community when necessary – with episcopal authority and that of its Superior General neatly delineated. The debates at the Lambeth Conference were to a great extent informed by the Society, which had taken soundings, led by Puller, from various communities of men and women;[40] and a paper published for the purpose by him in early 1897 had its origins in the Chapter discussions of 1893. Then he had opposed the motion to give the Bishop of Oxford and his successors the inherent right to be Visitor – "it might very easily happen that a bishop might be appointed who would use his power to destruction rather than to edification" – and now he applied the same argument to the broader picture. In addition, he noted,

[t]o say that religious obedience cannot be rightly paid to a religious superior, unless the community has been specially authorised by the Church, and unless ecclesiastical authority has been specially delegated to the Superior, appears to me to be a position fundamentally subversive of the religious life and absolutely unhistorical. It would mean that the religious life, when it was in its prime and in its glory, when it was subduing Europe to Christ, and handing down the torch of religious and learning, was based on a fundamental mistake [...] The Church does not possess religious jurisdiction. An ecumenical council cannot create religious jurisdiction. That can only come from the free donation of the religious, who have themselves been called by Christ to the life of obedience. That is the core of the matter.

He concluded that the episcopate *in toto* did not know enough about the religious life "to make it safe to subject ourselves indiscriminately to Bishops appointed by the Prime Minister of the day", and maintained that bishops were entitled only to "visitational jurisdiction" at the community's invitation.[41] Twenty years earlier, while he was still Vicar of Roath, Puller had included a similar "Caution against Episcopal Autocracy" in his *Duties and Rights of Parish Priests*, and reminded his readers that "Episcopal authority is limited by the Canons."[42]

While the Anglican bishops who attended the 1897 Lambeth Conference may have been generally ignorant of the needs of religious communities, and of the canonical limitations of their authority in respect of them, there were two notable exceptions: Hall and Grafton, of Vermont and Fond du Lac respectively, who had previously both been members of the SSJE. Grafton had been asked by the Archbishop of Canterbury to prepare a paper for discussion on the relation of religious communities with the bishops; and both he and Hall were appointed to the committee charged with producing Resolution XI. Eldridge Pendleton called it "a benchmark of acceptance in the history of Anglican religious life."[43]

---

40 Dunstan, "Bishops and Religious".
41 F. W. Puller SSJE, *The Relation of Religious to their Bishops*, printed privately (1897).
42 F. W. Puller SSJE, *The Duties and Rights of Parish Priests and the Limits of Obedience due from them to their Bishops*, London: Rivingtons (1877).
43 Pendleton, *Grafton*, 126.

For Grafton, the trip to England also served as an opportunity to heal some old wounds. Page invited him to stay at Cowley, and to preach in the new church. He was able to reconnect with his old community, which had grown significantly since his departure; and went for a long visit to Yorkshire, to stay with the Halifaxes at Hickleton. The growth Grafton found at Cowley was not unique. The SSJE provided spiritual succour to parish clergy and lay people up and down the country and overseas; and by its very existence and growth – and through the increasing expertise of some of its members in the spiritual gifts necessary to the fruitful living-out of the monastic vocation – it had also become the centre of the revival of the religious life for men. Of the enduring brotherhoods that had been established by 1900 the majority had concrete links with the Cowley Fathers in one way or another. The Rule of the Society of the Divine Compassion had been drawn up during a retreat led by Philip Waggett in 1894, for example; while the members of the community that eventually became the Benedictines of Caldey Island had lived alongside the SSJE in the course of their peregrinations in 1899.[44]

The Community of the Resurrection, the SSJE's most obvious counterpart, had many connections; although the experience of the founding brethren led them to form a distinctly different type of monastic life from that of Cowley. Leonard Prestige noted that the earliest members of the CR recoiled from the fact that after Page's election "the Cowley Society again was ruled by a Superior, who after his election held more or less autocratic powers for his period of office. Gore and his friends were aiming quite deliberately at form-ing a democratic spirit in their community."[45] Nevertheless, the model that the CR rejected in the 1890s continued to work well for the SSJE, and bore much fruit; while Geoffrey Curtis CR later observed that "the debt of my own Community of the Resurrection to Father Benson is beyond reckoning."[46]

The work at home continued to grow. The Infant School burgeoned to accommodate nearly 400 parish children, and plans were made to extend the Boys' School as well. Together with the Girls' School both received a glow-ing inspectors' report in September 1900, which Page presented with pride – while, of course, asking for an increase in subscriptions.[47] The houses occupied by the teaching Sisters of the Holy Childhood on Marston Street were knocked through: a small chapel was added at the back, and the Sisters soon began hosting retreats for schoolmistresses, led by members of the Society.

Simultaneously, a concerted effort was being made to pay off the balance on the new church. The Bursar of Keble, Colonel John Jervoise, who served as Treasurer of the fundraising committee, noted that "if those interested in the work of the Cowley Fathers would each agree to be responsible for a specified sum [the appeal was followed by his exact calculations for raising the final £2200] on condition the whole amount were raised or promised by the end of

---

44 Peter Anson, *Benedictines of Caldey*, Prinknash Abbey (1944).
45 Prestige, *Gore*, 111.
46 *CE* April 1951.
47 *CE* March 1901.

the year, it seems probable that the money might be provided without much difficulty".[48]

Jervoise was only slightly over-optimistic: the money was raised by May 1901, and the debt paid off. Without a moment's hesitation, he and the committee launched a new appeal for another £3000 to complete the west end of the building. Bodley had offered his services *gratis*, and the committee "hoped that this appeal will meet with a speedy and liberal response".[49] Its members were not disappointed: Halifax laid the foundation stone of the tower on 12 May 1902 – again within the octave of St John before the Latin Gate, and the anniversary of the dedication of the new building by William Stubbs in 1896.

Benson preached at High Mass, after which "the clergy and choir proceeded to the spot where the stone was to be laid, singing Ps. lxxxiv [*Quam dilecta*] with the Antiphon 'Other foundation can no man lay than that which is laid by Christ the Lord, Alleluia'." After the stone had been blessed and put in place, Halifax addressed the assembled company. He reminded his hearers that he had been present at the meeting in Reginald Tuke's rooms at St Mary's, Soho, in 1865 – shortly after which Benson, Grafton, and O'Neill had moved into the house on Magdalen Terrace.

> When he thought of those small and humble beginnings, and looked round and saw this beautiful church and cloister, and still more when he remembered how the Community had increased and flourished, how its members were now working, not only in Oxford and London, but in America, India, and South Africa, he felt that its history was indeed the exemplification of the parable of the grain of mustard seed, and that there was reason to exclaim: "This is the Lord's doing, and it is marvellous in our eyes."

He tactfully did not mention Benson's resignation as Superior, which had enabled the flourishing to take place. He dwelt instead on the establishment of the SSJE as part of the fulfilment of the work begun by Keble, Newman, and Pusey in recalling the Church of England to a supernatural relationship with Christ; and mentioned that aspect particularly because the congregation had gathered "to lay the stone of the tower which was to complete the Church of the Cowley Fathers, that society to which they owed so much, to the members of which they were so profoundly grateful, and whom they thanked most of all for that example of the supernatural life realized and lived, the lack of which was so great a source of weakness to the Church of England and to the whole Anglican Communion."[50]

By the autumn, the walls of the tower had risen to a height of sixteen feet, and the committee was once more working to keep the funds coming in. Bodley, by now a Royal Academician, was corralled into circulating his plans for the west end of the building; and had already presented a window in the Holy Spirit Chapel.

---

48 *CE* Dec 1898.
49 *CE* May 1901.
50 *Church Times*, 16 May 1902.

The work now commenced, comprises a quasi Tower the full width of the Nave, and a continuation of it. It will be an "engaged" Tower, if, indeed, it can be called a Tower at all, for it is only intended to rise just sufficiently to stop the ridge of the Nave roof [...] Like the rest of the buildings at S. John's, it will simple, indeed severe, in its character.

"It should be remembered", he continued, "that this is the first considerable monastic building that has been built for the use of the English Church for many centuries". Costs would be kept down: the tower would not contain a peal, only "one large, deep-toned bell [...] worthy of its companions at Oxford"; and Maynard would be Clerk of Works, which was a considerable saving. "The work is being well done," he pleaded. "It has made a good start. Is it to be continued?"

The bell could be paid for later, he thought; and so could the carving of the Crucifixion, facing the Iffley Road, the north and south porches, and the statue of St Michael set into the internal west wall. The cost of each was enumerated separately, should anyone wish to give them as an offering; but Bodley's priority was the completion of the nave: "I hope the building need not be stopped for lack of funds."[51] A helpful donation slip was included, with gaps for names, addresses, and the amount of money sent or promised.

By October the money was coming in, and the carved work had already been provided for; but the walls rose only as quickly as the funds would allow. By March 1903 a handful of workmen had been retained, and the *Cowley Evangelist* had another drive: it circulated a photograph of the ongoing work with an update on the progress and some gentle coercion.

At present only the sum subscribed, month by month, is being expended. Should any substantial increase take place in the funds at our disposal, the staff of workmen could immediately be increased and the work pushed on; in any case it will be possible to go on working, stone by stone, up to a point above the arch of the nave, where a temporary roof could be put. It would, however, be a great advantage to get so far as the temporary roof before the end of the summer.

In the end a view was taken that it would be better to push ahead regardless, and look for the money afterwards: "the additional expense which would have been incurred [by the temporary roof] and other serious inconveniences which would have arisen from further delay, seemed to make it desirable to complete it."[52] Francis Paget, who had been Bishop of Oxford since Stubbs' death in 1901 – and who, as Dean of Christ Church, had preached at the dedication of the church in 1896 – blessed the completed tower and aisles on December 6. He referred to it as the completion of "a work long ago commenced, patiently sustained, and now, by God's grace, happily finished".[53] The large bell that survives today was fixed in place twenty-five years later.[54]

---

51 *Completion of the Church, CE* Sept 1902.
52 *CE* Dec 1903.
53 *CE* Jan 1904.
54 SSJE/2/6/76.

A New Monastery

In early September 1897 Sr Louisa Katherine of the All Saints Sisters of the Poor wrote to Page to say that a friend of hers "who knows <u>one</u> of the Fathers very well" wished to know how much it would cost to build the hoped-for new house: "I mean the full amount, including interior fittings etc, and including the covered way to the Church that you spoke of [at the time of the building of the new Church]." This potential benefactor was willing, if possible, to give the whole sum; or if too large to be given in a lump sum, to contribute it over a few years, and wished it to be used "for <u>no other</u> purpose".[55]

"My dear Child", Page replied – as SSJE Superior General he was also Chaplain-General of the ASSP – "your letter rather takes my breath away. To think that it should have been put into the heart of anyone, by God, to desire to build our Monastery. *Deo Gratias.*" He swiftly named the price as £12,000, which was Bodley's quote for a plan that he had roughed out a year or two earlier. There was a stumbling block, however, as at that stage the new Church had not been paid off, and the fundraising committee for the long-awaited London house would soon be appealing for an identical sum. "It seems to me," he continued,

> therefore not quite modest to start another expensive building at this time, for which there is no immediate necessity. I should much prefer to wait for two or three years – and in the mean time, if there is a prospect of building, I can get plans from Mr Bodley and have all in readiness.[56]

Louisa Katherine responded immediately to say that she intended to propose to the benefactor, who was clearly determined to make the gift,

> to pay what can be managed into your Banker for that purpose, before the end of this year, and to go on doing so each year, letting it accumulate there until you think there is enough to begin with, and leaving instructions in the Will that the whole sum required shall be paid to you in case of the Donor's death before the completion of the Monastery.[57]

A couple of days later she wrote again to say that the donor had dismissed her idea of paying the money in instalments, and that she intended them to have the money at once.

> "Mrs Brown-Jones" (or whatever you like to call the Donor) wishes to offer £12,000, to build the monastery for the Cowley Fathers, and hopes to send the whole sum in a few months' time, and hopes also that the Building will be begun as soon as possible.

She was absolutely clear, however, that the gift was not to be used for the

---

55 Louisa Katherine ASSP, Sept 1897, SSJE/6/3/2/8/1ff.
56 Page, 11 Sept 1897, SSJE/6/3/2/8/5ff.
57 Page, 12 Sept 1897, SSJE/6/3/2/8/7.

London house, despite it being the same amount required: "Mrs Brown-Jones thinks London people ought to build that for the Fathers."[58]

By return of post Page asked Louisa Katherine to thank "Mrs Brown-Jones" for "her magnificent offer", but asked her to hold off sending the money until he had consulted his brethren. "I must bring the matter before my Council", he observed, "and perhaps the Chapter of the Society, which will all take time".[59] Louisa Katherine's response counselled haste, and demonstrated both women's solid grasp of finance:

> I think the good lady is anxious to transfer the money to you as soon as she can, in case of her own death. She wants to make sure that it comes to you, during her own lifetime. I think what she feels is that if it is paid into your Bank then it will be safe; and if you do not wish to use it immediately it will do no harm – it will only go on collecting interest which will help towards the furnishing, perhaps. Or at all events you are sure to be glad to have a margin to fall back upon, as buildings always run on into greater expense than one expects. So it will not be a bad thing to be able to nurse the £12,000 for a little while.

This was, of course, an enormous sum of money; and Louisa Katherine also advised discretion:

> Perhaps it would be well to say as little as possible about this offering. I know she would wish it kept as quiet as possible. And as you may not be ready to use it at once need it be known at all beyond yourselves, at all events at present? One is afraid it may damage the interest in the London Monastery.[60]

Page jumped at the idea, and wondered whether as "probably the money is already well invested" it might be easier for the Society to receive the securities. "It is delightful," he mused "to look forward to the building of our Monastery."[61] Naturally, he had also consulted Benson, who wrote from Boston in agreement – both to the acceptance of the legacy and the necessity of the work: "a good stone House would be a permanent gain" – although he favoured using Ninian Comper, with whose father he was on good terms.[62] Page had not yet consulted the SSJE Council when his letter to Louisa Katherine was posted by mistake. He recalled it by telegram immediately, and the next day told her how the meeting had progressed.

> It was thought by some that a better site could be found for the House, one which would not take up so much of our garden, and that if the present Mission House were considerably added to it would supply our wants. It was said that the cost would be less than Mr Bodley's plan, and therefore that we ought not to accept so much as £12,000.

The question was whether or not "Mrs Brown-Jones" wanted Bodley's design carried out, or whether she was willing simply to fund an extension.[63] Page

---

58 Louisa Katherine ASSP, 16 Sept 1897, SSJE/6/3/2/8/8ff.
59 Page, 18 Sept 1897, SSJE/6/3/2/8/10.
60 Louisa Katherine ASSP, 19 Sept 1897, SSJE/6/3/2/8/11.
61 Page, 20 Sept 1897, SSJE/6/3/2/8/13.
62 Benson, 20 Sept 1897, SSJE/6/3/2/8/15; Symondson & Bucknall, *Comper*, 97.
63 Page, 23 Sept 1897, SSJE/6/3/2/8/16.

sent the plans to be forwarded on, and received back the news that the donor was "quite willing to agree to the addition to the present Mission House or any such plan, as long as you have the kind of Monastery you <u>really</u> want at Cowley".[64]

There had, however, been disagreement over which of the offices should be recited in the conventual church, and therefore how large the new house chapel needed to be. This caused an impasse, and Page, who was aware that the Society might in any case elect another as Superior General in 1899, decided that it would be "more respectful to the Council and the Society by whom it is elected to delay building for the present; and the more so as [...] another Superior ought not to be embarrassed by finding the foundations laid of a building which might not have his approval".[65]

A year later the Chapter minutes noted that the disagreements had been overcome. "The site of the new Mission House had been determined upon: the plans approved of, and the work would be commenced at once." It was the last piece of business before the election of a Superior General: Page left the chapel at the top of the Mission House, and was duly elected for another term of office.

Bodley's unique project was finally under way. The new monastery was as elegant as it was austere – all dark wood and leaded lights – and very much in keeping with the style of the church. Michael Hall considers that it was designed to a great extent by Maynard, who again also acted as Clerk of Works. At the General Chapter of 1900 Page told the assembled brethren that "Mr. Bodley was responsible for the main outline of the Buildings, though he had accepted the co-operation of Brother Maynard as co-architect, and Brother Maynard had done nearly all the practical work."[66]

It had the all the hallmarks of a monastic building: a cloister joining the house to the community church; frosted glass in all the windows that looked onto the outside world; and a Lady Chapel with stalls for the brethren, decorated at frieze level with the Vulgate text of Revelation 3.21: "To him that overcometh". For the next eight decades, the new buildings would be the mother house of the Society of St John the Evangelist, with the original Mission House functioning as the guest house. The new building was blessed on 18 April 1901 by the Bishop of Reading, Leslie Randall; by which time "Mrs Brown-Jones" had died. Katharine Isabella Margaret Rennie had been a wealthy spinster, and her munificence was commemorated by a large brass plaque outside the chapel.

Requiem æternam dona Domine
Katharinæ Isabellæ Margaritæ Rennie
quæ has ædes cum sacello Beatæ Mariæ dicato
in usum Soc: Scti: Joannis Ev: exstrui curavit
et in Christo obdormivit
In Oct: Epiphiniæ MDCCCC

---

64 Louisa Katherine ASSP, 24 Sept 1897, SSJE/6/3/2/8/19.
65 SSJE/2/1/284.
66 SSJE/2/1/309.

THIS LONDON OF OURS

Nineveh continued to beckon, and plans for the London house also moved on apace. The Society had been informally present in London since 1892 – at 5 Margaret Street, right next to All Saints' Clergy House – so that brethren visiting the capital to preach or conduct retreats could be spared a late return to Oxford; but not the rigour of community discipline. To the general Rule was added a short list of points headed "London".

1. Members of the Society when engaged in work in London shall sleep at the house of the Society in 5 Margaret Street, unless they obtain permission to the contrary.

2. They shall not take meals in private houses without permission, except at the Priest's house where they may be staying.

3. They shall not pay visits to persons without permission, or at least without reporting the same to the Superior afterwards.

4. They should be careful, if it is necessary to speak with women alone out of the Confessional on spiritual matters that such interviews shall be brief and strictly confined to what is necessary.

5. Though it may be not possible for the Mission priest to keep the hours after returning and going to rest when away from home, as observed at the Mother House, he shall be careful not to transgress them unnecessarily, and specially avoid sitting up late with the Parochial clergy.[67]

It had always been intended that the SSJE should build a house of its own in the metropolis, as envisaged by Benson in his discussions with Samuel Wilberforce over thirty years earlier.[68] Like the Mission House at Cowley it would function as a retreat house; but the chapel would not be within the enclosure and would therefore be open to both men and women.[69] In 1897 Page asked the Bishop of London, Mandell Creighton, for his approval, which he received[70]; and a fundraising committee – to operate "without touching the work of the General Committee"[71] and including, naturally, Halifax – had been established to raise the necessary sum of £12,000.[72]

Of the "London people" whom Katharine Rennie had been keen should fund the work, the widowed Countess Grosvenor was among the first to contribute. Her father-in-law, the Duke of Westminster, was in regular contact with the committee, and Grosvenor House was frequently put at the Society's disposal

---

67 *London*, SSJE/7/1/1/8.
68 SSJE/2/1/192.
69 *CE* Dec 1897.
70 Page, 3 May 1897, SSJE/7/1/1/4/1; Mandell Creighton, 25 May 1897, SSJE/7/2/1/1.
71 *CE* June 1904.
72 SSJE/2/1/260.

for London meetings of its various Associations.[73] The list of subscribers soon grew to include Earl Beauchamp, Lord Aldenham, Lord Forbes, Sir Theodore & Lady Hope, Athelstan Riley, members of the Gurney and Hoare families, the Bishop of Argyll & the Isles, the Bishop of Nassau, and – perhaps sensing a canny investment – Charles Eamer Kempe; while the publisher Francis Hansard Rivington, whose family had been associated with the Society from its earliest days (Luke Rivington's secession to Rome in 1888 notwithstanding) served as one of the treasurers.[74] Henry Montagu Villiers, Vicar of St Paul's, Knightsbridge, served as Chairman, and his parish duly contributed to the fund. The Vicar of St Peter's, London Docks, Benjamin Dulley – a Keble man, who had served at Bombay and Poona in the 1870s – sent £50; while a poor curate sent in 5 shillings with a telling note.

> [I] wish my contribution was a larger one. It require some courage to send it when pounds are needed, but I think that you had better print it in your list of donations to give encouragement to others who, like myself, have the desire to help but are not largely blest with this world's means.[75]

Other smart parishes like Holy Trinity, Sloane Street, and St Saviour's, Pimlico, also made donations; and the Society was encouraged by a testimonial from 70 priests of the diocese – organised by Villiers and the Vicar of St Matthew's, Westminster, William Trevelyan (although Villiers credited Trevelyan for the lion's share of the work[76]) – which concluded that "we consider that the presence among us of such a body of Clergy, independent of parochial ties, would greatly strengthen our hands in our conflict with unbelief, indifference, and sin."[77]

The Society initially used 29 Great Titchfield Street as temporary residence; before moving to 19 Charles Street, off Berkeley Square, late in 1899[78] – its upkeep was particularly supported by donations from Adeline, Duchess of Bedford; her mother, the Countess Somers; Lady Harriet Duncombe, widow of the late Dean of York; and other aristocratic benefactors who had invited the SSJE to work in that part of the city in the hope that they might be able to assist at the Berkeley Chapel on John Street, a chapel-of-ease to St George's, Hanover Square.[79]

By May 1901 enough money had been raised for the SSJE to renovate and move into 13 Dartmouth Street, Westminster, and to add a temporary chapel at the back – the house had been bought as early as 1895. After Creighton's premature death in January 1901 his successor, Arthur Winnington-Ingram – another Keble man, who had previously indicated his support to the Committee[80] – gave permission for the chapel altar almost immediately after

---

73 SSJE/7/1/1/5. Sibell Grosvenor had continued to use the title after her second marriage in 1887 to the Conservative politician George Wyndham.
74 *CE* Nov 1898; SSJE/1/2/242.
75 SSJE/7/1/1/6/7.
76 Henry Montagu Villiers, 19 June 1896, SSJE/7/1/1/5/1.
77 *To the Superior and Fathers of the Society of St John the Evangelist*, SSJE/7/1/1/3.
78 Page, 6 Nov 1899, CUL, MS (Add.7651) WYON/9/3/97.
79 SSJE/1/2/309.
80 SSJE/7/1/1/5.

his translation from Stepney.[81] Hollings was sent to oversee this new sphere of ministry as plans were made for a new and permanent home on the site;[82] while Waggett took on the outward work: Benson thought he had "the ear and the welcome of the world", with "scientific and social characteristics" that made him particularly suited for ministry among the well-to-do.[83] Waggett's self-assurance was one of his great strengths: George Santayana noted that "had we been at a military mess or a duchess's table, he would have been the same";[84] while fifty years later Rose Macaulay recalled "Fr Waggett's social life in London and Cambridge, which did such immense good to people he met".[85]

A statement circulated at Christmas 1901 was clear that the existing building was unsuitable for further extension, and that the committee felt that "nothing but the erection of the permanent buildings will do anything to satisfy the needs of the work".[86] The architect Henry Wilson drew up plans for a mission house, and it was duly circulated to potential donors, who it was hoped would

> do all what lies in their power to assist a Brotherhood which can appeal to such manifest tokens of God's blessing resting upon it as can the Society of St John the Evangelist, and by a generous contribution at the present time provide the Fathers with a House where the regular Rule and life of the Community, the daily Celebration of the Holy Eucharist, and the recitation of the Divine Office, can be duly observed as in the Mother House at Oxford, while at the same time their efforts in deepening the spiritual life among all classes in the Metropolis will be rendered far more effective.[87]

By 1901 the Society had not only acquired 13 Dartmouth Street, but the whole row of nos. 9 to 15. It was understood that the University Mission to South Africa would use nos. 9 and 10 as its London offices, and that the SSJE house would be built on the land occupied by nos. 12 to 15. All seemed to be going well when disaster struck. The two sisters who had owned nos. 11 and 12 had been bought out in 1898, having insisted – significantly – that they would only sell if both houses were taken together. No 11 had therefore helpfully been bought by the Abbey Restoration Trust. Its trustees who had acted in the matter were now deemed to have exceeded their brief by their colleagues, and to have gone beyond the limits of the terms of the trust.

The trust moved to save the situation and sell the property immediately to protect its interests. This compromised the Dartmouth Street scheme considerably: the Society had wanted to retain no. 11 – which now appeared as it if might not be its outright property – in case an extension became necessary; and more pressingly so that the freeholder of no. 11 would not oppose the

---

81 Herbert Cronshaw, 25 April 1901, SSJE/7/1/1/4/3.

82 CE May 1901.

83 Benson, 9 Sept 1906, SSJE 6/1/2/2/210.

84 Santayana, My Host the World, 114.

85 Rose Macaulay (ed. Constance Babington Smith), Letters to a Friend 1950–52, London: Collins (1961), 184.

86 London House for the Society of St John the Evangelist, Christmas 1901, SSJE/7/1/1/2.

87 SSJE, 7/1/1/1.

proposed large building next door. Page felt that "a stranger in no. 11 would almost certainly object", and that the Society could not risk the gamble. The Dartmouth Street plans would have to be abandoned.

The official reason for the abandonment of Dartmouth Street was presented to the Committee – which was chaired by Halifax and had by then had grown to include the Earl of Shaftesbury; the Bishop of Stepney, Cosmo Gordon Lang; and Lord Victor Seymour, Vicar of St Stephen's, Gloucester Road, and brother of the Marquess of Hertford – was not terribly convincing; but was at least less embarrassing than the reality.

> Sir Theodore Hope said the Committee had been summoned to consider a proposal to get rid of the Dartmouth Street site owing to its proximity to the Imperial Theatre as the noise late at night made it quite unfitted for the purpose for which the House was intended.

The Committee did its duty: it resolved to acquire a different site that had become available in Great College Street, near Westminster Abbey; to find guarantors for the advance of the money; and to have new plans drawn up immediately.[88]

As fundraising would need to start again while the Dartmouth Street business was resolved, seven of the members immediately contributed £4,400 between them. Waggett had been summoned from retreat to attend the meeting,[89] and he set to work.[90] Legal advice taken by Page later showed that the decision was the right one: the Society's lawyer in the matter was of the clear opinion that no matter what had been intended, there was no way in which he could see that 11 Dartmouth Street belonged to anyone other than the Abbey Restoration Trust, whose trustees were therefore in an exclusive position to act in the matter.[91]

The ground at the new site was broken in February 1904; but the cost of the land and the house was expected to be in the region of £15,000 – a significant increase on the sum required for Dartmouth Street – and another fundraising drive was begun, led again by Adeline Bedford and Sibell Grosvenor.[92] Potential donors were urged to recognise that the building of a permanent London house for the SSJE meant that

> in the heart of this London of ours, in this centre of ambition, money-making, strife, sin and sorrow, a healing spring will break forth and perpetually grow. Here too the Holy Eucharist will be daily offered, and burdened souls may at all time seek help.

The new plans had also been circulated.[93] They included two libraries, "so that at all times it may be possible to arrange for the complete silence of retreat for

---

88 SSJE/7/2/1/1.
89 Trenholme, 26 Nov 1946, SSJE/7/1/2.
90 cf Waggett, 7 Dec 1903, SSJE/7/2/4.
91 *Case*, 21 Nov 1906; *Opinion*, 5 Jan 1907; SSJE/7/1/3.
92 SSJE/7/2/4/1; CE Dec 1904.
93 SSJE/7/2/4/6.

any one or more priests or laymen without long notice"; but the chapel would have to form part of the second phase of building.[94]

The Bishop of Stepney laid the foundation stone of the new house on 22 June 1904 – St Alban's Day – and the usual protagonists were present. Benson preached at High Mass at St Matthew's, Westminster; after which the company processed to the corner of Great College Street and Tufton Street, where Halifax asked Lang to lay the stone. A large number of priests of the diocese were in attendance; the Abbey clergy were led by the Dean and the Archdeacon of Westminster; and the Community of the Resurrection and Pusey House were also represented. Chief among the laymen were Sir Theodore Hope, Francis Rivington, and Athelstan Riley; while Sir Benjamin Stone MP brought his camera along and "added a picture of the event to his famous collection of photographs".[95] The laywomen were headed by the Dowager Duchesses of Bedford and Westminster, and the Countess Grosvenor. It was a Society gathering, in every sense.

Halifax echoed much of what he had said at the laying of the foundation-stone of the newly-completed tower at Cowley two years earlier; but after paying his compliments to Benson, he singled out Waggett for particular thanks: "to whom this particular work, we may say, owes its existence". In reply Lang spoke of "the debt of gratitude which we owe to the Society of St John the Evangelist, in the name of the whole English Church, not only in England, but abroad."

> We remember how in days of much worldliness and days of much confusion of thought and practice, they have quietly, steadily, and without obtrusion held to the great task which they have laid before themselves and given themselves entirely over in a manner which is of the deepest moment as an example to all the priesthood, to the great single task of saving and perfecting the souls of men and strengthening the faith of the Church of our Blessed Lord and Master.

Lang later became the first Anglo-Catholic to be preferred to the archbishopric of Canterbury, and he felt that the SSJE had "in a singular degree, exhibited all that was felt to be truest and best in the recovery by our English Church of its ancient heritage". To be able to perform what had been asked of him was, he declared, "a very great privilege".[96]

---

94 *CE* June 1904.

95 See Stephen Roberts, *Sir Benjamin Stone 1838–1914: photographer, traveller and politician,* Charleston, SC: Create Space (2014).

96 *The Guardian,* 22 June 1904.

9

FRUIT FORMED AND FORMING

We have planted two young cocoa-nut palms in our Compound, and we trust that Cowley Fathers, yet unborn, will eat the fruit which we shall never live to see.

—Edward Fenton Elwin SSJE[1]

When Queen Victoria died in 1901 the *Cowley Evangelist* lamented that "her last years have been disturbed by the wickedness and treachery which have made South Africa the seat of a miserable war" – Frederick Puller complained from Cape Town that the quiet service which he and George Congreve had arranged to usher in the new century at St Philip's was disturbed at midnight by the hooters of the numerous ships moored in Table Bay[2] – but rejoiced that "she had cause to be thankful for having such a mighty Empire entrusted to her care".[3]

That Empire continued to flourish as the new century progressed. Edward VII and Queen Alexandra were crowned in 1902, while in India preparations were being made for the Imperial Durbar at Delhi: the Society of St John the Evangelist anticipated it as "the mighty gathering of India's multitudes upon the historic scene of an Empire that has passed away; the exhibition no longer of the brute power of Islam, but the assembly of subject sovereigns with their attendant hosts coming in loyalty and love to acknowledge the beneficent supremacy whereby they are welded into one."

The jingoism continued: in Egypt the first Aswan Dam was moving towards completion, so "as the Nile once told of the honours which our great Admiral obtained in war, so its waters will henceforth flow with a mighty stream of wealth, bound by the skill of the British engineer, while they carry over Egypt the wealthy soil of the distant hills no longer to be wasted in unmanageable inundation". Further south, railways were beginning to criss-cross British Africa for the easier transport of goods and people; and the same was true as far away as Western Canada, for the better distribution of the harvest. Within such a system of diverse flourishing, the SSJE continued to work within its understanding of a God-given increase.

For all of this we cannot be too thankful, but we must remember that our position is not so much a matter of gratulation as of responsibility. God has not given

---

1 Elwin, 21 Aug 1898.
2 Puller, 2 Jan 1900.
3 *CE* Jan 1901.

us this mighty dominion for our own aggrandisement but for His own glory. We have to give Him an account.[4]

Part of that account was the dissemination of sound Catholic principles. The *Cowley Evangelist* was now widely distributed in the Anglican networks across the Empire, and the Society was in an ongoing and almost unique position to be able to teach and affirm – and to chastise. Its mission field was well-established and widely-flung, and despite secessions and uncertainty in the wider Anglo-Catholic movement the SSJE continued to plough an international furrow from its growing site at Oxford.

A new orphanage was being raised at Poona; and the Society was on the cusp of founding a mission at Yerendawana, to the south-west. In Bombay, the Church of the Holy Cross was built at Umarkhadi; while at the heart of Mazagon Gertrude Bradley – "not satisfied with the cares of her hospital and practice, and the work of the Night High School" – had opened St Andrew's Little School for [Hindu] Girls. It became so popular that only a few years later it had to move into much larger accommodation in the mission compound: "easily accessible to a densely crowded group of houses from which children can be drawn, and yet near enough to its old quarters for the present children to continue their attendance".[5]

At Prize Day at St Peter's School in December 1900 the prizes were presented by Lady Northcote, the wife of the Governor (Lady Hely-Hutchinson performed similar functions for the Society at Cape Town[6]), and the Archdeacon of Bombay – William Scott, another Keble man – noted approvingly Albert Tovey's work as headmaster.

> [T]here is in the school a most excellent tone. And, after all, that is why we find good people like the Cowley Fathers giving so much of their time and attention to school work – that they may seek to establish among their pupils that mysterious undefinable thing which we call a good tone. Without it you may instruct, but you cannot truly educate. You may fill your pupils full of the ability to pass examinations, or help them acquire very interesting accomplishments, but you cannot lay the foundation of good citizenship either of the kingdom of the world or of the kingdom of Heaven, if you have not that most important educational factor, a good tone in the school.[7]

In 1903 the Society noted with approval the establishment of the College of the Resurrection at Mirfield, to train men for the priesthood along Catholic lines within an Anglican monastic setting, and embarked on "a series of Instructions on some of the great fundamental truths of our holy religion". Starting with *I Believe in One God*, the course took in *The Holy Trinity; Creation; The Powers of Darkness; The Fall; The Incarnation; The Work of Christ on Earth, its Victory, and its continuation in Heaven;* and *The Sending of the Holy Ghost*.[8]

---

4 *CE* Jan 1903.
5 *CE* Aug 1903.
6 cf Congreve, 22 July 1902.
7 *CE* March 1901.
8 *CE* Sept 1903–June 1904.

It is thought that some teachers at home and in the mission field, as well as others among our readers, who have not access to a theological library, will be glad to have clear teaching on some of the great truths which constitute the foundation of the message which our Church is commissioned to proclaim.[9]

While the *Cowley Evangelist* was thundering for theological truth – "our object is purely practical, [and] we shall not scruple to use other people's words, when they express what we want to say" – Page went on a tour of inspection. In October 1902, he left Oxford to visit the missions in India and South Africa;[10] to see for himself the work that he had overseen from Cowley as Superior General over the previous thirteen years.

After a thorough inspection of the Panch Howds compound he wrote to Edward Elwin from Yerendawana to say that he thought it all "truly delightful", that sitting on the veranda of the Mission House he could just see the campanile of the church of the Holy Name above the trees in the distance, and that he intended to stay in India for longer than he had originally intended.[11] Bombay was harder work: he found himself drawn into the effort to buy a crowded and unsanitary *chawl* – a tenement building – next to the compound at Umarkhadi, evict the heathen residents, and erect a "native hostel" much in the manner of St Columba's Home on the site. He wanted to see the work "on a good footing" before he sailed for Africa, relied on "the readers of the C. E., who are so many and generous", and felt that "hitherto our Christianity has not been properly aggressive."[12]

The property was purchased before he had even left Bombay: it was a swift and effective takeover. The building was to be rented to the Bombay Municipality until the next year, to give the city time to rehouse the 600 or so Gujarati-speaking residents. As such it was thoroughly inspected by Page, as "we feel duty bound to do what we can for our new colony". A school was immediately established for the children; and a door was knocked through the wall of the compound so that the residents could have access to the church of the Holy Cross. They duly began coming to catechism and to Evensong. Next, a meeting was organised at which they were spoken to in Gujarati by an Indian Christian; and addresses by the Superior General and Henry Lord were interpreted. "Such is the beginning of the work with these people," wrote Page, before he boarded the steamer after five months in India. "Pray that it may be fruitful."[13] Shortly afterwards Hugh Nicholson wrote to say that the first conversions were taking place.[14]

Page sailed to East Africa in the company of "thirty-four fine specimens of camels", which joined the ship at Karachi and were destined to be put to work in Rhodesia. He went ashore at Mombasa to see the Bishop, his old friend William Peel; and Zanzibar, where he visited the cathedral and toured the numerous UMCA missions. On 6 May – St John before the Latin Gate – the ship

9 *CE* Sept 1903.
10 *CE* Oct 1902.
11 Page, 25 Nov 1902.
12 Page, 11 April 1903.
13 Page, 13 April 1903.
14 Nicholson, 2 May 1903.

arrived at Beira, in Mozambique, and the next morning he and the camels were put ashore. He set out for Pretoria a few days later, arriving at the cathedral to discover Bishop William Carter about to celebrate the opening mass of his diocesan synod.

Such was the reputation of the Cowley Fathers in South Africa – coupled with Carter's personal link to the SSJE through his uncle, Thomas Thellusson Carter – that Page was immediately invited to attend the synod. He was deeply impressed; and particularly so by "the evident enthusiasm of the lay representatives for the Church, and their able and generous action on questions of finance".[15] After visiting the Community of the Resurrection at Johannesburg, on Ascension Day he set out to stay with the Society of the Sacred Mission at Modderpoort; and by Pentecost he had reached the Mission House at Cape Town. His visit culminated in the Whitsunday baptisms at St Philip's, with the candidates going down into the full, deep font and "rising from their immersion beneath those waters with His Resurrection life".[16] A week later he boarded the *Walmer Castle*, and headed back to Cowley for the Society's annual fortnight's retreat.

Immediately on his return he issued an *ad populum* to the Society's friends and supporters, thanking them for their prayers during his journey.

> My journeyings have been a time of great spiritual refreshment and wonderful experiences of the progress of the Kingdom of God amid the opposition it encounters from the malice of Satan in heathen lands; and of the workings of the grace of Christ in individual souls who have surrendered themselves in obedience to His most gracious call, and have come out of the heathen darkness into Light, and are living in the blessed experience of the power of the love of Christ.

By the end of January 1904 Page was on his way to America.[17] He wrote excitedly that the *St Paul* was equipped with the latest communications technology – "Marconi's wireless telegraphy apparatus" – and marvelled at its use.

> Two days before our ship arrived in New York we played a game of chess with another ocean steamer bound for the same port. The game lasted about three hours, the vessels being at a distance varying from twenty to sixty miles apart, and it was finished after the vessels were out of sight of each other. By the same telegraphy Reuter's latest telegrams about the [Russo-Japanese] war were received five hours before we reached Plymouth; they were then printed on board and circulated amongst the passengers.

The world seemed to be getting smaller; and Page's itinerary was packed. The ship docked at 10 a.m. on the morning of Sunday 17 January, and within the hour the Superior General was at High Mass at St Mark's, Jersey City, where he was due to preach. The next day he met Edward Osborne, who was passing through New York on his way to Baltimore, and in the evening boarded the Fall River Line steamer for Boston. In the morning, Charles Field met

---

15 Page, 18 May 1903.
16 *CE* Aug 1903.
17 *CE* Feb 1904.

him and took him directly to St Augustine's Farm – "the Yerendawana of Boston", as he called it – where he spent the day before heading to the house on Bowdoin Street. Over the next couple of weeks, he met numerous friends and associates of the Society, chief among them Arthur Hall; visited St Clement's, Philadelphia; and called on a number of religious communities in the vicinity – including the American daughter houses of the All Saints Sisters of the Poor.[18]

In comparison to his trip to India and Africa, Page's visit to the United States was whistle-stop; but the American work was better-established and its needs more straightforwardly provided for. Its culmination meant that by the middle of 1904 the Superior General had visited and seen for himself almost every aspect of the SSJE's life on four continents. There was, however, one more star to be added to the Society's firmament.

NEW WORK IN SOUTH AFRICA

In October 1897, Philip Waggett had made the long journey from Cape Town to Umtata, in the Eastern Cape, to lead a retreat. The Bishop of St John's, Bransby Key – whose cathedral city Umtata was, if it could be called a city at all – asked him to stay a little longer and attend his diocesan synod as an observer. Among the clergy who attended the synod was Godfrey Callaway, to whom Waggett was naturally drawn. Over thirty years later Carter, by then Archbishop of Cape Town, wrote that "there are perhaps few Europeans who know more about the mind and thought of the Native people in South Africa than Father Callaway"; but in 1897 he was still relatively inexperienced. In 1891 he had gone to work at St Cuthbert's, Tsolo, a mission station nestling in the foothills a few miles away from Umtata. When Alan Gibson left in 1892 – he soon became Bishop Coadjutor of Cape Town, forging another tangible link between Tsolo and the SSJE in Africa – Callaway succeeded him as priest-in-charge of the mission.[19]

Both Callaway and his assistant Gerald Ley were Associates of the Society, and Sydney Wallis was already known to Puller.[20] After fire had swept through the mission in August 1897 Congreve had appealed for donations to support the rebuilding work;[21] and when Alfred Kettle visited in 1899 he noted with pleasure that Callaway had sung mass "vested in the old red chasuble, familiar in days gone by in the Iron Church at Cowley".[22] But, unlike Cape Town – where infrastructure and amenities, such as they were, at least existed – the area around Tsolo was completely wild. Waggett thought Umtata remote; but called it a "sophisticated metropolis" compared to St Cuthbert's.[23]

18 CE March 1904.
19 Godfrey Callaway SSJE, *Building for God in Africa*, London: SPCK (1936), 91.
20 Puller, 23 April 1901.
21 CE Oct 1897.
22 CE May 1899.
23 Waggett, 2 Nov 1879.

Arthur Pridham first went to St Cuthbert's to learn "more of the native ways and mind" than Henry Bull thought possible in Cape Town,[24] before being seconded to Mohales Hook in Basutoland, 250 miles to the north-east.[25] He wrote home with his first impressions of the mission at Tsolo in late 1902.

> The Mission is in the centre of innumerable kraals, all built either on the top or on the slope of a hill: this with an eye to their primitive drainage arrangements. The kraals round us consist for the most part of from five to eight huts, according to the number of the family. [Tsolo] is quite a small place, about nine miles from S. Cuthbert's, made up of an hotel and traders' stores.[26]

Furthermore, the weather could be terrifying. "The rivers were not bridged," recalled Edward Sedding,

> [...] and the summer rains kept them in flood, sometimes for days or even weeks together, and travelling was rendered exceedingly difficult, not to say danger-ous. It was not an unfamiliar sight to see a number of waggons outspanned by a drift on the main road, waiting for the river to go down and make a crossing possible. The missionary with his itinerary made out must cross. If there was no steel box suspended on a steel wire (which was usually available on the main road drifts, with the Africans on the spot to pull the box across), then he must strip and swim.[27]

Callaway's aptitude for hardship, coupled with his ability to survive on meagre rations, reflected to a great extent the privations that Benson had embraced in the SSJE's earliest days. Like Benson, he too saw the benefits that might be gained from the spiritual discipline of a religious community; and with advice taken from various members of the Society of which he was an associate – and particularly from Congreve – he founded the Society of St Cuthbert in 1900, "fully [aware of] the risks of small communities and [...] much alive to our own inexperience".[28] When Puller visited St Cuthbert's in early 1902 he found the community there "most kind and hospitable".

> One could see that they were living truly in the spirit of the religious life, and were at the same time carrying on a most hopeful missionary work among the Pondomisis and other tribes in the neighbourhood. The magnitude of their operations is shown by the fact that there are 2,000 native communicants belonging to the Mission; and large numbers are continually being admitted into the classes for Catechumens. All this good work is of course the outcome of long years of patient labour.[29]

---

24 Bull, 9 July 1902.
25 Pridham, 11 Aug; 19 Aug; 2 Sept; 28 Sept 1903.
26 Pridham, 8 Aug 1902.
27 E. D. Sedding SSJE (ed), *Godfrey Callaway: Missionary in Kaffraria 1892–1942*, London: SPCK (1945), 11–12.
28 Callaway, *Building for God*, 90.
29 Puller, 10 Jan 1902.

Later that year Callaway laid out his vision for the work at Tsolo in the *Cowley Evangelist*, in his series *Work among the Native Races of South Africa*. He was sharply aware of the importance of not separating his converts "from past obligations and old customs where there is nothing contrary to the mind of Christ". Just as Elwin had seen the teaching opportunities presented by the Diwali customs at Poona a few years earlier, Callaway clung to the dictum laid out by the Diocese of St John's: "Missionaries should be careful not to interfere needlessly with harmless customs, or to act towards them as though they partook of the nature of sin."[30]

But his community did not grow; and Callaway's health suffered. There was so much work in the surrounding area that when asked where his home was he would reply, "in the saddle".[31] By 1904 it was obvious that the Society of St Cuthbert – which by then only numbered Callaway himself, Ley, and Wallis – could no longer run the mission alone, and, after taking soundings from the Superior General, Key's successor as Bishop of St John's, Joseph Williams, invited the SSJE to step in. Williams had known the Society since his time at New College in the 1870s: "It will give me personally the very greatest pleasure", he wrote to Page, "to find myself once more in relation to the Society".[32]

Almost simultaneously, the new Bishop of Rangoon, Arthur Knight, approached Nicholson with a message for Page to see "if the Cowley Fathers can help us in the glorious, but very difficult, work of evangelizing Burma".[33] "He has a most depressing task", Nicholson wrote,

> with about nine priests, of which only two know the language well; he was anxious to know whether there was any prospect of the Society being able to take up permanent Mission work in Rangoon; he said that he should most warmly welcome the advent of the Society and do what he could for its support; he felt convinced that the work requiring to be done could not be accomplished without a brotherhood. I did not hold out any hopes, but said that I would of course write.[34]

The SSJE's reputation for "native work" preceded it – Knight's immediate predecessor, John Strachan, had made a similar approach[35] – and it is easy to see why a new bishop in Anglican Indo-China would be keen for its help. Although the Society "would gladly respond to the call if our numbers allowed of it", St Cuthbert's was already well-connected with the SSJE, and so Knight had to be disappointed.[36] The Chapter minutes record that it was regarded as "a venture of an alliance between two communities".[37]

The annexation of Tsolo was a significant part of a realignment of the SSJE's work in South Africa. Williams' request came soon after it had been decided

---

30 Callaway, *Work Among the Native Races of South Africa*, CE Oct 1902 ff.
31 Callaway, *Building for God*, 18.
32 Williams, 26 Jan 1904.
33 *CE* March 1904.
34 Nicholson, 25 Jan 1904.
35 Strachan to Page, 23 Oct 1896, SSJE/6/3/2/4.
36 *CE* March 1904.
37 SSJE/2/3/3ff.

that in Cape Town the parish work of St Philip's would be handed over to the diocese. This was to free the Society to work entirely among the black African community, which had increased tenfold in the two decades since the work began. Although the SSJE had been reluctant to give up the parish until it was provided with a church and schools, that point had been reached; and it was decided now "to give up the parochial work, so as to set us free to carry out with greater efficiency the growing missionary work among the Kaffirs".

> The two events are, so far as we are concerned, wholly independent the one of the other. But as the offer of S. Cuthbert's followed very quickly after our resignation of S. Philip's became a settled thing, we cannot help seeing in what has occurred an indication of God's providential ordering.

The new development also cemented the SSJE's resolution from 1904 that its work in South Africa should be concerned with mission-centres rather than parishes, and focussed among black Africans.

> There is every reason to think that our new Kaffir work at S. Cuthbert's will in many ways strengthen our work among the Kaffirs in Capetown and its neighbourhood. We had always felt that a mission among the Kaffirs in Kaffir-land [the Transkei] would, if it were possible to undertake such an addition to our responsibilities, be a great help to our Capetown Kaffir mission [...] Now God has put it into the hearts of the members of the Society of S. Cuthbert to offer not only their mission but also themselves to the S.S.J.E.[38]

The Archbishop had appointed Brett Guyer, who was serving at St Saviour's, Claremont, to replace Bull as priest-in-charge: this was "a great consolation", as before going to South Africa Guyer had been a curate at Cowley St John. And so, thought Bull, "twenty years have not ended, but come to their full blossom – as full as it has been permitted us to prosper it. And there is fruit formed and forming."[39] At the same time the Society took responsibility for supporting Lydia Williams in her old age – in recognition of her importance to the earliest days of its work in South Africa – and paid the rent "and a little over" on her evocative little cottage, in which she died a few years later.[40]

The Society could not send priests on the missions fast enough: Henry Chard was professed in August 1904, and already learning Xhosa.[41] By October he was on his way to Cape Town,[42] where, even without the parish, the SSJE's flock numbered about 7000 – divided between distinct spheres of work at Ndabeni, the Docks, Newlands, Simonstown, Somerset West, the Convict Stations, and "Elsewhere".

Seventy-five of those souls were resident at St Columba's Home. By 1904 the men paid two shillings a week for their bed, and the rules were relatively loose. The daily services were not compulsory (although about a third were

---

38 *CE* April 1904.
39 Bull, 7 Sept 1904.
40 Bull, 20 June 1910.
41 Bull, 7 Sept 1904.
42 *CE* Oct 1904.

communicants, and Evensong was usually well attended) and the "Sunday Afternoon Service" was only of obligation to those who happened to be in the house at the time. The thrice-weekly Night School was compulsory for all, however; and drink was forbidden. Bull was perfectly willing to levy fines, or even to administer a thrashing from time to time;[43] but the inevitable expulsion of incorrigible offenders always distressed him,[44] as he treasured "the happiness of being their father".[45] Nevertheless, as the modest rent was much lower than elsewhere in the city their places were filled soon enough.[46] The Home was always full, except when there was a slump in the market, when Bull regretted that "we cannot keep people who are out of work".[47]

Originally Page had intended to send Bull to take over at St Cuthbert's after the agreed date of St Philip's transfer in September[48]; but the Bishop asked for Puller, because of his "knowledge and experience of native work".[49] Puller duly returned to South Africa to take over at Tsolo, and Williams soon made him a Canon of his pro-Cathedral.[50] He was, as we have seen, highly regarded in Africa – Callaway described him as "a Missionary under whom all of us will feel privileged to work"[51] – and only a couple of years earlier he had helped lead the Order of Ethiopia out of factional chaos and into the Church of Southern Africa.[52] Then he had won the admiration and gratitude of West Jones and the Governor, Sir Walter Hely-Hutchinson – who was thereafter "quite convinced of the loyalty of the Church Ethiopians"[53] – and plaudits across the Province.[54] When Bull – wearing an identical white habit and black knotted girdle – met members of the Order near Umtata, they insisted on calling him "Fr Buller".

Bull thought that St Cuthbert's was "an ideal Mission",[55] and Puller was already deeply impressed with the work that Callaway had done there.

> It reproduces in the twentieth century the glorious missionary traditions of the great religious foundations of the seventh century in England. One could imagine that one was at Peterborough, or at Croyland, or at Ripon, in their modest beginnings, when they were really doing the work of evangelists for all the country roundabout. It must be an immense comfort to the Bishop to have such a beacon of light in the midst of his diocese.[56]

He sailed with Frederic Noel, then a priest-novice; Lawrence Walcot, a postulant; and Br Maynard. All three mugged up on their Xhosa on the journey, with

---

43 Bull, 10 May 1905.
44 Bull, 1 March 1905.
45 Bull, 10 May 1905.
46 *SSJE Native Mission, Cowley Evangelist*, June 1905.
47 Bull, 4 Oct 1905.
48 Page, 1 March 1904.
49 *CE* April 1904.
50 Puller, 25 Sept 1905.
51 *Report of St Cuthbert's Mission*, 1903.
52 See Hinchliffe, *Anglican Church in South Africa*, 220f.
53 West Jones, 7 Feb 1902; Puller, 12 Feb 1902.
54 cf *Vote of Thanks*, Missionary Conference of the Diocese of Grahamstown, 2 July 1902, in *CE* Sept 1902.
55 Bull, 23 April 1903.
56 Puller, 10 Jan 1902.

the help of Callaway's own "Kaffir-English Dictionary".[57] Also on the *Gaika* was "the little derrick crane [...] which hoisted up the stones in our Church Tower";[58] as Maynard was going to oversee the completion of the new mission church, the building of which had been under way for a number of years and was still not finished. Bull described the original building, in which worship was still taking place, as

> a thatched building, enlarged with iron-covered aisles of bricks; a strangely insignificant ill-assorted building, with broken windows in the aisles, for glass is not easily procurable. But inside you tread softly on the mud floor, and the pillars are the trunks of trees, and plain school forms for seats.

Bull realised that the old patchwork church would be sorely missed, "with its simplicity, its native character, and its true ring of first faith and love and worship"; but that as the work was "full of devotion", the same would be true of the new church in the fullness of time.[59]

When Puller and the other members of his party arrived at Tsolo late on the afternoon of 19 July 1904, they were driven straight to the old church, "which was packed with people".

> Fr Gerald [Ley] was at the door with a surplice, which he put on me as we entered, and we went straight up to the quasi-chancel. Fr Gerald said a service of welcome in Kaffir. Then we sang in the same language "*The King of love my Shepherd is.*" Then I said a few words to the people, and after the chanting of the *Te Deum* I pronounced the Blessing. Then we left the church and I went to the house to rest and get ready for a meal.[60]

Puller was less romantic than Bull: he thought the old church was little more than a "mud round hut". [61] Maynard wrote immediately to say that he was optimistic for the new building. "I have made friends with the carpenter; we shall work quite happily together [...] The stone-cutters do their work exceedingly well."[62] The incomplete shell was admired and approved of by Lord and Lady Halifax on their South African tour in 1905;[63] and the roof was made in Oxford to Maynard's specifications, carefully numbered, and sent out to be assembled on site – the "tiles" were made of steel, painted red, to guard against hailstones.[64] Photographs of Maynard at this time show him in habit and pith helmet, rule in hand, clearly in his element among the local workmen and enjoying the project. From Poona Elwin wrote that it was a "great joy" that Maynard had been able "to crown his building operations by building a Church in the Mission field".[65]

---

57 Puller, 9 June 1904.
58 *CE* May 1906.
59 Bull, 4 May 1903.
60 Puller, 21 July 1904.
61 Puller, 14 Dec 1905.
62 Maynard, 20 July 1904.
63 Maynard, 16 Nov 1905.
64 Witwatersrand Historical Papers, AB799/Ea4; Taylor, 10 June 1920.
65 Elwin, 9 May 1904.

The arrival of the Cowley Fathers brought to Tsolo not only spiritual and architectural benefits; but also, through its donors, a much-needed financial boon and an opening of networks.[66] Puller was soon advertising in the *Cowley Evangelist* for young priests to work on the mission – partly for its building-up for its own sake; partly to prevent the less well-served areas of the district from lapsing into heathenism; and partly to keep out the Presbyterians and Moravians – and for a schoolmaster to take charge of St Cuthbert's School.[67]

The SSJE also brought its connection with the Community of St Mary the Virgin, which sent sisters to help run the mission's ministry to the local women late in 1905,[68] after the retirement of the long-serving and devoted resident mission-worker Alice Blyth.[69] The Superior General had hoped that the Wantage Sisters might be able to accept this new sphere of work,[70] and Wallis – who was completing his novitiate at Cowley with the intention that he would be professed in the SSJE before returning to Tsolo – wrote to the Mother General that her sisters' arrival would "mean a great deal for the work at St Cuthbert's in the future".[71]

When Mother Lucy CSMV placed the invitation before her Council it was "carried unanimously". "It is a real joy to us all," she told Page, "that we are able to respond, and to do so heartily and enthusiastically".[72] By October Puller was in Cape Town, waiting for the first batch of sisters to arrive, so that he could escort them to East London and on to St Cuthbert's;[73] and by November, to his relief, they were established on the mission: "One is able to feel now that Miss Blyth's work among the girls and women will not fall to the ground."[74]

In August 1906, Callaway was invited to be professed in the Society of St John the Evangelist after a "nominal probation" *in situ* at St Cuthbert's.[75] It was an indication of the esteem in which he was held by the Society, and his already considerable experience of the religious life;[76] but Callaway's dispensation from the novitiate came after prolonged wrangling in Chapter over the possibility of such a step. Benson himself eventually proposed that the Society should consider treating his profession as a "translation from the Society of which he has been head" – subject to the approval of the Visitor – to avoid the complications of a suspension of the SSJE's Constitutions.[77]

Francis Paget approved wholeheartedly.[78] In the presence of the Bishop of St John's, Callaway duly made his vows to Puller – who as Provincial Superior deputised for Page in the unusual circumstances – during mass in St John's

---

66 cf *CE* June 1906.
67 Puller, 8 Sept 1904.
68 Puller, 9 Nov 1905.
69 Puller, 25 Feb 1905 (copy), Witwatersrand Historical Papers, AB1653/Eb2.
70 Page, 25 March 1905 (copy), ibid.
71 Wallis, 13 June 1905 (copy), ibid.
72 Mother Lucy CSMV, 13 June 1905.
73 Puller, 25 Sept 1905.
74 Puller, 9 Nov 1905.
75 SSJE/2/3/15.
76 SSJE/2/3/2ff.
77 SSJE/2/3/47.
78 Paget, 10 Aug 1906, SSJE/2/3/51.

Chapel of St Cuthbert's Church on 15 November: "not, strictly speaking, a profession", Puller emphasised, "but an admission of one already professed into our Society". Wallis was already serving his novitiate at Cowley, and was professed in January 1907; and both were joined by Ley in 1909.[79] Callaway saw that "in this way alone can our early efforts in the direction of brotherhood life at St Cuthbert's really live [...] We could feel that our little Community had never died."[80] Not long after, while the Society of the Sacred Mission was looking for ways of developing its own colonial mission-work, George Carleton SSM visited St Cuthbert's and called it "nearer the ideal Church mission than any other I saw".[81]

New work in India

Back at Poona, Elwin had been laying it on with a trowel in the pages of the *Cowley Evangelist*. "If April [1898] finds us without money", he wrote, "I suppose you will not be surprised to hear that the SSJE in India has become a mendicant order, and that we are begging our way with all the little St Pancras' boys in our train."[82] His pleading poverty was to some extent an exaggeration: the fact that Poona had the added support of the Wantage networks meant that it invariably did better than Bombay when it came to alms.

When two brothers turned up towards the end of 1899, one minus a leg at the hip, he was delighted. "I had long been wishing for some cripples to add to our collection," he enthused. "But they are so valuable in India for begging purposes that they are hard to get. And to get a boy with one leg entirely gone is an extraordinary stroke of luck. I know that patrons [the various boys' sponsors in England, sourced through *The Star in the East*] will rush for him so that I think we shall have to let him go to the highest bidder [...] We are all very fond of having such a genuine cripple in our collection."[83]

The monopod Giles – named, obviously, for the patron saint of cripples – soon became something of a mission mascot, and Elwin was swift to put him to use. "He walks at a great pace with his crutches," he noted. "He undertook the work of distributing Christmas cards, and excited great interest as he hopped about the street [...] Many people smilingly received a card from him who would not have taken one under other circumstances [...] Many people, especially kindly mothers, make sympathetic remarks as he passes [...] But he is an extremely happy little chap, and the loss of his leg was really the greatest benediction possible." Giles's thoughts on the matter remained unsolicited.

Elwin also noted the tendency of donors to muddy the waters by giving generously for specific projects or items. The *Cowley Evangelist*'s monthly list of subscribers, after all, frequently included offerings of individual items: sanctuary lamps for Bombay; altar frontals for Cape Town; an organ for Poona.

---

79 SSJE/1/4, 121ff; Puller, 15 Nov 1906.
80 Callaway to his father, 28 Aug 1906, in Sedding, *Callaway*, 179–80.
81 *Society of the Sacred Mission Quarterly*, Michaelmas 1915.
82 Elwin, 3 Mar 1898.
83 Elwin, 7 & 14 Nov 1899.

Poverty and wealth with us runs curiously side by side and I do not wonder that people are sometimes puzzled as to whether we are rich or poor. At the time when we say we are at our last rupee we spend Rs 500 on a new American Organ for the Church and people might naturally say – How inconsistent! But you see the good lady sends out £20 for this object, and we have in hand a little over Rs 200 invested towards a new organ – so get a really good American Organ. The Instrument is very sweet in tone and in all respects a sound and useful instrument. It is extraordinary what a difference it makes in the singing.[84]

In this lies the key to much of the SSJE's approach to its funds: money well-spent in the service of God was an investment well-made. When the Society came to build a Mission House at Yerendawana at the turn of the century, Elwin was adamant that it would be "much more satisfactory to build a pukka building" than to try to raise one on the cheap.[85] By the middle of 1901 the money had been raised, and there was a good deal of to-ing and fro-ing from Poona to get the house ready.[86] It was dedicated with full ceremonial on 2 June.

We came in Procession from our improvised vestries to the Bungalow, with cross, lights, incense, holy water, choir and clergy, and then visited the various parts of the little Mission House, saying suitable Prayers. We then sang solemn Evensong before the [temporary] Altar in the verandah.

But Elwin was not complacent, and he and Nicholson had already both said mass in the Chapel. "It is impossible ever to imagine the extent of the power of the Holy Sacrifice", he reflected, "pleaded in the midst of a heathen village, and the consternation which must be excited thereby amongst the evil spirits. We must expect that they will try their uttermost to pay us back in some way."[87] By the end of June 1901 he was permanently resident at Yerendawana with some of the orphans; and as the Bombay administration was by then in residence at Poona, Lady Northcote – who was "always very kind" – had called to look over the new building.[88] The Wantage Sisters were also making plans to settle there,[89] and a new church was being contemplated.[90] Elwin was clear that "we must try and devise something which will look Indian [...] Something really beautiful would make a great impression".[91]

While hospitalised with a serious attack of asthma during the monsoon season in 1901, Elwin was able to use some of his time being cared for by the Wantage Sisters at the Sassoon Hospital to flesh out his plans for the church at Yerendawana.

We must have something very Eastern, in which Indians will feel at home. It must also dominate over the Hindu temple close by, which has a hideous but

---

84 Elwin, 30 Oct 1898.
85 Elwin, 23 Sept 1900.
86 Elwin, 19 April 1901.
87 Elwin, 6 June 1901.
88 Elwin, 18 June 1901.
89 Moore, 23 Sept 1901.
90 Elwin, 26 Jan 1899.
91 Elwin, 13 Oct 1900.

rather lofty cone on its top. When you see the sketch you will think at the first glance that we want to build a second S. Paul's. But you will get at the scale by looking at our little bungalow alongside it, which is only sixty feet long. We should build of native brick, plastered inside and out with white plaster. And you know how well such buildings look and how durable they are in India. We have not put in any ornamentation, trusting to shape and proportion for its beauty.[92]

The sketch he mentioned had been drawn up by Edmund Kershaw, who was also serving on the Poona mission. Kershaw was a Cambridge man in his mid-forties, "of much vivacity and spiritual power",[93] who had been a barrister in Canada before being ordained in the United States and entering the Society. He was a talented draughtsman, and had been responsible for much of the design of Holy Cross, Umarkhadi, and some of the features at Holy Name, Poona.[94] Elwin casually noted that his "admirable" plan for the new church at Yerendawana would be delayed by illness – he did not at that stage know that Kershaw was already desperately ill with malaria.

Elwin was soon temporarily recalled to England in the hope that a drier European summer would alleviate his symptoms. After showing no signs of improvement, Kershaw was invalided home on the *Caledonia*. He sank steadily on the journey, and died not long after the vessel had left Aden. Elwin alighted at Plymouth on All Saints' Day 1901 – "very worn and weak [but] entirely free from Asthma"[95] – and on the same day Kershaw's mortal remains were interred in the Red Sea, with the captain reading the service and the crew mustered around.[96]

It was left to Sydney Moore, still at Poona with Charles Gardner, to usher in a new era in February 1902. "Today we made a new beginning", he wrote to Page, "using bicycles for the village work". He was thrilled with their efficiency: he and his catechist sent a *tonga* ahead of them and were able to overtake it after nine miles; and "to our surprise [we] came back eleven miles in three-quarters of an hour".[97]

Bicycles or not, demand in India continued to outstrip supply as the first years of the new century wore on. The Missionary Association launched a membership drive: "a great increase in the number of Members and Associates and zealous Secretaries is highly desirable." They would cover the whole country, and encourage new members and donors. Suggested rules for parochial associations were provided: they were to exist to pray for the prospering of missionary work in general and the Society's missions in particular; and to subscribe a regular sum of money to for their practical support. "India has a claim upon us such as no other country possesses," enthused the *Cowley Evangelist*. "Every Englishman should be doing something for Mission work in India."[98]

---

92 Elwin, 13 Aug 1901.
93 *CE* Jan 1901.
94 cf *Bishop Macarthur's Charge*, CE Dec 1903.
95 *CE* Dec 1901.
96 Biscoe, 10 Nov 1901.
97 Moore, 4 Feb 1901.
98 *CE* May 1902.

As monsoon approached in 1902, it was Moore's earnest wish that one of those Englishmen might come forward and foot the bill for repairs to the Mission House roof, which was on the point of collapse. "There was no help for it," he wrote in June, "I had to give the order for repairs to-day, and can only hope that some one may be led to help pay the bill, or else we shall be reduced [...] to our last rupee."[99] The readers of the *Cowley Evangelist* soon stepped up; but while continuing his recuperation in England Elwin received an anonymous donation of £500 towards the new church at Yerendawana, which put the necessary total "quite within range". He also finished and published his *Stories of Indian Boys* – in which Giles naturally played a leading role – to raise money for the Poona mission and increase interest in the work in general. Callaway published a similar series from Tsolo, called *Some of My Kafir Friends*, in the *Cowley Evangelist* in 1905 – it later appeared in book form as *Sketches of Kafir Life*.[100]

Soon after *Stories of Indian Boys* appeared, however, Panch Howds was briefly but fiercely hit once more by plague; and Moore recorded pitifully that "there is a sad appendix to some of Father Elwin's chapters." Some of the boys featured had already succumbed;[101] while at Yerendawana the Society had lost "our butler and his two boys, our cook (a Goanese), and his pupil Benedict, who was doing well".[102]

Even so, it was not all doom and gloom. In the light of Elwin's temporary absence and Kershaw's death, the Society had sent Richard Traill and Alfred Langmore to supplement the priestly work at Poona, along with Br Arthur to run St Joseph's; while at Cape Town Nalbro' Robinson's magic-lantern services for "our coloured children" had encouraged them to raise £12 over the year for the support of two orphans at Panch Howds. Bull thought that he had "drawn out the hearts of these little brownies well".[103]

In the spring of 1903 Elwin wrote from San Remo – the chaplaincy there was a regular recuperation spot for Cowley Fathers in need of a warm but temperate climate – to say that he was very much recovered and looking forward to returning to Poona; and that he was keeping up his Marathi by using it to communicate with the local children. He conceded that it left both parties "with rather vague ideas as to each other's sentiments".[104] The same could hardly be said of the children at Yerendawana: when Nicholson visited shortly after his return he noted that "Father Elwin has quite won the confidence of the Hindu village lads [...] and they come to see him and talk quite freely about all sorts of subjects."[105] Gerald Maxwell later commented on "how perfectly at home he is with the people, and how friendly they are".[106]

---

99 Moore, 20 June 1902.
100 Godfrey Callaway, *Sketches of Kafir Life*, Oxford: Mowbray (1905).
101 Moore, 4 March 1903.
102 Moore, 12 Feb 1903.
103 Bull, 21 Jan 1903.
104 Elwin, 19 March 1903.
105 Nicholson, 30 Oct 1903.
106 Maxwell, 17 Nov 1905.

By the end of 1903 the designs for St Crispin's Church – the first boy brought to the font at Yerendawana had taken "Crispin" as his baptismal name[107] – had been taken on and "skilfully devised" by the firm of Bucknall & Comper.[108] Having missed out on the commission for the new Mission House, Comper was at the time building a new vicarage for Ss Mary & John, Cowley;[109] and was in regular contact with the Society at home and abroad. "Mr & Mrs Comper send affectionate greetings", Benson told Traill in the summer of 1904.[110] Comper designed fittings for the chapel in the proposed house at Dartmouth Street in London;[111] and he had also produced the plans for the All Saints Sisters' magnificent new chapel in Oxford, the foundation stone of which was blessed by Page and laid by Benson on 11 May 1905. For St Crispin's he produced a remarkable modern Indo-Gothic design, about which Anthony Symondson and Stephen Bucknall's important book *Sir Ninian Comper* is disappointingly silent.[112]

Meanwhile, at Bombay Gertrude Bradley had been looking for a place to establish a House of Rest within easy reach of the city, where members of the wider Cowley family at Mazagon and Umarkhadi – "both Europeans and natives" – could go for rest. After a number of fruitless enquiries, she finally settled on the ruins of the old Portuguese fortress at Bassein, thirty miles to the north and on the mouth of the Ulhas River. St Francis Xavier had visited the area in 1548, and made a number of converts: now one of the large bungalows within the walls, with space for "quite a colony", was to serve as a place of respite from the bustle, noise, and heat of the city.[113]

The Society took a long lease on the fort in 1904: "we felt that the place possessed many advantages, amongst them a good water supply, an important point in India, beautiful scenery, productive soil, and ample scope for any possible developments." Rather than renovate one of the ruined churches, they added a small chapel to the bungalow, which was dedicated on 9 April. A whole party came by special train and most of the day – after the ceremonies were completed – was spent exploring the ruins and walking around the tops of the walls. Nicholson was optimistic that the Society would be able to raise a modest income from the renting of the "very fertile" farmable land that came with the property.[114] The Government soon realised the strategic position of Bassein, and bought the Society out;[115] but not before a tiger had taken up residence, prompting Dr Bradley to issue a general invitation through the local Collector "for any sportsmen who care to go over" to bag it.[116]

---

107 Elwin, "Crispin: The First Fruits of Yerendawana", *Stories of Indian Boys*, no.1, Oxford (1903).

108 Elwin, 6 Oct 1903.

109 *CE* Jan 1902.

110 Benson to Traill, 15 July 1904, SSJE/6/1/2/26/2.

111 *CE* Dec 1902.

112 *CE* June 1906; Anthony Symondson and Stephen Bucknall, *Sir Ninian Comper: An Introduction to his life and work*, London: The Ecclesiological Society (2006), 97ff.

113 Nicholson, May 30 1904.

114 *CE* June 1904; Nicholson, 16 April 1904.

115 Maxwell, Feb 15 1906.

116 Biscoe, 26 July 1905.

10

Wreaths of Empire

Our worldwide colonies look up to England with filial sympathy and recognise the fraternal association as superior to the rivalries of jarring interest.

—*Cowley Evangelist*[1]

As early as 1903 Edward Elwin had enthusiastically marked out "a ground plan of most beautifully harmonious proportions" for the church at Yerendawana.[2] While Br Maynard got on with his work at Tsolo, which included providing the mission with running water[3] – the mission worker Ethel Wallace was "tickled to death" to find Alan Young and Francis Rumsey timing the flow of water in the new school lavatories, with one counting the seconds on his watch and the other pulling the chain[4] – Elwin was "tempted to be envious" that Maynard was not working on his project.[5] The costs soon rose considerably; but Elwin insisted that the church would be worth waiting for, and defended the design.

> Mr Comper was not in any way to blame for designing the Church in excess of the proposed cost. He could not tell what would be the cost of labour and materials in India, and perhaps I gave him an exaggerated idea of their cheapness. He was careful to exclude all ornament, and to get its beauty out of its shape and proportions. It could not be modified without spoiling it. I would much sooner wait than build something inferior. My theory that India needs beautiful Churches, if only as object lessons for the people, remains unchanged.[6]

Temporary vestments for the looked-for church were beginning to arrive: in early 1905 Elwin reported that "we have now got all the colours, and though they are a very nondescript lot they quite suffice for present purposes. I daresay when the church is built someone will give us a plain but harmonious set such as Mr Comper will approve."[7] He knew that he had "strong ideas on such

---

1 *CE* Jan 1903.
2 Elwin, 8 Dec 1903.
3 Puller, 1 June 1905.
4 *NS* 2/87. Ethel Wallace died in England in 1992 at the age of 103, having been a member of the Fellowship of St John since 1911, and in which she remained active almost until the very end.
5 Elwin, 9 May 1904.
6 Elwin, 14 Sept 1904.
7 Elwin, 27 Feb 1905.

matters".[8] Books were next on the list, and he wondered if he might claim the next incoming novice's library for the house at Yerendawana. "Two or three hundred books of simple Theology, etc, would be very useful out here [...] Our library at present chiefly consists of Whittaker for 1902 and the *Times of India* Directory for 1900, and I do not know which of the two to select as that standard work which our rule says we are to study when at home."[9]

At the same time, Richard Traill was running a two-week mission encampment from Pirangut, "a very strong Brahmin centre" on the Mula River, ten miles north-west of Poona. After early Mass, breakfast, and Matins a gruelling day's work began.

> [W]e make a start for one of the neighbouring villages. If we are well received, we may spend a good time in preaching and chatting to the people, and, probably, we don't get back till between 1 and 2. Then we have our meal, and take a good rest in the heat of the day. We have tea at 4, and then Evensong, and then we pay an evening visit to another village, accompanied by our magic lantern, which excites great interest and surprise. We probably don't get back till 9 or later, and then we have our supper and are pretty ready for bed.

The welcome was not always warm; but even an inauspicious start could pay dividends: "we were expelled with ignominy from the village two nights ago, when we tried to shew our lantern; on the following morning we were invited by the town clerk to eat *pan-supari* [betel], in order to make amends. It was quite a little triumph."[10]

The more ordinary hardships were not easily dismissed – at the outset Traill declared that "physically this life suits me 'down to the ground'", but he conceded at the end of the fortnight that "happy though the time has been, I shall not be sorry to get within the *pukka* walls again".[11] But a spot of persecution from time to time was not necessarily unwelcome, either: when Bishop Jabez Whitley of Chota Nagpur was attacked while preaching in 1904, Hugh Nicholson thought that it was "quite refreshing to hear of a real live bishop in India being beaten for proclaiming Christian truth";[12] and later Sydney Moore and his catechist were "hustled and pelted in quite an apostolic manner" near Poona.[13]

In November 1905, a group of SSJE evangelists was arrested at one of their usual preaching spots in Poona City. When Traill and Moore arrived at the police station they demanded to see the senior officer in the district; but were told he would not be available until the next morning. They were allowed to take their men home, who seemed "a little sorry not to have the privilege of being locked up for the night, 'for the liberty of the Gospel'". It transpired that the sergeant who had performed the arrest was a Brahmin, and had been incensed to see a converted Brahmin preaching Christianity. Traill declined

---

8 *CE* May 1905.
9 Elwin, 11 May 1905.
10 Traill, 9 Feb 1905.
11 Traill, 14 Feb 1905.
12 Nicholson, 13 Jan 1904.
13 *CE* May 1904.

to lodge a formal complaint against the man, but felt that "the whole thing will be of use [...] It is evident that we are considered dangerous, and it is no longer safe to leave us alone." "I fancy the building of Yerendawana church will intensify the feeling very much," he concluded. "So much the better."[14]

It was with some relief that Elwin wrote on St Stephen's Day 1906 to say that *The Church has commenced. I began to fear that people at home would begin to think I was a fraud, and that the Church [at Yerendawana] was never going to be built."* He was tickled to discover that the contractor was the *patel* of a nearby Hindu stronghold, willing to build a church "for the sake of money". By the new year, the foundations were well under way;[15] and Gerald Maxwell laid the foundation stone on 23 February 1907. He delighted in telling the assembly "of the happy relations there will always be between Yerendawana and S.S.J.E."; and in pointing out that the centre of the carved cross of the foundation stone was "formed by a little stone that once was part of our church at home, and to tell them that a stone from Yerendawana has been built into the tower at Cowley".[16] Not to be outdone, the more devout Hindus at Yerendawana started to restore their temple: "they have painted it all sorts of colours, put on the gilded cone and re-tiled it". Elwin sensed something of an initial "encouraging" spirit of opposition in the village,[17] which soon died away.[18] In April the structure was complete, and being whitewashed;[19] and he thought it "an unexpected pleasure that I have been allowed to watch the building of the Church from the beginning to the end".[20]

At Tsolo, meanwhile, St Cuthbert's Church was dedicated on 9 May 1906 – within the Octave of St John *ante portam Latinam*.[21] Bishop Joseph Williams came from Umtata to carry out the consecration and to preside at the mass that followed; and various other services were also held. Maynard acted as crucifer in the morning, and followed the thurifer into his new building after Williams had knocked for entry. He had also made brightly-coloured pennants with the name of each of the outstations served from Tsolo, to be processed in by the people and then hung in the church for its consecration. They later came into their own as useful place-markers for the annual great St Cuthbert's Day festivities, when the hundreds of children found the pennant bearing the name of their village and duly sat under it until their group was called up to be fed.[22]

The heathen neighbours arrived after mass, "and arrived in their hundreds, in festal array. The men with bead and brass ornaments, and hair done up fantastically with grass plaits [...] the women in gay coloured handkerchiefs wound round their heads [...] their faces smeared with yellow clay".[23] In the course of Xhosa Evensong in the afternoon – it followed Evensong in English

14 Traill, 10 Nov 1905.
15 Elwin, 10 Jan 1906.
16 Maxwell, Feb 22 1906ff.
17 *CE* Aug 1906.
18 Elwin, 18 Sept 1906.
19 Elwin, 26 April 1907.
20 Elwin, 5 July, 1907.
21 Puller, 28 Dec 1905.
22 Ley, 9 Sept 1913.
23 Bull, 11 May 1906.

for a white congregation – eight men were baptised in the new full-immersion font, which had been copied from the original in Old St Philip's. The singing at all the services captivated him: "Of course", said Frederick Puller, "it was not the singing of Magdalen chapel nor the singing of St John's, Cowley, but it is the sort of singing which suits our native people, and Mfundisi Xaba had taken the greatest pains to train not only the St Cuthbert's choir, but also the choirs of the out-stations."

The visitors got through 150 cauldrons containing seven oxen, but also "mutton, goat's flesh, mealies, pumpkins, etc", produced by an "army of cooks": Puller estimated that there had been over 2000 people present, who he thought could not fail to have been struck by "the beauty and dignity which befit the worship of Almighty God".[24] Henry Bull thought that they rather enjoyed the feasting, too.

Difficulties had by this time presented themselves over the funding of some of the colonial work. In 1897 Edward Osborne had laid out, in an address to the Sisterhood of St John the Divine at Pietermaritzburg, various charisms belonging to – and works proceeding from – colonial religious life. It witnessed, he argued, to three purposes. First, it was a witness to a living faith; secondly it was a witness against the worldliness of life in the colonies, where "all go to get rich, and, if possible, quickly", and "the spirit of the world rules"; and thirdly it was a witness against covetousness, when it was "easy to acquire the habit of unwillingness to give up the shining gold or silver".[25]

To that end, some of the work was run on a shoestring; but in India the Society had access to some diocesan money, while at Poona and Yerendawana the missions – and particularly the orphanage work – had the support of a network of patrons for the boys, and the particular support, through the Wantage connection, of the readership of *The Star in the East*. It was a source of income of which Elwin rarely missed an opportunity to exploit; and while Nicholson was adamant that he was glad of it – "I do not grudge Poona a penny that it gets" – he nonetheless felt that "if we only got half what they do each year, the mission here would be practically provided with all it wants."[26] Elwin hated Bombay for its climate: he called it "one of the few places in India which does not suit me", and admired Nicholson's "quite wonderful" work in the heat, noise, and smell.[27] Maxwell later commented that "[Poona and Bombay] are so different, and each has its own delightful features [...] but the interest of a mission among people living as ordinary very poor Bombay people, and which has its members living mostly as other poor people do in *chawls* and lodgings, has, of course, its own very special features."[28]

Coupled with the developments in South Africa and the needs of Bombay – which seemed "to call for a more united effort" – the Society decided to consolidate its fundraising and intercession in a more clearly delineated manner; and to that end it established the Fellowship of St John in 1904.

---

24 Puller, 17 April 1906; 10 May 1906.
25 *The Religious Life in the Colonies, CE* Nov 1897.
26 Nicholson, 2 April 1904.
27 Elwin, 9 April 1904.
28 Maxwell, 1 Dec 1905.

Our present effort must be to co-ordinate the other works of the Society at Bombay, Capetown, S. Cuthbert's (Kaffraria), and our houses at Oxford and Westminster. [...] Belonging to the Fellowship will not prevent anyone from devoting alms and special efforts to any one or more of the Society's works [...] while it will unite in prayer those who are engaged in its various works.

Poona was excluded from its financial aims because of its distinct interest to the Cowley-Wantage Guild. The American work was also exempt, as it had its own supporters; although life at Boston could sometimes be a hand-to-mouth affair. At Epiphany 1904 Field reported that "we have had a very merry Christmas. On Christmas Eve, at 10 p.m., we had nothing for dinner the next day, and several guests expected who have no home ties. A goose came at 11 p.m., so we were well provided."[29]

The expectations placed on the members of the new Fellowship were serious: it existed "to gather up various works of the Society more unitedly and consciously under the supreme unity of Divine love".[30] Those who chose to support the SSJE through it were to pray daily for the Society and its work; to offer an unspecified annual donation, and practical help where possible; and to receive Holy Communion – in a state of grace – for the intention of the Society on the Feast of St John before the Latin Gate or in its Octave. Other regulations were laid out in the *Manual of the Fellowship of St John*. For those inclined to less pious commitment, the *Cowley Evangelist* was clear that "at the same time it will be quite open to any who help us in our work to do so without joining the Fellowship".[31]

A few months later the membership stood at "400 persons (Priests, Laymen, and Women)" and a number of branch meetings had been held. Page was at pains to emphasise that "none should be admitted who do not take a *lively* interest" but, with that condition fulfilled, anyone was eligible: "be he young or old, poor or rich, weak in health or strong". The chronically ill were encouraged to offer up their suffering for the Society: such an oblation would be "heartily welcomed, for suffering, as Father Benson teaches us 'is a discipline of God's love'".[32]

The Fellowship of St John engaged the Society's supporters in a way that went far beyond almsgiving and deep into spiritual matters. At about the same time George Hollings reminded the readers of the *Cowley Evangelist* of the dread work of his Association for Prayer on behalf of the Condemned – "it is our privilege to have part, by prayer and the pleading of the Holy Sacrifice, in winning back to God, through our Lord and Saviour Jesus Christ, those over whom Satan has won the most miserable victories" – and the whole SSJE network was asked to take part in the forthcoming Ascensiontide Novena: "continuous prayer-watch night and day for nine days, for the increase of priestly vocations and consecrated life".[33]

---

29 Field, 4 Jan 1905.
30 *CE* Sept 1904.
31 *CE* June 1904.
32 *CE* Feb 1906.
33 *CE* March 1906.

A Dissonant Note

Back in London, Philip Waggett appealed for *"small* gifts in large numbers" to provide for furnishings at the new house[34] – he calculated that the cost for each cell was £8 10s[35] – while Adeline Bedford and Sibell Grosvenor continued to collect funds. By March 1906 they had raised £3,000 towards the increased costs of the Westminster house; and in the course of their efforts "a benefactor who desires to remain strictly anonymous" had provided £3,500 for the cost of the chapel.[36] The ground rent was dealt with by the Earl of Shaftesbury – Sibell Grosvenor's son-in-law – who had put off his grandfather's low-churchmanship, become an enthusiastic supporter of the Society,[37] and later served as President of the English Church Union. The Bishop of London, Arthur Winnington-Ingram, duly blessed the nearly-finished house on 20 July, and laid the foundation stone of the new chapel.[38]

A year and a day later, Winnington-Ingram was back at Westminster to consecrate the finished work. It was a discreet and quiet affair; with none of the pomp associated with the laying of the original stone of the house. Osborne, visiting from the States, was present with about sixty local clergymen; as were "the donor of the Chapel, and his wife [...] and a large group of those who have taken a leading part in building the House." The chapel was dedicated to Ss Peter & John, "because of its situation between the great Abbey Church of St Peter, on whose ancient patrimony it stands, and the Church of St John the Evangelist [Smith Square], our own patron, in whose parish it is". After the conclusion of the service the bishop and the members of the Society present went to bless the house chapel, which overlooked the main chapel at the west end.[39]

Waggett was very pleased indeed with the new arrangements. "The work is more than the work of preaching and missions," he wrote.

That work has been maintained in London during the last year, and has been done lately with much greater ease in the healthy conditions of the new House.

But it is not for this alone that so large a building has been accepted as a trust from the generosity of Church people. A much smaller home would have been sufficient for the Fathers and from such a home they could have rendered that service to the parochial clergy for which they were invited to live in London by many incumbents and welcomed there by the Bishop of the Diocese. But the large house is for the purpose of receiving others, both priests and laymen, for retreat, and in the case of some of the younger laymen, we may venture to add, for instruction.[40]

---

34 *CE* March 1905.
35 *CE* Dec 1905.
36 *CE* May 1905.
37 SSJE/2/3/117ff.
38 *CE* Aug 1905.
39 *CE* Aug 1906.
40 *CE* May 1906.

There was one dissenting voice: that of Benson himself. In September 1906, he wrote bitterly to Page to complain that "I was not the Founder of the Society as it now is. What I contemplated would have been something very different."

> Its English development has become involved in union with the world which no doubt is working out God's great purposes, but, in a manner far different from what we set before ourselves at the original start.

"Humanly speaking", he continued "the building of the Westminster House was a great misfortune. The very site placed in the midst of what we had abjured. All its necessary surroundings are at variance with our aspirations." He thought that the House should now be given to the diocese as a residence "for a Society of Mission Preachers" – the direction in which Page had considered trying to lead the SSJE in 1896.

At this point in the Society's history it is tempting to regard Benson's letter as nothing more than the recriminatory ramblings of an irritable old man, increasingly rheumatic and nearly blind – the letter was almost illegible, and Page copied it out for ease of reference – who had lived longer and seen more than he might have wished. Even Mildred Woodgate, who comes closest to being his hagiographer, considered that as early as the 1880s Benson was effectively "cut off from the young and rapidly changing world around him"[41] – a factor that played no small part in his resignation from the Superiorship. Nevertheless, his concerns deserve to be considered carefully.

> The work in College Street is not merely an additional work. Its character is altogether different in kind from the energies which are the proper outcome of our life. It requires men who are thoroughly *au courant* with London Society. If I may say so, Liddon is the type of man that they want. Pusey exhibits the devotional retirement essential for ourselves.

"I should not so much object to our having a house in London like St Peter's in the East", he went on. "The circumstances of poverty and hardship would be such as we might heartily accept". "Do let us keep ourselves to live with the poor and as the poor", he concluded. "God bless you."[42]

He had earlier suggested that "it would be much better to have a couple of rooms over a coffee shop", rather than a retreat house.

> Instead of seeking facilities for giving retreats and missions, I think we need to have their number diminished, so as to have more time at home for study, contemplation and prayer [...] Who are we that people should want us so very much? Why should they build houses for us?[43]

It must be remembered that Benson, devout as he was, was not always right. His dealings with the early American brethren had been disastrous; and under his leadership it had been the sort of introspection that he was now advocating which had threatened to smother the Society in the late 1880s.

---

41 Woodgate, *Benson*, 151.
42 Benson, 9 Sept 1906, SSJE/6/1/2/2/209ff.
43 Woodgate, *Benson*, 170.

What Page had achieved in the intervening years was something that in 1890 Benson had accepted he could not do: make the Society of St John the Evangelist an attractive and dynamic option for capable priests who might wish to offer themselves heartily to the consecrated life. Furthermore, Liddon had been dead since 1890, and Pusey since 1882; and Benson seems to have been oblivious to the contradictions of his position. The idea for a London House dated back to the very foundation of the Society in 1866 – and at the laying of the foundation stone of the London house he had himself spoken of the work at Cowley as being "not only for one class of Society but for all".

Now that it had finally happened – after a huge effort on the part of the leadership of the SSJE and the upper-crust of its supporters – Benson seemed to think that it was in the wrong part of town, and all a great mistake. To some extent this was an echo of the issues raised in Council in 1896, and whether it was appropriate for the Society to accept costly oblations. The letter of Statute 76 seemed to forbid it; but the Statutes were liable to be broadly interpreted in the light of Benson's own discretion decades before, when he had been Master of the Brotherhood of the Holy Trinity.[44] In any case, Benson's own practice had also followed similar lines in the past: after Bull celebrated mass at Ndabeni on Easter Day 1904 he wrote to say that he had "used the chalice set with the jewels of Fr Benson's mother", which had by then found its way to the Cape Flats, six thousand miles away.[45]

Benson and his successor were fond of each other: Page had been one of his first novices; and he in turn had welcomed him back to Cowley in 1900, where the Founder had feared isolation but had instead found honour and affection – in Chapel he was allocated the stall immediately to the right of the Superior General's. It was Page who, when he realised how bad Benson's rheumatism had become, bought him a stick which the older man hated; but it was also Page who realised that from time to time Benson's mind was becoming "apt to wander",[46] a development on which George Congreve also commented.[47] Page now stuck to his course, and Benson was won over: Woodgate noted that just as he had grown to like the new buildings at Cowley, after the opening of the Westminster house, "he always loved an excuse to go to London".[48]

Spence Burton – an American novice who would later become Bishop of Nassau – took him to town in 1909 to be guest of honour at a dinner to celebrate the fiftieth anniversary of the consecration of All Saints', Margaret Street. Benson refused to stay at the hotel where it was held – as Page had arranged – and insisted on going to sleep at the house that he had detested only three years earlier. On that occasion Page's mistake had been not to put him under obedience. A few years later, when he had been absolutely forbidden to fast on what would be his last Good Friday – he had only begun eating at all on

---

44 BHT Minute Book 7, 181ff, PH.
45 Bull, 12 April 1904.
46 Woodgate, *Benson*, 163.
47 Congreve, 31 May 1912, SSJE/6/5/2/2/13/13ff.
48 Woodgate, *Benson*, 162; 170.

Wednesdays and Fridays at the age of 83[49] – he refused to eat fish and demanded chops instead, "which he ate with much enjoyment".[50]

But others, too, raised eyebrows. Herbert Kelly, the founder of the Society of the Sacred Mission, thought that the SSJE's London house was "all in the severest monastic style but all the same money no object"; and Alistair Mason, in seeking to emphasise the difference of means between the two communities, describes the "expensive and tasteful simplicities of the Cowley Fathers".[51] It is certainly true that in the summer of 1896 Page had mooted the idea of the SSJE adapting its vow of poverty to suit better the needs of a community of mission priests, rather than contemplative monastics. He felt "that the spirit of the Society had changed, and that the sort of postulants we were likely to attract now, were not men who aimed at the monastic life but rather men who wanted to join a congregation of mission clergy".

Page had been dissuaded from such a course by Puller and Congreve, who intimated that they would feel forced to withdraw from the Society if he went ahead.[52] When Osborne was consecrated to the episcopate, the Bishop of Springfield sought to make arrangements for the sending ahead of his books and furniture. When he discovered that his new suffragan had neither, he was "amazed". "He had not taken in the literalness of Poverty," observed Osborne, who duly received $1000 from the people of the diocese to enable him to buy some necessary new items.[53]

The fact that the SSJE used its connections to raise money for specific projects, however, is a pertinent distinction. Certainly it benefited from generous benefactions from time to time – when Benson's Christ Church contemporary Richard Randall retired as Dean of Chichester in 1901 he presented the SSJE with his theological library of several hundred books,[54] and an unsolicited windfall had provided for the building of the new Mission House at Cowley – but it nevertheless remained dependent on alms, at least in the strict sense. From the 1890s until most of the fundraising was subsumed into the Fellowship of St John the lists of subscribers at the back of each edition of the *Cowley Evangelist* had often been followed by a space-filler instructing readers how to make donations to the various works in hand.

DONATIONS AND SUBSCRIPTIONS for
    The India and Capetown Missions,
    The New Church,
    The Cowley S. John Schools,
    The General Fund of the Society,
should be sent to the Secretary, Mission House, Cowley S. John, Oxford. Cheques should be crossed "Oxford Old Bank," and made payable to the Rev. R. L. PAGE.

    Colonel JERVOISE, Keble College, Oxford, and Messrs. PARSONS, THOMSON & Co, Old Bank, Oxford, also receive donations for the New Church.

---

49 SSJE/6/5/2/2/9.
50 Woodgate, *Benson*, 170; 173; 180.
51 Mason, *SSM*, 120.
52 SSJE/6/9/1/2.
53 Osborne, 4 Nov 1904.
54 *CE* March 1902.

Donations sent for the LONDON HOUSE are forwarded to the Treasurer, F. H. Rivington, Esq., 44 Connaught Square, W., and will be acknowledged on his list.

MISSIONARY GUILD OF S. MARY AND S. JOHN in aid of the Mission of the Cowley Fathers and the Wantage Sisters, at Poona, India. General Organising Secretary Mrs. Bengough, 155 Sloane Street, London, S.W.

S. PHILIP'S MISSIONARY GUILD in aid of the Cowley Fathers' Mission at Capetown. General Secretary. Miss Briggs, 37 Tedworth Square, London S.W. Parcels for Capetown may be sent to the Secretary, 29 Great Titchfield Street, London.

More frequently, as it took up less space, a "Form of Bequest" appeared, which allowed sympathetic readers to leave some (or, even better, all) of their estate "to be applied to the general purposes or to any special work of the said Society"; while in 1907 the SSJE's fundraising efforts were well-enough known for the *Cowley Evangelist* to have to warn its readers that "persons have been discovered using the names of some of the Fathers for begging purposes".[55]

When the Bishop of Oxford agreed that the collections taken in the community church at Easter 1904 should be retained for the use of the Society, its needs were made clear.

> The cost of supporting the Mother House of the Society at Cowley S. John, with the Guest-house attached, is very considerable. In addition to the expenses of every household – for board, rates and taxes, clothing, washing, coals, gas, subscriptions, books, claims on charity – the nature of our work entails upon us exceptionally large outlay for travel, posting, stationery, &c; while the income from our invested capital and house rents is sufficient for *scarcely one quarter* of our annual expenditure.[56]

Statute 76 – with its stricture that "all costly gifts should be refused" – continued to trouble some of the brethren;[57] but Page made no apology for the links that his Society might have with the well-to-do. When he had addressed the Festival of the Society of the Sacred Mission at Michaelmas 1892 – the SSM had at that time only just begun to evolve out of the Corean Missionary Brotherhood – he had observed that the SSJE was able to draw on the talents and connections of men who had had the "great advantage of public school or college life".[58] The lists of names of subscribers in the *Cowley Evangelist* and *The Star in the East* to the Indian and African work – records of generous gifts and what would now be called "regular planned giving" – were constantly dotted with titles. When it came to fundraising, as we have seen, a duchess here and there did no harm at all.

By 1907 various projects were drawing to fulfilment. In London, August saw "the happy completion of the Building Fund" for the property at 22 Great College Street, and the Society commemorated the occasion by consciously deciding to refer to the building as "St Edward's House". To some extent this also solved the problem of the house being on a corner, with its front door in

---

55 *CE* July 1907.
56 *CE* May 1904.
57 SSJE/6/9/1/2.
58 *Journal of the Society of the Sacred Mission*, November 1892.

Tufton Street. For the avoidance of future doubt a brass plate engraved with "St Edward's House" would be fixed to the wall by the door, which Waggett hoped would make the house "sufficiently discoverable".[59] It was a cause of particular satisfaction to the Superior General that the house had been completed in time to be able receive visitors during the Lambeth Conference of 1908.[60]

At Cowley, Kempe's west windows in the community church depicted "four great missionary saints" – Martin, Ansgar, Patrick, and Birinus – whose vineyards lay "to the north, south, east and west of Oxford, at varying distances". The anticipated scheme to fill the clerestory windows with similar paragons of endeavour remained unfinished;[61] but the essential fabric of the building was finally completed in September 1907 with the addition of Bodley's porches, shortly before his own death in October. "We are happy in the thought", reported the *Cowley Evangelist*, "that our own church, upon which he bestowed such loving pains, was just completed before he was taken from us".[62]

Various loose ends were being tied up; and at General Chapter at the end of July 1907 Page asked to be allowed to step down, having discussed the matter with Benson and other senior members of the Society, including the overseas Provincials.[63] His own health had not been strong – he too had spent most of the winter of 1905 to 1906 at San Remo – and he was becoming increasingly deaf. At General Chapter he said that "he believed it was the Will of God that he should have been in Authority so many years, and also the Will of God that he should now retire".

Benson stopped him as he made to leave the Chapel, saying that "he would not like our Fr Superior to leave without expressing our sense of how he has watched over us, and of his intense self-sacrifice [...] We can look forward with confidence, because God has helped him do so in his long reign." After a discussion about whether it was even possible for a Superior General to resign before the normal end of his term of office, the Chapter voted – "with a grateful sense of indebtedness" – to accept his resignation.[64]

Loss & Gain

It is no exaggeration to say that during his seventeen years as Superior General, Page transfigured and transformed the SSJE into a community with a vibrant life and viable future – a situation far removed from the condition in which it was when he came into office. Over thirty men were professed in the course of his tenure, and the notices at the back of the *Cowley Evangelist* list the

---

59 *CE* Aug 1906. It made little difference, as forty years later the London fathers were still complaining that first-time visitors were using the tradesmen's entrance on College Street rather than the front door around the corner on Tufton Street: "Ladies have entered the kitchen more than once by that entrance." SSJE/3/3.

60 SSJE/2/3/88.

61 *CE* Aug 1905.

62 *CE* Oct 1907.

63 *CE* Aug 1907.

64 SSJE/2/3/59ff.

ever-increasing comings and goings of Cowley Fathers who were either off to the missions or coming home on furlough.

Not all of them had stayed the course. Walter Wyon was one of the brethren whose names had been subscribed to the ratified Statutes in 1884: an enthusiastic musician, he had been conductor of the Cowley St John Vocal Society; and had become a particular favourite of the ladies of the parish.[65] By 1891 concerns had been raised about his ongoing suitability for the community. Page removed him from his position as Director of the Holy Cross Sisters at Winchester, to the dismay of a number of members of the community there;[66] and at the end of the year he sent him to America, with the intention that he should break off his old worldly associations in England.

Page sent a firm letter after him to Liverpool, to be read aboard ship. "We all feel that you are getting out of touch with the letter and the spirit of the Religious Life", it said. The Superior General ordered Wyon, on the journey, to be diligent in saying his offices and observing daily meditation; and not to allow himself "the recreation of conversation until you have fulfilled these duties". As it was Advent, he was to "practise some abstinence at the table", and to keep the Vigil of St Thomas as preparation for his work in Boston.

"A Religious must not be ashamed to act as a Religious on a voyage," Page continued. We cannot set aside the responsibilities of our Vocation; and the reserve proper to our life, and identify ourselves with the secular element about us, without being guilty of a betrayal of our trust and disloyalty to our Lord." In Boston Wyon was to settle down to his work, and to life under the Rule. "Be very careful about your Meditation, Reading, and daily self-examination, and don't neglect the fortnightly confession which the rule requires." There were to be no social calls for tea, and he was not there "to see America and interest yourself in the novelties of the country, though of course that may come in in an altogether subordinate way".

Above all, Wyon was to "keep up the religious tone of the Community by great regularity and punctuality in the house, observing carefully the house rule." He had, thought Page, been "so lax about this at Cowley that it was felt to be a great hindrance in training the novices", and he instructed him to read and meditate on the Rule on the voyage. "You must by a great patience and perseverance make a marked difference in these matters before your return to Cowley."[67]

Page would not have been impressed to see Wyon's sailing-card for the Cunard Line's *Etruria*: he was travelling first-class, and had annotated the names of passengers who had caught his interest, particularly Miss De Morat ("Contralto"), and Mr A. L. Halliday ("Violinist").[68] Matters came to a head in 1892: it had also been felt that Wyon had become rather too close to some of the women who sought him out as a confessor and spiritual guide. Although in the end he was expelled "on account of grave indiscretions in dealing with female penitents", the process had been cumulative – and at its end Wyon had acknowledged the scandal, and himself asked to be dismissed.

---

65 Cambridge University Library, MS(Add.7651) Wyon 9/6/2; Wyon 9/3/147.
66 CUL, MS(Add.7651) Wyon 9/3/101;102;103.
67 Page, 11 Dec 1891, CUL MS(Add.7651) Wyon 9/3/91.
68 CUL, MS (Add.7651) Wyon 9/2/3.

The Chapter minutes made a point of noting that "the Fathers wished to express to their Brother their extreme sorrow at being obliged to take this step; their conviction that in the actual circumstances it is the kindest course towards him, as well as the wisest with reference to other interests; and their earnest and affectionate prayers for him, both now and in the future." Responding to Page's communication of the outcome, Wyon thanked the Chapter "for having acted expeditiously according to my request, and for having desired you should make provision for my immediate needs. I am deeply sensible of the injury my unguarded conduct has done, and may yet do, to the Church of Christ, and I ask the Society's forgiveness for the discredit it suffers from my weakness."[69]

Other Cowley Fathers put their long-distance travel to more suitable use. Some lengthy sea voyages became missions in themselves, and microcosms of mission life. When Bull returned to Cape Town in September 1905 he took on the mantle of chaplain to the *Kinfauns Castle*, engaging in pastoral conversations with the other passengers and taking services: "A great many came and sat around, of all classes, and many of the ship's crew, including the captain, who did not miss any service."

Most of the passengers were of other denominations – including ministers – and he did not robe or use any formal rite: "On board ship it seems best to be as simple as possible." He corralled the other clergy into preaching and Bible study; made friends with a Salvation Army commissioner; and shut down a gambling table after its players had kept him awake until 6 a.m. with a raucous game of cards.

> I dressed and went out in my shirt sleeves, and spoke to them of their inconsiderateness, the open scandal, and their personal sin. They listened altogether quietly, and promised to stop immediately, which they did. One of the Scotchmen was very much ashamed, and promised not to do it any more. Perhaps he was the one who had lost a sovereign, or more, but he may have remembered his boyish Sabbaths in Scotland.

As at St Columba's, Bull tempered his robustness with deep pastoral insight: complaining to the captain was "not a converting way for a chaplain to adopt"; while travelling in second class was undesirable, as "if the chaplain is at all to influence the third class men, he must be amongst them".[70]

On his way to India for the first time a month later, accompanying Nicholson, who had been at Cowley on furlough, Maxwell found on the *Rubattino* "Church people, Quakers, Goanese Romans, a Hindu of high caste, [and] a Plymouth Brother Colonel going out to preach". The Quakers shared his cabin; but his most regular interaction was with the Hindu.

> [He] generally consults me about the menu at each meal, to make sure that he is not breaking caste. It is an odd beginning of my Indian experience to be watching over the maintenance of caste, but Christian charity seems to demand it in this instance![71]

---

69 SSJE/2/1/181ff.
70 Bull, 27 Sept 1905.
71 Maxwell, 23 Oct 1905.

The SSJE's supporters had also increased: both in number and in means. St Edward's House was not built with the pennies of the poor, but through the efforts of well-to-do families with an interest in the Anglo-Catholic spirituality that the Society continued to offer; while the monthly subscription lists show kings' ransoms and widows' mites. An increasing number of parishes began to make regular contributions to the Society's work; and the Fellowship of St John grew steadily from its inception.

At Cowley the Society's schools continued to provide for local children; but far away in India and South Africa the churches at Yerendawana and Tsolo crowned its final pieces of major colonial expansion. By the close of the first decade of the twentieth century the SSJE was taking its part in the noise and din of Bombay, escaping the hustle and bustle of the city for higher and cooler ground when it was possible; and in and around Poona on the Deccan plains. The work that had originally centred on Cape Town – a bustling fleshpot like Bombay, but without monsoons – was now complemented by the extremes of the ministry at Tsolo, seven hundred miles away.

For the Cowley Fathers some sort of Indian work had been planned from the start; but the work in South Africa had developed more organically. In each place the work followed a distinct theme: schools, hostels, workshops, clinics, and a handsome new church. That was even true at Bombay after the Port Trust took over the site of old St Peter's for expansion in late 1905. "We feel sorry to leave the old Church," mused Nicholson, "but we cannot but be filled with gratitude to God for what he has permitted the Church to do for the Catholic faith and worship during the last 30 years."[72] With the compensation he oversaw the raising of the building that survives today – in its style and ornamentation it had much in common with Holy Name, Poona.

The foundation stone of new St Peter's was laid on 19 March 1907 by Lord Lamington, who had succeeded Lord Northcote as Governor of Bombay. He had visited the mission at Poona the previous year, and the relationship of the Society with the structures of the British Empire can hardly go unremarked. It is impossible to avoid the occasional impression that even Puller ran St Cuthbert's – which was by far the most indigenous and remote of the missions – much in the style of a English country parish. Certain imported traditions were non-negotiable: on 9 November 1905, the whole mission downed tools to celebrate the King's birthday. A party was laid on for the children – but with "mealies, pork, and *amarewu* (a sort of temperance Kafir-beer)" instead of sandwiches and barley water.[73]

FRIENDS & RELATIONS

Hilary Carey has observed that there has been "perennial debate" on the nature of the interaction between the churches and the colonial agenda of successive governments – from the days when Britain's imperial

---

72 Nicholson, 19 Dec 1905.

73 Puller, 9 Nov 1905. "Mealies" are corn-on-the-cob, and I am grateful to Jasper Hersov for this identification.

ambitions were expanding, through its heyday, and to the "uneasy memory" of the present; but in her important book *God's Empire*, she does not treat the Anglican religious orders.[74] Within the ongoing discussion – which is very far from over, as recent events have demonstrated at Cape Town, Oxford, and elsewhere – even from an entirely secular viewpoint it is impossible to depict British missionaries neatly as having been either perfect heroes or villains, as Andrew Porter emphasises in *Religion versus Empire?*[75]

Jeffrey Cox notes that many Anglican missionaries were committed to racial hierarchy: not necessarily deliberately; but with its presence on missions simply being an uncontroversial and tenacious reality of life.[76] The SSJE, however, valued the part played by its local co-workers, without whose cooperation its work would have been almost impossible – or at least as not nearly effective. As early as 1904 Bull was able to report that at Cape Town "largely the Mission depends on its native workers".[77]

Six decades later, as its closing days in South Africa drew near, the Society would rejoice in the profession of its first African member; and almost its last act was to attempt to found an indigenous brotherhood for work in the Diocese of St John's. Such a development had been looked for as early as 1900, when Callaway founded his Society of St Cuthbert. "One hopes", he wrote then, "that the minds of our African Christians may be turned towards such a life, and may see in it a possibly vocation for themselves and their children. All such hopes may be very, very far from realization, but every plant must have its seed."[78]

When Puller wrote to Benson from India in 1908 he told the Founder that "I have been welcomed here with great warmth of affection. Evidently the Native Christians here have a great love for our Society."[79] It would be hard for even the most dyed-in-the-wool anti-imperialist to assert that every missionary was an oppressive agent of empire; although, naturally, some were. The truth lies in between: across the whole Empire missionaries can be regarded in retrospect as a blessing and a curse, depending on against which criteria they are assessed; and the "surrogate imperialism" that Anna Johnston describes in *Missionary Writing and Empire* involves a kaleidoscope of nuance.[80] Even Simeon Wilberforce O'Neill, who effectively lived most of his life in India as a Christian *sadhu*, was prepared to use imperial structures to solve local problems from time to time; but when he died "the poor lifted up their voices and wept".[81]

When scholars have dealt with missionaries working in the British Empire, they have generally engaged with mission work that involved individuals working under the auspices of a missionary organisation, rather than those

74 Hilary M. Carey, *God's Empire: Religion and Colonialism in the British World, c.1801–1908*, Cambridge University Press (2011), 14.

75 Andrew Porter, *Religion versus Empire?: British Protestant Missionaries and Overseas Expansion, 1700–1914*, Manchester University Press (2004).

76 Cox, *British Missionary Enterprise*, 178–9.

77 *SSJE Native Mission*, CE June 1905.

78 Sedding, *Callaway*, 19.

79 Puller, 14 March 1908.

80 Anna Johnston, *Missionary Writing and Empire, 1800–1860*, Cambridge University Press (2003), 9.

81 cf Samuel Gopal, "Simeon Wilberforce O'Neill", *Nagpur Diocesan Quarterly*, July 1904.

working in and through a community. This model raises another problem of interpretation: individual missionaries were not under vows, and so there was nothing to stop them leaving their organisations and setting up on their own.[82] Of these David Livingstone was the most respectable, and retained his missionary interests. Others were not very far from what Sydney Smith called "little detachments of maniacs" as early as 1808, and left to pursue secular interests.[83] Some caused grave scandal; and the exploits of Noël Coward's Uncle Harry were not entirely fictional, even if he himself was.[84]

Emily J. Manktelow's phrase "the missionary family" applies to the same model, and relates to the work of the travelling nuclear family of wife and children that would often accompany and succour independent travelling missionaries. It may be easily and usefully co-opted to describe the support network of the myriad people who regarded the SSJE missions in India and South Africa as a family affair, to which many of them contributed liberally.[85] Most immediately these included the sisterhoods who assisted on the ground – and in some cases there was a literal connection, with members of the SSJE having biological sisters in the women's communities.[86] As Deborah Gaitskell noted, in the context of women missionaries, a high doctrine of celibate priesthood was "far more noticeably coupled with extensive use of unmarried female labor".[87] Other families became prominent through the pages of the *Cowley Evangelist* as labourers on the Society's behalf – the Rivingtons, Rumseys, and Callaways, to name but a handful – they were often those whose association with the SSJE had led a clerical son to profession at Cowley, or *vice versa*.

Certainly the SSJE's active colonial work would have been very nearly impossible without the cooperation of the All Saints Sisters of the Poor at Bombay and at Cape Town; and the Community of St Mary the Virgin at Poona and at Tsolo, where they enlarged the mission work by opening St Lucy's Hospital in July 1906.[88] Their members undertook the work of teachers and nurses, and enabled the SSJE to extend an effective pastoral ministry to both men and women; and in return the Cowley Fathers provided the women's orders with their sacraments and spiritual counsel. But the effectiveness of other women-workers like Gertrude Bradley, Edith Pellatt, and Alice Blyth cannot be underestimated; and the same is true of the quiet but crucial support given by laywomen as diverse as Lydia Williams, Paula von Blomberg, Lilian Rousby, and the unnamed lepers on Robben Island.

---

82 Adrian Hastings, *The Church in Africa: 1450–1950*, Oxford: OUP (1994).

83 Sydney Smith, "Indian Missions", *Edinburgh Review* 12 (April 1808), 172; Johnston, *Missionary Writing*, 7.

84 "Poor Uncle Harry got a bit gay and longed to tarry. This, Aunt Mary couldn't quite allow. She lectured him severely on a number of church affairs – but when she'd gone to bed he made a getaway down the stairs, for he longed to find the answer to a few of the maidens' prayers. Uncle Harry's not a missionary now." *I'll See You Again* (1954).

85 Emily J. Manktelow, *Missionary Families: Race, gender and generation on the spiritual frontier*, Manchester University Press (2013).

86 cf Sr Fidelia Maturin, Sr Johanna Maturin, and Sr Selina Congreve: all CSJB. Bonham, *A Place in Life*, 127.

87 Deborah Gaitskell, "Rethinking Gender Roles", in Andrew Porter (ed), *The Imperial Horizons of British Protestant Missions, 1880–1914*, Grand Rapids, MI: Eerdmans (2003), 150.

88 Callaway to his mother, 18 July 1906, in Sedding, *Callaway*, 178–9.

By the time the Cowley Fathers arrived in Bombay and Cape Town, Livingstone's caricature of the missionary as "a dumpy sort of man with a Bible under his arm" had to a great extent passed from the scene; although its memory lingered long enough for G. K. Chesterton to reference "the modern missionary, with his palm-leaf hat and his umbrella, [who] has become rather a figure of fun".[89] The foundation of the Universities' Mission to Central Africa in 1857 had been the beginning of a new phase of mission work which pointed to "a significant widening in those responding to the missionary call". Cox observes that "the overwhelming majority of missionary recruits [in the first half of the nineteenth-century] were from relatively plebeian if not working-class backgrounds. Even in the Anglican CMS [Church Missionary Society], graduates were not a majority at the turn of the century, and the anxiety that CMS recruits were 'not quite gentlemen' continued to plague a society committed to social respectability but serving as an avenue of upward mobility, a back door into the status of gentlemen."[90] But the first UMCA missionaries were the contemporaries of the members of the Brotherhood of the Holy Trinity, and the fact that they included men from the Cambridge First Eight is not insignificant.[91]

Johnston notes that "the role of missionary provided young men, frequently limited by class and education in England, opportunities for social advancement, community standing, and a challenging and exotic career."[92] But public schoolboys who became university men with vocations also became, sooner or later, the sort of priests who were professed in the Society of St John the Evangelist in the 1890s. They did not need an introduction into polite society, and nor did their sisters. A number of women professed into the Community of St John the Baptist at Clewer from the 1860s onwards, for example, had discarded their aristocratic titles – but not necessarily their social standing – when they assumed the veil.[93]

Mother Jane Frances CSJB was the granddaughter of the 8th Lord Erskine; a kinswoman by marriage of the Duke of Argyll; and a cousin of the Countess of Dufferin, the wife of the Viceroy of India. When Clewer later sent Sisters back to India to work in Calcutta and Darjeeling, inevitably they landed at Mazagon and rested with the All Saints Sisters of the Poor. When Jane Frances herself arrived with a group of sisters on the *Clyde* in January 1888, she wrote home that "Fr Page most kindly appeared with one of his native boys from their mission, and a little wherry to take us and our goods on shore. We found Sr Gladys, the All Saints' Superior [in Bombay], waiting for us with a gharrie [carriage]."[94] Not long after her arrival she was collected from the compound and taken to tea at Government House – a nun in full habit and veil riding in

89 George Seaver, *David Livingstone: his life and letters*, London: Lutterworth Press (1957), 285; G. K. Chesterton, *The Everlasting Man*, London: Hodder & Stoughton (1925).

90 Cox, *British Missionary Enterprise*, 186.

91 Ibid, 252.

92 Johnston, *Missionary Writing*, 8.

93 Bonham, *A Place in Life*, 127ff.

94 Valerie Bonham, *Sisters of the Raj: The Clewer Sisters in India*, Clewer: CSJB (1997), 63.

the Vicereine's carriage, "in state, with a mounted native bodyguard in gorgeous uniforms".[95]

The priests who joined the Cowley Fathers in the decades after its establishment were gentlemen already. Congreve and Puller were both Old Etonians; and when Frederic Noel died in 1929 his obituary described him as having been of "good family – he was able to trace up a descent of fifteen generations to Edmund Langley, Duke of York, and younger son of King Edward III, and then on to Dukes of Normandy and by collateral lines, as he would merrily recount, to Alfred the Great."[96] Almost all of those who were intended for the work of the English congregation were public-school men who had been to Oxford or Cambridge; and their contemporaries – or at least men of the same generations with similar backgrounds – took up positions in public service, often leading into colonial administration in both India and South Africa.

Benson's own encouragement was that "God has spoken to us, giving us a great Empire. God speaks to us that we may give ourselves to him in the development of all this material wealth."[97] Others were more cynically confident that the work of the Cowley Fathers and similar mission-bodies would help to produce more biddable locals.[98] Either way, what the SSJE offered was an opportunity for clergymen to carry out missionary work within a context of genteel respectability and a support structure that ranged from the donations of committed benefactors to the practical domestic assistance of the lay brothers – some of whom were later sent to the Cowley outposts in India and Africa as missionaries themselves. Nicholson was delighted when a visitor to Poona declared himself "impressed with the religious atmosphere"; and went away feeling "that we laid more stress upon the religious side of Christianity and less upon the mere imparting of the blessings of civilization than is sometimes the case".[99]

Rowan Strong has observed that more work needs to be done to furnish "a more complete and critical understanding of the Anglican missions that derived from the Oxford Movement". He notes that a neglect of a proper understanding of theological motivations has led many writers to fall into "the reductionist trap that mission theologies were merely a screen for more nefarious and worldly motives"; and argues that "missions need to be understood in their own terms before they are subjected to necessary critical scrutiny and assessment."[100] Cox, meanwhile, describes the successes of other missionary organisations as having been "the triumph of bricks and mortar".[101] Mindful of Strong's *caveat lector*, it may not seem unreasonable to regard the Society of St John the Evangelist's corresponding colonial efforts under Robert Page as the triumph of marble and lively stones.

---

95 Bonham, *Sisters of the Raj*, 65.
96 *CE* Aug 1929.
97 *CE* April 1910.
98 cf Sir J. Johnstone, *Berrow's Worcester Journal*, 24 Dec 1887.
99 Nicholson, 10 Aug 1915.
100 Rowan Strong, "The Oxford Movement and Missions", in Stewart J. Brown, Peter B. Nockles, and James Pereiro (eds), *The Oxford Handbook of the Oxford Movement*, Oxford: OUP (2017), 497.
101 Cox, *British Missionary Enterprise*, 213ff.

11

ONE BIG FAMILY

*The world values Religious Communities for
their work: Christ values them for their love.*

—Henry Power Bull SSJE[1]

obert Lay Page was succeeded as Superior General of the Society of St
John the Evangelist by Gerald Speirs Maxwell.[2] In many ways Maxwell
was a reluctant ruler: he later described himself as "one who [...] has
a natural dislike of responsibility and feels little qualified for the position he
has to fill".[3] Nevertheless, to his brethren he was an obvious choice: although
he had not been professed until 1899, he had served as Novice Master and
Assistant Superior, and already had much of the intricacies of the Society's
work at his fingertips.

By the time of Maxwell's election, in and around Bombay alone the SSJE was
running work among Europeans, Indian Christians, and non-Christians; and
four separate schools – and it was not until 1905 that Gertrude Bradley had
gained the assistance of another doctor, Janet Vaughan.[4] At the other mission
centres in India and South Africa the burden was similar, and at each location
there was a handsome new church and a mission house of variable size and
elegance. Retreats were organised, mission-journeys undertaken, visits made
to the sick, and Viaticum carried to the dying.

At the same time, the SSJE's integration of the local people into the life of all
their missions marked it out from many others who had attempted to pursue
similar ventures. They were modern missionaries, spread over a wide area.
When Maxwell visited Poona in 1905 as Assistant Superior he told Page that
one of the local welcoming party had said in his speech that "just as the King
had sent the Prince because he could not come himself, so you had sent me".

After these speeches came on the garlanding [...] It was really all so nice and
cordial, and they seemed so entirely to grasp the idea of S.S.J.E. as a society, and
to feel that welcoming it in the person of your representative was quite an event,
that we felt like one big family.

---

1 *CE* Aug 1920.
2 GenC 1907, SSJE/2/3/59ff.
3 SSJE/2/5/204.
4 *CE* Jan 1905.

George Congreve made the same point when he addressed the Fellowship of St John a few years later. "India and Africa are no mere geographical names for you," he emphasised.

> As you pray for the various provinces of Christ's empire throughout the world, you find your own idea of home extending; you cannot be a stranger among people for whom you pray, and among whom Christ reigns. There are good people who are just as much at home on Table Mountain, Ndabeni, St Cuthbert's, Poona, Boston, as in their own flat in London.[5]

Maxwell was particularly taken with the attention paid to SSJE's day-to-day life at Yerendawana by the Hindu locals. He was not a strong singer, and so at Terce on his first morning he and Edward Elwin recited the office hymn. Afterwards he found "a small heathen boy in the verandah [who] wanted to know why we had not sung; he had always noticed that hitherto when a second Father was here there was always the singing of the hymn".[6]

In the course of his tour of the Indian missions he was equally impressed by the local identities of the Christian homes he visited. "They were plainly Christian, and many had a crucifix in the shrine originally designated for the household idol, but, except for the absence of anything suggesting an idol and the presence of some Christian symbol, there was nothing to mark any connexion with England or Europe."[7] The same applied elsewhere: Godfrey Callaway had similarly warned against the evils of "unnecessary Europeanism" in African mission work;[8] while Philip Waggett insisted that it should be entirely possible for the members of the Society to be "true servants of English traditions in the Catholic Church, and yet keen in building up a true native Church" in the colonies.[9] At Poona the new font had an inscription from Psalm 119, carved in Marathi; while at Tsolo the pulpit had been made big enough to accommodate both preacher and interpreter, and the best super-frontal had been embroidered with the opening of the Magnificat in Xhosa.

Congreve was clear that prayer and vigilance were essential to the life of missionaries, and particularly those ministering among the heathen: "no minister needs his daily meditation and occasional retreat so much as the Missionary who lives where Satan's seat is."[10] As the mission work continued to increase, Benson urged those members of the Society serving away from Cowley to remember that because they belonged to the same religious community they "must realise the unity of this life, and as the love of God rests upon us His eye beholds us wheresoever we are. Every part of the community is living, working, in the full brightness of His love, even though we are separated".[11] No edition of the *Cowley Evangelist* at this time opened with anything

---

5 *CE* Jan 1911.
6 Maxwell, 17 Nov 1905.
7 Maxwell, 12 Jan 1906.
8 *CE* Jan 1905.
9 *CE* June 1905.
10 *A Paper read at the Conference of Delegates of the Federation of Junior Clergy Missionary Associations, 1906, Cowley Evangelist,* Aug & Sept 1906.
11 *The Spiritual Unity of our Common Life not Injured by Necessary Separation, Cowley Evangelist,* Oct 1906.

other than a theological reflection on the liturgical season or a pressing issue of the day.

As many of the brethren as were in England took part in the Society's general retreat each July – which ended with the annual Chapter – and the others joined themselves to it spiritually by prayer, sending their votes with their Provincial Superior.[12] All individual members of the Society undertook regular retreats themselves, and most led them for others. They also prayed the same daily offices, with appropriate concessions to the local languages in their public worship. The liturgical *Supplementary* produced in 1904 contained "The *Songs of Syon*, together with Introits, Graduals, Sequences and Antiphons as used in the church of the Society of St John the Evangelist", compiled by George Ratcliffe Woodward. A second edition, of the same year, included the *Cowley Carol Book* of 1901.

Woodward had previously collaborated with the Society's old friend George Herbert Palmer, the plainsong expert, and the liturgical texts of the *Supplementary* demonstrate the richness of the SSJE's worship: the deeply sacramental nature of its corporate theology interwoven with its intricate plainsong, and translated in the colonies as well as possible into Marathi and Xhosa – at Bombay, for example, Hugh Nicholson had some of the translated mission hymns put onto slides, so that they could be used at the magic-lantern services.[13]

Dom Anselm Hughes recalled the worship at Cowley at the end of the first decade of the twentieth century in his memoir *The Rivers of the Flood*.

> The singing at Cowley in those days was as good as anything I have heard since. A choir-school, with its small band of volunteer choirmen trained by Cedric [he meant Basil] Bucknall, sang the service, all in plainsong except for some hymns; and *Salve festa dies*, the verses by five boys in the rood loft, was quite unearthly in its beauty. The back view of Father Benson, then in extreme old age, could be seen in the return stalls.[14]

Songs of Syon was deliberately Catholic without being Roman, and Anglican without being Protestant – although Woodward conceded a few Lutheran tunes. Most of the translations not by Woodward himself were by John Mason Neale: these included his rendering of Thomas à Kempis' *In domo Patris*, with its evocation of the many mansions of heaven mentioned in St John's Gospel, and each containing the neatly-ordered ranks of the redeemed.

> My Father's home eternal,
> Which all dear pleasures share,
> Hath many divers mansions,
> And each surpassing fair:
>
> They are the victors' guerdon,
> Who, through the hard-won fight,

---

12 cf Nicholson, 30 July 1904.
13 Chard, 8 March 1909.
14 Dom Anselm Hughes, *The Rivers of the Flood*, London: Faith Press (1961), 42.

Have followed in my footsteps,
And reign with me in light.

The monastics came between Doctors and Hermits; with the ascetic life set against the promise of glory yet to come.

The brave Religious Orders,
Their self-denial ceased,
Sit down with me and banquet
At my eternal Feast.

The heady imagery of the SSJE's self-understanding of its life and mission at the start of the twentieth century was a far cry from the days of the late 1880s, when Benson's community had seemed to a number of its leading members to be on the brink of collapse. By 1907, Page's leadership had transformed it into a well-resourced practical and spiritual powerhouse unlike anything the Church of England had ever seen. In America it was dedicated to the raising up of the downtrodden, in India and Africa to the conversion of the heathen, and at home to the advancement of the Catholic faith as it understood the Church of England to have received it. Its work had won the warm approval of the SPG and other sympathetic missionary bodies;[15] and even the personal commendation of the President of the United States.

Meanwhile, the Society's life of corporate prayer was constantly informed and sustained by its Anglo-Catholic spirituality. In 1907, for example, it discussed in great detail which saints should be kept when, and how: the matter of kalendrical revision had been brought to General Chapter to have the attention of Society's collected wisdom, but naturally Frederick Puller came to the fore. He approved of keeping St Hilary as a Doctor; but objected to St Valentine being observed as a Priest – "as in Sarum and Roman Use, not Bishop as in the Prayer book". Nalbro' Robinson contended that the Sarum Use Valentine was a different Valentine from the one commemorated in the Prayer Book, which was justified in calling him a Bishop. St Dominic and St Francis were to be kept as Confessors, not as Abbots as before; but King Charles the Martyr did not make the cut, as the Chapter was divided. George Hollings withdrew his proposal that he be included "in deference to the wish of the Fr Superior, who felt that the day ought not to be observed unless the Society were unanimously in favour of it". The martyred Companions of St Denis, however, joined his liturgical observance on 9 October.

St Cuthbert was admitted after the takeover at Tsolo: the feast of the Translation of his Relics on 4 September was kept at the mission as a Greater Double with Octave, and at the other houses as a Simple Feast with full office; while the commemoration of his death on 20 March was observed at Tsolo as a Lesser Double, and a Simple Memorial everywhere else. As the Society had also recently committed itself to a permanent presence on Iona, the house there was also directed to keep St Blathmac of Iona & Companions, Martyrs, as a Simple Feast on 19 Jan; and the various Memorials of St Bride, St Oran,

---

15 *Jackson's Oxford Journal*, 10 Dec 1887.

and St Donan & the Martyrs of Eigg.[16] The discussions went on for nearly two days; then continued in subcommittee for much of the next year, and on into the General Chapter of 1908.

When the new version of the day hours was published in 1908, edited by Edward Trenholme – whose liturgical scholarship came close to that of Puller[17] – the *Cowley Evangelist* described it as broadly following the Sarum breviary, "with some practical modifications, and with some liturgical enrichment from other sources".[18] Liturgical observance was an important matter, because, as Elwin observed, the Society was "a very scattered Community";[19] and its Kalendar was a spiritual tool by which the dispersed mission-centres could feel particularly bound to one another in prayer. Gerald Ley wrote from Tsolo on 6 May 1913, having remembered that St Cuthbert's had not sent greetings ahead of time to Cowley for the feast of St John before the Latin Gate; but reassuring the brethren at home that nevertheless "we all had you very much in our thoughts this morning".[20]

No Surrender

Catholic spirituality also, naturally, infused the Society's understanding of its ministration of the sacraments. By the turn of the century Anglo-Catholicism was generally accepted as an increasingly normative expression of Anglican church life – John Henry Overton observed in 1897 that it was "perfectly marvellous to observe how things are now accepted which once provoked suspicion"[21] – but an unwelcome development in India towards the end of Page's time as Superior General led the SSJE to take a public and spirited stand for an orthodox interpretation of Eucharistic doctrine as it perceived the Church of England to have received it.

The Society's friend Louis Mylne had retired from Bombay in 1898, although he continued a doughty supporter of the Indian work; his successor James Macarthur had been translated to Southampton in 1903; and Macarthur had been succeeded by Walter Pym, who had been translated from Mauritius. Mylne had taught at Keble, and Macarthur had been trained at Cuddesdon; but Pym was a Cambridge man, and came from a very different theological stable. In a *Charge* delivered in the course of his Primary Visitation of the diocese in 1907 he ostensibly sought to regularise a number of aspects of worship and practice across the see. In practice, he meant to curb Anglo-Catholicism in his diocese.

Among the practices he objected to were the use of holy water; the burning of incense, except in a static censer to sweeten the air; the blessing of palms on Palm Sunday; and the liturgical observation of any feast not mentioned in the BCP. As he intended to abolish the keeping of All Souls' Day and the offering

16 SSJE/2/3/72ff.
17 cf "The Development of the Divine Office", *Cowley Evangelist*, Sept 1912.
18 *CE* Nov 1908.
19 Elwin, 8 June 1904.
20 Ley, 6 May 1913.
21 J. H. Overton, *The Anglican Revival*, London: Blackie & Son (1897), 199ff.

of requiems, he also suggested that the Guild of All Souls – which had been founded in 1873 by Arthur Tooth, one of the "ritualist martyrs" imprisoned in the wake of the Public Worship Regulation Act of 1874 – ought to "disappear".

Although he was willing to allow the Cowley Fathers and other clergymen who wore Eucharistic vestments to "benefit by the doubt" surrounding the interpretation of the Ornaments Rubric, Pym also contended that "ritual and practices which represent Roman teaching are the very ritual and practices which in our own Church are at the root of our present trouble". Accordingly, he sought to suppress the reservation of the Blessed Sacrament and any gestures that might suggest adoration of the consecrated elements at mass – he particularly advised "the discontinuation of such *pauses* even for the sake of your private devotion as materially interrupt the prayer, and suggest that you are secretly reciting the Roman Canon of the Mass".

This all led up to the main points of the *Charge*: that the offering of bread and wine was not more than a commemoration of the Sacrifice of Calvary; and that the Real Presence was effected in the reception of Holy Communion by the devout believer. "The consecration prayer", he argued, "works no such miracle in the bread and wine."[22] He also forbade the celebration of mass when there were fewer than three communicants present; and the attendance of unconfirmed children, except those who "on some *one* Sunday before they make their first Communion, may be allowed to attend".

Pym effectively took up a theme that was by then seven decades old: that those who advanced a fuller understanding of theology and liturgical practice than that which seemed to be explicitly laid down in the letter of the BCP were not loyal sons of the Reformation. It was an accusation almost as old as the Oxford Movement itself, with its crucible in Newman and Keble's publication of Froude's *Remains* in the late 1830s.[23] "They ignore or repudiate the religious changes of the Reformation," wrote Pym, "and speak of them with hatred and contempt." He singled out Viscount Halifax and the English Church Union for particular criticism.

> [W]hen Lord Halifax speaks on such a subject, we cannot regard his utterance as that of an individual Layman, for he is the President of the *English Church Union*, a powerful organisation within the Church, composed of a large number of Clergy as well as of Laymen, who undoubtedly whole the same views of their President.

In attacking Halifax and the ECU, Pym also attacked – through its leading patron and overlapping membership – the SSJE. "We ought to be very thankful for having such a man as Lord Halifax," Benson had written, during the ritual controversies of 1899.

> If he were gone, who could we look to? No one could take his place. His position is very difficult. He has to speak as a lay pope. It is not his incline but his position

---

22 Pym, *Charge*, 1907.

23 John Henry Newman & John Keble (eds), *Remains of the late Reverend Richard Hurrell Froude*, London: J. G. and F. Rivington (1838–39). Cf, *inter alia*, Piers Brendon, "Newman, Keble, and *Froude's Remains*", *The English Historical Review*, vol.87, no.345 (Oct 1972), 697ff.

which necessitates it. It is a great mercy that he speaks so firmly and yet does not slip into mere self-will [...] To strengthen him and stand by him is to help forward the eventual triumph of order and harmony.[24]

The brethren in India received the *Charge* with horror. Elwin wrote home urgently to say that "till you have read it, you will not be able to realise how critical the situation is". He pleaded for "a most earnest consideration" by the members of the Society in Oxford as to what sort of stand should be taken. As early as 1866 the *Church Times* had trumpeted that "the Real Presence and the Unbloody Sacrifice are the two hinges of that mystic rite";[25] but now he was clear that "the whole of the Indian work may be in jeopardy".

On certain points concessions might be made. The Society was not prepared to go to the stake over the thurible, for example – even if Godfrey Callaway later felt that in South Africa that "we really needed the fragrant smoke of incense. There is no outward symbol in the Church's worship which appeals to me more."[26] In 1899 it had briefly ceased to be used during High Mass at Cowley, after Bishop William Stubbs had asked the Society to defer for the moment to the negative *Opinion* of the Archbishops of Canterbury and York on the matter.[27] During its suspension the community church was instead "perfumed with incense by the Deacon and Subdeacon" beforehand, which Puller thought "a slight modification of the usage of the Eastern Church".[28] Pym's *Charge*, however – while in places echoing the earlier Archbishops' *Opinion* – was now so "distinctly against that doctrine concerning the Blessed Sacrament, for which the Church has suffered so much" that there could be no desertion, and no surrender.[29]

The *Cowley Evangelist* immediately laid out the grounds on which the Society would now have to proceed, and "the truth for which we wish to contend". It united itself with the statement issued by prominent Tractarians in the wake of the Denison case of 1856,[30] and to the same constituency's *Letter to the Archbishop of Canterbury* of 1867;[31] and its position boiled down to two main points.

We believe that, as in heaven, Christ, our Great High Priest, ever offers Himself before the Eternal Father, pleading by His presence His Sacrifice of Himself once offered on the Cross; so on earth, in the Holy Eucharist, that same Body, once for all sacrificed for us, and that same Blood, once for all shed for us, sacramentally present, are offered and pleaded before the Father by the priest, as our Lord ordained to be done in remembrance of Himself, when He instituted the Blessed Sacrament of his Body and Blood.

24 Benson, 17 Feb 1900, CUL MS(Add.7651) Wyon/9/3/34.
25 *Church Times*, 10 Nov 1866.
26 Callaway, 31 March 1926.
27 Frederick Temple & William Maclagan, *The Archbishops on the Lawfulness of the Liturgical Use of Incense and the Carrying of Lights in Procession*, London: Macmillan & Co. (1899).
28 Puller, 2 Oct 1899, CUL, MS (Add.7651) WYON/9/3/99.
29 Elwin, 8 Feb 1907.
30 Chadwick, *Victorian Church*, i:493ff.
31 Reed, *Glorious Battle*, 64.

We believe that Christ Himself, really and truly, but spiritually and ineffably, present in the Sacrament, is therein to be adored.[32]

Benson voiced his own opposition to Pym in a letter to Richard Traill, reassuring him that "it is by the power of the Holy Ghost descending from Heaven at Pentecost that we are called to consecrate the Bread and Wine, and make them channels of mediatorial grace by their Identification with the Mediatorial Head of the Covenant. If we do not realise the supernatural character of this Presence we cannot believe in the spiritual glory of the ascended Saviour."[33]

"It will require all the collective wisdom of the Society, under God's good guidance, to steer us through these troubled waters," thought Elwin;[34] and it was the necessity of consultation that precipitated the next stage of the business. As men in religious vows the brethren in India – and it affected all of them, as the SSJE's permanent Indian work was entirely based in the Diocese of Bombay – could not take a personal view of whether or not they would or could accede to Pym's requirement. Any decision would have to be taken at Cowley; and the response would have to be a corporate one, led by the Superior General.

Elwin's instinct was that Pym would not "budge an inch", and that the matter would come down to opposing him outright on two points: "the exclusion of our children from mass"; and the enforcement of the three-communicants rule, which in some places "would deprive many souls of the communions which are to them their very life". The ritual proscriptions would also have to be resisted, "on the ground that they symbolise a doctrine which he will not tolerate". He feared that Pym would withdraw the licence of any priest who refused to comply with the directions of the *Charge*, but that whatever happened the Cowley Fathers must stay with their people "at whatever spiritual sacrifice for ourselves"; and that there was already enough support in the wider Church for the day to be won. "If we hold on, even if we have to go for our communions to one of the cantonment churches, we must win."[35]

Far away in Boston, even the members of the Tuesday-evening Bible Class at Bowdoin Street were outraged, and sent an alms-offering to Bombay "as a token of sympathy with the S.S.J.E. there in its present difficulties".[36] Nicholson wanted it to be generally made known that "we have not got any extravagances of ritual in our Churches" – and as we have seen, the Society's liturgy had lagged behind the developing ritualism of more advanced establishments. Furthermore, any ritual practices that existed had "been in long use and sanctioned by previous Bishops" – although, knowing these defences were likely to be used, Pym had made a point of dismissing them at the outset.[37]

---

32 *CE* April 1907.
33 Benson, 29 April 1907.
34 Elwin, 17 Feb 1907.
35 Elwin, 22 Feb 1907.
36 Field, 11 April 1907.
37 Nicholson, 23 March 1907.

REQUIREMENT 24

In May 1907 the *Cowley Evangelist* thanked its readers for the support the Society was receiving from its "many kind friends", and gave a flavour of its feelings on the matter by reproducing William Draper's poem "Die Fighting". It also gave a reassurance that the Society was confident of a satisfactory outcome, "though it is not possible to say much now".[38] Page had in fact taken advice from Darwell Stone, the Principal of Pusey House, which was later published as an open letter.

Stone considered that Pym had overreached himself: that he had misunderstood the obligations placed on the clergy by their oath of allegiance to the Crown, on which he had rested much of his case; that he had misinterpreted Reformation-era practices through want of knowledge, and made errors "which could hardly have been made by anyone who had the facts clearly before his mind"; that he had misunderstood the position of the Anglican divines, particularly Richard Hooker; that he had presented as mere Receptionism the rich and ancient theology of the concept of Spiritual Communion; and, effectively, that his arguments against allowing children to be present at mass might as well have been plucked out of thin air.

All these historical and theological points, thought Stone, might well be placed before Pym to see if he could be persuaded to pursue a different course. But he also made the point that if the Society's licences were withdrawn, with "the eventual result of the break up of your native congregations and the removal from the diocese of your clergy and of the Sisters who belong to the Communities of All Saints and of St Mary's, Wantage", then "such results might have disastrous consequences in the way of destroying the confidence and shaking the faith of native Christians, and even some of the native clergy".

"The harm which may thus be done", wrote Stone, "might not be confined to the diocese of Bombay or even to India". This widened the scope of the controversy considerably, and in itself called for action from the Indian bench.

> I cannot think that decisions so far reaching in their consequences ought to be wholly at the discretion of an individual Bishop, especially when the form in which they come is that of the reversal of a very deliberate policy of eminent predecessors, who knew India well [...]

> [T]he Indian Bishops other than the Bishop of Bombay cannot be regarded as without concern in the matter. As Bishops of the Catholic Church they have an indefeasible right to a share in the rule of Church affairs throughout the Province. On no sound principle of Church government can such matters be determined in one diocese in independence of what is done in the other dioceses of which the Province is made up.

Stone also suggested that Pym might be well-advised to consult the Archbishop of Canterbury, Randall Davidson, on the prudence of "whether a sudden

---

38 *CE* May 1907.

prohibition of what has long been allowed ought to be pushed to extremes by an individual Bishop" before the 1908 Lambeth Conference had met.[39]

Puller was impressed by Stone's letter, and thought that Pym was "very much at sea". From his own scholarship he rejected the instruction, which Pym had also made, for mass to be said on Good Friday and Easter Eve. Although he favoured a more pacific course, he was also adamant that the matter of the children's exclusion had to be fought all the way;[40] and "Requirement 24" soon became the mast to which the Society fastened its colours.

After a heated meeting with a number of the Indian brethren on 17 June, Pym wrote an angry letter to Nicholson, as Provincial Superior, which he also released to the newspapers. He accused the SSJE of having been ringleaders of "agitation" against him in his own diocese; and stated that while many of the clergy had acquiesced in his demands, "it has rested with your own Community and those closely associated with you to persist in refusing me obedience". He was also furious that "it was admitted by you and the others that you must be guided, not by the wishes and directions of your Bishop, but by the advice of friends in England [...] What right Mr Darwell Stone has to interfere in the affairs of this Diocese, or what claim he has upon your obedience compared with the claim which I have as your bishop, I am at a loss to understand."

Pym did not grasp – or refused to acknowledge – the fact that Stone's part in the matter was incidental: he had merely advised Page, albeit publicly, on the matter. Colin Stephenson later observed that Stone was "consulted by everyone in the Church of England like a Delphic oracle",[41] and on the basis of his advice Page had instructed the Indian brethren in the course they were to take. Now their obedience to their Superior General – whether or not it aligned with their personal views on the matter, which of course it did – brought them, Pym claimed, "under ecclesiastical censure". On that basis he was resolved to treat the Society's work as "extra diocesan", and so terminate its eligibility for access to diocesan funds.

The *Cowley Evangelist* responded robustly, pointing out the obligations relating to canonical obedience dealt with in the first and second of the Society's Statutes.

> Our Fathers in India are, therefore, doubly pledged, both as priests of the Church of England, and as members of the Society of St John the Evangelist, to acknowledge the Bishop of Bombay's authority [...] The Bishop's authority is, however, not an unlimited authority, but a constitutional authority; and our Fathers in India hold that in his recent Charge the Bishop has made certain requirements, and given certain orders, in regard to which he had no authority to demand the obedience of his clergy.

---

39 Darwell Stone, *Letter to the Rev. R. L. Page, Father Superior General of the Society of St John the Evangelist*, 12 March 1907.

40 Puller, 4 April 1907.

41 Colin Stephenson, *Merrily on High: An Anglo-Catholic Memoir*, London: Darton, Longman & Todd (1972), 63.

It also called Pym's teaching on the Eucharist "very inadequate and, in some of its negations, grievously erroneous". As such, there would be no change in the way in which mass was celebrated, or to who was allowed to attend, in the Society's churches in the Diocese of Bombay until the Indian brethren "can feel certain that this or that requirement is not based on a view of the Holy Eucharist which contradicts the teachings of Our Lord". The Society therefore intended to take the matter to the Bishop of Calcutta, Reginald Copleston, for adjudication in his capacity as Metropolitan of India.

> Our Fathers will be quite ready to vindicate their orthodoxy and the legitimacy of their practice before any properly arranged tribunal which the Metropolitan of India and his Suffragans may see fit to constitute. Our Fathers do not claim to be judges of their own cause. They belong to a Diocese which forms part of a Province, and that Province has for its chief ruler a Metropolitan, to whom the Bishop of Bombay has presumably taken an Oath of Due Obedience.[42]

Otherwise, business continued as usual. Elwin got on with overseeing the final touches to St Crispin's; Traill found a permanent spot for a mission room in Poona City; and Nicholson continued working on the plans for new St Peter's.[43] But the issue at stake was not only the preservation of the Society's day-to-day work in India. As the Superior General observed at General Chapter in 1907, it was, more than anything, an opportunity for the SSJE to have "the privilege of bearing witness to true Eucharistic doctrine".[44]

Pym soon realised that Society was in no mood to compromise on Requirement 24, the matter of the attendance of children at mass. He therefore played his trump card, and refused to countenance consecrating new St Peter's at Mazagon until his instructions had been effected. At this stage the appeal to the Metropolitan became crucial; and Puller – who was on furlough at Cowley – was duly despatched to Bombay to help.[45]

Nicholson's appeal – "To the Most Reverend Father in God Reginald Stephen, by Divine Permission Lord Bishop of Calcutta, and Metropolitan of the Province of India and Ceylon"[46] – claimed that Pym had "taken divers coercive measures to enforce obedience to the said requirements, insisting that he has legal authority to impose the same". The appeal centred round Requirement 24: it was submitted to be "illegal and *ultra vires*" and that "in making and insisting upon obedience to the same" Pym had exceeded his lawful authority. An associated submission, relating to Requirement 35, was that no priest should be coerced to say mass on Good Friday and Easter Eve.

The appeal argued that "in the matters hereafter set forth, the Lord Bishop has misused his lawful powers and authority as Bishop of Bombay, and has conducted himself unlawfully and oppressively towards your Petitioner and

---

42 *CE* Aug 1907.

43 Ibid; Nicholson, 3 Aug 1907; Traill, 11 July 1907.

44 SSJE/2/3/60.

45 *CE* Nov 1907. Puller's contribution to the proceedings was later published as *Non-Communicating Attendance*.

46 SSJE/9/1/5/8/2.

others of his Clergy", causing "great scandal and dismay" in the diocese and in the Church at large.

Nicholson then summarised Pym's offences in seven points.

1. In associating the established custom and practice of much of the diocese with "strange doctrine" he had held up to public opprobrium not only the present clergy who practised it, but also his predecessors in the See.
2. He had made in public "divers grievous unfounded charges" against Nicholson and his brethren:
   (a) That they had sought to tarnish Pym's reputation.
   (b) That they had taken orders from Darwell Stone rather than himself.
   (c) That they had refused to acknowledge his episcopal authority.
   (d) That they had been antagonistic towards him.
   (e) That he had placed them under ecclesiastical censure.
3. He had cut off the rights of the Cowley Fathers to benefit from diocesan funds.
4. He had said he would not license any more members of the SSJE for work in the diocese, "threatening in effect to destroy and bring to an end" the Society's work in India.
5. He had refused to consecrate new St Peter's, "for the purpose of coercing".
6. He had threatened to deprive Nicholson of the cure of Mazagon.
7. He had intimated that he would see to it that the S.P.C.K. withdrew its grant for Gertrude Bradley's medical work in Bombay.

Nicholson concluded his petition by asking Copleston to act on a number of points. He wanted:

1. The revocation of Requirement 24, relating to the presence of unconfirmed children at mass.
2. A declaration that Requirement 35, which imposed the compulsory celebration of mass on Good Friday and Easter Eve, was non-binding.
3. A ruling on whether or not the presence of unconfirmed children at mass was a representation of "strange doctrine".
4. A ruling on the accusations made by Pym against the Society.
5. A public recantation from Pym, should the accusations be unfounded.
6. A declaration of whether or not the Cowley Fathers in Bombay could be under ecclesiastical censure given that none of them had been convicted of any ecclesiastical offence by an Ecclesiastical Court; and a public statement to that effect.
7. A cancellation of any kind of censure that Pym had purported to pass, and a direction that in future he "proceed in all matters of Ecclesiastical discipline in due form of law".
8. A declaration that Pym was wrong to have declared that the Cowley Fathers in his diocese were "extra-diocesan"; a statement of their restoration to the full rights and privileges of the diocesan clergy; and a direction that Pym was to act as bishop in the Society's churches as in any other in the diocese.

9. A decree that Pym would "consecrate, dedicate, or license" new St Peter's as soon as it was completed.
10. A declaration that Pym could not refuse to grant licenses to qualified clergymen on whim.
11. An inquiry into whether or not Pym had attempted to influence the SPCK to the detriment of the SSJE medical work.
12. An absolute ruling "that it is unlawful for the Lord Bishop to use his episcopal powers and authority for the correction of the Clergy or Laity of his Diocese, expect in the manner and for the purposes provided by law".

The hearing was originally fixed for 7 January, 1908. Puller was to argue the theological and liturgical points and the Society's lawyer in Bombay was to present the legal case. Pym, however, was known to be in poor health; and with the agreements of all parties it was postponed to 18 February. But things began to look bright, as with the announcement of the postponement Copleston directed that Nicholson should not in the interim be hindered in any way in his work at St Peter's. "We shall patiently await the judgment which the Metropolitan will deliver," noted the *Cowley Evangelist*, "confident that we shall not fail to obtain whatever is just."

The Society received with relief a telegram from Nicholson a few days after the hearing had begun, "telling us of the happy ending of our anxiety".[47] Details would have to wait until the letters arrived from India a couple of weeks later; but the *Times* reported that "the Bishop of Calcutta, Metropolitan of India, has decided that the attendance of unconfirmed children at Holy Communion does not necessarily imply a strange doctrine, and cannot legally be prohibited."[48] It soon became clear that "the three points which our Fathers brought before [the Metropolitan] have been one and all decided in our favour."[49]

TRIUMPH & DISASTER

By the time he was defeated Pym had already repented of much of his hot-headedness. He wrote a conciliatory letter to Henry Lord, who was by then ministering in the Konkan, recanting his former accusation of disloyalty to the diocese because of his association with, and support of, the SSJE: "I write to say that as far as I associated you with that Society in the expression 'Extra Diocesan' [...] that expression is withdrawn." He closed "with the prayer that a smoother course now lies before us all". The Indian brethren were also "looking forward hopefully and happily to the peaceful development of their Mission Work" in the diocese; but any concerns they might have harboured about their relationship with the bishop in the future were swept away on 2 March, when he conveniently died.

47 CE March 1908.
48 *The Times*, 22 Feb 1908.
49 CE April 1908.

Pym had been seriously ill for some time; and, keen to demonstrate that all was forgiven, the *Cowley Evangelist* paid him fulsome tribute and praised his determination to work until the very end. "We wait in prayer and hope," it concluded, "that such an appointment may be made to the vacant Diocese as shall ensure the peace thus inaugurated being carried on to the fullest realisation."[50] It was a sign of things to come that, after his ruling in the Society's favour, Copleston chose to spend Easter Day at Poona.[51]

Herbert Asquith, only just in office, did not disappoint. Edwin Palmer was Chaplain of Balliol, and his father had been Archdeacon of Oxford. Among his uncles were William Palmer, the celebrated High Churchman, and Roundell Palmer, twice Lord Chancellor under Gladstone, and 1st Earl of Selborne. He was known for being "moderate in opinion and accommodating in all things except where basic beliefs and principles were involved";[52] and the Society could hardly have asked for a more satisfactory outcome. When Maxwell addressed the General Chapter for the first time as Superior General later in the year, he spoke of "the thankfulness which we feel for the ending of our troubles in India, and for the appointment of the new Bishop of Bombay."[53]

The Society that Maxwell came to govern was firmly established as an institution well able to use its pooled wisdom and resources to overcome local difficulties, and one with significant international interests and sympathisers – at Dedication Festival at St Edward's House in Petertide 1908 the guests included the Bishops of Pittsburg, Los Angeles, Milwaukee, Pretoria, and Zanzibar, and the Bishop in Madagascar, all of whom were in England for the Lambeth Conference.[54]

The triumph in Bombay had also marked out the SSJE as a champion of the advancement of the Catholic Church, in its broad sense, through its mission of service, prayer, and teaching; but the new Superior General knew well that a wise course would have to be steered between the ongoing demands placed upon his community, and what was practically possible with the men available. If Bombay represented the Society's overseas success on a grand scale, almost simultaneously Iona spoke of smaller disappointment nearer home.

The House of Retreat on Iona had been something of a white elephant since the SSJE had received its care in 1896. Mindful of St Columba's prophecy that permanent monastic life would be destroyed and then restored on the island, Alexander Chinnery-Haldane had hoped that the SSJE "might be called to take its share in so glorious a restoration".[55] Benson had echoed the sentiment, and wondered whether Iona might become "a centre of future Missionary effort, as of old".[56] But the Society had only been able to maintain a summer presence on the island, when most visitors came, and after Chinnery-Haldane's death

50 Ibid.
51 Traill, 18 March 1908
52 *The Times*, 30 March 1954.
53 SSJE/2/3/88.
54 *CE* Aug 1908.
55 *CE* Oct 1906.
56 Benson, 7 June 1900, SSJE/6/1/2/3/4/8ff.

in 1906 Page had lamented that he could not but have been "disappointed at the little progress the Society was able to make in response to so high a call".[57]

As usual, funds came in immediately; but it may be that the timing of Page's appeal was not coincidental. Although he had overcome Benson's objections to St Edward's House, he can hardly have disregarded them entirely. The House of Retreat represented an opportunity for brethren more suited to the deep contemplative side of religious life to be able to engage more deeply with a life of prayer and reflection, far away from the hustle and bustle of the towns and cities in which the SSJE now mainly operated.

Thomas Bignold was duly sent to take charge at Iona at the start of September 1906, "primarily to live in retirement and prayer" with Br Robert, a newly-professed lay brother.[58] As winter drew on, the reasons for the island's out-of-season quietness began to present themselves. Not only was it far away from the SSJE's urban centres; it was far away from almost anywhere. Although Bignold was able to keep the Rule, offer mass daily, and to pray regularly and for longer unbroken periods than at Cowley,[59] the Glasgow steamer could only dock and unload fresh food when the sea was calm enough. By the end of November, the brethren were "feeding on old cow salted and pickled pig".[60]

When Trenholme went to join them for Christmas, the *Fingal* was "tossed like an egg-shell" on its way across from Mull. A message arrived soon after his arrival from the neighbouring Maclaine of Lochbuie, "asking us to give them Christmas Services".[61] He duly returned to Mull, expecting to return on St Stephen's Day; but was foiled by "a raging snow-storm [that] has been going on all day, blowing and snowing and drifting". Iona was "bitterly cold with a gale from the N.W., about the worst storm we have had yet", and the island was covered with snow to a depth of several inches. "Our poor Father Trenholme", shivered Bignold. "When shall we get him back?"[62] He finally returned on 4 January: ten days after he had left, and having been snowed in at Lochbuie Castle for a week.[63]

A year later new stoves had been installed at the House of Retreat, and coke for them was being delivered by steamer from Greenock; but the roof still leaked.[64] Page and Kenneth Mackenzie, Chinnery-Haldane's successor as Bishop of Argyll & the Isles, both went to Iona to keep St Columba's Day on 9 June 1907. The Superior General preached, and said that "he believed that God had called the S.S.J.E. to revive that work which S. Columba had carried on". It was a lofty ambition; but in more immediate terms the Society saw the "special object" of their presence on Iona as being "to afford the members of the Society an opportunity of greater retirement and to allow of more prolonged and uninterrupted prayer and intercession".

---

57 *CE* Oct 1906.
58 Bignold, 9 Jan 1907; *CE* July 1941.
59 Bignold, 21 & 23 Nov 1906.
60 Bignold, 3 Dec 1906.
61 Trenholme, 22 Dec 1906.
62 Bignold, 26 Dec 1906.
63 Trenholme, 16 Jan 1907.
64 Bignold, 9 Jan 1908.

If in some of our Houses there is a call to exercise more largely our calling as "Mission Priests", it seems desirable that in other houses there should be special facilities for the exercise of the more retired side of our life as Priests of a religious community. In this way we can make provision for the needs of all.[65]

The development was not a success. Maxwell decided not to make the brethren on Iona endure another freezing winter on the island, explaining at the General Chapter of 1908 that the island was lonely, and too remote for effective mission work. Experience had shown that the weather might easily leave the brethren "imprisoned", and unable to fulfil engagements they had undertaken; while for most visitors it was "too inaccessible to be of any great use".

It is disappointing to have to acknowledge this, but it is evident that however suitable the house might be for a Religious Order whose Vocation demanded not only inward separation but outward seclusion from the world it is very little suited to be the home of a body of Religious who are also Mission Priests.

Iona represented, he said, "a life so unlike the normal vocation of our Society" that he had decided to bring the experiment to a close.[66] Apologising for the disappointment that it would cause the supporters of the Scottish work, the *Cowley Evangelist* announced that "it has been decided to give up the attempt to occupy our House in Iona permanently."[67] The property was handed over to Mackenzie, as per the conditions of the original deed of gift,[68] in the hope "that some day [Chinnery-Haldane's] House may be the home of faithful Religious, who will be not wholly unworthy followers of those who so many centuries ago filled the Island with the odour of sanctity".[69]

LIFE & GROWTH

It was a sign of the buoyancy of the overseas work that in 1906 the Statutes had been amended to allow the setting-up of Provincial Finance committees – with the strict injunctions that no individual mission should spend over £100 on a single item without consulting the Provincial Chapter; and that any proposed expenditure over £2000 was to be referred to General Chapter.[70] Money, however, was less of a problem than manpower; and the rate of attrition among the lay novices had become a cause of concern. At General Chapter in 1908, Lucius Cary – who had succeeded Maxwell as Assistant Superior – laid the issues bare.

Cary thought that the Rule, inasmuch as it pertained to the lay brothers, needed to be altered, as not enough laymen who came as postulants were

65 *CE* June 1907.
66 SSJE/2/3/91ff.
67 *CE* Oct 1908.
68 SSJE/2/3/129.
69 *CE* June 1909.
70 SSJE/2/3/18.

proceeding to profession. "The Brothers are dedicated to God side by side with us by Vows as complete as our own," he noted.

> It is impossible to foresee what the future may bring, but since they themselves are dumb amongst us, and absolutely in our hands for all governance and all changes, any question bearing upon their undertaking on this life needs to be treated with the greatest consideration.

Unlike the choir brethren, who returned to their priestly functions after their own novitiate – "while we were learning the meaning of self-suppression and consecration" – a lay brother, "instead of consecrating his antecedents that he may receive back his life enlarged and amplified", fully left his old life behind when he entered the novitiate. Cary thought he had at that stage "no certain prospect before him of any occupation more inspiring than a routine of house work". The opportunity for a lay brother to work in the colonies might be a more interesting prospect, but he noted that "these openings are not numerous".

> They are not sufficiently definitely contemplated in the organisation of our Mission to justify, at least at present, the *promise* of such prospects to individual aspirants [my italics].[71] Ordinarily therefore he has still the same 'daily round and common task' of work in the house, and ministering to our comforts.

The sacrifice for the lay brothers was greater: a priest who left the Society could simply return to being a secular priest, as Walter Wyon had done; but a lay brother who was not elected to profession could find himself "stranded, having cut himself off from his old life". There were, Cary lamented, "several recent examples of Lay Novices who have left us, and have found it as a very serious matter to have spent some years among us". Br Maynard was an obvious exception – but he had entered the Society before the regulations had been drawn up. Now any layman who came with "possibilities and abilities" was liable to be set to housework, without any opportunity for continuing to practise his trade or other skills to benefit the life of the house.

Others fared better. Br Michael came to Cowley from service in 1902, and was set to work in the kitchen – during Lent he relied heavily on letters from his godmother, filled with suggestions for vegetarian dishes. As his profession approached he was trained for missionary work, given a part in the local pastoral work, the Sunday School, and the Catechism classes. He also helped train the servers – it was as a sacristan that he had first encountered Benson, and through his work in the sanctuary that he had first come to feel called to the religious life. He was professed in 1907, and was sent to take charge of the domestic arrangements at St Edward's House a year later; where he was also given a large amount of outside work to do, including assisting successive chaplains at the nearby Refuge for Girls in Tufton Street.[72]

Michael entered the Society with no formal qualifications, and his progress was indicative of what might be achieved if postulants and novices were given

---

71 Br Arthur was already working at Poona, and Br John at Tsolo; whereas Br Maynard's had been a special case.
72 Taylor, *Brother Michael*, 10ff.

the right support. But that could frequently be lacking; and the deliberate distinction between the choir and lay brethren in the Rule could make some of the choir brethren appear cold and unfriendly: "Brothers have complained that for month after month they have not been once spoken to by one of the Fathers except for the necessary demands to supply household needs." The converse, however, could also be true – a series of long and affectionate letters exchanged between Congreve and Br John, for example, demonstrate the deep bond that had developed between them despite the considerable disparity in their age and backgrounds.[73]

Cary proposed renewable three-year vows, with the possibility of life vows after special applications, and "after an additional testing such as a foreign service". Congreve agreed with the Assistant Superior that the lay brothers' sacrifice was greater; but in consequence was unsure whether it was fair to expect the lay brothers to take life vows at all. At Greater Chapter 1913 it was agreed that the lay brethren's novitiate should be reduced to two years, followed by a five-year period of renewable annual vows (or a three-year period if a man was over thirty); after which life vows might be taken.[74]

Congreve was sanguine about the fact that the Rule had been a long time in its development: "We have had our lessons to learn and we are not surprised at some mistakes and failures."[75] Nearly twenty years later the Society was still discussing how best to retain lay brothers after the attrition of the First World War – in 1920 the Home Provincial Chapter resolved that "they should be encouraged to look forward to the exercise of any natural or spiritual gifts that they may possess, *provided* [my italics] that the Religious basis of this life be always presented"[76] – and it was not until 1923 that definitive action was taken.[77]

At the beginning of 1909 Congreve set out his thoughts on some of the benefits of the revived religious life in the Church of England; both for the individual making religious profession, and for the Church at large.

Our special joy is the recovery of a treasure that was supposed lost to us for ever. Here is a power of the life of Christ re-discovered among us, a long-forgotten force breaking out to our surprise in the Church. It is an encouragement to find by experience that God can do, and is doing for us still, what no one expected, or what was supposed impossible. In our childhood who are old, the idea that Houses of men and of women living religiously under monastic rule might ever again come to be in the English Church was quite unthinkable. To-day they exist; their number is considerable, and their work and character acknowledged.

In this, the Cowley Fathers had been the harbingers of the stable men's communities; and in addition to their set-apart life of prayer they had also played their part in mitigating various social needs – as the ancient monasteries had done in days of yore – through their schools, clinics, and workshops, both at

---

73 SSJE/6/5/2/2.
74 SSJE/2/5.
75 SSJE/2/3/95ff.
76 SSJE/3/1/73.
77 SSJE/2/5/1.

home and in the colonies: they were "poor for Christ's sake, in order to help the poor, the sick, the children, and the sinful".

Congreve particularly dwelt on the raising up of new members of the Society; at this point not necessarily in numerical terms – although that was an ongoing consideration – but in the implication of fresh professions.

> For us who have followed in this service, however imperfectly, for many years, each new Profession is a renewal of our youth. We remember that once we were kneeling to receive this grace [...] We who are seniors must support and encourage the younger by the brave sincerity of our religious aim. The youngest should be able to recognise in us as we grow in years the deepening tide of the same grace which has brought them here.[78]

This was no empty sentimentality. Charles Gardner's death at Poona in 1908 had underlined two aspects of the situation in which the SSJE found itself. The first was the SSJE's longstanding international character. Gardner was an American, who had come to Society as a postulant through the house at Boston in 1870. He had weathered the storm of the 1880s and had kept faith with Cowley; but had since spent two-thirds of his time in India, which he loved, and where he had always hoped to die.[79]

The second was more immediately pressing. Gardner had never enjoyed particularly good health; but he had become increasingly frail and had spent much of the year before his death in hospital, recovering from a fall. A number of the early members of the Society, including some of its stalwarts, were now well-advanced in years. Gardner was replaced at Poona by Page, whose own health was beginning to fail, and who returned to the work from which he had been called in 1890 and in which he was expert – although he never quite managed to master Marathi.[80]

When Alfred Langmore died at Bombay at the end of 1911, however, there were not enough brethren at home for him to be replaced. As the *Cowley Evangelist* observed, numbers were dependent on the movement of the Holy Spirit.

> [I]t would be quite contrary to the principles upon which our Society has been founded to seek to add to our numbers by suggesting to anyone that he should join us. Those who come to us come because God has spoken to their hearts and has given them grace to recognise His call to the Religious life, as it is realised in our Society.[81]

The Indian work was further compromised when Oswald Barton fell and broke his hip at Yerendawana at about the same time, and was confined to bed for twelve weeks.[82] Congreve, too, was beginning to feel his age; and towards the end of 1912 his recollections of the early days of the Oxford Movement

---

78 *CE* Jan 1909.
79 *CE* July 1908.
80 Elwin, 1 Nov 1912.
81 *CE* Jan 1912.
82 Moore, 1 Dec 1911.

appeared in the pages of the *Cowley Evangelist*. When his trusty razor began to fail – "its handle is broken, and the blade wearing out" – he told John that he thought himself "so dilapidated that I do not feel that I am worth keeping in repair".[83] He and his sister at Clewer had decided to follow the convent doctor's advice to "make friends of your limitations".[84]

Despite these setbacks and concerns about numbers, there nevertheless remained life and growth in the Society as Maxwell's term of office progressed. The work of the London house thrived; and the colonial work continued to bloom.[85] The development of the lay novitiate bore particular fruit; and by 1916 there were a dozen professed lay brothers. By then Br Maynard had been reduced to hobbling around on two sticks, and Br James was in poor health; but Br William served as sacristan, Br Robert took care of the house linen and oversaw the servers, and Br John looked after the kitchens. Br Michael was working in London; Br Arthur ran the workshop at Poona and looked after the servers at Holy Name; while Br Herbert looked after the domestic affairs of the house in Cape Town, and ran the boys' club at St Philip's.[86]

The Society had also entered a new phase of confidence after its recent victory in Bombay. At Mazagon the new St Peter's Church was dedicated by Palmer with full pomp and ceremony on 25 January 1909, the feast of the Conversion of St Paul. With the clergy of his diocese he "proceeded to different parts of the Church, the altar, the font, the lectern, the pulpit, etc, making a station at each and saying appropriate prayers."[87] The strictures and threats of his unhappy predecessor, like their instigator, were dead and buried.

---

83 Congreve, 25 Oct 1912, SSJE/6/5/2/2/13/26a.
84 Congreve, 20 Sept 1912, SSJE/6/5/2/2/13/21a.
85 *CE* Feb 1912.
86 Bull, 29 June 1916, SSJE/2/5/1.
87 Nicholson, 30 Jan 1909.

12

FAITH AND WORKS

From many an ancient river, from many a palmy plain,
They call us to deliver their land from error's chain.

—Reginald Heber[1]

Minor setbacks notwithstanding, the Society of St John the Evangelist's work under Gerald Maxwell continued to flourish. Edward Trenholme even managed to salvage something from the disappointment of Iona with a well-received book on the history of the island, which he had begun "with the scenes before my eyes day by day".[2] The Society's ecclesiological position had come to be acknowledged as an authentic expression of part of the life of the Church of England; and it had thoroughly defeated an attempt to see its eucharistic theology constrained. It also continued to be well-supported by the Fellowship of St John and other donors, although Edward Elwin thought – after he had mentioned in a letter how useful the gift of a regular copy of *The Sphere* had been – that some of the Society's benefactors had perhaps more money than sense.

> The moral of this, if it had a moral at all, was that a similar publication, sent with the same care, would be equally useful. But the moral which quite a number of people drew from this chance remark was that, if one *Sphere* was useful, several *Spheres* would be more useful, and so we were inundated with stray *Spheres*, and even bundles of *Spheres*, which we had already seen.[3]

The new Mission House at Mazagon was completed by May 1909, and the Superior General took advantage of the definitive break with the old site to reorganise the Indian work – sending Hugh Nicholson to take over at Poona, John Biscoe to succeed him at Bombay, and transferring Sydney Moore to work at Umarkhadi.[4] Letters home sending greetings at Patronal Festival that year related a flurry of packing and moving; although Nicholson reported that all that actual lifting and carrying was being done by "coolies, supervised by the Peon".[5]

---

1 Reginald Heber, "From Greenland's Icy Mountains", 1819.
2 Edward Craig Trenholme SSJE, *The Story of Iona*, Edinburgh: David Douglas (1909), vii.
3 *CE* March 1912.
4 *CE* June 1909.
5 Nicholson, 14 May 1909.

By June the rains had flooded the chapel, but Biscoe was optimistic: "a first monsoon is sure to manifest the weak places in a building, and the rest of the house has not suffered much." He was less impressed with the fact that the coolies had dumped the books from the library in their new home "in great heaps, irrespective of classification", and Henry Chard, who by then had been sent to India, was trying to sort them out.[6]

A friend of the Society wrote to Cowley from Poona at the end of 1908 to say that he thought the finished work at Yerendawana had "absolute simplicity, and yet wonderful beauty and dignity". To his delight, he had found Elwin in the Compound, supervising the orphans in a game of cricket.[7] The village *patel* had been persuaded to give a plot of land just outside the village to serve as the mission cemetery, and Elwin intended to raise a large cross there – partly to mark out its intention, and partly because it was "a very conspicuous spot, from which the Cross will be seen from the high road if it is large enough". He was conscious of the rare opportunity of "putting up a Cross in the midst of heathen India";[8] and shortly afterwards he hung a number of William Hole's scenes from the life of Christ around the interior of St Crispin's, "framed and hung something after the fashion of the Stations of the Cross".

> [T]he Stations do not suit for a church which is to educate Hindus, because they only represent the suffering aspect of our Lord's life and leave Him dead and buried. But our pictures begin with the Nativity and end with the Ascension, and I can travel round the church with a Hindu and show him our Lord's life in a series of delightful typical pictures. They are immensely appreciated by all Indians, young and old, Christian and heathen.[9]

Elwin was utterly convinced of the value of pictures as a tool for conversion. His most constant appeal in the *Cowley Evangelist* was for postcards and old Christmas cards with religious themes, which he took with him whenever he travelled and distributed to almost anyone he could – while his more discerning clients among the local children called at the Mission House to augment their own collections. "To give pictures to all these stray people", he thought, "may seem so small an act that it might be thought hardly worth the doing. Nevertheless, it brings us into touch, and makes some sort of bond […], and may make it a little easier for those who may be able to follow up the work."[10]

When Chard visited Elwin shortly after his arrival in Bombay, the latter wrote to Cowley to say it had been a joy to see him "before he has become a jaded old Indian, and while everything is still a wonder and delight".[11] The hotchpotch of life in India continued to impress itself upon the Society: when in June 1909 Alfred Langmore returned by train to Bombay having led a retreat for the Sisters of the Church at Ootacamund, he was struck by the diversity of his travelling companions.

---

6 Biscoe, 4 June 1909.
7 Potts, 5 Nov 1908.
8 Elwin, 28 Dec 1908.
9 Elwin, 6 June 1909.
10 Elwin, 14 Jan 1913.
11 Elwin, 6 June 1909.

[A] Portuguese doctor going to Goa, and anxious to know a great deal through the medium of a minimum of English; a Roman Catholic engine driver, a mixture of Irish, Dutch and Portuguese, keen to become a Freemason, but told by his priest that it was wicked; three stalwart European miners (English) going to the goldfields at Kolar, so tender to me as they thought I was ill; an ex-Tommy who had lately joined the police, a quite superior fellow from London; an ex-choirman from the Madras Cathedral, devout and good; a French priest going to their sanatorium in the hills. He was surprised to hear we had native priests.[12]

In South Africa, the variety of life also continued. At Tsolo Frederick Puller oversaw the installation of two new stained-glass windows in the church, which spoke eloquently of the SSJE's ongoing mission-priorities there: the first depicted St Philip's baptism of the Numidian eunuch in Acts 8, which tied the mission at St Cuthbert's firmly to that of St Philip's at Cape Town; while the second was a memorial to the first black Anglican to be ordained to the priesthood in South Africa, Peter Masiza, and depicted Simon of Cyrene helping to carry the cross. "Personally", explained Puller, "I am inclined to identify S. Simon of Cyrene with the 'Symeon that was called Niger,' who is joined with Lucius of Cyrene in Acts 13.1. If the identification is correct, and there is, I think, a good deal to be said in favour of it, S. Simon of Cyrene must have been not only a man of Africa, which of course he was, but also a black native of Africa."[13] Like Elwin's cemetery cross, nothing was ever without its significance.

At St Cuthbert's School Br John – the lay brethren had begun to be sent overseas, as per Lucius Cary's suggestion in the General Chapter of 1908 – was busy organising the construction of a new hut to serve as a boarding house for the smallest boys for whom the mission was now home;[14] while the work of St Lucy's Hospital also grew. The foundation stone of its new building was carved with *Lendlu yakelwe uzuko lu-ka Tixo* – "practically the Xhosa equivalent of A.M.D.G." – while Kenneth McMurtrie, the new mission doctor, used the local heathen children's interest in his dog and the tools of his trade to win their early confidence, and to try and mitigate Godfrey Callaway's observation that "it is often only when everything they can try has failed that they come to the European doctor."[15] McMurtrie himself once had to carry a dangerously sick boy the four miles to St Lucy's, after his family had repeatedly failed to bring him for check-ups. It was too late to save him, and he died the next day; but the family was grateful for his efforts: "They brought a big can of milk for the boy, and when he was dead they told us to keep it for ourselves."[16]

Like all newcomers, McMurtrie was dependent on an interpreter, his "faithful Solomon";[17] but even long-serving missioners like Nicholson continued to value the input of their local co-workers. When it came to confirmation at Poona, and reception of Holy Communion for the first time, he observed that

---

12 Langmore, 4 June 1909.
13 Puller, 24 Oct 1908.
14 *CE* Feb 1909.
15 Callaway, 25 Jan 1909.
16 McMurtrie, 29 April 1909.
17 McMurtrie, 2 June 1909.

"Mr [Reuben] Dhawle gave the instruction to the children. One was much struck by it, and felt that the children would never forget how to behave, or how to believe about the Blessed Sacrament, after they had listened to what he taught them."[18]

Back in England, the work of the Fellowship of St John continued unabated; although Maxwell was keen to emphasise that its existence was not a reason for others to be less generous – he particularly singled out parishes who asked for missions to be preached and offered only travel expenses.[19] The special office for the Fellowship's work was prayed in the community church regularly – "at 5 p.m. on the second Monday of every month"[20] – before it gave way to quarterly gatherings in Oxford and in London at All Saints', Margaret Street, in addition to its annual retreat. At Cowley it supported the Society's schools, and maintained a nearby house as a "Fellowship Room" – it moved a number of times – which provided a small lending library, board and lodging for members when required, and an address for the reception of gifts. "Will Members kindly note that no parcels should be sent to the General Secretary's own residence?" pleaded the *Cowley Evangelist* in April 1910.

George Congreve summed up the Fellowship's work as twofold: it was made up of people who gave "of their substance and energy" to further the work of the SSJE; but who also wished "to have their part in the prayers and other good works" that the Society offered corporately to God.[21] To that end, and in addition to the Fellowship's sizeable grants of money, its days of perpetual intercession for the SSJE – on which each member of the Fellowship was asked to undertake a designated half-hour of prayer for the Society's work – and its annual retreat in Oxford, various Working Parties collected or made items, "always in the best taste",[22] either to be sold in the Fellowship's frequent Sales of Work, or to be sent directly to the missions in one of the large packing-cases that was shipped out from time to time. Those full of gifts for the mission children were a regular and much-looked-for Christmas treat.

The members provided a full stock of linen to furnish the new Mission House at Mazagon,[23] clothes for the boys at Poona,[24] and cassocks for the catechists at Tsolo;[25] while at Cape Town Henry Bull was delighted to find, among "a most generous abundance" of items, a ping-pong set for the young ones, which was put into "immediate, joyful and most boisterous use".[26] A number of "useful things" had also arrived at St Cuthbert's – whose boxes were overseen personally by Callaway's sister – including "vestments for our out-station churches and altar ornaments for the same, and pictures and cassocks for our native preachers", for which Puller wished to convey "our most hearty thanks".[27]

---

18 Nicholson, 1 April 1910.
19 *CE* March 1912.
20 *CE* July 1909.
21 *CE* Jan 1911.
22 Biscoe, 12 June 1910.
23 Biscoe, 4 June 1909.
24 Nicholson, 10 June 1910.
25 Ley, 27 Sept 1915.
26 Bull, June 30 1909.
27 *CE* April 1909.

A few years later the Weaving School at Tsolo was producing its own vestments: Frederic Noel wrote to say that some had been used when the Bishop of St John's presided at High Mass during the Whitsun Octave in 1916.

> Fr Ley and a native priest were deacon and sub-deacon, their red dalmatic and tunicle being the manufacture of our native weaving school, as well as the red cope used in procession. Again there was the striking effect of the multitude that filled the church falling on their knees as the procession passed for the Bishop's blessing, as he walked in cope and mitre, carrying his staff.[28]

The vestments were particularly significant, because of the Society's consistently high doctrine of the sacraments. When he preached at the diocesan ordinations at Umtata on All Saints' Day 1908, Puller was clear that the men to be ordained were set apart to receive "a share in the Apostolic commission or [in the case of the new priests] an increased measure of that commission".

> Consider well what it is that is going to happen to you. Outwardly you will hear the solemn words of prayer which the Bishop will utter, and you will feel the touch of his consecrating hands. But inwardly you must be lifting up your hearts to the throne of God on high. There you will see with the eyes of faith Jesus your Saviour bending down over you, and stretching out his pierced hands over you to impart to you from on high the gift of His Holy Spirit.

"It is the Holy Ghost who will really consecrate you to be Presbyters and Deacons," he went on. "It is the Holy Ghost who will give to you that measure of Apostolic authority, which appertains to the office which you are receiving. It is the Holy Ghost who will pour out upon you further gifts of sanctifying grace to enable you to use your Presbyteral or Diaconal authority in a right way, so that it may help forward the souls of your people and extend the bounds of Christ's Kingdom, and promote the Glory of God."[29]

Hard on the heels of his return from the resolution of the Indian controversy, Puller had also taken up cudgels in the "Deceased Wife's Sister" marriage question in the Church in South Africa, after the passing of the associated Act at Westminster in 1907 and what Bull called "the lamentable division of opinion in the English Episcopate" on the issue.[30] A proposal to admit to Holy Communion anyone who had entered into such an arrangement in a civil union was thrown out in Provincial Synod in 1909 after Puller made a lengthy speech against it in the course of a three-day debate, and demanded a vote by houses.[31] He later published his thoughts on the whole business in the unequivocal *Marriage with a Deceased Wife's Sister Forbidden by the Laws of God and of the Church*.[32]

---

28 Noel, 29 May 1917.
29 *CE* May 1909.
30 Bull, 24 Nov 1909.
31 Puller, 26 Oct 1909.
32 Frederick William Puller SSJE, *Marriage with a deceased wife's sister: forbidden by the laws of God and of the Church*, London: Longmans, Green & Co. (1912).

Meanwhile, Bull was tied up with less-theological concerns. The mission at Ndabeni had developed a reputation as a place where help could be found during the economic downturn that hit South Africa towards the end of the 1900s: it was already home to "six native lads, one of whom pays, another being supposed to pay, the others working in various ways as a contribution to expenses". He found himself on the wrong side of the law after "two heathen natives" appeared unexpectedly asking for "Fr Buller": they wanted him to ascertain whether they might safely claim "the reward usually given to natives on the spot who find and give up diamonds", and gave him "twelve sparkling stones" for safekeeping.

On consulting the local magistrate, Bull learned that by holding on to them he was himself liable to a £500 fine and seven years in prison – "he hoped I should not appear before him the following morning!" He duly handed the stones over to the police, and waited for the strangers' return. "I fancy they would get into no trouble, and would probably get half-a-crown per pound", he thought, and – having met others who had been to prison after less-successful outcomes – called it "a fascinating game to play, with high stakes".[33]

Far away in America, Frederic Powell travelled to Hawaii, to help the Bishop of Honolulu, Henry Restarick, with mission work among the Japanese, Chinese, and Korean populations – which outnumbered the Hawaiians by nearly two to one. He observed the same priorities of language as characterised the Cowley missions: "a Japanese mass at 5.30, then a Chinese Mass at 6.15 [...] At 7.45 the Hawaiians sang Mass in their own language, and at 10 the Bishop celebrated in English"; but he also noted that as almost everyone also spoke at least some English he was able to preach without an interpreter. He was received by ex-Queen Liluokalani; and attended his first traditional Japanese dinner.

> The Bishop got very stiff from sitting on the floor. He tried sitting on his heels, like our hosts, and various other positions, that made us all merry, but he could find no comfort in it [...] We managed the chop-sticks and the raw fish and various fruits and rice and soups and spices fairly well, and then a little girl came in and strummed on an instrument like a guitar with two strings. Then there was a sword-dance, and after that we got up to go. I could hardly stand or move, I was so stiff.[34]

The local clergy were keen that Powell should see as much of Hawaiian life as possible during his visit. By the time he left, he had taken in the flora and fauna, observed the disposal of a washed-up whale carcass by a combination of sharks and Japanese fishermen, and met the islands' last surviving player of the nose-flute.[35]

Not long afterwards Callaway met a lady in South Africa while leading a mission at Mount Fletcher, north of Umtata, who had known Powell during her childhood in Canada. "She was very anxious to hear all I could tell of

---

33 Bull, 14 April 1909.
34 Powell, 6 Oct 1908.
35 Powell, 16 Oct 1908; 17 Nov 1908.

him," he noted.[36] Certainly his trip to Hawaii was a world away from Canada: when Powell went on retreat to Pembroke, near Ottawa, in January 1910 he nearly froze; but he was at least able to minister unexpectedly to a group of lumbermen who lived forty miles from the nearest church and of whom "not one" had been able to get to mass at Christmas.[37]

Hawaii was far-removed from Boston, too, where the SSJE black missions of St Martin and St Augustine in the deprived South End were finally brought together in the new church of Ss Augustine & Martin on Lenox Street – as at Cape Town the dedications were hardly coincidental. Soon after its inauguration Field reported that it was also being used by the local Russian Orthodox community, much as old St Philip's had given house room to the Greeks in Cape Town. Such "acts of courtesy" were, he felt, a means of furthering the cause of union with the Eastern Churches.[38]

SPICY BREEZES

From Cowley, Maxwell cautiously continued to ring the changes. He allowed Philip Waggett to take up the headship of the new House of Theological Study at Cambridge: the *Cowley Evangelist* emphasised that it was not a branch house of the Society, but that the fact it was to be run by a member of the SSJE made it "certain that our interest in its welfare and our prayers for its right ordering will be constant and full of sympathy".[39] Puller was recalled to succeed him at St Edward's House; and Gerald Ley sailed to replace him at St Cuthbert's, "packed like herrings" onto the *Saxon*.[40] Arthur Pridham left Mohales Hoek to serve as Chaplain to the Wantage Sisters at Irene, near Pretoria; while Br Arthur was invalided home from Poona.[41] Br Leslie was sent out in his place, and soon distinguished himself on the cricket field – to the delight of the mission schoolboys.[42]

By the end of 1909 Nicholson was under canvas outside Poona, "in the centre of some dozen villages some three or four miles from our encampment", from where he was leading a mission in the usual manner: preaching in one village in the morning, and going to another in the evening "to show the magic lantern pictures of the life of our Lord".[43] On 8 December Chard sang mass for the Wantage Sisters, before finding himself caught up in "a surging mass of idol-worshippers" who were keeping a festival of their own;[44] while from his new posting at Umarkhadi Moore soon wrote to say that he had met the local rabbi – "a Jew from Aden" – and visited the synagogue. He noted that a number of impoverished "dock boys" had entered the catechumenate; and

---

36 Callaway, 27 Nov 1909.
37 Powell, 18 Jan 1910.
38 Field, 23 Nov 1909.
39 *CE* Sept 1909.
40 Ley, 10 Jan 1910.
41 *CE* Dec 1909.
42 Nicholson, 5 Aug 1910.
43 Nicholson, 3 Dec 1909.
44 Chard, 8 Dec 1909.

that he was better understood in Marathi than at Poona – but only because the self-confessed poorness of his pronunciation seemed to align with the "corruptions" of the language in multi-cultural Bombay.[45]

In early 1910 the Society further widened its scope in Bombay by opening "a hostel for Indian Christian lads" in the compound at Mazagon, and Br John immediately set about working alongside the first intake of boys as they did their domestic chores, to get to know them better. Chard noted that his approach worked well: "it rather surprises the people around to see a 'Sab' washing down the floor and doing what they call 'coolie work'."[46] Simultaneously, at Tsolo the work of the new hospital was beginning to thrive, and had become something of a recruiting ground for the mission school, to the delight of Ley. "The photographs I had seen of the hospital", he wrote, "excellent as they are, failed altogether to present the picture as I saw it."

> The sun was shining brightly, and as I came in front of the hospital and saw the beds, with their bright red blankets, and the patients, some up and about, others in bed, and the doctor and nurse at work, I began to realise, I think, what a really big thing it is, and how full of promise for the future.[47]

Callaway was also planning for the future with the debates that he encouraged among the schoolboys at St Cuthbert's. Public disputation formed part of traditional conflict-resolution methods among the local people, and he felt that some of the boys might in time use a skill that was to many of them second-nature "for the pulpit and for educational purposes". When the benefits of hospital-nursing over home-nursing formed the subject of one of the debates – it was chosen as an experiment "to see how far the natural prejudices against a hospital had died away in face of experience" – he and McMurtrie were surprised that it was voted down by the smaller boys, despite having been vigorously supported by their elders. Nonetheless, Callaway was particularly satisfied that the boys had felt able to vote as they wished, and not simply to please him.[48]

Elsewhere, there remained seemingly endless movement: Cary was sent on furlough to North America and Canada, where he joined Charles Field and wrote a series of evocative letters home as they travelled from Montreal to San Francisco, taking in Toronto, New Westminster, Vancouver, and Seattle, the Niagara Falls, the Rockies, the Golden Gate Bridge, and the Grand Canyon – "our last and greatest spectacle" – as they went.[49] He returned to hold the fort at Cowley before Maxwell sailed for South Africa in December 1910, to inspect the work there. With the Superior General went Charles Turner, who was going to work at Tsolo, and Thomas Bignold, who would succeed Bull when he was transferred to Boston as Provincial Superior.

Maxwell had a thorough tour of Cape Town, where he met the lepers on Robben Island, and had tea at Bishopscourt with Archbishop William Carter,

---

45 Moore, 18 Nov 1909.
46 Chard, 25 Feb 1910.
47 Ley, 16 Feb 1910.
48 Callaway, 3 Aug 1910.
49 Cary, 30 Aug 1910ff; 5 Oct 1910.

who had been translated from Pretoria after William West Jones's death in 1908; but he was particularly moved by the Christmas services at Ndabeni and St Philip's, after which he and the brethren had dinner with the residents of St Columba's Home. He was welcomed warmly at their new church by members of the Greek Orthodox community, who had not forgotten the Society's hospitality in their earliest days in Cape Town; and soon afterwards he had travelled to the Transkei and thrown himself into the round of life at St Cuthbert's. He thought the mission "a new world", with "a sort of atmosphere of freedom and self-respect", and called Easter there "the crowning point" of his tour. He was overwhelmed by the High Mass on Easter Day – "I have never in my life been at one single service with such a number of people receiving the Holy Communion" – and was delighted by what he had seen of his Society's efforts. He insisted that he had "enjoyed every thing that I have done as much as anyone could possibly have wished me to".[50]

Elwin, meanwhile, had been in Ceylon – "a most wonderful place" – preaching and leading retreats, with perhaps an inkling that the SSJE might in time be called to establish a house there as an offshoot of the Indian work.[51] "As you walk amongst the wealth of wondrous vegetation", he wrote, "the air is literally laden with what is admirably expressed by 'spicy breezes' – and the warm, steamy air 'blows soft'." He was making reference to Reginald Heber's missionary hymn "From Greenland's Icy Mountains", and thought that the advances of Christianity on the island "would rejoice the heart of Bishop Heber if he could visit Ceylon again".[52]

By quoting Heber, Elwin hinted – probably quite consciously – at a narrative of self-sacrificing mission-work in which the SSJE was very deeply invested. Of the eight members of the Society who had died by 1911, six had either expired or contracted their final illness in India. When Ernest Hollings, one of the Society's priest co-workers in the schools at Poona, was invalided home in 1911, Nicholson accompanied him; but a couple of weeks into the journey he was obliged to bury him at sea off Cape St Vincent.[53] In both India and Africa the brethren were frequently laid low with illness brought on either by the local weather or by contact with the dangerously sick; and many letters home were written from hospital wards. "We do not doubt", intoned the *Cowley Evangelist*, "that the lives and deaths of our Brethren have borne and will continue to bear fruit".[54]

Even for the healthy, mission journeys could also be dangerous. Oswald Barton – who had by then recovered from his accident of the previous year – wrote from Khandala at the end of 1912 with news of the mission to the temporary labourers at the Tata works around Lonavla, where massive dams were being constructed to power the cotton mills at Bombay. The magic lantern was used as usual to great effect, and the party camped alongside the coolies – but in the course of one evening they were robbed.

---

50 Maxwell, 26 Dec 1910; 13 Jan 1911; 1 Mar 1911; 19 April 1911.
51 *A Statement concerning the development of the Religious Life in Ceylon by the SSJE*, Gen., SSJE/2/5/448.
52 Elwin, 5 Oct 1910.
53 *CE* June 1911.
54 *CE* Jan 1912.

My cassock had disappeared, with all my money for the fortnight's expedition, and Brother Arthur's purse had also been stolen, with both our watches [...] The thieves had seized the box of altar linen, etc, and taken it outside, thinking, I suppose, that it contained our valuables. The strange thing is that no one of us heard the slightest sound.

Comparing notes, the party came to the conclusion that their dinner had been drugged to induce stupor. They decided to sleep under cover: "we are continuing our work under less romantic conditions. The thieves must have been very expert and daring."[55] Such setbacks notwithstanding, the Indian work still continued to grow: Barton later described the more mundane work of the mission as "much like the ordinary routine of an English curacy, visiting and classes and regular services".[56] A larger mission house was begun at Poona, with the foundation stone laid by Biscoe – who was by then the doyen of the Indian work – at Candlemas 1913. He conducted the entire ceremony in Marathi, using the new Occasional Offices book that the SSJE had produced for its Indian missions; and that it included a rite for the laying of foundation stones speaks of the hopes the Society had for what lay ahead.[57]

Away from Poona, the Cowley Fathers had their eyes on other prizes. Through Nicholson the SSJE continued to take an interest in the Oxford Mission to Calcutta's successes in Bengal, where from Barisal the OMC and the Clewer Sisters ran a large mission station with outposts in a number of surrounding villages – rather like the SSJE mission at Tsolo, but on a much larger scale. Unlike the SSJE, the OMC had established the Bengali Brotherhood of St Andrew; and Nicholson noted approvingly of its early successes.

The Oxford Mission seems to be successful in inspiring some of their lads with a desire to dedicate their lives to God. Their Bengali Community of St Andrew has now two Indian priests and three others. The Metropolitan has given a commission to the priests to evangelise the country in which there is a hill tribe called the Garos, who seem willing to be taught Christianity, and there are now some 200 catechumens. The work is done by Indians, who employ their own methods and raise money for their own support, Rs 100 a month, from Indians.

The question that faced the SSJE generally, and Nicholson in particular, was whether or not it might be possible for the Society to establish a similar community at Poona. He was convinced that several of the Indians on the mission at Panch Howds wished to live the religious life in some way. "What its exact form will be we cannot tell, but such a brotherhood would find great scope for both mission and educational work," he wrote, noting that "one would wish it to develop on purely Indian lines, but it would at any rate require help from us for some time. One's whole desire is to welcome and encourage all who are drawn to the life."[58]

---

55 Barton, 13 Dec 1912.
56 Barton, 17 Feb 1914.
57 Nicholson, 30 Jan & 7 Feb 1913; Biscoe, 7 Feb 1913.
58 Nicholson, 30 Jan 1913.

The Community of St Mary the Virgin had already established an Indian community;[59] but soon both the Cowley and Wantage efforts were set back gravely by the deaths of the first aspirants to both communities: Sr Krupabai, who had already entered the novitiate, and Stephen Bhaskar. The demise of the latter was a particular blow to Nicholson, who had seen in him the clear signs of vocation both to the priesthood and to the religious life.[60] "It seems strange", he lamented "that God should have called our first postulant";[61] while the Greater Chapter of 1913 made a point of expressing its "profound interest and sympathy" in this aspect of his work and its apparent frustration.[62] Chard was more hopeful: "No doubt God means some great blessing to fall on those who are inspired to fill their places."[63]

CHALLENGES IN COMMON

The idiosyncrasies of life in India still presented themselves – Nicholson called it "the most inexplicable country"[64] – and issues of caste continued to frustrate. In the course of a preaching tour Chard inadvertently defiled a man's food one morning when he moved a bag so that he might sit down. He paid for its replacement, rather than see the man go without his midday meal. "Some day I trust that they will learn that a priest's hand does not defile bread", he wrote, "but is empowered by God to bless it".[65] Occasionally the brethren were disheartened by the falling-away of convert-boys at the mission, lured back to caste by their families.[66] At other times family members attempted to claim them back, in which case permission for them to leave was refused without a magistrate's order – against which the Society would then appeal.[67]

The return to caste was a particular local symptom of a far wider problem for missionaries in the Empire. It was an issue on which Michael Newbolt, Principal of the Dorchester Missionary College – to which the SSJE was close, both literally and figuratively – elaborated later that year. "The heathen have not only to be taught the Faith, they have to unlearn quickly a vast body of inherited tradition of moral evil. This can only be fought by dealing with individual souls one by one."[68] A similar problem applied to witchcraft at Tsolo: when Ley found that two schoolteachers at one of the outstations had returned to its practices towards the end of 1914, he gave them both immediate notice of dismissal and suspended them from Communion.[69] In other cases, those who

---

59 *The Indian Church and Community Life*, CE April 1910.
60 Nicholson, 28 Feb 1913.
61 Nicholson, 7 March 1913.
62 GreC 1913, SSJE/2/5/66.
63 Chard, 6 March 1913.
64 Nicholson, 16 Jul 1912.
65 Chard, 23 July 1913.
66 cf Nicholson, 4 July 1913.
67 cf Moore, 13 Nov 1901.
68 *A Sermon Preached on behalf of the Dorchester Missionary College*, 23 Nov 1913 (CE Feb 1914).
69 Ley, 16 Nov 1914.

repented of their backsliding were sent to the penitents' class to prepare for readmission to the sacraments.[70]

More practically pressing at Poona was the fact that most of the city was filthy, with "open cesspools, open gutters with the refuse lying in them, [and] the most appalling odours from the Municipal carts";[71] which in turn made cholera an ever-present threat. At Bombay, which was even more crowded, plague came and went. Too many people, thought Nicholson, were "feckless about sanitary matters; they overcrowd their rooms and fill them with boxes and things which harbour rats and vermin, and then they are surprised when plague comes."[72]

Elwin, who had in 1912 completed his history of the SSJE in India, protested that he was "commonly supposed to be a keeper of cats". "It would be truer to say that the cats keep me," he argued. "Anyhow, in a country in which doors and windows are open night and day, I do not know how one is to prevent two cats living with one if they choose to do so."[73] The felines entered into Cowley legend; and by the time Bull visited in 1920 the elder had just died[74] – he noted that "Fr Elwin showed me the grave of his famous cat"; and that he had also met its kitten, which was by then fully grown.[75]

At Mazagon the mission compound seemed to be always full of songbirds[76]; but other animals – quite apart from Dr Bradley's tiger – could be more problematic. A mongoose found its way into the Mission House at Poona, and two wildcats got into church through the roof to hunt the sparrows in their nests at the top of the pillars – dislodging plaster and making so much mess below that they had to be shot.[77] Far away in the Transkei, at Upper Mjika Turner found himself obliged to share a hut with "a hen sitting on her eggs."

> [I]t seemed impossible to suggest moving [her], as she sat there in all the dignity of motherhood. But she had no scruples in arousing me long before light, when she wanted to stretch her legs a bit, and would make a tremendous clucking till I got out of bed to open the door for her.

Sometimes it was invaded by goats; and when a colony of ants broke through the mud floor they were immediately set upon by chickens.[78] Snakes came and went in all the mission outposts – at Yerendawana Elwin had to corner and kill a cobra, "rearing himself up and spreading out his hood", behind the altar in the All Souls' Chapel at St Crispin's[79] – and in Bombay Nicholson was attacked by a monkey.[80] Barton called the sight of vultures picking over the

---

70 Ley, 19 Nov 1914.
71 Nicholson, 20 Feb 1913.
72 Nicholson, 4 July 1913.
73 Elwin, 14 Jan 1913.
74 Elwin, 5 Nov 1920.
75 Bull, 12 Oct 1920.
76 Nicholson, 16 May 1913.
77 Nicholson, 11 Oct 1909; 26 Aug 1910.
78 Turner, 12 June 1913.
79 Elwin, 13 Oct 1919.
80 Nicholson, 8 April 1913.

carcass of a freshly-dead dog "about the most disgusting sight I ever saw";[81] while Nicholson later countered with a buffalo that had run amok near Poona: "with one of his great horns he severed a man's head from his body."[82]

From Tsolo Ley wrote to say that he was "thankful to Mrs Norris for replacing the bible eaten by the cow" – it had also devoured a cassock after wandering into the outstation church at Elunyaweni.[83] He was delighted by the arrival of a duplicator, "capable of doing 100 copies of printed matter";[84] but even as St Cuthbert's embraced new technology it remained at the mercy of the weather. In March 1912 a new hospital horse, bought as an investment for £15, was struck by lightning and killed within two weeks of its arrival.[85]

By November the thunderstorms had given way to drought: so severe that Ley was "feeling bound to refuse boys who are offered to us now, lest we should be unable to feed them". Ploughing was impossible, and the mission cattle began to die from hunger.[86] A month later the weather turned and the veld was lush again; but the heavy rain came at a price. A *rondavel* was destroyed by lightning, and its occupant killed: once the fire was out Callaway and Turner went to lead prayers and to recover the body – "much burnt and unrecognisable" – for burial.[87] In Cape Town, Noel took comfort in the buffeting of the fierce winds in the knowledge that they would carry rain to the Eastern Cape; while he rejoiced in the baptism of "four of my afflicted men" at Ndabeni. "Two were blind, one minus a leg, and one dumb and partly paralysed. I managed on this occasion to get through nearly the whole service in Sixosa [Xhosa], having the help of the catechist in the rest."[88]

Soon there was too much rain at St Cuthbert's, and the surrounding area was flooded. Although the locals were used to taking their boots and socks off to paddle across the veld, the rivers continued to be treacherous. Turner was just able to drive his horse, Cato, across so that he could visit the outstations, although he had anticipated "a great effort and heroic plans. I was glad it was not necessary, as I was again carrying the Blessed Sacrament."[89] When on another trip Cato slipped and got stuck in a narrow stream, Turner resigned himself to a long wait and sat down to say Matins until some passing "'Red' [heathen] lads" passed by and helped extricate him.[90] Visitors to Tsolo took similar risks: when the new Bishop of Kimberley & Kuruman, Wilfrid Gore Browne, visited in March 1913 his horses were forced to swim; and the bishop soon found himself in the water. "On the whole there was very little damage," observed Ley after Gore Browne had been fished out. "I think he enjoyed the experience."[91]

---

81 Barton, 19 Oct 1918.
82 Nicholson, 15 Sept 1921.
83 Ley, 1 Feb 1915; 6 May 1915.
84 Ley, 4 April 1913.
85 Ley, 2 May 1913.
86 Ley, 12 Nov 1912.
87 Ley, 14 Dec 1912.
88 Noel, 1 Jan 1913.
89 Turner, 4 Jan 1913.
90 Turner, 29 June 1912.
91 Ley, 14 March 1913.

Like the Oxford Mission to Calcutta, the Sisters of the Community of the Resurrection at Grahamstown were open to the idea of founding a community for African women, and Ley visited them "to talk over the outlines of a Rule, etc, for the native women who desire to test their Vocation to the Religious Life".[92] The Wantage Sisters were already engaged in the same work, and admitted their first African postulants at Candlemas 1914. Turner turned his attention to building a new church at Mhlakulo – where mass was being said in the hut that also served as the village school – and to doing something about the heathen husbands of some of members of the congregation: a problem, he reflected, not entirely confined to the mission at Tsolo.

> The headman came up and said they were gathered together for a little *amarewu*, which one understood quite as clearly as if one met a party of confirmed topers and they said they were gathered together to drink ginger beer, the equivalent [...] It is a strange experience to find oneself presiding at a meeting of merry-hearted gentlemen, all clothed in red blankets. They are an extraordinary contrast to their wives and children, who are nearly all Christians. But I believe there are other places besides S. Africa where men are glad that their wives and children should go to Church, but themselves prefer to potter about the garden and to wind up the clocks, etc, on Sunday.[93]

By the middle of 1913 it must have seemed to the members of the Society that – in both India and South Africa, and despite significant challenges – there remained irrepressible growth, and always more work to be done. "In some ways everything seems to be at sixes and sevens", wrote Nicholson from India – where a year later the SSJE further increased its workload when it took over the Church Missionary Society work in Parel[94] – "and one wonders how progress can be possible. Our work as missionaries seems so feeble, and apparently without results, and then, on the other hand, one comes across incidents full of encouragement."[95]

At about the same time Turner mused from Tsolo that "a great many things come to him who waits, in S. Africa";[96] although his letters home frequently betrayed the exasperation he often felt at the apparent and "hardly credible" indolence of some of the local people, as well as many of the men's tendency towards drunkenness.[97] When the new church walls at Mhlakulo collapsed because the roof had not been raised before the heavy rains arrived, he was livid.[98] Nevertheless, he attended a *mjikelo* to raise funds for the new school at Nongxola, and willingly took part in the fun.

> One man offered a he-goat for the Chief [Mtshazi] to take off his hat, and another 10 shillings for him to put it back on again [...] The rule is that what is paid holds good unless someone offers a larger sum to counteract it. Sixpence was offered to me to take my spectacles off. I obeyed, but said it prevented me seeing his very

---

92 Ley, 27 Jan 1913.
93 Turner, 22 April 1913.
94 Barton, 10 April 1914.
95 Nicholson, 31 May 1913.
96 Turner, 12 June 1913.
97 cf Turner 1 Aug 1913; 23 Sept 1913.
98 Turner, 4 Nov 1913.

handsome countenance, and a shilling was promptly given so that I might put them on again.[99]

The seemingly-incessant work continued to be balanced by the homeliness of purely practical needs: the *Cowley Evangelist* reported that "our Brethren both in India and S. Cuthbert's are constantly crying out for a supply of old tennis balls and of bats. The need seems to be quite inexhaustible. It is of the greatest importance to be able to provide games for our large families of boys."[100]

There were shades of home almost everywhere: from Tsolo the Society worked to revitalise the Mothers' Union in the outstations round about;[101] and at Yerendawana the self-regulating scout-pack looked to Elwin as its final arbiter of discipline, while otherwise getting on with making themselves useful in the local area. He noted with pride that "they are to the Catholic Faith and all that it brings to them as to the manner born."[102] At Umarkhadi, the entertainments after High Mass on Holy Cross Day 1912 included a performance by the resident boys of Br Leslie's rendering of *Jack and the Bean Stalk*, "with Indian songs and by-play, at which some of them were really very clever".[103]

The various Cowley "families" were not isolated from each other, either, despite the great distances between them. At Whitsun 1913 the collection taken at Tsolo, which amounted to not quite two pounds, was sent to Poona to help with the building of the new Mission House there.[104] This munificence, modest as it was, was not entirely spontaneous. There was certainly an element – for Callaway, at least – of a need to demonstrate to the local people that white people in South Africa *could* inculcate generosity, and encourage it in others. He was adamant that

> the white man [...] shows his least good side to the native. In his own home he is perhaps generous, kindly and hospitable. He loves nothing better than to receive white strangers gladly and to give them of his best [...] But we must never forget that of all this the native sees and knows nothing [...] Towards himself the native only sees a closed door.

There was much of which to be repented, he thought: "we have been spoilers as well as sowers."[105]

At Patronal Festival in September 1913 distinctions of colour were evident. The black population all came for St Cuthbert's Day: "over a 1000 people sat down to dinner to negotiate three-and-a-half bags of grain, i.e. 700lbs, and three cows, which had been cooking since the early hours in some forty large three-legged pots." It was all eaten after High Mass, before the benign chaos of the sports and singing competitions began. The European neighbours came on the Sunday in the Octave, had sandwiches, and went away again.[106] A year

---

99 Turner, 27 Aug 1912.
100 *CE* July 1913.
101 Turner, 6 June 1912.
102 Elwin, 22 July 1913.
103 Moore, 18 Sept 1912.
104 Ley, 22 May 1913.
105 *CE* Sept 1913.
106 Ley, 9 Sept 1913.

later the *Cowley Evangelist* launched an appeal to build a school for the relatively small number of coloured children in and around Tsolo, in an attempt to answer the vexed question of how to care for a group that was "disliked and despised by the white people, and perhaps equally so by the natives".[107]

There was, however, an ongoing element of integration at Tsolo, as at the other Cowley missions. At Christmas 1913 Ley noted that: "at the High Mass Fr Callaway was deacon, and Mr Cornner was thurifer, but otherwise it was delightfully African—Mr Xaba the celebrant [John Xaba, the catechist who had worked with Puller at Cape Town, and who had since entered Holy Orders], the two African deacons administering the chalice, and the African acolytes."[108] He was particularly proud of Jemuel Pamla, formed by the Society and soon to be ordained to the priesthood: "one's thoughts go back to the boy who some fifteen or twenty years ago used to cook our food, but after a time the cook returned to school, then he came as catechist and teacher, then as deacon."[109] Simultaneously, in India, Nicholson was looking forward to the ordination of the first Indians whose vocations had been nurtured through the Society's work at Poona.[110]

The vignettes that arrived at Cowley from Tsolo in the second decade of the twentieth century, notwithstanding the weather, had something of an idyllic quality to them – in early 1914 Ley wrote to say that Hester Carter, the Archbishop's wife, had given him the root of a white agapanthus to plant alongside the blue ones that grew in abundance around the mission[111] – but in the bustle of Cape Town the SSJE experience could be very different. Not long after the St Cuthbert's Day ceremonies Bignold wrote from the metropolis to say that he had attended the impressive dedication ceremony of the new St George's Cathedral; but with the sombre news that Sydney Wallis was ministering to four men under sentence of death.

> He is quite hopeful about their spiritual condition. They are to be baptized tomorrow (Friday): the poor fellows are to be executed on Thursday next. The Archbishop is being asked to confirm them. Two of them are Zulus. It is little more than three weeks since the last native was executed. He was baptized by Father Wallis, and received his first Communion and Viaticum only a few minutes before death.[112]

Wallis's corporal works of mercy did not end at the gallows – he claimed the bodies afterwards, and buried them himself.[113] He valued his prison ministry greatly: "I don't think one ever realizes the happiness and the privilege of being a priest so much as when ministering at the House of Correction."[114] Life in the colonies was not all white habits and High Mass.

---

107 *CE* Aug 1914.
108 Ley, "In the Christmas Octave" 1913.
109 Ley, 21 July 1914.
110 Nicholson, 1 July 1914.
111 Ley, 3 Feb 1914.
112 Bignold, 27 Sept 1913.
113 Ley, 27 Jan 1914.
114 Wallis, 15 April 1914.

High Summer

When King Edward VII died in 1910, Puller – who was by then back in England – preached at the Solemn Requiem in the community church on 20 May, the day of the great funeral at Windsor. He did not shy away from mentioning "some things in our late King's earlier life, before he came to the throne, which might reasonably cause anxiety when he was called to take up the tremendous burden of kingship". But God had turned him away from his former predilections, Puller thought, and into "a great gift" to the nation – not that the country over which he had ruled had been grateful for it.

> Is not the public recognition of God less than it was fifty years ago? Has it not been the tendency in very many quarters to break down the sanctity of the Lord's Day, to leave unfulfilled the duties of public worship, to turn week-ends into times of mere worldly festivity and enjoyment? Is there not a tendency to break down the sanctity of marriage? Is there not a powerful movement to multiply opportunities for divorce, and to make breaches and so to weaken the whole structure of the laws against incest? Is not our public provision of education being gradually divorced from all effective teaching of the Christian religion? Are not immense efforts being made to rob the Church of God of her schools, and set before the rising generation a washed-out undenominationalism, which has lost all the power which belongs to the full Gospel of Christ?

Puller sealed the message by urging his hearers devoutly to join "in offering this holy Sacrifice" for their dead king. "Let us beseech God to cleanse his soul from all stains of sin", he concluded, "washing it in the Precious Blood of our Lord."

To a great extent, Puller had become the Society's theological mouthpiece – a position he shared with Congreve, while the latter lived. He would go on to spend several months in Russia in 1912, when he was invited to travel to St Petersburg to deliver a series of lectures on the Church of England to a new society established by the Most Holy Governing Synod "for the purpose of cultivating friendly relations", an important step in the establishment of relations between the two churches;[115] but now he laid out from the community's central pulpit, and later in the pages of the *Cowley Evangelist*, the SSJE's manifesto for its work under Maxwell.

It contained everything for which the Society had fought for in the preceding years: most particularly for true Eucharistic doctrine and the efficacy of the holy sacrifice of the mass; the wholesale rejection of marriage-with-deceased-wife's-sister; and proper Christian schooling at Cowley and in the colonies – fundraising to continue to support and improve the Society's schools at home had been a constant theme in the background.[116] Under Maxwell's leadership the SSJE had made great gains on all these points, and when John Biscoe – "our old friend and Associate" – preached in the community church for the feast of

---

115 *CE* April 1912.
116 *CE* June 1910.

St John before the Latin Gate in May 1913, he summed up what the Society had come to mean to very many people:

> You, my Fathers, must please forgive me if even here I cannot help saying why it is those who, like myself, have had the privilege of association with the Society, as it seems now for many years – why it is we feel we owe to you a debt beyond all words. Our own failure is ever with us; our own broken, faltering witness; service; the circumstances of religion we know best are dull and disheartening; there is not much to assure us of the victory of Faith and the triumph of the Cross. But we have always to help us the thought of Cowley, your holy and peaceful House, this solemn Church, your work of praise and prayer, your missions throughout the world, all the very highest work done in the very highest way. Above all, we know that in you, in your Society, may always be found, in no inadequate presentation, those high gifts and beautiful graces which St John received from Jesus Christ – the spirit of Contemplation; the spirit of Love; the spirit of Sacrifice.[117]

When Page breathed his last at Poona in at the end of October 1912, after having sunk steadily over the preceding months, Nicholson was with him – he was glad to have been able to say the appropriate prayers "as provided in the form for the commendation of a Brother in the Article of Death". As the news spread, the men of the Poona congregation gathered at the hospital and insisted on carrying Page's simple coffin through the darkening streets to the Church of the Holy Name. After the obsequies of the next day, he was buried in the new cemetery, next to Gardner.[118] Waggett recalled that under him "we who began our Community life under his rule, and those others, our elders, who saw him take up, in obedience, the burden of our affairs, learnt in him quite plainly the fact that rule is service."[119]

The well-documented overseas adventures of the SSJE under Maxwell continued to build on Page's vision and bedrock; and they helped to shape the Society's image as a provider of mission-work on an international scale. In the years ahead its buildings would be adorned or enlarged as necessary – a more permanent church of St Cyprian was raised at Ndabeni in 1912, with the altar a copy of that in the Mission House chapel at Cowley[120] – but the arrival of Ninian Comper's "perfectly beautiful" pulpit for St Crispin's at Yerendawana, the design of which, with that of the lectern (it included two desks at different levels to provide for what Elwin called "my boy and man readers"), Comper had given as an alms-offering, marked the completion of the final major building raised by the SSJE, now firmly established on four continents.[121] Thereafter the churches built by the Society were relatively modest, conceived of as outstations to be served from Poona and Tsolo respectively.

At home, the essential work of the Society also flourished. Its scholarship expanded: more books were published, and Cary was sent to Moscow and

---

117 *CE* June 1913.
118 Nicholson, 24 Oct 1912.
119 *CE* Dec 1912.
120 Noel, 7 Aug 1912.
121 Elwin, 13 May 1913.

St Petersburg to gain experience of the Orthodox Church;[122] while in March 1913 the *Cowley Evangelist* advertised several forthcoming residential three- or four-day retreats for clergy and laymen at both Cowley and Westminster. Congreve perhaps had the widely-flung and diverse nature of SSJE's work in mind when he wrote about the Communion of Saints later that year.

> However God may lead us in our prayer to realise the Communion of Saints, as we pray with them and rejoice with them in the Holy Eucharist, we will consider how faith in their solidarity with us in Christ lifts the horizon of our life. Think how this little forsaken pool in the sand, our life in England today, the faith of the Catholic Church brings the sound of the great sea, rising all along the shore, and overflowing our banks: how the life of all the Saints flows in, and we know that we are one with the unity, holiness, joy, of the glorious Body of Christ. Think how this capacity for fellowship for communion with all Saints, this passion of brotherhood in Christ, is meant to grow.[123]

Shortly afterwards, the empty niches in the reredos at St John's, Bowdoin Street, were populated with figures from Oberammergau, painted by Ralph Adams Cram. "So now", wrote Bull from Boston, "we have a very full and inspiring set of saints set before our eyes, and we before theirs."[124] When he later travelled to Nassau he was pleasantly surprised to find that "a number of coloured people inquire after Father Benson with great affection, and remember even his first visit with Father O'Neill."[125]

The American work had occupied much of the discussions of Greater Chapter since 1910: it had been proposed to grant independence to the American congregation to try and iron out the many historic and continuing anomalies of the Society's attempt to run a daughter house in an independent country with an independent church.[126] Benson had opposed this development from the beginning – it had formed the bedrock of the rupture with Charles Grafton – and as late as 1905 he was still railing against the idea. "It makes me quite uncomfortable," he told Page, "to think of [...] the idea of perpetuating the House at Boston. It is not a Religious House, and never can be." He wanted the house closed, and the church given to the Sisters of St Margaret.[127] It may well be that Benson was the unnamed "one member of the Chapter [who] did not vote", when the others present voted wholeheartedly to grant independence to the American congregation of the Society as soon as the house in Boston numbered seven professed priests. It was clear that although a full administrative rupture would necessarily take place, the Society hoped and intended that the usual warmth of relations and regularity of contact would remain unaffected.[128]

---

122 Cary, 1 April (Old Calendar), 1913ff.
123 *CE* November 1913.
124 Bull, 6 Jan 1914.
125 Bull, 5 Mar 1914.
126 GreC 1910, SSJE/2/3/165.
127 Benson, 22 Aug 1905, SSJE/6/1/2/192ff.
128 GreC 1913, SSJE/2/5/34ff.

The various arrangements were laid out in a newly-cast Statute, which was adopted at a special General Chapter held directly after the Annual Chapter of 1914; and ratified by the Visitor at the end of July.[129] Maxwell visited shortly afterwards: he preached at, and particularly approved of, the new St Augustine's Church for "our colored congregation" in South Boston;[130] but his visit was a short one. By September 1913 he was on his way to inspect the Indian missions. He was travelling with Moore and Br Walter Frederick, and wrote to say that they had met a Maronite priest in Cairo, who had been "a little puzzled at my account of ourselves as being Catholics without the Pope, for to him obviously the Pope was the whole thing". He had taken a great interest in the knots in their girdles – he turned out to be a monk of Mount Lebanon – and was delighted to find that they were monks also. "'*Alors!*' he exclaimed, '*nous sommes confrères*'."

The whole Cowley contingent was drawn up on Mazagon pier when the Superior General and his companions landed at Bombay. They would shortly be under canvas, leading missions in the countryside around Poona; but on the morning after their arrival they were formally welcomed in the mission compound by the people.[131] "We were all duly garlanded", wrote Maxwell. "I do not know what Brother Walter Frederick felt like in wreaths of roses for the first time." They had sailed with the Austrian-Lloyd line, which he thought "one of the best ways of coming, and wonderfully quick".[132]

Maxwell had sailed to America on the *Lusitania*;[133] while the vessel of the line which carried Walter Frederick to India to start his mission-work for the Society was called the *Habsburg*. Soon enough an announcement in the *Cowley Evangelist* spoke of a new state of affairs at the Mission House.

> Father Waggett writes very cheerfully from the front, but attention to the requirement of the Censor prevents our having much news. Father Conran will no doubt already be in France when our November *Cowley Evangelist* appears in print.[134]

The Cowley Fathers had gone to war.

---

129 Special GenC 1914, SSJE/2/5/163ff.
130 Maxwell, 9 Oct 1912.
131 Maxwell, 3 Dec 1913.
132 Maxwell, 3 October 1913.
133 *CE* Sept 1912.
134 *CE* November 1914.

13

BROTHERS IN ARMS

The great change comes, and the great testing.

—Philip Napier Waggett SSJE[1]

M any people – including the Archbishop of Canterbury, Randall Davidson – had hoped in the summer of 1914 that the gathering storm in Europe might pass Great Britain by. Germany's violation of neutral Belgium in early August made a declaration of war inevitable, however; and, as Davidson's latest biographer observes, he himself became "fundamentally committed to the idea that Britain was fighting a virtuous war against tyranny".[2] Among the leaders of the Anglo-Catholic party both Charles Gore, who was by then Bishop of Oxford, and Cosmo Gordon Lang, who had been translated to York, also concluded after no little soul-searching that Britain's entry into the conflict was the only right and honourable course of action in defence of the defenceless.[3]

Albert Marrin does not treat the work of the religious orders in *The Last Crusade: The Church of England in the First World War*, despite the fact that the leading men's orders all had members serving at the front at one time or another.[4] Even Alan Wilkinson, in his updated and definitive work *The Church of England and the First World War* only mentions them in passing[5] – although he devotes a whole chapter to the period in his history of the Community of the Resurrection.[6] Edward Madigan, in *Faith under Fire: Anglican Army Chaplains and The Great War*, mentions the CR and the Society of the Sacred Mission; but only in the context of the chaplains who had received their priestly formation at Mirfield or Kelham.[7]

The Society of St John the Evangelist rallied to the cause as soon as war was declared. "A great change has come over all our lives", observed Philip

---

1 *CE* Sept 1914.

2 Michael Hughes, *Archbishop Randall Davidson*, Abingdon: Routledge (2018), 5.

3 Stuart Bell, "The Church and the First World War", in Stephen G. Parker and Tom Lawson (eds), *God and War: The Church of England and Armed Conflict in the Twentieth Century*, Burlington: Ashgate (2012), 33ff.

4 Albert Marrin, *The Last Crusade: The Church of England in the First World War*, Durham, NC: Duke University Press (1974).

5 Alan Wilkinson, *The Church of England and the First World War*, Cambridge: Lutterworth Press (2014).

6 Alan Wilkinson, *The Community of the Resurrection*, London: SCM Press (1992), 129ff.

7 Edward Madigan, *Faith under Fire: Anglican Army Chaplains and the First World War*, Basingstoke: Palgrave Macmillan (2011).

Waggett in the *Cowley Evangelist*. "We were forced to face the dread of war, and a little later we faced the dread of peace, a peace which would have been purchased by the desertion of duty, and the fatal acknowledgement that might is right."[8]

The Superior General immediately increased the number of newspapers delivered – in addition to those regular subscriptions paid for by donors[9] – and instructed for them to be placed in the common rooms earlier in the day than had been the custom, so that the brethren's private prayers might be better informed. At the General Chapter of 1915 he spoke of "the sacredness of the causes for which we are fighting"; which included, among other considerations, "for our very existence as a free country and Empire".[10] Brian Taylor considered Gerald Maxwell to have shared "the views of most thoughtful patriots";[11] and by July 1915 the Society had invested £1700 in war bonds.[12]

George Congreve sought wisdom in James Mozley's thoughts about the Franco-Prussian War – four decades earlier, but well within the memory of most of his brethren. In 1871 Mozley had channelled Augustine and Aquinas on the "startling and extraordinary" idea of Christians killing other Christians, and drawn the conclusion that

> "Resist not evil" cannot be a law for a nation, or even for a family. An individual may be free to submit to injuries that affect himself alone; he is not free to allow his wife and children, or a poor neighbour, to be brutally ill-used by a tyrant, or a friendly but weaker State to be crushed by a stronger, through selfish ambition. A humble individual may surrender his own personal rights; he may not out of humility surrender the rights of other people. There are natural rights, and questions of life and death of nations, which nations must be left to decide as well as they can.

He now concurred with Mozley that "the Church was not *'made a judge and divider'* in such questions. She stands neutral, and takes in both sides; both sides fight within the bond of Christian unity. The Church contemplates war as a mode of settling national questions, which is justified by the want of any other way of settling them. This *judicial* character of war, as a way of obtaining justice, gives war its morality."

Congreve came from a distinguished military family, of course; but in publishing his analysis in the pages of the *Cowley Evangelist*, the Society effectively adopted his theology of self-sacrifice as an offering to God as its own position. It was a stand that found favour far beyond the SSJE, which would itself be called to live out the spirit of sacrifice soon enough. In practical terms, it was immediately obvious that the SSJE would have to cut its cloth. All fresh building work was postponed – the Hostel that the Society was hoping to raise in Bombay, to mirror St Columba's Home in Cape Town, would have to wait –

8 *CE* Sept 1914.
9 SSJE/3/1/111.
10 SSJE/2/5/192ff.
11 Brian Taylor, "The Cowley Fathers and the First World War" in *The Church and War, Studies in Church History*, 20, Oxford: Blackwell (1983), 384.
12 SSJE/2/5/196.

and the Superior General was clear that there would be no fundraising for any new endeavours.

The brethren in India and South Africa were already more isolated, because the normally efficient postal service was seriously disrupted by the outbreak of hostilities. "We do not know when we shall get letters from England," lamented Hugh Nicholson, from Poona. He was clear, however, that "war or no war, the work of the Mission goes on, and we must try and pay our way."[13] At Mazagon Oswald Barton was more sanguine, and realised that "we shall have to economize as much as possible".[14] He also noted "a crammed meeting of all creeds and castes of Indians at the Town Hall here to express their loyalty to the British Empire, and to offer their service to the Emperor."[15]

There were also obvious physical inconveniences. John Biscoe, home on furlough, was obliged to abandon his return ticket with Maxwell's hitherto favoured Austrian-Lloyd line. He took his chance instead on the Ellerman's Hall line, along with Frederick Playne and Br Leslie.[16] Their original vessel, the *City of Nagpur*, was requisitioned by the Admiralty; and so they had to wait and sail on the *Karachi*. When Lucius Cary made his way to Cape Town at the end of August, the *Gascon* – "the slowest vessel in the Union Castle fleet" – had to outmanoeuvre mines in the Solent and torpedo-boats in the Channel, and take a longer route than usual.[17] After a couple of days at the Mission House on Chapel Street, he pressed on to Bloemfontein, where he received the news of the German bombardment of the cathedral at Rheims. He was outraged: "I am hoping that S. Remigius will do something drastic to-day to avenge his Cathedral."[18]

The weather was wreaking its usual havoc; but to Gerald Ley it all seemed "dreadfully small talk compared with all the horror of war going on in Europe".[19] The South African bishops had appointed special prayers, and the Resident Magistrates had called together the local headmen to tell them that Europe was at war. "The natives are talking much about it, [but they] of course do not in the least take in where the seat of war is, or the vastness of the operations. Some are asking if the Government will need them."[20] The school for coloured children was nearly ready, and Ley and Godfrey Callaway had decided – the Society's moratorium on new work notwithstanding – that as it had been so long in the planning it should be opened nonetheless, but with all due "care and economy".[21] When Cary finally arrived at St Cuthbert's the whole mission turned out to greet him – in the course of the speeches he thought it "a new and welcome suggestion to find that my successful evasion of the Germanic peril was a proof of my own strategic skill and tact, and of my devotion to the Pondomisi".[22]

---

13 Nicholson, 11 Aug 1914.
14 Barton, 7 Aug 1914.
15 Barton, 14 Aug 1914.
16 *CE* Oct 1914.
17 Cary, 28 Aug 1914.
18 Cary, 1 Oct 1914.
19 Ley, 18 Aug 1914.
20 Ley, 24 Aug 1914.
21 Ley, 27 Aug 1914.
22 Cary, 28 Dec 1914.

By Christmas 1914 the war was not over. As the nations continued to rage, for the SSJE to some extent it was still business as usual; although under altered circumstances. Congreve had earlier written of "the perpetual beat of a regular life, like the never ceasing ticking of the clock – the bell that calls you almost every hour to one duty after another, and from this a sense of perpetual gentle strain of attention to order and discipline".[23] The same offices were sung, retreats were led – these now included those for teenagers, or "Junior Laymen" – and the Fellowship of St John continued to provide some of the means to keep it all going.

In India, there were troops camping on the Bombay maidans *en route* to the battlefields of Europe, and imported goods were in short supply; but both there and in South Africa the daily round continued: the monastic offices were prayed, brethren redeployed, masses offered, missions led, orphans fed, and children catechised. The mission children were of particular concern, and Maxwell was particularly adamant that the Society could not and would not "turn the orphan children adrift in a heathen country".[24] While he acknowledged that he was "well aware that our own numerous friends and helpers will be among the foremost to respond to what our country asks of them", he nevertheless emphasised the importance of keeping the existing work going.

> By far the greater part of our work is not such as can be retrenched without causing much suffering, and without crippling our efforts in the future. The Wantage and All Saints' Sisters", he went on, "as well as our own Society, have a very large number of children under their care, for whose support they are responsible [...] It is impossible to send them away; it is equally impossible to ask them to put off their next meal till after the war is over.

"It is not necessary to labour the point", he concluded: the Society needed to be able to continue to rely on a steady income from its regular supporters if its colonial mission work was to survive.[25] By Easter 1916, however, almsgiving was down by "several hundred pounds", and Maxwell renewed his appeal.[26]

Soon afterwards – to the Society's particular satisfaction and gratification – Field Marshals Lords Roberts, Grenfell, and Methuen issued a letter encouraging their brother officers serving in the colonies to make friends of the missionaries they found on the spot.

> [Y]ou will almost certainly come into contact with the representatives of various Christian missionary societies, whose special work it is to show to non-Christian peoples the love of the Christ Whom we profess to serve. We commend these missionaries to you as a body of men and women who are working helpfully with the Government, and contributing to the elevation of the people in a way impossible to official action.

---

23 Congreve, 12 Jan 1912, SSJE/6/5/2/2/13/3.
24 SSJE/2/5/200.
25 *CE* Oct 1914.
26 *CE* April 1915.

They reminded their readers of their responsibility to be ambassadors for the Church – "our personal lives materially affect the estimation in which the claims of Christianity are held by numbers of natives around us" – and that those who objected to mission work could only do so out of ignorance. "We would suggest that you will use all opportunities in making yourself personally acquainted with the work they are doing," they wrote, "and the character of the converts. Most Missions will bear looking into, and we are convinced that if you do this you will never afterwards condemn or belittle them." At the very least, such links would show "a fellow-countryman's sympathy" in the difficulties that lay ahead.[27]

Death of the Founder

The Society's first great blow of the war years occurred not at the front but at home; when, in the small hours of 14 January 1915, Richard Meux Benson died quietly in his sleep. "Somehow", wrote Edward Elwin, "it gave us a great sense of stability while we had the Founder still visibly with us;"[28] but Mildred Woodgate's general intimation that Benson's body had failed while his mind remained sharp was more discreet than accurate.

Maxwell was frank about the fact that Benson had not necessarily been fully aware of recent world events: Congreve wrote to Br John that it was "as if his part of life was written on a page that is turned over for ever, and the affairs of today belong to a fresh page in which he has no part".[29] He was alert enough, however, to be wheeled to the Sheldonian Theatre in 1913 to vote against the proposal to award degrees in Theology to "men of all religions and no religion", where his appearance "made the historical highlight in the scene";[30] and to descry the German east-coast bombardment in December 1914.

During his address to Greater Chapter in 1915 the Superior General alluded to "the curtailment, in one direction after another, of [Benson's] outward life of sense";[31] and both Robert Page and Congreve had earlier noted his mind's wanderings – in his last years he had taken to speaking "at all times and in all places, regardless of the rule of silence, and to all people including himself". Spence Burton observed that he had begun to sing "violently, to the complete overthrow of the plainsong"; although when the younger man prayed for King Edward and not King George in the course of the office, he "got well sat on". He had not preached to the Society since 1908; and soon afterwards Maxwell had taken his name off the mass-list, having observed him fumbling and stumbling about the altar in the course of one of his "terrifying" celebrations.[32]

Telegrams were sent far and wide announcing Benson's death, and soon the priest brethren scattered across the world began to offer requiems. Biscoe had

27 CE July 1915.
28 Elwin, 19 Jan 1915.
29 Congreve, 14 Feb 1913, SSJE/6/5/2/2/14/3a.
30 Congreve, SSJE/6/5/2/2/14/8a.
31 SSJE/2/5/190.
32 Woodgate, Father Benson, 175ff.

only just landed in Bombay when the news arrived: he wrote from Magazon of "Requiem Masses at all our altars"; and to say that the *Times of India* had contacted the Mission House for an obituary.[33] Benson's death, in his ninety-first year, was hardly a surprise; but it effectively severed the Catholic Movement's physical links with its founders. Benson had known Pusey and Liddon, and had heard Newman preach before the University; while the *Church Times* noted that "a new generation has arisen since Fr. Benson held sway at Cowley".

> To many, therefore, his is but a name in the long roll of those who have taken part in the hard fight for winning for the Church of England its full Catholic heritage. But to those who can carry back to the 'fifties and 'sixties of the last century his name will be placed in the very forefront of the leaders in the struggle.[34]

The frail Congreve preached at the Solemn Requiem in the community church: in his eightieth year, he was now the senior surviving member of the Society, and was himself obliged to enter a nursing home a few weeks later.[35] He took as his text Mark 8.35 – the *Cowley Evangelist* of February 1915 reproduced it under the title *Loss and Gain* – and after the obsequies Benson's body was laid to rest in the Society's plot in the churchyard of Ss Mary & John. Lord Halifax and Frederick Puller contributed their own encomia: Halifax reminisced about the SSJE's earliest days, while Puller wrote – tactfully – about Benson's life within the community. "He outlived all his contemporaries," he wrote, "and now he himself has been taken".

> It belongs to us who belong to his Society and for the Church at large to treasure his memory, and to cultivate the spirit of faith, self-surrender and un-worldliness which shone out so conspicuously in him. We shall thus be able to transmit to future generations all the best results of the movement which were so mightily wrought in him and in the work which he was enabled to accomplish.[36]

The memorial edition continued as normal with the usual letters and notices; but afterwards the *Cowley Evangelist* ran a series of meditations, reprinted – without irony – from Benson's *Life Beyond the Grave* of 1883. William Longridge and Congreve soon began preparing a volume of his letters;[37] while a memorial Calvary was commissioned from Ninian Comper for the parish churchyard, and dedicated in November 1917.[38]

Benson's memory would be long-lasting and far-reaching – and, in some cases, eclectic. Only a few years after his death a mural was added to the walls of St Michael & All Angels, Walsall – alongside images of Charles I and William Laud – depicting him wrapped dramatically in a cloak, with his right hand raised in blessing and his left holding a model of Bodley's community

33 Biscoe, 22 Jan 1915.
34 *Church Times*, 15 Jan 1915, 55.
35 *CE* April 1915.
36 *CE* Feb 1915.
37 G. Congreve SSJE & W. H. Longridge SSJE, *Letters of Richard Meux Benson*, London: A. R. Mowbray (1916).
38 *CE* Nov 1917.

church.[39] He later appeared in stained glass at All Saints', Clifton; and between St Francis of Assisi and St Ignatius Loyola in the nave of the Cathedral of St John the Divine in New York. Closer to home, the legacy of the Father Founder would continue to haunt the English congregation of the SSJE for the rest of its active life.

Only three of the brethren nominally resident at Cowley were absent from the funeral: Cary, who had made his way to St Cuthbert's through a colony under martial law;[40] and Waggett and Marcell Conran, who were serving in France. It may well be argued that the wide scope of the SSJE's work and its local responses to the effects of the war form a modest part of a wider correc- tive to a recent over-emphasis on the fighting in Flanders to the exclusion of the conflict on a number of other fronts.

The fighting in Mesopotamia, for example, brought the war in the Middle East particularly close to the Indian missions. The 16th Indian Infantry Brigade, which formed part of the Indian Expeditionary Force, included men from the Dorsetshire Regiment who had previously been stationed at Poona. They took part in the Fao Landing and the Battle of Basra in November 1914, after which Nicholson noted that of the men known to the SSJE by their church attendance, at least one had been killed – but also that the devout sergeant "who was the leader in all that was good" had been promoted. One of their officers later offered a chalice and paten to the mission for the new outstation church of St Michael & All Angels, Rasta Peth: the chalice in memory of his men who had died, and the paten in thanksgiving for his own safe return.[41] The Wantage Sisters, meanwhile, were bracing themselves for the arrival of the wounded at the Sassoon Hospital.

At Poona Nicholson worried about the fate of the newly-qualified carpen- ters, who would find it difficult to find work while the war continued; and soon afterwards the workshop at Mazagon was closed for the duration.[42] The Indian organist at Holy Name left Poona with the officer whose batman he was; but Sydney Moore continued painstakingly to compile his plainsong Marathi psalter.[43] Nicholson's letters sometimes betrayed a wistful sense of patriotism. From time to time the police visited the mission to ask whether there were any German or Austrian members in the community, as there might be in some of the Roman Catholic orders, and each time they left assured by him that the SSJE was "a purely English article".[44] When he went to lead a retreat at Ootacamund at the start of January 1915 he made a point of noting that "Ooty is one of those places where arum lilies grow like weeds; there is a wonderful show of white flowers on the Sisters' Altar for the festival of the Epiphany. In this part of India one sees the old English flowers that one loves so well."[45]

All the same, India and England were deeply bound each to the other – the *Cowley Evangelist* told its readers that "our hearts have been deeply stirred by

---

39 SSJE/11/2/1/60.
40 Cary, 21 Dec 1914.
41 Nicholson, 7 Oct 1915.
42 Barton, 29 Oct 1915.
43 Nicholson, 30 Oct 1914; 6 Nov 1914; 19 Nov 1914.
44 Nicholson, 4 Dec 1914; 19 Dec 1914.
45 Nicholson, 5 Jan 1915.

the thought of Indian regiments fighting in Europe side by side with soldiers from every part of the Empire, and by the thought of the place which India is finding for herself in the Empire's life"[46] – and there was general rejoicing when the first vocations to holy orders among the Society's Indian boys came to fruition. Nicholson called the ordinations "a great event in the history of our mission",[47] and soon afterwards the Mission House at Poona added a separate retreat for Indian laymen to those it already ran for catechists, ordinands, and priests.[48]

Louis Botha's brief campaign to neutralise German South-West Africa made its presence felt in Cape Town; and Charles Turner observed from Ndabeni that "it is not always realized what a lot of hidden work is being done in this war by the natives." He felt that many local people were "sometimes treated with little more consideration than the mules": by April 1915 the usually quiet location hospital was packed with workers who had either fallen ill or been injured in accidents, and the matron was run off her feet.[49] It was the Indian missions, however, where the effect was more easily observed day by day: by the middle of 1915 Nicholson was regularly receiving letters from "our lads who have gone to the front either in France or Persia". Not all of them had been the easiest with whom to deal: he noted that "several of our black sheep have gone, and the discipline of the life will be excellent for them" – although he was pleased that they wanted to keep in touch.[50]

CONSECRATION & SACRIFICE

Before his death Benson had forgiven the modernism of Charles Gore, who had become both his diocesan bishop and the Society's Visitor, and who professed to have "loved and honoured him with all my heart".[51] Preaching in the community church at Sexagesima 1915 – he had been abroad when Benson had died, and so had been unable to preside at the funeral – Gore reflected on the spirit of sacrifice in relation to the religious life, and in the context of the ongoing international strife. "It does not take a good Christian to make a good soldier," he declaimed, "but it does take a good soldier to be a good Christian".[52]

Congreve had entered upon a similar theme in 1914. "There is one side of the moral character of war in special harmony with the Christian type," he emphasised, "namely, the spirit of sacrifice which it develops – the individual faces death for his country. There is a mediatorial function which goes through the whole dispensation of God's natural providence, by which men have to suffer for each other, and one member of the nation has to bear the burden and share the grief of another. And it is this serious and sacred function which

---

46 *CE* May 1915.
47 Nicholson, 25 Feb 1915.
48 Nicholson, 26 March 1915.
49 Turner, 20 April 1915.
50 Nicholson, 9 July 1915.
51 Woodgate, *Benson*, 175ff.
52 *Church Times*, 12 Feb 1915.

consecrates war."[53] The ideal of a life of consecration and sacrifice was not strange to the SSJE; and by the time of the Founder's death the Society's ranks encompassed a number of men who had gained distinction not only as practitioners, but also as theologians and masters of the spiritual life.

Page, while he lived, had been instrumental in the early life of the Community of the Holy Rood when he was Vicar of Coatham, and had remained its Warden long after being professed in the SSJE; while with Maxwell, who was then about to step down as Sub-Warden at Wantage in order to join the Society, he had helped to revise the Rule and Constitutions of the Community of St Mary the Virgin in 1896. He had remained devoted to the All Saints Sisters, both while he was Chaplain-General and afterwards; and in due course the sanctuary of the sisters' new chapel at Khandala was given in his memory by various friends.

When George Hollings dropped dead at the altar of the Convent of the Incarnation on Holy Wednesday 1914, just after the Fourth Commandment, he fell surrounded by the Sisters of the Love of God, whose community he had founded in 1906 and nurtured since[54] – the SSJE later contributed £250 towards the sisters' new buildings at Fairacres, citing their "special claims" on the Society's attention.[55] He was the first priest of the Society to be buried in the SSJE plot in the parish churchyard, where he joined Br Walter. "One by one", Benson wrote at the time, "the number of the elect is being made complete".[56] It was further testament to the SSJE's international character that not long afterwards the Founder himself was only the third member of the Society to die and be buried at home.

Maxwell spent some of 1915 trying to help bring order to Denys Prideaux's chaotic community of Benedictines at Pershore,[57] and Longridge had developed a particular interest in reviving the Ignatian method of retreat-giving;[58] but the SSJE's particular expertise – apart from its own ministry of retreat-giving and spiritual guidance – had become the direction and care of the women's communities who depended upon the Cowley Fathers either for their foundation, or their sacraments, or both – with the exception of baptism, which the nursing sisters were empowered to administer in urgent cases, following the ancient practice of the Church.[59]

In such matters Luke Miller considers Congreve to have been preeminent: not just within the Society, but also in the wider Church of England. At the Pan-Anglican Congress of 1908 he had been the only male speaker to speak in the sessions on "Sisters, their Vocation and Special Work"; but the publication of *Audi Filia* by Cary – who had succeeded Hollings as Director of the Sisters of the Love of God, and who became Chaplain to Burnham Abbey in

---

53 *CE* Sept 1914.

54 Anson, *Call of the Cloister*, 251; 371ff; 497ff; 530.

55 SSJE/2/5/131; "The Enclosed Life", *CE* Feb 1920.

56 *CE* May 1914.

57 Petà Dunstan, *The Labour of Obedience: The Benedictines of Pershore, Nashdom and Elmore*, Norwich: Canterbury Press (2009), 30.

58 *CE* June 1916.

59 cf Nicholson, 7 Oct 1915.

1916 – indicated the presence of a competent successor.[60] In the same year William O'Brien became Chaplain of the Sisters of Our Saviour at Chesterfield; and Thomas Bignold became Warden of the Community of All Hallows at Ditchingham.[61]

Puller's liturgical work was also being supplemented by Cary, who spent much of the 1910s working on the Society's new office book, which would complement Edward Trenholme's *Day Hours* of 1908; and by Nalbro' Robinson. The *Cowley Evangelist* observed in September 1915 that "as the terrible war in Europe is bringing the East and West into a closer moral and spiritual union, on account of the [controversial] alliance with Russia, the interest in the rites and ceremonies of the Eastern Church that already exists is likely to be further increased", and that the latest must-have book on the subject was Robinson's *Monasticism in the Orthodox Churches*, which would, conveniently, be published soon.[62]

The spectre of death in war had by then already begun to impinge on the Society's life and work. Frederick Brown, who had trained at Dorchester and was due to have spent his deacon's year at Tsolo, joined the Army Medical Corps in 1914 and went straight to the front – he was killed ten months later, in an attempt to bring in some wounded men.[63] When the *Lusitania* was sunk on 7 May 1915, Basil Maturin – who was by then Roman Catholic Chaplain to the University – went down with the ship. The later accounts of its final minutes accorded him a posthumous place among its heroes, calmly hearing last confessions on deck and trying to reunite a child with its mother.[64]

Maturin had never fully abandoned his former life. "I don't think I shall ever cease to love Cowley and all that belongs to it", he wrote after his secession. "I say the old prayer every day."[65] His death affected Congreve particularly – their shared Irish provenance had brought them close as confrères, and they had remained in regular contact. Congreve wrote affectionately to Maturin's sister, Sr Fidelia CSJB, of "all the vitality of intelligence and affection, all the light and joy and beauty of his soul".

> I refuse to dwell in thought on the sorrow of the end, for that is passed and over for ever, and one thinks of the Infinite Love that has welcomed him home. And of all the hope and happiness he has brought to numberless souls in this world, whom he has taught to look through it, to our Lord.[66]

At the same time Conran was serving with the 25th Field Ambulance in France. He was probably near Loos, but the demands of the censor precluded any solid

---

60 Lucius Cary SSJE, *Audi Filia: Notes of Addresses given in Retreat*, Oxford: A. R. Mowbray & Co. (1915).

61 Bull, 29 June 1916, SSJE/2/5/1.

62 Nalbro' Frazier Robinson SSJE, *Monasticism in the Orthodox Churches* London: Cope & Fenwick (1916).

63 Ley, 2 July 1915.

64 Maisie Ward, *Father Maturin, A Memoir: with Selected Letters*, London: Longmans, Green & Co. (1920).

65 Gertrude Donald, *Men Who Left the Movement*, London: Burns Oates & Washbourne Ltd (1933), 367.

66 Maisie Ward, *Father Maturin*, 60.

information. His particular charism was to encourage others to attend to the development of their holiness of life: in 1914 he began to distribute his *Chaplets of Prayer* to the men who sought him out, and taught them the prayers.

Conran wrote towards the end of 1915 to say that he had been preparing some of his men for confirmation, but that in many cases the teaching on matters of faith was at a remedial level, and the vagaries of war meant that life was frequently haphazard: "often I rode for miles to only to find my men off to bathe, or drill, or dig, or some duty or other, and so my afternoon was practically lost." The ceremony, when it came, was equally chaotic.

> The time had to be changed to an hour earlier the day before. I was afraid the change would upset things, but at 2 p.m. 126 of those I had prepared were there, marched down by their n.c.o.'s, but no Bishop; then a wire to say 'motor broken down,' but he was coming on […] the men were getting uneasy; they had to be back in their trenches.

In the end the Bishop arrived in time for a truncated service: there was "no time for address or hymns", the questions were put and answers given, and then all the men knelt down to have the sacrament conferred upon them. After the final blessing, they formed up and were marched off again – "I fear some to death, and some to be wounded", thought Conran, as heavy fighting had resumed almost immediately. He comforted himself with the thought that they had at least been given "the gift of the Holy Ghost to strengthen them through what was to come the following day; a day I shall never forget as long as I live, or any, I think, who went through it".

One "poor fellow" particularly claimed his prayers: he had been ordered to his machine gun just before the ceremony, so had remained unconfirmed in the face of the onslaught. "He was killed, but I feel happy about him", Conran emphasised. "It wasn't his fault."[67] He himself was as deep in the action as any of his men: by February 1916 he had been mentioned in despatches and had won the Military Cross.[68] In June the *Cowley Evangelist* announced with pride that he had received his medal "from the King's hands at Buckingham Palace, on Saturday, May 20";[69] but Conran's service had been costly, and he was declared medically unfit to return to the front.[70]

Nearer home, Br Michael was helping the military chaplains at St Thomas's Hospital, just across the Thames from St Edward's House. There he led ward services, and shared in the pastoral work; while he also ministered to "individual servicemen, who learnt to turn to St Edward's House in increasing numbers". From these beginnings he developed an immense ministry of correspondence with soldiers on active service and in military hospitals, and with the families of many who were killed.

His work took on a new dimension when some of his correspondents asked if they might be sent crucifixes to wear under their uniforms, "to show that they believed and trusted in Christ Crucified, and resolved to walk in the right

---

67 Conran, 11 Oct 1915.
68 Taylor, "The Cowley Fathers and the First World War", 385.
69 *CE* June 1916.
70 *CE* July 1916.

way, realizing that before them lay many trials, temptations, and dangers". Soon there was such demand – "once comrade telling, or bringing, another" – that he could hardly keep up, and kept a stock of pre-blessed crosses in preparation.

Michael came to think of those who undertook to wear the crucifix in this way as modern-day knights, and the giving of the crucifix at St Edward's House developed a ritual of its own.

> [T]he military details of each recipient were noted down, and with all who came in person I had a short talk about the Crucifix, and what the wearing of it involved; then I took them into the Chapel and prayed with them, giving each his Crucifix from the Altar, and saying a few encouraging words as I placed it with its cord around his neck. [I]n each case the Knight's earnestness and gratitude has much impressed me.

Others were sent crucifixes by post, with a general letter to which Michael added "a personal postscript". The only obligation laid upon the "Knights of the Crucifix" was that each should be baptised, and should strive to live out his baptismal promises. To that end, as the war progressed, each knight was sent four booklets "intended to form a line of practical, instructive thought". Although Michael was keen to emphasise that the essence of the work was rooted in the Church of England, by 1918 the 6000 or so knights included Roman Catholics, Presbyterians, and Nonconformists of all kinds of shade and hue. To these, from 1916, were added the "Beadsmen", who undertook to pray daily for a number of enrolled Knights – and who later included a number of women whose husbands had been killed.[71]

At the end of the war the Knights of the Crucifix had members as far away as Australia, the West Indies, Canada, Newfoundland, New Zealand and South Africa. "The work now practically embraces the Imperial Army," wrote its founder; and to this number was added those knights in the Royal Navy and the young Royal Air Force. In all three services the members came from all ranks. Michael was present when the Unknown Warrior was buried at Westminster Abbey on Armistice Day 1920, and later added the anonymous man to the roll of knights. On the grave he placed a crucifix that had formed part of his ministry to wounded and dying soldiers at St Thomas's Hospital; and when the marble slab was laid in place a year later, the Dean of Westminster, Herbert Ryle, placed Michael's cross underneath it at the head of the grave.

Both Conran and Michael's activities were inextricably linked to the ideals of self-sacrifice and righteous toil which underpinned the SSJE's spirituality in the war years. In October 1915 the *Cowley Evangelist* particularly underlined the importance of "the Life of Wisdom, as regulated by Hope",[72] and soon afterwards it urged its friends to pray earnestly for the success of the "Novena of Prayer in the Present Time of Trouble", which it had arranged to be observed by religious communities in England and overseas either side of the new year:

---

71 Taylor, *Brother Michael*, 13ff.
72 *CE* Oct 1915.

"There is no Christian who may not help the Novena by one Lord's Prayer for God's blessing upon it."[73]

LOVE & LOSS

The life of sacrifice continued. Callaway's brother Robert – who had been in charge of Holy Cross Mission, Eastern Pondoland, and was a frequent visitor to Tsolo, where he had served at the start of his ministry – was killed on the Somme in September 1916.[74] "Thank you for your cable about dear Robert," wrote Callaway from Tsolo shortly afterwards. "He made a very willing and generous offering of his life, and very touching are the tributes of his many friends."[75] At the same time a number of young men from Pondoland and Tsolo had answered the call to serve with the controversial South African Native Labour Corps.[76] When the new mission church was dedicated on Holy Cross Day ten years later, St Cuthbert's was out in force: Francis Rumsey noted that hanging in the new building, "set in the middle of a solid wooden cross, [was] the pyx used in the war by the Rev. Robert Callaway (founder of the mission) which was found on his dead body on the battlefield".[77]

Congreve had numerous nephews and cousins serving with the forces: not least Walter and his son Billy – "I don't know any parents and children more devoted to each other".[78] He wrote to comfort and encourage Billy's fiancée when he returned to the front in April 1916: Pamela Maude thanked him for helping her to understand "the security of duty known, and the love of God".[79] Miller notes that Billy himself had imbibed his great-uncle's faith and spirituality. "I could not ever have a swelled head", he wrote from the front, "because I know it is not me who does well. I remember in that little book Uncle George gave me, and which I always carry, came the words 'I cannot do this unless Thou enablest me' and often have I said those words to God, knowing their truth".[80] Congreve needed all his resolve a few months later, when on 20 July – after having spent several weeks in the thick of the fighting around Longueval, leading reconnaissance missions and recovering casualties under heavy fire – the young Major Congreve was once more risking his life in no-man's land when a sniper's bullet ripped through his throat.

"My dear boy killed at the front!", wrote Congreve. "Everything is happy about him. He was – and remains, not only a very gallant gentleman, but he possesses the best of all qualities that go to make the 'happy warrior' [a

---

73 CE Dec 1915.

74 Alan Wilkinson, *The Church of England and the First World War*, London: SPCK (1978), 42.

75 Callaway, 23 Sept 1916.

76 cf Ley, 16 Oct 1917; B. P. Willan, "The South African Native Labour Contingent, 1916–1918", *Journal of African History*, v.19 no.1 (1978), 61ff.

77 Rumsey, 26 Sept 1926.

78 Congreve, 8 Aug 1913, SSJE/6/5/2/2/14/16ff.

79 Congreve, 6 Nov 1915, SSJE/6/5/2/6/5.

80 L. H. Thornton & Pamela Fraser, *The Congreves*, London: John Murray (1930), 330ff. Luke Miller notes that the book was Br Lawrence's (c.1614–91) *The Practice of the Presence of God*.

reference to Wordsworth]: the love of God – a habit of prayer."[81] During the Boer War he had mused that those who died in war were particularly blessed, "because they have the grace to do their duty to God and to their country at great cost, which is worth more than to die on a feather bed"[82] – Miller observes that for Congreve "the call is not to mere loss of life and limb, but to sacrifice and consecration." For his gallantry in the weeks leading up to his death Billy was awarded a posthumous Victoria Cross.[83] He and Pamela had been married for all of seven weeks, and she was already pregnant.

Waggett later commented that "Some of the very old people have hardly been able to 'feel' the War. Fr Congreve was *in* it utterly";[84] and it was the Congreves' link with Cowley that took Waggett himself to France. Both Marrin and Wilkinson, in their studies on the Church of England and the First World War, point out the various links that inevitably existed between a number of distinguished churchmen and officers. These were usually ties of blood or schooling, but not exclusively so. The Congreves belonged to the wider Cowley diaspora whose family life was linked to the Society, and at the start of the war Walter Congreve was in command of the 6th Infantry Division. While waiting to go to the front they were camped on Midsomer Common in Cambridge, which happened to be just opposite Waggett's house on Chesterton Lane.

The soldier and the priest discussed at length the possibility of the latter finding some "useful work", and when the troops were mobilised in early September 1914, Waggett went with them as their chaplain. The disarray in chaplaincy arrangements at the start of the war meant that many priests were able to redeploy themselves when they realised a need; and when Waggett came upon a large field hospital near the front with no spiritual provision, he stayed put – he was not officially attached to the Royal Army Chaplains' Department until December.[85] His letters at the time talk of the constant stream of wounded men, the desperate state of some of the injuries, the burial of the dead, and the constant artillery bombardment – at one point early on he

---

81 Congreve, 17 Aug 1916, SSJE/6/5/2/6.

82 Congreve, 22 Dec 1899, SSJE/6/5/2/4/34.

83 "For most conspicuous bravery during a period of fourteen days preceding his death in action. This officer constantly performed acts of gallantry and showed the greatest devotion to duty, and by his personal example inspired all those around him with confidence at critical periods of the operations. During preliminary preparations for the attack he carried out personal reconnaissance of the enemy lines, taking out parties of officers and non-commissioned officers for over 1,000 yards in front of our line, in order to acquaint them with the ground. All these preparations were made under fire. Later, by night, Major Congreve conducted a battalion to its position of employment, afterwards returning to it to ascertain the situation after assault. He established himself in an exposed forward position from where he successfully observed the enemy, and gave orders necessary to drive them from their position. Two days later, when Brigade Headquarters was heavily shelled and many casualties resulted, he went out and assisted the medical officer to remove the wounded to places of safety, although he was himself suffering severely from gas and other shell effects. He again on a subsequent occasion showed supreme courage in tending wounded under heavy shell fire. He finally returned to the front line to ascertain the situation after an unsuccessful attack, and whilst in the act of writing his report, was shot and killed instantly." *London Gazette*, 24 Oct 1916.

84 *CE* June 1918.

85 Taylor, "The Cowley Fathers and the First World War", 384.

had a near miss, and was forced to abandon a service after a shell exploded nearby.

Waggett actively engaged with the theology of self-sacrifice advanced by the Society, of course; but his deep reflection on the subject and the reality of life at the front sometimes led him to difficult ground.

> [S]o *much* suffering; such *processions* and masses of hurt men: so many dear dear friends who *can't* stay with us. I am convinced all the lives are laid down for a mysterious purpose of regeneration, and I *understand* sometimes, without ever being able to explain, why the Death of the Lord was necessary for our salvation. I understand sometimes quite well. But it surprisingly little I can say to the poor wounded.

As the war drew on, it began to take its toll on him. "Every death is to me *more* grievous than the last, not less," he wrote, "and people keep writing to me from home of the fun I must be having and the interesting life. I cannot tell *how* these poor widows are to bear the grief hearing of death as the first definitive news of their husband". He recovered his equilibrium after some much-needed leave; and later drew the conclusion that "you can't have the Crucified *with* you, if you're not in the smallest degree being crucified yourself".

He was mentioned in despatches after the Battle of Ypres, where he assisted in the evacuation of the wounded under fire – after which he had to contend with the seemingly interminable mud, and the "pitiful" sight of displaced villagers whose homes had been destroyed. He wrote letters home for wounded soldiers, tried to keep up his reading, and – like Conran – prepared men for confirmation when he could. In short, his life was much like that of any other chaplain, except for his unusual – if not unique – status as an Anglican chaplain who was also a professed religious.

By June 1916 he had been appointed a senior chaplain, and found himself "extraordinarily busy" – a situation not helped by a bout of trench fever. He was billeted in an abandoned house, where he celebrated a daily early mass in his bedroom for the eight chaplains in his charge,[86] before their work began. Being now a little further from the front meant that he was even able to organise day retreats for his clerical colleagues; and by the autumn he had turned his mind to the possibility of planting seeds to be harvested when the war was over. "The best part of young male England is *here*," he wrote. "We have also got here [...] the *whole* of the future clergy."

> So if there ever *does* come a possibility of quiet speaking here, it must be taken. And it is fine for the chaplains to have something more positive to do than the consolation of suffering, and fine for them to have something more definite to do than the encouragement of the troops.

He was mentioned in despatches again in November, before being recalled to lead the chaplaincy to the soldiers at and around Tidworth. By then he was 58, and he was delighted to find enthusiasm for Christian formation among the

---

86 Bull, 29 June 1916, SSJE/2/5/1.

young men he found there: "that God should have given me such sons in my old age!"[87]

A Terrible Season

In January 1916 the two handymen who worked at the Mission House were given notice, and "advised of the expediency of seeking munitions, or other work, for the Country".[88] After the Derby Scheme and the consequent Military Service Act in March, the *Cowley Evangelist* was at pains to stress that several of the younger lay brothers had been permitted to volunteer "before it was compulsory, and are faithfully at work on the Western Front at the moment".[89] In addition to the priests serving as chaplains – which included a number of mission co-workers and Priest Associates of the Society – they were joined by men who had been educated in the Society's schools; had taken their part in the community church as musicians or altar boys; had worshipped with the community as students; or who had other connections with the Society through their families.

All were remembered daily after Nones in the Lady Chapel, and the General Chapter of 1916 made a point of sending particular "affectionate greeting" and encouragement to the members of the Society serving with the forces.[90] Scattered excerpts from letters home show that correspondence was kept up as best as possible with all sorts of men with Cowley connections: prisoners of war wrote with expressions of thanks for books sent; while others sent encouraging letters from the trenches, but were dead before they arrived.[91] The wounded wrote from hospital, while Br Giles's letters spoke evocatively of the conditions at the front.

> The mention of woods usually brings to mind pictures of peaceful loveliness, but here for many of us the places of undisturbed growth will raise scenes of horror and desolation. Little remains but places where woods once were. The trees that remain standing are torn branch from branch; the leaves still on them are wizened and burnt. A terrible season has overtaken them.[92]

Others wrote with more homely messages. Sheltering from a "very wet and cold" afternoon, beside the stove in his tent near Paris, Basil Bucknall, the organist of the community church, wrote with a brief description of his work – "we have never carried so many very badly wounded as we have here. It seems to us more and more terrible as the war goes on" – but his thoughts were much of what he had left behind. "I should much like to have news of you all and of the choir."[93] Cary was doing his best to keep things going, having been

---

87 Nias, *Waggett*, 138ff.
88 SSJE/3/1/7.
89 *CE* April 1917.
90 cf *CE* August 1916.
91 cf *CE* July 1916; *CE* Oct 1916.
92 Giles, 17 Aug 1916.
93 Bucknall, 2 August 1917.

urged by the Superior General "to simplify the music for the time being".[94] In November 1916 the elderly George Palmer returned to Cowley – twenty years after he had overseen the music at the opening of the new church, and a year before he received a Lambeth Doctorate of Music for his contribution to liturgical scholarship[95] – to act as organist and salvage what he could of the plainsong.[96]

By mid-August 1916 Giles was somewhere in the thick of the various Somme offensives. That month's *Cowley Evangelist* had arrived at his dugout in time for him to read it during what he called "a very 'hot' time". He noted that a sermon by Congreve on "The Beauty of God" had "helped one immensely to meet calmly" the pressure of work under fire; while observing that a Calvary in the remains of a nearby copse had remained untouched, and that the corpus of another nearby had been dislodged, and was now held in place by bandages.

The mention – either consciously or unconsciously – of the Calvaries among the wreckage of the countryside fed, again, into the SSJE's theology of self-sacrifice and union with the Cross. Giles followed it with the reassurance that the "unspeakably horrible affair" was at least "bringing to light the noblest qualities of self-sacrifice and endurance".

> We, in the R.A.M.C., have had some casualties – six wounded, and three have been killed. The last act of one of the killed was to take off his tunic and place it over a wounded man in his charge; the other two had volunteered to take down to the dressing station under very heavy shell fire an urgent case.

"These three have set us all a very high example", he ended. *"Laus Deo."*[97]

Congreve explored the theology of self-sacrifice again at Easter 1916, when in the pages of the *Cowley Evangelist* he told a parable of a tradesman who went to war – "a very average man who had led an ordinary kind of life". The story had first appeared in *The Spectator*; but it served his purpose well.[98] This man's faith was only a veneer of establishment respectability: his morals were practical and opportunistic, and he went to church only to please his mother and to reassure his clients. "Then," said Congreve, "came the bewildering change of circumstance", and he found himself spirited from his comfortable office chair, and serving in France.

Amid the terrifying reality of frontline trench-warfare, he resigned himself not to God but to Fate – which would surely deal him an inescapable hand, and leave him either dead, maimed, or blinded. Such a destiny had befallen others, and his turn must surely come. The waiting was agony, and the conditions terrible. Then, after months of intolerable suspense, he was ordered to take the place of one of his N.C.O.s, who had fallen ill.

He knew from having seen it done by others that his task was now to be constantly with the men: to encourage and calm those in the trenches; to reassure the sentries on night-watch; to steady the nerves of the soldiers whenever

---

94 SSJE/2/5/202.
95 http://www.lambethpalacelibrary.org/files/lambeth_degrees_date.pdf
96 SSJE/2/5/1.
97 Giles, 17 Aug 1916.
98 *Spectator*, 30 Oct 1915.

one of their comrades was killed; and to tend urgently to the treatment of the wounded. This cycle continued until the battalion was relieved a couple of weeks later, and away from the front he found himself with time to reflect on what had passed.

"It suddenly struck him", continued Congreve, "that all the time he had actually forgotten to be afraid, or even nervous. He had been so anxious about his men that he had forgotten all about himself. Then he realised that he had stumbled up against something like a discovery; that he had hit upon the secret of courage and indeed of every other virtue: and the secret was unselfishness, the will to lose your life in others."

> But it was not a discovery at all, for the solution of all the puzzles with which the war had confronted him was in that very religion in which he had been brought up, and yet he had missed the solution all these years. It was there all the time in the Cross of Jesus Christ [...] Faith was the higher form of self-confidence. Love was the only spring of selflessness. All through the years the Holy Spirit had been touching his spirit and he knew it not. Now at last he knew. In the din of battle, amid the shriek of shells, he had heard the still small voice.

"When loss was everywhere", he went on, "he had found something for which Christ died – his own soul. Civilization might fail, but not religion, the religion of the Cross. Amid all the ruin the Cross stood, revealing the heart of the Father that alone had not failed. But it took the war to convince him of it."[99]

Such then, for the Society of St John the Evangelist, was the summit and whole meaning of the work of those of its members and friends who were serving at the front, and the deaths of those had been killed. Of the former, the Superior General was clear – in the context of chaplaincy – that "we feel glad and proud that they should be helping our soldiers and we pray that they may be helped and guided in the very difficult and honourable work in which they are engaged".[100] Of the latter, thought O'Brien – who was serving as Novice Master – "we can but say that we are giving of our best. May God accept their sacrifice, and make us less unworthy of it."[101]

---

99 *CE* April 1916.
100 SSJE/2/5/194.
101 *CE* Nov 1916.

14

IN THE FURNACE

The war with Satan and his angels on the one side and a very full sacramental life on the other is in full swing, and as in any other war it is marked with some disaster and also many gallant deeds.

—Edward Fenton Elwin SSJE[1]

The ideal of the consecrated offering of self-sacrifice, united with the ultimate triumph of the Cross, continued to pervade the public orisons of the Society of St John the Evangelist as the First World War progressed. The war itself and its concomitant losses were a constant presence in the pages of the *Cowley Evangelist*, in which news of fallen friends became a regular feature; and from its theological vantage-point the SSJE was able to point, through the memory of the serried ranks of the dead, to a consummation of the highest ideals of the Christian life. There was general shock throughout the Society at the end of 1915, however, when the SSJE was "called to face the loss that it would seem to us that we could least afford".[2]

It had been obvious to the brethren at Cowley that the burden of leading the Society through the war had wearied the Superior General; and Gerald Maxwell had already made it clear that, although he would feel bound to accept the will of his brethren, he did not wish to be re-elected at the next Greater Chapter: "it would be a great relief to take my natural place [among the ordinary brethren] in the Society".[3] Early on the morning of 3 December he came downstairs as usual, intending to say the 6 a.m. mass in the Holy Spirit Chapel on the south side of the community church. As was his custom he went to pray in the Lady Chapel first, but as he left to cross the cloister he felt a sudden attack of pain and a general loss of strength, and struggled back to bed instead. Twenty-four hours later, he was dead.

> It seems that the strain of unremitting work had exhausted all the nervous strength, and the collapse that had come over him was complete. All through the day the restlessness and the sleeplessness at night witnessed to the utter loss of power and control, though there was still no sign to give warning of that moment when, on Saturday morning at dawn, just as the first Mass of the day was being finished, with no word spoken but only one glance upwards and a smile, the Father gave back his soul to God.[4]

---

1 *CE* July 1909.
2 *CE* Jan 1916.
3 SSJE/2/5/205ff.
4 *CE* Jan 1916.

Maxwell had been at Cowley for almost twenty years, and had led the Society for nearly eight of them. He was 57 when he died, and he had buried his two predecessors; but now it fell – characteristically – to Frederick Puller and George Congreve to try to trim the boat. "We cannot help sorrowing", said Puller, from the pulpit of the community church the next morning – which Maxwell had himself occupied on Advent Sunday, only the week before – "Our Father was so dear to us, and seemed to be so necessary for us."

> He was kind and considerate and courteous, and extraordinarily unselfish. He was an eminently just and equitable man, and he was the soul of honour and truthfulness. For that very reason he was loyal to all those who were in any position over him; when he was in a subordinate position in our Society, he was loyal to his religious Superiors; as a priest and as a member of the Church, he was loyal to his Bishop and to his mother the Church of England, and to her Prayer-book; and as a patriotic Englishman he was loyal to his King and Country, taking the greatest interest in the ups and downs of the present war, firmly convinced of the righteousness of our cause, and full of bright assurance of our ultimate victory.

"All of these virtues", he thought, "were sanctified and nourished by the genuineness of his life as a Religious." After drawing comfort from Scripture, he charged his hearers to pray for Maxwell – "we must still offer the Holy Sacrifice on his behalf" – and for the Society in general, "that, when the time for election comes, a wise and holy successor shall be chosen, who shall carry on the work of our Father and of his two beloved and saintly predecessors, to the sanctification of souls, the edifying of the Church, and to His own greater glory".

Congreve had more time to collate his thoughts, and in the *Cowley Evangelist* of January 1916 he wove a theological view of love and loss from the strands of Maxwell's sudden death and the grim realities of the ongoing conflict. He wrote of sudden death as "a chasm [that] suddenly opens in our life [...] then the thought occurs, is there no way back to the life as we knew it only so lately? Might we not sleep and awake and find things as before?

> How often must this vague desire be in the hearts of the friends of those people whose portraits meet us week after week in the illustrated papers under the heading of the Roll of Honour. Every one of them is the son, or husband, or brother of somebody. It breaks one's heart to think how they are missed at home today; are they really lost to us?

To bring something out of the general shock and sense of loss, Congreve urged his readers to try to strive "resolutely to die to the natural sense of isolation and discouragement that presents itself in bereavement, and to reassert the risen life that is ours by courageous acts of life, acts of faith, of hope and of love".[5] "I use at last with reality the expression 'I cannot at all realize it'," wrote Philip Waggett from the front. "Fr Maxwell was a rock man, absolutely straight, full of goodness. I shall miss him terribly."[6]

---

5 *CE* Jan 1916.
6 Nias, *Waggett*, 136.

The necessity of the election of a new Superior General broke new ground for the SSJE. His two predecessors had both retired from office and been replaced immediately; but Maxwell had died with time left to serve of his latest term, and at a time when the members of the Society were more dispersed than ever before. The American congregation was starting out, in Maxwell's own words of a few months earlier, "on its new venture";[7] while the war had compromised the arrival of the post and greatly compounded the perils of sea travel.

A flurry of administrative correspondence followed, exchanged between the various houses of the Society. Led by Lucius Cary, as Assistant Superior General, and Puller, Frederic Powell, and Henry Bull, it discussed whether or not the election of the Society's fourth Superior General would have to wait until the customary General Chapter of July 1916; whether a Special Chapter could be called immediately; and whether in itself the presence of the election of a Superior General on the agenda of any chapter meeting turned it *de facto* into a meeting of the Greater Chapter. If the last were true, then it seemed as though the Statutes might forbid another Greater Chapter meeting until 1919 – the customary three-year gap – which, given the war, would be far too long to wait.

The American brethren favoured waiting until July, or at least renewing any imminent election in the course of the normal Greater Chapter; but Puller was adamant that it was important that "there should be no needless prolongation of a vacancy in the office of Superior General". While legislative business – such as was usually discussed at the Greater Chapter – might benefit from the physical presence of as many brethren as possible, and the customary fortnight's retreat that preceded it, elections were a matter of silent voting with "no discussion whatsoever". The Society's Council decided that a new Superior General should be elected as soon as possible, with the overseas brethren sending in their votes as per the Statutes. The Visitor agreed: Charles Gore ruled from Cuddesdon that the course was the right one, and that a Greater Chapter should be held in August 1916; but that a change of wording in the Statutes was desirable "as to make explicit provision for a situation which may arise again".[8]

On 7 March the votes were counted in a Special Chapter convened for the sole purpose of electing a Superior General: of the thirty-three Cowley Fathers eligible to vote, fifteen were present – including Waggett, who had been granted a brief period of leave to allow him to attend[9] – and the others had sent in their ballot papers. The first round was inconclusive; but the second ballot gave a clear majority, *in absentia*, to Henry Bull. As he could not be immediately installed, the meeting was adjourned.[10]

Bull had been prominent in the Society's South African work for many years, before being transferred to oversee the house at Boston. In the course of the discussions relating to the American congregation at Chapter in 1913,

7 SSJE/2/5/198.
8 Puller, 27 March 1916; Powell, 12 Jan 1916; Bull, 25 Feb 1916; Gore, 4 April 1916, SSJE/1/7.
9 Nias, *Waggett*, 127ff.
10 SSJE/2/5/256.

Powell had declared that he "could guess a little of what it must have cost the Fr Superior to send Fr Bull out to them", but, as the Chapter Book recorded, "words failed him to tell what he had been to them in America."

> In the Diocese of Massachusetts and in the whole country he had been a champion of Truth. In Convention he had done what no other man could have done for the Catholic Faith, and he had upheld amongst Americans the very best traditions of the Society of St John the Evangelist.

"But – he had come from England";[11] and so the election of March 1916 not only saw a strong candidate elected to lead the Society, but also solved the problem of an Englishman being the senior member of the American congregation as it moved towards independence. Everything about Bull's election was different: he was the first Superior General to be elected with none of his predecessors still living; and it took him nearly two months to return to Cowley to be installed – a delay caused by the danger to shipping in the Atlantic, and the reduction in passages caused by the cancellation of the Holland-Amerika boats.

Bull finally arrived at Cowley on 11 May – just in time to address the annual festival of the Fellowship of St John, which had been arranged for the following day.[12] On the morning of 12 May the Special General Chapter that had been adjourned on 7 March reconvened: Bull took the necessary oath and was installed with the usual minimal ceremony by the Assistant Superior. All was done in order: he spoke to the whole gathering first; and then, when the novices and lay brothers had withdrawn from the chapel, he spoke briefly to the professed members, and confirmed the various office-holders in their appointments.[13]

The new Superior General addressed himself to the wider Cowley family in the *Cowley Evangelist* of June 1916. "In the Providence of God", he wrote, "I am called to succeed to the office of Superior General in our Society at a time when, beyond all crises of which we have had any experience, Religion and Life are being strained and tested to the uttermost."

> It is not that our day is really darker than many another through which the Church and the world have passed. Only we had hoped that the worst things were passed, that mankind had improved, that we might hope for an orderly reasonable development of civilization, that Christianity had so far made good its claim.

He, too, emphasised the call to sacrifice – which "was never so loud as now" – and laid it out in deeply theological terms: "Our covenant with death is disannulled: our agreement with hell is at an end. 'The foundations are cast down, and what hath the righteous done?'"[14]

---

11 SSJE/2/5/46.
12 *CE* May 1917.
13 SSJE/2/5/258.
14 Psalm 11.3.

It is the hope of the world that the sacrifice of to-day on the field of battle will lead to a new national and international life. The 'high resolve' to which we have to consecrate ourselves is not simply that this scene of slaughter shall not be again, but that national life and relationships shall be so ordered that what is happening now shall not be again. We must consecrate ourselves to repentance, to righteousness, to charity, to bearing the burdens of others, to letting the oppressed go free. We must consecrate ourselves to a liberty which we can only achieve in the recognition, and worship, and love of God. The lives that are being sacrificed now are the price—when shall it be full?—of a world set free from godless selfishness.

Such an existence was far from easy; but it was the SSJE's bread and butter: "the work of a Religious Order at such a crisis is evident."[15] Not unnaturally, Bull closed by asking for his readers' prayers for the Society: for its sustenance and for an increase of vocations. He also held up the forthcoming National Mission of Repentance and Hope – in which the SSJE was deeply invested – as a pertinent and timely means of renewing people's desire to live "lives of sacrifice, of worship, and of love".

Repentance & Hope

Alan Wilkinson has called the National Mission of 1916 "an attempt by the Church of England to respond to the spiritual needs of the nation; an attempt to discharge its sense of vocation to act as the Christian conscience of the nation". It was nominally led by the Bishop of London, Arthur Winnington-Ingram, with the help of a number of Secretaries. Among them was the former Headmaster of Repton William Temple, who had returned to parish ministry as Rector of St James's, Piccadilly, and would soon begin his ascent towards the archbishoprics of York and Canterbury.

Wilkinson observes that Winnington-Ingram "united the Victorian, romantic, and chivalric images of war with themes of sacrifice and fellowship from the Gospels";[16] but his jingoistic rhetoric led many to question how successful the National Mission could be under his leadership. A slogan coined by Field Marshal Sir William Robertson, the Chief of the Imperial General Staff – which appeared on posters all over London – read "some put their trust in horses, and some in chariots, but I am old-fashioned enough to put my trust in the Lord God." Others felt that the parameters of the National Mission meant that it would only appeal to people who were churchgoers already.

There was confusion from the outset over "whether the aim of the National Mission was to convert the individual or to christianize the social order"; and about what was the sort of repentance to which the nation was being called. Winnington-Ingram's list of offences included discord in industry, antagonism between the sexes as evinced by the suffragette movement, neglect of the Sabbath, drink, and – as the SSJE chaplains had themselves discovered – the

---

15 *CE* June 1916.
16 Wilkinson, *The Church of England and the First World War* (1978), 251.

middle-of-the-road clergy's general abnegation of the theological formation of their people. Cosmo Gordon Lang, as Archbishop of York, presented his own understanding of the National Mission to Convocation in 1916: "Repentance because we are called to repent of the sins which have stained our civilisation and brought upon it the manifest judgment of God; and Hope because, during the closing period of this terrific ordeal in the midst of increasing strain and sorrow, our people will need the strength of Hope."[17]

Herbert Kelly felt that much was lacking. When his pamphlet *The National Mission and the Church* was issued in 1916, the imprimatur of his successor as Director of the Society of Sacred Mission, David Jenks, effectively amounted to the SSM's endorsement of his criticisms. He was clear that "the political and social condition of England before the war and her condition now is amply sufficient to prove the need of a National Repentance, for nobody can deny that somehow or other the whole political and social system is wrong." The situation called for a more far-reaching self-examination than he thought was anticipated.

> We all know that to ask for National Repentance is to ask a very big thing indeed. We ask Tom, Dick and Harry to repent of getting drunk, stealing, neglecting their children, and other recognised offences; but to ask Messrs. Respectable & Co. to repent of a deal in shares, to ask the Carlton and the Reform Clubs to repent of thinking about votes, is quite another matter. To ask Church-goers to repent of buying their frocks too cheap, or playing golf on Sundays, is one thing; to ask our Church leaders to repent is also another.[18]

Only two months after his nephew Billy's death, Congreve was clear that in terms of the conflict "we are more sure to-day than ever that we are on the side of love, truth and honour in carrying the war through, at whatever cost". That cost, he conceded, might be great: "we may be beaten, but we will never be traitors to God, and to all honest men, by repudiating engagements of honour and friendship to save our skin."

> Thousands of men have been killed already; they volunteered, they left home with songs, and prayers, and blessings: they went to offer their lives to God for a cause they were sure of, that was worth it. Their conviction of a supreme duty – their sense of personal loyalty and affection – was the meaning of those light hearts. There sacrifice was not made to an abstraction, or a name, but to Christ, King of Kings.

Congreve was adamant that "there is nothing in that to repent of" – Winnington-Ingram thought the same, but in his case because he believed the war to have been solely Germany's fault – but nevertheless echoed Kelly's sentiments in other aspects of contemporary affairs.

17 Ibid, 70ff.
18 Herbert H. Kelly SSM, *The National Mission and the Church*, London: Longmans, Green & Co. (1916), 27ff.

We confess to national crimes that have shamed the Kingdom of Christ among us, such as the existence in our towns of slums where millions of our brethren live under conditions that seem to make Christian life impossible; the existence of criminal classes; the social isolation of the rich and of the poor; the mass of the neglected; the open and secret corruption of morals; the exclusion of religion from schools; the feebleness of our missionary endeavour; the divisions of Christendom.[19]

Much of this recast Puller's observations in the wake of the death of Edward VII in 1910, and his view of an ungrateful nation that had forgotten its duty to God; while focussing on some of the issues on Congreve's list has led Simon Heffer to call the decades that led up to the First World War "the Age of Decadence".[20]

"All this evil has accumulated", Congreve continued, "and we grow indifferent to it. We do so little to overcome because through our own personal sins we have so little spiritual power to help others." Any sense of national repentance, however, had to begin with the individual. This approach linked him with the emphasis laid on the National Mission by those on the evangelical wing of the Church; and he made a point of emphasising that "the worst feature of religion in England today is the loss of the deep sense of sin, and the brave self-discipline that produced such noble Christian lives in the Evangelical movement, and the Oxford revival of the last century."

"In our preparation for the Mission", he continued, "we bring first our own personal sinfulness to God in confession, asking the grace of a deeper penitence, that we may be able to join with the Church in a public and national return to God." This was "the surest way to help our country in a national repentance." For those at home the call to repentance was their chance to take a part in the sacrifice of those at the front.

We cannot be proud or happy in the sacrifice of our men buried on the field of battle, or sunk with their ship at sea for so great a cause, while we at home have no part in it […] It is only as penitents, as united to Christ that we have any real part in the sacrifice of those souls who have given their lives to God in the war, whose sacrifice has been accepted through the Blood of the Lamb.

The mission was one of Repentance and Hope, he noted; and the latter was a natural sequitur: "in my repentance, my sins confessed and renounced, I come back to God in Christ […] Here then, Hope awakes."[21] He later called it "Hope that Saves",[22] and longed to see the time, after the war was over, when "history may have to tell that to the very end of this war our cause suffered no stain, but the conduct of the allied nations was marked throughout not only by unprecedented courage and self-sacrifice, but also by rare self-control, cheerful discipline, and Christ-like mercy to the vanquished."[23] As we have already

---

19 CE Sept 1916.
20 Simon Heffer, *The Age of Decadence: Britain 1880–1914*, London: Random House (2017).
21 CE Sept 1916.
22 CE Oct 1917.
23 CE Sept 1916.

seen, he thought that the experience of the war had in many cases made men out of mice, and knights out of knaves.

The Church in the Furnace of 1917, a collection of essays by military chaplains reflecting on their experience of ministry at the front, opened with the same point. "The Church is in the furnace," observed its editor, Frederick MacNutt. "We have felt the scorching of the purgatorial fires. And we Chaplains not least, who have moved where the flames are hottest and have seen the pure metal dropping apart from the dross."[24] It was certainly not a low-church book; and although Peter Howson has described it as an "insular" volume written by Anglicans, it was partisan even within its own denomination.[25] The foreword was written by the Bishop of Khartoum, Llewellyn Gwynne – who in 1915 had been called to serve as Deputy Chaplain-General to mitigate the extreme and well-known anti-Catholicism of the Chaplain-General, Bishop John Taylor Smith – and among its contributors were Eric Milner-White, Kenneth Kirk, and Geoffrey Studdert Kennedy.

Marcell Conran – one of seven contributors to have been awarded the MC or DSO for his war service – contributed a piece called "Instruction in Prayer", in which he laid out some means by which soldiers who had been baptised and raised in the Church of England as boys, but whose faith had been either dulled or obliterated since, might be led to a life of prayer that would sustain them in the heat of battle. He drew on his own experience of using his *Chaplets of Prayer* at the front, and of preparing men for confirmation: "we have taken too much for granted [...] God has become to our people an abstract idea, or a mere Fate."

"What then are we to do?" For him the answer lay in emulating St Paul, who "took pains and laboured to vitalise Gospel truth by his teaching, so that it became a living power in the lives of the men and women who learned it, not a mere intellectual formula to be put to no use and soon forgotten, as it is by the greater number of those whom we teach today." The vigour and zeal of the Catholic-minded chaplains at the front needed to be carried on: "very much more needs to be done if, when our men come back after the war, those who have learnt to wish for religion and to go forward are to find what they need in their Church."[26]

Conran had also concentrated on resourcing the National Mission with his thoughts on how it could be conducted "on a Basis of 'Calling upon the Name of the Lord'". This was aptly summarised by Winnington-Ingram in an introduction to the new edition of the *Chaplets of Prayer*, which had "proved a wonderful blessing to many". He noted at the same time that "if one tried to sum up in a sentence what was the aim of the National Mission, one could not do better than by saying its aim is that every man, woman, and child in the nation shall in the fullest sense 'call upon the name of the Lord'."

---

24 H. B. Macnutt (ed), *The Church in the Furnace: Essays by Seventeen Temporary Church of England Chaplains on Active Service in France and Flanders*, London: Macmillan & Co. (1917).

25 Peter Howson, "Visions from the Front: Discourse on the Post-war World among Anglican Army Chaplains in 1918", in Michael Snape & Edward Madigan (eds), *The Clergy in Khaki: New Perspectives on British Army Chaplaincy in the First World War*, Farnham: Ashgate (2013), 176.

26 Ibid, 237ff.

For his part, Conran was clear that "England, as Rome of old, can be saved from sin, from drunkenness, impurity, disunion, and godlessness, the forces which drive nations to destruction. Sodom would have been saved had there been ten righteous within her." He followed a series of instructions to parish priests about best practice when leading a mission with his "Method" for approaching prayer, and a series of fifteen reflections "on the Sacred Mysteries of Our Lord's Life" – effectively it amounted to a manual of how to lead a parish mission for those for whom it might be unfamiliar. His advice ranged from the spiritual – "no parish priest will be ever be able to lead his people in prayer unless he practises *the same prayer* himself" – to the practical: "I think the service, as a rule, should not last more than an hour."[27]

The National Mission led the new Superior General to reflect on the future of mission work in general – the Society gladly sent its best young men to the overseas missions, but the need at home was "as great as ever". Lang felt that although "a great effort and an important witness had been made", it had not achieved much of what he had hoped for.[28] In the end, the National Mission pointed unequivocally to a number of areas in which the Church of England was already on the back foot in terms of its hold over people's loyalty and lives – a situation which, in the fullness of time, would come to affect the SSJE also.

FORWARD INTO BATTLE

The chaos into which the Society had been thrown by the war was amply demonstrated when, shortly after his installation, Bull had to preside over a meeting to approve Br William John's renewal of annual vows. The Master of the Lay Brothers, Leonard Strong, reported that he was satisfied that "though serving with the R.A.M.C. [he] had been living in accordance with his vows".[29] A year later he was working in the accounting office at the part of the military hospital operating in the old Cowley Workhouse;[30] and so was at least "now sleeping at the Mission House", even if he was absent from the monastery the rest of the time.[31]

Circumstances occasionally had a more congenial side: Charles Turner wrote from Cape Town in June 1916 to say that a former choir-boy from Cowley had turned up at the Mission House on his way to join the flying corps in East Africa, and been given dinner; at Matheran John Biscoe found himself ministering to a shell-shocked young officer who had been one of the Society's altar-boys; and when Percy Wigram took over the care of a Field Ambulance unit in 1918, he found Br Maxwell John among its men – from then on he "had the privilege of saying Mass daily, served by the good Brother".[32]

---

27 Marcell W. T. Conran SSJE, *The National Mission: How it may be conducted on a Basis of 'Calling upon the Name of the Lord', With Notes on Fifteen Addresses on the Mysteries of Our Lord's Life, together with Instructions for use in the Mission*, London & Brighton: SPCK (1916).

28 Wilkinson, *The Church of England and the First World War* (1978), 76.

29 SSJE/2/5/259.

30 Bull, 29 June 1916, SSJE/2/5/1.

31 SSJE/2/5/279.

32 Turner, 20 June 1916; Biscoe, 25 April 1917; Wigram, 14 July 1918.

The war also played havoc with the General Chapter meeting of 1917, and the minutes recorded that "the dangers of travelling have made it unadvisable for any of our Fathers outside England to cross the seas, and the delays, and possibly the loss, of the mails have prevented us receiving the[ir] opinions, or votes". Decisive legislative action was therefore impossible. In April 1918, a Special Provincial Chapter was summoned, to discuss the implications of the final Military Service Act, which had been passed earlier in the year after a good deal of wrangling between Church and State over whether or not the clergy would be conscripted as combatants.

In the end the threat of clerical conscription passed; but Bull observed that now that the clergy were no longer liable to be conscripted, the Church had to be seen to take definitive action "lest the Clergy should seem to take advantage of their exemption". He was well aware that "some of the Fathers and Novices were feeling deeply the call under present circumstances to volunteer for non-combatant service at the front where they could share the risks and sacrifices of our soldiers."

The matter of whether or not the clergy should be allowed to serve at all, or whether they should be conscripted as regular combatants, had been a political hot potato almost since the war began; and the compromise that had been reached seemed to oblige the young clergy to volunteer for non-combatant service. Strong and John Williams spoke to this effect, while Wigram had sent a letter expressing his consonant sentiments on the matter. Gore, meanwhile, had made it clear that although he would have preferred his clergy to stay at their posts to minister to the spiritual needs of their people – which by 1918 had in many cases become very considerable – he "would not refuse permission to those who could be spared to volunteer for Non-Combatant Service".

Waggett – who was by then stationed at Tidworth, and so had been easily able to attend the hastily-called meeting – was uninterested in how things might look to the outside world, and feared instead "actual slackness". He felt that many of the clergy would be influenced by the Society, if some of its members led the way by enlisting with the RAMC; and, if some of them found themselves transferred against their will (which was technically possible, as Edward Trenholme pointed out), then "they would in such a case be canonically justified in fighting". Puller also supported the idea of "a certain number of the eligible members of the Community offering themselves for service".[33] In May 1918 the *Cowley Evangelist* announced that

> the Home Chapter of the Society has decided to give all whom it can spare, and who are fitted for it, to work in the Army. Fr Strong, Fr Wigram, and of our Novices Mr Peacey, Mr Balcomb, and Mr Ballard will volunteer for work as Chaplains, or in the R.A.M.C. [34]

In the end the three priest novices ended up serving with the YMCA. Harold Peacey had been a regular soldier before being ordained, and had served in South Africa during the Boer War. He had volunteered as soon as war had been declared, and in 1915 he was serving in France when the incorrigible

---

33 SSJE/3/1/49ff.
34 *CE* May 1918.

Taylor Smith discovered that he was hearing the men's confessions, and sent him home. He joined the Society shortly afterwards, and returned to work in France and Belgium.

Lee Ballard, although an Englishman, was a novice in the American congregation. He had come to England in the hope of obtaining a chaplaincy; but had been unsuccessful. He became instead a YMCA secretary, and was sent to Mesopotamia – where he essentially functioned as non-official chaplain until the end of the war. Arthur Balcomb, like Ballard, was also sent to Mesopotamia by way of India; but ended up staying there, and later left the Society to join the Oxford Mission to Calcutta.

Strong was infirmarian at the Mission House, and in 1917 began assisting with rehabilitation work with wounded soldiers at the Base Hospital at Cowley[35] – his work there, like William John's, had been part of the Society's active response to the "Call to the Clergy and Religious for National Service" earlier in the year.[36] He was sent straight to 43 General Hospital at Salonica, where – after narrowly avoiding being killed in a railway accident just short of his destination[37] – his work included ministry among members of the newly-created Royal Air Force. At Bombay Oswald Barton was already serving as a chaplain at the Alexandra War Hospital; and the brethren at Cape Town took their part in ministering to the wounded from Jan Smuts' campaign against German East Africa. Wigram went to serve with the Highland Light Infantry; and by October had been hit in the face by shrapnel while leading the retrieval of casualties near Le Cateau. As he walked to the rear to have his wound dressed he was hit again, but saved by his helmet. By November he was recovering in hospital in Oxford; and he was back in France by January 1919. For his "fine example of coolness and absolute disregard of danger" he, too, was awarded the Military Cross.[38]

In the States the American novitiate was burgeoning – it had been established at Cambridge, not very far from Bowdoin Street, in a house dedicated to St Francis, with Spence Burton as Novice Master – to the extent that by the end of 1917 another property had had to be rented to meet the number of postulants. Powell, meanwhile, was exploring the possibility of branching out into China in the future.[39]

The brethren at Cowley took a great interest in these developments – and most of them remembered Burton well from the days of his own novitiate. When he submitted a list of the American novices – with brief biographical notes – to be read out in Provincial Chapter at Christmas 1917 it contained four choir novices, one lay novice, and five postulants about to be clothed. The Society's will to grant independence to its American congregation seemed to have worked wonders; while Bull noted with approval "that Fr Burton is seeking to link on the new with the old, and keep it in close contact".[40]

---

35 PC 1917, SSJE/3/1.
36 *CE* April 1917.
37 Strong, 18 June 1918.
38 Barton, 15 Jan & 10 April 1917; Taylor, "The Cowley Fathers and the First World War", 388; *CE* Nov 1918.
39 Powell, 8 Aug 1917.
40 Superior General's Address, PC 1917, SSJE/2/5/1.

The bonds of shared experience were forged yet closer after the United States entered the war, on Good Friday 1917. By 1918 a number of the American novices were serving in various parts in Europe and Mesopotamia, alongside their English confrères[41] – the lay novices at Boston had been subject to the military draft. Powell was refused a passport to travel to England for General Chapter later in the year, but bore it patiently. He wrote from Boston to say that "men have often gone to Europe about this time of the year, but never before in such steady, stalwart stream, and for such a splendid purpose. I gladly surrender the place that I might have occupied on board a ship to some fighting man."[42]

Other journeys were possible, if perilous. When Charles Field returned from the West Indies in 1916, having been invited by the Bishop of Antigua to lead missions in his diocese to coincide with the National Mission, he noted that the *Guiana* was bound for New York – "if we ever get there. Everyone is more or less nervous of submarines. No lighthouses show their lights. No lights are allowed on the ship, but thank God we are safe so far."[43]

In 1918 William O'Brien went to relieve Hugh Nicholson, who was struggling with ill-health, the long way round: across the Atlantic to Boston, overland to San Francisco, up the coast to Nova Scotia, across the Pacific to China, and then on to Bombay. It was a more expensive way of travelling, but a quicker journey given the restrictions of the West-to-East passage. Bull was later candid that although it had "seemed the safer way", the reality had been just as bad: the ship was attacked by submarines anyway, and ended up grounded in the dark on rocks off Newfoundland. After a worrying night, it had settled enough for the crew to serve breakfast – "which was served with the printed menu, and only one item scratched off" – and for the passengers to pack their bags. O'Brien wrote home cheerfully to say that they had all had "a wonderful escape, with no loss of anything except the poor ship itself".[44] Several weeks later he was being garlanded in the traditional manner at each of the Indian outposts.[45]

Waggett was not so fortunate: very early one morning in May 1918 he found himself sitting in hastily-donned shirt and trousers, dripping wet in a lifeboat after his ship was torpedoed before dawn in the Mediterranean; and being circled all the while by the hostile vessel responsible, letting off depth charges "like a terrier with a rat". He lost all his belongings; but was able to proceed with his journey after having been picked up and delivered safely to Malta. He was on his way to the Holy Land to join the Egyptian Expeditionary Force as a political officer with the rank of Major, to bring his scholarship to bear on helping to improve relationships with the various groups who were jostling for dominance in the region. As John Nias pointed out, "how he came to be chosen for this delicate task of pacification was, no doubt, one of the many well-guarded secrets of the war years; it remains a mystery to this day."[46]

---

41 Taylor, "The Cowley Fathers and the First World War", 386.
42 GenC 1918, SSJE/2/5/1.
43 *CE* August 1917.
44 O'Brien, 16 June 1918.
45 O'Brien, 19 Nov 1918.
46 Nias, *Waggett*, 141ff.

TRUE & CERTAIN HOPE

Inevitably, many of the Cowley men serving at the front were not to return. Henry Dunn had joined the choir as a boy and risen to be assistant organist of the community church. In November 1916, he was serving as a Lieutenant with the West Kent Regiment, and was killed by a shot through the head while leading a reconnaissance party in no-man's land.[47] William Nettleingham was an accomplished woodcarver who had produced a number of items for the Society's use, and had been an active member of the young men's League of St Francis at Cowley. When he found work near Peterborough he soon founded a local League for Lads along similar lines, and at the front he actively tried to keep the daily office going among like-minded men – "I need hardly say they belong to the Catholic section […] We do it all on our own account, but we have informed the chaplain."

After Christmas 1915 he wrote to say that "we sang Cowley Carols at a certain village in France."

> We did our best, and they did a good deal towards giving us an atmosphere of Christmas and something to think about. We sang them round the village aided by a paraffin lamp out of our barn hung on a pitchfork. We sang "The Noble Stem of Jesse" [Woodward's rendering of *Es ist ein Ros entsprungen*], "Nowell", and "Good King Wenceslas." At the Officers' Mess they were highly delighted. It was hard work copying out the music and training the chaps.[48]

He was killed at the Somme a few months later. On hearing of his death Turner, who had helped prepare him for confirmation several years before, wrote from South Africa recalling "his consistent faithfulness to his religious duties and his high ideals".

"Dear Will", he ended, "in the better land and the fuller life, there will surely be some service to accomplish after all this practice. There will not much be carving needed to fit him for his place in a niche in the walls of the new Jerusalem." His mother later sent £30, which amounted to her son's life savings, to help build the new St Augustine's schoolroom at St Cuthbert's.[49] To Turner's letter O'Brien added the observation that five other members of the League of St Francis had also fallen. "For each one there is some memory for which we thank God", he observed, "and which fills our minds with hope and gladness as we plead for them at the Altar".[50]

A printer's apprentice from Leeds, Ernest Turner had been a regular visitor to Cowley. Over the years leading up to the war he had been testing his vocation to the Society while serving at St Hilda's: the vicar there wrote of "the desire of his heart – going to Cowley". His letters show both a punctilious approach to prayer and the sacraments; how the faith of a Catholic-minded Anglican might

---

47 *CE* Jan 1918.
48 *CE* Dec 1916.
49 Ley, 30 Aug 1917.
50 *CE* Nov 1916.

be nurtured by sympathetic chaplains in the field; and how deep the Society's ethos could take root in fertile ground. He was fortunate to have found himself in proximity to chaplains whom he thought "true Catholics in practice and teaching"; but had dissuaded them from writing to his Captain to excuse him early duties so that he could get to Mass instead – "it is unfair, another chap having another man's work to do".

When he was not on early duties, he invariably asked a chaplain to say an early mass, at which he served – one later called him a "soldier Saint", who had endured and overcome the jeering of his comrades, "some of the most vicious and profane in the British Army" – which designation the Society took up with enthusiasm. Ernest Turner maintained a Rule of Life as best a busy signaller could; and as this involved daily Communion when possible, the chaplains at headquarters – who clearly recognised the advanced state of his spiritual discipline – allowed him to communicate himself from the Reserved Sacrament whenever they were away. He tried to keep up short daily meditation and reading when he could, and thought that the daily death toll "makes one prepare as a real Christian ought always to" – he was regularly able to make his confession, which he said "makes me feel a new lad every time I go".

He had with him the Society's office book – on St Stephen's Day 1915 he made a particular point of praying First Vespers of St John "to join with those I love at Cowley in keeping the festival of the Patron of the Society". In Lent 1916 he wondered if he might soon be at Cowley, serving his novitiate. At Michaelmas, as the fighting began to close in, he was delighted to meet a fellow-server from St Hilda's, George Calverley. Knowing that he would be in the thick of the battle shortly, he asked him to look after his prayer books and his member's medal of the Confraternity of the Blessed Sacrament, in case he was killed in the coming days. He was blown apart by a shell on 12 October, at the age of 20. "The grain of wheat has fallen into the ground and died," the *Cowley Evangelist* noted – with immediate echoes of John 12.24 – "and it will not abide alone".[51]

To Ernest Turner's story must also be added the fate of Br Walter Frederick. He had been admitted to the novitiate in 1912, and had gone to India shortly afterwards, in the wake of the Society's decision to attempt to make the life of the lay brothers more appealing to would-be postulants. He had returned in 1915 to take first vows, but had instead felt duty bound to enlist. Having failed to meet the requirements for the RAMC he enlisted as an ordinary combatant with the Royal Fusiliers, and by early 1917 was serving with his regiment near Arras, with the rank of Lance-Sergeant.

In many ways Walter Frederick's death was a stark contrast to that of Ernest Turner. Early on 23 April, the first day of the Second Battle of the Scarpe, he was with his men on the Arras-Cambrai road. They were sheltering in a crater when he was hit by a stray piece of shell, which shattered his left arm. He managed to make his way to the rear, but the speed at which the offensive was moving forward meant that there was no time for his wound to be dressed. Aged 27, he probably either bled to death shortly afterwards or died of shock later that day.

---

51 *CE* Dec 1916.

Only a few years earlier Waggett had argued that St George should be given particular observance in the Society's Kalendar, as "the patron saint of our Army";[52] and in 1917 the Cape Town brethren turned out to support the St George's Day recruitment rally, led by William Carter. Turner noted that "the Archbishop, in Convocation robes with a purple Laudian cap, and carrying his pastoral staff, (he also wore some medals,) gave one a real sense that the English Church was at home at the Cape."[53]

Walter Frederick's death on the same St George's Day, on the other side of the planet, was steeped in pathos. Had anyone been able to attend to his injuries he would almost certainly have returned to Cowley – without his arm, but at least alive – to be professed. The *Cowley Evangelist* noted that his letters home spoke of his loneliness at being away from the Society; but also of his tenacious hold on his faith, and his care of his men. When the Society sent him money to buy winter supplies at the end of 1915, he spent half of it on two of the men in his Company, as they were "sons of labourers, and their parents could not afford to send them any money". His time at the front "only increased his desire for the renewal of his life in Religion".

Ernest Turner clearly went to his death, as the Prayer Book has it, "in sure and certain hope of the Resurrection to eternal life", and so was more easily eulogised. Without his letters – they do not survive in the SSJE archive, and may well have been sent on to his family – it would be only too easy to regard Walter Frederick's death as an avoidable waste of life. Nevertheless, the *Cowley Evangelist* warmly and proudly gazetted him as "the first of our Society to give his life in the war" – although by then the particulars had not been received.[54]

Bull was at pains to emphasise that "we have been taking, I believe, as much share as we are capable of taking in the burdens laid on all by the War". It had taken weeks for news of Walter Frederick's death to reach Cowley; and so the High Mass of Requiem for him had been delayed until the brethren gathered for Chapter – but he noted that "as soon as we heard the news we said our Masses for him in the Church with thanksgiving, as well as with sorrow."[55]

Even had the Society been in possession of the sorry details of Walter Frederick's death, it would hardly have recorded it in any other way. Its position stood as a bulwark against the nihilistic fatalism that had found a foothold in contemporary society – a tendency that Conran had observed in many of the troops at the front[56] – and which by 1916 had led some, like Arthur Conan Doyle, to dabble in Spiritualism and other forms of heterodoxy.[57] The difference for the SSJE between death as a squandering of life, and death as a sacrifice well-pleasing to God in the shadow of the Cross, was everything.

52 SSJE/2/3/73.

53 Turner, 1 May 1917.

54 *CE* July 1917; Oct 1917.

55 Superior General's Address, GenC 1917, SSJE/2/5/1.

56 "Religion and the War", *CE* Feb 1916.

57 cf "The Courage of Faith", *CE* Jan 1920.

THE SHADOW OF THE CROSS

The idea of placing a permanent set of Stations of the Cross in the community church as the Society's war memorial was first raised in 1917, after the grieving parents of Gordon Bradley – another member of the League of St Francis, who had been killed while serving with the Oxfordshire and Buckinghamshire Light Infantry a year earlier – offered the Society £100 for the purpose in their son's memory. The Society had used a set of temporary images since 1915 – first as a teaching aid for the children, and later as a devotional office for adults with Gore's approval – but Bull felt that £100 would not go far enough for a suitable permanent set; and so it was tactfully suggested that the Bradleys might like their son's memorial to form part of the whole. A committee was duly constituted to take the matter forward.[58]

By Easter 1918, Edward Fellowes Prynne had been approached to undertake the creation of the new images. He felt that the church "afforded a unique opportunity by reason of its splendid wall-space" – Bull was more direct, and spoke of "the blank, windowless walls of our nave"[59] – but there was dissent among the Chapter, led by Conran and Puller, as to whether the Society should follow the customary practice, or include only the images to which there was explicit scriptural reference. Bull was determined, however, that the whole scheme should be carried out; and after a long argument in Provincial Chapter observed that to introduce a set of Stations of the Cross that differed from those widely in use elsewhere "would increase the sense of our external divisions and lack of coherence with one another", and that no member of the Society would be compelled to use the full devotion against his will. Puller proposed an amendment, in opposition to the Superior General, that only ten stations should be put up; but found himself in a minority of one.

Fellowes Prynne regarded his commission as "a very great pleasure and high privilege",[60] and over the next two years he and Bull wrangled over the details of what he thought was "a record set".[61] The striking – if not entirely unproblematic[62] – set of images was finally installed in St John's Church in 1921.[63] Fellowes Prynne died shortly afterwards, and it represents the pinnacle of his devotional work. That the images stand as the Society's war memorial speaks of the developments in the Society's life and theology as the war years progressed; and the obvious project in St John's Church for which funds might have been given – the completion of the projected series of great missionary saints in the windows of the clerestory – appears to have been allowed to lapse in the Stations' favour.

---

58 PC Dec 1917, SSJE/3/1/27;31.

59 *CE* July 1918.

60 Fellowes Prynne, 4 May 1918, SSJE/6/20/1/2/1.

61 Fellowes Prynne, 8 May 1918, SSJE/6/20/2/1/3.

62 Jo Moffatt Levy, *Anti-Jewish imagery in a WW1 memorial: the Stations of the Cross in an Oxford Church*, "Faith and the First World War" conference, Glasgow, June 2016.

63 All the Stations were originally hung in the nave, but the opening up of the wall into the new Blessed Sacrament chapel in 1935 complicated matters. They were eventually respaced in 1950, with the first two being placed in the Holy Name Chapel. PC 1950, SSJE/3/2.

"Our War Memorial", stated the Superior General, "will thus be no mere decoration of the Church, but rather, by its constant use, will become a perpetual stimulus of devotion."

> Let us pray that our pictures may not only keep alive our gratitude, and our prayers for our dead, but may raise up amongst us in generation after generation soldiers of Christ, who will glory and rejoice in the way of His Cross, and devote themselves to His service wholly, Who is our only hope of healing, and of peace.

"The Cross", he concluded, "must be the inspiration as well as the hope, the strength as well as the consolation of our lives, as it has been to so many who have nobly lived, and generously died, in this War."[64]

In his first public address after his installation in 1916, Bull had been clear – referring to the need of a life of sacrifice that the demands of the war had presented to the world – that "in the Church we need the same awakening. There is no newness of life, no escape from self-seeking, indifference, selfish antagonisms, formality, lukewarmness, pride, but by way of sacrifice." The *beau idéal* of this sacrifice was a life "surrendered to God in Christ, given to him in penitence, in devotion, in service, separated off by the voluntary dedication of poverty, chastity, and obedience, spent freely in the exercises of charity, consecrated wholly in adoration, reparation, intercession".[65]

This was the life that the SSJE was called to lead, in both war and peace, as a witness to which others might seek to aspire. Bull observed that First World War, in the course of which the SSJE had walked its own *via crucis*, had "served to accentuate and bring into greater force the reality of the Spiritual Vocation, whereby we serve the deepest necessities of our day, and subserve every other form of useful action".[66] The basic hospital work that many of the brethren had undertaken in 1917, for example, had been "just what as Religious we might have desired [...] to bring us more directly to God in scrubbing hospital floors than ever we found Him before at the Altar or in the Cell."[67]

The SSJE's call, then, was to service and sacrifice. It was no coincidence that when it came to commemorating Br Walter Frederick, the Society retained the second of the Stations – "Jesus Receives His Cross" – as his memorial.[68] In his dual identity as a member of the SSJE and as a soldier who had fallen in battle, he had lived out a double vocation. Within the Society of St John the Evangelist's eschatological metanarrative of spiritual warfare refined in the furnace of immolative self-sacrifice united to the Cross, Walter Frederick represented at once both its apogee and its consummation.

---

64 *CE* July 1918.
65 *CE* June 1916.
66 GenC 1918, SSJE/2/5/1.
67 *CE* April 1917.
68 The first station was reserved for Gordon Bradley.

Richard Meux Benson.
1 As Student of Christ Church
   and Vicar of Cowley.
2 At the height of his powers
   as Superior General of
   the Society of St John the
   Evangelist.
3 In amiable decrepitude
   towards the end of his life.

4 Charles Chapman Grafton
disagreed with Benson over
the direction of the early
American work, and left the
SSJE in 1882. He ended his
days as Bishop of Fond Du
Lac in Wisconsin.

5 Simeon Wilberforce
O'Neill was an early
advocate of the religious
life for men in the Church
of England. He went to live
in consecrated poverty in
India, where he died in 1882.

6 'The Iron Church', shortly after its construction in 1859.

7 Lord Halifax laying the foundation stone of the tower at Cowley in May 1902.
Benson is just visible, seated to the right of the large gentleman holding his top hat.

8 The paschal candle came into liturgical use at Cowley in 1928. A new tester and reredos were set in place in 1934, and the original alabaster gradine reworked to include a carved relief of the Resurrection. The sanctuary survived in this form until the liturgical reforms of the late 1960s.

9 The community church and cloister: G. F. Bodley's masterpiece.

10 The Mission House of 1868, with the original chapel and belfry perched on top, photographed at some point after the replacement of the shovel-hat with the beret in 1952 and before the major renovations of 1961.

11 Br Maynard – whose craftsmanship was almost everywhere the SSJE looked – photographed in Philadelphia in the 1880s, where he was decorating the interior of St Clement's.

12 George Congreve.

Both Old Etonians, George
Congreve and Frederick Puller
brought the SSJE back from
the brink of disaster in the
late 1880s.

13 Frederick Puller.

14 Like Congreve and Puller, Philip Waggett brought his considerable distinction to the SSJE on his profession in 1896; in the following decades he became its leading public theologian.

15 Lucius Cary became an authority on the regulation, practice, and purpose of the religious life in the wider Church of England, publishing his seminal *Called of God* in 1937.

16 Three Superiors General: L-R, Gerald Speirs Maxwell (1907–15), Richard Meux Benson (1866–90), and Robert Lay Page (1890–1907), in the cloister garden at Cowley in 1907.

17 A rare photograph of a bearded Benson in Boston in the 1890s, surrounded by the choirboys of old St Augustine's, with Fr Field – the doyen of the early American work – behind him, and Fr Longridge in the doorway.

18 The Indian brethren with their co-workers at Panch Howds at the turn of the twentieth century. Standing, L-R: Reuben Dhawle, Edmund Kershaw, Robert Smart, Samuel Lolitkar, Fr Moore, Fr Nicholson, Ernest Hollings; seated: Fr Tovey, Fr Gardner, Fr Biscoe, Fr Elwin. Kershaw and Hollings both succumbed to the climate soon afterwards.

19 L-R: Br Walter Frederick, Br Arthur, and Br Leslie in Bombay in 1914. Walter Frederick would die at Arras three years later.

20 Wooden scaffolding surrounding the nearly completed new campanile at Holy Name, Poona, in 1896. In the foreground are two of the water tanks from which the location took its name.

GLORY TO GOD IN THE HIGHEST.

21 Ninian Comper's 'Indo-Gothic' St Crispin's being built at Yerendawana in 1906, with its intent of purpose vividly displayed.

22 L-R: Gregory, Wasant, and Paul, three of Fr Elwin's 'Indian Boys', learning about the mass in front of St Crispin's.

23 A group with Fr Elwin at the door of the mission bungalow at Yerendawana in 1903.

24 Holy Name, Poona, after the addition of Ninian Comper's baldacchino and other embellishments in the mid-1930s.

25 Fr Wilkins' Mission Band at Poona in the 1930s.

26 The new mission house at Cape Town in the late 1890s, with Table Mountain behind.

27 The men of St Columba's Home in the late 1880s, with Fr Puller and Paula von Blomberg. Bernard Mizeki is seated fifth from left on the front row.

28 L-R: Fr Dakers, Fr Savage, and the towering Fr Gardner in the mission house garden at Cape Town in 1949, all wearing over-hemmed habits in the parsimonious Cowley style.

29 St Cuthbert's, Tsolo, shortly after the completion of Br Maynard's new church in 1906, with the original mission house on the left.

30 L-R: Fr Bull, Fr Callaway, and their friend and catechist the Revd John Xaba, all in old age at St Cuthbert's in July 1940.

31 Fr Rumsey with mission staff and resident boys at St Cuthbert's in 1922.

32 Most of the brethren gathered for General Chapter in 1928, the year Parliament rejected the revised *Book of Common Prayer*. From back, L-R: Br John, Fr Pulley, Fr Dakers, Fr Turner, Br Francis, Fr Sedding, and Fr Williams; Br James, Br William, Fr Cary, Fr Moore, Fr Wallis, Fr Tovey, Fr Trenholme, Fr Waggett, Fr Noel in splendid bath chair, and Fr Adams, who later became C. S. Lewis's confessor; Fr Bignold, Fr Puller, Fr O'Brien (SG 1931–49), Fr Bull (SG 1916–31), Fr Ley, and Fr Longridge.

33 1958. From back, L-R: Br Anselm, Fr Campbell (SG 1976–91), Fr Huntley, Br Laurence, Fr Pulley, Fr Slade, Fr Young, and Br Raymond; Fr Cotgrove (SG 2000–2002), Fr Naters (SG 1991–2000), Fr Cooper, Fr Thomas, Fr Manson, Fr Beasley-Robinson, Fr Rose, Fr Sedding, Fr Fitch, Fr Gibbard, and Br Alban; Fr Playne, Fr Pridham, Fr Triffitt (SG 1964–76), Fr Hemming, Fr Dalby (SG 1949–64), Fr Thomson, Fr Bryant, Fr O'Brien (SG 1931–49), and Fr Dakers; Novices Br David, Fr Phalo, Br Cyril, Fr Bovey, and Fr Nomlala.

'IN THE PRIME OF HIS LIFE'

So brave and so smiling, he went with them all,
Oh just as we've seen him so many a time;
So brave and so smiling; to fight and to fall
In the trenches of France the dear lad *in his prime*!

Oh, why did he go! and why did he die!
Just he of them all—in the springtime of youth?
He went for dear England with heart beating high,
He died, thank the Lord, for her honour and truth.

But *'dead in his prime'*—is there answer to give?
Kind Christ! lift our eyes and grant us to see
In the garden of God he's *beginning to live*,
And 'the *prime of his life*' is the *Life that's to be*!

W. H. D.[69]

---

69 *CE* Dec 1923.

15

Re-Pitching the Tent

One feels the love which draws and pardons and accepts.

—Godfrey Callaway SSJE[1]

As the Society of St John the Evangelist's fiftieth year drew to a close, its new Superior General foresaw a devolution of governance which saw the Provincial Chapters in each place dealing with local matters – including at the mother house – and the General Chapter "dealing with the larger questions, which affect the Society as a whole". Henry Power Bull was determined not to govern the Society in isolation – Gerald Maxwell had begun to feel the strain considerably in the lead-up to his death[2] – and wished to see brought into Provincial Chapter meetings "a full freedom of discussion, a real interest in one another's concerns, and a real sense of responsibility for all that is done in the name of our Society."

> I do not desire to act alone. The ultimate decision must no doubt rest on the Superior in the great mass of practical detail, but it will be of the greatest consequence to him, and to the Society, a safeguard and security to both, that such decisions should be made in the light of opinions freely, and fully, and if necessary formally expressed.[3]

That said, Bull had none of Maxwell's reticence. He was every inch a Superior General, and in 1918 the custom in Chapel of the brethren waiting for him to rise before commencing the offices – it had become the practice for all to stand together at a single stroke of the bell – was restored. He served for fifteen years, and oversaw a number of major developments which crystallised the identity of the SSJE for decades to come. It was not until 1921 that General Chapter met with no major legislative matters to discuss – but, as he then observed, "our life happily does not consist in, or depend on legislation".[4]

Among Bull's first priorities was a practical rearrangement of many of the Society's affairs, in as much as could be reasonably accomplished within the restrictions placed upon communications by the war. At the mother house, various sub-committees were set up to deal with domestic issues, and by the end of his second term of office over £1000 had been spent on improvements

---

1 Callaway, 22 March 1923.
2 SSJE/2/5/204.
3 Bull, 29 Dec 1916, SSJE/2/5/1.
4 SSJE/2/5/1.

to the buildings. The upper library was overhauled – for a number of years it had doubled as the infirmary – new volumes were acquired on a regular basis from the London Library and the Times Book Club, and a "Suggestions Book" was introduced. New bathrooms and a smoking-room were provided in the guest house; a new heating system was fitted; and all the external wood and leadwork was repainted. Even the linen room was reorganised: from 1916 each member of the Society had his own separate pile of items, and "a supply of underclothing, &c" was provided for brethren visiting from other houses who might find themselves short.[5] Electric lighting was installed in the domestic range and the cloister, and by 1921 telegrams for members of the Society could be addressed to "Evangelist, Oxford".[6]

Bull's first major official act was to preside over the General Chapter of 1916; and almost immediately, with the support of Frederick Puller and William Longridge, he proposed that the method of recording Chapter business should be amended. It had previously been the custom for any debates – and therefore also the names and words of the brethren who either supported or opposed any motions that might be brought – to be written down in the Chapter Book. Bull moved "that the debates in Chapter be excluded from the Official Minutes and be recorded separately". The motion was passed: from then on the Chapter Books included only the bare facts of what had been agreed; and the minutes of debates were written down elsewhere, as were the Superior General's addresses.

This streamlined Chapter business considerably; but significantly complicates the work of the historian who would seek to analyse the tensions and disagreements that may have existed thereafter behind a presented veneer of decisive unanimity – and not least because the Superior General's addresses of Bull's successors are now missing. What the documents that do survive make clear, however, is that even without the First World War, the SSJE would have approached the 1920s as a changed institution. Enough of its members had died for a form of cumulative memorial to be erected; and from 1918 the names of the departed brethren began to be carved into the panels of the Lady Chapel.

George Congreve died in April 1918, and with his passing the Society lost one of its most influential figures. Bull paid him warm tribute from the pulpit on the Sunday after his death.

> It is the secret of countless souls what Fr Congreve has been to them, a multitude even that never saw him in the flesh, yet who found in his books an unfailing source of hope, of inspiration, of encouragement, of cheer, because so full of human sympathy and so full of the realisation of Divine things.

Soon afterwards the Society began the task of collating Congreve's correspondence for publication, as it had done for Benson: "we should be very grateful if friends who have letters from him, which they have treasured, and which they feel would be of blessing and a joy to others, would lend them for

5 PC 1916, SSJE/3/1.
6 *CE* Jan 1921.

this purpose. The Father Superior will gladly receive them, and take every care that they are returned uninjured."[7]

Others followed in short order. On the morning of 24 May Br Maynard, who had been an invalid for some time, was found unconscious on the floor of his cell: he had suffered a massive stroke, and died soon afterwards. The fruits of his skills as an architect, draughtsman, and artist, had been almost everywhere the Society looked: from the magnificent ceiling in the community church to the simple domesticity of the mother house; from St Clement's, Philadelphia, to St Cuthbert's, Tsolo – where his "training of the native stone masons and builders, who did the great mass of the work under his supervision, meant a real rise in native capacity and reputation".[8]

In India John Biscoe had been sinking for some time: by the end of September he was in the hills at Panchgani on doctor's orders; but at Michaelmas he became "the third member of our Society to be gathered this one year 'to our store in Paradise'." He had served on the Indian missions for thirty-four years, after serving curacies under Arthur Tooth at St James's, Hatcham, and Charles Lowder at St Peter's, London Docks, where "the priests possessed neither the favour of the world, nor of the Church. They had but one aim, the Kingdom of Christ and the salvation of souls."[9] "I suppose I miss him most," wrote Albert Tovey, "because I have been with him longest [...] I am sorry that he should have died away from us and has been buried away from Bombay, but I don't suppose it much matters."[10]

The work in Bombay had already suffered an "incalculable loss" with the death of the redoubtable Gertrude Bradley in March 1917, which Congreve had observed at the time could "only be recorded in terms of thanksgiving to God for a life of sacrifice so generous and complete".[11] She had refused help as her own health had declined and had finally collapsed in her dispensary in early March, dying two days later. Hugh Nicholson observed that it was the end of "a wonderful life and work".[12] Her medical facilities were closed, as she had inspired "plenty of other such institutions"; but her schools, which she had funded with the income from her private medical work in Bombay, were taken over by the Society[13] – as were the two orphan boys for whom she cared, who entered St Peter's School.[14]

The deaths of Bradley and Biscoe, compounded by Nicholson's ongoing ill-health and Edward Elwin's advancing years – when Bull visited him at Yerendawana on his Indian tour in 1920 he described him as "much aged since I last saw him eight years ago at Cowley, with white hair now"[15] – precipitated a number of difficult questions about the Indian work. Bull wondered in 1918 whether it had in fact reached its zenith. The war had increased costs

---

7 *CE* June 1918.
8 *CE* July 1918.
9 *CE* Nov 1918.
10 Tovey, 5 Oct 1918.
11 *CE* April 1917.
12 Nicholson, 10 March 1917.
13 Barton, 13 March 1917.
14 Nicholson, 1 May 1917.
15 Bull, 12 Oct 1920.

considerably, and had depressed the value of the sovereign against the rupee. As early 1916 he had realised that the SSJE might have to start outsourcing some of its work, and raised the idea of "paid clerical help" in the form of a priest who really knew India well to undertake preaching engagements and fundraising lecture-tours.[16]

The situation at Cowley was not much rosier. Shortage of paper and the increase of general costs meant that by 1918 the letters pages of the *Cowley Evangelist* – which by then had a circulation of some 3000 regular readers – were being produced in small print.[17] At the same time the absence of so many brethren, compounded by the rationing of coal, had obliged the Society to stop conducting retreats at the Mission House. This was a very serious under-taking; but with the paid help gone and the active brethren away, despite Br John's best efforts in the kitchen there was no way in which large numbers of guests could be accommodated or fed. Instead priests were invited to make private retreats, which Bull hoped might be "even more fruitful and powerful in their lives than the public gatherings".[18]

Ten novices advanced to profession between 1914 and 1919; but by the end of that period the novitiate had become seriously depleted "and likely, so far as we can see at present, to be few in numbers for some time". Bull's address to General Chapter that year noted that "the three years now closing [since the last Greater Chapter] have been years of stress, and they leave us with many marks of the strain". Part of it reads like an intercessions sick-list of various members of the Society who were either in hospital, chronically ill, or con-valescing. Philip Waggett and Leonard Strong were still absent on ongoing military work – although at Salonica the latter had been helping the Air Corps mechanics to pack up various pieces of aeronautical ephemera into crates to be shipped back to England, so would be home soon enough. More worryingly, Br William John had developed late-onset shellshock, and was "in a really serious condition".[19]

But it was not all doom and gloom. The "coming of peace and of summer" had enabled the Mission House to start hosting public retreats once more. The numerous parish missions, which had also been in abeyance, were also resumed;[20] and the Society intended to precede Michaelmas Term at the University with "a large undergraduate retreat", led by the Superior General,[21] which would in turn lead to the resumption of the retreats for laymen. The most promising news, however, came from the United States.

The hostilities in Europe had ended relatively shortly after the conscription of the American novitiate, and by August 1919 its members were either back at Boston already or on their way to rejoin Spence Burton on the banks of the Charles River, where plans were afoot to build a permanent replacement to St Francis House. A year later the novitiate moved to St Augustine's Farm at Foxboro; and by 1921 the American growth had been so impressive that it had

---

16 PC 1916, SSJE/3/1.
17 "Cowley Evangelist, 1918", insert.
18 GenC 1917, SSJE/2/5/1.
19 GenC 1919, SSJE/2/5/1.
20 cf *CE* Feb 1920.
21 *CE* Oct 1919.

fulfilled the conditions laid down in 1914 "to entitle them to the full establishment of the Congregation". Bull was delighted, and urged the members of what had now become the English congregation to "rejoice heartily with them".[22]

A branch house was opened at San Francisco almost immediately, with Charles Field – who had by then been naturalised[23] – as its Superior. "It is about as far from Boston to San Francisco over land as it is from Oxford to Boston over sea," noted Bull. "The tide of American life flows west, and there is an immense need for the Society's life and work in the great western cities and universities."[24] By 1923 a house had been set up in colonial Korea, which effectively established the American congregation's Japanese work of the following decades;[25] the Sisterhood of St Anne had been founded out of the work at Boston;[26] and a Canadian congregation would soon be established at Elmsdale and Bracebridge, in Ontario.[27]

In the English congregation the chantry list continued to grow. Elwin and Nalbro' Robinson died in January and February 1921 respectively: Robinson had been instrumental in the early efforts among the coloured community at Cape Town; while Elwin had built up the work at Yerendawana from scratch, and made it his later life's work. "His own boys will not forget", thought Bull, "the English Father, who wore sandals, and talked in rather broken Marathi, and lived among them as a friend, and as a Christian priest."[28] Frederick Playne took over some of the work at St Crispin's; but was clear to him from the outset that "of course one cannot be a second Father Elwin".[29] The Society eventually withdrew from Yerendawana in 1930.[30]

Br John, Congreve's friend and faithful correspondent, died in August: in the course of forty-five years he had been cook-housekeeper at Cowley, Philadelphia, and Cape Town; had cared for the boarder boys at Tsolo; and had returned to Cowley and taken up his former work. But he was "much more than a serving brother": one of his former charges recalled that he had a knack for "a tremendous amount of genuine missionary work with us boys without our really knowing it".[31] Bull mourned him as the "most faithful and devoted of brothers and servant of all in Christ";[32] while the lengthy tribute he received in the *Cowley Evangelist* showed how, when the conditions were right, an unskilled but devout "simple lay brother" might overcome the challenges of the life about which the members of Chapter had worried from time to time, and thrive.[33] Br Herbert's life in the Society was similarly lasting and fruitful,

---

22 GenC 1921, SSJE/2/5/1.

23 *CE* Feb 1929.

24 *CE* Dec 1921.

25 *CE* Sept 1921.

26 GenC 1923, SSJE/2/5/1.

27 GenC 1928, SSJE/2/5/1.

28 Bull, 20 Jan 1921.

29 Playne, 8 Sept 1921.

30 B. D. Wilkins SSJE, *With Wings As Eagles*, London: Cowley, Wantage & All Saints Missionary Association (1953), 28.

31 *CE* Oct 1921.

32 GenC 1921, SSJE/2/5/1.

33 *CE* Sept 1921.

although, as his obituary noted "it cannot have been easy for a professional football player to accept the discipline of the Novitiate, and then to complete the spiritual adventure which he had begun by binding himself for life to the worship and service of God under the restraints of the Religious State."[34]

TABERNACLES & TRIBULATIONS

One of Bull's aims was to try and align the life of the house at Cowley with the wider Catholic Movement, and through it with the Church of England as a whole. In the course of a general discussion about the refurbishment of the Lady Chapel during Provincial Chapter in 1917 – in which the unadorned space was complained of as too plain, bare, lacking in devotional character, and in need of a splash of colour – he ventured his hope "that the time would come when both the Bishop of the Diocese and the Society would be willing that the Blessed Sacrament might be reserved".[35]

The suggestion was not without controversy, and a series of debates followed. Puller presented a paper to General Chapter in 1920 saying that while the whole Society surely agreed that "the Presence of our Lord in the Blessed Sacrament of the Altar is adorable and ought to be adored" he felt that the contemporary enthusiasm for reservation of the Sacrament was the result of "a wave of fashion", and that while the Founder would have allowed it for the purpose of sick communions he would have deplored the idea of it being reserved for worship.

> I most devoutly hope that we, who belong to the Society which [Benson] founded, shall not introduce into our Mother House a practice which he would have regarded as so supremely undesirable.[36]

For the second time in recent memory the General Chapter disregarded Puller's advice – he had also spoken against the installation of the unabridged Stations of the Cross – and then voted in favour of a formal proposal that the Superior General should proceed in consultation with the Bishops of Oxford and London (a tabernacle was also intended for St Edward's House). It is likely that the two dissenting votes were those of Puller and George Hodge.

Bull noted in the following Provincial Chapter that the Society was divided on the matter; and as such the Sacrament would be reserved in a way that avoided "the strain of perfectly real conscientious difficulties". At the same time, however, he did not think it right that the needs of the minority should "entirely override" the desire of the members of the Society who wanted to see the Sacrament permanently reserved; and that as far as he was concerned it was "really intolerable that there should be no provision for Reservation". If anything, it was required for emergency Viaticum, "for no one could foretell the hour of his need of it"; and in Congreve's last weeks "the Reserved Sacrament

---

34 *CE* July 1933.
35 PC 1916, SSJE/3/1/35ff.
36 Puller, *Address on Reservation for purposes of worship*, GenC 1920, SSJE/2/5/1.

[had] afforded him the opportunity of a communion that was almost daily, till the call came that sealed his life's profession."[37] He now proposed, therefore, that the forthcoming tabernacles should be placed in the house chapels not used for the singing of the office. It was a compromise with which he was not entirely happy, and he alluded to his dissatisfaction.

> This would lay no burden on the consciences of those who desired to say their offices as heretofore, while it would give opportunity for the devotion of those who found in Visits to the Blessed Sacrament every direct exercise of devotion towards our Lord, and a great means of spiritual advance. Those who had been trained on other lines found it difficult to sympathize with this, or even wholly disapproved of it.

"But", he continued, "it is a fact in the life not only of the Church, but of members of the Society. Our common actions must be governed by consideration for individual consciences; but for this very reason provision must be made for private, individual freedom."[38]

Puller wished to be loyal to his interpretation of the wishes of the dead Founder; while Bull wanted to reflect contemporary practice – a situation brought about to some extent, as Robert Beaken has observed, by an increased devotion to the Blessed Sacrament that had grown out of many people's experience of the First World War.[39] In 1917 Viscount Halifax himself, addressing the Church Union in his fiftieth year as its President, said that he felt that those who "create obstacles in the way of perpetual Reservation of the Blessed Sacrament [...] deprive us of all that makes a church where the Blessed Sacrament is reserved so different from one that is not".[40]

For the SSJE, however, the introduction of its tabernacles was a peremptory moment of shibboleth. Despite the respective bishops' permission for the Blessed Sacrament to be reserved at the Mission House and St Edward's House – and Bull's reflection that "what a Bishop is willing to authorise should not be considered illegitimate for members of the Society in their individual capacity[41] – Hodge saw it as the point of no return, and entered into a lengthy and heated correspondence on the subject. He left the Society – or, rather, refused to return to Cowley from a leave of absence – after a series of tortuous meetings of a Special General Chapter in 1921, citing his difficulties of conscience, and to his brethren's "extreme sorrow".[42]

The controversy was curious, because it did not necessarily relate to the principle of Reservation of the Blessed Sacrament. The Society's practice varied across its work, and was not necessarily delineated by generation. Robert Page had overseen the installation of an enormous tabernacle on the high altar of

---

37 *CE* May 1918.

38 SSJE/3/1/79ff.

39 Robert Beaken, *The Church of England and the Home Front 1914–1918*, Woodbridge: The Boydell Press (2015), 142ff.

40 Viscount Halifax, *Reservation of the Blessed Sacrament*, London: English Church Union (1917), 15.

41 *A Statement on Reservation of the Blessed Sacrament*, Special GenC 1921, SSJE/2/5/387.

42 SSJE/2/5/390ff; *Memorandum* etc, SSJE/2/5.

Holy Name, Poona, a full twenty years earlier; while as a curate Biscoe had been trained by two of the leading ritualists of his day in the heat of the controversy that led up to the Public Worship Regulation Act, and was known to have a "deep and reverent love for the Blessed Sacrament".[43] Reservation was already practised at St Cuthbert's; while in France, one of Br Maxwell John's tasks had been to care for the key of the tabernacle during Percy Wigram's absence, as the latter had been "able to reserve the Blessed Sacrament continuously" since his arrival.[44] Strong, still at Salonica, had maintained a tabernacle in the tent that functioned as his church from the start, and led a Watch of Thanksgiving before it through the freezing night when the end of hostilities was announced.[45]

The question was not, then, whether the SSJE should reserve the Blessed Sacrament in its churches; or whether members of the Society should avail themselves of the opportunity to approach it as a devotional aid, and encourage others to do likewise. The issue at stake was only whether it should permanently be reserved in the English houses of the Society at Oxford and London. At St Edward's House it pertained particularly to Br Michael, and through the discussions leading up to his eventual separation from the SSJE we glean a sense of the broader thought and general direction of the Society in the matter.

Michael's biographer, Brian Taylor, notes that in his departure from the Society there was to some extent "on both sides a lack of understanding".[46] In this the war had played its part – because of the importance of his work with the Knights of the Crucifix Michael had been given more freedom outside St Edward's House than he might reasonably have been expected to receive in ordinary circumstances. He found it hard to return to "normality" when peace came; but in turn Taylor felt that he had to a great extent lost touch with developments in the community. He wanted to establish the Knights in a less overtly ecclesiastical setting than St Edward's House; and felt the work "was hindered in some measure by his monastic habit, and the fact that he was organising it from a religious house".

It may be that the Society did not entirely appreciate the depths of Michael's ecclesiastical conservatism – Taylor thought that "the introduction of devotions to the reserved Sacrament were to him very serious alterations in the churchmanship of the Society". For his own part he advanced the view that the SSJE was now "increasingly diverging in doctrine and practice from what he regarded as the Reformation standpoint, especially in regard to the Invocation of the Saints and the Reservation of the Blessed Sacrament".[47] His brethren were, in fact, willing to give him as much leeway as they felt they could: Chapter was nominally in favour of freeing him from the obligation of the habit;[48] but "on the other hand, he was never very conciliatory, and allowed himself to become bitter". It was this bitterness that compounded the Society's attempts to find a way out of Michael's difficulties; and by the end

43 *CE* Jan 1919.
44 Wigram, 14 July 1918.
45 Strong, 16 Nov 1918.
46 Taylor, *Br Michael*, 17ff.
47 SSJE/2/5/478.
48 SSJE/3/1/113ff.

of 1924 he had stopped communicating with the Superior General and any of his brethren.[49]

In the end he was released; but only because the Society feared for his health. It was felt that "Br Michael's discourtesy to the Superior General in not answering letters was due mainly to his defective manners and mental strain, rather than to deliberate intention, and that at the present time he was not able to speak or think sanely on the subject of the Society". The Chapter's decision, then, was taken on compassionate grounds – it was not because of Michael's theological difficulties, which in his case Chapter did not think serious enough to merit a dispensation for voluntary exclaustration.

The Chapter's decision, which was ratified by Charles Gore, was clear that "while the vow of obedience is *ipso facto* voided, the obligations of the vow of Poverty and Chastity shall be held binding, and that there is a real purpose to observe them."[50] Michael effectively became a professed religious without a community – and when the Knights' Hostel he had envisioned floundered he continued to function as a lay-worker in successive parish churches. In his old age he resumed cordial relations with the SSJE; and received a pension from the Society, "which was valued both for its own value, and for the link it preserved with the community".[51]

The discussions in the Special Chapter of Epiphany 1925 about Michael's situation reinforce the point that, as we have seen, theological differences on various subjects existed among individual brethren. Bull's major challenge as Superior General was to find a way of enabling the Society to present a united front that would chime with the general direction of the Catholic Movement within the Church of England – of which it was part, and which it sought in turn to serve. In Michael's regard Edward Trenholme had observed that the Society had mechanisms for dealing with theological differences, and although he was later persuaded that charity demanded his release, he helpfully laid out the Society's official position on such matters.

> The Statute [lxxi] did not sanction release on conscientious grounds at all. In London, Brother Michael's objections had been against Reservation, and the way some of the Fathers celebrated, and such like things. When there were objections the Society must either own that the things are wrong and alter them, or maintain as we do that they are not wrong. And in the latter case the objector must either submit or be *ipso facto* dismissed. Release on grounds of conscience is unstatutory and encourages disobedience.[52]

In retrospect Longridge was quite clear that the decision had been taken on account of Michael's "mental condition and the probably serious consequences of trying to retain him in the Society any longer, and not on the ground of his own alleged difficulties of conscience";[53] which would, as Thomas Bignold had also observed, have essentially amounted to the indulging of a member of the

---

49 SSJE/2/5/480.

50 SSJE/2/5/481ff.

51 Taylor, *Br Michael*, 18n.

52 SSJE/2/5/482.

53 Longridge to Bull, 7 Jan 1925, loose opposite SSJE/2/5/482.

Society whose vocation to obedience had failed. Once more, Puller seems to have been a lone dissenting voice: Longridge called his advocacy to allow a member of the Society to be released on grounds of conscience "erroneous and very dangerous doctrine".[54]

COMMON CONCERNS

The overseas work continued to worry the Superior General as time drew on. Bull seems to have made a conscious effort for the SSJE to engage more with service of the Church in England, rather than continue to bear the heavy administrative burden of the work in the colonies, which he felt did not properly belong to the religious life.

> Is this the true work of the Society? In England we have withdrawn to a large extent from parochial organisations; abroad we develop them to the greatest activity. I am genuinely afraid of the scale of our mission work abroad. I do not think our numbers justify it, and the claim the maintenance and support of business organisation makes on the Fathers both abroad and at home, seems to me to interfere with the truer work of the Society, on its intensive as well on its diffusive sides, for individuals and for the Church.

The Indian work, as we have already seen, was a cause of concern. Bull visited in 1921 – "we must support the weak, or they will certainly fall, but we must seek their strength, and rejoice to be able to see them walk alone". With the brethren leading the work in India he concluded that the moment had not yet come to hand over the various missionary endeavours being run from Poona; but that the time might come as the diocese's corporate life grew – although he acknowledged that "perhaps it never really will till it is divorced from State control".[55] Nicholson's experience was that "Hindus respect all missionaries and religious communities working in India, however opposed in their own hearts they may be to Christianity." The Indian Church therefore benefitted from their presence – and he also felt that an enclosed community, dedicated to solely to prayer, "might do much for the conversion of India, and would present to Hindus such an ideal of absolute devotion to God as would undoubtedly impress them".[56]

Waggett was among the priests and "women messengers" who assisted the Bishop of Peterborough, Theodore Woods, in his Mission of Help to India in 1922 and 1923.[57] Although William O'Brien had been delighted, after his own arrival, to be recognised as a Cowley Father by "a gentleman who was Father Page's cabin mate in the passage from England in '78",[58] in 1924 the Society marked the fiftieth anniversary of its ministry in Bombay with thanksgiving tinged with trepidation.

---

54 SSJE/2/5/484.
55 GenC 1921, SSJE/2/5/1.
56 "The Place of Religious Communities in the Indian Church", CE Nov 1920.
57 CE Nov 1922.
58 O'Brien, 17 June 1920.

Our mission has been singularly blessed in the number of men and women who have worked with us in the most devoted way [...] The future of the mission, if it is to be blessed, must depend upon a close co-operation and sympathy between Indian and European workers. Each have their own part to play, and each have their own contribution to make to the building-up of the Church in this land. Each make their own mistakes; each have a different outlook; but it is evident that it is the Divine will that both should work together for a common cause, and mutual love will be the solvent of all difficulties.[59]

Meanwhile, more churches were rising around Tsolo, where the Society's success in training local priests in its image – "bred wholly with us as a boy and owing everything to us" – had outstripped its efforts elsewhere.[60] The new church at Ncembu was being built, pleasingly, by one of the men who had learned stone-cutting under Maynard in the course of the building of new St Cuthbert's in 1905:[61] Jonathan Zondani was still carrying out work for the SSJE forty years later.[62] But the constant growth – as welcome as it was – increased the work of the brethren, and the administrative pressure placed upon the Society. "St Cuthbert's is becoming a bigger and bigger mission," noted the Superior General. "How soon will it outgrow our capacity to take care of it?"[63] In many ways his was a prophetic voice; but it would be another fifty years before the Society heeded his advice.

Bull's plan to rationalise the devotional and financial aspects of the various bodies associated with the Society came to fruition relatively swiftly: in 1918 the original Cowley-Wantage Guild was subsumed into the Cowley, Wantage, & All Saints Missionary Association, with a dedicated office in London at 50 St Anne's Gate, and its remit taking in both the Indian and South African work from then on; while the St John the Evangelist Trust Association was formed in 1919 to deal with the interests of the Society's property and investments.[64] By 1924 Bull was satisfied that the necessary transfers had taken place, and that Chapter was itself "free from the difficulties which arose from trustees being absent abroad, or dying and being just forgotten".[65]

On the new Missionary Association and the Fellowship of St John, Bull announced the former's change of name and the Society's decision to "bring the two organisations into more definite relationship with one another" in February 1919. He pointed out that the original Missionary Association had concerned itself with India; and that the Fellowship of St John "adding alms to prayer, and its members desiring to work as well as pray for the Society" had developed its own missionary character, focussing on the South African work.

Our proposal now is that the Missionary Association should include the South African as well as the Indian Missions, and should be the one Association for organising the financial support of our Missions. This will leave the Fellowship

59 "The Jubilee of the SSJE Mission in India", *CE* April 1924.
60 GenC 1921, SSJE/2/5/1.
61 Ley, 17 April 1917.
62 Callaway, 20 Aug 1939.
63 GenC 1920, SSJE/2/5/1.
64 GenC 1921, SSJE/2/5/1.
65 GenC 1924, SSJE/2/5/1.

free to give itself to the spiritual side of its work, and to gather into itself all who wish for closer communion of prayer and life with the Society.

"The Missionary Association", he went on, "will always be the wider body. The Fellowship will only consist of those who desire special union with the Society of St John the Evangelist." Its obligations were kept deliberately light, so that it did not interfere with membership of parish guilds – "the members only covenant to pray for the Society daily, to give an offering for its works, and to communicate on the Feast of May 6th [St John before the Latin Gate], or as near it as possible, for the intentions of the Society"[66] – but there was a Voluntary Rule for those who desired it, to be used "in whole or in part, as may seem most helpful to themselves, or as they may arrange with the Priest, whose spiritual advice they ordinarily seek".[67]

The changes would be a means of developing the SSJE's system of Associates – essentially its Oblates – and Bull intended "soon to take in hand the necessary revision of the Devotional Forms of the Association."[68] By 1921 the Rule of Life for Priest and Lay Associates of the Society had been overhauled, after a discussion of the appropriate level of rigour and expectation: it was generally agreed that some matters were best left to pastoral care, rather than a laying-down of rules. Waggett particularly "deprecated the inclusion of duties which were binding upon people by the Moral Law and the Ten Commandments or Ordination Vows and that anything further should be accepted as Counsels of Perfection". This particularly applied to "conjugal relations" – although the "great number of letters asking for advice in this matter received by the Fr Superior General" has not survived.[69]

Conjugal relations had already caused a major scandal within the Society itself. Having returned from Salonica, Strong had been deployed to St Edward's House, whence he absconded at the end of August 1922. After a "considerable correspondence" with the Superior General and the Bishop of London he horrified his brethren by marrying in December. A Special Chapter was summoned in January 1923 – as early as it could be summoned to allow the overseas Father to have formal notice – "when the Father Superior General will propose the formal dismissal of the Rev. Leonard Thomas Strong from the Society".[70]

It was the first time that Statute LXXII had ever needed to be enacted in its formal sense. Walter Wyon's departure in 1892 had been "with the full concurrence of the Father concerned, to avoid what was thought to be a probable occasion of open scandal to the Church and to the Society; and there was no doubt as to the penitence of the Father concerned". "We may be thankful," thought Bull, "that, in the fifty-seven years which have elapsed since the inception of the Society, there has been a stability which has given confidence to the many and steadfast friends of the Society in the Church, as well as to ourselves".

---

66 *CE* Dec 1927.
67 *CE* Jan 1925.
68 *CE* Feb 1919.
69 SSJE/3/1/93.
70 SSJE/2/5/427.

A Special Chapter met "to propose summarily to dismiss one of the Fathers of the Society for the open abandonment of his Religious Profession".[71] The facts were bad enough – Bull spoke of the Society's "abhorrence at what he has done" – but they were further compounded by the circumstances. It emerged that since his return from Salonica Strong had kept up a correspondence with a number of young women; and although this was not necessarily remarkable for a member of a religious community that had developed a charism of spiritual direction, a large number of letters had not been strictly confined to ghostly counsel.

A loose note in the Chapter Book records that Bull presented to the Chapter "for their own help some reflections which had come to him in the reading of some 500-odd letters addressed to Strong. These had come from penitents and others since he left the Society, and at Strong's request he had opened, read, and dealt with them." The Superior General had been struck "in the first place, by the remarkable variety and character of the souls he had helped" – they were "precisely the people who needed help, either from loss, or confusion of faith, or entanglement of sin".

> But I am equally struck, in the second place, by the excessive personal element which pervades them. It appears to me an exceedingly dangerous position for a Religious Priest to occupy, especially with women. Some letters are hardly distinguishable from love letters. Others involve intimacies of personal spiritual life which the writers apparently have received from him or given to him; there are complaints that he has not come for a long time to lunch, to tea, to dinner, or to supper; interest in every kind of family concern belonging to the writers is assumed; one or two are so unreserved as lacking in respect; from all sorts of women, it seems, letters end "Your affectionate – or loving – Child", or "daughter", or "yours affectionately only", and the signature is sometimes a Christian name only. I feel bound to say that this seems to me an extremely dangerous method of correspondence with unmarried women.

While Bull was willing to take at face value Strong's good intentions and "the complete sincerity of his desire to bring real help to people in mental and spiritual distress" – he could also see that there were "a large number of cases" in which he had been effective – he felt that many of his penitents' "whole reliance has been on himself – and with his failure has come a collapse of faith and hope in those who leant upon him".

> The most extreme, and most distressing example came to my notice only 2 days ago – an aspirant after religious life, devoted to Fr Strong, lost her reason altogether when she heard of his failure, and in conjunction with another circumstance which contributed directly to the result but which would not have arisen had not this occurred, the end was suicide. This is of course possible with unbalanced souls, at any time and with anyone – however careful. I fear however most gravely that the method and the want of reason, and habit of communicating his own personal feelings and needs to women have been full of danger.

---

71 SSJE/2/5/428.

"There is continually danger in our path," Bull concluded, "of giving ourselves without reserve to the works we are given to undertake, without reserve to persons or to things – and the more ardent any soul is, the greater the need of watchfulness". Strong's path was already set, and even had he repented he could hardly have disposed of his new wife. "Having forsaken his life and work in the Society by his own will, and having openly declared his renunciation of his Religious vows by his marriage", he was duly expelled.[72]

"We must renew our strength," exhorted the Superior General, "because of this manifestation of weakness in our midst".

We must renew our union one with another, because of this excision of one member – by fidelity to our rule of life, by watchfulness over our personal character, by recollection of the Presence of God in our midst in the Community, at our office, in our dealings with souls, we shall be safe ourselves, and shall really save others. The exercise of our Priesthood is now governed by our Religious dedication. It is this to which we have to be true, and to which we have to bear witness in the Church and in the world.[73]

CATHOLIC CONSOLIDATION

The SSJE's witness in the Church and in the world – to which in the face of calamity Bull urged his Society to be true – remained a very serious commitment. A glance at the notices section of the *Cowley Evangelist* shows that in the autumn and early winter of 1921–1922 the Society ran about forty three-day or four-day retreats from the mother house. Most were external, and the great bulk were for women's communities up and down the country. Next in frequency were those for priests, usually held at Cowley or Westminster; then in decreasing order those for laymen, for members of other male communities, and "for women and girls".

In the same period the Society also ran six two-week parish missions; and while such a small sample cannot not be taken to be a general overview of the SSJE's general workload, it points to how busy the Society remained in the years following Benson's death – and how quickly it had resumed its work after the chaos of the First World War. The shock and scandal that attended Strong's departure – which was, of course, never mentioned in any of the Society's published material – was in no small part because of the rarity of such an event. By the 1920s it had further consolidated its position; and although long-standing and key members had died; others had continued to distinguish themselves.

When Waggett returned from Palestine he went straight to Cambridge to prepare his Hulsean Lectures – "the most weighty of his published works" – which he had been appointed to give in 1914, before the war intervened. He eventually delivered them in 1921 on the subject of "Knowledge and Virtue"; and in the same year he was made a Doctor of Divinity *honoris causa* at Oxford.[74]

---

72 SSJE/2/5/432.
73 Special Chapter 1923, SSJE/2/5.
74 Nias, *Waggett*, 165ff.

It is worth briefly setting Waggett's public distinction against the other obvious surviving SSJE scholar, Puller. By the 1920s it seems that Waggett's work continued to engage the academy in ways that Puller's did not. In a previous generation, he had been one of the Society's brightest stars – to the extent of declining a mitre on more than one occasion in order to remain a Cowley Father. He had recently, however – as borne out in the discussions about the Stations of the Cross and the Reservation of the Blessed Sacrament – become a dissenting voice in Chapter.

That there was diversity of belief and practice within the membership of the Society is certain. We have already seen how the views of individual Cowley Fathers differed in relation to Reservation; while in 1915 a discussion about the Invocation of the Saints in Chapter had indicated that not all of the brethren were in favour of its use.[75] Nevertheless, by Advent 1919 at least some of the Society's churches were used to the recitation of the Angelus as part of regular public worship. From South Africa Charles Turner thought nothing of telling the readers of the *Cowley Evangelist* that at the dedication of the new Lady Altar at Ndabeni he had "censed the Altar and the Statue of Our Lady over it, and then said the *Angelus*".[76]

Other indicators present the Society's general public shift towards a mainstream expression of life in the Catholic Movement of the Church of England. The Society had already embraced the Eucharistic sacrifice as efficacious for the living and the departed,[77] and when Francis Rumsey sailed for Cape Town early in 1920 he openly described in his letters the "daily mass" that he had managed to arrange on board;[78] while on his way to India Oliver Carter "utterly shocked" a Baptist minister on his ship "by telling him plainly what we believe and practise".[79] The men who were professed in the Society in the course of Bull's tenure as Superior General had been formed in a phase of the Catholic Movement whose expression and outlook was very far removed from the reserve of that of their early predecessors; and Bull himself was cast in a similar mould.

In 1921 the readership of the *Cowley Evangelist* found the Superior General of the Cowley Fathers, as the setting sun glinted off the gold mosaic-work of St Mark's in Venice, admiring approvingly a picture of "our Lady, a kind of eikon, in a gorgeous gold frame with an immense quantity of jewels, emeralds, rubies, diamonds, rows of pearls, &c". He was on his way to inspect the work in India and South Africa, and called Pontifical Mass on Sunday morning – at which the Cardinal Patriarch presided, with concomitant ritual and vested flunkeys – "the most delightful organised confusion".[80]

Puller, however, was committed to a line of supporting practices of which Benson would have approved – and opposing anything he might have deprecated. As early as 1901, long before the Founder's death, he had opposed

---

75 SSJE/2/5/206ff.
76 Turner, 19 Jan 1920.
77 cf *CE* Nov 1916.
78 Rumsey, 14 Feb 1920.
79 Carter, 14 Jan 1920.
80 Bull, 11/12 Sept 1920.

Longridge's suggestion that the custom of the brethren reciting Lauds and Vespers in addition to Matins and Evensong be abandoned. Benson had appointed the whole of the Day Hours to be said by his Society; and the liturgical overlap arose because of the choir brethren's obligation as clergy of the Church of England to say their Prayer Book offices.

Puller's reasoning for retaining the cumbersome practice had been that "the history of religious communities in the past shows how important it is to guard and hand on unimpaired the fundamental rules given by founders. They ought normally to be held sacred."[81] Three decades later, however, the members of the Society attached to the colonial houses had been dispensed from the Prayer Book offices, and recited only the Day Hours as a matter of obligation.[82] Although it could not be said that under Bull the Founder's memory was not held sacred – Benson's writings continued to appear regularly in the *Cowley Evangelist*, and the Society marked particularly the centenary year of his birth in 1924 – his death enabled his Society to move towards what had become a more mainstream expression of Catholic Movement witness, both at home and in the colonies.

Although he had himself played a major part in the revivication of the Society in the 1890s, it may be that Puller was the SSJE's last member to remain consciously mindful of his early forebears' thoughts on theological Reserve, which had begun with men like Pusey and had been passed onto Benson and his contemporaries. In Tract 87 Isaac Williams had urged his readers to "not seek to remedy by external effects, that which can only be from within; to think less of appearance, more of the reality".[83] Within the Catholic Movement there were those, as George Herring notes, who – not unreasonably – asked whether those who approved of such overt practices as the Reservation of the Blessed Sacrament had "contradicted the character of Reserve and so hollowed out one of the core principles of the Oxford Movement".[84]

The doctrine of Reserve had effectively dissipated, however, as succeeding generations developed other ideas of what it meant in practice – rather than in theory – to contend for Catholic truth in the Church of England. By the 1920s there could be hardly any question of the SSJE's view of the Real Presence, given that the "Holy Eucharist" section of *Songs of Syon*, the Society's hymnal, included renderings by John Mason Neale and others of the ancient texts of *O Salutaris Hostia; Tantum Ergo Sacramentum; Pange Lingua* – "Word made Flesh, by word he maketh / Very bread his Flesh to be"; *Adoro Te Devote* – "O most sweet Memorial of his death and woe / Living Bread, which givest life to man below"; *Ecce Panis Angelorum* – "Very Bread, good Shepherd, tend us"; *Iesus Christus Nostra Salus* – "O how pure this Bread, and holy! / It is thou, my Saviour, wholly"; *O Esca Viatorum* – "O Jesu Christ, whom hidden / 'Neath form of bread, as bidden, / On earth we magnify"; and *Ave Verum Corpus*.

---

81 *Reasons Liturgical and Practical for the Omission of Lauds and Vespers from the Daily Office of the Community, &c*, SSJE/2/1/332a.

82 SSJE/2/6/372.

83 Isaac Williams, *On Reserve in Communicating Religious Knowledge (continued)* [Tract 87], Oxford: Parker (1840).

84 Herring, *The Oxford Movement in Practice*, 222.

Ave! very, real Body, born of blessed maid Marie;
From whose riven side, forth-welling, blood and water mingled free:
Truly smitten, freely offer'd for mankind upon the Tree:
Be our antepast of heaven, in our dying agony."[85]

When the new chapel of the Convent of the Incarnation was completed in 1923, Lucius Cary noted both publicly and approvingly that "the reredos consists of a large panel of cipollino with alabaster pilasters and pediment and frieze with the legend 'Hic est panis de caelo.' The tabernacle on this altar has a silver front with the sacred monogram and the words 'Ecce panis angelorum.'"[86]

When he visited Cowley for the first time in 1934, Colin Stephenson – whose 1972 memoir *Merrily on High* is perhaps the Catholic Movement's most open and human record of its days of summer – confessed to having "nearly swooned with delight" to see the Fathers' distinctive shovel-hats hanging in a row in the hall; but he was shocked and disappointed to find that the Blessed Sacrament was still not reserved in the community church. He could not have known that plans were at that stage already in hand for the conversion of the Song School to serve as a designated Blessed Sacrament chapel, in accordance with the Chapter's decision that the tabernacle should not be placed on an altar which was already in use for regular public worship.[87]

The tabernacles at Cowley joined the other external signs of the SSJE's quiet corporate Catholicity. In St John's Church, under Kempe's ornate and allegorical east window, the main act of worship on Sunday was the High Mass, offered with incense and vestments, to the accompaniment of plainchant led by the choirboys in the rood loft, and cantors from the enormous carved music desk in the middle of the monastic choir. Confession and spiritual advice continued to be offered; while Fellowes Prynne's masterpiece Stations of the Cross now added colour to the previously bare walls of the nave.

It was a long way from the linen chasuble in the Iron Church on Stockmore Street; but it was not far enough for some: Stephenson noted in *Walsingham Way* that Alfred Hope Patten thought the SSJE "represented a rather restrained form of Catholicism which he did not find attractive", even though it had by then modified what Dom Anselm Hughes called its "old-fashioned Sarum" phase of the turn of the century and made its style of worship its own;[88] and was by the 1930s able to congratulate itself, in the light of Dom Cuthbert Butler's *Ways of Christian Life*[89] – in which he referred to Popes Pius X and XI's comments on the participation of the faithful at mass – as practising "what is now being urged in the Roman Church as the ideal thing to be done in public worship".[90]

---

85 *Songs of Syon*, no.139.
86 *CE* Nov 1923.
87 SSJE/2/6/300.
88 Hughes, *Rivers of the Flood*, 42.
89 Dom Cuthbert Butler, *Ways of Christian Life*, London: Sheed & Ward (1932).
90 *CE* May 1933.

Nevertheless, Bull was the "monastic oracle" whom Patten consulted about whether or not he should accept the "potty little parish" of Walsingham in 1921, and it was he who persuaded him to accept the living. Patten restored the Holy House in 1931, and so it is that the Shrine of Our Lady of Walsingham in its sleepy corner of Norfolk partly owes its existence to the Cowley Fathers.[91]

"Our faith must proclaim the Incarnate God," wrote Bull at the start of 1922. "The faith remains constant, the witness of God's love and of man's redemption, the challenge of the condescension of God to man so sorely stricken, yet so strangely heedless and wilful." The loss – in one way or another – of a number of key members of the Society had presented its own challenges, and had caused Bull to worry about the sustainability of some of the overseas work. The American congregation was thriving in its new independence, however; and by the middle of the 1920s he had been able to preside over a process of ecclesiological realignment at home. Under Bull's leadership, the Society of St John the Evangelist caught up with the prevailing mood of the Catholic Movement of which it was a part – and which, crucially, it sought to serve. It was a direction in which he was able to proceed, after the death of the Father Founder, by using the Society's system of internal governance. That in itself reflected the churchmanship of the members of the Chapter in the decade that followed the outbreak of the First World War, and by the mid-1920s its new course was set. There was, however – as Bull had reminded his brethren in the wake of Strong's disgrace – no room for complacency.

[O]n those who worship rests a tremendous responsibility. The claim to hold the Catholic Faith involves that we should live a life in accord with the Catholic Tradition. We may so easily, and so certainly, obscure and discredit the faith we profess and proclaim [...] We cannot be in indifferent to the practice of our religion; we must seek the grace of Jesus Christ, frequent the Sacraments, be found in His house, uphold the law and order of His Church, reverence His sanctuary and the place of His Name, the tabernacle of His glory, where He meets with His people in the Blessed Sacrament of the Altar.[92]

---

91 Colin Stephenson, *Walsingham Way*, London: Darton, Longman & Todd (1970), 104ff.
92 *CE* Jan 1922.

LAUDEMUS CORPUS CHRISTI

Hail! Feast of God's sure Love,
　　Reflecting Heaven above—
Sweet Food of souls, True Life sustaining life:
　　Foretaste of future bliss,
　　Stored Grace of God—ah, this
We crave for, sorely need amid this strife.

Hail! Mystery Divine,
　　Wherein Earth's bread and wine
Yield men the Body and the Blood of Christ:
　　Be Thou our Staff, each day
　　Throughout life's pilgrim way,
Viaticum and Shield;—all needs sufficed!

Christ's Body and Christ's Blood!
　　Unpraised on Holy Rood
For remedy of sin-wrecked man's estate:
　　Celestial watchers gazed,
　　Awe-stricken, sore amazed,
As, 'Victor e'en in death,' Love conquered hate.

Now, with that heav'nly choir,
　　Up-reaching ever higher
We lift our hearts—lo, meet and right it is:
　　Our bounden duty too,
　　To take, in credence true,
And laud and magnify Love's Sanctities.

In-oned with God, we raise
　　Triumphant songs of praise;
Surrend'ring wills and lives, we Love acclaim:
　　Love inexpressible,
　　Benign, accessible—
Sure, boundless Love—aye hallow'd be His Name!

　　　　　　　　　　　　S. J. WALLIS SSJE[93]

---

93 *CE* June 1925.

16

CATHOLIC AND EVANGELISTIC

Shall we be sufficient for these things?
—Henry Power Bull SSJE[1]

When the *Graz* docked at Mazagon in October 1920, in the course of Henry Bull's tour of the colonial missions, the Superior General of the Society of St John the Evangelist had to find his Bombay brethren among a large crowd of supporters of the Islamic Khilafat Movement. Mohammad Ali Jouhar and other of its leaders had joined the ship at Brindisi, on their way back from an unsuccessful attempt to petition the British Government to help shore up the position of the Caliph in the wake of Mustafa Kemal Atatürk's dismantling of the Ottoman Empire as part of his policy of secular nationalism in Turkey:[2] their reception was marshalled by "troops of khaki-clad volunteers with red flags with the crescent on them." The Khilafat Movement would go on to instigate Muslim opposition to British rule in India; and although it would itself fail in the wake of the fall of the Caliphate, its numerous presence as Bull made his way down the gangway presaged something of events to come in both the short and long term.[3]

Bull remained adamant that the colonial work needed to be considered carefully: "we have to keep continually before us the danger of a work that goes beyond our strength, and not only our strength but our true objective in work". To run missions and schools in the colonies was one thing; but "we have to take care that we do not sacrifice our spiritual and pastoral care for merely technical and institutional work; and we have to seek in every possible way the development of native responsibility for spheres and departments of work which are really proportioned to ordinary capacity." He looked for a time when "native agency" might be given responsibility "in the development and care of limited but real pastorates"; but after his colonial tour conceded that the time was not yet fully come – although there were encouraging signs at Poona, where the cure of Rasta Peth had been given to the SSJE's priest co-worker Bashkar Savant. He was able to call on the support of the Society when he needed it, and Bull thought of the development as "the kind of way in which real Indian Church life will grow, and as the kind of relationship which

---

1 *CE* Jan 1920.

2 Maria Misra, *Vishnu's Crowded Temple: India since the Great Rebellion*, London: Allen Lane (2007), 140.

3 Bull, 8 Oct 1920.

we should wish to encourage". His successor, however, was not a success; and by 1928 Rasta Peth was being run once more from the Mission House at Poona.[4]

In South Africa Bull felt that the onus was on the bishops of the Province to make the districts within their dioceses "small enough to be served reasonably by one priest"; although the temptation was for mission-providers like the SSJE – which had already raised up many local vocations – to try to oversee the whole need themselves.

> Immense care is needed, therefore, that we should attempt not what is desirable but what is unavoidable; not what we should like to do, but what God gives us the capacity for: not what the circumstances of the case by themselves seem to demand, but what the Providence of God seems clearly to call us to by providing us with the means to do it. We must measure our enterprises ultimately by our spiritual resources.

He conceded, however, that this was a difficult lesson to learn, and that most of the strain fell on the local Superiors. He commended them particularly to their brethren's consideration: "that their inability to meet the demands made upon them may not hinder their prayers, injure their lives, discourage their devotion, or embitter their hearts. We must not fret ourselves against bonds that we have not bound ourselves with. We must very gladly and contentedly leave in God's hands what we cannot by His will accomplish. That is not a feeble resource, but an act of faith."[5]

It was in the same spirit that when the General Chapter of 1923 discussed the possibility of expanding into Ceylon it resolved that while the SSJE was "prepared at the present time to receive Ceylonese Postulants, to train them in the Society, and to receive them to annual vows", it should be made clear that "the Society cannot as yet pledge itself as to the form in which it will be most desirable that the Religious Life should be established in Ceylon, and for that reason is not as yet prepared to receive them to full profession".[6]

There were also other, more pressing, issues relating to profession within the Society. In the same year, Bull used his address at Chapter to chastise his brethren for their intransigence in having declined to elect a novice, David Procter, to life profession because he was a chronic invalid after having suffered a serious stroke.

> I am driven to the conclusion that the only reason why he has been rejected is that he is stricken with an illness which will prevent him, so far as we see, from ever taking part in the active life of the Community, and that in spite of his great, and indeed unquestioned, personal spiritual qualities and desire for Profession, this disqualifies him.

Bull was frank about the fact that Procter's case had affected him "more deeply than anything else" in his time as Superior General. "On what grounds", he

---

4 GenC 1928, SSJE/2/5/1.
5 GenC 1921, SSJE/2/5/1.
6 SSJE/2/5/450.

asked, "have Fathers determined that the reason of health must necessarily make them vote against the election of one who otherwise has seemed so thoroughly qualified and apparently called of God, and who for so many years has held to his vocation?"

Although he did "not wish to impugn the conscientiousness or the active charity of any Father, or to separate myself from the Constitutional result of our requirements for election", he felt that an error had been made. His comments made it clear that he thought his brethren had misread the Rule, and had interpreted the original stricture – that "sick and weakly persons shall not be admitted as members of the Society, if their infirmity is of such a nature as to render them habitually incapable of observing the ordinary rules" – as binding in all cases without exception.

The statement had appeared in the original Rule of the 1870s, but had not appeared when the Rule had been printed with the Statutes in 1884: "I submit that the only conclusion we can draw is that the Fr Founder, and if you will the Chapter that agreed upon the new draft of the Rule and the Statutes, desired to give, and that our present constitution does give freedom to us to deal with sick persons as may seem best." He followed it with the concrete examples of those who had been professed while Benson was Superior General, despite having been chronically ill.

> Have we not a firm and definite tradition, and clear commentary on the mind of the Fr Founder, that the call to the Religious Life must be our primary consideration, and that we may not reject a person merely on the ground of ill-health, if the call is clear and it is evident that there is spiritual life and power countervailing the physical disability?

Bull felt that the members of Chapter had been overzealous in trying to observe the spirit of the Founder – what Frederick Puller had already spoken of as guarding and handing on "unimpaired the fundamental rules"[7] – and that in returning to first principles they had failed to appreciate their later developments and the occasions upon which Benson had himself practised latitude in their application. He now urged a similar approach in Procter's case.

> Can we not abandon ourselves, in such a case as this, to the pure giving of joy? I am quite certain that numbers of our own friends would welcome it as wholeheartedly as now they are somewhat saddened and perplexed by an unexpected impossibility. I am sure that such an action would bring to us all a great reaction of spiritual values recognized, and grace triumphant over Sickness.

He had decided to extend Procter's novitiate, as his doctor felt that his rejection after "many disappointments in a crowded life" had been significantly detrimental to his health, and the Superior General did "not think that any of you would wish to feel that your action was actually becoming fatal to him". Although he himself had accepted the result with resignation, he was

---

7 *Reasons Liturgical and Practical for the Omission of Lauds and Vespers from the Daily Office of the Community, &c*, SSJE/2/1/332a.

delighted "that there was hope again", and his condition began to improve. "I am then keeping him for further 'probation' for you," Bull told the Chapter.

> Here is evidence I suggest to you. A novice who can bear what seemed the final and crushing disappointment of his life-long hope, in perfect silence and self-restraint, who only breaks out again into words when the light has come back, is a novice whom it seems to me we ought to be most thankful to Almighty God to receive, to whom to minister will be a perpetual blessing, and whose prayers, example, and self-oblation will indeed bring 'much grace'.[8]

Chapter did not have an opportunity to reconsider and vote again: Procter soon worsened, and died in November 1923. He was buried in the Society's plot in the parish churchyard; and the unusually frank obituary notice that appeared in the *Cowley Evangelist* – "for us it has been our privilege and our blessing to have had the care of so sweet a life, and to have it entrusted to our Religious fellowship" – perhaps indicated the frustration felt by the Superior General at governing a Society still haunted by the ghost of its Founder.[9] Bull had paid Benson fulsome and pious tribute at the centenary of his birth in January 1924: "may his prayers ever ascend and prevail for us on high";[10] but as early as 1922 he had wondered whether some of the unreformed Statutes were "really a hindrance, not a help".[11]

DEBTS OF NATURE

There had been other problems, too. In 1922 Bull had noted that the infirmity of some of his increasingly elderly brethren would have to be attended to in the near future: "the sickness of one involves the strain of all". At that point he had associated the burden with "our poverty of numbers, and on the whole diminished natural strength"; but by 1928 the situation was more acute.

> [T]he number of Fathers available to meet the demands made upon us by the Church diminishes as age and sickness take toll of us – and this creates a real difficulty of community life, if we are to accept as freely as in the past the invitations which come to us and which do not diminish. These carry off the still active brethren into frequent absences, and those that remain have hardly strength to carry the burden of the daily life and are in danger of being lonely.[12]

An annual Novena of Prayer for the Increase of the Religious Life was established in 1925 to try and build up the religious communities in the Church of England. During the Society's preparation for it in 1929 William O'Brien, in his capacity as Assistant Superior General – he had replaced Lucius Cary, whose health had collapsed, and Bull was absent once more in India – noted that "the

8 GenC 1923, SSJE/2/5/1.
9 *CE* Dec 1923.
10 *CE* Jan 1924.
11 GenC 1922, SSJE/2/5/1.
12 GenC 1928, SSJE/2/5/1.

stream of vocations to the Religious Life, at any rate among men, flows very feebly". He referred to Benson's paper of four decades earlier, *The Desirableness of Reviving the Common Religious Life among Men*, which was simultaneously serialised in the *Cowley Evangelist*.

> Since that time there has been considerable development among women of the Religious Life but the actual number of men to-day dedicated to the Religious Life must be very little above what it was then. This very large disproportion between women living under Life-vows and Priests in the same condition is serious.

The secular clergy could not, thought O'Brien, supply all the needs of the women's communities "now flourishing in the Church of England over the world". His argument laid bare the ongoing symbiotic relationships between the men's and women's communities in general, and by extension those of the SSJE with the All Saints Sisters of the Poor and the Community of St Mary the Virgin in particular. Even if the needs of the women's communities could practically be supplied with ordinary priests, "we could not be satisfied with the spiritual vigour of a Church which for so vital an element in its life could only find vocations amongst its women."

At the same time, while there might be "a natural tendency to desire new Orders, for men to seek something which gives expression to their own predilections", there was a need "to maintain that which has been founded"; and anyone thinking of starting afresh ought "to think well by what spirit they are led". He suggested to his readers that – while the general purpose of the novena ranged wide – those who had received the relevant papers and prayer intentions "might also keep as a daily intention for our prayer the increase of Religious Vocations among men".

> The power of the Holy Spirit calling men to the Religious Life will not be found so much in new orders usefully designed for what are felt to be special needs of the time, but in the call to men to submit themselves to be trained and ordered in places where the Religious Life is established, so that they may learn to do God's will instead of their own.

"Mere human zeal", he continued, "is often enough the occasion of confusion, but it is the work of the Holy Spirit to draw men gently, but with a wonderful attraction, into ways of hiddenness and self-renunciation, where their happiness is not to see the end for which they are called but only to know that He has called them."[13]

Only six men had been professed in the English congregation of the SSJE since 1920, and alongside the need for fresh blood was the matter of the ongoing ill-health of a number of prominent members of the Society – chief among them Cary and Philip Waggett at home, Sydney Moore in India, and Godfrey Callaway in South Africa. The Society was also beginning to feel its age: Charles Field and Frederic Noel both died in 1929; to be followed in 1930

---

13 *CE* Nov 1929.

by Hugh Nicholson, William Longridge, and Bishop Arthur Hall of Vermont. Charles Turner's death in the same year came as a shock, however, saving a boy from drowning at Broadstairs: "a life devoted to saving boys crowned with the symbolic act of a successful rescue by the surrender of his own life."[14] He was later honoured by the Carnegie Hero Fund Trustees.[15]

The increasing infirmity of the older members of the Society at Cowley precipitated the considerable enlargement of the infirmary in 1929; but the period that preceded the building work, while one of what Bull called "straitness at home", was at the same time remarkably one of "somewhat remarkable elasticity abroad". The SSJE's colonial work continued to develop, despite the Superior General's caution of the preceding years. The ongoing financial difficulties caused by the rate of exchange between the sovereign and the rupee seemed to call for a cutting of the Society's cloth in India; but as Bull himself observed, "when a Mission has the charge of many institutions and numbers of children and the responsibility of many out-stations – to say nothing of the evangelistic enterprise – minor economies may be made but, but serious retrenchments are held over in hope of increased support."[16]

The Indian work soon grew to include a farm at Nanded, a few miles south-west of Poona, under the charge of Br Arthur; and soon afterwards a medical mission was established in the Konkan, run by Frederick Playne.[17] At Cape Town the people at Ndabeni were being displaced to Langa, which soon became a new and ongoing concern;[18] and the mission buildings at St Cuthbert's were considerably enlarged with the addition of a new and airy library.[19]

The international to-ing and fro-ing of the active brethren continued as usual, and the constant letters home were as full of hopes and fears, triumphs and disasters, as they had ever been; while outstation churches continued to be built as the need arose. When Nicholson's health had plummeted at the end of 1925 it was felt by Provincial Chapter that the situation made "a special visit of the Superior General to India justifiable and even necessary".

Bull's letters home underlined the serious financial situation; and after his return he noted that the meetings of the Missionary Association had been full of "a real enthusiasm of affection and loyalty in those who follow and help our course at home and abroad by their prayers, their sympathy, and their alms",[20] and acknowledged a stream of "generous gifts" which had poured in.[21]

Perhaps in the end the overseas work was irresistible, both to its supporters and to the Society itself. In 1926 Callaway brought out his popular *The Fellowship of the Veld: Sketches of Native Life in South Africa*, and followed it with a number of similar publications about life in South Africa as the years went by. His letters and articles were, after Edward Elwin's death, the literary high-

---

14 *CE* Sept 1930.
15 *CE* Feb 1931.
16 *CE* Feb 1926.
17 *CE* Sept 1928.
18 GenC 1928, SSJE/2/5/1.
19 *CE* Dec 1929.
20 "Our Indian Mission", *CE* June 1926.
21 *CE* June 1926.

light of almost every edition of the *Cowley Evangelist*; and in 1927 the Superior General returned to South Africa to inspect in person the ongoing new work there.[22]

By the end of the 1920s the missions at Poona, Bombay, and Tsolo had all been provided with cars; while the Cape Town brethren had to make do with a motorbike and sidecar. The Superior General hoped that, while the colonial work benefited from these "apostolic equipments", Cowley would "retain an old-fashioned simplicity and leave it to the daughter houses to adopt the new fashions".[23]

THE CONGRESS MOVEMENT

The world was changing, and so were the parameters of the Society's work. In 1922 Bull had been particularly struck by "the special call to work amongst priests under the special circumstances of the day, the opportunity of awakening and inspiring and developing and guiding into deep channels of personal life and devotion the body of those who call themselves Catholic."

> Spiritual questionings and spiritual movement are all around us – in the world and in individuals – and that the priesthood of the Church should be really alive to them, responsive, understanding, able to take part in them, able to help in them, is in a peculiar degree a special responsibility resting on ourselves and our religious brethren of other Societies. We are expected to be able to help, we are definitely asked for help; what we have received is precisely that which those outside of us look for, feel their need of, and would most thankfully partake of.

It was with this in aim in mind that the Superior General, and by extension the whole Society, became involved in the Anglo-Catholic Congress Movement. As William Davage has observed – channelling Geoffrey Rowell, Kenneth Stevenson, and Rowan Williams[24] – the meetings of Catholic-minded Anglicans, both clerical and lay, which took place in the 1920s and 1930s may be "conventionally regarded as the high-water mark of Anglo-Catholicism".

> They fired enthusiasm, captured the imagination of thousands, expanded the reach of the Catholic faith and practice beyond the bounds of Anglo-Catholicism and made it appear possible that that Catholic principles, doctrine, and cere-monial practice would triumph in the Church a century after John Keble had preached his sermon on the National Apostasy in the University Church [...] These were heady days for the participants and for the wider Anglo-Catholic community.[25]

---

22 Bull, 26 Oct 1927 ff.
23 GenC 1927, SSJE/2/5/1.
24 Rowell *et al*, *Love's Redeeming Work*, 372ff.
25 William Davage, "The Congress Movement", *The Oxford Handbook of the Oxford Movement*, 517.

When Bull addressed the first Congress in July 1920, his vision of the restored religious life in the Church of England was clear. He had already enthused about the Community of the Sisters of the Love of God's new buildings at Fairacres earlier in the year, and spoken about the enclosed life as "the vocation of the hidden, sacrificial, intercessory life of a perfect self-oblation in love" – in contrast to the other "mostly active" communities, which had "multiplied wonderfully and happily". There had been some discussion, even in SSJE Chapter, about how useful such communities could be in the life of the Church; but Bull was clear that he wished "to commend now most earnestly" such efforts – and apart from the SLG, he cited particularly the contemplative Benedictines at Malling Abbey:[26] "It is no self-centred idle life, no dream of prayer, or following of self-will. It is a burning desire of love to die to self and to live to God, in great humility, and with an ever increasing intensity of worship and self-oblation."[27]

Fr Davage's faultless nose for a congenial and well-heeled dinner party leads him to the observation that the Congresses "grew from modest beginnings in conversations among Anglo-Catholic clerical dining groups", and had the support and patronage of a number of the Society's own benefactors – not least Viscount Halifax and the Duke of Newcastle.[28] Among the other speakers at the Congress who had close links with the SSJE were Darwell Stone, Frank Weston, Walter Frere, and Charles Gore. Bull noted that he had himself to speak on the subject of "a definite form or mode of spiritual life, within the common life of the Church; a form of life which enshrines in a special development the root principles of the common Christian life, but which has a marked character of its own".

> The Religious Life is that state, or form, of life in which, obediently to the inspiration or call of God, a soul is consecrated to God in Jesus Christ under perpetual vows of Poverty, Chastity, and Obedience. There are many forms of this consecration, as there are also many objects with which is it is undertaken; and the Church has need of all. But strictly for the Religious state, as it exists in the Catholic Church, there is required the entire and permanent surrender of self, according to some fixed and recognised rule based upon the Evangelical Counsels, that is, upon the observance of a real spirit of Poverty, Chastity, and Obedience.

After a brief overview of the idea of the Religious life in the life and history of the Church, he then talked about "the permanence of the Religious life and our own need of it". He was quite clear that no plans made, resolutions passed, legislation enacted, or gifts given – and he had in no uncertain terms told the readers of the *Cowley Evangelist* earlier in the year that they needed to increase their almsgiving[29] – could make the "heavenly plant" grow.

---

26 Anson, *Call of the Cloister*, 426.
27 "The Enclosed Life", CE Feb 1920.
28 Davage, "The Congress Movement", 517ff.
29 *CE* April 1920.

Care we must take – the expert gardener is the friend of the plant. Gifts must be made – for the plant must be nurtured. Enthusiasm we need – we have been too long treading the easy paths of convention, or respectability, and have called too little for sacrifice and fire of love. Official recognition we hope is on the way. But we want the recognition of the life, not of the works.

"The plant itself", he went on, "is the growth of the seed of fervent love, and personal devotion to Jesus Christ, springing up in chosen ardent souls." It is not difficult to trace the Society's theology of consecrated sacrifice through his words: the Religious life needed to be encouraged in the Church partly so that its work could be increased – he enumerated retreats, spiritual direction, missions, nursing, teaching as obvious examples of its outwards service to the world – but also so that its spiritual gifts could be more widely distributed.

[T]he work of prayer, and of sacred study; for the development of spiritual power; for the inspiration that springs from souls that have left all for Christ; for the maintenance of the great ideals and standards of faith, and love, and worship, of purity and humility, of self sacrifice and self-surrender; for the manifestation in the world of a brotherhood, that, if only it be true to itself, has 'love and joy and peace' as its evident life.

"We dare not", he concluded, "leave anything undone which might fill this school of perfection with disciples. To aim at perfection is to do the best service of which we are capable to our neighbour as to ourselves; to aim at perfection is to do the best service we can render to our Lord himself. The way of Religion is our Lord's own way of perfection commended to those who seek Him supremely."[30]

The second Congress, in July 1923, was regarded by the Society as "deliberately planned as part of a campaign, Catholic and Evangelistic, personal and corporate". Halifax and Cardinal Mercier's ecumenical Malines Conversations were underway; while in England Bull felt that real progress had been made since 1920: "it is then in a new atmosphere, and with the sense of a fresh responsibility, that the second Albert Hall Congress meets."

Its programme seeks once more to cover, so far as it may in three days, the Catholic Faith in its main outlines, but it deals with it in its implications of life, of service, and of devotion, and it has as its aim the renewed evangelization of England, Wales, Scotland, of whatever country may be the home base of those who are present. It is a bold phrase, but the evangelization of England means the evangelization of the district, the town, the village, the hamlet, where each one lives and is set to be a Christian. Each parish, and each home in it, each priest and each communicant, young as well as old, must catch the fire, and flame with the faith, and feel the responsibility, and take part in the enterprise.[31]

The aims of the second Anglo-Catholic Congress, then, were very much the aims of the SSJE's early missions; but now writ large and conceived of on a

---

30 *Report of the First Anglo-Catholic Congress, London, 1920*, London: SPCK (1920), 183ff.
31 *CE* July 1923.

national level. The Society's parish-by-parish work of the preceding decades had been as a means of converting individual souls, and the principles of its operations had been taken up by the Catholic movement as a whole. "Catholic and Evangelistic", summarised the Superior General, "personal and corporate, these are its marks".

> It is Catholic, for it presents the faith of Our Lord Jesus Christ in its full and defi-nite content. It is Evangelistic, because it seeks to relate this faith to the needs, and inquiries, and perplexities of our present day, and to bring it home to those who have never quite realized it. It is personal, for it invites the aid of every individual and calls on each to share the enterprise of prayer, or of work, or of witness. It is corporate, for it bids us come together, and work together, and worship together, parish with parish, soul with soul, and reveal in the Church a living body, an active society, a fellowship of worship, of service and of sacri-fice. This perfected would indeed be the revelation of Jesus Christ, and His true witness to those who desire Him.

The seed planted by Benson's first mission to Bedminster in 1862, which Rowan Strong has called an "early move into discreet Anglo-Catholic domes-tic missions by the inheritors of Tractarianism", had yielded a rich harvest.[32] Sixty years on the SSJE was no longer the only tree in the orchard; and others were growing quickly. As the years passed members of other religious com-munities, notably the Community of the Resurrection and the Society of the Sacred Mission, would take a more active role in the Congress movement, and indeed in the wider international aims of the SSJE itself.

John Betjeman wrote later of those "who remember the Faith, the grey-headed ones, / Of those Anglo Catholic-Congresses swinging along, / Who [...] surged to the Albert Hall in our thousands strong / With 'extreme' colonial bishops leading in song."[33] When Arthur Hall had donated a pectoral cross as an offering at the Congress of 1920, it was redeemed by the congregation of the community church and presented to Stanley Haynes SSM, the newly consecrated Assistant Bishop for Basutoland in the Diocese of Blomfontein. "It is a very happy thing," noted the *Cowley Evangelist*, "that this Cross, given for missions abroad, should now find an active employment in the mission field, and that we should have been enabled to give it to the first member of the Society of the Sacred Mission, known as the Kelham Fathers, to be appointed a Bishop."[34]

Preaching in the community church after the second Congress had met, Bull told his hearers of the "three great foundation principles [which] may be picked out as having received special emphasis, meeting three great needs of our day".

---

32 Rowan Strong, "The Oxford Movement and Missions", *The Oxford Handbook of the Oxford Movement*, 487.

33 John Betjeman, "Anglo-Catholic Congresses", *High & Low*, London: John Murray (1966), 37.

34 *CE* Aug 1923.

They were the Catholic doctrine of the Incarnation, the centrality of the Cross, and the necessity of carrying the redemptive power of the love of God into all relationships of life. These are principles of the faith of the Gospel for which we have to strive, and in union with which we must strive, as inspired and moulded by them.[35]

The Congresses were, to some extent, a yardstick by which to measure the progress of the Catholic Movement's aims. In preparation for the Congress of 1927 an overview was published: *An Illustrated Record of Work for the Three Years 1923–1926*, in which the Society had taken its own part. It was, for example, one of the 48 religious communities to be associated with the Fiery Cross movement,[36] which sought to maintain "unceasing prayer for the conversion of our country"; while the revival of pilgrimages – "a noteworthy result of the Congress Movement"[37] – had been at the forefront of Marcell Conran's thoughts a whole decade earlier. Appropriately enough, given the Society's more recent controversies, the Congress of 1927 focussed especially on the Eucharist. Waggett gave the opening paper, on "The Christian View of the World"; while Bull – who called it "in effect a Eucharistic Congress"[38] – was noted, almost characteristically, to have "made the appeal for contributions to the Congress funds".[39]

CORPORATE CONSOLIDATION

Stands had also been taken. When the Bishop of Birmingham, the liberal and controversial Ernest Barnes – "an active persecutor of the [Anglo-Catholic] movement"[40] and a leading eugenicist[41] – moved to ban Eucharistic reservation in his diocese, the Society countered robustly with an exposition by the Superior General on the Blessed Sacrament entitled "Our Defence of the Catholic Faith".

> [T]he controversy which at the present moment distracts and distresses us in the Diocese of Birmingham is really identical with that for which Dr Pusey and his fellow priests suffered at the beginning of the great revival. It was the Catholic doctrine of the Sacrament of the Altar which was attacked then even as it is now.

"The circumstances have changed", conceded Bull. "Then there was nothing of Ritual as we understand it now. That controversy developed and came to its height in the Public Worship Regulation Act of 1874. There was nothing about

---

35 *CE* Aug 1923.

36 *CE* November 1925.

37 *The Anglo-Catholic Congress: An Illustrated Record of Work for the Three Years 1923–1926*, London: ACC (1927), 6ff.

38 *CE* Jan 1927.

39 *Report of the Anglo-Catholic Congress* [1927], London: Society of Ss Peter & Paul (1927).

40 Barry Spurr, *Anglo-Catholic in Religion: T. S. Eliot and Christianity*, Cambridge: Lutterworth Press (2010), 92.

41 Patrick T. Merricks, *Should Such a Faith Offend? Bishop Barnes and the British Eugenics Movement, c.1924–1953*, PhD Thesis: Oxford Brookes (2014).

Reservation of the Blessed Sacrament. Those were days of rare Celebrations and infrequent Communions. But the doctrine of the Blessed Sacrament was fearlessly set forth, with its glorious implications for sinners and for saints."

He referred to Pusey's University preaching ban of 1843 – "because it was an adorable Presence that he taught" – and to his and Keble's respective works on the Real Presence and Eucharistic Adoration, which he felt had in turn influenced Sir Robert Phillimore, the then Dean of the Arches, in his judgement of 1870 in respect of the controversy surrounding W. J. E. Bennett and St Barnabas, Pimlico, that "to describe the mode of Presence as Objective, Real, Actual, and Spiritual, is certainly not contrary to the law." The judgement had in turn been confirmed by the Judicial Committee of the Privy Council, "and though Catholics have always protested against the assumption of jurisdiction by this Court in questions of doctrine, this remains the expressed 'law' of the Church of England".

The Superior General urged patience, although he acknowledged "justification for a feeling of resentment when those who are wont to take their 'law' from the Ecclesiastical Courts yet bring accusations of false or unlawful doctrine against Priests, and the faithful who hold this Eucharistic Doctrine. But saints are not made out of resentment, nor is the faith thus advanced."

> The truth of God demands the intellect and worshipful surrender of man's whole being. It brings forth its fruit in us as we live by it; it is commended by our practice of it. Humility, patience, forbearance, charity, willingness to suffer, determination to persevere, fuller consecration to the service of Christ in the Church and in his members, thanksgiving for His grace, and praise for His mercy, these are ever our best defence of the Catholic Faith.[42]

Barnes was still in post a decade later, and the Provincial Chapter noted that "there was grave strain and discouragement amongst those who were holding out", and that "help from outside was urgently needed". It wished the Church Union, which was supporting Anglo-Catholic clergy in the Diocese of Birmingham, to know "of our own willingness to help in any manner which might prove possible".[43]

Meanwhile, controversy over the Book of Common Prayer loomed large. As John Maiden has observed, it had its origins in "an intensive period of Protestant agitation over Anglo-Catholic 'indiscipline' from the mid-1890s" – with which the SSJE had itself been associated through Walter Walsh's scathing criticism of the Society of the Holy Cross in *The Secret History of the Oxford Movement* of 1897 – and the discussions relating to proposed changes had ranged far and wide in the wake of the First World War and "shifting wartime spiritualities".[44]

The infamous Ornaments Rubric, with its injunction that "such ornaments of the Church and of the ministers thereof shall be retained and be in use as were in this Church of England by the authority of Parliament in the Second

---

42 "Our Defence of the Catholic Faith", *CE* Jan 1926.
43 PC 1936, SSJE/3/1.
44 John Maiden, "The Prayer Book Controversy", *The Oxford Handbook of the Oxford Movement*, Oxford: OUP (2017), 530ff.

Year of the Reign of King Edward the Sixth", meant that for many Anglo-Catholics the 1662 Prayer Book could be used with enough latitude to cover a range of liturgical practices. Mass at the Society's altars – with plainchant, incense, and vestments "of English shape"[45] – was, at least in its essentials, a celebration of Holy Communion according to the Book of Common Prayer.

After lengthy discussion in Convocation, the book that was approved for parliamentary consideration in 1927 did not command the united support of the broad sweep of Anglo-Catholics. In his March message to the readers of the *Cowley Evangelist*, Bull called the situation "a wild gateway to Lent";[46] and much of the heat surrounded the proposed restrictions upon Reservation of the Blessed Sacrament, in which "many Anglo-Catholic sensed a strong whiff of ecclesiastical tyranny".[47] The delegates at the 1927 Anglo-Catholic Congress deliberately refrained from discussing the proposed book;[48] but Bull's position was quite clear.

> This Congress marks a definite stage in the development of the Oxford Movement. The conception of the Catholic Church as the living Body of Christ, and of the Church of England as an integral portion of it, brought men's minds to the realisation of the treasures of Sacramental grace in her, which had been so little heeded or explored [...] With the new conception of the Church came a new understanding of the Sacraments, and a new vision of worship.

"So Masses have multiplied," he went on, "and Communions have multiplied, and an increasing sense of reverence, awe, joy and devotion have gathered round the Altar. And this has not been confined to the Liturgy itself. The Holy Sacrament [...] is still the shrine of the Divinely Covenanted Presence. It is still the Body and the Blood of Christ. It is still His Sacramental Presence."[49] Preaching during the Congress itself he pressed the point further: "The Blessed Sacrament is the pledge of future glory. Let us make it more and more the foundation of all our life."[50]

Parliament returned the 1927 book to the bishops, after a wide-ranging discussion that Maiden describes as having been "among the great parliamentary set-piece debates of the twentieth century".[51] Their response, the proposed 1928 Prayer Book, was generally deemed by the Anglo-Catholic party to be even less satisfactory than its predecessor – it banned tabernacles outright – and Bull observed in General Chapter that he had told the Diocesan Conference that "if the Deposited Book became law I could only see ahead of us a fresh period of strife and confusion". He favoured, however reluctantly, passive resistance in the spirit of William Connor Magee's oft-misquoted view that he would rather see "England free than compulsorily sober".

---

45 *CE* Nov 1927.
46 *CE* March 1927.
47 Maiden, "The Prayer Book Controversy", 538.
48 Davage, "The Congress Movement", 525.
49 *CE* July 1927.
50 *CE* August 1927.
51 Maiden, "The Prayer Book Controversy", 530.

We would rather see the Church of England Catholic than disciplined. The Archbishop [Magee] wanted to preserve liberty at the risk of some drunkenness; those with whom I agree want to preserve Catholic faith and development at the risk of some disorder [...] What the Church really teaches and her living work is far more influential than the external fact of her discipline and unity.[52]

The new Bishop of Oxford was in favour of the 1928 book, a fact of which Bull did not approve.[53] Thomas Strong was a former Dean of Christ Church, who had been translated from Ripon; whereas when Hubert Burge had died in 1925 the *Cowley Evangelist* lamented that "the Catholic cause of the Church of England loses in our late Bishop a true friend and interpreter in circles often unfavourable to it by prejudice or simple ignorance".[54] Nevertheless Strong was generally supportive of the Anglo-Catholics in his diocese, whom he treated with self-effacing good humour.[55]

After what Bull called "disastrously persistent attempts" to persuade Parliament to approve "a revision of the Prayer Book, that bore on its face only too patently the marks of compromise", the proposed version of 1928 was in turn thrown out; but not before the possibility of its passing into law had played havoc with the Society's attempts to revise, once more, its own liturgical observances. In the end the long-looked for new edition of the *Hours of Prayer* came to fruition after another round of kalendrical wrangling: St Simeon of Jerusalem was added, St Gregory the Great promoted to a greater simple feast, St Mary Magdalene raised to the rank of a double feast, and St Procopius the Martyr voted down: "not very well known". In the wake of accusations of Anglo-Catholic indiscipline and disloyalty, the raising of the Conception of the Blessed Virgin Mary to a double feast was discussed and rejected, on Puller's now-heeded advice.[56]

A few years later, while settling with sixteen hostel boys into a new retreat bungalow provided for the Poona mission through the munificence of Sir Ness Wadia, Cyril Whitworth met a Goanese priest nearby, "a most pleasant man and very intelligent", who pressed him on the issue.

[W]hen I told him I belonged to the *ecclesia anglicana* he said you have had many innovations of late years but do you accept the Immaculate Conception? [...] I told him in the English Church – like the Roman Communion of not so very long ago – it was not a matter of *de fide* but we were left free to accept it or not.[57]

The feast finally received its due promotion in 1938;[58] but from 1927 the Angelus was rung "at the usual times" at the mother house, with the agreement in Provincial Chapter that it should be tolled "sufficiently slowly to allow of the due recitation of the words, and of the observance of the customary silence

---

52 GenC 1927, SSJE/2/5/1.
53 Ibid.
54 *CE* July 1925.
55 Stephenson, *Walsingham Way*, 61.
56 SSJE/2/6/62ff.
57 Whitworth, 17 May 1934.
58 SSJE/2/6/464.

and attention when in the midst of work or conversation".[59] In 1928 the same body resolved *nem con* to ask the Superior General, "if he consider it right, for the use of the Paschal Candle at Easter". Strong consented to its use, and also to the ceremonies pertaining to its hallowing on Easter Eve. Shortly afterwards, electric light was installed in the church itself.[60]

Perhaps Bull's most significant achievement as Superior General, however, was the overhaul of the Statutes relating to the life of the lay brothers. The need for their revision had been precipitated by the arrival of Br Basil, who as a lay-man was technically a Lay Novice; but was also a Choir Novice in that he was a candidate for Holy Orders. The development, noted the Superior General, "raises the question not only of the distinction of laymen and priests in our Choir Noviciate, but suggests afresh the consideration of our whole attitude to laymen".

He described the subject as having been "under discussion amongst us for certainly 30 years", since when "every attempt has hitherto failed", and "attempts at consolidation other than by profession in the same way and under the same vows have also been made and died away".

> It was recognized again and again in Chapter debates that some sort of con-solidation of life was necessary, if lay professed were to be able to maintain any reality of religious life in community. To be professed in the same society, with the same vows, seems indeed to demand some real community of life.

"It seems that at one time lay brothers sat at a different table in the Refectory," he went on. "Allusion to this is made in [the Chapter minutes of] 1909. That at least has ceased."[61] There were other obvious problems, however, which had "not tended to peace".

> While Father Congreve was Master no one would be likely to complain much of separation from the centre of the Society's life. But has time has gone on the tendency has been perforce to appoint as Master of the Lay Brothers one of the younger and more active Fathers [...] Of late – perhaps I might say since I became Superior General – it has seemed to me impossible to carry out the Statutes strictly in respect of the Master of the Lay Brothers' control of the older Brothers.

Furthermore, the office of Master of the Lay Brothers was not extant in any of the other houses, which meant that a distinction had come into being since lay brothers had begun to be sent on overseas mission work after the minor reforms of 1909.

> Abroad – that is outside the Mother House – the lay brother, or brothers, are directly under the Superior, and if they are minded to do so can share the family life quite freely. When they return to the Mother House this family life gets a sudden check; they are suddenly disconnected with the central life.

---

59 SSJE/3/1/168.
60 SSJE/3/1/177–179.
61 GenC 1922, SSJE/2/5/1.

He thought the subject was once more "worth our fresh consideration".[62] By 1926 he was adamant that the professed members "must make their fellowship in our life the basis of our rules."

> Difference of function does not imply lack of fellowship. It is rather the condition of a true fellowship if properly limited. If fellowship in the religious state in daily life is amply and generously secured, the functions which differentiate priests and laymen in our Society may be bonds of union [...] Much of what I have been saying to-day need not necessarily have been addressed to the Fathers only.

The greater involvement of the lay brethren in meetings of the Society might be "a possible way of helping forward that sense of corporate fellowship and obligation which is so difficult of realization, and yet so essential to harmony".[63] In 1927, after over two decades of angst and wrangling, Chapter finally instructed a committee to consider the matter, directing it to be "guided by the following principles" – of which the first three were the most significant.

> (a) That the Lay Brothers shall observe the same Rule of Life as the Fathers, except in such matters as are of special obligation for Priests, and subject to such regulations as may from time to time be determined by authority.

> (b) That the Lay Novices shall form part of one novitiate of Choir and Lay Novices, under the charge of the Master of the Novices [the Office of Master of the Lay Brothers had been unfilled since 1922].[64]

> (c) That the Lay Novices shall have a novitiate of three years at least, and after the completion of this novitiate they shall be proposed for election to temporary vows renewable from year to year for a further period of three years, after which they shall be put forward for Profession, if they shall have reached the age of thirty.

A year later the committee presented its report, with the necessary changes to the Statutes which the development would entail. O'Brien presented each in turn for the Chapter's consideration and vote of approval.[65] By the end of Chapter business in 1928 the lay brothers were nominally more fully integrated into the life of the Society, less segregated from the community at large, and no longer liable to undergo what had in the past seemed at times to be an interminable test period. It had taken nearly 30 years, and the near-collapse of the novitiate – in which the war had been an overarching external factor – to bring the Society to this point.

---

62 GreC 1922, SSJE/2/5/1.
63 GenC 1926, SSJE/2/5/1.
64 SSJE/2/5/540.
65 SSJE/2/6/2ff.

HIGH PRAISE

W hen Bull addressed the readers of the *Cowley Evangelist* in June 1930, just ahead of the fourth Anglo-Catholic Congress, he was at the height of his powers as the Superior General of the senior men's community in the Church of England; and he spoke with the all authority of an established leader of the Catholic Movement.

I invite all who are able to become Members of the Congress by applying to the Congress Office, 235 Abbey House, Victoria Street, London, S.W.1, and sending 2s 6d; and I invite all, whether able to become members or not, to unite in prayer to God for His blessing on the Congress. Its purpose, as set forth in the Handbook, is 'to set forth the nature of the Church and to define the obedience due to her from her children'.

"The Congress Movement", he continued, "has become the rallying point for those who rejoice to call themselves Catholics in the Church of England, on its definitely evangelistic side." Nicholson, dying in the Sassoon Hospital, specifically asked John Williams to bring him a copy of the *Church Times* with the account of the Congress, two days before he breathed his last. His death, coupled with that of Turner, elicited affectionate tributes from the Bishops of Bombay and London,[66] the Archbishop of Cape Town,[67] and the Archbishop of Canterbury himself[68] – indicating, once more, the high regard in which the Society was held in the various spheres of its work at home and abroad.

It was decided that the Boys' Senior School at Cowley should be renovated in memory of Turner and to commemorate his heroic death: this was part of an appeal for £10,000 to overhaul the Society's schools in preparation for an anticipated raising of the school-leaving age in the near future. The appeal as a whole was led in the pages of *The Times* by the Earl of Shaftesbury, the Dean of Westminster, Lord Victor Seymour, and Athelstan Riley. It had been a while since the Society had employed a similar strategy; but the need was great: "these Senior Schools will be the largest Church Schools in Oxford",[69] and the future of church schools coexisting alongside those run by the state was by no means clear. Still, as Bull put it, "If we believe that religious education, based on definite Church principles, is worth having, it is worth fighting for."[70] At the other end of the educational spectrum, St Edward's House continued to host the Retreat for Public School Boys established by Turner;[71] although Edward Trenholme later thought it a shame that the Society had not been able to attract working-class men in the same way.[72]

In the course of his address to Greater Chapter in 1931 Bull referred to the various goings-on outside the enclosure that made for a bleak worldview:

66 Acland, 5 Aug 1930; Winnington-Ingram, 24 Aug 1930.
67 Carter, 22 Aug 1930.
68 Lang, 2 Sept 1930.
69 *CE* Jan 1931.
70 *CE* Nov 1930.
71 *CE* March 1931.
72 *CE* Feb 1933.

the Great Depression at home; the volatile political situation in India, which had once more effectively "crippled" the resources of the missions there; and increasing poverty among the indigenous population in South Africa. He also referred to a circular letter that he had sent to the members of Chapter a few weeks earlier. The letter does not seem to have survived; but after fifteen years at the helm he had announced his wish to retire as Superior General.

As Halifax had observed as early as 1915 – referring to the Society's growth and influence since its inception – the SSJE's praise was in all the churches,[73] and under Bull's leadership its reputation had continued to grow. In India in 1923 O'Brien was asked to lead a retreat for Syrian Jacobite women at Kundara, which he recounted in great detail in his letters home. He noted with particular approval his retreatants' devotion to the Blessed Sacrament. "It is ludicrous to think", he wrote, "of what Protestants called ritualistic in some timid Anglican church when the clergyman has dared to bow to the altar compared with the ceaseless movement and vigour of the Eastern ritual".[74]

Relations with the Eastern Churches had come to the fore in the wake of the controversy surrounding the Jerusalem Bishopric in the 1840s, although, as Mark Chapman has noted, they had mainly been cultivated by "enthusiasts".[75] Many of those enthusiasts, however, were members of the SSJE – among them Puller and Nalbro' Robinson – and Charles Grafton's ties with the Russian Orthodox Church had been particularly strong in the days before historical events "smash[ed] the unity of Eastern Orthodoxy into many fragments".[76]

When a large official delegation of senior Orthodox clergy came to London in 1925 for the celebrations of the sixteen-hundredth anniversary of the Council of Nicæa they stayed for three weeks at St Edward's House. As all the bishops were also monks, "they were very glad to be in a Religious House"; and the Patriarch of Alexandria left so impressed that he "said he wished it known that now that whenever the Orthodox were away from their own ministrations they should go to our priests, and in like manner Anglicans could make use of their sacraments".[77]

To a great extent, Bull had loosened some – but by no means all – of the bonds of a community constrained by deference to the memory of its Founder and its original Statutes, and had led it into a new phase of life: out of the First World War, through the uncertain days of domestic and international realignment that had followed – in the midst of which the Society had lamented the "unutterably horrible" Armenian atrocities[78] – and on into an era of buoyant self-confidence for the Catholic Movement in the Church of England. He was an uncompromising Anglo-Catholic, and under his leadership the SSJE had followed closely and corporately espoused the movement's developments as time drew on; but, as we have seen, he had not necessarily overseen a private-

---

73 *CE* Feb 1915; cf 2 Corinthians 8.18.

74 O'Brien, 27 & 28 Aug 1923.

75 Mark D. Chapman, *The Fantasy of Reunion: Anglicans, Catholics, and Ecumenism, 1833–1882*, Oxford: OUP (2014), 208.

76 Pendleton, *Grafton*, 157.

77 *CE* Aug 1925.

78 cf *CE* July 1925.

ly united Society. The election that followed his withdrawal from the Lady Chapel was chaotic.

The now-aged Puller, as one of the scrutineers, first observed that in the past "it had come to his knowledge that in one case a Father entitled to vote had given both his A and B votes for the same name. This would nullify the B vote." After the numbers were read out after two inconclusive ballots, however, Albert Tovey contended that in the past the giving of both votes to the same name had been allowed. O'Brien was duly despatched to Bull's cell, to ask his advice. Nothing could be found in the Chapter's minutes; but Bull felt that Puller's position was sound – and as he was still technically Superior General, his advice was heeded and the voting continued.

A third ballot also resulted in stalemate, after which the meeting adjourned for Sext, lunch, and Nones. The fourth ballot failed similarly to produce a majority; after which, according to procedure, a committee of seven professed members – four *ex officio* and three elected by Chapter – voted "according to the method prescribed" in favour of O'Brien, the Assistant Superior General. Bull was finally readmitted to the Chapel, and his successor duly took the oaths and was installed. It was an unconventional means of achieving a result; and by the next morning Bull had found the reference to which Tovey had alluded – a motion brought by Robinson in 1904, which had failed.[79] If there was any general dissatisfaction among the Chapter as to the means of the election, however, there was none about the result. At his brethren's pleasure William O'Brien ruled the Society of St John the Evangelist for the next eighteen years.

---

79 SSJE/2/6/126.

17

LIFE AND VIGOUR

We make the best of what we have, and thank God for it.
—Edward Charles Trenholme SSJE[1]

Villiam Braithwaite O'Brien had seen at close quarters the various developments and concerns that the Society of St John the Evangelist had needed to balance in the years following the First World War; and had himself been sent to India to try and alleviate the pressure there in the early 1920s. When he addressed the Society's Associates and the members of the Fellowship of St John immediately after his election as Superior General, he was clear that "the first concern of a Religious Community is to live its life and cultivate personal holiness in its members through the discipline of the Holy Rule." It was, as he knew at close quarters, no easy undertaking.

[I]t is a Rule which makes a great demand upon us, and it is in no careless way that we look for the support of your prayers and sympathy that we may fulfil our vocation. There are some who will always regard a life of renunciation as morbid or Manichean, but our friends who share our ideals will understand how joyful and abundantly satisfying is a life which is lived in obedience to the call of God.

The life of the Society continued to need careful tending and pruning, and his task was plain: "faithful and progressive response to God's call is not child's play or the work of a day. One of the first concerns of a Superior must be the maintenance of the life of the Society in its distinctive character and claim."

The SSJE's trust was in God first: "it is one of our first principles that we should depend absolutely on the call of God for the growth of our Society." While that trust – viewed objectively – ought to have alleviated anxiety about the active work, at the same time "we have undertaken work, for example in the Mission Field, which we could not abandon without grave loss to Dioceses already strained and harassed under heavy burdens." He maintained, however, that "it is always a wonder to see what responsibilities and labours come to us in our life as Religious, manifestly beyond our natural capacities and in some cases in defiance of physical weakness."

"It is a real encouragement to find the grace of our vocation thus manifested," thought O'Brien. Nevertheless, for roughly each man who had been

---

1 *CE* June 1933.

professed under his predecessor another had died. O'Brien's first *ad populum* openly referred to the state of the Society's numbers, at a time when the life of the Catholic movement in general was burgeoning.

> [I]t does seem as though too often the line is held by those worn down by age or climate or disease, where surely we should expect to see the young and strong. Somehow our Congresses and Conventions, with their crowded and enthusiastic audiences, have not evoked those vocations to lives of sacrifice which we might have hoped for.

He closed with Robert Page's observations from nearly forty years earlier, that the Society needed to guard against too many external engagements, to preserve its interior life of "quietness, order, and discipline".[2]

The overseas work had to be kept up, of course. Following the custom of sending the outgoing Superior General away from Cowley, Bull returned to South Africa, "where he will bring strength to our work at Cape Town, where at present we have only two, extremely busy, fathers".[3] The brethren who went to meet him at the docks found him already "clothed in a white habit beaming with joy at being again in (sometimes) sunny South Africa".[4] Time moved on apace: at St Cuthbert's the new Archbishop of Cape Town, Francis Phelps – a Keble man – preached at the High Mass of Thanksgiving for the fiftieth anniversary of the establishment of the mission;[5] while Godfrey Callaway noted with resignation the coming of "the telephone which is to link us with Tsolo (ten miles) and through Tsolo with the great, busy world". He was not best pleased – "to me a telephone is an abomination" – but saw that it might "prove more and more useful".[6] He continued to insist on others making calls for him, reading out pre-written messages down the line, and noting down the responses for him to read.[7]

From India, John Williams had already noted that, while "from the spiritual point of view it is all important that neither our pastoral nor our educational work should be curtailed", if the Society was forced to choose between the two then it would be the schools that would suffer. It would be "a serious blow" if the SSJE was only able to educate the children of families able to pay full fees; but the alternative was to dispense with some of the Indian clergy, or to reduce their stipends – which, after decades spent raising up indigenous vocations to function on a par with the English brethren, would be worse. "Where, then, can we economise?"

The evangelistic work was under particular pressure from the volatile domestic situation; and although the usual round of missions continued, "in the present time of political unrest, when everything considered in any way to be connected with foreign domination is suspect, it is often difficult to get

---

2 *CE* Sept 1931.
3 *CE* Oct 1931.
4 Robert, 5 Nov 1931.
5 *CE* Aug 1931ff.
6 Callaway, 23 Sept 1931.
7 Callaway, 9 Aug 1932.

non-Christians even to listen to the presentation of a faith which they regard as the religion of the British Empire."

He, too, echoed the Superior General's concerns about the fruits – or rather the lack of them, in so far as they related to the reinvigoration of the religious life – of the Congress Movement, and particularly in the light of the forthcoming celebrations of the centenary of John Keble's Assize Sermon of 1833, which John Henry Newman had famously "ever considered and kept" as the Oxford Movement's primary catalyst.[8]

> The glory of that great work of the Holy Ghost was that it restored to our Communion not only Catholic doctrine and Catholic ceremonial, but the ancient Catholic ideals of sacrifice and renunciation. There are those, and they are not unfriendly critics, who tell us that it is just this element – the ascetic element – which is wanting in much of the Anglo-Catholicism of today. If so, the call for sacrifice that comes from the Church overseas comes at an opportune moment.

"By all means let us have our great congresses," he went on, "and make our thanksgivings for what God has wrought in us, but may there also be the note of penitence and self accusation, of serious examination into our weaknesses and unrealities, and an earnest desire to return to that way of the Cross which Our Lord Himself trod for us."[9]

The way of the Cross came again soon enough to Bombay: in November 1931 the All Saints Sisters lost almost all their contingent at Holy Cross to cholera, which O'Brien called "an overwhelming trouble to the Indian congregation at Umarkhadi, who will for a time feel themselves truly orphaned".[10] From Mazagon, Bernard Wilkins – who had administered the sisters' last rites – called it "a grievous blow".[11]

PERFECT ORTHODOXY

In 1932 O'Brien called the generally still-sluggish growth of the men's communities "miserably poor and inadequate", and although there had been modest discernible growth at Cowley he at the same time emphasised that "Religious *Life* is not increased or developed merely by numbers".[12] It is worth observing that while the various improvements instigated by Bull had improved the domestic aspect of the life of the mother house, the spiritual aspect of the Cowley Fathers' lives was as rigorous as ever. Lucius Cary felt that "it was most important that as generations pass the essential character of the Father Founder's creation should not be jeopardized."[13]

William Longridge's posthumous *Meditations for a Month's Retreat* of 1931 gives an ample overview of the kind of interior life that the individual members

---

8 Newman, *Apologia*, 122.
9 *CE* Aug 1931.
10 *CE* Jan 1932.
11 Wilkins, 21 & 24 Nov 1932.
12 *CE* Nov 1932.
13 SSJE/2/6/230.

of the Society were still expected to cultivate. As well as the shorter retreats that the members of the Society might lead or undertake, they represented the model for the month's corporate retreat that preceded Greater Chapter each year, and which each novice undertook before his profession.[14]

Longridge had based his *Meditations* on the Spiritual Exercises of St Ignatius Loyola – the study and championing of which had become his life's work. The *Cowley Evangelist* noted with satisfaction that the Belgian *Bulletin des retraites fermées* had approved of its publication, with a Jesuit reviewer describing him as "an Anglican advocate of strict retreats", and commending the book in glowing terms.

> We have nothing like this in French, and it would be interesting, and the fulfilment of a desire we have long had to publish a manual of the Exercises of S. Ignatius on the model of Fr Longridge's work. An intimate friend of several Jesuits, especially Fr Darlington and Fr Rickaby, Fr Longridge, who had corresponded on various occasions with Fr Watrigant and Fr Peypoch, had entered fully into the spirit and thought of St Ignatius.[15]

On his way back to India after Greater Chapter in 1931, Williams found some Jesuits aboard the *Orsova* who were "very friendly, and speak appreciatively of Fr Longridge".[16] St Ignatius's feast day on 31 July was added to the Society's calendar in 1939,[17] and it may be that it was through Longridge's well-published interest in the devotional structures of the Society of Jesus – and his brethren's embracing of his work in the spiritual life of their own Society – that earned the SSJE the moniker (which was not entirely complimentary, depending where one stood) of "the Secret Society of Jesus in England".[18]

The *Civiltà Cattolica* had praised Longridge for "the very exact knowledge and perfect orthodoxy of the book;[19] all that was written in it could have been signed by a Catholic"; and at the end of the year the *Cowley Evangelist* commended to its readers Kenneth Mackenzie's *Anglo-Catholic Ideals*[20] as "a useful attempt to express the distinctive element in Anglo-Catholicism".

> It should help us understand better our own ideals, and stir us up to strive more faithfully for them. It would be a suitable book to put into the hands of those who are outside the movement, but who wish to learn about it and to hear what can be said reasonably and persuasively in answer to critics.[21]

O'Brien had contributed a series of articles of his own to the *Cowley Evangelist* shortly before his election as Superior General, called "I believe in One Holy Catholic and Apostolic Church";[22] and it was the Anglo-Catholic ideals on

---

14 SSJE/2/6/472.
15 *CE* Aug 1931.
16 Williams, 3 Sept 1931.
17 GenC 1939, SSJE/2/7/5.
18 cf *The Living Church*, 15 Aug 1954.
19 *CE* Aug 1931.
20 Kenneth D. Mackenzie, *Anglo-Catholic Ideals*, London: SCM Press (1931).
21 *CE* Dec 1931.
22 *CE* Jan 1931ff.

which they were based that led the Society into the next Anglo-ecclesiological controversy, the matter of the Church of South India.

In 1920 the Lambeth Conference had debated the matter of the South India Scheme – which essentially amounted to the secession of the four southern dioceses of the Church of India, Burma, & Ceylon into a new, non-episcopal denomination, into which episcopacy would be introduced at a later juncture – and there had been limited, but not insignificant, support.[23] It was discussed again at the Lambeth Conference of 1930, after which Darwell Stone enumerated the English Church Union's concerns about the Conference's resolutions.[24]

The SSJE appealed for "prayers and vigorous support, not on behalf of the Society, but on behalf of the Catholic principle of the Divine institution of the Church's Ministry, on which the Oxford Movement was based, and which is now more seriously threatened than at perhaps any time in the past century." Williams wrote from Poona about "the determination of the [Anglican] advocates of reunion to go their own way regardless of Catholic tradition and of the wound and scandal they are causing their fellow Churchmen". He was "anxiously waiting for [an] authoritative opinion from England concerning the line of action we ought to take".[25] The *Cowley Evangelist* called the proposals "charity gone rancid".

> [W]e might well ask ourselves what we should think our duty to be if we were told that the Southern Indian Re-union Scheme was to become operative in England also [...] The great Catholic principle that the Eucharist may only be offered by those who share in the ministry which [Christ] founded and transmitted through His Apostles, a principle which the Church of India itself clearly professes, should be thus obscured and flouted (as a mere Anglican prejudice) for the sake of a unity so unreal.[26]

Charles Gore had noted the "profound disquiet" that had stemmed from the discussions at the Lambeth Conference;[27] and elements of the Society's identity were thrown once more into focus with his death in January 1932. While he lived, Gore had represented a tangible link with Benson, and had himself been among the great monastic founders of the Church of England. Although his relationship with his own Community of the Resurrection had been eclectic since he had accepted consecration to the episcopate in 1902, his later translation to Oxford had been a distinct boon to the SSJE, as Frederick Puller observed.

> [W]e of the Society of St John the Evangelist had every reason to rejoice at the advent of Bishop Gore to Oxford [...] in electing Bishop Gore as our Visitor, and in his acceptance of that position, we knew that our Visitor had made a

23 Michael Yelton, *The South India Controversy and the Converts of 1955–56: An Episode in Recent Anglo-Catholic History*, Anglo-Catholic History Society, Occasional Papers no.11 (2010), 7.

24 Darwell Stone, *The English Church Union and the Lambeth Conference: The Report of the Committee of the Council*, London: ECU (1931).

25 Williams, 1 July 1932.

26 *CE* August 1932.

27 Yelton, *South India*, 7.

study of the principles of the religious life, and that he had personally put those principles in to practice and that he was thoroughly convinced of their value [...] And our joyous expectations have been verified by more than twenty years of experience.[28]

The Bishop of Oxford, Thomas Strong, was approached to succeed Gore as Visitor. He had no experience of the religious life, and accepted the Visitorship "with considerable hesitation owing to my very serious ignorance"; but assured O'Brien that "if you are willing that I should act in spite of this defect, I should be glad to do my best." He immediately approved various revised Statutes that had been under discussion since the days of Bull's tenure.[29]

The controversies over *Lux Mundi* notwithstanding, Gore had been a towering presence in the development of the Catholic Movement in general and the religious life in particular. He had been unable to accept the South Indian proposals "without greater safeguards for Catholic principles"; and some of the best of the Society's scholarship was brought to bear on an erudite discussion of the matter in the course of General Chapter in 1932, with Albert Tovey coming to the fore.

[T]he decisive factor in the in the Council of Jerusalem was St Peter's speech convincing them that his action was the work of the Holy Ghost, and he claimed three miracles to prove that is was so. The United Church of South India might convince us too, if they would assure us (1) that the Bishop of Dornakal had seen an angel who told him to send to the Metropolitan of India who would tell him what to do. (2) That the Metropolitan of India had a visitation thrice repeated and heard the Spirit telling him to accede to the request and (3) that at the meeting of the delegates the Holy Ghost fell on all of them so that they spake with tongues. But they do not allege that any such thing happened. That they themselves think that they were moved by the Holy Ghost is what all people who desire to make religious changes think.[30]

The matter would simmer on for another two decades; but by 1933 the discussions had "steadily deteriorated" to the extent that they were regarded by O'Brien as "the most serious menace to Anglican unity that has risen for many years".

It has been compared to the situation in which the Church of England found itself on the eve of the Oxford Movement. Our great Societies, the English Church Union, the Confraternity of the Blessed Sacrament, and the Federation of Catholic Priests, are uncompromisingly arrayed against it. Undoubtedly we have just the same need to-day, as we had a hundred years ago, to assert that the Church of England is Catholic, that our whole allegiance is based on this fact.[31]

Dom Anselm Hughes mused that "the pens scarcely dry from correcting the mistakes of the Prayer Book revision campaign were taken up afresh to

28 *CE* February 1932.
29 Thomas Strong to O'Brien, 12 July 1932, SSJE/2/6/177.
30 SSJE/2/6/198.
31 *CE* Jan 1933.

warn the English Church of danger on a new front".[32] Williams, as Provincial Superior in India, wanted to be able to speak "with the authority of the Society behind him";[33] and by 1936 its official position was "that the South India Scheme breaks with Church order", and that therefore it was, "unless effectively checked by Catholics, a menace to the peace and unity of the Anglican Communion".[34]

Even at a time of uncertainty, however, Edward Trenholme thought that "we can join in the celebration, if not without some anxieties yet with thankful hope, based on the experience of these hundred years."

> The fruit of the Tractarian seed in a hundred years is truly astonishing, but it has germinated in its own way. The Movement began as one of Church defence, and has resulted in Church regeneration. It was to have been outward, against State encroachment; instead, it became primarily inward, as a revival of Catholic life [...] The fruit of the Movement has been internal, in Church, and has in fact changed the face of the Anglican Communion.

Among those fruits, of course, had been the revival of the religious life; but in the straitened circumstances to which O'Brien had alluded when he became Superior General, Trenholme sounded a cautious note.

> It cannot be supposed that a hundred years have taught all that time and experience can teach us practically of the Religious Life. It appears unlikely that Religious Orders of men can ever again hold their old place amongst us, such as they occupied in the great centralized and celibate ecclesiastical system of the pre-Reformation Church.

"But neither is it easy", he went on, "to believe that there is no place any more for dedicated societies of priests and laymen. There does manifestly seem places for such, in the Church's normal life."[35] Cary took up a similar theme in a sermon later in the year. "We cannot leave the story of that which has come to pass incomplete, as though all that was asked or needed was already accomplished."

> Must we not fear lest our thanksgiving might fade into complacency and self-gratulation, instead of stirring us to a mightily increased energy of effort, kindling within us a purer flame of self-devotion and desire? What God has wrought is true evidence that He is working, but where are those who should be flocking to His call? If it is His sovereignty that is worshipped, why are there not hundreds hastening to His standard? If it is the claim of the eternal as a present possession that is calling, why does the world still detain those who should 'lay hold on eternal life'? If it is, as it may well be, simply the claim and challenge of the Cross that is sounding, where is the response of generous sacrifice? That which has been restored to us needs to be amplified and strengthened by us not a hundred but a thousand fold!

---

32 Hughes, *Rivers of the Flood*, 103.
33 PC 1935, SSJE/3/1.
34 *CE* March 1936.
35 *CE* March 1933.

"A hundred years are passed," he continued, "years of life restored, of faith rekindled, of hope enlarged: but this is only the beginning. We have not mere dreams but a divinely-given vision of the Church of the living God *united*, of a victorious Church against which the gates of Hell shall not prevail."[36]

For all his hearty tub-thumping, Cary had gone to the very heart of the matter. The restoration of the religious life was one of the many triumphs of the Oxford Movement: in *The King's Highway* George Carleton SSM contended that "in no way has the Church in England shown its true catholicity more clearly";[37] while Evelyn Underhill called it "perhaps the greatest achievement of the Anglican revival, when seen in spiritual regard".[38] By the time of the centenary celebrations, however, it had not flourished with the seemingly-boundless vigour of other aspects of Anglo-Catholicism. The SSJE itself was continuing to feel the pinch: in July, August, and September respectively Brs James, Herbert, and William – "our three oldest lay brothers" – all paid the debt of nature.[39]

At the other end of the social spectrum, Viscount Halifax died in January 1934. His association with the Society went back to the days of its earliest beginnings, and had still been coming to the Mission House for retreats in his nineties. He had served as President of the English Church Union from 1868 until 1919 – when one of the Society's other noble benefactors, the Earl of Shaftesbury, had held the office – and then again from 1927 until his death. "Was there any sincere phase or effort of the Catholic revival of which he was not the warm friend and supporter?" asked O'Brien.

> [T]hough he returned to the enjoyment of wealth and position, his life was to be one of unremitting service to the Church up to the very day of his death, and to be marked as surely by renunciation, simplicity, humility, and deep spirituality as it could have been had he remained in the obscurity which he sought.[40]

Halifax had outlived by many years his friends who had formed the nucleus of the SSJE and made its preliminary arrangements seven decades earlier. For the Society, as for the Catholic Movement as a whole, his death – particularly in the afterglow of the centenary celebrations and the triumphant 1933 Anglo-Catholic Congress[41] – marked the end of an era.

LEAPS & BOUNDS

When Muirhead Bone produced his illustration for the Oxford University Almanack of 1934, which depicted the crowds arriving at Christ Church for the centenary thanksgiving service in the Cathedral on 18 July 1933, all the

---

36 *CE* Aug 1933.

37 George D. Carleton, *The King's Highway*, London: Anglo-Catholic Congress Committee (1924), 240.

38 Evelyn Underhill, *Worship*, London: Nisbet & Co. (1936), 333.

39 *CE* July/Aug/Sept 1933.

40 *CE* Feb 1934.

41 cf Yates, *Anglican Ritualism*, 374.

figures were nearly half life-size. It was a sleight of hand employed by many ecclesiastical engravers down the centuries; but gives the impression of a procession that was more densely packed with priests, monks, nuns, and friars than was probably the case. The three Franciscans in the foreground may speak of the new prominence of what Trenholme called "humble followers of the friar-life in ministry among the vagrant poor"[42] – a reference to the developing work of the Society of St Francis.[43]

O'Brien felt that in the end the novenas had at least "not been fruitless". There had been growth overseas, and it was "a matter of no small interest also to see how indigenous Communities are springing up in the Mission Field".

> There has been a marked increase in vocations to the Religious Life, not least among men [...] Our prayers are needed that the increase in vocations may be maintained and extended; and that new and strong foundations of Communities for men may in God's good time be raised up. This is indeed a great need.[44]

There had also been gentle growth and development at Cowley. By 1933 numbers were large enough at the mother house to justify the annexation of the Lower Library as a Common Room, with a bay window being added on the south side to improve the light;[45] and by 1935 a new chapel had been added to the infirmary wing. A Della Robbia plaque of the Virgin and Child was placed on its east wall, to complement the huge Calvary of the guest-house gable above.[46] Although only five men had proceeded from the novitiate to profession in the years of the novenas, O'Brien thought that there was "good hope" that all the colonial work might be able to be properly staffed by the end of 1936.[47]

Meanwhile, the SSJE's various external ministries continued unabated. The inside cover of the *Cowley Evangelist* for January 1934 listed no fewer than thirty-seven published works by members of the Society – most of whom were still alive – which could be obtained for the edification of individuals who wished to acquire them. In India, Wilkins – whom William Slade later described as having "with infinite patience persuaded music out of boys and instruments which would have defeated the efforts of anyone else"[48] – convinced the officer commanding the Royal Bombay Sappers & Miners at Poona to lend his Pipe Major, "a nice and friendly Panjabi Mussulman", to teach some of the mission boys to play the bagpipes.[49]

On the edge of Cape Town, the Earl of Clarendon laid the foundation stone of the new St Cyprian's Church at Langa in May 1934: "announcing in loud ringing tones that it was done in the Name of the Father, the Son and the Holy Ghost". The inscription was in Xhosa, and Charles Savage felt that "the

---

42 *CE* March 1933.
43 Dunstan, *This Poor Sort*, 46ff.
44 *CE* Nov 1933.
45 SSJE/2/6/242.
46 PC 1934, SSJE/3/1.
47 SSJE/2/6/314.
48 Slade, *A Work Begun*, 70ff.
49 Wilkins, 5 Feb 1934.

great cheering when the Governor General departed showed how Langa felt about it".[50] The building was ready two months early – "a rare occurrence in the experience of those who have to do with buildings and their builders"[51] – thanks to the efforts of the builder, the "most appropriately named Mr Cowley". The altar in its Chapel of the African Martyrs was inscribed with *Bernard Mizeki Sitandazele* – "Bernard Mizeki, pray for us" – while its reredos was a copy in alabaster of that in the ante-chapel of St Edward's House.[52]

Soon afterwards the Society received back the cure of St Philip's, at the request of Archbishop Phelps. Sydney Wallis worried that it would place a great strain on the Mission House, but "knew well that the proposal would be a great delight to the church people of Cape Town". There was general enthusiasm for the suggestion in Chapter, and the Superior General felt that in the context of modestly increasing numbers it would be "cowardly to refuse". The formal proposal was passed unanimously, and the Cowley Fathers resumed their parish work in Cape Town, three decades after they had given it up.[53]

At St Cuthbert's the brethren had become "much concerned" about an increase in witchcraft in the area: Francis Rumsey urged his readers to "be careful to think rightly of those who succumb, and let us help them in any way we can";[54] while the dread work of caring for the condemned also went on, as it had for decades. In June 1934 Williams wrote home from Panch Howds with a description of the execution of two prisoners to whom he had been ministering: a vignette of how deeply integrated the Cowley Fathers were – and how normative their presence was – in the day-to-day lives of some of the local institutions.

> By the kindness of the Superintendent I was able to celebrate mass in one of the cells, so they had their Viaticum just before the execution [...] The end followed very quickly. They were wonderfully calm and brave to the last, repeating prayers after me as long as it was possible. We were all supported by a great volume of intercession that was being offered by many who were remembering us at the moment.

"The goodness of the Prison authorities", he emphasised, "was a thing to be very thankful for. The Superintendent, a big-hearted man, has always been ready to take any trouble to make things easy for us [...] Just before the Mass a Hindu warder came hurrying up with two little vases of freshly picked flowers to be put on the altar."[55]

In cheerier vein, the mission band came on in leaps and bounds under the direction of Wilkins, ably assisted by the borrowed Pipe Major, Ali Hussein. When the Bishop of Bombay, Richard Acland – another Keble man – consecrated the new chapel at Kirkee later in the year, its members turned out "with

50 *CE* July 1934.
51 *CE* Dec 1934.
52 *CE* Feb 1935.
53 SSJE/2/6/312.
54 Rumsey, 20 Sept 1934.
55 Williams, 21 June 1934.

uniforms and instruments complete" to play at the bunfight after the ceremony. Frederick Playne wrote home to describe the performance.

> At present the pipers can only manage the Appen Stuarts' march, but by playing
> over once or twice and then letting the drummers have a turn by themselves,
> and then the same tune on the whistles it did not seem too monotonous. The
> whistlers also played *Baa, Baa, Black Sheep*, which was last year's standby. They
> know various other tunes, but at present the chief difficulty is to get them to
> play together.[56]

Back at Cowley, the Song School on the north side of the community church was
repurposed for a Blessed Sacrament Chapel in 1935. Strong had given permission; and after his objections to reserving the Sacrament at all in 1920, fifteen
years later Puller was greatly in favour of the scheme, as "certain ceremonial
books of the Roman Catholic Church said that the Sacrament should always be
reserved in some separate Chapel".[57] "We shall all be very thankful to have the
Blessed Sacrament reserved in the Society's Church," wrote O'Brien.[58]

There was considerable discussion about the details before the final plans
were approved, not least about whether or not the proposed baldacchino –
Ninian Comper was at that point designing one for the neo-Classical Church
of the Holy Name at Poona[59] – was at all "permissible in a Gothic Church".[60]
When it was completed, the richly-carved screen that formed the new entrance
from the nave bore the memorial of the Incarnation from the first chapter of
St John's Gospel in large letters: *Et Verbum Caro factum est, et habitavit in nobis.*

As part of the scheme a Servers' Sacristy was added at the east end of the
church, so that "the Fathers will no longer be in danger of treading upon small
boys crouched on the floor exchanging boots for slippers", and a new Church
Hall, Fellowship Room, and Song School built. The last was built away from
the Church, with a covered cloister linking it with the Chapel of the Holy
Name.

> It has been found that while the Song School has a door directly into the Church
> and is separated only from it by the intervening wall, any kind of practice in
> the Song School is over heard in the Church; this is embarrassing to those who
> worship, and sometimes also to those who want to practise.[61]

A year later the choir was done away with altogether, and Basil Bucknall –
"to whom we feel so grateful, and for whom we have so much respect and
affection" – was pensioned off.[62] The Society took "into its own hands the
rendering of the music for the liturgical parts of the service"; although O'Brien

---

56 Playne, 2 Sept 1934. 'The Cowley Fathers' Mission in India' features Wilkins conducting the band – complete with baton and solar topee – and is available on the British Film
Institute website.
57 SSJE/2/6/300.
58 *CE* Feb 1935. The aumbry for the Oil of the Sick was added in 1950. PC 1950, SSJE/3/2.
59 SSJE/2/6/311.
60 SSJE/2/6/301ff.
61 *CE* Feb 1935.
62 *CE* Sept 1936.

was at pains to point out that "plainsong is the musical expression of worship springing out of the Church's life of prayer."

> There was something incongruous in the fact that the Community was almost silent in that expression of its worship, it was all done for us [...] Now circumstances have made it more possible for us to take a really responsible and controlling part in the music of the liturgy [...] We have returned to our original ideal, when the plainchant was first introduced here, that of being ourselves the exponents of the music we use.[63]

By 1941 it was generally agreed that the institution of a weekly choir practice for any members of the Society in residence had become an urgent and necessary development.[64]

Other domestic changes also took place. From 1935 the guest-house Chapel became known as the "Founder's Chapel" – after a typical spat in Chapter, with Sydney Moore proposing the new nomenclature, "since it was designed and built by [Benson], and would always be associated with his teaching"; Marcell Conran objecting to the change, "since [Benson] was strongly against the reservation of the Blessed Sacrament for purposes of devotion, and the chapel was now used for that purpose"; Puller being appealed to as arbitrator, and pronouncing that he "did not think it would be a reason for withholding the name of the Father Founder from the Chapel"; and the Superior General musing that "if the Father Founder had lived in this generation he would probably have thought differently", anyway.[65]

FURTHER DEVELOPMENTS

The memory of the Founder was still never very far away. By 1937 Cary had wondered whether Benson's name was held in the reverence that it deserved. In Greater Chapter he pointed out that while the Society's benefactors were commemorated with plaques here and there, the Founder had no memorial of his own.

> [T]here was nothing to commemorate for strangers and for succeeding generations the name which above all others deserved to be remembered and honoured. Even to a large number of the members of the Society the Father Founder was little more than a name and a legend; to a growing number even of catholic-minded churchpeople his very name was almost unknown.

He wondered whether the "architectural solecism" of the old Song School door, "with its exquisite moulding and the figure of St John our patron" might be transformed into some kind of memorial to Benson. He had already prepared an inscription – "a rough draft from which a better form could be made".

---

63 *CE* Nov 1936.
64 SSJE/2/7/37.
65 SSJE/2/6/342.

In memoriam perpetuam vitæ et exempli fundatoris nostri Ricardi Meux Benson iste ab infantia dedicates sese vitæ et doctrinæ verbi incarnati ita devovit ut jam gratia sacerdotali praeditus societatem sacerdotum discipulo dilecto S. Joanni Evangelistæ dedicatam instauraverit.

There was an immediate flurry of enthusiasm. Conran suggested an altar-tomb with a recumbent figure; while Frederic Powell wanted "a kneeling figure in low relief". Harold Peacey was adamant that "we must get a first-class architect" and suggested Comper. O'Brien welcomed the proposal, as Comper "had known Fr Benson and was devoted to him and Fr Congreve";[66] but as Luke Miller has observed, although Comper had been a regular visitor to the Mission House from an early age he had not necessarily found the atmosphere congenial, and he had appreciated Benson's qualities only after he had come to know and like George Congreve.[67]

Comper now proposed placing "a kneeling figure in bronze of the Fr Founder" on the north side of the church sanctuary – a suggestion from whose "magnificence" Cary recoiled. In Provincial Chapter in 1937 Spence Burton, who was visiting from the United States, "felt that the proposal concerned the American Congregation as much as the English", and favoured a chantry chapel with a recumbent figure under the altar – "more in keeping with the spirit of the Founder, as the central object of the memorial would be the altar rather than the figure".

Peacey countered with the observation that "a recumbent figure would not express the spirit of the Founder with his keen sense of spiritual warfare". Douglas Sedding and others "spoke of kneeling figures of great beauty and suitability which they had seen in various churches"; and O'Brien observed that while he felt that "the figure kneeling in the sanctuary would give us a sense of the Fr Founder praying with us", the exact details could be discussed later. The proposal that some sort of memorial should be erected was carried unanimously.

A number of liturgical emendations had also received approval as the 1930s had progressed. In the community church altar cards had been introduced and the ringing of the Sanctus bell at the consecration of the elements: "the centre and heart of the Canon, and of the whole liturgy".[68] Holy water stoups were provided in the Lady Chapel and its sacristies; at Greater Festivals the officiant at Solemn Evensong began to be attended by two other priests in copes; and the former practice of the Superior General assuming a cope for processions was revived.[69]

When a new bell arrived for the church tower in 1933, one much larger and deeper than that which hung in the belfry on the western gable of the Chapel of the Holy Name, the *Cowley Evangelist* rejoiced that "it will mean much to have a bell more worthy of the Church, [and] we shall welcome the deeper and more solemn tone as it rings for the Consecration and for the Angelus

---

66 SSJE/2/6/442.
67 Miller, *Congreve.*
68 *CE* June 1933.
69 PC 1931, SSJE/3/1.

at the end of the Sunday High Mass."[70] The Mass of the Pre-sanctified was introduced on Good Friday 1935, and private votive masses were authorised "without special leave". From 1936 the singing of the Kyries at High Mass was elided with that of the Introit, as in the Tridentine Rite; both First and Second Evensongs of Sundays were treated solemnly; and "it was agreed that birettas might be worn" – which suggests that they had slipped out of use since the days of Benson and Page.[71]

All these developments brought the Society's worship more closely in line with a number of external marks of contemporary Anglo-Catholic practice; but its rite remained eclectic, and "quite unlike the use of any other church"[72] – the actions of High Mass shoehorned into the words of the Prayer Book Communion Service. In 1936 the SSJE Altar Missal appeared in print, but not before an argument with Mowbray's, its publishers, who pointed out that while monastic detachment was all very well, "the missals in use were all connected with some well-known person or Society." Much of the appeal of the book would be that it had been prepared by Trenholme and approved for use by the SSJE, and the firm "did not wish that this book should appear to be edited, as well as published, by Messrs Mowbray".[73] In the end the missal, with its options for Sarum and Roman tones, appeared with the inscription "edited by a priest of the Society of St John the Evangelist with the general approval of the Society".[74]

Other developments were also in train. In 1935 the Society entered enthusiastically into the Octave of Prayer for Christian Unity, and by the end of the decade – at the request of Malcolm Mackay, Archdeacon of Magila in Tanganyika – it had lifted the restriction placed on Priest Associates prohibiting them from attending "places of worship inconsistent with the discipline of the Church of England". St Edward's House was extended in 1937,[75] and by 1938 the English congregation's own work was set to expand even further: it accepted from Francis Brown, the Bishop in Jerusalem, the use of a house at Ein Karem – primarily so that the Society could continue to minister to the Sisters of the Love of God who were in the process of establishing a branch house there, but "also that we may study the Community life of the Oriental Churches in the Holy Land".[76]

Puller died in February 1938, in the ninety-fifth year of his life and the fifty-fifth year of his profession; but the proposed work in Jerusalem would have gladdened his heart. Although he had been an invalid for his last year, his stature within the Society and far beyond had remained undiminished, and tributes poured in from around the globe, led by the Archbishop of Canterbury.[77] He was buried in the grave that had long been reserved for him

---

70 *CE* Feb 1933.
71 PC 1935, SSJE/3/1.
72 PC 1938, SSJE/3/2.
73 SSJE/2/6/340.
74 *Altar Missal*, London: A.C. Mowbray & Co (1936).
75 *CE* Sept 1937.
76 SSJE/2/6/478.
77 Lang, 12 Feb 1938.

next to the Father Founder's: the grave on the other side was filled by Philip Waggett eighteen months later.[78]

That Puller had been a man of principle was beyond dispute; but as O'Brien freely recalled, there had been times when "in Liturgical matters, his consistency was embarrassing". Although he was "always charitable to those who did not feel obliged to conform themselves so starkly as he did to the requirements of the Book of Common Prayer"[79] – from South Africa Savage mourned "his aristocratic courtesy"[80] – he would certainly have deprecated the advances of 1939, after which the Society began observing the Feasts of the Sacred Heart, the Precious Blood, and Christ the King; and started calling the feast of the Blessed Virgin Mary on 15 August "the Assumption". The changes were part of another large kalendrical overhaul; and although some eyebrows were raised at "the omission of certain saints' days from the 1662 calendar",[81] the proposals all received large majorities in Chapter.[82]

Puller's example also was a timely reminder of the necessity of defence of Catholic principles at a time when they seemed once more under assault.

> In the more vital matters which are the cause of so much anxiety among us in the present day, and about which the Anglican trumpet certainly gives a very uncertain sound, his call to prepare for the battle was unmistakeable. There was no vagueness in his principles, no hesitation in accepting the consequences they entailed. We must pray God we may not lose that clearness and steadfastness of principle in which, so largely through his influence, our Society has stood united, where so many even amongst Catholics falter and are perplexed.[83]

The Archbishop of Wales – Charles Green, yet another Keble man – observed that the Society would "really miss one whom it will be difficult to replace".[84] Waggett's eventual release from his lengthy incapacitation in 1939 deprived the Society of another of its theologians;[85] but as we have seen, others had already risen in their stead. Cary's *Called of God* of 1937 was a major exposition of the essence of the religious life, as well as a *vade mecum* for those charged with its direction.

Cary was by then a member of the Church of England's Advisory Council on the Relations of Bishops and Religious Communities. He had himself had become a "well-known authority" on the religious life;[86] and the Council's very existence demonstrated how much had changed in the six decades since Benson, Grafton, and O'Neill had taken their vows. Its Chairman – James Seaton, the Bishop of Wakefield – thought that *Called by God* demonstrated its author's "wide knowledge and deep experience" of the religious life; and at the

78 *CE* Aug 1939.
79 *CE* March 1938.
80 Savage, 13 Feb 1938.
81 PC 1938, SSJE/3/2.
82 SSJE/2/7/9.
83 *CE* March 1938.
84 Green, 12 Feb 1938.
85 *CE* Aug 1939.
86 J. W. C. Wand, *Anglicanism in History and Today,* London: Weidenfeld & Nicholson (1961), 189.

same time professed his view that "the whole life of the Church is raised and quickened by the inner life of well-ordered Religious Communities." Seaton also quoted approvingly from Evelyn Underhill's recently-published *Worship*.

[T]he Religious Life sums up, and expresses in a living symbolism, the ideal consummation of all worship: the total oblation of the creature to the purposes of God. No Church within which these sacrificial dispositions are not produced and which does not possess its hidden power-house of surrendered personalities, the consecrated channels of its adoring and redeeming love, has risen to the full possibilities of the Christian call: or proclaimed, in the only language which carries conviction, the unlimited demands of God upon the soul.

"This is the knowledge", Underhill continued, "by which the founders of the Anglican Orders were inspired, and this is the truth which these Orders continue to declare".[87]

No Anglican bishop could have dreamed of associating himself with such a view in 1866. In turn, Cary expressed his gratitude "to the Society which for close on forty years has given him his spiritual home and been his guardian and his teacher". He dedicated the book to the memory of Benson, and with the inscription beginning *Patris nostri memoriæ venerandæ* he may have intended to cast the attribution beyond the SSJE and on to the other numerous men's communities of which it was now the doyen.[88]

WIDER STILL & WIDER

A carved stone statue of the Virgin and Child was placed in the Lady Chapel at Cowley in 1937,[89] and a question soon arose over whether the space was really suitable for what the community now needed as its domestic chapel. Trenholme observed that when he had entered the Society nearly forty years earlier, "we had comparatively few Masses and each Priest was far from celebrating daily. All this has changed, we all say Mass, [and] we have many Altars".[90] A few months later O'Brien sought his brethren's approval of the cost of Comper's plans for an extension of the Lady Chapel: as it came to over £2000, the decision belonged to the General Chapter.

From Cape Town, Bull, on behalf of the other South African brethren appears to have questioned the wisdom of spending such a large sum on what was effectively a private chapel, and to have suggested that the missions were more deserving of the expenditure. O'Brien was clearly irked by his predecessor's intervention – when in office himself he had not been averse to spending large sums on necessary work at the mother house – and addressed it at length.

---

87 Underhill, *Worship*, 333.

88 Lucius Cary SSJE, *Called of God: Notes on some Questions concerning the Religious Life; with an Introductory Essay on the Meaning of the Religious State*, London: A. R. Mowbray & Co. (1937), vii ff.

89 PC 1936, SSJE/3/1.

90 GreC 1937, SSJE/2/6/430.

"I do not know of any request for help from any of the Missions", O'Brien observed, "which I have refused for lack of money, nor do I know of any works they have begun and been unable to complete because we failed at home to find means to support them." Early on in his tenure he had made a point of instructing his brethren to make the Fellowship of St John known widely on missions and retreats, and among their private penitents;[91] and by 1935 it had sixteen branch chaplains and secretaries spread across England alone – of which, not insignificantly, a quarter were those with responsibility for the Anglo-Catholic bastions of Brighton, Bournemouth, Worthing, and St Leonard's-on-Sea.[92]

O'Brien pointed out that, in the context of "brighter prospects in the business world",[93] the Society had received the enormous total of £50,000 in the preceding half-decade – "but the fact that it is spread over five years has made it less startling to us" – and that the clear policy of the Finance Committee had been based on two principles: "(1) That we do not desire to accumulate an income by investments large enough to supply us securely for all our needs; we wish to remain in part dependent on the alms of the faithful. (2) That the needs of the Mission Field always come first."

To that end, £19,000 had been set aside and invested to provide an income for the missions; but "the remainder of the sums received has been spent on a variety of needs at home and abroad. The truth is not only that we have expended large sums at home but that we have expended very large sums in every part of the Society [...] I think I can venture to say that during all the years I have been in the Society there never has been a period of five years during which anything like so large has gone to the support of the work in the Mission Field."

Domestic expenditure had not been insignificant, but had included the remodelling of the new Common Room; new dossals for the Founder's Chapel and the community church, the latter being permanent and richly stencilled and ornamented with figures of Christ in Majesty, Our Lady, and St John; the conversion of the old Song School into the Blessed Sacrament chapel; the building of a new Song School, church hall, and sacristy extension – and the creation of a little covered cloister to join them all together, "thus enabling our guests to go dryshod to the services"; the new oratory for the Infirmary wing; and the purchase of a cottage at Westcote in the Cotswolds, to serve as the rest-house for which the Society had been looking "for a good many years".

"There is not one of these developments which I regret," O'Brien continued, "not one of which it can be said that experience proves it to be without value. Indeed without going into detail I believe the use of these various additions abundantly justifies them."

I have no reason to think that any of the Fathers at home or those who have come from abroad, would question what I have said. I have heard much of appreciation and very little of criticism and certainly no criticism at all on the grounds which the South African fathers have stated. It is of course impossible to make

91 PC 1932, SSJE/3/1.
92 CE Jan 1935.
93 CE Oct 1934.

additions either to this house or to our church which are not in keeping with that to which they are added. It is this which makes them costly and this which necessitates the large sum we are proposing to spend on the chapel.

By the end of his statement the Superior General was very cross indeed. "I think our South African fathers have taken a somewhat parochial view of this and should realise that we did not embark on our plans without considering the points they put forward."

> There is indeed one exception. It did not occur to me that our Missions after the record of the last five years could have thought themselves neglected, but I think it is only Cape Town which has put that consideration forward [...] I do most certainly think that this Chapter need not feel that the Missions have suffered by what we have done for our home needs. The further question, whether the suggested addition to the chapel is suitable, and possible, having regard to our resources, is for this Chapter to decide.[94]

Perhaps not unsurprisingly, "it was unanimously agreed by those present to authorise the expenditure".[95] A committee was duly appointed to oversee the work, which was given the additional and curious remit "to decide whether or not the proposed Ciborium Magnum, about which there had been a good deal of discussion, should be accepted".[96]

For O'Brien, there was much more than just a practical aspect to the proposed development: the house at Cowley was now the hub of a very large wheel indeed. To that end, he felt that the developments at Cowley had "a significance and a value psychologically".

> They are an evidence of vitality and they are a not inconsiderable help to its preservation [...] I believe there is a higher value in our recent developments than Father Bull or the other fathers in South Africa have been able to appreciate. They are not merely for convenience and beauty; they are consonant with the life and spirit of the Society at this present time. I believe the evidence of life and vigour which they bring has really been welcomed by the members of the Society who have seen them, and by our friends who have known the Society for many years.

"We are the nerve centre of the Society," he continued. "We need a vigour of life and hopefulness here at the centre. We have now immense responsibilities spread over a very wide area. As I think of the many fine churches the Society owns in the Mission Field; of our big mission centres with their large organization; houses, hostels, workshops, hospitals and schools I cannot think that the provision we have made at home and are purposing to make is anything but suitable to the Mother House."[97]

---

94 SSJE/2/6/452ff.
95 SSJE/2/6/448.
96 SSJE/2/6/450.
97 SSJE/2/6/455ff.

In the wake of the controversy the *Cowley Evangelist* was distinctly coy about the plans for the extension to the Lady Chapel: "Mr Comper has designed for us a new Sanctuary which will add some sixteen feet to the length of the Chapel and also provide transepts in which two additional altars can be placed".[98] Taken as a whole, however, the work of 1938 was an elaborate expression of community identity and aspiration.

The north altar was made from stinkwood and wild cherry in the workshop at St Cuthbert's, and dedicated to St Cyprian of Carthage: its creation and dedication linking the long-established work in the Transkei with the latest developments at Cape Town. The south altar was made from Indian teak in the workshop at Poona, and was dedicated to St Thomas, the patron of India. Both were enclosed with hangings in the English style, and their embroidered superfrontals were worked with the Ter Sanctus in Xhosa and Marathi respectively.[99] Such deliberate care over the fittings effectively turned the domestic chapel at Cowley, with its multiplicity of masses and the regular chanting of the offices, into the beating heart of the English congregation's work.[100]

It is worth noting that at its mother house the SSJE utilised Bodley at his most austere, and Comper at his most restrained – the ornateness of the new ciborium above the main altar was undercut by the total lack of any of the latter's trademark gilding.[101] The gilt-papier-mâché extravagances of Martin Travers never found favour at Cowley, despite his long association with Sedding's architect-brother, George;[102] but when the flamboyant Kenneth Kirk was named to succeed Strong as Bishop of Oxford in 1937, the Society was so delighted that it sent him loyal greetings.

Strong was Establishment to his very core; but he had dealt tolerantly and patiently with the Anglo-Catholics in his diocese. Kirk was an out-and-out Ritualist; and a doughty champion of Catholic principles.

> The fathers of the Society of St John the Evangelist assembled in their Triennial Greater Chapter desire to offer their most respectful greeting to Dr Kenneth Escourt Kirk on the occasion of his nomination to the bishopric and diocese of Oxford. As they have been privileged to be associated with him in the past in the defence of fundamental principles of catholic order so they look forward to a future in which they will tender him their confidence and loyalty.[103]

At Christ Church Kirk celebrated High Mass in full pontificals, down to the gauntlets; and elsewhere was often to be seen in *cappa magna* with purple biretta, dripping in Brussels lace.[104] He duly professed himself "greatly honoured" to accept the Visitorship of the Society,[105] which Strong – already in the early grip of the severe dementia that would eventually overwhelm him

---

98 *CE* March 1938.

99 SSJE/11/2/7/71.

100 *Cowley*, SSJE (1958).

101 Symondson and Bucknall, *Sir Ninian Comper*, 173.

102 Rodney Warrener & Michael Yelton, *Martin Travers 1886–1948: An Appreciation*, London: Unicorn Press (2002), 7ff.

103 SSJE/2/6/444.

104 Stephenson, *Merrily on High*, 61; 86.

105 Kirk, 28 Jan 1938, SSJE/2/6/457.

entirely[106] – had relinquished after Chapter had agreed that O'Brien should tactfully "suggest to him that as he was now resigning his see he might be glad to be relieved of his office".[107]

The SSJE seemed to be on the cusp of a new period of consolidation at home and expansion abroad. Numbers were increasing, and particularly in North America. In 1939 the Canadian work was organised into a separate province, and in Boston Burton was consecrated to the episcopate to serve as bishop suffragan of Haiti and the Dominican Republic[108] – the first of his brethren to become a bishop and remain a member of the Society.[109] The Society presented him with the pectoral cross that had been Edward Osborne's, his predecessor in the episcopate by thirty-five years, which he accepted "with the understanding that I shall pass it on to the Cowley Father to be consecrated a Bishop after me".[110]

In all the areas of the Society's activity there were ongoing and encouraging signs of growth that had by no means been inevitable ten years earlier. A scheme for Oblates of the Society was drawn up – "for those who desire to make a life-long oblation of themselves under the protection and guidance of the Society while still living in their natural spheres of duty"[111] – and plans were well underway for the establishment of the looked-to house in Jerusalem.[112] Furthermore, a Central Council had been established so that links might be maintained more effectively with the Society's ever-further-flung activities, and to counteract the great distances – both physical and psychological – between the various branches of the SSJE across the world.

The intention of the establishment of the Central Council was to root the dispersed Society at Cowley: "the Central Council shall meet [every five years] at the Mother House in England"; and to give prominence to the English congregation as the senior branch: "the Superior General shall preside at all meetings of the Council and shall have a casting vote in addition to his vote as the representative of the English Congregation". There was also an element of ongoing devolution, in that the Council would have "no power to compel a Congregation to accept for itself any decision to which its own Chapter has not given consent".[113]

By the end of the 1930s the SSJE had become an international concern with a concrete system of governance, and it enjoyed the approval and support of a broad swathe of the leadership of the Church of England. The Cowley Fathers remained in great demand as preachers and spiritual guides; and through the Society's published works it continued to influence the life of the Catholic Movement across the Anglican Communion. It was now possible for a man to be professed in the American or Canadian congregations without having met

---

106 Stephenson, *Walsingham Way*, 61; Harold Anson, *T. B. Strong*, London: SPCK (1949), 89ff.
107 SSJE/2/6/444.
108 *CE* June 1939.
109 *CE* May 1939.
110 Burton, 15 Aug 1939.
111 *CE* March 1939.
112 *CE* Aug 1939.
113 SSJE/2/6/419.

any of his English brethren; and so the Central Council was also intended "to serve as a bond between the Congregations of the Society, for the preservation of its unity and its well-being", across the work that was now firmly established in India, South Africa, the United States, Canada, Korea, and Japan.

After the usual review and discussion of the general state of the Society's affairs, the Superior General confirmed and signed the minutes of the last General Chapter of the decade on 4 August 1939. Germany invaded Poland four weeks later.

18

Battle on Two Fronts

We are glad to know that the Fathers and Brothers of the English
Congregation are carrying on with united and unswerving fidelity.

—SSJE American Congregation, 1940[1]

On the last Sunday of peace the Superior General preached at High
Mass in the community church. "The world's sorrow," he lamented,
"is the work of human sin."

We look around astonished to see that in the power of one man lies the awful
decision as to whether our European world is to be plunged into the inconceivable miseries of modern warfare. We look aghast at the cynical contempt
for truth and for the plighted word of nations, at the appalling indifference to
human suffering, but it is our godless pagan civilization which has brought
us to this pass. It is we have who have fashioned the instrument by which the
harvest we have sown is to be reaped.[2]

The Society of St John the Evangelist had not existed in a vacuum as the
storm clouds of the 1930s had gathered over Europe. In the course of a Special
General Chapter meeting in January 1938 its plans for a memorial to the Father
Founder were quietly shelved, "in view of the widespread needs and distresses
of the present time". The purpose remained, but it was agreed "to await a more
suitable opportunity, when an appeal could be made without conflicting with
such urgent need".[3]

Under the robust leadership of William O'Brien the SSJE had continued to
prick ecclesiastical consciences as the decade progressed. When the Upper
House of the Convocation of the Province of Canterbury prevaricated about
assenting to a petition signed by 9,000 clergy inviting the bishops to affirm
the Church of England's affirmation of the Nicene Creed "in that sense only in
which it has ever been held throughout the history of the Church", the *Cowley
Evangelist* was quick to thunder.

Our Bishops therefore have no comfort to give to their petitioners and the faithful
people committed to their charge. Yet there are Clergymen holding positions of
great dignity and responsibility who, while reciting the Nicene Creed in public
worship, deny in the pulpit and in their published writings the truths which the

---

1 Williams, Otis, Viall, Banner, 15 July 1940.
2 *CE* Sept 1939.
3 SSJE/2/6/450.

Creed affirms about the Virgin Birth of our Lord, His bodily resurrection from the tomb and His bodily ascension into heaven.

To a great extent these unsatisfactory developments were part of the ongoing working-out of the liberal theology that Benson had deprecated while he lived. O'Brien thought its latest manifestation "a very grave matter".

> [T]here is clearly here a *matter for controversy*. Controversy need not mean bitterness, or loss of charity, or lack of respect to the Episcopal office. We may be hard pressed to maintain the right spirit, but one thing is very certain: the matter cannot rest where it is. There is no need for panic or desertions to Rome. But we must all, Catholic and Evangelical alike, demand that there shall be no uncertainty as to what the Church's teaching is about the ineffable mystery of the Incarnation.[4]

Such an approach was not new. As early as 1934 the Superior General had protested strongly the ongoing massacres of Assyrians at the hands of the Iraqi army: "we need to have our conscience stirred about this little people, our allies in the Great War, whom our statesmen have so unaccountably left to the mercy of their enemies."

> Why there should be a conspiracy of silence I do not know. The *Church Times* has refused to be silenced, otherwise their sufferings and our Country's faithlessness would be completely forgotten. Why no statesman, no Archbishop or Bishop, no other newspaper, except on one occasion the *Times*, has raised the voice of protest I do not know. The facts of their grave need are not disputed. It is a sin to desert our friends, to leave them helpless in the hands of ruthless and bitter oppressors, and this sin lies on the conscience of England. Such sins God will not fail to visit in the day when He makes up His account.[5]

Furthermore, when Francis Downton had preached in the community church on Armistice Day that year, on the general subject of the League of Nations, he emphasised that O'Brien had wanted "the main thought of the service to be the needs of our Country to-day and thankfulness for the great mercy of our deliverance from the German domination".

> [T]hat thought gains fresh point from the sufferings of the Jews in Germany and from the great stand which our Evangelical fellow Christians have had to make, and, thank God, have made so nobly and successfully for their spiritual liberties today.[6]

The Evangelical resistance came at a high price. Dietrich Bonhoeffer stayed at the mother house in 1935 as part of a tour of religious houses with his friend Julius Rieger, before he returned to Germany to found his preachers' seminary at Finkenwalde.[7] The visits were organised by the Bishop of Chichester, George

---

4 *CE* Feb 1939.
5 *CE* Oct 1934.
6 *CE* Dec 1934.
7 Ferdinand Schlingensiepen, *Dietrich Bonhoeffer 1906–1945*, London: T. & T. Clark (2010), 175ff.

Bell, who introduced him as "very anxious to have some acquaintance with our methods in England, both with regard to training for the Ministry and with regard to Community life".[8]

Bonhoeffer returned to Germany and martyrdom most particularly impressed by the spiritual and recreational aspects of life of the Community of the Resurrection, where he had both prayed and played ping-pong: in his search for what he called "a new kind of monasticism" to counter the ever-increasing malevolence of German National Socialism, "he seemed as thrilled by the sight of Anglican monks enjoying sport [...] in the afternoon as by the solemnities of compline."

A heavy smoker himself, Bonhoeffer observed that smoking was forbidden at Cowley, optional at Mirfield, and seemed to be compulsory at Kelham – Herbert Kelly was a notorious chain-smoker whose habit "appeared permanently covered in grey ash".[9] At Cowley he reached for a cigarette only to be told to put it away; but this well-known vignette needs a little unpacking. It demonstrates, effectively, that the members of the SSJE had taken Bonhoeffer into their bosom for the short time he was with them. The exchange must have taken place in the community enclosure, at the heart of the Society's common life; because had he been staying in the guest house as an ordinary visitor he would have been free to smoke at will.[10]

Inevitably, of course, the war would call for a renewed spirit of self-denial and service. In Advent 1939 O'Brien urged the contemplative nuns at Malling Abbey to "endeavour to maintain very deeply the spirit of charity and mutual forebearance, and of quiet confidence and unshaken trust in God";[11] but he realised that "the most obvious sacrifices, though not always the greatest suffering, will fall upon the young, and indeed very great are the sacrifices which their Country asks of them."

There were also "millions of smaller plans of varying importance" that were also thrown into disarray, "from the loss of a much needed holiday to the hindering or destroying of plans for the advancement of God's Kingdom".[12] Among the latter was the house in Jerusalem, the plans for which now foundered; and the Missionary Association conference that had been intended for Michaelmas was cancelled: "it seemed useless under present conditions to discuss plans for developing our home work."[13]

From October 1939, the *Cowley Evangelist* appeared in small print once more, to save paper. Other economies would need to be made, but for this the Society was already prepared. In the wake of the recent major expenditure at the mother house – coupled with the Society's commitment to living on alms rather the income from its investments,[14] and with the general desire of

---

8 Keith Clements, *Bonhoeffer and Britain*, London: Churches Together in Britain (2006), 83.

9 Charles Marsh, *Strange Glory: A life of Dietrich Bonhoeffer*, London: SPCK (2014), 217ff.

10 Smoking was permitted in the American congregation: a photograph from 1929 shows Frs Williams and Johnson enjoying a cigarette together outside St Francis's House. SSJE/11/2/1/38.

11 *CE* Jan 1940.

12 *CE* Sept 1939.

13 *CE* Oct 1939.

14 SSJE/2/6/452ff.

the Chapter that "stricter regulations with regard to our practice of fasting and abstinence are desirable"[15] – a committee had been established to look into economies that might be made in the day-to-day running of the house. Its wide consultation within the Society yielded enthusiastic responses, and in the light of necessary economies that would be imposed by the outbreak of war, it was a useful exercise ahead of its time.

Three main points guided the Economy Committee's advice pertaining to individual members of the Society, of which the first two were purely practical. The brethren were to "be careful in the use of all stores"; and each was "to accommodate himself to that which is in ordinary use so that special items need not be obtained". The last, however, was more strictly monastic: the Cowley Fathers were "to give up the use of such things for their personal use as poor people cannot afford". As early as 1932 the Chapter had actively looked for jobs that needed doing about the mother house that might provide employment for men out of work during the winter;[16] but this application of strict poverty within the community itself spoke of an attempt – once more – to return to first principles.

The Society took to the exercise with gusto, and the suggestions ranged from the practical – "garden [...] to be re-designed in part, and a greater proportion to be used to grow food"; "jam or lettuce at supper"; "wash up own cup after afternoon tea" – to the masochistic: "cold water [baths] only"; "carbolic soap for shaving"; "chalk and salt instead of toothpaste". With the second category came the risk of a return to the days when "holy poverty became deliberate discomfort"[17] and to the morbidity of life that the Society had thrown off in the 1890s.

Unsurprisingly, much of the discussion centred on the refectory. The brethren at St Edward's House produced a thorough paper based on British Medical Council guidelines, which was as much an insight into the table-practice of the Society as it was a reflection of the British diet at the end of the long Imperial summer. Canned food had come into its own: it was "safe and economical as well as labour-saving (at times an important matter): vitamins are not interfered with. Salmon, pilchards, herring roes (sardines are expensive) tomatoes, spinach, peas, plums, apples, pears, pine-apples, may be used freely: in general they will provide all that could be given by fresh products, and they are a great help to variety". As St Edward's House only had its ornamental roof garden for outside space this was an important consideration.

Other practicalities also presented themselves: "beef sausages are half the price of pork"; "boiling bacon at 6d or 7d the lb is half or less than half the cost of more expensive cuts". By 1942 hens had been acquired at the mother house, and in 1943 they produced a saving of £13 on eggs. However "the purchase of unsexed day-old chicks had proved a failure, most of the chicks proving to be cockerels". They duly atoned for the deficiencies of their sex by appearing for Christmas dinner.[18]

15 SSJE/2/7/15.
16 PC 1932, SSJE/3/1.
17 Miller, *Congreve*.
18 PC 1943, SSJE/2/3.

Anticipating the inevitable question of diet within the charism of religious communities, the report of 1939 also pointed out that "the most expensive constituent in the dietary is protein".

> Over this the most acute controversies have raged and are not settled. Some religious communities are vegetarian, others prohibit meat but allow fish and poultry. It is a safe and moderate position to say that meat is a great help [...] but it cannot be called a necessity. It is uncertain as to how far vegetable proteins (peas, lentils, &c,) can replace animal proteins (meat, fish, eggs, cheese). Many people would be unable or unwilling to eat the amount of peas or lentils which would contain the same amount of protein as 5oz of meat.

It was a merciful caveat for life lived at close quarters. The rest of the report continued in a similar vein, and strove for a balanced diet based on the latest nutritional science: "a supper of rice pudding supplemented with bread and jam (all carbohydrates) would not be satisfactory". It sensibly concluded that psychological factors could not be reasonably taken into account in a large community eating at a common table; but, while provision would obviously need to be made for those with strictly medical requirements, "most people have an astonishing power of accommodating themselves to change of diet, of overcoming 'dislikes', and of becoming able to deal with the food which they had thought disagreed with them. These are clearly important questions for those who live any kind of common life."[19]

The bonds of the common life were underlined once more by the various collateral consequences of the outbreak of war. From Poona John Williams noted that the Indian nationalists hated Adolf Hitler for his odious views of non-Europeans laid out in *Mein Kampf*; but that they remained reluctant to support the Government "in any circumstances whatever". Prices had soared, which was "likely to add to our financial difficulties";[20] although the need for munitions had provided increased opportunity of employment for the people at Kirkee.[21]

By the end of 1940 the mission had "about twenty-five of our young men and boys" in military service: they turn up from time to time looking very robust and smart in their uniforms, and generally with a great deal of saluting and clicking of heels". As in the First World War, military service was the making of some of the Society's more troublesome charges.

> It is a fine thing for them – good food, good pay, plenty of exercise and the discipline that they so much need. Some of our most insoluble 'problems' have been solved in this way. The 'problem' disappears for some months to Bangalore or Karachi or somewhere, and the 'solution' reappears one day in the form of a cheerful and well-drilled young soldier.[22]

19 SSJE/2/6/1.
20 Williams, 3 Sept 1939; 12 Sept 1939.
21 Williams, 5 Oct 1939.
22 Williams, 4 Dec 1940.

Meanwhile, one of the boys in Bernard Wilkins's band, Jacob Patolé, had joined the Mahratta Light Infantry as a bass drummer, and "soon found himself in all the glory of a tiger-skin apron on Viceroy's Guard at New Delhi". After being taken prisoner in North Africa he was taken first to Italy and then to a prison camp in Germany: "a terrible experience for a young Indian of barely twenty"; but after leading five other prisoners in a daring and successful escape, when he next visited Panch Howds "it was with the three stripes of a 'havildar' (sergeant) on his sleeve".[23]

In the Transkei Godfrey Callaway, as Provincial Superior, was already looking to economise "in every possible direction. I remember so well the 'slump' after the 1914–18 war." Br Gordon also remembered it well: he had lost an arm at the Battle of the Somme, but soldiered on at the organ at St Cuthbert's, where "he insisted on playing the hymns at English Evensong [...] with one hand and a hook".[24] Nevertheless, when George Dakers visited in early October he found the brethren all "fit and smiling". Frank Cornner had only just returned from Cape Town, where he had found the atmosphere strange: "one feels that if the world can be rid of Hitlerism our sacrifices are a blessed offering."[25]

At home, however, things were deeply discombobulated: "the disorganization of life under lighting restrictions and evacuation is complete [and] one of its immediate effects is the embarrassing cessation of the flow of subscriptions and collections for Church purposes." Evening meetings in London were difficult, if not impossible, in the blackout; while the various retreat houses at which the brethren customarily ministered were soon given over to evacuees. Although in October 1939 the community was "all still together at the Mission House", it seemed inevitable that sooner or later "some will be called up to serve as Chaplains and that our lay brothers will be called up according to their age class for service".[26]

Midnight Mass in the community church at Christmas 1939 was necessarily cancelled because of the blackout; but the fewer windows in the Lady Chapel were more easily covered, and so High Mass took place there instead, with "any Laymen in the neighbourhood" invited to signify their intention of attending.[27] It would be the home brethren's last Christmas together.

MARCHING AS TO WAR

Reginald Podmore was soon "serving as Chaplain to the Forces in the same way that during the last war Father Waggett, Father Conran and Father Wigram were allowed to serve". His appointment as a Chaplain appeared in the *London Gazette* in January 1940; by early February he was "somewhere in England" preaching, teaching, and getting to know his men;[28] and by May

23 Wilkins, *With Wings As Eagles*, 30.
24 Mark Woodruff (ed), *True Man a Long Season: Poems of Gordon Shrive SSJE*, London: FSJ (2016), 8.
25 Dakers, 7 Oct 1939.
26 *CE* Oct 1939.
27 *CE* Dec 1939.
28 Podmore, 3 Feb 1940.

he was with the B.E.F. in France. Podmore soon wrote to the community at Cowley to say that casualties were building up, and that "the sadder side of my ministry to the men is likely to be in demand soon". He was working alongside the medics, and had acquired the necessary material to construct a portable altar that would fit in the back of his car. The lady with whom he was billeted had made him a dossal and frontal for it; and he had also persuaded a local café owner to let him hold services at her establishment, having overcome her qualms about his not being in communion with the Pope.

Poignantly, he also remarked that "we have one of the smaller English cemeteries outside this village. It is a beautifully peaceful spot, though unspeakably sad with its long straight rows of head-stones".[29] His letter was dated 14 May 1940: by the time the community received his letter he was already dead; but it would be several weeks before they would know for certain, and over a year before they learned anything of the circumstances. O'Brien asked for prayers for him in July, noting that "we have no news of Father Podmore and are of course extremely anxious about him, but it may still be a considerable time before we can expect to hear whether he is a prisoner in the hands of the Germans or whether he has fallen with the troops he was serving".[30]

By the end of August, the community was still desperate for information; but O'Brien had heard from Podmore's colonel.

> We still have no news about Father Podmore, except that on May 20 he was sent into Belgium with the troops to which he was attached. On that day or some subsequent day he was driving back to a village he had just left to fetch some stores from the canteen. It was learned subsequently that the Germans had reached the village. His Colonel thinks that he is a prisoner. Enquiries are being made from various quarters, but it is a slow work.

His batman had certainly been taken prisoner, for he managed to make contact in September 1940. The *Church Times*, which had been following the *Cowley Evangelist*, announced that "News that the Rev. Reginald Thompson Podmore was killed in action has been received from his batman, who is a prisoner of war. Fr. Podmore, of the Society of St. John the Evangelist, Cowley, has been reported missing since the withdrawal from Dunkirk."[31]

Podmore's brethren were deeply affected. In the *Cowley Evangelist* of October 1940 O'Brien announced his death in the customary formal way on the first page, before noting that he had "died in Belgium [as the community then still thought] probably in May, 1940, while acting as a Chaplain to His Majesty's forces, in the thirty-ninth year of his age and the seventh year of his profession".

> We have no details of Father Podmore's death. His batman writing to his own mother said 'The padre is dead, I must tell you more when I get home.' We do not know the date, place, or any of the circumstances of his passing. He went to his new and unfamiliar work as an army Chaplain like many other Chaplains with

---

29 Podmore, 14 May 1940.
30 *CE* July 1940.
31 *Church Times*, 20 Sept 1940.

not a little trepidation, but with a clear sense of duty. I think he was happy in the work. His Colonel wrote of the appreciation he gained from those amongst whom he worked.

In February 1941, the batman – "G. W. Randall, Driver, R.A.S.C." – managed to get a letter to the British Red Cross, a copy of which was sent on to Cowley. Like Br Walter Frederick's death in 1917, the tale of Podmore's end was full of pathos.

> I regret to inform you that this officer is dead. He was in a British Army car, driven by myself on the morning of May 23rd, 1940, he had just passed Bruny, travelling towards S. Pol, Pas de Calais, when we ran into a German machine gun ambush. The Padre was hit four times in each leg, and, in spite of all efforts by the German stretcher-bearers (their Ambulance which was immediately sent for was delayed by other German transport blocking the road and arrived too late) died four hours later from shock and loss of blood. He was conscious for the first hour only, and then passed peacefully and imperceptibly from coma to death. I buried him myself with the aid of two French civilians. A German officer later told me that he believed us to the start of a British attack; had he known it was a Chaplain his men would not have fired.[32]

After the war, a letter written in French arrived at St Edward's House in London addressed to "Monsieur Le Directeur" – one of "special interest and value".

> Dear Sir,
>
> I have in my possession some priestly vestments of embroidered silk, which belonged to Captain Reginald Thomson Podmore, Chaplain, who was killed at my house on May 23, 1940. Perhaps you have already received details concerning his death from his batman, George Randall, who succeeded in escaping while the Germans were occupied in burying the Captain in our garden [see below]. He had been attacked on the road and mortally wounded. On the morrow, when the German force which occupied my house had left, I had a grave made for the Captain with a plaque, and contrived to give him a worthy burial. Some months later, when permission could be obtained, I had the body moved to the little English cemetery near at hand, and had a cross of cement placed upon his tomb, on which I fashioned his helmet and a plaque of copper upon which I had his name engraved, together with a religious form of expression [pensée] found in this prayer-book, written upon the photograph of a grave which I presumed to be that of his mother. Knowing that his family and friends were still ignorant of his death, I had Masses said and prayers offered for him in our own church [...].
>
> On leaving my house for the Dunkirk front on the 24th of May, 1940, the Germans took away Captain Podmore's motor, after emptying it and throwing into the garden all that at that moment was no use to them. After their departure I collected all these objects, so that the family might eventually recover them. Unfortunately in 1942 the Germans came to arrest me, and before taking me away they ransacked the whole house. In this way they discovered all the Captain's belongings and those of his batman, and carried them off. If I have

---

32 Randall, 24 Feb 1941.

been able to keep in safety the sacred vestments to which I referred, it is only because my wife, finding them to be too fragile to be left with the objects of a military nature, had wrapped them up and placed them in a special cupboard.

Believe me, dear Sir, Yours sincerely,
E. MATHON, Chief Engineer of Mines,
Route Nationale, Divion, Pas-de-Calais

O'Brien forwarded the letter to Podmore's father, the Revd Claude Podmore, who wrote in the same issue of the *Cowley Evangelist* that he had himself met Randall.

[I] had a long talk with him, about 3 hours. He gave me full details of the attack. He and my son left the car and took shelter in a ditch before Reg was hit. There is one discrepancy between his account and M. Mathon's. He (Randall) with the help of two Frenchmen buried Reg. He did not escape, but was made prisoner. I am very glad to know that the grave is so well marked. I hope you will eventually receive the vestments safely.[33]

Podmore "went out and became our first sacrifice":[34] the Society of which he was a member had already laid out its theology of battle in the First World War, and did not stint itself in the Second. Podmore was 39, and had been professed for seven years: he had been instrumental in the Society's work among schoolboys, and "it was appropriate that he should have been called to share in the toils and risks of the young among whom he had worked so faithfully and to seal his work by the supreme sacrifice".[35]

Others followed Podmore to war; but all returned. The junior lay brothers were the first to go: General Chapter was consulted and "considered that no impediment should be made".[36] Another Br Michael joined the South African Medical Corps and was posted to the Middle East; while Brs Andrew, Raymond, and another William John all joined the Royal Air Force. Various breathless letters home as their postings took them to India and the Mediterranean spoke of unfamiliar sights and sounds, and of the attempt to maintain a vestige of the religious life in rough-and-ready surroundings. When Raymond used his Office Book to follow Solemn Vespers in the cathedral at Carthage in 1943 he found that "the chanting, in some respects, was a trifle disappointing, as there was a tendency to hurry the endings"; but all the same thought it "a great joy to hear *the* chant once again" after three years away.[37]

The younger priests soon went as chaplains: William Slade joined the fray from Cowley; in India Wilkins returned to service as a hospital chaplain, while George Huntley sailed with the troops to the Far East; and a young priest-novice, Alan Bean, was posted to Burma. Bean would later become the last member of the Society resident in Oxford, and one of his letters amply

---

33 *CE* Aug 1940.
34 PC 1942, SSJE/3/2.
35 *CE* Oct 1940.
36 SSJE/2/7/27.
37 Raymond, 30 Aug 1943.

illustrates the challenges faced by a chaplain in the field. His tropical habit had had to be dyed khaki, "as nothing white is permitted on this job", and other compromises had to be made.

> The question of fasting Communion in the Army is extremely difficult, especially during a campaign like this. On one occasion I was visiting one of my batteries for a long week-end. As it turned out they were firing for about 6 hours from 9.30 a.m. on the Sunday and several who wanted to make their Communion at 7 had been unable to do so. So, for the first time in my life, I celebrated non-fasting for the people at about 4 in the afternoon.

"I finally came to the conclusion", he went on, "that I ought (after a lot of thought while the guns were going) to celebrate, rather than give them Holy Communion from the reserved Sacrament, since it was a Sunday". He had been carrying the Blessed Sacrament in a chamois washbag since he arrived, and although he had not used it yet, "others have, and it might happen at any time. I also carry the Oil of Unction." He had decided, having conferred with a field-hospital chaplain of whom he approved, that "it is not essential for a patient to be an instructed Catholic before Unction can be given";[38] and later proposed that the Oil of the Sick should be reserved at Cowley "for speed and convenience of administration and for the better instruction of both adults and children".[39] An aumbry for the purpose was installed in the Blessed Sacrament Chapel in 1950.[40]

In 1943 Slade was serving with the 83rd Field Regiment of the Royal Artillery somewhere near the south coast, and had taken over his Camp Quiet Room for a chapel with "a little casuistry".

> To begin with, no one, except the camp spaniel, has ever used it since I came here; and he only sleeps there on cold, wet nights. Then, as a member of the camp, I have as much right as any of the men, let alone the spaniel, to use it. So I got the men to help me take possession. The quartermaster gave me a blanket, the men made me a cross, and I found a table [...] and now I am waiting to be evicted. That in the army is no easy thing where possession is more than nine points of the law.

He was confident that the Quiet Room would go on serving as the Camp Church, and since he was "willing to allow that spaniel a place in it on cold, wet nights, there is no one who can grumble". But his optimistic good humour had a practical side: in his new church he could start saying mass with relative dignity – he later persuaded one of the sergeants to hang up a picture of the Virgin and Child for him, "knowing that no one would dare interfere with his work"[41] – and from it he could carry out his "most responsible of all duties", and take the Blessed Sacrament to the men unable to leave their posts at the Coastal Batteries: "I have communicated several of the men in this way, and

---

38 Bean, undated, 1943/4.
39 PC 1949, SSJE/3/2.
40 PC 1950, SSJE/3/2.
41 Slade, 13 Dec 1943.

they have been grateful for the opportunity, and most reverent in their use of it."[42]

In India Huntley "had the unheard-of experience of men coming to me and saying, 'Padre, may I serve Mass tomorrow?'"[43] There was a marked difference between the practical experiences of the Cowley Fathers who served as Chaplains in the Second World War, and those of their predecessors who had served in the First – much of this was a result of the growth of Anglo-Catholicism as a normative expression of Anglicanism in the years following 1918 – although Wilkins remained unconvinced of the general development. But there were differences between the conflicts at home, too; and not least as the Luftwaffe began to visit *Blitzkrieg* on mainland Britain.

When George Gater and David Hemming took the Boys' Club to Gloucestershire on camp in August 1940, bombs were heard in the distance shortly after lights-out on the first night, and "the Senior tent – with a promptness which was very efficient – began to sing the latest rag-time at the tops of their horribly loud voices, in order to prevent the youngsters in their tents from hearing the sound".[44] In September, reflecting on "the deadliest peril [England] had ever known", O'Brien reserved the greatest revulsion not for defeat or even invasion, but for "the foulness and uncleanness of the evil thing which threatened to overwhelm us". The Canadian congregation had offered to house any brethren who might need to be evacuated to Canada; while the American congregation wrote "with mingled feelings of admiration and deepest sorrow", and assurance of an abundance of masses and prayers.[45] The *Cowley Evangelist* noted that "the kindly thought of the two other Congregations of the Society for the English Congregation is one more instance of the close bonds which unite us both within the British Empire and beyond it to the free nations of the world."

WEATHERING THE STORM

Even in the depth of war the Society's life went on: and there were other opportunities for thanksgiving. After the evacuation of Dunkirk "we were compelled to sing our *Te Deum* as if it had been a great victory"; and in the Battle of Britain the young had proved themselves worthy of the burden that had been laid upon them.

> Youth has found its opportunity, and added another chapter of glory to the history of our Empire by the magnificent defence of our homes, and the intrepid unceasing attacks on the enemy made by the gallantry of our Air Force. We recall too the amazing efficiency and steadfast endurance of our Navy and dauntless leadership of our great Prime Minister.

---

42 Slade, 23 Jan 1943.
43 Huntley, 24 June 1943.
44 *CE* Sept 1940.
45 Williams, Otis, Viall, Banner, 15 July 1940.

For all his oratory, O'Brien still wished that in the context of Dunkirk and the onset of blanket bombing, "our experiences of judgment and warning, of humiliation and deliverance, we may recognize the Voice of God calling His people to penitence and amendment".[46]

As in the previous conflict, the Society remained alert to the opportunities for the spiritual development of individuals in the face of adversity, and for moments of transfiguration in the face of undesirable circumstances – the "Souls made Great by Sacrifice" of the Stations of the Cross in the community church at Cowley. In anticipation of the National Day of Prayer on 3 September 1942, the anniversary of the start of the war, the Superior General urged on his readers the confidence that "there still remains at the heart of the nation a vague, inarticulate, sense of God".

"Men can be as inconsistent to false and perverted aims as to good and true aims," he went on. "Human nature is always a strange mixture of heights and depths. There are the heights of heroism and endurance, of almost unconscious but sublime self-sacrifice, as well as the depths of the unspeakable atrocities of war." He cited particular examples, just as Henry Bull had done a quarter-century earlier.

> You would not necessarily look for heroism in a man whose trade was to push a tricycle selling ice-creams, but there was one who became a stoker in the Merchant Navy, a small frail man who was so exhausted at the end of his day's work that he could not even reach his bunk. Yet he was always grinning and cheerful, continually calling out his old cry, 'Ices, ices, stop me and buy one'. When the ship was torpedoed he gave his lifebelt to the cabin boy and was last seen in the water still uttering the old cry to cheer his mates.

"Or think of the endurance of the poor in London during the period of continual air raids," he mused. "Night after night they could be seen tramping to the shelters with their bedding and returning in the morning to see if there was anything left of their homes."

> During one of these raids, amongst many who sought shelter in the Convent of S. Saviour, Hoxton [one of the houses of John Mason Neale's Society of St Margaret], was an old woman. Hearing her murmuring to herself one of the sisters thought she was saying her prayers but soon she caught the words, 'O Churchill, Churchill, it's mighty hard, but we'll stick it, we'll stick it'. Surely it was this element of height and depth in human nature which brought our Saviour down from Heaven.

O'Brien closed with an exposition of the battle of the powers of the Kingdom of Heaven against the powers of Evil, in the context of conditions that must have seemed for many people caught up the heavy fire-bombing of the major cities as if they had stumbled through the very gates of Hell. "Evil can never ultimately prevail against good, but God gives to his servants the task of overthrowing evil and it is our privilege, undeserving as we are, to take our part in the conflict together with the Heavenly host, we on earth as they in Heaven."[47]

---

46 *CE* Sept 1940.
47 *CE* Sept 1942.

The battle of good and evil was the broad subject of the back-to-front spiritual direction of *The Screwtape Letters*, which C. S. Lewis had begun writing shortly after he first began coming to Walter Adams for confession in 1940.[48] "Let us therefore think", wrote Screwtape to Wormwood, "how to use, than how to enjoy, this European war".

> For it has certain tendencies inherent in it, which are, in themselves, by no means in our favour. We may hope for a good deal of cruelty and unchastity. But, if we are not careful, we shall see thousands turning in this tribulation to the Enemy, while tens of thousands who do not go so far will have their attention diverted from themselves to values and causes which they believe to be higher than the self.[49]

The London brethren spent the nights of the Blitz visiting the air-raid shelters;[50] but after the bombing of the Houses of Parliament in May 1941, a worried Cyril Whitworth wrote from Bombay to ask for urgent reassurance.

> With the news of the Abbey and Parliament Houses being damaged one cannot help being anxious about S. Edward's House and the Fathers in London. I wonder how long it will be before we get news and whether you are to cable to us if there is bad news? How people can live these days who have no Faith in the Sovereignty of God I cannot imagine.[51]

Despite the loss of life, however, and the serious damage done in the surrounding streets – not least to Westminster School, just across the road – St Edward's House had several very near misses and came through the bombing relatively unscathed. The House of Commons moved from its burnt-out chamber into Church House, directly opposite, and the *Cowley Evangelist* announced that "The Executive Committee of the Cowley, Wantage, & All Saints' Missionary Association have courageously decided that our Annual Festival in London shall be held as usual." For a moment in the midst of the chaos it was almost business as usual; and after High Mass at St Matthew's, Westminster, which was also still usable, O'Brien hoped that the slides which had become a regular part of such meetings – "which last year were so disappointing because of the deficiencies of the Blackout" – would give "just that intimate view of our Mission work which it is often difficult for speakers to convey".[52]

One of the most compelling interpreters of the mission work in Africa had been Godfrey Callaway; and almost the whole attention of the Society turned briefly to St Cuthbert's, Tsolo, in the autumn of 1942, where early on the morning of 4 September he died quietly in his sleep. The symbolism could hardly have been richer: it was the morning of the Feast of the Translation of the Relics of St Cuthbert, the patronal festival of the mission and of the original Society of

48 Walter Hooper (ed), *C. S. Lewis: Selected Letters*, Volume II, London: Harper Collins (2004), 453.

49 C. S. Lewis, *The Screwtape Letters*, London: Geoffrey Bles (1942), 31.

50 PC 1941, SSJE/3/2; *CE* June 1948.

51 Whitworth, 13 May 1941.

52 *CE* May 1941.

St Cuthbert which he had founded and led into the SSJE. The crowds who had gathered for the High Mass and celebrations instead found themselves attending his funeral; with the burial after the solemn requiem "attended by a very large concourse of people, European and African [and] Coloured".[53]

Callaway was another Cowley Father who narrowly escaped a mitre: he would almost certainly have been elected Bishop of St John's in 1923, had he been fitter. O'Brien noted that he had struggled with increasingly ill health for decades; and in his final years he had been confined to his cell.

> Yet none who read his letters in the *Cowley Evangelist* could have guessed the conditions under which they were written, this seeming frustration of his missionary activities, the cough for which no relief could be found, the deafness and latterly the threat of blindness, the increasing exhaustion of the body which longed for the release of death. His spirit was unconquerable, humour, gaiety, vivid interest in life, love for the Africans and shrewd appreciation both of their weaknesses and (far more) of their virtues, give his letters their unique charm.

"There was no suppression of interest, love and care for his people in his self-effacement", continued the Superior General; "he was really great, really wise, really humble, really holy."[54] Not long before his death he had observed the faith and fortitude of a local woman in the face of personal calamity, and "realised that I came out here to *learn*".[55]

The *Cowley Evangelist* for the rest of the year was full of tributes from various quarters; and Callaway's death perhaps marked something of the closure of a chapter. Although Gerald Ley and Sydney Wallis survived him at St Cuthbert's – to whose number had been added various other Cowley Fathers as time had gone on – he had been very much a giant in the manner of George Congreve, Frederick Puller, Philip Waggett, Hugh Nicholson, and Edward Elwin; and he had been one of the Society's pioneers in the years following its reinvigoration in the 1890s.

Their successors, however, continued to rise. A dozen men were professed in the course of the war; and among them were names that retain familiarity: David Hemming, Terence Manson, William Slade, Francis Dalby, and Anselm Chiverton. They joined others like Lonsdale Wain and Christopher Bryant, who had been professed in the 1930s. In the Transkei, the foundation stone of yet another SSJE outstation church was laid "in the blazing sun of a cloudless day" in the Christmas Octave of 1940;[56] and in 1943 the Society accepted from the Bishop of St Andrews, Dunkeld & Dunblane, Lumsden Barkway, the cure of Doune in Perthshire. Arthur Pridham was to be Rector, assisted by Gerrard Pulley and Dalby: the *Scottish Guardian* reported that "the many reminders in the countryside of the coming spring were a suitable symbol of the new life which will flow into the veins of the Church in Scotland with the arrival in our midst of the Cowley Fathers."[57]

---

53 *CE* Nov 1942.
54 *CE* Oct 1942.
55 Callaway, 21 June 1941.
56 Rumsey, 18 Jan 1941.
57 *Scottish Guardian*, 26 Feb 1943.

By the time of the opening of the new Scottish house the blackout had come to Cape Town: the library and kitchen windows were made lightproof, which Bull called "warnings to us of dangers ahead".[58] Meanwhile, at Panch Howds a large air-raid siren was installed on the roof of the Mission House "after much struggling and shouting and panting": Williams noted that "it will be operated from another part of Poona, and will be another disturbance in addition to the many that already exist."[59]

The large movements of troops once more brought some congenial encounters: when Whitworth took the Bombay boys camping, they found a large detachment already in place on a neighbouring field.

> Every night at our Sing-Song soldiers up to about twenty came and joined with us and made tremendous friends with the boys. The Regiment was a Scotch Regiment with a Presbyterian Chaplain who did not come near us. But two officers asked me to give them Holy Communion, which was delightful [...] Another Regiment arrived with a delightful Chaplain, Father Sparrow, a Priest Associate of ours whom you know well. He at once got his Church Tent up and said his Mass daily and quite obviously has a splendid influence.

Elsewhere, while being given tea "in a strange Mess", Slade met an officer who introduced himself as having been a chorister in the community church in the days of G. H. Palmer: "meetings like this are like water in dry places".[60]

Once more the wider Cowley family was spread across the globe; but some were isolated by the war: in 1942 General Chapter had sent a message of greeting to Callaway to express sympathy at the state of his health, but "at the same time to explain that it was most undesirable to attempt any communication with the Japanese Fathers to whom he had desired to be remembered".[61] Other experiences were harrowing: Slade later wrote frankly from Holland of "our most difficult day, when all the light seemed gone, and joy something only to be remembered. It was the day we lost seven men in one morning, besides a great many injured, and a young officer I had been preparing for confirmation"; and of the "mud and shells doing their utmost to submerge me in despondency and fear". Nevertheless, on St John's Day 1944 he wrote to his brethren to reassure them that had found some comfort.

> I cannot allow this day to pass without sending my love and best wishes. You were my intention this morning at Mass, and I think my driver realised that this was a day of special importance, for he arrived almost punctually to assist me. This separation and this conflict have not divided our family nor destroyed its peace. Each day brings me fresh experience of the living unity and the past-all-understanding peace which not only survives but grows on the face of this deep.[62]

---

58 Page, 3 July 1942.
59 Williams, 29 Sept 1942.
60 Slade, 13 Dec 1943.
61 SSJE/2/7/55.
62 Slade, 30 Oct; 16 Dec; 27 Dec 1944.

All around there were dangers of the soul as well as of the body. "Because so few men are actively Christian, hope is a treasure known and guarded by a few; and they do so with almost everything against them. There is the enemy on one side, the weather and mud, and, worse still, that awful souring cynicism which takes possession of so many."[63] Hemming had noted the same from the pulpit.

> A young fellow in the Forces finds himself surrounded by a pervading atmosphere of complete absorption in the task of prosecuting the war. Everything is done, and rightly so, to make for efficiency; his training is normally rigorous and he is kept hard at it. As a result of this, and also of the indifference of the great majority to Christianity, there all too easily creeps in the feeling that compared to this gigantic task religion and the observance of Catholic practices are trifles. It must require great fortitude to resist this ever-present anaesthetic.

Prayer, then, was an absolute necessity. "As fellow members in Christ and in the congregation", he asked his hearers, "you will bear in your hearts, won't you? all those who have gone out into the Forces from this Church."

> [T]hey are our special care and responsibility. You may not know them; but their names are before you in the Blessed Sacrament Chapel and on the lists at the back of the Church; you have knelt with them at Communion often in the past; you have seen them serving, or coming out of the early Mass as you were coming into this one. They are boys and girls and men and women who, like many of you, look to this Church as their spiritual home; and, as it is their home, they have a right to love of all of us who with them make up the Family of Christ in this place.[64]

There was, then, spiritual warfare as well as physical conflict to be taken into account. From 1940 the Society began to observe the anniversary of the death of the Founder with a special commemoration and sermon;[65] but in its prosecution it also looked beyond its own hedges. In the early months of the war the Superiors of the three leading men's communities – O'Brien, Edward Keble Talbot CR, and Reginald Tribe SSM – circulated a letter in which they treated "the problem of winning back to Christ masses of folk who live in distressed areas under dehumanising conditions, and [...] the monstrous growth of housing estates which threaten to become new centres of heathendom". Just as the organisers of the National Mission of 1916 had hoped that the war would help focus people's minds on spiritual matters, now was a moment "to start to consider how the Church can effectively set about rebuilding a Christian order of society in the modern world".

---

63 Slade, 1 Dec 1944.
64 CE Nov 1943.
65 SSJE/2/7/25.

The Unity of the Faith

In March 1940 the three Superiors were "convinced that a supreme spiritual opportunity is offered to the Church in this day when mere secularism and humanism stand manifestly bankrupt". Their appeal to their readers – it was printed in the *Cowley Evangelist* particularly for the information of the Society's Priest Associates – was for single clergymen to go and serve with one or two others where the need was deemed to be greatest: "the ideal at which we should aim is that of a parish staffed by a vicar and curates living a common life and sharing a common purse".

> Our aim is to stimulate a movement among such priests, and to organise such an association of them as may help them to find some practical expression of the spirit of sacrifice and service, as well as the added strength that comes to a priest through a spiritual bond with others who share his spiritual vision. It is to the spirit of service and nothing else that this appeal is addressed.

Cosmo Gordon Lang, by then at Lambeth Palace, was firmly in favour of the scheme; and the signatories were pleased to be able "to append to this letter a commendation by His Grace the Archbishop of Canterbury". It was hoped that the appeal would "elicit a response from very diverse quarters"; and its originators were not to be disappointed.[66] Percy Wigram served as the first Warden of the Company of Mission Priests that it inspired, whose work continues today.[67]

Paul Couturier's Week of Prayer for Christian Unity had also met with the Society's "enthusiastic support". O'Brien thought it was "Universal in its appeal and in its scope";[68] and a prayer in which the SSJE was able "to unite with all our separated Brethren without the slightest compromise of principle and thus to find an anticipation of union as our several prayers and wills meet in the Sacred Heart of Jesus".[69] However, he was clear that it was also an antidote to fractious plans.

> We cannot have schemes of union or federation, we cannot have united services and general communions without grieving and wounding the consciences of many, but we can all, Romans, Orthodox, Anglican or Protestant, pray for that Unity which is the will of our Lord.[70]

The *Cowley Evangelist* encouraged its readers to engage more seriously with the prayer: it deprecated the fact although it had gained considerable traction on the Continent, it yet remained "unhappily unknown to the majority of our fellow Christians in these Provinces"; and urged them to have "an honest and untiring effort to understand each other's convictions, and a conscientious determination that mere prejudice shall never be allowed to pass for

---

66 *CE* March 1940.
67 *CE* March 1941.
68 *CE* Jan 1941.
69 *CE* Jan 1943.
70 *CE* Jan 1941.

conviction" – which might be all the easier in the context of "the spectacle of a world at war and the complete bankruptcy of all merely human panaceas for the healing of our wounds". It was in the context of the Week of Prayer for Christian Unity, however, that the Society took its next stand.

> Outside the domain of prayer [for Christian Unity] we cannot so easily avoid controversy and there are controversial issues before us at this time which it is our bounden duty not to avoid. Obviously it is when action is threatened which affects our most sacred and cherished convictions and seems to us to be in contradiction to the teaching and practice of the Catholic Church as it has been held through nearly two thousand years of Christian life, that we have to do our utmost to resist it.[71]

Resist they did: by 1943 the discussions that had disquieted the Anglo-Catholic party ten years earlier had come to a head. The new Archbishop of Canterbury, William Temple, laid out the South India plans in Convocation in May: not only would four dioceses cede from the Church of India, Burma, & Ceylon, but "the establishment of the new church [of South India] was intended to involve the continuation in office and function of non-episcopally ordained ministers who already held positions in the existing body".

> It was this part of the scheme, rather than unprecedented release of the four dioceses, which galvanised Anglo-Catholics and in particular made them seek to ensure that such a body was not officially recognised as being in any way a constituent part of the Anglican Communion, since to do so would carry with it the clear implication that episcopal ordination was not a necessary requirement of priesthood.[72]

Many feared that this scheme might be used to lay the ground for a similar arrangement in England;[73] and Michael Yelton has observed that "the Anglo-Catholic attack was led on this occasion by the male religious orders" with O'Brien at their head. In noting that "this was probably to only occasion upon which the SSJE adopted such a belligerent tone" he discounts its triumph over Walter Pym in Bombay thirty-five years earlier and its less vocal stand against Ernest Barnes in the diocese of Birmingham; but the disagreements with Pym and with Barnes, although they had been *causes célèbres* at the time, had essentially been local diocesan matters. The South India business was a matter of universal interest, even in the middle of the war.

In the course of the Christmastide Provincial Chapter in 1942 the meeting adjourned "in order to hold a conference in the Library on the South Indian Church Union scheme".

> The result of this discussion was that, while postponing the formulation of any course of action which the Society as a whole might feel itself bound to take

---

71 *CE* Jan 1943.
72 Yelton, *South India*, 8ff.
73 Eric Waldram Kemp, *The Life and Letters of Kenneth Escott Kirk*, London: Hodder and Stoughton (1959), 150ff.

in the event of the scheme being finally adopted, the conference affirmed its whole-hearted desire that the Society should give its immediate support to all efforts made to combat not only the South Indian scheme but all other such endeavours which compromise the teaching of the English Church as set forth in her Prayer Book and Ordinal.

The Chapter duly voted to give a grant of up to £250 "towards the defence of Faith and Order in the English Church and the support of the organisation formed for this purpose".[74] Lucius Cary explained the SSJE's concerns in the *Cowley Evangelist* a week later.

In what is known as the South India scheme [...] the privilege of intercommunion is to be granted to separated bodies whose ministers do not possess the priestly powers derived by ordination through Apostolic succession, and whose members do not profess the faith in the Eucharistic sacrifice or in the Real Presence in the Blessed Sacrament, the tradition of which the Anglican Church has retained in her formularies. The Scheme goes even further to admit the right of intercelebration to ministers of the non-conforming bodies, though there is no safeguard provided to secure that such ministers shall even have been baptised.

By February 1943 the Council for the Defence of Church Principles had been established, with the Superior General at its helm, and the support of the Priest Associates of the Society had been canvassed.[75] In August O'Brien was re-elected to office,[76] and the Greater Chapter adopted a formal motion of support.

[I]n view of the gravity of the issues involved in the present crisis, in which the Catholic tradition of the English Church and its principles are at stake, the Fathers present in Chapter wish respectfully to offer the Fr Superior their sympathy in the grave responsibility which circumstances have imposed on him, and their wholehearted offer of such support as they may be able to give.[77]

It was a remarkable development. Yelton notes that the Cowley Fathers "were generally regarded as impeccably loyal" to the Church of England;[78] and the former Bishop of London William Wand considered them to have a "rather specially Anglican character", in contrast to some of the other men's communities.[79] Now Arthur Taylor wrote from Cape Town to say that his only hesitation in choosing to test his vocation at Cowley rather than anywhere else had been that "Cowley seemed to me to be holding back and not joining in the forefront with those Catholic priests and others who were in the vanguard of the fight for Catholic faith and practice. Now this can no longer be said."[80]

A Day of Prayer was held on 15 December for "the triumph of the Church over the many perils and problems by which it is beset today". Slade was

---

74 PC 1942, SSJE/2/3.
75 *CE* Feb 1943.
76 SSJE/2/7/61.
77 SSJE/2/7/70.
78 Yelton, *South India*, 8.
79 J. W. C. Wand (ed), *The Anglican Communion: A Survey*, Oxford: OUP (1948), 308.
80 Taylor, 4 Oct 1943.

delighted to find that three officers of his regiment came to mass in the church hut to unite themselves to the effort: "I know this is not a very big response, but at least it is a response, and I was very grateful [...] There is indeed among the few a real love for the Church." At Cowley the Litany was sung in procession before High Mass, and the intention was specially made "for the bringing together of all Christians into *'the unity of the faith,'* of which St Paul speaks".

The Unity of the Faith was an open letter addressed to the Archbishop of Canterbury by the superiors of the Community of the Resurrection, the Society of the Divine Compassion, the Benedictines at Nashdom, the Society of St Francis, the Order of St Paul at Alton, and the Cowley Fathers – "Your Grace's sons *in Dño*". It laid before Temple a number of "essential and minimum" safeguards "without the observance of which by ourselves all thought of future Reunion with that three-quarters of Christendom represented by the historic Eastern and Western Churches must forever be laid aside"; and foretold dire consequences should they not be observed. Yelton argues that the author was probably Gregory Dix: "a master of English prose and in particular of the cutting phrase".[81]

> Your Grace knows that in this country there are many hundreds, we might say thousands, of loyal clergy, with strong lay support, who could not in conscience continue in communion, mediately or immediately, with a Church in which these or equivalent guarantees of right belief were not observed. And it is certain that it if they were driven to choose between their conscience and their present ecclesiastical allegiance (which God forbid!) they would receive from other parts of the Anglican Communion not only sympathy but aid in reestablishing a body which could claim with justice to be the legitimate heir of the authentic principles of our Church of England.[82]

It amounted to a threat that if the South India scheme went ahead then it might precipitate a non-Juring Church of England along Anglo-Papalist lines. The Director of the Society of the Sacred Mission, Stephen Bedale – who had also been present at the meeting – declined to sign, as he thought its inclusion intemperate; but he was also implacably imposed to the proposals before Convocation and noted that "the fact that my name does not appear amongst those of the signatories to this letter should not be taken to imply either my Society's or my own approval of the South India Scheme"."

Temple thought that *The Unity of the Faith* was little more than blackmail;[83] but such was the perceived depth of the crisis that O'Brien urged the participation in the Day of Prayer of "all our Associates and the members of the Fellowship of St John and all our friends"; and closed his appeal with a startling observation.

---

81 Yelton, *South India*, 9.

82 W. B. O'Brien SSJE *et al.*, *The Unity of the Faith: An Open Letter to His Grace the Lord Archbishop of Canterbury from the Superiors of Certain Religious Communities*, London: Dacre Press (1943).

83 Petà Dunstan, *The Labour of Obedience: The Benedictines of Pershore, Nashdom and Elmore*, Norwich: Canterbury Press (2009), 136ff.

The need is tremendous, for a very vital choice lies before the Church of England in the immediate future; a choice which also a multitude of individual Church people may have to make for themselves.[84]

Yelton observes that the vigorous campaigning of the Council for the Defence of Church Principles was criticised by some who thought it "inappropriate that this should be happening during a World War"; but at the same time makes the obvious point that "on the other hand the proposals for a United Church [of South India] could themselves have been delayed until hostilities were over". Either way, for the Society of St John the Evangelist the closing years of the Second World War effectively became a battle on two fronts.

---

84 *CE* Dec 1943.

19

WINDS OF CHANGE

"You must never forget, Laurie, that dissenters are often excellent Christian people. You must never be narrow minded." I promised that I never would. "Though of course," my aunt added, "you must always remember that we are right."

—Rose Macaulay, *The Towers of Trebizond*[1]

The Second World War was over by the time General Chapter met in the summer of 1945; although the world remained in a state of turmoil. The meeting resolved, among other things, to send letters to the members of the Society of St John the Evangelist who were still serving with the Forces, "assuring them of our loving remembrance and the hope that they may soon be able to return home".[2] It was later decided that military service should not count against any member of the Society in annual vows when it came to life profession: "the lay brothers who return after absence on service with the Forces should on profession take their places in the community according to their seniority when entering on first vows". The same privilege was also unanimously extended to the choir novice, Alan Bean.[3]

Lucius Cary's counsel was that "the world, barely saved from appalling disaster, remains the world; and in it stands, for witness and salvation, the militant and suffering Church, the mystical body of the Exalted Christ";[4] and a glance at the minutes gives an idea of the diet of the Society's internal affairs at the end of the years of conflict. Even in the heat of the battle against the powers of darkness in both the world and – as the Society regarded them – in the Church, there had been an element of continuity. The General Chapter had carried on tweaking the SSJE's Statutes and altering its liturgical observances, while at the more homely end of the scale the Provincial Chapter had bickered about bicycles and the state of the garden.

Three items of Chapter business in 1945 pointed to the position that the Society occupied within the Church of England, and the mind of Anglo-Catholics particularly, at the end of the war. The first was an acknowledgement of the publication of Dom Gregory Dix's *The Shape of the Liturgy*, which had originally been delivered as retreat addresses at Cowley: he dedicated the

---

1 Rose Macaulay, *The Towers of Trebizond*, London: Collins (1956), 10.
2 SSJE/2/7/87.
3 PC 1946, SSJE/3/2.
4 *CE* July 1945.

book to the SSJE, calling it "the oldest, the most respected and in more ways than one the greatest of our Anglican communities."[5]

The second was an unusual request from Miss Lily Breckon, who intended to leave a large sum of money to St Alban's, Manchester, "provided that at the time of my death the said church maintain the same Anglo-Catholic teaching as in the Rev E. A. Glenday's time". If it did not, the money was to go to the Community of the Resurrection, and the Superior General "for the time being" of the SSJE was to be umpire. The Chapter granted Miss Breckon's desire, and agreed "that the Superior General should undertake this small responsibility". The responsibility may have been small in its substance, but in its essence it spoke volumes: the Superior General of the Cowley Fathers was an ecclesiastical luminary whom at least one pious spinster was able to regard as a supreme arbiter – whoever might fill the office – in matters of Catholic faith and order.

The third was the golden jubilee of the dedication of the Church of St John the Evangelist, which would fall in the coming year. It was a happy coincidence that 12 May 1946 was the Sunday in the Octave of St John before the Latin Gate, and so the Bishop of Oxford, Kenneth Kirk, would preside and preach. The *Cowley Evangelist* hoped that "there will be many of our friends in many parts of the world who will be in spirit with us, as we keep our festival with its special note of thanksgiving for 50 years of worship in our beautiful House of Prayer and for its preservation through the recent perils of war".[6]

The celebration itself was a set-piece example of where the Society's liturgical practice had come to rest by the 1940s. The brethren met Kirk at the west end of the church, as their predecessors had met William Stubbs in 1896; but on this occasion the ceremonies of the Solemn Reception of a Bishop were lifted straight out of the Latin-rite *pontificalia*. After being vested he presided over High Mass at the Throne, attended by two deacons-of-honour; the Superior General as assistant priest; four chaplains in the form of students seconded from St Stephen's House; and their Principal, Arthur Couratin, as master of ceremonies. It was to Couratin that the *Cowley Evangelist* thought was due credit for "the order and reverence of a most impressive service".[7]

In his sermon Kirk invited his hearers to "think of the external values of the Tractarian Movement, the Catholic revival, the religious life in the Church of England and all that these things stand for, summarised for us to-day in this church in which we gather around the Altar". He emphasised the place of the religious life in the ongoing "conversion of England"; which he thought now "passes through three stages, so that not one, but three conversions are needed". The first was to do with "the way in which the natural law of God is being set aside".

---

5 Gregory Dix, *The Shape of the Liturgy*, Westminster: Dacre Press (1943), ix.

6 *CE* May 1946.

7 I am grateful to Fr William Davage for pointing out that the folklore of St Stephen's House holds that Couratin and his team – who were a regular fixture at episcopal functions during Kirk's tenure of the see – were known in certain quarters of the diocese as "Arthur's Flying Circus". Shortly afterwards Bull wrote of the Archbishop of Cape Town coming to Langa to ordain one of the SSJE's former catechists to the priesthood "with his galaxy of attendants for whom we have to borrow vestments from the Cathedral". Bull, 22 June 1946.

The evidence of profligacy, licence, almost promiscuity between the sexes, the horrifying figures of the arrears of divorces which cannot find enough judges to hear the causes – these things show that the law, 'Thou shalt not commit adultery' has passed almost under the shadow of darkness in England. The increase in juvenile crime, again, the widespread dishonesty of our times – here too is matter for earnest thought and grave anxiety. Is it not clear as day that until the country is converted to the simple principles, I will not say of Christian morality but of natural morality, we are very far indeed from anything that can be called religion?

The second conversion was that of those who wanted to lead what his predecessor Charles Gore had called "the good life"; but who only turned to prayer when their own strength failed. "They take God as their helper, their aide-de-camp, their resource to whom they can turn in time of need. It seems to me that this is the way in which the thought of religion comes to many people; it is not entirely a caricature of normal English religious life." At least, though Kirk, it brought prayer into the foreground, but meant that society was still "only on the threshold of the Christian revelation".

The third conversion was the consummation of the other two: "the Catholic Faith revealed by our Lord Jesus Christ, handed down by His Church, continually renewed by the outpouring of the Spirit, made fervent by the Grace which is given in the Sacraments; the faith which insists that we must turn our whole thought of God and man into another pattern altogether, remembering that this life is not the life that really matters."

Here we live in a world of temporal, finite experience, but our true home is in the world invisible, eternal, supernatural, infinite. To that we must always turn, living throughout a life of humble yet grateful worship. From it we must derive the directives of our lives. To it we must turn for the saving and gracious mercy of God in the forgiveness of our sins, for the renewal of our strength, for the inspiration of supernatural ambitions to live a life according to His Will.

The punchline, perhaps inevitably, was that the religious life – and that of the SSJE in particular, given the occasion – was the epitome of the last. Kirk's conclusion was that the Society, five decades after the dedication of its church, and eight after its foundation, proclaimed to the world "that which it really needs – the third conversion, the conversion from this-worldliness to other-worldliness".

This is the Catholic Faith; this is the thing for which, above all else, the religious life stands. In the religious life the cares of this world are reduced to a minimum so that those who have received the call to enter it may stand as witnesses for the truth the whole Church proclaims.[8]

A day earlier William O'Brien had taken a similar view of the Fellowship of St John; meditating on its purposes in the course of its annual meeting. It was, he emphasised, "a *fellowship* binding its members together in a spiritual bond";

---

8 *CE* June 1946.

and particularly in the context of "devotion to the mystery of the Incarnation in a life of consistent witness to its truth". He spoke of the significance of the Fellowship's patronage, which immediately "associated [it] with the profoundest and most sublime truths of our Christian faith".

> You will not think I am belittling the practical side of the fellowship, or the immensely valuable help given to the Society by its generous alms, but it is your joy to feel that your membership implies an intimate tie with the Society of S. John the Evangelist in that devotion to the mystery of the Incarnation which is our special characteristic.

"Thus we must think of our membership in the Fellowship of S. John", he concluded, "as a precious gift to help us to become capable of a fellowship hereafter which will be incomparably more intimate, more satisfying, more blessed, than anything which we can know here."

The part played by the Society in presenting to the nation "that which it really needs" was emphasised further in early October 1946, when a Catechism Service, led by David Hemming, was broadcast from the community church. "All except those actually taking part in the service will be rigidly excluded from the Church", warned O'Brien, "but many of our friends will, I expect, be glad of the opportunity of listening in by lawful methods".[9]

In his introduction to *Cowley Sermons*, a volume of selected sermons preached in the community church since 1896, The Bishop of Brechin, Eric Graham, wrote of the renewal of the Anglican religious life as "one of the happiest and most significant results of the Catholic Revival". This was not an isolated sentiment; and nor was his view that "the recent Jubilee of the Cowley Fathers' church at Oxford reminds us how sound and steady the growth has been" – only three years earlier the Advisory Council for Religious Communities had brought out its *Directory of the Religious Life* for the Church of England.[10] He also noted, however, "how great is our debt to that wonderful pioneer, the Father-Founder of the Society of St John the Evangelist";[11] and the jubilee was inevitably bound up with the resurgent and controversial business of the proposed memorial to Benson.

By the end of 1944 Ninian Comper had been approached to draw up plans, which had been circulated to the professed members. Comper appears to have proposed removing the tester and figures on the east wall – which Pevsner in any case thought to be "a disappointment"[12] – piercing the dossal, and creating a raised memorial chapel above the sacristies and foundation stone. One of his huge trademark ciboria would be placed over the high altar, which would frame the new arch and the altar and east window beyond.

The arguments began all over again. Percy Wigram was all in favour of the scheme, "which while leaving the present church untouched, added something

---

9 *CE* Oct 1946.

10 Advisory Council for Religious Communities, *A Directory of the Religious Life*, London: SPCK (1943).

11 *Cowley Sermons: The Jubilee Volume of the Conventual Church of St John the Evangelist, Oxford*, London: Mowbray (1947), 11.

12 Sherwood & Pevsner, *Oxfordshire*, 341.

to it of great value". Edward Trenholme felt that "an Italian ciborium would be architecturally incongruous in a gothic church". David Gardner and Douglas Sedding objected to the expenditure; while Henry Thomson felt that "a scheme of this kind required a liberal expenditure and should not be hampered by undue economy". Walter Adams "deprecated having a memorial chapel which would not be accessible to the public" – it would be entirely within the enclosure – but O'Brien noted that "the important feature was the view of the extended east end disclosing through the ciborium and the chancel arch the memorial window".

Frederick Playne thought that the plans were "a real vision of architectural genius", while Leonard Wilks wanted the whole thing dropped, reusing with consistency his argument that he thought "a memorial of this kind as not in keeping with the poverty and hiddenness of the Father Founder's life". Discussions continued at a conference in the Common Room a few days later – the Society was still in its Christmastide retreat – along much the same lines, although Cary opened up the field by suggesting that the Society might abandon the plan altogether and instead provide the funds to build a new church in one of the planned post-war urban areas, where "by holding the advowson the Society should ensure that there should always be a priest in charge there who would teach the whole Catholic Faith".

In terms of strategy Cary's suggestion combined the two pressing needs of the moment: urban evangelisation and the defence of Catholic order. Terence Manson was in favour, but pointed out that the new building work would take years to materialise – he suggested instead the establishment of Benson Memorial Bursaries at selected theological colleges. Others, however, reaffirmed their approval of the scheme: Harold Peacey "desired that the great message of the Father Founder should be enshrined as it were in stone in the Society's church", and "did not think there could be a better way of doing this than in the beautiful design which Mr Comper had given us". The recently professed Mark Gibbard, however, thought that Bodley's original scheme of a triptych behind the high altar might be better – and also questioned the suitability of the ciborium "in our church, with its general gothic style and screen".

Comper himself addressed some of the concerns in a letter to O'Brien early in 1945: if the Society wanted the ciborium "to be more elaborate and gothic, I can make it so".[13] Tantalisingly, the designs – of which numerous copies must have been made, for distribution among the members of the Chapter – do not appear to have survived either in the SSJE archive at Lambeth or the RIBA archives at the Victoria & Albert Museum. In the end, the plans came to nothing; and the disagreements over the memorial chapel represented in a very particular way the maelstrom at the heart of the Society over whether the life and teachings of the Father Founder were to be preserved in aspic for the edification of his spiritual children, or to be used as a broad base for an evolving expression of the religious life in the Church of England.

The Society effectively practised the latter: Henry Parry Liddon thought that "the silent eloquence of [its] rule is worth more than a thousand sermons";[14] but,

---

13 PC 1944, SSJE/3/2.
14 Johnston, *Liddon*, 333.

as we have seen, the Statutes and Rule were frequently recast as part of a process that Luke Miller has called "nuancing the teaching of the Father Founder", which he traces back to the days of George Congreve.[15] Rose Macaulay, in a burst of maudlin piety, did not hesitate to ascribe the process to the work of "the Holy Spirit, always on the move, [which] expanded it continually, suiting it and making it possible to the times it had reached." Macaulay also observed that "the S.S.J.E. has developed, hasn't it? I expect Fr Benson is watching it with approval and pleasure";[16] which was not a view shared universally by the members of Chapter. In the end Playne went to the nub of the issue when he contended, in the face of opposition in Provincial Chapter, that "it was not so much a question of what we thought the Father Founder would have wished, as our unceasing sense of his greatness which we wished to memorialise."[17] By the time of the jubilee he was forced to concede that "on more than one occasion the question of a memorial to the Father Founder in the Church has been debated in the Society, but so far no scheme has met with full approval."[18]

Developments in Scotland soon bore out a similar tension. Chapter had approved of the idea of a new Scottish house two years before its establishment in 1943;[19] but by the end of 1945 the Society had decided to withdraw from Doune and move to Joppa, on the eastern outskirts of Edinburgh. The general view was while there were those who appreciated the SSJE's "work of prayer and hiddenness"; others felt that the Society belonged in "the centres of population". Francis Dalby – who had himself been based at Doune – felt that a house near Edinburgh would help the Society "get within reach of the right contacts such as university and theological students", and that in practical terms of retreats, "there was more likelihood of people coming to us if we were near Edinburgh".[20] To some extent it was Iona all over again – the ideal of the prayerful contemplative life in a quiet and secluded location set against what seemed to be the reality of the Cowley Fathers' irresistible attraction to active ministry in the life of the wider Church. A house was acquired at Joppa in early 1946, and dedicated later in the year.[21]

SOUTH INDIA AGAIN

One point on which the Society appeared to be united, however, was matters of church order. In 1943 the Greater Chapter had thrown itself wholeheartedly behind the Superior General when he and his fellow superiors had broken ranks and openly criticised the South India Scheme; and by the start of 1945 the situation was an ongoing cause of grave concern.

15 Miller, *Congreve*.
16 Rose Macaulay (ed. Constance Babington Smith), *Letters to a Friend 1950–52*, London: Collins (1961), 220ff.
17 PC 1944, SSJE/3/2.
18 *CE* May 1946.
19 SSJE/2/7/39.
20 PC 1945, SSJE/3/2.
21 *CE* Feb 1946; Oct 1946.

O'Brien regarded the plans – which had rumbled on after Archbishop Temple's sudden death in October 1944 – "with the utmost dismay". As he saw it, a controversy "on those very fundamentals which must bring confusion and distress to every part [of the Anglican Communion], and may compel many of its faithful children to choose between their ecclesiastical allegiance and their loyalty to truth" had come at the very worst time – "just at the moment when all the spiritual forces of mankind are needed for recovery from the evil which is devastating the world".[22]

The SSJE's standard had long been raised in India; and its practice, by its own lights, was unabashedly Catholic. When the low-church Bishop of Tinnevelly, Stephen Neill, visited Mazagon to administer confirmation in 1944, Cyril Whitworth was impressed with his zeal and the way "he talked to all my boys quite splendidly"; but also felt that Neill's eyes had been opened by his visit to St Peter's.

> He dined with us at the Mission House and saw all the hostels, and I think he was very glad to have been with us, although I think our church left him speechless when I showed him the altars, tabernacle and confessionals, etc [...] I do not think the bishop had ever come face to face with a fully equipped catholic church within the Anglican Communion.

Anglo-Catholicism, despite having been in the ascendancy in the Church of England in the 1920s and 1930s, had by no means become the only expression of Anglicanism either at home or in the Empire. Whitworth noted astutely that "the moment one leaves England and comes to the mission field, one realises there is going to be a great Protestant Evangelical Church quite capable of standing up to the Roman Catholicism spreading equally through the world."

> [I]f we are asked to judge them by the words of Our Lord— 'by their fruits shall ye know them' it would be impossible to give an answer. I still feel that before re-union can take place Evangelicals must come face to face with the catholic faith within the Church, and we have to make some further understanding concerning Protestant Christianity which we know here is not dying but living.[23]

It fell to John Williams, as Provincial Superior in India, to lead the charge on the ground. After the Anglican representatives on a joint committee set up to consider proposed amendments to the Scheme failed to insist that Methodist and Free Church ministers be episcopally ordained before being allowed to minister in the new United Church, he was exasperated. "I feel more and more convinced of this", he wrote. "People do not listen to arguments; and very few are capable of understanding the points at issue."

> Personally I could not remain in communion with a Church that actually *consummated* the union which is now contemplated in the Scheme [...] I believe the time has now come for setting up the necessary machinery for 're-establishing a body which could claim with justice to be the legitimate heir of the authentic

---

22 *CE* March 1945.
23 Whitworth, 16 Aug 1944.

principles of our Church of England' [i.e. the non-Juring body alluded to in *The Unity of the Faith*].

Essentially the issue revolved around the fact that one aspect of the Scheme as it stood "would undoubtedly make it possible even for an unbaptized minister to celebrate Holy Communion in the United Church. There is no safeguard against it." O'Brien railed against "the final and complete surrender of principle" by the Anglican representatives on the joint committee. He spoke of "how grievously those Catholic principles by which alone the Anglican Communion has been held together have been betrayed"; and prophesied that the Scheme would have the effect of "introducing into the Anglican Communion a seed of disintegration and decay which whether slowly or swiftly will surely do its work".[24]

The now-elderly Cary was differently robust, and sought to apply to the present crisis the past lessons of the religious life.

> It is *constancy* to the very deepest of its secret principles that the Church is needing if she is to mediate Salvation and divine Peace to the world. As in the Religious Life constancy to the Community tradition is one of the main sources of strength to ensure stability, so in the larger field of the Catholic Church strict fidelity to the Apostolic tradition of Faith and Order is an essential element needed to secure health and life.[25]

As O'Brien observed, the subject was of "additional importance to those who have, or support, missionary work in India" – and not least for the SSJE and its Missionary Association.[26] The stakes were high: the work of the Society's missions, to say nothing of that of its associated sisterhoods, was enormous. The profession in 1940 of Albert Rangaswamy had been the small fulfilment of six decades' prayerful longing for the raising up of indigenous vocations to the Society – despite the fact that he had himself originally come to India from Mauritius.[27] It was not lightly, then, that Williams and Lonsdale Wain wrote to the Bishop of Bombay, Richard Acland, to protest that they seemed to be "in the tragic situation of finding that our Church has committed itself to a doctrinal position which we believe is contrary to Catholic Faith and Order".[28] Williams foresaw disaster.

> [A]n authority like Bishop Gore taught that the Anglican Communion would break up if it departed from its traditional practice in this matter of the ministry, and now a province of the Anglican Communion has committed itself to a complete approval of a departure from this practice and consequently to the doctrine behind that departure.[29]

---

24 *CE* March 1945.
25 *CE* July 1945.
26 W. B. O'Brien SSJE, *Vital Issues*, Pax House (1944).
27 Slade, *A Work Begun*, 76; *CE* Sept 1968.
28 Williams, 7 March 1945.
29 Williams, 21 March 1945.

There would be other consequences, too. Marcell Conran, whose work among soldiers in the First World War had borne rich fruit in the context of his promotion of his *Chaplets of Prayer*, and whose letters home from the front had been full of the challenges and horrors of the warfare in France, died at the end of the year.[30] By the time of his death the Society had already turned its thoughts to how it might effectively minister to soldiers returning from the conflict; and Bernard Wilkins – who, like Conran and Wigram, was awarded the Military Cross – felt that, despite the positive experiences of some of his brethren in the field, the actual statistics made for generally depressing reading.

> The thousands of British soldiers who have passed through the Hospitals in which the Society has sent me to minister, may fairly be considered a cross-section of British society in almost all stations of life. About 75% of those who pass through are marked as 'C. of E.' Of these, so far as I have been able to judge, a very small number indeed make any practice of prayer or worship, and a still smaller number frequent the Sacraments.

He noted further that "many are so occupied with their own cares, that they have no interest in religious thought; a very large number seem to be entirely uninstructed in the facts of the Christian faith. A very small minority seem to have any active connection with parish life in England."

At the same time, Wilkins saw clearly that almost to a man his patients were "friendly and responsive to the visits of a priest"; that many spoke warmly of the chaplains they had encountered at the front; and that they were "for the most part kind and unselfish to one another". They were, he felt, on the whole receptive to the truths of Christian faith; he could see "no future for the Church in England, if those who present Her to their people do not show Her at the height of Her beauty and glory, with the supernatural life of prayer and Sacraments placed most firmly in the foreground".

> It is true that disunion must always be a great obstacle to the acceptance of the Faith. But unity built upon compromise, or surrender of what is the essence of the Catholic Faith can be no true unity [...] To give away one fact, in order to secure some degree of agreement with other workers in the same field, is, I believe, wholly unsound.

That the Society was committed to Christian Unity in its broader sense was not in question: year after year the January edition of the *Cowley Evangelist* introduced the Week of Prayer of Christian Unity with an exposition or a sermon on the subject, and its readers were exhorted to enter wholeheartedly into the intention. But there was a world of difference between unity and compromise.

> If the Church is to be shown as She is, the Body of Christ, in-dwelt by the Holy Ghost, to our men of the Services, I feel quite certain we need to strengthen and not to weaken our hold on every revealed article of belief. To my mind, the first step must be, not the lowering of our standards of faith and practice, to meet the

---

30 *CE* Dec 1945.

expressed wish of those who, however sincerely, reject certain portions of what we believe to be revealed truth, but the raising of those standards.[31]

The situation in Bombay had been serious enough for the Superior General to spend the first part of 1947 in India. When the Captain invited him onto the bridge of the *Strathmore* on his way out he was bowled over by the advance of technology.

> [I]t is indeed a place of wonders. *Without leaving the bridge* the depth of the sea can be ascertained at any point, or continuously traced on paper, showing the contour of the ocean bed. If fire breaks out it can be ascertained where it is and if I remember rightly the proper sprinkler valve set working. The ship can be set on its course and kept on it without touching the wheel by some contrivance which is affected by the rotation of the earth. Perhaps the most interesting object was the indicator, which shows the working of Radar.[32]

In South Africa, meanwhile, the introduction of general airmail was making its mark. Writing from St Cuthbert's, Arthur Hill noted that "we are brought very close through the airmail; Father Superior General's last letter, written on December 30th, reached us on Jan. 8th. A letter from an adjoining parish, arriving on the same day, was written on Dec. 14th."[33] When Forbes Bishop returned to Cowley on furlough in 1948 he was taken to Santa Cruz airport by George Huntley, who saw him "safely emplaned on his trip to England in a B.O.A.C. Lancaster".[34] Wain returned similarly: "it took him only twenty-one hours. What a revolution in transport methods."[35]

On the other side of the Atlantic, Wilkins found himself in Boston at the same time as some of the brethren from the house at Oyama: "I can now say good-night in Japanese."[36] When Francis Rumsey sailed on the *Queen Mary* in 1949 the journey took only 5 days. He stayed at the Wentworth for a couple of days as the guest of Miss Arnold, "a good lady who lives there and shows great kindness to any of our Society who happen to visit New York"; and while waiting for the train to Boston at Penn Station he was captivated "by a wonder that I cannot refrain from mentioning".

> The waiting passenger can step behind a curtain into a small and brightly lit recess, where he (or she) sits down and places a coin (in value about 1s) into a slot and looks straight forward. At the end of about one minute three copies of his photograph slip out of the machine into his lap. There's no one there. It's all done by 'Photomatic'. What *would* be the effect of having one of these machines at S. Cuthbert's.[37]

The world was changing; but although at Poona on the feast of the Holy Name the local Methodist minister was spotted "joining heartily in the hymn as we

---

31 *CE* Aug 1945.
32 O'Brien, 11 Jan 1947.
33 Hill, 9 Jan 1947.
34 Huntley, 25 June 1948.
35 Huntley, 23 Nov 1948.
36 Wilkins, 14 Sept 1948.
37 Rumsey, 24 Feb 1949.

went round in procession",[38] in matters of ecclesiology the SSJE continued to hold fast to its principles. After the General Council of the Province of India, Burma & Ceylon approved the South India scheme in early 1947, the Superior General thought that "the moral responsibility of our English authorities for their inadequate criticisms of the provisions of the scheme, their lack of warning as to the consequences of its departure from Catholic principles, their positive encouragement of their supporters and for their gravely misleading assurances that Anglican principles were safeguarded is beyond denial."[39]

FRATERNAL CORRECTION

In General Chapter just before the impending inauguration of the new Church of South India, it was declared that "under no circumstances can members of the Society accept, or counsel others to accept, the ministry of any Bishop, Presbyter or Deacon of the proposed Church."[40] The *Cowley Evangelist* went as far as to provide a form of words drawn up by the Council for the Defence of Church Principles, which "we should recommend to all to all parish priests who share our convictions that they should insert in their parish magazines, and display in a prominent place on their Church Notice Board".

IT IS WRONG

for any communicant of the Church of England to receive Communion from one known not to have been ordained by a Bishop. To allow this is contrary to the principles of the Church of England as found in the Prayer Book.

FOUR DIOCESAN BISHOPS HAVE LEFT THE ANGLICAN COMMUNION TO ENTER THE NEW 'CHURCH OF SOUTH INDIA'

In this body it is allowed to receive Communion from those who are not priests. The four Bishops are leading their dioceses into this body. They have publicly stated that they will themselves receive Communion from ministers not ordained by a Bishop.

THEREFORE NO BISHOP OR PRIEST OF THIS BODY CAN BE ALLOWED TO MINISTER THE WORD OR SACRAMENTS IN THIS CHURCH.

Signed.....................................
Rector or Vicar.

"The need at the present moment", concluded O'Brien, "is that all Catholics should unite in a firm stand for the principles of the Church which are threatened. There are times when it is cowardly to avoid controversy. Timidity and silence when we ought to speak may be as unfaithful to the cause of truth as acquiescence in error."[41] Paul Couturier himself concurred from Lyon, and wrote to the Superior General assuring him that "I have suffered with you in

---

38 Williams, 28 Aug 1948.
39 *CE* Oct 1947.
40 GenC 1947, SSJE/2/7/103ff.
41 *CE* October 1947.

all that is sorrowful in the affair of the United Church of South India. Your suffering is our suffering. Every union of compromise works against true union among Christians."[42]

In the end, however, the Church of South India came into being without the Church of England having decided whether it recognised it as part of the Church Catholic; and the Lambeth Conference of 1948 failed to come to any clear understanding on the matter. Michael Yelton notes that "the outcome in this country was a classic compromise designed to get all those involved, particularly those who had threatened to leave if intercommunion were established between the two churches"; and, although there was some protest on the ground,[43] the threat of general secession in England receded as time passed.[44]

Furthermore, when the Central Council of the Society finally met – after the vicissitudes of war had delayed the preparations for its first meeting until 1948 – it was clear that, while the English congregation of the SSJE had been willing to take a firm stand in the matter of the South India Scheme, some – or rather, one – of its public pronouncements had caused considerable controversy. The American Superior, Granville Williams, was "most grateful for the efforts which had been made by the English congregation, and in particular by the Superior General, to avoid the tragedy they feared". Although he did not think that the members of the Society should feel bound to shrink from controversy, he cited "special dangers".

> If a Father were involved, especially a Superior, care needed to be taken that it was quite clear that it was an individual Priest who was speaking and that he did not speak for the Society as a whole. Therefore the greater was the necessity for members of the Society to play their parts in these matters, the greater was the need for safeguards in order that pronouncements on such matters should be in accord with the mind of the Society.

His concerns, perhaps inevitably, revolved around the threat of secession implied by *The Unity of the Faith*, and he felt that "on such occasions a Father should feel obliged to consult his Superior, and a Superior to consult his Council." O'Brien laid out his own position clearly, noting that a Superior could neither "escape the responsibility of his position nor always be free to consult continually with his chapter".

> It was impossible to be always bringing up these delicate and controversial questions to the brethren; but he had summoned a conference for this purpose [in 1942] so that they should not be left in ignorance; and at this the whole subject was fully and frankly discussed.

The Superior General was not, then, entirely free to act unchallenged – either in his nominal oversight of the Society as a whole, or in his *de facto* governance of the English congregation – a principle that went back to the framing of the Statutes for the first time in 1884, and to Congreve's teaching that the

---

42 Paul Couturier, 1 March 1948: *CE* April 1948.
43 *CE* June 1948; Huntley, 7 Dec 1948; Williams, 3 March 1949.
44 Yelton, *South India*, 12ff.

questioning of a Superior was acceptable because it was "within the framework of helping the brethren to grow in holiness that authority must be exercised, not simply in an arbitrary fashion because the Superior has authority".[45]

The proceedings seemed to suggest that the other congregations felt that
O'Brien had exceeded even the authority of the Superior General in the South
India business, and in the end the Central Council decided that a statement
should be circulated to the whole Society on the matter, which – although it
was passed unanimously – effectively distanced the SSJE from the thunder of
the preceding years.

> There must always be differences of opinion within the Society itself as to the
> wisdom or safety of the particular plans brought forward, and for this reason
> it is important that members of the Society involved in such discussions should
> make it plain that they speak only as individuals and not as official representa-
> tives of the Society [...]
>
> The Father Superior if engaged in such discussions would do well to consult his
> Council as to any measure to be taken or statement to be issued, as well as other
> members of the Society whose opinion would carry weight [...]
>
> If the occasion should ever arise where in any Congregation of the Society it
> should be thought necessary to withdraw from communion with a part of the
> Anglican Communion (which God forbid) [...] a meeting of the Central Council
> shall be called.[46]

Only eight years after Williams had led the American congregation in praising their English brethren for "united and unswerving fidelity",[47] in the first
meeting of the Society's wider governing body – a forum which O'Brien had
himself nursed into being ten years earlier – he had stood on his rights and
exercised fraternal correction of the Superior General.

The English congregation had effectively emerged from the years following
the Second World War as the senior branch of the Society in name only. In terms
of the wider Society's governance and direction it had become only *primus
inter pares*; while the Superior General's precedence in relation to the other
congregations had become one of honour, rather than authority. It might be
argued that the situation was merely a restating of the complicated and sometimes strained nature of the relationship between the English and American
houses that had first been manifested in the late 1870s. Five years later, the
second Central Council – which had on its establishment been intended to
meet at Cowley[48] – met in America instead.[49]

Anglo-Catholicism, too, was itself at a point of flux. The horrors of the
Second World War did not drive people into church in the numbers that
had been observed in the years after 1918; and the Anglo-Catholic Congress
Movement, which had been the rallying-point of the 1920s and 1930s quietly

---

45 Miller, *Congreve.*
46 CC 1948, SSJE/4/1.
47 Williams, Otis, Viall, Banner, 15 July 1940.
48 SSJE/2/6/419.
49 *CE* Aug 1953.

fizzled out. Even within the SSJE the decline was palpable: in August 1946 five branches of the Cowley, Wantage & All Saints Missionary Association were without Secretaries – including Oxford Central and Oxford South-East – and fourteen were defunct. The latter category included some in areas that had in the past been Anglo-Catholic strongholds, most notably in London and on the south coast – parishes which John Betjeman described as having been in the vanguard of the Congresses, with their "South Coast salvo of incense-guns".[50]

As William Davage has observed, "that there was a Congress in 1948 at all, albeit more modest in scale and ambition, might be regarded as a notable achievement"; but in the end the movement's parameters and purpose had shifted so significantly that the 1948 Congress was the last.

> The world had changed and so had the relationship between Anglo Catholicism and the Church of England. Liturgical and ceremonial innovations, or recoveries, and not least in vesture, had permeated into parishes of relatively moderate churchmanship. The parish communion was becoming more established as the principal act of Sunday worship. What had once seemed extreme and contentious achieved greater acceptance. More priests of some degree of Catholic sympathy were appointed bishops. Others did not see the point of fighting old battles in a new context and extended a degree of toleration and, sometimes, tacit acceptance. It appeared that working within the Church establishment brought greater benefits than defying it.

He concludes that "by accepting a tolerated place within a comprehensive economy, falling into an establishment embrace, the Anglo-Catholic missionary edge was blunted; its aims were watered down, [and its] practices and disciplines became increasingly compromised".[51] It was left to some in the Society to make their own stand over the Church of South India: Edmund Ruck-Keene's name disappeared from the Chapter Book between the Provincial Chapter at the end of 1945 and the Greater Chapter of summer 1946, and from Crockford's in 1947.

Others, however, found that their bluff had been called. In India Williams stayed at his post and died in communion with the Archbishop of Canterbury in 1951; but his adaptability had extended beyond spiritual qualms and into the temporal. In August 1948, he was the only European guest at a luncheon party at Government House at Poona – "a stately mansion built in the full glory of late Victorian imperialism" – after which he noted that "the old order has given place to the new".

> The entertainment was strictly vegetarian and non-alcoholic. It was odd to sit in the great banqueting hall, with the portraits of British sovereigns, and viceroys and governors, looking as though they did not quite know what to make of it all.[52]

While other members of the Society struggled to reconcile themselves with an independent India, however, he "accepted the changes wholeheartedly and

---

50 *CE* Aug 1946; Betjeman, *High & Low*, 37.
51 Davage, "The Congress Movement", 528.
52 Williams, 28 Aug 1948.

gave himself to the work of giving a Christian interpretation to the new and popular concepts of independence, freedom, and the right demands of God and Caesar".[53]

O'Brien, meanwhile, retired as Superior General in 1949 "at his own request".[54] He was the longest serving of any of his predecessors or successors, and the Greater Chapter expressed its gratitude for his "long and unremitting service".

> The period has included both the years of the recent world war with all their special difficulties and problems, and the years of perhaps even heavier difficulty which have followed. The Society owes to him, under God, a very great debt of gratitude for his service and prays that God's blessing may rest upon him in richest measure during the years that he may be spared to us.

ROWING BACK

Francis Bruce Dalby was duly elected in O'Brien's place. He had served as Master of the Novices since 1947, was one of the English congregation's assessors on the Central Council, and came to lead the Society at a time of change and realignment. Although Colin Stephenson described the SSJE as "a society, which, to the astonishment of many Roman Catholics, managed to combine the special virtues of both their active and contemplative orders in one packet",[55] Dalby had not recently shrunk from regarding it as "an active community".[56] When Gerrard Pulley, whom he had appointed Assistant Superior General, was sent on a tour of the missions in 1950, he observed that "we are bidden to go out from our cell to our external work as from the place where God dwells with us in the assurance that he goes out with us to that work undertaken for his glory."

Although towards the end of O'Brien's tenure the Superior General's office had been proved to be no longer one of unlimited jurisdiction, it had nevertheless become a position of international significance within the life of the Anglican Communion; and through its new Central Council the SSJE's life had maintained a tangible breadth of action by the time Dalby assumed office. Pulley's tour was part of that breadth: he was going "to visit and encourage our brethren in the mission field, struggling to maintain their life in threes and fours, amidst the problems and perplexities of their surroundings".[57]

The subjects discussed by the first Central Council had been wide-ranging and ambitious: they included whether the former custom of the brethren moving cells at Christmas in honour of the Incarnation should be resumed; the procedures to be followed in future when members of the Society might be called to the episcopate; whether or not the English brethren should resume the practice of adding a fourth knot at the opposite ends of their girdles from

---

53 Slade, *A Work Begun*, 28.
54 *CE* Oct 1949.
55 Stephenson, *Walsingham Way*, 104.
56 PC 1945, SSJE/3/2.
57 *CE* Dec 1950.

the other three once they were professed – a custom "given up as meaningless" years earlier, but still practised faithfully in America and Canada; and the desirability of giving the lay brothers a vote in the election of their Superior.

The Central Council resolved to recommend that "vote and place in the election chapter for the Superior of the Congregation should be given to lay-brothers, with the provision that the number of lay-brothers permitted to vote should not exceed one quarter of the professed fathers". The English congregation adopted the proposal in Greater Chapter of 1949, shortly after electing Dalby to the Superior Generalship. He had himself been vocal in favour of the development, arguing that "a religious community was a family governed by their elected Father. Therefore all ought to be gathered together to take their full share in the election."[58]

It also fell to Dalby to temper O'Brien's belligerence on the ongoing matter of the Church of South India, whose relationship to the Church of England had yet to be settled by Convocation; although his position on the matter was essentially the same, and he upheld the ban on those Anglican clergy who had chosen to enter the Church of South India from ministering in the Society's churches, "believing that they have made a grave error of judgement".[59] At the same time he was clear that "it is not our business to sit in judgment on our fellow priests. It is simply a matter of applying certain inescapable principles of Church Order, which do in fact exist, whether people recognize their existence or not."

He emphasised that "it is absolutely essential we should get our minds perfectly clear on this most momentous question, and not be sidetracked from the main issue by muddled thinking or misplaced enthusiasm. The whole future of the Anglican Church is at stake."[60]

> This is the truly momentous and far-reaching issue, with which the whole Anglican Church throughout the world will be confronted in a matter of months. It demands the earnest prayer of all faithful Church people. Presumably there are none of us who do not desire whole-heartedly the reintegration into one whole of the sundered fragments of Christ's Body, the Church; but we do not desire ill-advised short cuts to that great objective, which would involve the surrender of fundamental principle, and only make confusion worse confounded. This is the great danger that faces us.[61]

By October 1954 the danger was drawing ever closer as Convocation prepared to discuss the matter. The issues had not changed: "however favourable a view competent theologians may take of the present Episcopal Orders of the C.S.I. and however much one may admire the work that the Church is doing in India, [or] the high hearted idealism that inspires its leaders, the fact remains that ministers who have not received episcopal ordination do at present perform the same functions and are regarded as on an equality with those who have."

---

58 CC 1948, SSJE/4/1.
59 *CE* June 1950.
60 *CE* July 1950.
61 *CE* Aug 1950.

If therefore the Church of England enters into a relationship of full communion with it, it will proclaim for the first time in its history to the whole world that it does not regard episcopal ordination as necessary, but only expedient. This may be the private opinion of many of our clergy now; but it has never hitherto been the official teaching of our Church, as set out in the Prayer Book Ordinal. It is important we should all get our minds quite clear on this point; and we must be prepared to maintain our position both with firmness and charity.[62]

In March 1955 the Anglo-Catholic Council released, through the Church Union, a statement printed on card for churches to display "in view of what appears to be a campaign waged at the present time to secure that the Church of England should enter into full communion with the Church of South India". It stated clearly that "in no circumstances [...] could we acquiesce in a situation in which the Church of England was in full communion with any Christian body, the ministry of which was not exclusively commissioned by episcopal ordination." Both the Superior General and his predecessor urged "our Priest Associates, members of the Fellowship of St John and other friends" to stand fast and explain to others "the need for the assertion of this fundamental Anglican principle which is so gravely jeopardized at this time".

Yelton has called the course steered through Convocation in July 1955 by the committee charged with presenting a report on the South India business "a careful path through treacherous waters". The committee was chaired by the elderly George Bell: it included prominent members such as the Bishops of Durham and Exeter, Michael Ramsey and Robert Mortimer; Eric Kemp; and – significantly – the Superior of the Community of the Resurrection, Raymond Raynes.

Raynes had himself signed *The Unity of the Faith*; but the committee's conclusion was, in the end, "likely to be acceptable to most of those involved". Yelton summarises its position in five points.

   (i) full intercommunion was not possible until 1975;
 (ii) the orders conferred by the CSI since 1947, that is by bishops, should be regarded as valid;
(iii) the bishops and presbyters of the CSI, when in England, should choose between church or chapel and not move between the two;
(iv) no presbyter of the CSI could celebrate at an altar in the Church of England unless he had been episcopally ordained.
 (v) no difference would be made between those who prior to 1947 had been Anglicans and those who had not: this was the most significant change introduced in 1955.

This effectively "provided a means whereby those who had originally been so opposed to the CSI could get themselves off the hook on which they had hung themselves"; even though really "nothing had changed between 1947 or 1950 and 1955 when the committee reported, save that tempers had had time to calm".[63]

---

62 *CE* Oct 1954.
63 Yelton, *South India*, 18ff.

Dalby was relieved that there would be no immediate intercommunion, and now noted that "as far as can be discerned, no essential principle of catholic order has been abandoned".[64] A new letter, subscribed to by the Superiors of the same communities who had signed *The Unity of the Faith*, was circulated at the end of 1955.

> We do not think that, reviewing the whole situation, there is reasonable ground for thinking that the Convocation decisions represent a weak betrayal of either Catholic or Evangelical aims; certainly they do not in any way promote the idea of Protestant Federation. Rather it is a delicately balanced temporary solution to avert disaster. Its unsatisfactory nature is inevitable in the present difficult condition of the Church of England. Judged in this way, we would assert our conviction that it leaves Catholics in a stronger position than they have been in since the negotiations for union in South India began.[65]

Other remained unconvinced. O'Brien was soon challenged by Walton Hannah – who would himself become a Roman Catholic shortly afterwards – to act upon his vigorous public statements of the 1940s. Hannah claimed that by then O'Brien "had no intention of seceding", and summarised their conversation in *The Anglican Crisis: The Church of South India* in 1957. "When asked in what way circumstances had changed since the pamphlets were published", wrote Hannah, "he replied, after a long pause, 'I suppose I've changed my mind.'"[66]

Whether Hannah can be relied upon on this point is open to interpretation: Henry Brandreth OGS noted in his personal copy of *The Anglican Crisis* that he "would be sorry to trust the author of this tract with my pocket book, or to have to trust at any point to his personal integrity."[67] Nevertheless, Hannah's wider point stood. Much of the fire had been taken out of the Council for the Defence of Church Principles with the early death of Dom Gregory Dix in 1952, after which it had been subsumed by the Church Union;[68] and while O'Brien had thundered in the heat of the battle, along with many others he had in the end failed to enact any of the consequences that had been threatened a decade earlier.

In the opening stages of the South India controversy the Society had joined the fray clad in the shining armour of Catholic faith and order, with its Superior General at its head – the Bishop of Kensington, Cyril Easthaugh, declared in 1950 that "God alone can know how much the Church of England, and indeed the whole Anglican Communion, owe under Him to the Society of St John the Evangelist"[69] – but at the end of what had become the defining crisis of Anglo-Catholicism in the 1940s and 1950s, the SSJE left the field, with many of its comrades, as something of a paper tiger.

---

64 *CE* Aug 1955.
65 *CE* Dec 1955.
66 Walton Hannah, *The Anglican Crisis: The Church of South India*, London: Catholic Truth Society (1957), 16.
67 PH.
68 *CE* Sept 1953.
69 "The Great Commandment", *CE* January 1951.

20

COMINGS AND GOINGS

Contemplation and action; the heavenward gaze of prayer, the earthward gaze of compassion; these must be the marks of the Cowley Father and Brother who is trying to walk in the steps of St John.

—Bernard Dashwood Wilkins SSJE[1]

At Cowley the various ups and downs of the domestic aspects of the life of the Society of St John the Evangelist went on as usual as the 1950s dawned. The church was redecorated and retiled, after an appeal was made to the "numbers of people throughout the world who would be glad to associate themselves with this task of redecoration of a church that has had and continues to have contacts all over the world with people from many different lands".[2] Fluorescent lights were installed – the local authority had condemned the ancient wiring[3] – and soon afterwards the domestic quarters were rewired, with plug sockets being introduced into individual cells.[4] The Librarian pleaded for his brethren to "show a more complete knowledge of the alphabet than is always apparent" when they returned their books; and the garden continued to flourish – although there was concern about the future of the bees when the elderly local enthusiast who had faithfully tended the Society's hives left Oxford after having inherited a baronetcy.[5]

In the midst of the ongoing busyness, however, the passage of time could hardly be ignored as the Society entered its ninth decade. Godfrey Callaway's death in 1942 had been followed only a few years later by that of Gerald Ley, which severed another link with the original Society of St Cuthbert at Tsolo. Thomas Bignold, Marcell Conran, Henry Bull and Henry Chard all went to their reward as the 1940s progressed; and the chantry list for the years that followed the Second World War was crowned by Edward Trenholme's death in 1949, and that of Lucius Cary in 1950. Another generation had passed from the scene: and a discussion at Provincial Chapter in 1952 – presided over by the newly-appointed Assistant Superior General, Christopher Bryant, Francis Dalby being in India – touched on the burial arrangements for members of the Society who died at home.

---

1 Wilkins, *With Wings As Eagles*, 3.
2 *CE* Feb 1956.
3 PC 1951, SSJE/3/2.
4 PC 1952, SSJE/3/2.
5 PC 1952, SSJE/3/2; Sir James Thorold, Bt (1887–1965).

It had already been decided that when the plot in the parish churchyard was full the brethren would be buried at the Rose Hill cemetery in East Oxford; and by 1952 the pented crosses that marked the Society's graves in the parish churchyard were in urgent need of preservation from decay. Replacements were now expensive to commission, but it was agreed that the matter would be reviewed when the new plot began to be used. The cross to mark Callaway's grave at Tsolo had been carved in the mission workshop to be identical with those at home;[6] and by the time a letter from Ley appeared in the *Cowley Evangelist*, describing its dedication on All Souls' Day 1945, his own was being prepared.

Ley had been a novice with William O'Brien, who spoke of his "precious memories" of the "mature disciplined religious" with whom he had shared the novitiate after his community had been subsumed into the SSJE four decades earlier.[7] Br Maynard's church at St Cuthbert's was extended in Callaway and Ley's memory, with the addition of "an apsidal chancel and vestries".[8] After Bull died in early 1947 the new church of St John the Evangelist at Kaya Mandi, in the suburbs of Stellenbosch, was dedicated as his memorial by Archbishop Russell Darbyshire.[9] Since 1935 the SSJE had buried its members at a rate of about one a year – to which attrition had also been added the small number of those who had left.

In hindsight, it may be tempting to view what must have appeared at the time a relatively mundane piece of business – coupled with the deaths in the 1940s of some of the Society's leading lights of its second generation – as an easy indication of decline. The numbers of voting brethren in fact remained just shy of 40 for most of the 1940s and 1950s; although when in 1952 an elderly Priest Associate wrote to ask whether the Society might resume its former practice of calling on associates in any neighbourhood they might be visiting, which had in the past been encouraged, it was felt to be impracticable.[10] Decline had set in; but at this stage it was not manifested obviously in the professed members. It lurked – far more dangerously – in the novitiate, which by the end of 1952 numbered only four.

Three Chapter decisions at the turn of the decade pointed to an increased elasticity in the Society's approach to its requirements for membership. The first was the admission in 1949 of Claude Beasley-Robinson as an oblate. He had taught Percy Wigram's nephews at Eton, and in retirement had been clothed as a novice. O'Brien felt that he had been an ideal postulant: "a person of quite outstanding humility. It was remarkable that when he might have gone into honourable retirement, after many years' service at Eton, with ample resources and many interests and occupations, he had set all that aside." He had, however – in the course of his long Ignatian retreat before his clothing – discerned that Beasley-Robinson was not at that stage called to the Society. At the same time the Superior General felt that he was certainly called to the priesthood, and quite genuine in his desire to live "a special life of prayer and

---

6 Hill, 5 Nov 1954.
7 *CE* March 1946.
8 *CE* Aug 1951.
9 Savage, 29 Dec 1947.
10 PC 1953, SSJE/3/2.

355

hardship in ministry to the rich". It was decided that he should be admitted as "an Oblate of the Society, living under the three vows, in dependence on the Society, but with a greater freedom of movement and manner of life than would be possible for a professed Father". His not-inconsiderable Eton pension would be handed over to the Society, which "would provide him with a home and such pecuniary assistance as was needed and would be consonant with his vow of poverty".[11] By then a priest, Beasley-Robinson eventually received regular profession in the Society in 1958.[12]

The second decision concerned Br Gordon. As the minutes of the Provincial Chapter of 1950 noted, "hitherto it had always been taken for granted that Br Gordon's disabilities made it impossible to be ordained". Miller observes that Benson might well have called the situation "an opportunity for humiliation and emptiness";[13] but despite his missing arm his brethren felt that Gordon continued to demonstrate a vocation to the priesthood. Eventually the Society had approached the Bishop of Oxford "to ask whether such disability was an absolute ban or not". Kenneth Kirk had replied, channelling Joseph Phillimore, to say that "the Canon Law enjoins that if the man in question be not afflicted with disabilities of such a kind as to make it impossible for him to exercise his ministry without grave risks, then he can be dispensed by the Bishop." The South African brethren were all in favour of his being allowed to proceed; and the Bishop of St John's, Theodore Gibson, was satisfied that despite his missing limb he would be able to say mass safely and decently, and wished to call him to Holy Orders if the Society consented. His suggestion was welcomed unanimously by Chapter, and soon afterwards Br Gordon emerged from his layman's chrysalis as Fr Shrive.[14]

The third decision was almost invisible, and yet most remarkable of all. In the course of the General Chapter of 1948 a discussion was introduced on Statute LXXV – it had also been on the Central Council agenda that year[15] – relating to cases of readmission. It was agreed that it should be recast to read:

If a Professed Father or Brother should ask to be allowed to return after release or dismissal, he shall be readmitted to the Society only after a period of probation in the Mother House, or in some other House of the Society, as the Superior may direct; and by consent of the Chapter of the Congregation as expressed by a majority of those present in person, or deemed present by their votes. A Father thus received back shall be incapable of holding office or attending Chapter, unless the Chapter at some future date determine otherwise.

It was hardly the return of the Prodigal Son. During his probationary period the returning man would effectively live in penitence – "according to the Rule of the Society, though not wearing the habit, taking his place next below the junior professed Father or Brother [in the case of returning lay brothers] present" – and although he would resume the habit if readmitted to the Society,

11 PC 1949, SSJE/3/2.
12 SSJE/2/7/206.
13 Miller, *Congreve.*
14 PC 1950, SSJE/3/2; *CE* Dec 1950; Horton-Smith, 10 Dec 1950.
15 CC 1948, SSJE/4/1.

a returning priest would not necessarily be given a place in Chapter; and even if he was, he would not necessarily be granted a vote.[16]

The Central Council minutes suggest that the discussion had its origins in Canada, and that the matter had also been discussed by the American congregation;[17] but the outcome had an immediate application in England. In the 1949–50 edition of Crockford's, Leonard Strong – the same man who had been expelled from the Society in 1923 after his disappearance from St Edward's House, the suicide of one of his penitents, and his marriage to another – appeared with permission to officiate in the Diocese of Oxford, with his given address as "The Mission House, Marston Street". The circumstances of his return – and not least the question of what had become of his wife – remain unclear, and were probably dealt with by O'Brien in his later Superior General's addresses, which do not survive.

Strong's obituary tactfully only referred to "a long period during which he was separated from community life"; and he had still not been readmitted to Chapter when he died ten years later.[18] The accusations laid against him by the then Superior General had been very grave indeed; and his return to Cowley seems to have been mooted only after Bull's death in 1947. Coupled with the sensitive handling of Beasley-Robinson's situation and the Society's championing of Shrive, the readmission of Strong pointed to a developing generosity of latitude which in previous decades had been absent.

More obvious change presented itself in 1952, when the Greater Chapter approved – by no means unanimously – the wearing of a black scapular to protect the habit, but not to be considered part of it; and also removed the obligation of wearing "the regulation hat",[19] the sight of rows of which in the hall had delighted Colin Stephenson on his first visit twenty years earlier.[20] Over a decade later the *Oxford Mail* observed that although "the old, and often-battered, shallow-crowned hats have given place to more rakishly-worn berets" – they had been chosen with Dalby's encouragement[21] – the Cowley Fathers still retained "their noted 'do it yourself' hairstyles".[22]

The memory of the Founder continued to cast its spell. When Mildred Woodgate was commissioned to write her biography of Benson, concern for his reputation was paramount: O'Brien noted that "as it was the story of Fr Founder, she need not insert details of the early difficulties and dissensions in the Society's development". Although Bryant felt that Woodgate should be provided with all the relevant material, which could be "used with discretion"; Dalby had to reassure the Chapter that in any case "nothing would be published without our full agreement beforehand".[23]

In 1952 the Superior of the Community of the Resurrection, Raymond Raynes, approached the Society with the suggestion that Geoffrey Curtis CR

16 SSJE/2/7/108.
17 CC 1948, SSJE/4/1.
18 *CE* Dec 1959.
19 SSJE/2/7/154.
20 Stephenson, *Merrily on High*, 52.
21 *NS* 9/90.
22 *Oxford Mail*, 6 May 1966.
23 PC 1950, SSJE/3/2.

might write a study of Benson's theology. Dalby and Bryant were enthusiastic; but Chapter disagreed – Sydney Wallis particularly recoiled from the idea of a member of another community undertaking such a work – and moved that "in regard to the enquiry about a possible theological study of Fr Benson by Fr Curtis, C.R., the Chapter would very much prefer that the Fr Superior General, if he should see fit, should urge Fr Wain to undertake this work".[24] Bryant had already pointed out that Lonsdale Wain could not be spared from India; and no book appeared. It was not until 1980 that Martin Smith brought out *Benson of Cowley*.

Meanwhile, the death of Walter Adams deprived C. S. Lewis of his confessor – he had been one of his penitents since 1940, and dramatised the experience of his first confession in *Perelandra* in 1943.[25] As A. N. Wilson has adroitly noted, "not much imagination is needed to guess what Father Adams would have said about the arrival in Oxford of a 37-year-old married woman from New York" earlier in the year – Joy Gresham, who would soon become the love of his life.[26] As Jack Lewis drifted away, however, Rose Macaulay was returning in the other direction.

Macaulay had first come into contact with the Society through Philip Waggett. Constance Babington Smith described him as "a stimulating and cheering influence" and, "for Rose, the starting point of an enduring [although interrupted] connection with the Cowley Fathers".[27] The "charismatic" Waggett provided epigraphs for Macaulay's novels *The Valley Captives* (1911) and *The Lee Shore* (1913), and Sara LeFanu goes as far as to describe him as her "mentor" at that stage in her life.[28] Through him she had become a regular penitent of Cary in the early years of the First World War; but she had later entered into a relationship with a married former Roman Catholic priest, Gerald O'Donovan, and had scrupulously separated herself from the sacraments.[29] After his death she kept up a correspondence with Hamilton Johnson, whom she had known slightly at St Edward's House, but who had been in America since 1916. Its effect was to bring her back to the Church of England in general, and to the Cowley Fathers in particular.

Until her death in 1958 Macaulay and Johnson corresponded on wide-ranging matters, but frequently their letters – or at least hers, which alone survive – dealt with spiritual affairs. Edited by Constance Babington Smith and published as *Letters to a Friend* and *Last Letters to a Friend* in 1961 and 1962 respectively,[30] they cover a relatively brief period of eight years. Nearly forty years after she had last been to St Edward's House, Macaulay was able to write that "I feel I belong to the S.S.J.E.", and was soon using the Hours of Prayer for her personal devotions. She felt that the Society had "long dogged her steps";

---

24 PC 1952, SSJE/3/2.

25 C. S. Lewis, *Perelandra: a novel*, London: Bodley Head (1943).

26 A. N. Wilson, *C.S. Lewis: A Biography*, London: Collins (1990), 175; 239.

27 Constance Babington Smith, *Rose Macaulay*, London: Collins (1972), 74.

28 Sarah LeFanu, *Rose Macaulay*, London: Virago (2003), 85; 95.

29 cf J. V. Guerinot, "The Pleasures of Rose Macaulay", *Twentieth Century Literature*, 33:1 (Spring, 1987).

30 Rose Macaulay (ed. Constance Babington Smith), *Letters to a Friend 1950–1952*, London: Collins (1961); *Last Letters to a Friend*, London: Collins (1962).

and was soon speaking of her duty to read more Benson: "I suppose I ought to, being S.S.J.E. myself."

Her return to the fold was complete: comments later included "I'm glad I belong to the S.S.J.E."; "has the S.S.J.E ever produced a Father *not* generous, good and full of human kindness?";[31] and the protest that "if I had been church-minded at Oxford, I should have gone to Cowley".[32] She did not necessarily find favour with the whole Society: William Slade read *The World my Wilderness* (1950) on a train, and found himself "so irritated by it that I decided to complete the journey on foot".[33] The correspondence, however, represents the only surviving example of letters written to a member of the Society by one receiving ghostly counsel – of which there must have been thousands – although it must be noted that by the time of their writing Johnson was a member of the American congregation, and that Rose Macaulay may hardly be regarded as an average sample.

THE MIXED LIFE

The dispensation from the shovel-hat may be viewed as part of a process of deepening self-awareness in the Society's life as the 1950s progressed. Bernard Wilkins produced his little work *With Wings As Eagles* in 1953, which amounted to the first analysis of the Society's activity since its foundation. He claimed as his muse the "privilege of being allowed to see almost every Province of our Society, *per orbem terrarum*", and it built on his pamphlet of 1950, *The Trumpet Shall Sound*. Like Dalby and Frederick Puller, he emphasised that the SSJE was called to engage in active work alongside its life of prayer.

> Cowley Fathers are not monks nor are they friars; they are mission priests. A monk is a religious who belongs to an order given to contemplation, to the worship of God, expressed in the Liturgy and Divine Office, the "Opus Dei", the work of God, and to such labour of the head or hands as may be allotted to him in his abbey. The friar is more "mobile" then the monk, and gives himself to mission preaching and a strict observance of corporate poverty.

"A vocation to the Society of St John the Evangelist", he contended, "is a call to what is known as the "mixed life", to works missionary and educational at home and abroad, securely founded upon the spirit of prayer and contemplation, the Liturgy and Divine Office, which are to be the source of all power and spiritual energy, and the foundation of all active labour".

Through *With Wings as Eagles* we glean an idea of the day-to-day life of the SSJE as lived from the inside in the 1950s. The mother house was the symbolic centre of the whole Society: brethren came and went to lead retreats or to preach; those serving overseas came on furlough for long periods of rest; and

---

31 Macaulay, *Letters to a Friend*, 109; 112; 148; 126; 198.
32 Macaulay, *Last Letters to a Friend*, 40.
33 Slade, 4 Aug 1950.

"here, too, at Oxford, the older and more infirm Fathers are cared for". It was also the home of the English congregation's novitiate.

A man aspiring to enter the Society would spend a few months as a postulant, during which time he would live and work alongside the novices as directed by their Master. If at the end of that period he seemed suited to the life, then he would undertake a month's retreat – which was based on the Ignatian Exercises – at the end of which he would be clothed in the habit. He would remain in the novitiate for at least two years, saying mass daily if he was a priest; or, if a layman, serving at the altar having usually received a new name.

A novice at Cowley in the 1950s kept to a "carefully planned" timetable of the offices, long periods of silent prayer, reading, housework, "walks on certain days", and recreation in the Common Room. None of this could be departed from without the permission of the Novice Master: in this way "the great principles of the Religious Life are learned in the most practical way, by living them". It was training for the Society's diet of "retreats, missions, sermons and the ministry of the Sacraments [...] all founded on the interior life of prayer and recollection".

After profession, his sphere of work would be allotted by the Superior General; but Wilkins was keen to underline opportunity for activity in the local area as well as overseas. This was not only spiritual work, but also involved a large amount of outreach to the local children – although inevitably all the youth work had its "roots in Church life". The Society's schools were by now Secondary Moderns; there was a Catechism class; and a number of clubs continued to meet in the enlarged St John's Hall. With this development Wilkins was particularly pleased.

> No longer are table tennis players unwittingly involved in a boxing match which has somehow strayed from its own side of the room; no longer does ringcraft – if you can be said to have it without a ring – consist in dodging the stove, and trying not to hit non-combatants.

A little way down the Iffley Road, the Gladiator Club had also come into its own. Founded shortly after the end of the war to help the various members of the boys' and girls' clubs who had been away with the Forces "to re-settle into the life of the Church on their return", it was now functioning as what David Hemming called "an experiment in Christian witness". Full membership was limited to regular communicants who accepted "the obligation of attending Mass on Sundays and the Greater Holy Days"; while associate membership was "open to other young adults who have no connexion with any Christian body at all". It was hoped that in the course of the club's numerous recreations the former category would exert influence on the latter by example, shored up by "the presence from time to time of the vicar or a father or brother of the Society in one of the rooms – as likely as not bent low over the dominoes board".

> Again and again, sometimes sooner, sometimes later, first one and then another begin to show interest in this religion which had previously never come their way but which now they see means a lot to a crowd of ordinary friendly people who are in most ways much like themselves. From this it is only a series of small

steps to join the discussions on religion to come now and again with a full member to church, and in time to ask one of the priests who are now well known to them for instruction or preparation for confirmation.

It was, thought Hemming, "a field of real though hidden missionary activity", despite "its somewhat fearsome name" – which had come with the building when it was purchased for the purpose.[34]

The rest of *With Wings As Eagles* provided a potted history of each of the areas of the Society's work, and in the case of India and South Africa a vignette of what its next steps might be. Wilkins observed that "it has always been our aim in the Indian Mission work to encourage Christians to bear responsibility, and stand on their own feet".

> A development to be expected, both in Bombay and Poona, is the placing of Indian parishes directly under the Diocese of Bombay. For years we have been working with the clergy of that Diocese, always in close touch with the Bishop in regard to Mission affairs; now the time seems to have come for our people to take their full share in Church life, not so much as children of a mission, but as responsible members of the Diocese.[35]

It had been a while coming, of course. When disaffected members of the Indian Navy had half-heartedly mutinied at Bombay in February 1946, John Williams and George Huntley had had a bird's-eye view of the action from the flat in which the latter had taken up residence, for ease of ministry in the dockyards, at the top of the headquarters of the Missions to Seamen on the Ballard Estate.

> They had hauled down the White Ensign, and some of them had hoisted the Congress flag [although the leaders of the Congress party were quick to disassociate themselves from the mutineers[36]]. They had their guns trained on the Taj Mahal Hotel and the Bombay Yacht Club. Meanwhile the naval barracks and shore establishments in Bombay had gone on strike in sympathy with the ships. They were besieged by British troops, and desultory firing was going on.

On his way back to the Mission House Williams was among the many Europeans to be jostled by hostile crowds, and had his topee snatched; but the unrest ended relatively quickly.[37] The next day he lunched with both the Bishop and Archdeacon at the Yacht Club.

> There were all the poor little ships of the Indian Navy – sloops, mine-sweepers, and so forth, and each of them was displaying a very large black flag, as a sign of unconditional surrender. There was something mournful and rather sinister about all this funereal drapery in the brilliant sunshine; the club people

---

34 *CE* Feb 1956.

35 Wilkins, *With Wings As Eagles*, 2; 6ff; 34.

36 Percy S. Gourgey, *The Indian Naval Revolt of 1946*, Hyderabad: Orient Longman Ltd (1996), 57.

37 Anirudh Deshpande, *Hope and Despair: Mutiny, Rebellion and Death in India, 1946*, Delhi: Primus Books (2016), 66ff.

sitting about sipping their after luncheon coffee, and few hundred yards away the Indian Navy doing penance for its folly.

He shuddered to think "what a horrible tragedy there would have been if owing to some mistake, or failure in the negotiations, these deluded young men had begun blazing away at the city". He noted that "most people seem to feel that the ratings had real grievances"; but laid the blame firmly at the feet of Jawaharlal Nehru: "because of his violent and provocative attacks on the Government, and his wild threats of revolution, unless India is immediately granted independence". He was also quite clear that the events had "a very tragic side for anyone who loves India and Indians, and hopes to see this great country independent and strong and happy".[38]

The unrest in Bombay had continued: when the community at Mazagon spent a week at Marve Sands for the short Michaelmas holiday in 1946 it was the "largest Camp we have ever had"; and in addition to the entire contingent of 90 boys – "we allowed no boys to go home for this short holiday owing to the disturbances in the city" – and Monty the mission dog, the brethren took the additional precaution of taking with them the house cat, Barnabas, "who thoroughly enjoyed it".[39] At patronal festival at Poona in August, while Viscount Wavell was encouraging Nehru to form a government "composed wholly of Indians" in preparation for the impending separation of India and Pakistan, the three sacred ministers at High Mass were all Indians who had been formed by the Society;[40] but when the see of Bombay fell vacant in 1947, Richard Acland having resigned "saying he realised how unhappy he would be under the new changes which must come", Wilkins was clear that "we cannot think of any Indian priest who would be equal to so high an office".[41]

Indian independence came into being on 15 August 1947, and Wain wrote from Poona to say that "the new flag was solemnly unfurled and saluted" at Panch Howds.

> At midnight the church bells were rung, joining in with sirens and hooters all over the city; and then they rang out the new National Anthem, *Wande Mataram*. The tower was lit up with electric bulbs, right to the top, it must have been seen for a great distance and the flag was flying from the lightening conductor on top. The flag is almost the same as the old Congress flag – horizontal stripes of saffron, white, and green.

All across India a similar ceremony was repeated: Paul Scott described the fictional scene at Pankot in *Staying On*, the coda to his *Raj Quartet*. Lily Smalley cried "all through that terribly, lovely moment when the Jack was hauled down inch by inch in utter, utter silence";[42] while the non-fictional Wain told of "one old lady who came to condole with me and assure me that it was all wrong! From the days of Queen Victoria the 'sahibs' had been so kind to her.

---

38 Williams, 16 March 1946.
39 Whitworth, 8 Oct 1946.
40 Williams, 18 Aug 1946.
41 Wilkins, 5 Nov 1946.
42 Paul Scott, *Staying On*, London: Heinemann (1977), 171.

She actually wept!"[43] Cyril Whitworth took a dim view of the approach to independence taken by the local Jesuits, with whom he was on otherwise good terms, but who were "frightfully sensitive on the question of patriotism".

> [T]hey want the schools to have ceremonies of hoisting the new national flag. I pointed out to them that as it was not our custom to hoist the Union Jack, it would be rather pointless suddenly to develop an enthusiasm for flag-waving, but they assured me they were having the flags made. When I suggested that Independence Day might overshadow the Assumption, they seemed quite indifferent; at all costs they want to win the approval of the Congress leaders.[44]

There was no such prevarication at Mazagon, where on 15 August the new Bishop of Bombay, Bill Lash, was received early and solemnly at St Peter's before presiding over High Mass at the Throne. Like so many of his predecessors he was no stranger to the Society: he had worked at Poona since 1932. Lash had asked for a school holiday throughout the diocese in celebration of his enthronement a few days earlier, and was roundly cheered by the boys on his way to breakfast in the Mission House.[45] Whitworth later had to deny "stoutly" the boys' suggestion that a new mission dog, William, had been deliberately called after his episcopal namesake.[46]

The Society watched the development of the new India closely. After Mahatma Gandhi was assassinated at the end of January 1948 Williams wrote of the plumes of smoke visible from the roof of the Mission House at Poona, where at Sadashiv Peth the Brahmin quarter was ablaze.[47] "When will this sad country be happy and prosperous?" asked Huntley, who had attended the memorial service for Gandhi in the Cathedral the day after his death.[48] Whitworth's observation on the cusp of Holy Week was that the imposition of civil discipline following the assassination had led to "the best Lent that I can remember during these years in India, and this has been the experience of all the English-speaking Churches", coupled with "the awakening of the people as regards the necessity to support their own Churches now that Government have withdrawn all grants".[49]

To many Indians the Cowley Fathers remained a welcome presence: Whitworth noted that while two years earlier "Quit India" notices had been everywhere, since independence "there is not the slightest doubt that there is a great reaction towards Britain and I think all hatred of English people has simply died".[50] Williams found the first Indian Governor of Bombay, Raja Sir Maharaj Singh – who had spent his formative years at Harrow and Balliol – to be "a genial person, and very 'broad-minded'". He was sympathetic towards the Society; and his wife, the Rani Saheba, who was given to "sudden kindly impulses" – which sometimes manifested themselves in impromptu visits

---

43 Wain, 18 Aug 1947.
44 Whitworth, 19 July 1947.
45 Whitworth, 15 Aug 1947.
46 Huntley, 13 May 1948,
47 Williams, 8 Feb 1948.
48 Huntley, 3 Feb 1948.
49 Whitworth, 20 March 1948.
50 Whitworth, 15 April 1948.

to the mission hospital at Poona – made a point of establishing connections with the Wantage Sisters. When she attended High Mass "most devoutly" for patronal festival at Panch Howds in 1948, Williams' description of the service could easily have been written by Charles Gardner five decades earlier.

> The Church of the Holy Name is always a wonderful sight on a great festival, with all the altars shining with candles, and the gorgeous colours of the women's best saris, and the crowds of servers and acolytes. The singing, with the organ reinforced by violins, trumpet and saxophone, was tremendous, and whenever there was an interval one could hear the crowing and wailing of numbers of babies in their mothers' arms.[51]

One of the "friendly and homely" Governor's hobbies particularly endeared him to the brethren: "he keeps a ventriloquial doll, as does Wilkins, for the amusement of the young".[52] When he visited the mission in September 1948 the boys were "a little disappointed not to see any uniform, and no sign of a sword"; but he "left us all with a feeling that we really were a part of this newly born India and had some recognised work to do in it".[53] By the end of the year the gubernatorial visits to the missions had become "quite informal"; and Whitworth was enjoying the use of the Governor's Bathing Box at Malabar Point, to the consternation of the new Indian Comptroller of the Household.[54]

A world away from Government House, on a packed train from Bombay to Poona, Slade was struck by the friendliness of his travelling companions; and when he was trodden on by "a none too clean foot", which left a footprint on his white habit, he was "pleased at the way so many brown hands stretched out to clean me".[55] His own interest in Hinduism led him to the observation that well-schooled Hindu children were encouraged "towards a spiritual and self-sacrificing ideal of manhood". His conclusion that "they certainly have not got the Seed; but there seems no reason why God should not be using them to break up and deepen and water our hard Indian soil for the day when He shall be pleased to place it here" put him firmly within the canon of the SSJE's approach to much of its Indian work, which went back to Nehemiah Goreh, and beyond him to Simeon Wilberforce O'Neill.[56]

With the advent of Indian independence also came what Slade later called "a growing movement for independence among Indian Christians".

> Parish priests were no longer content to act as dependent curates to wealthy missionary societies. In schools and hospitals, it became increasingly clear that the staff should be led by one of their own country and the pressure towards this kind of independence grew.

In 1900, with remarkable prescience, Edward Elwin had observed that "fifty years is far enough to look forward in this country [...] by the end of 50 years

---

51 Williams, 28 Aug 1948.
52 Williams, 5 July; 26 July 1948.
53 Slade, 9 Sept 1948.
54 Whitworth, 30 Nov 1948.
55 Slade, 8 Feb 1948.
56 Slade, 22 March 1948.

everything will have changed";[57] while Bull had anticipated the Society's withdrawal from India as early as 1920.[58] Alan Bean became the last member of the English congregation to be sent to serve on the Indian missions, shortly after the recall of Whitworth and before the death of Williams. In 1951 General Chapter had "a considerable discussion" about the Indian work;[59] and in 1953 the Superior General sailed to India once more to take stock of the situation on the ground.[60] Thereafter the Society pursued an active policy of transferring its Indian interests into other hands.

In 1955 St Peter's School was handed over to a board of Indian governors; and in the course of 1956 the brethren in India withdrew to Poona, handing over the Mission House to the school as well. Soon afterwards the SSJE parishes were all transferred to the Diocese of Bombay, with an endowment fund established for their support – at patronal festival at Holy Name on 7 August Forbes Bishop was "asked by the parish priest and Church Council to speak at High Mass on Diocesanization and explain it to the people".[61]

At the start of 1957 Walter Fitch, who had returned from India a decade earlier, felt that in general "those missions which have been successful in developing an Indian ministry, and in which the local church has developed a sense of responsibility for evangelistic zeal, will be the best off." A received tradition of the Society was that Fitch, when serving with the Indian Army before his profession, had arrived at Mazagon "complete with batman, personal servant, and a string of dogs";[62] but now he thought that, if the idea of withdrawal from India was unsettling, "we should ask ourselves whether our heavy paternalism is the cause".[63]

The remaining property belonging to the Society was eventually transferred to the Bombay Diocesan Trust Association on 1 June 1965,[64] along with £10,000 to establish an endowment for its upkeep.[65] It was not for nothing that Slade called his account of the Society's Indian activities *A Work Begun*, for towards its close he presented the Society's withdrawal as part of God's plan for India.

> So came to fruition a slowly-maturing plan by which the Society allowed its own work in India to decrease in order that our Lord's work might increase. By laying down what formed the heart of its life for more than eighty years it prepared itself to respond to the new tasks which we can be sure our Lord will give.[66]

In that light, the winding-up of the SSJE's work in India could be presented as a seed dying in order to live, rather than as the felling of a mighty tree.

---

57 Elwin, 20 March 1900; "Aspirations of the Indian Church", *CE* Sept 1916.
58 Superior General's Address, GenC 1920, SSJE/2/5/1.
59 SSJE/2/7/141.
60 *CE* Oct 1952.
61 *CE* Sept 1956.
62 *NS* 6/81.
63 *CE* Jan 1957.
64 See *S.S.J.E. Work in India: Transfer to the Diocese of Bombay*, Cowley, Wantage & All Saints Missionary Association, no.8: Winter 1966.
65 SSJE/2/8/275.
66 Slade, *A Work Begun*, 123.

But even had independence not come when it did, the Society could hardly have maintained its Indian presence for much longer. Part of this, of course – and Slade himself acknowledged it – was that in the end the attempt to found an Indian religious community had failed, which itself "arose from the fact that the Society never succeeded in attracting a sufficient number of Indian members which would have justified such a modification of its life and rule".[67] Albert Rangaswamy returned to Cowley with the others – "though not without misgivings" – where he died in 1968.[68]

Gathering Clouds

Wilkins also noted, pertinently, that "India has her independence, while African people have as yet but little voice in questions of government".

> Thus our Brethren of the South African Province of Cowley have the delicate task of helping young Africans to their full stature of soul and body, and yet guiding them in the exercise of patience and endurance, so that they may be free from bitterness of spirit.[69]

At the end of 1950 Dalby had spoken of "the various perplexing problems of our work overseas";[70] and in South Africa, where the situation was in many ways more complicated than in India, things were coming to a head. F. L. Cross observed that "a necessary corollary of Incarnationalism is Sacramentalism";[71] and it naturally followed that a necessary corollary of Sacramentalism was Incarnationalism. In India the SSJE had contended for the Sacraments; but in South Africa it soon found itself championing the doctrine of the Incarnation in the face of government policy that came to deny the essential dignity of the human person.

As early as 1905 – the year of the General Pass Regulations Act, which denied the vote to black Africans – William Bevan, an elderly priest-associate of the Society with long experience in South Africa,[72] wrote a doleful letter to his SSJE friends from his post at Kimberley, in the Northern Cape.

> I am beginning to grow old now, and my missionary life is probably drawing to its natural close. South Africa is wonderfully changed since I first came out in 1869. From a very quiet pastoral country, it has become suddenly a place full of speculators and land-grabbers. I cannot say that I like the change – yet, no doubt, it is all over-ruled to the spread of the Gospel and the advance of the Kingdom of God.

---

67 Slade, *A Work Begun*, 118.
68 *CE* Sept 1968.
69 Wilkins, *With Wings As Eagles*, 45.
70 *CE* Dec 1950.
71 "Anglo-Catholicism and the Twentieth Century", in G. L. H. Harvey (ed), *The Church and the Twentieth Century*, London: Macmillan & Co. (1936), 308.
72 See *Life and Work of William Henry Rawlinson Bevan, Canon of Kimberly & Kuruman*, Kimberley: Robert B. Creer and Co. (1919[?]).

Bevan, although he preferred the old rural ways, thought that the result of an increased European presence in South Africa would be the increase of the spread of Christianity; and although this may discomfit modern sensibilities, it was a widely-shared view. What is remarkable about his letter, however, is his comments about what the future might hold.

> What I fear most is the antipathy between black and white men, and the selfishness which tries to get everything for itself and to leave none for anyone else.[73]

At about the same time, the *Cowley Evangelist* lamented "the numerous rash and superficial (and frequently, we regret to say, prejudiced) opinions which are now-a-days so often heard on the subject of the South African native";[74] while George Congreve noted presciently that "the 'Colour Question' begins to loom. It seems to me quite insoluble and to contain future terrible things".[75] Nearly thirty years later Callaway took up a similar theme in his book *The Soul of An African Padre*.[76]

When the Prime Minister, J. B. M. Hertzog, visited St Cuthbert's in 1925 Francis Rumsey mused that "he was given a rousing welcome and send-off; but at the bottom of our hearts there was, mingled with these loud expressions of enthusiasm, a real sense of uneasiness in view of the Native policy of the present Government, of which this great man is the leader";[77] while in 1926 Callaway advocated "an 'Open Door'".

> It may be reasonable to urge that conditions are not yet ripe for any large extension of political rights to the Native, but surely would be unwise, and certainly unchristian, to write in large letters over the future of any people, "Abandon hope, all ye who enter here." Nothing is more certain to incite the spirit of revolt and to keep alive the temper of hostility.[78]

On his way back to South Africa after furlough at Cowley in 1948, Br Gordon (as he then still was) was asked by a fellow-passenger on the *Winchester Castle* what was the sort of mission work in which he was engaged. He was roused by his terms of reference: "I made him realise he had made a mistake when he asked me if I was working among the 'niggers'." It transpired that his interlocutor was on his way to study race relations, so "it seemed a necessary preliminary that he should realise the Africans are people."[79]

The Bishop of Masasi, Leslie Stradling, took a similar position in the pulpit of the community church a few months later. The opportunities for missionary work across Africa – he was making an appeal on behalf of the Universities Mission to Central Africa – demonstrated, he thought, that God was "offering us the chance to make reparation for the evils that Africa has suffered".

---

73 *CE* Sept 1905.
74 *CE* May 1905.
75 Congreve, in Miller, *Congreve*.
76 Godfrey Callaway SSJE, *The Soul of an African Padre*, London: A. R. Mowbray (1932).
77 Rumsey, 25 Aug 1925.
78 "The Native Problem in South Africa and its Challenge to Christianity", *CE* Aug 1926.
79 Gordon, 3 June 1948.

Mr C. S. Forrester, in his latest novel [*The Sky and the Forest*, 1948], has reminded us of the frightful wrongs done to Africa by the cruelties of the slave trade and by the even greater cruelties of European exploitation. In the great modern schemes for the development of Africa [...] God is giving us the opportunity to see that this time the African is put first; that his development, physical, mental, and above all spiritual, is more important than the advantages of his labour to the white man. God give us the faith to recognise His presence and His challenge in these events.[80]

Congreve's grim prophecy about South Africa came to full realisation in May 1948, when the National Party came to power. By the early 1950s the implications of its introduction of apartheid – and particularly the passing of the 1953 Bantu Education Act – had come to dominate the correspondence between South Africa and Oxford. Writing from St Cuthbert's, Alan Young begged for prayers: "the chief need of intercessions just now seems to be with regard to the New Education Act. The leaders of the Church need help to make wise decisions – to buy up what opportunities are left".[81] The Act was roundly condemned at Provincial Chapter in 1954.

The Bantu Education Act, being based on apartheid and racial discrimination, seems to offer just that kind of education which the Bishops, in their Synod of 1953, referred to as being morally wrong [...]

We [...] find ourselves unable to see how the Church can rightly co-operate with the Government in implementing the said Act, either by leasing its buildings for the purpose or in any other way.

We cannot foresee the consequences of our proposed non-co-operation, though we fully realize that they may be very serious.[82]

It was a world away from Congreve's description of the Society's schools in Cape Town only fifty years earlier.

On entering our Schools you are struck with the curiously various sorts of humanity that look up into your face – English, Dutch, German, Jew, African pure Native, Cape coloured folk, and Malay. All these sit side by side, join in the school-prayers and sing together 'Fair waved the golden corn,' with the delicate accent of children to whom English is a new accomplishment.[83]

Apart from the moral issue, the situation was pressing because the SSJE's work in South Africa continued to grow: it had recently opened schools at Nomhala, a few miles to the north of St Cuthbert's, and at Kensington, near Cape Town; and had plans for new churches at Upper Mjika, a few miles south-east of Tsolo, and at Nyanga East, a black township on the Cape Flats. The brethren in

---

80 *CE* Dec 1948.
81 Young, 11 Nov 1953.
82 PC (South Africa) 1954, Witwatersrand Historical Papers, AB1886/P.1.35.1(4).
83 *St Philip's Mission*, 10.

South Africa conferred with others in a similar position,[84] but Dalby noted his concerns in the *Cowley Evangelist* in November 1954.

> A very serious situation has arisen in South Africa through the passing of the new Education Act, which puts all education of Africans under the Ministry of Native Affairs [...] Our own Fathers have conferred about it at St Cuthbert's, and sent us the result of their deliberations [...] There seem to be two possible policies only – either to refuse all cooperation with the Government plan as being fundamentally un-Christian; or to give such a limited cooperation as may seem possible without a surrender of principle. Either way, the situation is most unhappy.[85]

The decision needed to be reached by the end of the year, and by the time Dalby's statement appeared he was already on board the *Richmond Castle* on his way to South Africa. A letter home from Shrive noted that many institutions seemed willing to lease their buildings to the government: "they cannot bear to contemplate all the buildings, on which so many thousands have been spent, standing empty whilst the parents of the children who have been students of these institutions, are taxed to pay for the erection of new buildings".[86]

Dalby was pragmatic: if the buildings in busier areas were not leased to the government, then other schools would be built – and the Society's own buildings would be left vacant.[87] If the Society closed all its schools and refused to lease the buildings, there were places where the government would not bother to build any – and so it became a question of whether nominally segregated education for African children was better than no education at all.[88] In the event, the decision was taken to close the school at St Cuthbert's in protest – being so close to Umtata it was clear that the government would replace it, and the children would still be able to come to the mission as they liked – but to agree to lease the outstation schools and the schools around Cape Town, with the exception of the factory school at Brakenfeld.[89]

Dalby thought, however, that "circumstances alter cases; and each school should be decided on separately."[90] As the Weaving School, which continued to thrive, and the Carpentry Shop, which had declined, were within the mission boundary and liable to government inspection, they were also closed. "We are not prepared", wrote Eric Horton-Smith in April 1955, "to have government control in the Mission [...] We have finally decided to shut the Carpentry and Weaving Schools, and to refuse to co-operate with the Government even in these things". However, permission was sought and granted for the Weaving School and the Sisters' Needlework School to continue in a private capacity.[91] Horton-Smith was resigned to the fact that the Society's educational work in

---

84 Dakers, 1 Sept 1954.
85 *CE* Nov 1954.
86 Shrive, 22 Oct 1954.
87 *CE* Feb 1955.
88 Dalby, 14 Dec 1954.
89 *CE* March 1955. The oversight of the factory school was shared with the factory management, who decided to redevelop the land.
90 Dalby, 14 Dec 1954.
91 *CE* Aug 1955.

South Africa was coming to an end; but that the parochial work run from St Cuthbert's would flourish for the time being. A new church, designed by Shrive himself, had been opened at Ngcele in 1948, increasing the number of outstations to five;[92] and as he wrote, Br Maynard's building at St Cuthbert's was itself being extended and adorned.[93]

The fudge was not ideal, and it was a softening of the robust position taken by the Provincial Chapter; but in the event it was the lesser of two evils in a situation over which the SSJE had no control. It reflected the general position of the Church in the Province of South Africa – with the exception of Johannesburg, where Ambrose Reeves oversaw a wholesale closure of church schools, which Dalby thought "terrifically drastic action"[94] – and the widely-held hope that the government's proposals would be unworkable, and that therefore in the meantime it would be better for the schools to have some link with the Church by which children could continue to receive religious instruction.

The community at Tsolo was heartened by the visit of Geoffrey Clayton, Archbishop of Cape Town, and four other bishops (the rest went to other near-by mission stations) during Provincial Synod at Umtata in November 1954, and their visit gives a glimpse of what the liturgical life of the mission was like: "we had a short solemn evensong [it was a Sunday] and a sermon from the Archbishop. The sanctuary with the five bishops in their copes and golden mitres. Fr Young singing the Office, the six tall candles burning on the altar, the crowded church and the hearty singing of the hymns – all contributed to a solemn and joyful act of worship."[95] The photograph albums deposited at the University of the Witwatersrand show similar contemporary scenes: huge congregations; long processions led by white-robed servers; clergy in vestments and birettas; and clouds of incense wafting through the air.[96]

Inevitably, however, the political situation caused the Superior General – and by extension the Society as a whole – to reflect on the future of the SSJE in South Africa. The announcement of the closure of the mission school had caused a good deal of consternation locally, and Dalby noted that this was because for the first time the local people had been asked to organise themselves into action. The South African brethren felt that "this was a good and necessary test of their ability to develop to adult status in the Faith, instead of having to be nurtured like children."[97] This theme permeated the 1950s: the outlying parishes served from St Cuthbert's were handed over to the diocese, with a long-term plan to hand over the mission itself at some point in the future.

Life in South Africa had been transformed since the days of Puller, Osborne, Waggett, and Congreve; and the effort that it took to reach the outstations from Tsolo had been alleviated to some extent by the acquisition of a Land Rover. But the difficulties of balancing community life with active work that had dogged the Society's early days in Cape Town remained an issue, and the SSJE

92 *CE* March 1948,
93 Horton-Smith, 21 Apr 1955.
94 Dalby, 14 Dec 1954.
95 *CE* June 1955.
96 Witwatersrand Historical Papers, AB1653/Ee1.
97 *CE* May 1955.

now took steps to put its parish work in the Transkei under diocesan over-sight. Nevertheless, Dalby was clear that this "would not necessarily mean our withdrawal if we were still needed to make our contribution to the life of the Church as Religious".[98] The *Cowley Evangelist* wondered in the middle of 1955 whether the schools situation might in some way be a blessing in disguise.

> For over fifty years, both at St Cuthbert's and at Cape Town the management of our schools has been done by successive Fathers of our Society, and it has taken up a large amount of our time and energy. If we lament the loss of our schools, we welcome the time and energy thereby saved, which may now be devoted to occupations more definitively ministerial and pastoral. And we welcome it the more because the situation, in both our Missions, while gloomy now regarding schools, is bright regarding progress in the life of the Church.[99]

The death of Wallis in England at the start of February 1956 severed the last priestly link with the original Society of St Cuthbert at Tsolo – it was handed down that he used to announce his arrival in far-flung locations by blowing a trumpet[100] – but Shrive's description of a retreat at about the same time spoke vividly of African successes since Callaway's work had been absorbed into the SSJE: "Africans, Coloureds and Europeans making the retreat together but more significant still [...] the same mixture of races were in retreat with an African priest conductor".[101] Most eloquent of all was the admission as a postulant of Nelson Nomlala, a black priest who had spent his boyhood at the mission, in May.[102]

The political situation, however, was becoming more sinister. When Clayton preached at Umtata Cathedral's golden-jubilee celebrations later that year and insisted that the Cathedral was the mother church of Christians in the whole diocese, regardless of colour, he was followed by police observers.[103] After Charles Savage died suddenly in December – he had been in Africa for almost all his adult life – his funeral emphasised the mission of the SSJE there: Rumsey wrote that "I did not notice it at the time, but, on reflection, I realize that the Europeans present [...] must have stood back from the grave, to allow the Africans to crowd round it. It was a very moving sight – the striking figure of the Archbishop, in black cope and white mitre, standing at the head of the grave and surrounded by such a dense crowd of Africans [...] Not only did the people ask (and they were allowed) to fill in the grave, but every African present wanted, as they always do, to throw in a little earth."[104]

By Christmas 1956 Shrive and Nomlala were at Oxford: the former once more on furlough, and the latter to begin his novitiate. A comically bad piece of doggerel was read out at recreation on Christmas Day which contained more than a grain of truth:

98 *CE* May 1955.
99 *CE* Aug 1955.
100 *CE* May 1965.
101 Shrive, 7 April 1956.
102 *CE* Aug 1956.
103 Shrive, 8 Sept 1956.
104 Rumsey, 11 Dec 1956.

Of us, the elder is coming back
To tread again an ancient track,
But the younger starts with courage true
To plough for himself a furrow new.

So travellers, to our Oxford home
We bid you both a warm welcome,
And may your coming invigorate
Our House and our Noviciate.[105]

The Society looked to Nomlala to be the first of many indigenous vocations in Africa: in the ever-deteriorating political situation, and after the closure of St Cuthbert's School, the long-term future of the South African province had been thrown into sharp focus.

When the National Government proposed legislation to segregate church attendance in 1957, the bishops of the Province realised that a stand needed to be made. On Ash Wednesday Clayton wrote his now-famous letter to the Prime Minister, Hans Strydom, stating that he and the entire South African bench were "bound to state that if the bill were to become law in its present form we should find ourselves unable to obey it or to counsel our clergy and people to do so. We therefore appeal to you, Sir, not to put us in a position in which we should have to choose between obeying our conscience and obeying the law of the land". Clayton possibly believed that the letter would lead to his imprisonment: he duly signed it, and soon afterwards suffered a fatal heart attack.[106] The people of St Philip's took their turn in keeping watch by his body on the night before the funeral, and the SSJE brethren in Cape Town joined them.[107]

The Society mourned Clayton deeply, but business went on. The church at St Cuthbert's was finally completed, and the Bishop of St John's, James Schuster, consecrated it with full and colourful ceremonial on 24 March.[108] Rumsey made no mention of the gathering clouds in his sermon, but looked to the future with hope.[109] Meanwhile, a pleasing development spoke louder than words when the new church of the Holy Cross at Nyanga East was consecrated three months later by the elderly Sidney Lavis, Coadjutor Bishop of Cape Town. Lavis had been present at the opening of St Cyprian's at Ndabeni in 1901, and had himself consecrated its successor at Langa in 1934. On the latter occasion one of his cope-bearers had been "a small boy called Stanley Qabazi". The same small boy, now a priest, was to be given the cure of Holy Cross, Nyanga East.[110]

---

105 CE Jan 1957.
106 Alan Paton, *Apartheid and the Archbishop: The Life and Times of Geoffrey Clayton*, London: Jonathan Cape Ltd (1973), 280ff.
107 CE May 1957.
108 CE June 1957.
109 CE May 1957.
110 CE Aug 1957.

21

AXES AND HAMMERS

I dare say that some Cowley Fathers of the distant future will cut down the two cocoa-nut palms, and will boast of the great improvement that they have made.

—Edward Fenton Elwin SSJE[1]

In May 1960 the large cherry tree in the south-west corner of the cloister at Cowley, which had always blossomed faithfully in time for patronal festival on 6 May, failed to flower. It was soon found to be dead, and was cut down.[2] To the Superior General the tree's demise must have seemed a portent, for – as a glance at the Profession Book demonstrates – the English congregation of the Society of St John the Evangelist had entered a period of steep decline.

It is impossible to avoid the impression that *With Wings As Eagles* amounted to an attempt to make the work of the Society better known, in the hope of attracting postulants. Bernard Wilkins closed his little book with "a prayer for the increase of numbers of the SSJE", with its proper versicle and response.

> *Ant.* There is no restraint to the Lord to save by many or by few. [Alleluia]
>   V The Lord gave the word.
>   R Great was the company of the preachers. [Alleluia]
>   Grant, O Lord, unto the Society of St John the Evangelist such an increase of numbers as may best enable us to carry out the purposes of our vocation; and whether we be many or few, grant that Thy word may have free course amongst us and be glorified; through Jesus Christ our Lord. *Amen.*

An appendix laid out how people might better unite themselves to the life of the Society: either as one of the new Oblates – a state now firmly established since the admission of Claude Beasley-Robinson – each of whom lived by a rigid private rule "adapted to his conditions of life"; as one of the long-established Associates; as a member of the Fellowship of St John; or as one of the Followers of St John, "who desire to live under a simple rule of life according to the vows of their baptism, in the spirit of St John the beloved disciple".[3]

With Wings As Eagles was followed in 1960 by a prospectus full of photographs taken inside the enclosure: "to take you in imagination over the house and whole establishment and perhaps give you a glimpse here and there of the life that is going on inside". As an exposition of what the house looked like,

---

1 Elwin, 21 Aug 1898.
2 *CE* Feb 1961.
3 Wilkins, *With Wings As Eagles*, 51ff.

how the Society operated within it, and how its day-to-day life was ordered in the late 1950s, it is invaluable. In its own day it amounted to advertising, and Benson would have been horrified;[4] but, as Wilkins openly admitted, the Society was by now "all too few in numbers".[5]

The house at Joppa had closed in 1954, just over a decade after the Society's return to Scotland;[6] and by Michaelmas 1957 it had become clear to Francis Dalby that the SSJE was going to have to cut its cloth in a number of ways. Writing in the *Cowley Evangelist*, he noted that the Society was receiving, as ever, more requests for assistance than it could hope to accede to.

The position at the Mother House, Oxford, is this:

1. We have a considerable number of regular duties in our own church and in convents. Thus we have to provide for roughly ten altars daily and fourteen on Sundays.
2. There are always fathers away from the house on missions, retreats, preaching engagements, etc.
3. Most of our elderly fathers are in residence at Oxford, and these are liable to be too infirm to be used for outside work.
4. Our own chief act of corporate worship is the High Mass at 11 on Sundays.

For all these reasons we are unlikely to have priests to spare for mere supply-duty during interregnums, holiday periods, etc.; and the first two reasons apply similarly to our branch houses in other places.

The continuing busyness of the members of the Society is borne out in the *Cowley Evangelist*'s monthly notices of missions, retreats, and preaching engagements being undertaken, and Dalby was concerned that the SSJE was in danger of losing sight of its essential vocation – a concern that went right back to George Congreve and Basil Maturin's worries in the 1880s.

[W]e are vowed to a life which is very firmly rooted in the daily round of common worship and work within the enclosure of our various houses. From this hidden and partially enclosed life, we are sent out to fulfil diverse works, evangelistic, missionary, teaching and pastoral; and from these works we return to take our place again in the corporate life of the Society. We should be untrue to our vocation if we allowed ourselves or others to assume that we used our houses merely as places from which to go to perform an active ministry. The most vital part of our work is the offering of our lives in prayer and sacrifice within the enclosure. All our outside activities have to be regulated so as to preserve a true balance. So, although we may not be occupied on external works at some given moment, it does not follow that we are therefore free to go out on supply work. We are 'on duty', so to speak, within our own houses.[7]

Local emergencies were another matter, of course, but Dalby's priorities as Superior General were to re-balance the various strands of the Society's work

---

4 cf *CE* Feb 1915.
5 Wilkins, *With Wings As Eagles*, 4.
6 SSJE/2/7/176.
7 *CE* Oct 1957.

within its needs as a whole. The world was changing – Dalby was the first Superior General to use aeroplanes as a regular means of travel to the far-flung SSJE missions – and so, to some extent, was the Church. Individual brethren began to embrace various innovations, and some found them to their taste: these included evening masses[8] and west-facing celebrations;[9] and at the same time the Society embraced the revised Roman Catholic regulations relating to fasting.[10] Meanwhile, the Fellowship of St John was reconstituted and subdivided to place much of the administrative onus of its organisation on its own lay members.[11]

Privately, some of the brethren recognised the fact that the mother house was "dangerously low in numbers" and that consequently "there was a real danger of losing that tranquillity which was important for both guests and novices, especially for the novices who should not feel an atmosphere of hurry and strain". Many wondered whether the support being offered to sundry women's communities might be scaled back – these included the Community of St John the Divine, of later *Call the Midwife* fame[12] – as most now had their own chaplains; and felt that the time had come to be "firm" with communities who scheduled their daily masses so that the celebrant was obliged to miss saying his office in choir: "the small numbers at Evensong and early Office were a matter of concern [which] needed to be considered in its effect on novices and guests". Most radical of all was David Campbell's suggestion that one of the branch houses might need to be closed to shore up the numbers at home.[13]

If Campbell was contemplating the closure of St Edward's House, then the prospect was unthinkable "except as a desperate measure".[14] In any case, arrangements there would soon be reorganised "to make it possible for others to live in the house who wish to share in the worship, fellowship and spiritual enquiry of the community";[15] after which the *Church Times* would describe it as having been transformed into "the best hotel in London for Anglican clergy".[16]

The situation in South Africa, however, had become a seriously pressing matter. The Society's history there was long and impressive – by way of reminder in July 1950 the reading in the refectory at Cape Town was being taken from Philip Waggett's letters home in the 1890s[17] – but as early as 1913 Godfrey Callaway had identified three "urgent necessities" for the development of the South African work: "(1) Concentration and intensive effort. (2) A carefully-trained Priesthood. (3) Self support."[18]

---

8 *CE* June 1958.
9 Naters, 11 Feb 1960.
10 *CE* Feb 1959.
11 *CE* March 1960; PC 1960, SSJE/3/2.
12 Helen Batten, *Sisters of the East End*, London: Ebury Press (2013), 131.
13 PC 1961, SSJE/3/2.
14 *The Bishop of Oxford's Visitation Charge to the Society of St John the Evangelist*, 28 December 1963, SSJE/2/8 (loose).
15 *Society of St John the Evangelist*, Oxford: S&S Press (1969), 19.
16 "The Changing Face of Cowley", *Church Times*, 8 Dec 1967.
17 Rumsey, 1 July 1950.
18 *CE* Dec 1913.

The vignette of the man whom Dalby called "our Stanley Qabazi"[19] at Nyanga East spoke more clearly than words of the SSJE's tangible success: a new church in Cape Town being run by an African priest whose vocation had been found in and nurtured by the Society's ministry to the local population – and it is worth noting that baptisms at St Cuthbert's in the 1950s were administered in exactly the same way as they had been at Old St Philip's in the 1880s.[20] But the greatest successes had perhaps been at St Columba's Home, and by the middle of 1957 it was in the National government's sights as a "native institution".[21]

Nearly ten years earlier Gordon Shrive had thought that "it does not look very hopeful for the future of St Columba's".[22] The Church of the Province of South Africa, under the leadership of the new Archbishop of Cape Town, Joost de Blank, remained a thorn in the side of the government: when Shrive went to de Blank's summer garden-party at Bishopscourt at the end of January 1958 there were police observers in attendance, and the members of the Cabinet had conspicuously declined their invitations.[23]

Arthur Phalo was clothed as a novice in June 1958, the second African priest testing his vocation with the Society; and a few months later George Dakers – who had spent most of his life in the Society in Cape Town – died. By the start of 1959 the effects of further legislation meant that in Cape Town Francis Rumsey was busy trying to coordinate support for families who were being displaced to the new Native Townships;[24] and soon afterwards the indigenous Sisters of St John the Baptist reopened the Weaving School at Tsolo.[25] Frank Cornner's death later in the year – he had been a lay missionary at St Cuthbert's since 1897 – was another moment for reflection.[26] With two African novices at Cowley, African sisters taking a hand in the oversight at St Cuthbert's, and increasing political tensions across the country, it was obvious that a realignment of the Society's life in South Africa would soon take place.

DRASTIC ACTION

Matters were precipitated by the national demonstrations against the Pass Laws organised by the Pan-African Congress on 21 March 1960; and the fatal shootings of protesters at Sharpeville, and at Langa – where the people of St Cyprian's were cared for by the Society. David Gardner, who was by then Provincial Superior, noted that "those who have been aware of this state of tension have realized for a long time that sooner or later the strain would become intolerable, and resistance on a large scale would manifest itself."

---

19 Dalby, 28 Dec 1954.
20 CE Aug 1958.
21 Rumsey, 18 July 1957.
22 Gordon, 3 June 1948.
23 Shrive, 7 Feb 1958.
24 Rumsey, 24 Feb 1959.
25 Shrive, 22 May 1959.
26 CE Oct 1959.

Part of the resistance – it was unclear whether it was part of PAC policy or the work of individual hotheads – now involved attacks on churches with white connections: the buildings at Kensington had been targeted, and "at Nyanga threats were made that if services were held in the churches on a certain Sunday, churches and parsonages would be destroyed." Qabazi stood firm: he sang mass as usual and the church was full. If nothing else, "the steadfastness and endurance of our African clergy, catechists and people" was encouraging;[27] and at Nyanga East on Good Friday the congregation stood at six hundred.[28]

Dalby was deeply disturbed by the turn of events, and as Superior General it fell to him to decide what course to take. He wrote on behalf of the Society in May 1960.

We are very greatly distressed by the news from South Africa. The disorder affects our work in the locations of Nyanga and Langa outside Cape Town. It is a time of great testing for African Christians of all denominations. They are liable to suffer violence from the police for being African, and violence from intimidators for being connected with Europeans [...]

A considerable number of people both European and Coloured are under arrest simply for holding liberal views and having pro-African sympathies, and under the Emergency Regulations they can be held without trial, without explanation, and without time limit [...] this is an appalling state of affairs in a country of the British Commonwealth, only too reminiscent of Nazi Germany [...]

Until this tyranny is overpast, our prayer needs to be continuous and unremitting, interwoven with all our devotions and activities.[29]

Nelson Nomlala returned to Africa in July 1960. He visited his family at Nyanga before heading to St Cuthbert's: he was seen very much as part of some "definite answers to our prayers for the Mission".[30]

Life at Tsolo continued much as normal: in October James Schuster confirmed 164 candidates at Upper Mjika and 200 at St Cuthbert's on the same day. In Cape Town, however, Leonard Wilks noted that it had been a quieter Christmas than usual, with no bands in the streets or carnival processions.[31] This, as it turned out, was a token of things to come; but in the Transkei things remained buoyant: the churches were packed as usual, and on 14 January Qolombana church – it was served from St Cuthbert's – was consecrated by Alphaeus Zulu, Bishop of Zululand and the first black bishop on the South African bench.[32]

On Good Friday 1961 Rumsey attended the Three Hours at Stellenbosch, and was pleasantly surprised to encounter a familiar face: "Near the front I saw Florence Jwara, now Mrs Ndlebe, wife of the churchwarden. She was a little

27 Gardner, 8 May 1960.
28 Rumsey, 22 April 1960.
29 CE May 1960.
30 CE Sept 1960.
31 Wilks, 26 Dec 1960.
32 Naters, 25 Jan 1961.

girl of twelve in a well-known family at St Cuthbert's when I first arrived there. She is now a grandmother, and after the service she invited me to her house to see the three generations." But the forced removals from Kensington and Windermere meant that the congregation there was greatly depleted on Easter Day.[33] A further readjustment to circumstances became necessary when the South African Republic was constituted on 31 May 1961. James Naters mused that "for many of us it seems sad that we no longer owe any allegiance to the Crown, and even more sad that we are outside the British Commonwealth."[34] In August Phalo returned to Tsolo to take over the outstation work from Shrive,[35] work that continued to increase with the impending completion of yet another new church at Xabane.[36]

Back in Cape Town, at Nyanga West the new church of St Mary Magdalene was consecrated by de Blank with full pomp and ceremony in early November: the SSJE was making its presence felt in the new township, where its church was the first to be built. Even after the people's displacement from their homes, Rumsey was able to describe a rosy picture of the party after the first mass in the new church, with the people enjoying the traditional singing and dancing that attended any African celebration.

> There goes little old Mrs Kali, who was married by Father Bull in Cape Town nearly sixty years ago, attaching herself to almost every group, and merrily and vigorously taking her part in its song and dance. And here comes Mr Alfred Coto, ninety years of age [...] well known to the Fathers in Cape Town for over fifty years; leaning on the arm of his friend, with sparkling eyes, he totters round keeping time with the others of his group, but once only; exhausted, he gets back to his young wife, his third wife, who appears to think perhaps she should not have allowed him to do it.

He noted that they sang *Sak' umz' omtsha* over and over again – "We are building a new home".[37] In the same year Bishop William Wand brought out his *Anglicanism in History and Today*, in which he contended that Richard Meux Benson's "original missionary intention" for the SSJE had been "amply fulfilled".[38]

Devolution soon became a continuing theme, as it had become clear that in South Africa the handing over of the missons' organisation into local hands was becoming increasingly desirable. David Hemming emphasised the point when he visited Tsolo in March 1962: "I tried to underline that as they became independent our relationship would become more and more one between parents and grown up sons and daughters and that God was giving them the great call to manage their own affairs and that he never called people without giving them power to answer the call." But he observed that, as the race laws meant that there was little chance of well-paid employment, they could hardly

---

33 Rumsey, 3 Apr 1961.
34 Naters, 2 June 1961.
35 *CE* Aug 1961.
36 Shrive, 10 Sept 1961.
37 *CE* Feb 1962.
38 J. W. C. Wand, *Anglicanism in History and Today*, London: Weidenfeld & Nicolson (1961), 190.

be expected to be totally financially independent.[39] At the end of the month Nomlala succeeded Rumsey at Nyanga West.

By October 1962, having returned from his visit, Hemming thought that the Society was making a huge contribution to the easing of the racial problems in South Africa. He reminded the Fellowship of St John that "in both the SSJE houses in South Africa there is a fully professed African Father [Nomlala at Cape Town, and Phalo at Tsolo] living alongside and sharing the life and work of the European Fathers", and also that as the Mission House in Cape Town was in a Coloured district, "in its life and ministry we are equally concerned with Africans, Coloureds, and Europeans, irrespective of race".[40] Congregations in the Cape were dwindling as more and more people were moved to the townships; and at about the same time it was announced that St Cyprian's, Langa, and Holy Cross, Nyanga East, were to be set up as independent parishes, and no longer run from the Mission House. "Father Callaway used constantly to say", wrote Rumsey, "that we should always be aiming at handing church work over to the Africans gradually – until entirely [...] If Nyanga West follows, as well it may before long, we shall then have little African work left on our hands, possibly none, and that may be just as it should be."[41]

This was a noble sentiment, certainly, but it cannot be ignored that combined with the difficulties of the political situation was a decrease in vocations to the Society in general, and the increasing age of the still-active brethren. When the Indian and African Provincial Superiors returned to Cowley in November 1963 to discuss the future of the work in their respective provinces, it was in the context of concerns at home that stemmed from a decreasing number of vocations to the Society and a conscious reining-in of its non-essential work. By the time of Gardner's arrival at the mother house to take part in the discussions, the situation in Cape Town had deteriorated still further. Although out in the new townships church life remained vibrant – "when we have a procession we really have a procession", noted Alan Young in October 1963[42] – the large-scale removals to the townships had seriously affected the numbers attending the chapel at St Columba's Home.[43]

A further crisis arose when, in January 1964, and shortly after his return from Oxford, Gardner suddenly died. He was another priest whose heart was in Africa: he had ministered in Gauteng before his profession, had been Superior at Cape Town and at St Cuthbert's, and had been Provincial Superior since 1958. Rumsey described his loss as "a grievous shock": he had been only 54, and the Society might reasonably have expected to have had two more decades' active work from him. The community found some comfort in the fact that he had died on his return to South Africa, and not while he had been in England: "it is not without significance to our African brethren that he should have died in their country: for a priest to lay down his bones in their midst is a real sign that our work is not just that of all migrant visitors but of real friends."

39 Hemming, 3 March 1962.
40 CE Nov 1962.
41 Rumsey, 26 Oct 1962.
42 CE Dec 1963.
43 Rumsey, 7 Oct 1963.

The letters home from Naters, Shrive, Nomlala, and Young give some idea of how deeply shaken the African brethren were by Gardner's death. Again, it is significant that after Naters had sung the High Mass of Requiem at St Cuthbert's on 29 January, the burial service was read in Xhosa, with Phalo reading the lesson, Bishop Zulu leading the committal, and Nomlala reading the prayers.[44] William Slade observed that "it was clear that the time for drastic action had come"; and the Superior General urgently left Oxford for the Transkei, where he intended to discuss with the brethren the future of the Society's work there.[45]

Dalby found St Cuthbert's thriving; but by the end of the discussions it was clear that the Society would have to modify its work in South Africa. "We all agreed we ought now to concentrate our resources on St Cuthbert's and make it a real centre of SSJE life, to serve the needs of the whole Province, as well as doing some pastoral work in and around St Cuthbert's," he wrote in the *Cowley Evangelist* of April 1964.[46] Young would oversee the transition as the new Provincial Superior; and at this stage it was hoped that the Mission House might continue to function in some capacity.[47] Difficulties grew in Cape Town, however, as apartheid took further hold: the brethren were no longer able to board the *nie-blankes* buses to the townships; and so visiting came to involve longer distances covered on foot.[48] Five men from St Cuthbert's fell foul of the authorities, and were imprisoned; and so the SSJE's ministry to Robben Island began again.[49] It soon had to extend its ministry to other prisons also.[50]

Having served as Superior General for fifteen years, Dalby was succeeded in July 1964 by Gerald Carrington Triffitt.[51] Within a fortnight of the election Arthur Pridham was dead; and this juxtaposition perhaps spoke loudly of the situation in which the Society now found itself. Pridham was 94 and had been in vows for 63 years: he had been professed in 1901 and so had been a member of the Society well before the Founder's death. The new Superior General would have to attempt to steer a course between faithfulness to the original ideals of Benson's Society and the practical need for survival in a world that was unrecognisably transformed, and within a Church poised on the brink of a new reformation.

Triffitt saw the same problems as his predecessor, and was candid about the difficulties facing the overseas work.

> Many of our friends will know of the problems which still face us in our work abroad. This is partly due to our shortage of numbers, and partly to the changing situation and the kind of work now needed [...] We ask you to pray especially for the overseas work of the SSJE at this time.[52]

---

44 *CE* Feb 1964.
45 Slade, *A Work Begun*, 122.
46 *CE* April 1964.
47 Wilks, 3 Aug 1964.
48 Rumsey, 5 Aug 1964.
49 Rumsey, 21 Nov 1964.
50 Rumsey, 21 Feb 1965.
51 SSJE/2/8/268.
52 *CE* Dec 1964.

At the same time Campbell arrived in South Africa to see the state of affairs for himself. He was no stranger to the African missions, having previously worked in Cape Town; now he came to judge whether it might be feasible to establish a novitiate at St Cuthbert's, rather than require any African postulants to spend their formational years in Oxford. He was "much impressed" by what he saw, hoped that it might be possible, and compared notes with the Mirfield brethren at Johannesburg.[53]

The future of St Columba's Home remained a pressing issue. Back in 1898 Waggett, in the context of the outbreak of plague in Cape Town and the forced removals that accompanied it, had been quite certain that St Columba's would come through unscathed.

> Whatever happens, and I fancy nothing at all will happen for a long time, the interests of our Home are perfectly safe. For there never can be a *compulsory* moving of the natives, and while they are free to do so, there will always be a perfectly sufficient number of them wishing to enter the Home.[54]

As it turned out, this was wishful thinking. By February 1965 it was clear that the Home would fall foul of the ongoing amendments of the government's Group Areas Act, and would have to be closed – it was decided to sell the site to the local Roman Catholic archdiocese.[55] The chapel was by then the only place in Cape Town which still provided a place of worship for African Anglicans, and Rumsey negotiated an ecumenical arrangement with the Vicar-General, who was only too glad to help.[56] It was a far cry from the heady days of the turn of the century, and in June the new Superior General found it necessary to travel urgently to South Africa for more discussions about the future.

Triffitt returned with the news that had been looming for a while: "we expect to withdraw from the Cape Town house during August."[57] A combination of the ever-intensifying race laws and paucity of numbers meant that the continuation of the work in Cape Town had become impossible: over eighty years after Frederick Puller had arrived on the *Conway Castle* – and while the brethren at Tsolo were baptising babies whose parents had also been baptised there, in some cases by the same priests[58] – the Mission House on Chapel Street was to be closed.

Writing to Bishop Harry Carpenter of Oxford, the new Archbishop of Cape Town, Robert Selby Taylor – himself a quasi-religious, being a member of the Oratory of the Good Shepherd – lamented the impending departure of the SSJE from Cape Town as a "very sad blow to the Church in this Diocese", and asked for Carpenter's advice on a possible replacement men's community to complement the continuing work of the Holy Paraclete Sisters. The Nashdom Benedictines had been suggested, but he worried that they might still be "a

---

53 Campbell, 24 May 1964.
54 Waggett, 10 Aug 1898.
55 SSJE/2/8/273.
56 Rumsey, 21 Feb 1965.
57 *CE* August 1965.
58 Rumsey, 12 July 1965.

little exotic".[59] In the end he asked the Franciscans to come, as "the Diocese has become very dependent upon having a Religious Community of Men, and the loss of the Fathers is going to be a matter of very grievous concern".[60]

The Father Minister General held out little hope of the Franciscans' being able help; but that he could "well imagine how very sad you must all be at the withdrawal of the beloved Cowley Fathers. They must have done a tremendous job – but, apart from that, just being themselves and being there is something that I believe no other Community can replace".[61] By the time of its withdrawal the SSJE had oversight of some thirty outstation churches in and around Cape Town, which they ran with the help of African priests and numbers of catechists and preachers – the successors of the loyal and indispensable men who had helped the Society since the beginning of its work in South Africa.[62]

Some had long links with the SSJE: at False Bay the catechist, Elijah Ngedle, had been a boy at St Cuthbert's thirty years earlier.[63] Frederick Playne thought that the Society was "tremendously indebted to the catechists and preachers who shepherd the various groups"; but also that "it must be difficult for our friends and supporters at home to visualise the vastness of the undertaking which has been developing in the diocese of Cape Town during the course of sixty years."[64] Reflecting on the SSJE's contribution, Archbishop Emeritus Desmond Tutu's recollection in 2016 was that "they did remarkable work".[65]

Schuster hoped that the Society's work around Umtata might be saved by its introduction of a novitiate "to assist and encourage the development of an indigenous South African Order for men rather than to graft on to the existing English Order such vocations as are to be found here". He felt it would be "a tragedy" if the SSJE were not given support in this field, but admitted that he was motivated by his wish to keep the Society in his diocese.[66] Triffitt felt the same. The reason for withdrawing from Cape Town and not from Tsolo was that the Society hoped that "before [the] non-African Fathers withdraw from South Africa there might be a nucleus of an African men's community. At present [January 1966] Fr Nomlala and Fr Phalo are our only African Fathers. The starting of a novitiate at St Cuthbert's was therefore part of our plan."[67]

Nomlala left the Society a couple of years later, however[68] – he reappeared as a member of the Fellowship of St John[69] – while Phalo, echoing Albert Rangaswamy, ended his days in England, having had "no wish to be left as

59 Selby Taylor, 26 Jan 1965, Witwatersrand Historical Papers, AB1363/R20.1
60 Selby Taylor, 17 Feb 1965, ibid.
61 Br David SSF, 23 Feb 1965, ibid.
62 Wilkins, *With Wings As Eagles*, 39.
63 "South African View", *CE* July 1951.
64 "Visits to Cape Town Outstations", *CE* June 1951.
65 Conversation with the author, 26 Feb 2016.
66 Schuster, Feb 1965, Witwatersrand Historical Papers, AB1363/R20.1.
67 Triffitt, 21 Jan 1966, Witwatersrand Historical Papers, AB1363/R20.2.
68 GenC 1967, SSJE/2/8/302; Ramsey, 31 Jan 1968, SSJE/1/4/loose.
69 *NS* 1&2/81.

the sole member of the Society in South Africa".[70] Soon enough, Triffitt was at St Cuthbert's once more to oversee the handing over of the parish work to the diocese, and to admit the first two postulants to the putative Brotherhood of St Joseph.[71]

In December 1968, Christopher Gregorowski was instituted as the first non-SSJE priest-in-charge of St Cuthbert's since 1904,[72] after which Rumsey and Naters both returned to Cowley; while Dalby, who had been sent to St Cuthbert's after leaving office, stayed behind to oversee what little SSJE work remained. Rumsey had been in South Africa for nearly fifty years: he had arrived at St Cuthbert's by ox-cart, but returned to Cowley by motor-car and aeroplane.[73]

SHIFTING SANDS

Benson had contended in 1900 that "the British Empire exists for the benefit of all that come under her sway";[74] but by 1965 his Society had handed its work in India and South Africa to the relevant diocesan authorities, while retaining a modest presence at Poona and Tsolo.[75] Slade was frank about "the events within the Society itself which removed finally all uncertainty about timing" in relation to the end of the Indian work.[76] Even had circumstances in India and South Africa not taken the turn that they did, with hindsight it seems inevitable that the Society would have had to withdraw sooner rather than later.

Although Chapter numbers remained relatively respectable, by the early 1950s the decline in the novitiate at Cowley could hardly have been ignored. There were constant pleas in the *Cowley Evangelist* for prayer for an increase of vocations; and although by 1958 David Campbell, Alan Cotgrove, and James Naters – all of whom would later serve as Superior General in the SSJE's twilight years – had taken their life vows, there were no professions at all between 1952 and 1957. The Novenas for the Increase and Development of the Religious Life continued.

To try and increase the appeal of Cowley to those in the wider church, a number of dramatic reforms were instituted at the mother house. In October 1961 the Society embarked on a thorough and expensive renovation of the guest house:[77] the pointed windows that were very much part of the original building were replaced with the larger square windows that survive today, and the statue of St John the Evangelist – which Mildred Woodgate con-

---

70 *NS* 7/97.
71 *CE* March 1968.
72 *CE* Dec 1968.
73 *CE* April 1968.
74 *CE* April 1900.
75 SSJE/2/8/274.
76 Slade, *A Work Begun*, 122.
77 SSJE/2/7/234; 246.

sidered "the only sign to the passer-by that here was a religious house"[78] – was removed from its niche above the front door.[79]

John Betjeman knew the building well: he had made a point of mentioning his regular visits as an undergraduate in his verse-autobiography, *Summoned by Bells*, only a year earlier: "Failed in Divinity! Oh count the hours / Spent on my knees in Cowley".[80] The *Cowley Evangelist* mused sheepishly that Betjeman "might if he knew what was going on regard us as Vandals"[81]; but as the aim was to let in more light, then perhaps it is fair to say that what was an architectural blunder was at least a practical success on its own terms. The entrance hall was modernised and a new wrought iron staircase introduced, incorporated into which was "SSJE" in large golden letters. In the same year, the mother house finally acquired a small car, for the use of those brethren "who had to travel a good deal where public transport was not convenient".[82]

An approving article in the *Church Times* about the various changes bore the headline "Cowley Fathers are austere, not grim", and in the course of the piece Alan Shadwick emphasised that "everybody who knows anything at all about such things expects the highest quality from a Cowley Father in his particular line of country – best quality goods, though it comes in a plain wrapper with no trimmings." Shadwick made a point of noting that "contrary to report the food is plentiful and good", which perhaps was something of an overstatement; and that everyone seemed to enjoy the lack of easy-chairs at community recreation.[83]

In the wider Church the Second Vatican Council loomed large. From Cowley the Society regarded it as "a matter of vital concern for all Christians everywhere".[84] Dalby himself had been in Rome in January 1962, lecturing on the World Council of Churches – another organisation in which the Society took great interest – and engaging in discussion with members of Roman Catholic religious orders.[85] Reflecting on the stirring events of the year, in Christmastide Slade opined from the pulpit that "future historians may very well look back on this period of Church history as a time when the Church was particularly concerned with her structure, the problem of divisions in her life and the attainment of unity." He went on to say that although those issues were "concerns of great moment", at the same time the "mystery of Bethlehem is a reassuring proof that the Church can function when outwardly all seems against her".[86]

In March 1962 Hemming wrote from Cape Town that the Sunday-evening service at St Philip's was "rather like the sort of Evensong-cum-Benediction that you *used* [my italics] to get in an East-End Catholic Church in London".[87]

---

78 Woodgate, *Benson*, 98.
79 Oxford Planning Department Reference 61/10588/AH: received 14 Feb 1961, approved 11 Apr 1961.
80 John Betjeman, *Summoned by Bells*, London: John Murray (1960), 108.
81 *CE* Oct 1961.
82 SSJE/2/7/235.
83 *Church Times*, 19 Jan 1962.
84 *CE* Nov 1961.
85 *CE* March 1962.
86 *CE* Feb 1963.
87 *CE* Mar 1962.

Liturgical emphases at Cowley had already shifted – and not least in the matter of Sunday morning worship. Home on furlough in October 1959, Rumsey had recalled that

> [t]ime was when, at least in term time, the men's side at the High Mass was quite full; I recollect the sight of a short and slender undergraduate, who later became a famous Monsignor, arriving late, and cap in hand creeping up the nave, peering along each row in search of a vacant place. To-day the vacant seats are by far the more numerous [...] But the people's Mass, with Communion at 9.30, a growth of comparatively recent years, is remarkably well attended with a large percentage of young people, and parents with their children, all taking a lively part in the service.[88]

The "famous Monsignor" was almost certainly Ronald Knox, who recorded that he did "not suppose that there were a dozen Sundays in all my undergraduate time when I did not attend St John Cowley at 11";[89] and who Evelyn Waugh contended was drawn to Cowley in no small part by "the restrained ritual – more sumptuous than Pusey House but still in strong contrast to the profusion of St Barnabas [Jericho]".[90] The verse attributed to Knox about the SSJE may still draw a smile: "The rather-rathers / Go to the Cowley Fathers; / But the whole-hoggers / Go to Allowoggers."[91]

As we have seen, liturgical experimentation had begun already within the Society; but at Michaelmas 1960 the death of Marjorie Close (a pupil of G. H. Palmer's who was herself a distinguished practitioner and teacher of plainchant, and who had studied at Solesmes) stirred memories in some of the older brethren of the days up to the mid-1930s, when St John's Church – both the Sunday High Mass and Evensong on several days a week – had been served by a choir of men and boys.[92] Similar memories were stirred in 1962 when the death Mother Annie of the Sisterhood of the Holy Childhood, ten years after she had gone to a nursing home, brought to an end the witness of her community, which had been intimately associated with the mother house since 1894.[93]

In 1897 the French ecclesiastic Albert Houtin recalled a visit to Cowley, after an acquaintance of his – "[un] ritualiste fervent" – had introduced him to "une communauté anglicane, 'la Société de saint Jean-l'Évangéliste', qu'on appelle souvent 'Pères de Cowley', d'après le faubourg d'Oxford dans leqeul ils sont établis." He attended mass in the community church and was deeply impressed by what he saw.

> Je vis chez eux une liturgie assez digne, presque aussi belle que celle de Solemnes [...] Pour la première fois de ma vie, je sentis que la sainteté existait en dehors de mon Église. Cowley était probablement l'institution la plus mystique de toute l'Église anglicane.[94]

---

88 CE Oct 1959.

89 Ronald Knox, A Spiritual Aeneid, London: Burns Oates (1950), 59.

90 Evelyn Waugh, Life of Rt Revd Ronald Knox, London: Penguin Classics (2011), 112.

91 St Aloysius Gonzaga on St Giles' – then in the hands of the Jesuits, and now the Oxford Oratory.

92 CE Nov 1960.

93 CE July 1962.

94 Albert Houtin, Une Vie de Prêtre 1867–1912, Paris: Rieder (1928), 164. "I saw with them a very worthy liturgy, as good as anything at Solesmes [...] For the first time in my life, I

Thirty years later Henry Bull, as Superior General, advanced the view in Provincial Chapter that High Mass in the community church was "unique, and that it was not possible to alter it much without spoiling it";[95] but by the 1960s the work of the Liturgical Movement loomed large. In 1961 the General Chapter carried a motion "that the Fr Superior General be asked to appoint a committee to explore in further detail, architecturally, musically, and liturgically the possibilities of a conventual mass at a central altar; and that this committee should request Messrs Seeley & Paget, our architects, to create a model with moveable pieces to demonstrate the reconstruction of the choir that would be needed."[96] Shortly afterwards at High Mass the celebrant adopted the practice of only ascending to the altar at the Offertory; and the use of the humeral veil by the subdeacon was abandoned.[97]

Campbell – who the Chapter minutes demonstrate as having been very much in the vanguard of the reforms, first as Novice Master and later as Assistant Superior – gave an idea of some of the other changes that the Society might adopt at Cowley. He approved of a west-facing celebration in the centre of the church – a nave altar was in use for children's masses by the late 1950s[98] – with changes in ceremonial and posture to reflect "a unity of offering, rather than the celebrant standing at the head of the congregation and offering on their behalf". He conceded that that was his personal view, and the *Cowley Evangelist* was at pains to point out that his position was not at that time that of the Society as a whole.[99]

This was something of an understatement. At a conference held in the course Provincial Chapter at the end of 1960 there had been a heated discussion about whether the congregation should be permitted to receive communion at High Mass on Sundays. Dalby observed at its outset that "it was notorious that in Communities, discussion of liturgical problems caused more dissention than even aesthetic questions, but he hoped there would be an amicable as well as a profitable discussion" – which in itself perhaps indicates a tension in the house about the proposed changes.

The thrust was that general communion was desirable; but the discussion also touched on the suitability of High Mass as a corporate act of worship – not to mention the place within it of the plainsong propers – because it might cause people to have "difficulty in following". It was not a universally convincing suggestion: Terence Manson was quick to point out that the children who came to High Mass in the community church managed perfectly well;[100] but the matter of the accessibility of the Society's liturgy being raised in 1960 is all the more remarkable when one considers that only seven years earlier it had wholeheartedly embraced the 1952 Roman Rite Paschal Ceremonies in the community church, which was "substantially the medieval mass" translated

---

felt that holiness existed outside my own Church. Cowley was probably the most mystical institution in the whole of the Church of England."

95 PC Jan 1927, SSJE/3/1/170.
96 SSJE/2/8/241.
97 SSJE/2/8/248.
98 cf PC 1956, SSJE/3/2; *Cowley* (1960).
99 *CE* Oct 1962.
100 *Conference Report*, PC 1960, SSJE/3/2.

into English. "The 'Gloria in Excelsis' is intoned festally", noted the Chapter minutes of 1953, "with bell ringing, if desired."[101] The 1952 changes in themselves, however, were a truncated version of the Tridentine ceremonies; and the General Chapter of 1956 had noted "the simplification of liturgical services, which is being so widely considered now", and begun jettisoning octaves – including that of St John in Christmastide.[102] The Maundy Ceremonies were transferred to the evening in 1964; with Tenebrae being abandoned.[103]

At Easter 1963 a large wooden table replaced the small temporary nave altar, and the Society eventually combined the congregations of the 9.30 a.m. Sung Mass and the 11 a.m. High Mass into one service. Although Campbell felt that the "the elaborate and dignified ceremonial [of the High Mass], and the ancient plainchant music sung by a choir but not by the people as a whole, all help to create an atmosphere of the supernatural", he nevertheless thought that such an atmosphere might obscure the divine immanence. Conversely, the informal character of the Sung Mass might present "the homely Gospel truth" while obscuring some of the mystery. The experiment effectively meant that the only service on Sunday mornings would be Sung Mass celebrated at the nave altar at 10 a.m. Some of the plainsong Propers would be replaced by congregational hymns, the Ordinary would be sung to the Merbecke *Communion Service*, and the members of the community would sit in the nave.[104]

After Seeley & Paget had submitted their report, in General Chapter 1963 Campbell proposed a motion, seconded by Slade, that their plans be adopted. These included the transfer of the high altar to the west of the rood screen, and the discarding of its dossal and tester; the panelling of the east end of the choir in wood and the setting up of a large chair on the top step of the sanctuary, behind a new freestanding altar; and the removal of a number of the return stalls, to enable the organ console to be placed in the choir.[105] After what was tactfully described in the minutes as "a long discussion" Campbell and Slade withdrew the motion, although the Chapter was clear that it was broadly in favour of some changes being made.[106]

It is impossible not to see in these suggestions the influence of mid-twentieth liturgical innovators like Dom Gregory Dix: the copy of *The Shape of the Liturgy* that he inscribed for the SSJE "with fraternal affection" survives in the library at St Stephen's House. At about the same time as Campbell was expounding the possible shape of things to come at Cowley, Dix's own community at Nashdom Abbey set in train a process that saw it abandon Martin Travers's sumptuous baroque high altar with its six tricolour candlesticks and embrace worship around a polygonal wooden table.[107] Campbell conceded that "to many this experiment will appear to be a revolutionary one, and some may be shocked at the prospect of a High Mass at Cowley without plainchant." He reassured his hearers that even if the new service became permanent, daily

---

101 SSJE/2/7/161.
102 SSJE/2/7/192.
103 SSJE/2/8/271.
104 SSJE/2/8/266.
105 SSJE/2/8/247ff.
106 SSJE/2/8/260.
107 With thanks to Dr Petà Dunstan.

Evensong would continue unchanged. He was clear that in the fullness of time the Society would have to weigh very carefully whether such liturgical changes brought about more gains than losses.[108]

Temporary three-year vows were introduced in 1961 for both priests and laymen;[109] and the fully-professed lay brothers were given votes in Chapter in 1963, except on "matters declared by the Superior General, in consultation with his Council, to involve the Faith and Order of the Church".[110] When Richard Burn was clothed as a novice in February 1963, however, he was, as the *Cowley Evangelist* put it, the first for "a considerable time".[111] It is perhaps impossible to avoid pondering whether the liturgical changes of the early 1960s – the offices were also completely overhauled from 1965[112] – were also part of an agenda to make the Society more attractive to potential postulants. At the same time the cover of the *Cowley Evangelist* discarded its calligraphy and rising eagle with wings displayed and expanded in favour of a modern font and abstract artwork,[113] while Hemming reminded readers of the piously vague prayer – "whether we be many or few" – for the increase of vocations to the Society.[114]

As the community prepared for the first festival of the Fellowship of St John with the new liturgical arrangements in place – at which the people were invited to present themselves for communion, as long as they had fasted beforehand; and at which the preacher was Robert Runcie, then Principal of Cuddesdon – Dalby emphasised that "no decision has yet been taken except to make certain experiments", and pointed out that he would welcome "considered comments" from members of the congregation.[115] By Christmas there was also a free-standing altar in the quire;[116] and by September 1963 the single mass on Sunday mornings had become a permanent fixture. The temporary altar continued its peregrinations; but while the General Chapter in July 1965 was preceded by "a Solemn Mass of the Holy Ghost", a year later it was replaced by "a concelebrated Mass of the Holy Spirit with general communion".[117] In the same intervening period Triffitt stopped suffixing his name with "Superior General" in the *Cowley Evangelist*; and the following month the phrase "making Eucharist together" was used for the first time as a synonym for "attending mass".[118] By May 1967 "St John before the Latin Gate" had been displaced by "St John in Eastertide".[119]

"This age does not want flamboyant and baroque architecture," observed Triffitt, a couple of years after his election. "It does not want florid music. It

---

108 *CE* March 1963.

109 SSJE/2/8/242.

110 SSJE/2/8/258; 269.

111 *CE* March 1963.

112 PC 1965, SSJE/3/2.

113 *CE* April 1963. The two-tone artwork was done by Frank Roper (1914–2000), who went on to become a prolific producer of ecclesiastical pieces. It was more expensive than the previous version, which had been in black and white. Ibid.

114 *CE* March 1963.

115 *CE* May 1963.

116 *CE* Dec 1964.

117 SSJE/2/8/276; 284.

118 *CE* Nov 1965.

119 *CE* June 1967.

does not want the ceremonial of a Byzantine or Spanish court [...] It wants the strong simplicity which speaks of the home at Nazareth, of the stark reality of the Cross, and of the Breaking of Bread at Emmaus and of the call 'Follow thou me'."

> [It] is certain that some of the liturgical insights, especially those in which the Roman Church and our own Church have followed the work of great modern liturgical experts, will be for the deepening of worship, and will give a new reality both for ourselves and our congregations.[120]

The Revised Standard Version was introduced at the mother house in 1965; and at the same time the "cursing verses" were excised: the Liturgical Committee was "asked to prepare a list of passages to be omitted from the public worship of the Community". Simultaneously, the brethren engaged with Carpenter's comments about nomenclature; and it was decided that "members of the Society may feel free to use their titles and names as seems appropriate to the occasion."[121]

Nor were the dead exempt from change: the pented crosses in varying states of decay which marked the Society's graves in the parish churchyard were finally removed in 1964, with a general stone marker-cross being placed over Benson's.[122] From 1966 the Society's funerary rites no longer included Matins and Lauds of the Dead, the *Dies Iræ*, or the final Absolutions;[123] while a Chapter motion in 1968 to change the liturgical colour of requiems from black to violet was headed off by Campbell, who successfully moved an amendment that they should instead be celebrated in white.[124]

In all things the influence of "the great modern liturgical experts" prevailed. "There is a changed atmosphere", remarked one of the older brethren a few years later, "and one that is very noticeable to an old priest. I prefer the holy mysteries in the far distance – and now we have brought the altar down! My Christ was Christ the King and now my Christ has to be Christ the Carpenter."[125] Eventually, so that mass could be celebrated facing the people in the choir of the community church, G. F. Bodley's high altar – a signal of the confidence placed in the SSJE by the sympathetic bishops who had subscribed to its cost six decades earlier – was removed. Its enormous and richly-carved alabaster gradine was demolished, and its soaring fittings discarded. In one fell swoop the sightlines and architectural unity of the entire building – in which, thought Peter Anson, "no detail could offend the sensitive taste"[126] – were destroyed.

---

120 *CE* Sept 1966.
121 SSJE/2/8/280.
122 SSJE/2/8/266.
123 SSJE/2/8/286.
124 SSJE/2/8/308.
125 Ronald Blythe, *The View in Winter: Reflections on Old Age*, London: Allen Lane (1979), 303ff.
126 Peter F. Anson, *Fashions in English Church Furnishings 1840–1960*, London: Faith Press (1960), 234.

22

A New Look

Coats and trousers in the street
Form a vesture all complete,
Masking from our wondering eyes
Cowley Fathers in disguise.

—S. L. Forrest, *Parson's Play-pen*

At the start of 1963 Terence Manson complained that the cloaks worn by the members of the Society of St John the Evangelist had an "unfortunate tendency to make members of our Society unduly conspicuous in public".[1] He may well have had in mind the Founder's warning that "the real danger and wretchedness of the religious community is when its dress has become a mark of honour in the world."[2] Nevertheless, when Christopher Bryant raised the question of the wearing of the habit at all in General Chapter a few years later, "a considerable discussion" – a discreet minute-book euphemism – ensued.[3] William Slade had hoped that the cloaks might be replaced by raincoats;[4] which, combined with the Society's parsimonious practice of hemming fraying habits ever-higher, caused the ecclesiastical humourist Stanley Forrest – who was also Chaplain to the Sisters of Bethany – to refer to it in his *Parson's Play-pen* of 1968,[5] after the *Church Times* reported that two Cowley Fathers had been seen "in coats and trousers in the street".[6]

Change had been in the offing, and by the end of the year the Superior General had invited the Bishop of Oxford to make a Visitation of the mother house, and by extension – and from a distance – also of St Edward's House. Harry Carpenter was impressed by "the Society's mood of self-criticism, [which] seems an entirely healthy one", and opened his remarks with what had become an almost customary episcopal panegyric.

> We should like in the first place to express our appreciation of the unique part played by the Society in initiating, developing and deepening the Religious Life for men in the Church of England, and indeed in many parts of the Anglican Communion. A very high standard of Religious observance has been set.

---

1 PC 1963, SSJE/3/2.
2 Benson, *Instructions on the Religious Life*, ii:34.
3 SSJE/2/8/288.
4 PC 1963, SSJE/3/2.
5 S. L. Forrest, *Parson's Play-Pen*, London: A. R. Mowbray & Co. Ltd (1968), 11ff.
6 "The Changing Face of Cowley", *Church Times*, 8 Dec 1967.

Carpenter had shared the worry about "the shortage of novices, postulants and aspirants, though we do not consider that this is yet a matter of grave concern". However, it was perhaps Carpenter's comments, more than any other, which spurred the Society on to further amendment of life.

> [T]he very small number of aspirants in the last two or three years inevitably raises the question why this should be so. One reason, no doubt, is the more clearly defined ethos of other men's communities. Those called to the active life are attracted to the Community of the Resurrection and the Society of St Francis, those to the contemplative life to [the Servants of the Will of God at] Crawley Down. As the oldest community for men, the Society has tended to stand for the Religious Life as such, without further definition.

Carpenter's Assessors for the Visitation were Eric Kemp, the Chaplain of Exeter; and David Allen, who had recently succeeded Arthur Couratin as Principal of St Stephen's House. He went on to observe that in order for the Society "to deepen its own religious life and family unity", the number of outside commitments needed to be reduced. These included preaching engagements, "except for specific purposes in connection with the fostering of the religious life, or in real emergency"; retreat work away from Cowley, "which might be lessened, if the Society could take steps to train suitable secular priests for this work"; and the extensive ministry to the sisterhoods, which could be similarly outsourced. He also suggested that from time to time brethren could be withdrawn from outside work for a year or two, simply to live at the mother house "in order to strengthen its corporate life and family feeling".

Most of all, however, he noted that "it may be that other communities belong more obviously to the twentieth century", and that there was "evidently the feeling that the Rule is rather Victorian and perhaps Puritanical in character, that it may help to create an excessive reserve and isolation".[7] In a letter to Francis Dalby he mentioned that "it would seem more in keeping with present day practice and the usage of other communities if the Fathers and Brothers were known by their Christian names among themselves". Above all he wondered whether the time had come to act upon "the general willingness shown by the brethren for some revision of the Rule".[8]

Although Carpenter did not want "to concentrate attention on the 'image' of the Society presented to the Church and world at large", he thought that there ought to be serious "further consideration of the ways in which the Society's missionary and educational vocation can be lived out in the years to come. The new guest house could well become a focal point of the Society's 'new look'." He also thought that the school buildings, which were now empty – the schools having been combined into the new Cowley St John Secondary Modern Mixed School, of which the SSJE retained the chaplaincy – might even become a conference centre.

> The Society should sponsor conferences for the clergy and for groups of laypeople, e.g. students and schoolboys. Outside help could be called in for this

---

7 *Bishop of Oxford's Visitation Charge*, 28 Dec 1963, SSJE/2/8 (loose).
8 Carpenter, 24 Feb 1964, SSJE/2/8 (loose).

purpose. The Society is particularly well placed in Oxford and should be able to call on University Professors, college Chaplains, and members of Theological College staffs to assist for a morning, afternoon or evening at such conferences.

"This", he thought, "would help to concentrate the Society's missionary and educational work on the spot, by the training of priests and laymen in theology, the spiritual life, and in pastoral and evangelistic concerns. In this way members of the Society would also be brought in touch with current movements in the Church, e.g. adult education, liturgical reform, patterns of spirituality."[9]

By 1963 an active ecumenical agenda had also emerged. The Society was represented at the Requiem for Pope John XXIII at Greyfriars in June;[10] and a number of articles that year dealt with matters relating to ecumenism. Chief among them, unsurprisingly, was the Society's response to the ultimately doomed discussions in Convocation on Anglican-Methodist reunion: Dalby advocated conditional ordination for Methodist ministers, and prayed "that discussion in both churches at all levels may lead us to increasing understanding of one another, and a real desire to be reconciled in Christ, as brothers in the Faith, though now unhappily separated on matters of Order".

Members of the Society visited other denominations: as the *Church Times* noted, "Cowley Fathers do get about".[11] Gerald Triffitt represented the SSJE at the millenary anniversary celebrations at Mount Athos,[12] and later took Arthur Phalo with him to Assisi to attend a joint conference of Anglican and Roman Catholic religious;[13] while George Huntley went to Løgumkloster in Denmark to experience the post-war revival of the Danish Lutheran tradition there.[14] At the start of 1964 the Society was firmly committed to this new agenda.

> Christians everywhere have united in thanking God for the work done by Pope John XXIII and Anglicans have watched the progress of the Vatican Council on one hand and found themselves faced with considering the Anglican-Methodist report at parish level on the other. We are all tending to live in each other's front rooms at present and praying earnestly too, that we shall soon be in the dining-room together.[15]

As the Society embarked upon its agenda of liturgical innovation and active ecumenism, however, the beginning of the final drying-up of vocations was already upon it – although it was not necessarily obvious at the time. In December 1962 Triffitt rebutted a tendency of people to think that the religious life was some sort of waste – a question that "rises to the lips of faithful church people as well as to those of unbelievers".

---

9 *Visitation Charge*, 28 Dec 1963.
10 *CE* July 1963.
11 *Church Times*, 6 Jan 1967.
12 *CE* Aug 1963.
13 *CE* June 1966.
14 *CE* Aug 1963.
15 *CE* Jan 1964.

How hard it is to describe that essential character which alone gives life and reality to a religious community. It is a grace, a spirit, a breath of the heavenly, a glimpse of the eternal [...]

In a real sense they lose all to find all. The life of dedication, of the vows, is necessarily a life of self-oblation. It is, if you like, a pouring out upon the altar. God gives in return good measure, pressed down and running over. If generous sacrifice is a waste, then this is. That was what Judas said of the ointment poured out upon our Lord before his Passion, but the fragrance of that anointing has filled the whole house, and the memory of that waste has filled the world.[16]

But words alone were not enough: it was also becoming increasingly difficult to find suitable domestic staff, let alone professed religious. As early as 1951 it had been "not easy to find the right men through the local Labour exchange",[17] and by September 1963 Bryant was writing plaintively from London to say that he was short of laymen to help with the domestic running of St Edward's House.

We try to make conditions as attractive as possible: Each man has his own room which is centrally heated; the staff room is newly decorated and has TV; five and a half day week; fortnight's holiday in the summer, five days near Christmas and Easter, all with pay; board and lodging provided and starting wage of £6 10s cash. We require men who can do a simple job efficiently and faithfully; a man could also see it as a real work for God. If any of our friends should know of a suitable man would he please write to the Father Housemaster.[18]

David Hemming – he had been at Boston and Bracebridge the previous year and had observed their novitiates as part of his visits – felt that part of the dearth of vocations to the English congregation was because in the past most of the priests of the Society had already been priests when they entered the novitiate; whereas most of the lay brethren had entered as young men and had not sought holy orders.[19]

The advantage of receiving into the community men who are already priests is that they have practical experience of parish life which should be a great help to them in the giving of retreats and the taking of parish missions. The disadvantage is that it necessarily heightens the age at which the great majority of our postulants in England come to try their vocation.

This was a particularly pertinent point; for many of the most distinguished members of the Society in the past – Congreve, Puller, Waggett, to name just a few – had brought their distinctions to the community, rather than having

---

16 *CE* Dec 1962.

17 *CE* Dec 1951.

18 *CE* Sept 1963.

19 An obvious exception to this was Raymond Molyneux, whose late vocation to the priesthood after twenty-five years as a lay brother had been supported by the Society. He was, however, in the final stages of terminal illness when Carpenter ordained him to the priesthood in the Lady Chapel on Easter Tuesday 1963; and his first mass was also his last. *CE* May & Aug 1963.

achieved them through it. It could not be ignored that the English congregation as it stood in 1963 was aging – a lift had to be installed at the mother house in 1967[20] – but Hemming noted that in both the American and Canadian novitiates there was an element of "youth and vitality"; although he felt that "it would be a disaster if we ceased to receive as postulants mature men who were already priests of experience, for they have much to give".

He suggested that the way forward at Cowley was to encourage *"young* laymen who feel the call of this glorious life; and to let it be understood that there would be nothing to prevent any who so wished from offering themselves at a later date for Ordination, though the decision would rest not just with themselves but with the judgement of the Society and of the appropriate Church authorities". In short, Hemming wanted the SSJE novitiate in England to reflect the historic and contemporary models of postulancy found in European monastic life: "Youth is the time for spiritual as well as any other form of adventure, and the Community would benefit by the fresh air that young and enthusiastic postulants would bring in with them."[21]

This was all very far from Richard Meux Benson's ideal of a community of priests living in common, with their domestic needs met by a bevy of professed laymen; but the 1960s were years of flux for both the Church and the world, and the Society was trying to balance its work of expert spiritual guidance with its need for perpetuation and survival. It may have occurred to many that the Founder's own maxim – to which Rosemary Kemsley SLG alluded in *Benson of Cowley*[22] – that no community should survive beyond two generations, lest it lose sight of its original purpose, was prescient.

It is hard – because to his mind the Church of England was Catholic in and of itself – to imagine Benson endorsing the Society's public approval of a young man who "had been to the Orthodox Liturgy on Sunday morning, the Mission House on Sunday evening and Campion Hall on Monday. He was being a typical student and, as a Baptist Ministerial, quite typical of those concerned for Christian unity".[23] In April 1964 Dalby attended the ecumenical conference at Saltley which discussed questions of faith and order, and was attended by "Baptists, Anglicans, Churches of Christ, Congregrationalists, Independent Methodists, Methodists, Presbyterians, Salvation Army and Society of Friends", and Roman Catholic observers. Dalby felt it to have been "well worth while, and a real occasion for thankfulness".[24] Rose Macaulay's Aunt Dot, with her "firm and missionary Anglicanism, with strong prejudices against Roman Catholics, continental Protestantism, Scotch Presbyterianism, British Dissent, and all American religious bodies except Protestant Episcopalianism", would scarcely have agreed.[25]

Elsewhere, concessions were made: in October 1963 the obligation laid upon the Associates of the Society of wearing their distinctive badge was lifted; and in June 1964 their mandatory formal reporting back to Cowley ceased: Dalby

---

20 PC 1967, SSJE/3/2.
21 *CE* Oct 1963.
22 Smith, *Benson of Cowley*, 98.
23 *CE* Jan 1964.
24 *CE* May 1964.
25 Macaulay, *The Towers of Trebizond*, 8.

had been clear that he would "much prefer a personal letter from each associate giving some news of himself and reporting very briefly and generally on the Rule".[26] The Community of the Resurrection followed an identical course for its Companions almost immediately.[27] The regional branches of the Fellowship of St John were further subdivided: area secretaries were appointed, and members were encouraged to approach their respective secretaries as "a first link between themselves and the General Secretary in Oxford". Increased lay leadership (or at least non-professed-lay leadership) within the wider Society seems to have become a guiding principle.[28]

A Turning Point

When Triffitt assumed the Superior Generalship in 1964, things might well have appeared still to be rosy. On 6 August Christ Church was packed with men and women in religious habits, who had come together for the first gathering of representatives of all the religious communities in the Church of England: High Mass was sung in the Cathedral; the Sisters at Wantage provided the choir; and Bishop Robert Mortimer of Exeter preached. Afterwards the Abbot of Nashdom gave a lecture on the modern Benedictine life, and Jonathan Graham CR led an open forum on "The Religious Life and Christian Unity": the enthusiasm for ecumenism and the interest in the ongoing Vatican Council was not confined to the Cowley Fathers.

Triffitt's election, however, had not been straightforward. He had received fourteen votes to Dalby's fifteen in the first round; had just overtaken him in the second ballot; but had only achieved the necessary statutory majority at the third vote. There had been a clear division in the Chapter between those who wished Dalby to continue in office, and those who wanted a change.[29] That change now came quickly. "Most of our communities", mused David Campbell, "were founded in the Victorian age, and still bear something of a Victorian stamp. It is most important that there should be a thorough re-thinking under the guidance of the Holy Spirit of the religious vocation in the church and world of today."

Carpenter's Charge had been heeded; and Campbell's prayer was that "what has already started may lead to a renewal of the religious life among us according to God's will and the needs of the present day world".[30] To a similar end, at the start of 1965 Triffitt outlined his vision for the preparations for the Society's forthcoming centenary. The brethren would reduce their outside commitments and effectively enter into a year-long retreat from June, in order to "give much prayer and thought and discussion to our vocation as a community and to the fulfilment of what may be God's purposes for us in this modern world [...] we shall be for a time specially waiting upon God".

---

26 CE June 1964.

27 Alan Wilkinson, *The Community of the Resurrection: A Centenary History*, London: SCM Press (1992), 334.

28 CE Jan 1964. The area secretary for London was Lady Fiennes, Sir Ranulph's mother.

29 SSJE/2/8/268.

30 CE Sept 1964.

Two elements underpinned this idea: the centenary in 1966 was an obvious milestone at which the community might pause and take stock; while the prevailing ecclesiastical mood of the mid-1960s called for reflection and response. The new Superior General's priorities were clear:

> This will involve much consideration of the theological basis of our life, of our prayer and worship, and of the form which our 'mission' should take in the world of today. In all this we shall be in step (perhaps at times in the lead) with liturgical, ecumenical and social movements of the present time.[31]

The reports of the annual novitiate outings from this period were cheerful; and in March 1965 Campbell asked for the Fellowship of St John's prayers for one existing novice, two postulants, and a number of aspirants to the Society: he hoped, borrowing from Newman, for "a second spring as it enters on its centenary".[32] It was a happier outlook than a decade earlier; and certainly the community's view of its own calling remained robust. When Bishop John Robinson seemed to question the value of the religious life in *The New Reformation?*[33] he earned a gentle rebuke from the Superior General, which also set out the parameters for the consideration of the process of discernment that lay ahead:

> [C]ommunities are more than compact units directed towards efficient evangelisation. Their witness is not solely, and not primarily, their external activity. For our own Society as for others it is the fact that we are bound to a common life in brotherhood under the vows of poverty, chastity and obedience. The energy of this life has a two-fold beat, like the contraction and dilation of the heart. It draws us first to God, and our prayer and worship are the foundation for what follows. Then the energy dilates and presses outwards in union with the love and compassion of our Lord for all men [...] In our small community there is also a two-fold action: some members who go out on mission and other work outside, while our houses are centres to which others come for prayer and spiritual renewal.
>
> We need mobile, unencumbered men in the front line (*avant garde* or not), but we must not let our centres of monastic life be dissolved. It is the life that counts. The brightness and goodness in a true community will speak for themselves. It is not an artificial attempt to reproduce an obsolete medieval pattern. The life of a true religious vocation is an ever renewed response to a real and genuine action of God. It is for us to see that our response is itself real and genuine.[34]

Campbell took up the theme in his sermon at the festival mass of the Fellowship of St John later that year, introducing the year of prayer and reflection that would begin in July. He reflected on what it meant to be "A Society of Mission Priests" as described by Benson, and felt that "the ways of carrying out the work of mission today must be very different from those of a hundred or fifty or even twenty years ago."[35]

---

31 *CE* Jan 1965.
32 *CE* April 1965.
33 John A. T. Robinson, *The New Reformation?* London: SCM Press (1965).
34 *CE* May 1965.
35 *CE* June 1965.

The wider life of the Fellowship remained important to the Society: the changes in the community's liturgical books continued to be relayed to the members so that their prayers – they were still expected to say the offices – might correspond to those of the mother house;[36] although the Fellowship's lending-library was wound up in 1966, and the books dispersed.[37] By the middle of 1967 steps were being taken to modernise its rules and obligations, as it was now "called to live in a revolutionary changed world" and could not avoid "a process of growth and adjustment to these profound changes in its environment".[38] A year later Slade described the disciplines of the Fellowship as "suggestions rather than rules", and suggested that individuals might form their own rules of life, which would lead to "an adult freedom in the Christian life".[39]

At the same time a steady stream of visitors seemed to continue to come to Cowley and Westminster from all over the world, and this Triffitt also took for a sign: "In these ecumenical days and times of world travel, we are continually finding ourselves forging links with many parts of Christendom and of the world."[40] The Superior General's message to commemorate the centenary of Benson, Grafton, and O'Neill's living in common, which fell halfway through the community's year of reflection, contained two particularly significant points.

> Fr Benson was sufficiently conscious of the needs and demands of his own age to ensure that in forming the Society of St John the Evangelist he would make it suitable for the century in which he was living. That is why he preferred, while drawing on the rules of the ancient orders, not to make the new community a revival of a medieval one.

> [W]e cannot tell what the future holds any more than Fr Benson and his companions, Fr Grafton and Fr O'Neill, a century ago. We can look forward in faith as our Father Founder did, and to quote his words: "God has purposes for us, and very real purposes, which are still hidden from us. We know not what God is calling us to yet. The future is dark, and he reveals it to us step by step only."[41]

The various changes in the life of the Society, then, and those that were still to come, could be presented as a hermeneutic of continuity in which the example and teachings of the Father Founder – whose presence and then memory had been something of a conflicted lodestar for the Society as time passed – could be appealed to as both the inspiration and justification for any new directions in which the Society intended to travel.

By Christmas 1965 those directions were already clear. It is no surprise, given the community's commitment to liturgical innovations from the early 1960s onwards, that when the Archbishops of Canterbury and York brought out *Alternative Services* in 1965 they were welcomed warmly by the Superior

36 *CE* Sept 1965.
37 *CE* Jan 1966.
38 *CE* June 1967.
39 *CE* March 1968.
40 *CE* Oct 1965.
41 *CE* Dec 1965.

General as "genuinely Catholic as a whole". He hoped that they would be "welcomed and given a fair trial by the Church";[42] but when they were introduced to the SSJE's church and chapels in 1967 he was more forthright.

> There is cause for thankfulness that the Church is in this way preparing to meet the challenge of a world which drifts towards unbelief and despair. Because there is greater simplicity and a greater emphasis on the participation of all who are taking part in this worship, it does not cease to be a Catholic liturgy.

"Our attitude", he thought, "should be one of welcome and interest";[43] although in June 1968 the *Cowley Evangelist* conceded that the introduction of the Series II Communion Service "represented a considerable change".[44]

Meanwhile, Carpenter had given permission for the Mother Superior of the Sisters of the Love of God to leave her own enclosure at Fairacres and to give a talk to the SSJE brethren in their own common-room: and so Mother Mary Clare SLG became the first woman to enter the Society's enclosure at Cowley, nearly a century after its establishment. Almost simultaneously, Victor de Waal pointed out that the new universities were unable to bring groups to Cowley because half of their number was inevitably female; and immediately it was resolved to open the guest house to members of both sexes.

It was made clear that women would not be admitted to the enclosure as a matter of course, and that there would not normally be mixed residential retreats, nor individual retreats for women, "for which there are already plenty of other retreat houses".[45] Chapter also remained adamant that under no circumstances would women be admitted as Oblates of the Society;[46] but only a few years later the guest house was opened to men and women and "boys and girls from Bible class age upwards" – with the caveat that "in parties where girls under the age of 17 are resident, a woman shall be in residence".[47] Mark Gibbard felt that the basic principle to open the guest house to women at all was a step towards the "new look" that Carpenter had alluded to in his Visitation the previous year.

Furthermore, the community no longer wished to reside at "The Mission House": it now preferred to be "known simply as the Society of St John the Evangelist, Marston Street". The last change altered definitively the identity of the Society as described by William Stubbs when he had laid the foundation stone of the church in 1894. The SSJE's path forward seemed to be set. It had taken advice from many quarters, and had renewed its links with the University: Gibbard particularly noted a paper delivered to the brethren by David Jenkins – then Chaplain of Queen's and later Bishop of Durham – "on the whole purpose of community life under vows today". At the same time Campbell wrote that many of the brethren felt that the decisions taken at Christmas 1965 "may be the turning point in the history of our society".[48]

---

42 *CE* Jan 1966.
43 *CE* Sept 1967.
44 *CE* June 1968.
45 *CE* Feb 1966.
46 SSJE/2/8/281.
47 SSJE/2/8/317.
48 *CE* Feb 1966.

In March 1966, the SSJE was able to name and expound some of the new challenges it faced in the *Cowley Evangelist*, maintaining that "the religious community has its place and function within the Church, not as an odd excrescence, but as a vital part of the whole"; and that "it presents in bold relief values and characteristics of the whole people of God." In the previous century, stable Anglican religious life had sprung up not as "an antiquarian restoration or a fanciful copying of medieval models", but "from those perennial sources of dedication and obedience to Christ which in varying forms have always been at work in Christendom". There was, inevitably, an element of uncertainty in a rapidly changing world and Church.

> What the communities are asking themselves today is, In what form is a special life and work asked of us at this time? This is not wholly clear. There is a fruitful searching after and experimenting in new ways both in this country and abroad. What we can be sure of is that those who enter religious orders with a genuine commitment to Christ at his call will both receive and give a rich gift in corporate dedication to prayer and work for the kingdom of God.[49]

The centenary provided an opportunity for the Society to reflect further on "the radical and confusingly rapid changes which have affected the world and the Western European culture of which we are a part, since Richard Meux Benson and his two companions gave themselves in renewed Baptismal dedication to God and their fellow-men in 1866".

> Such looking to the past is not only part of the pleasure proper to an important anniversary, but an essential and sometimes salutary element in the re-appraisal upon which we are engaged. We look to the past so that we may learn how best to face the future and find our place as a relevant structure in the life of the Church which, through eucharist and foot-washing, seeks always to be renewed in combined adoration of God and self-denying service to man.[50]

It was in the quest for relevance that the high altar had been removed from the community church; and at the thanksgiving mass on 6 May "Father Superior presided over the liturgy from a seat at the east end of the church facing across the free standing altar to the assembly". Members of over thirty religious communities were present, with one of each of the men's communities sitting in choir; the numerous ecumenical guests were led by the Abbot of Caldey; and the University was represented by the Dean of Christ Church, Cuthbert Simpson, whose robes "provided more than a splash of scarlet at his return stall". The Bishop of Oxford preached: he "looked back to the foundations of the Society, examined its early growth and pointed to the ways in which we may learn to serve the needs of our present open and mobile society".

A day later the ceremonies were repeated for the benefit of the members of the Fellowship of St John "from all parts of the country" – the first service had been for the Society's Oblates, Priest Associates, and invited guests – with the exception that Carpenter celebrated the mass, and the preacher was the

---

49 *CE* March 1966.
50 *CE* May 1966.

Archbishop of Canterbury, Michael Ramsey, "flanked by our two African Fathers [Nomlala and Phalo] acting as his Deacons".

> The archbishop spoke of Fr Benson's theology and its practical character as it grew out of his own deep conviction and was not limited to any particular system or school of theological thought. We were shewn a man of patience who was willing to wait for his own vocation to be disclosed and who calls us to be patient now in prayer and humble waiting upon God. [...] Here was a picture of the Founder, a 'man of the moment' who calls us to be men of our own age, a picture most of all of a man in whom joy was deep rooted and who reminds us of our own vocation to be joyful now.[51]

Ramsey returned to church after lunch to speak on "Vocation and Prayer", and noted that "a shortage of priests and a shortage of monks and a shortage of nuns" was linked to the state of society.

> It isn't only that we're short of priests and short of monks and short of nuns. It is also that the country is short of men and women called to be doctors and men and women called to be teachers and of the spirit of choosing your job in life with the motive of serving, whether serving God or serving your fellows. It is that that is very much in shortage and we have a society all too dominated with the motive of enjoying yourself and getting and grabbing.

He noted, however, what he identified as a revival of the contemplative spirit in the Church of England: "a revival among Christian people of the sense that the contemplation of God is not so very queer or *outré* but is a wholesome Christian thing and a very part of man's prerogative as God's child." Quoting St Dominic – "the meaning of the Christian life is *Contemplare et contemplata aliis tradere*, to contemplate and to pass on to others the things contemplated" – his optimistic conclusion was that growth was on its way.

> If in our Church we can try to be faithful to those things God will do the rest and will give a wonderful increase in the coming years to the whole of our Church and not least in the granting of vocations to the religious life, including, no doubt, the Cowley Fathers among the rest.[52]

Triffitt, meanwhile – after associating Benson's name with those of Ss Antony, Benedict, Francis, Dominic, and Ignatius, "founders of new families within the Church" – laid out his own vision for the SSJE's path in the coming years.

> [W]hile the principles of our life remain the same, there is a spirit of renewal, a new spirit of freshening, invigorating and (sometimes) alarming force. Christians are learning to avoid a masterful, didactic or over-paternal attitude. Rather there is a loving sharing in the life and thought of other people, a placing oneself with and among them, a readiness to learn as well as to teach.

---

51 *CE* June 1966.
52 *CE* July 1966.

This, he thought, would involve reaching out to "non-Christians as well as Christians, non-practising as well as the faithful. The deep realities of the Faith and of the Creeds remain, but we shall try to interpret them in ways which attract rather than repel the enquirer and the half-believer."

He noted with thankfulness the work that had been done in a hundred years on five continents; but also that now "we have been able to hand over to others a good deal of the Society's former work in schools and in the clubs here in Oxford – the greater part of out-station work in South Africa – the hostels, schools, and parishes in India". He also identified new openings for work that might now reasonably form the core of the SSJE's life and work as it entered its second century.

(a) Both in Oxford and at St Edward's House the gathering round us for useful dialogue and discussion Christians, both clergy and laymen, who find in a religious community a stable centre. It is our hope that this may issue in time papers, publications and guidance in spirituality.

(b) Being available in Oxford and Westminster and possibly elsewhere for students, sixth-formers, university men and women, both junior and senior, and for ordinary mortals – especially for retreats, conferences, and talk. The 'presence' of a religious community can be used by God we believe in a special way.

(c) Maintaining our ecumenical interests and relations.

(d) Always wherever we are our firm basis of prayer.

Perhaps not unsurprisingly, Triffitt thought that the last was "a vital need of the world to-day", and "a genuine expression of the Church reaching out both in prayer and action". "First there is the contemplation of God and of the things of God", he concluded, "and then there is the going out in the light and grace of this vision to an apostolate in the world".[53]

Other spheres of activity had already presented themselves as the overseas work had diminished. In particular Br Cyril had concentrated on the SSJE's ongoing ministry to the young: the links with the local schools went on, and conferences for schoolboys continued to be organised;[54] but by the 1960s the Society had also branched out into the much more challenging work of borstal ministry,[55] as well as into chaplaincy work in the local youth hostels and at "a hospital for mentally deficient children".[56] A piece in the *Oxford Mail* commemorating the centenary in May 1966 noted that the SSJE had been "one of the greatest spiritual forces in the English Church", and that its "greatest work was done among young people".[57]

A new prospectus, published less than a decade after its predecessor, set forth clearly what the monastic round was like at Cowley by the end of the 1960s.[58] The early starts continued – although the chapel bell was no longer

---

53 *CE* July 1966.
54 cf *CE* Dec 1965.
55 *CE* April 1961.
56 *Society of St John the Evangelist*, Oxford: S&S Press (1968), 19.
57 *Oxford Mail*, 6 May 1966.
58 *NS* 1/70.

rung before Matins "for the sake of sleeping guests" – and the daily rhythm of the Society's life remained to a great extent unaltered, divided as it was between prayer, work, and recreation. Here and there the liturgical developments presented themselves: "we are trying to use [the community church] according to the new insights of the day". The brethren still processed into church through the little doors in the east wall of the sanctuary, but now "those who are concelebrating follow and stand on either side of the chief celebrant, behind the altar, facing west"; while the accompanying photographs demonstrated the extent of the alterations.

The prospectus also laid out the SSJE's vision for the future: "the ideal which lies before us is of a closely knit body of men, trying sincerely to follow Christ and his call, learning to live together in an affectionate brotherhood, ready to stay at home or go out on mission as shall seem necessary."

> In fact the community should, as a kind of microcosm, reflect what a modern theologian has given as his concept of the Church, "a community that lives in openness and fidelity of friendship, in mutual respect and forbearance, in *Sobornost*, in humility under the judgement of truth." This is by no means always easy for us, and every community knows the gap between ideal and achievement, yet by persevering with such an aim and ideal before us, a great work may be done by a small company.

"S.S.J.E. does not aim at great numbers", it insisted, "but hopes for a sufficiency to accomplish what God asks. Through the darkness of this age of violence and confusion there gleam bright rays of faith and self-consecration. There are and will be great opportunities for religious communities to fulfil. So we should have a spirit of expectation and readiness."[59]

EXPLORATION & EXPERIMENT

The *Cowley Evangelist* finally folded in December 1968.[60] Its demise brought to an end the organ which had kept the Society's supporters in touch with the community's life since 1891, and beyond that to 1867 and the original *Cowley St John Parish Magazine*. Without the letters from India and South Africa that had been its backbone it had become a shadow of its former self; although news from St Cuthbert's had continued to trickle in, and the lists of engagements at the end continued to present a full round of quiet days, parish missions, sermons and retreats. Of the last, between March and November 1968 members of the Society expected to lead no fewer than thirty-seven of varying length: for priests, laymen, women, and for men and women together; at Cowley, Westminster, and further afield.[61]

A thin monthly newsletter, edited by Slade, succeeded the *Cowley Evangelist*; but from its ashes also rose the Society's most significant contribution to the

---

59 *Society of St John the Evangelist* (1969), 5; 10; 22.
60 *CE* Oct 1968.
61 *CE* March 1968.

theological life of the Church of England in its latter days: *New Fire*. Edited by Bryant, who had by now effectively become the Society's official theologian, *New Fire* was launched at the end of 1969. It was conceived "as an instrument of mission and as a way of serving the Church and our world".

> We have a special responsibility as a community for people who look to us for guidance; and I am thinking not only of religious sisters and devout church people but also for the many young people, students, and others with whom some of us are in touch. It may be that by speaking to their condition we may be able to say something that many others will be glad to listen to.

He was adamant that *New Fire* was not to be a means "of circulating news about the Society among its friends"; but that it was to be "an extension of our preaching under a different mode". He identified three particular "over-lapping of interests" with which the journal would try to engage.

(1) First, there is the gospel itself; explaining what it means and shewing its relevance in the world today; shewing how it is being translated into action. We shall expect to say something about prayer and contemplation, about communal living, about the style of Christian living in the seventies.

(2) Second, there is the world itself which God has made, redeemed and loves. We shall take to heart the current saying that the world provides the agenda for the Church's mission. We shall aim to keep before our readers' eyes some of the problems of our times: the population problem, the exploitation of the earth and the pollution of our air, rivers, and soil; war, racialism, the care of drug addicts and other drop outs.

(3) Third, we shall I trust concern ourselves with the problem of communications. We shall be interested in new education methods, of learning by doing; for example, in ways of training lay men and women. We ought to write about non-verbal methods of communication; through the arts, painting, music, architecture, sculpture, to say nothing of the goggle box. These are ways in which people are being influenced far more effectively than by the printed word.

"Who is sufficient for these things?" asked the Editor. He looked to his brethren to supply at least some articles, and a number of book reviews; but at the same time intended to do his best to be firm when it came to standards: "obviously we do not want the contributions by members of the Society to stick out like a sore thumb for their bad or boring qualities."[62]

Similar themes of engagement had emerged in Campbell's proposed alterations to the Society's intercessions after Terce – "many of which are dated". As a general principle the Provincial Chapter of 1965 agreed a new basic structure that reflected the needs of the day, in addition to the daily petitions for the needs of the Society itself.

MONDAY: For a revival of faith among men in a divine purpose for mankind. For the Press, BBC, ITV. Politicians and all who have positions of influence

---

62 PC 1969, SSJE/3/2.

and responsibility in public life. For a solution of racial and colour problems throughout the world.

TUESDAY: For all engaged in the work of education, especially the universities and theological colleges [...].

WEDNESDAY: For all efforts to foster a spirit of mutual confidence among the nations. For a just and peaceful settlement of social problems on the continents of Asia and Africa.

THURSDAY: For Christians suffering persecution. For refugees and displaced persons, and for all working for their rehabilitation [...].

FRIDAY: For the work of hospitals, doctors and nurses; and for all engaged in the work of scientific research.

SATURDAY: For all our relations, friends and benefactors. For Christian family life.[63]

The Society was seeking new ways of being a presence within the Church of England, and Bryant's exposition of the part that he hoped *New Fire* might play in that process spoke to the English congregation's realignment of its identity at the end of a period that had seen its withdrawal from most of its historic channels of active work.

Although it maintained loose links in India after the return of the last members of the Society in June 1967[64] – individual brethren returned each year "for regular tours of duty which the Bishop of Bombay has asked us to undertake"[65] – and stronger ones at St Cuthbert's, where Gordon Shrive and Arthur Phalo were actively engaged in the building up of "the indigenous community of St Joseph"[66] and in continuing to raise outstation churches,[67] the SSJE's future for the most part now lay in England. To that end, a house in Reading was acquired in 1966 as part of a venture that Triffitt called "Dagenham".[68]

"Dagenham" is a code-word for the idea of a small detachment (say three) taking up simple quarters in a flat or rented house, working alongside Sisters in a nearby house, sharing in work and worship, and providing a simple centre – for (say) two years or so – possibly in an area where a modern university, schools, and other folk could find what we hope would be a real expression of a modern mission – the presence of this community available for all [who] should be drawn towards it.[69]

In tandem with the Clewer Sisters, the SSJE sought to provide "a centre from which they can go out among students and others, and to which they can welcome those who come for discussions, conference, individual talks, and

63 PC 1965, SSJE/3/2.
64 *CE* June 1967.
65 *CE* Jan 1967.
66 *Society of St John the Evangelist* (1969), 19.
67 cf *CE* April 1967.
68 SSJE/2/8/290.
69 *CE* Sept 1966.

so on."[70] The putative community at Reading – where the coats-and-trousers incident was claimed to have occurred[71] – used St Giles's Church for worship, "through the ready cooperation of the vicar and his mother".[72]

After much publicity in the *Cowley Evangelist*, however, the "Venture", as Triffitt called it, did not last long.[73] The house was sold in 1970,[74] and its ethos should not be conflated with the Community of the Resurrection's Emmaus venture, begun by Augustine Hoey CR a few years later in Hulme and Sunderland; which focused more on an enclosed life of intercessory prayer amid far grittier surroundings and yielded greater and longer-lasting dividends.[75]

Other schemes were also put into action. As early as 1966, to reflect the Society's desire to engage more fully in ecumenical work, Gibbard had begun running retreats for Roman Catholic undergraduates – and later for other Nonconformists – at the mother house.[76] After the SSJE had withdrawn from India, however, Slade had regretted "that there was not [in the preceding years] greater freedom to experiment with forms of prayer more suited to the needs of the Society of its Indian environment and that more attention was not given to Indian forms of contemplative prayer".

He conceded that "in those days the hour for this adventure had not come and it was sufficient that the Fathers should have been found faithful"; but felt that that past faithfulness had laid the ground for the Society's "present adventurous growth in new ways of prayer".[77] At the end of the decade a lama, exiled from Tibet, visited Cowley "with some anxiety that perhaps we might, as he put it, want to change him."

> When we had reassured him on that point, he quickly became a member of the family, insisted on taking his share in the community life and was obviously at home. Before he left he was asked to lead the family in meditation. Without any words, he sat in perfect stillness in our chapel and for a half-hour took us into the centre of his prayer and revealed to us how such silence not only discloses the incomprehensible God but also binds to him in love.

Slade thought that the Society's Buddhist guest had "opened a door which was already ajar and shewing through that opening a road which may well lead to the continuation of a work begun and eventually to its completion". Shortly afterwards a delegation of Japanese Buddhists visited St Edward's House;[78] and at the end of January 1969 the Society opened the Anchorhold at Haywards Heath as a centre of "exploratory ventures in new forms of community and prayer", led by Slade himself.

---

70 *CE* Jan 1967.
71 "The Changing Face of Cowley", *Church Times*, 8 Dec 1967.
72 *CE* March 1967.
73 *CE* May 1968; Valerie Bonham, *A Joyous Service: The Clewer Sisters and their Work*, Clewer: CSJB (1989), 136.
74 GreC 1970; GenC 1971, SSJE/2/8.
75 Wilkinson, *The Community of the Resurrection*, 338ff.
76 *CE* July 1966.
77 Slade, *A Work Begun*, 119.
78 *Church Times*, 21 June 1968.

The community form of life aims at producing the conditions of a Christian home, made up of a small nucleus of permanent members, living under the spirit of poverty, chastity, and obedience with what might be called a fluctuating perimeter of all kinds of people. Those who have lived in India will see in this pattern something resembling the Indian type of community called an Ashram.

At the Anchorhold the round of prayer was drawn, as Slade described it in 1970, "from both non-Christian and Christian sources".

The main non-Christian source is the eightfold path to contemplation outlined in the Yoga-sutras of Patanjali. This has been adapted and supplied with suitable images for western people and is proving a valuable guideline for growth in contemplative prayer by many who are learning to use it. The main Christian source of prayer is the growing theology of the Catholic Church, as prayerfully expressed in the divine office and the eucharist. Again there is in this prayer an attempt to explore the ways of contemplation used in India and to harmonize them, as far as is possible, with the many and various forms of this prayer in the West.[79]

It is no exaggeration to say that in the space of five years from 1965 – which is to say immediately after it gave up almost all its overseas work – the English congregation of the SSJE overhauled itself swiftly along the lines of what had come to be regarded as best practice in the wake of the Second Vatican Council, effectively directed by Campbell. Six decades earlier Benson had observed that "the twentieth century is not likely to be wanting in visions [...] The simple truth which we have received from the beginning is not what satisfies the present day."[80] A puff-piece in the *Church Times* by Desmond Bean, however – which he based on St Edward's House – approved entirely of the changes.

Even twenty-five years ago life at any of their houses was tough and austere. The food at the mother house at Cowley, Oxford, for example, was notoriously grim, and in winter the rooms rather cold. Nevertheless, students used to visit despite these hardships. To enter St Edward's today is quite a different thing [...] There are no hard seats or worn-out chairs, and in the guest-room and library are comfortable and even new arm-chairs, even carpets; and, of course, the whole building is centrally heated. Each guest has a bed-sitting-room with hot and cold water.

"During dinner," he continued, "in place of a holy or serious book, one is entertained by readings, for example, from Francis Chichester's writings, or, for a change, recordings of Elgar's music played on the Hacker. To crown it all, the Fathers are letting their hair grow: one wonders how long." The various liturgical changes seemed to follow naturally: "after all this one would naturally expect Series II, the altar pushed forward for the 'westward position', no cross on the altar and night-light candles; and so it is."

---

79 Slade, *A Work Begun*, 125.
80 Benson, 8 April 1903, *Letters of Richard Meux Benson*, 94.

Soon afterwards women were admitted to the chapel and the lower part of St Edward's House – in addition to the regular male visitors who ranged "from Archbishop to schoolboy"[81] – and the Society hoped that there might soon be "a few laymen residing permanently in the house who will go out to work day by day, who will at the same time have a close share in the community life and witness and prayer." Campbell took over the London work as it entered this period of "exploration and experiment".[82] In Chapter a year later he moved successfully that Superiors of branch houses should instead be known as Priors; and duly attended the next Chapter meeting as "Fr Prior".[83]

"Cowley conservative and behind the times?", Bean asked. "A few hours in St. Edward's House soon shatters that false image."[84] Reviewing Simon Phipps's *God on Monday*[85] towards the end of 1967, Campbell pointed to "falling congregations, frustrated clergy, shortage of ordinands, lack of vocations to the religious life, a church increasingly out of date and ineffective in the life of the nation".

> This is the picture that most honest people see. The Bishops warn us not to lose our nerve, and point to places where the church still flourishes, and to group or team ministries and to other experiments, but the total picture presented is one of disintegration which nothing is likely to stop.

"The theology of the church", he went on, "as well as its structures, is geared to the situation of centuries long past which is not our own. In short the gospel can only begin to have effect in the secular city when the theology of the church ceases to be ecclesiastically centred and becomes secular based." Campbell identified a church carrying on "regardless in the same old ways, playing its little ecclesiastical games which seem to have no bearing on the life of the world at all". He concluded by asking, in the religious communities' attempt to engage with the world, "ought we not once and for all to drop the world 'religious' as a descriptive label?"[86]

At the end of 1967 the Society brought to an end the Association for Intercessory Prayer, which Benson had founded exactly a century before; and with it the Association for Prayer on Behalf of Prisoners: "the prayer leaflet will no longer be issued". At about the same time the Fellowship of St John met for its London Festival at Holy Trinity, Brompton; and the on-message sermon preached by the Vicar of St George's, Bloomsbury, Gordon Phillips, might well suggest that not every member of the Fellowship was thrilled by the Society's new arrangements. "Has the Society become soft and disobedient?", he asked.

> The 'many changes' we find at Cowley and indeed all over Christendom are not changes in the direction of softness and disobedience. They are the signs of the hardest kind of discipline we are called to accept – the abandonment of what we

---

81 *NS* 3/69.
82 *CE* Jan 1968.
83 SSJE/2/8/317ff.
84 "The Changing Face of Cowley", *Church Times*, 8 Dec 1967.
85 Simon Phipps, *God on Monday*, London: Hodder & Stoughton (1966).
86 *CE* Nov 1967.

cherish as known and familiar even when ineffective and outmoded, and it is based upon an obedience to things as they are and not as we would have them to be.

Phillips thought that the church was now "stirring to life",[87] and Campbell mused that "the church will be most truly alive just in those places where the old established structures are most dead".[88] Preaching to the same constituency in May 1968, the latter's cheerful observation, channelling Richard Baxter, was that "everyone of us in this church is dying."

> Not only is this true of us as individuals; it is true of the organisations and societies to which we belong. F.S.J. is dying, S.S.J.E. is dying, the church is dying, the world is dying. All that will remain is God and His kingdom. The trouble with us is that we do not want to die, we try to resist dying, we try to hold on, we try to cling, but we can't – at least we can't for long – for death catches up with us in the end.

"Much better", he thought, "to learn to live a dying life, to live each day as if it were the last, than to imagine that somehow or other we are going to go on as we are for ever and ever."

After Apollo 8 orbited the moon in December 1968 the first of the new monthly newsletters noted that the world had changed forever.[89] The Archbishop of Canterbury had foretold growth, and the Superior General had looked for renewal;[90] while the Society's prospectus of 1969 mused that "it may be that the storms and disturbances of our times, and the unsettlement affecting family and social life will draw many to life in community".[91] In the end, however, the widespread ecclesiastical reforms of the 1960s refilled neither the churches nor the cloisters.

In the context of those reforms, and in an attempt to make its life more relevant to the needs of the modern world and more appealing to the tastes of the age, from 1965 the English congregation of the Society of St John the Evangelist removed the high altar from its conventual church; transformed its liturgies; reordered its domestic affairs; began to look to non-Christian sources to reinvigorate its life of prayer; and established an ashram in the leafy suburbs of West Sussex for the purpose of "learning what the East can teach us".[92] Despite the steady growth of the novitiate, it would be a full ten years before another man was professed into life-vows at Cowley.[93]

---

87 CE Dec 1967.
88 CE June 1968.
89 NS 1/69.
90 CE July 1966.
91 Society of St John the Evangelist (1969), 2ff.
92 Ibid, 19.
93 Gerald Perkins, a lay brother. SSJE/1/4; NS 5/75.

23

BACK TO THE FUTURE

This is the time of flower arrangements and other such decorative experiments.

—Herbert Edward William Slade SSJE[1]

Developments within the Society of St John the Evangelist continued as the 1970s progressed. In the Transkei the Society withdrew from St Cuthbert's and moved its house to Upper Mjika, where it stayed for a few years before moving to Umtata – appropriately enough, to a house on Callaway Street – whence it returned after a few unsatisfactory months in the noise and bustle of the town.[2] At home the annual retreats began to take place away from the mother house, having themselves gone through their "minor revolution";[3] occasional pilgrimages to the Holy Land were led by some of the priests; and members of the Fellowship of St John continued frequently to be invited to spend quiet days in the country at Lodsworth in Sussex, as the guests of Audrey, Lady Fiennes.

By 1971 Alan Cotgrove had become "Kitchen Father"; and a year later his brethren had been so well-trained in efficient washing-up that "without a special course and much practice the casual helper is left feeling very much like a beginner of the T'ai Chi Chu'an."[4] Alan Bean continued to run the garden, and after a bumper crop of apples in the autumn he "followed the Novices' sugges-tion to make cider";[5] while the Anchorhold acquired two tortoises, Augustine and Monica.[6] They soon moved to Oxford, and the latter was nearly renamed Monicus, after "a person skilled in these things" explained the difference; but it was felt by then to be too late, and "he doesn't mind, so why should we?"[7] In less-bucolic vein it was also decided to permit cremation for those members of the community who had expressed a desire for it.[8]

Francis Rumsey died quietly at the end of May 1969, and was buried. Although "his heart was obviously still in South Africa, he [had] achieved the remarkable feat of growing a new one which he shared so generously with the members of the Mother House and an assortment of relations and friends".[9]

---

1 *NS* 8/70.
2 GreC 1970, SSJE/2/8; GenC 1976, SSJE/2/8; *NS* 2/76; *NS* 10/76.
3 cf PC 1971, SSJE/3/2.
4 *NS* 11/72.
5 PC 1970/1971, SSJE/3/2.
6 *NS* 7/72.
7 *NS* 12/72.
8 GreC 1970, SSJE/2/8.
9 *NS* 6/69.

By the time of his death the brethren at Upper Mjika were living alongside the two African postulants in the Brotherhood of St Joseph, Josiah Tafeni and Zachariah Mpati – whom Francis Dalby hoped would "prove to be the nucleus of a South African community here" – and a priest-doctor, John Chitty. "This rather curious collection of people", he thought, "by living a common life together, is demonstrating that in Christ differences of race, culture, language, and social background can be transcended, though not eliminated."[10]

The conditions at Upper Mjika were primitive; but Dalby wondered whether this might be a boon.

> People sometimes rightly complain of the portentousness of the buildings occupied by religious communities, which are usually an overhang from the spacious days of Queen Victoria, but no one viewing Fr Shrive's present habitation could make any such complaint; they would be more likely to echo the immortal words of Trevor Huddleston, 'Naught for your comfort'. It may well be that this new plan will provide the right sort of setting for a religious life suitably adapted to the circumstances of the Transkei countryside.

Br Zachariah soon withdrew, leaving Br Josiah as the only member of the Brotherhood of St Joseph – he was professed in March 1973[11] – with Gordon Shrive as its director.[12] Work was soon underway on the modest *Umzi Womtandaze* – "House of Prayer" – which would become the Brotherhood's permanent home, while Shrive served as curate to the African priest-in-charge, Michael Ndakisa.[13] Shrive soon became the sole remaining SSJE presence in South Africa;[14] although other members of the Society continued to visit as the political situation deteriorated.

On 29 October 1969 the Society had kept a day of prayer for racial harmony in the community church, "in sympathy with the day of prayer being kept on the same day in South Africa";[15] but after Idi Amin expelled the Ugandan Asians in August 1972 its priorities extended to the makeshift arrangements at Maresfield, where the refugees became "the most dependent community we have at present". On visiting the camp a Muslim boy who wanted to take A-Levels presented himself: shortly afterwards he was resident at the mother house, at school nearby, and "a delightful addition to our home, with a smile which opens the heart and makes our small service a great reward".[16]

The SSJE also applied its developed awareness of sensitivities of race to the appointment of a new Vicar of Cowley St John after the incumbent, Leslie Arnold, was killed in a road accident in January 1975.[17] Arnold had been in post since 1946, and in the intervening years immigration – mainly from the West Indies – had transformed the demography of the parish. Its solicitous

---

10 *NS* 3/69.
11 *NS* 5/73.
12 *NS* 4/70.
13 *NS* 7/70.
14 *NS* 9/70.
15 *NS* 10/69.
16 *NS* 12/72.
17 *NS* 2/75.

presentation of Michael Brotherton to the living was in no small part due to the fact that Fr Brotherton had spent the preceding decade in the West Indies; although, as he himself has observed, the appointment did not necessarily take into account the not-inconsiderable nuance that most of the black parishioners had come from Jamaica, while he had served on Trinidad.[18]

In the wider Church the circulation of *New Fire* continued to grow; and significant realignments in the Society's ecclesiology also came to the fore. After the ecumenical agenda of the preceding years, in a statement released in the *News Sheet* in advance of the formation of the Churches of North India and of Pakistan in November 1970 – which amounted to an amalgamation of Anglicans and other Reformed churches, much along the lines of the Church of South India – the Society adopted a distinctly qualified view.

> In our own church we have as yet to wait for our own adventure into unity, but as we wait we may remember our brethren in these churches and grow in courage and flexibility of mind for the day when we ourselves go forward on the path which God is preparing.

Such a position would have been unthinkable only twenty years earlier. After the Church of North India came into being on Advent Sunday the *News Sheet* called it "a matter for thanksgiving and prayer even though at the last moment the Episcopal Methodists declined to come in".[19] When he arrived in India shortly before the outbreak of the brief Indo-Pakistani War of December 1971, Bean found that St Peter's School was "in very good heart and grows under its freedom";[20] while the Wantage Sisters, who were at that time still in Bombay, had "wisely made their presence felt in the new set-up, being at all the inauguration ceremonies [of the CNI] and many committees". He thought that after their own reforms, however, "a less nunnish headgear makes them difficult to identify".[21]

When the Church Assembly was replaced by the General Synod at about the same time – to which Christopher Bryant was soon elected[22] – the *News Sheet* mused that "those of us who have sometimes looked in on its debates in the past [Church House being literally across the road from St Edward's House] will not be entirely sorry that this transformation has taken place." The Society hoped that "in its new form there is a chance that it will be able to handle more than the mere administrative problems of the Church and will become an instrument of evangelisation."

Meanwhile, a well-wisher had "sculptured a pair of open hands and given them to the Anchorhold for use as a focus of prayer". William Slade's response to the gift demonstrates how elastic the Society's approach to worship had now become.

---

18 Conversation with the author, 17 April 2015.
19 *NS* 12/70.
20 *NS* 4/72.
21 *NS* 11/71.
22 *NS* 8/71.

Sometimes we place in them a lighted candle, sometimes a glass of water, sometimes the paten, and a few days ago I found them holding three sunflowers
[...] As an image of the heart in prayer they marvellously express what must
be beyond words and are an inspiration to many who meditate around them.[23]

Members of the Society later attended a "Festival of New Forms of Worship"
– which included Tai Chi – at St James's, Piccadilly;[24] but perhaps not everyone was as immediately enthusiastic as Slade about the new approach. In the
autumn, the *News Sheet* scolded the members of the Fellowship of St John for a
poor turnout at its London meeting.

The F.S.J. meeting in London was discouraging. On September 19 Fr Campbell
and his staff made arrangements to welcome a large number and instead a
handful turned up [...] It was all a little anti-climax compared with the visit of
thirty-five women from the Methodist church who came to the Anchorhold a
few days previously and sat in profound silence for more than twenty minutes.

"Next year", it chided, "we shall hope for a more enthusiastic support".[25]
Although it took very seriously its own developments, at the same time the
Society was not above finding humour in other emerging trends. A "buzz-
word" generator parodied modern approaches to theological engagement
with the gospels, compiled by an unnamed woman religious, which was "a
warning to us all".

Buzz-word generator for students of the Gospels in the Twentieth Century
(inspired by a course of lectures on the subject).

0	eschatological	midrashic	punch-line	0
1	geschichtlich	proleptical	kerygma	1
2	existentialist	figural	pericope	2
3	typological	redactive	doublet	3
4	allegorical	telelogical	sitz im leben	4
5	haggidic	apocryphal	paradigm	5
6	polysemous	deontological	plurisign	6
7	cosmological	demythologised	didache	7
8	ur-Marcan	suprahistorical	conflation	8
9	paracletic	apocalyptic	hermeneutics	9

(666 is a notable expression, this is no doubt significant. I regret there was not
room for *basileia* with a footnote 'not meaning Kingdom').[26]

---

23 *NS* 8/70.
24 *NS* 7/73.
25 *NS* 10/70.
26 *NS* 5/70.

MASSAGE, DANCE & MEDITATION

Other trends came in for more serious comment. The Society deprecated the "meal of grass" that Christian Aid organised in Trafalgar Square in May 1971, for example, which it thought that some must have found "difficult to understand".

> No one doubts the obligation of all Christians to help others through Christian Aid, but this meal and the care taken to photograph some of the participants, and the description of it as symbolic, made it all appear as yet another fund-raising gimmick which when it comes to Christians doing their duty to their starving brothers would seem to be the kind of advertising which the gospel so clearly condemns.

"The Church needs money to carry out the Lord's work" – the SSJE knew that as well as anyone else – "but surely something nearer the simply Buddhist begging bowl would be more appropriate than this ostentatious and to many offensive gesture."[27] Christian Aid came in for considerable criticism as time went on. The *News Sheet* soon accused its means of bringing water to Maharashtra in 1973 during drought in India – at the cost of £50,000 – as having "marks of superiority".

> We must share in regretting this way of doing things, partly because this is in practice such a minute contribution to the alleviation of the suffering of some twenty-five million people and mostly because it is presented in the triumphal tones of western technological expertise. The effort was called a 'giant Halco 625 drill rig' instead of the adequate expression of western Christians' compassion for their suffering brethren in India.[28]

When the organisation altered the tone of its appeals a couple of months later, the Society remained unimpressed.

> We may be glad that the 'starving-child' image has been abandoned but some of us cannot help feeling that there are signs of an almost cynical expediency in this approach. Raising larger sums for the hungry by Christians should be based on scriptural principles and images and then these sudden changes or 'ditching' of images will not be needed.[29]

The Society had not, of course, been reticent about spending its own small fortunes in India in the preceding century; but its trajectory had now changed. In 1973 it rejoiced in the inauguration of the Christa Prema Ashram at Poona, an ecumenical venture under the auspices of the Wantage Sisters and the Bombay-based Roman Catholic Sisters of the Society of the Sacred Heart, which had been opened as part of an ongoing attempt "to bring Indian and

---

27 *NS* 6/71.
28 *NS* 3/73.
29 *NS* 6/73.

Christian spirituality more closely together";[30] and it took particular pleasure when Indira Gandhi addressed the crowds in New Delhi at the celebrations of the 1900th anniversary of the death of St Thomas.

Gandhi spoke of how, after the European conquest of India, "Christianity came to be erroneously associated with foreign rule". She also took the opportunity to pay tribute to "the men and women who believed and the men and women who gave themselves in dedication and who have added to wisdom".

> Contentment does not come from conquest, from possessions or even from knowledge, but from something far more subtle and at the same time more concrete – the ability to give, to give oneself to a large cause, a large purpose.

"There are many", thought Slade, "who have spent themselves in India whose hearts will glow from this wonderful tribute from a great leader of the country they served."[31]

The Indian engagement continued at the Anchorhold: in early 1974 a description of an "initiation rite" gives an idea of the community life there, which by now involved craftwork as well: "we used for the three sacraments materials made in the workshop: a mixing bowl for the baptism, a pottery chalice and paten for the eucharist, and a prayer mat made in the weavery."[32] The young man being "initiated" had spent some time in India, where he had sat at the feet of Dom Henri Le Saux – the French Benedictine known in later life as Swami Abhishiktananda,[33] – an account of whose death the *News Sheet* reproduced with approval.

> Swami Abhishiktananda has experienced his final Awakening [...] 'Died' hardly describes what happened. He went to the Father. Dear Swamji thus had his desire of many years fulfilled, he has at last become truly a-cosmic, thus realising to the full the vocation which the Spirit through Hindu *sannyasa* had put deep inside him.[34]

Again, many of the Society's people seem to have remained unimpressed by such developments. The *News Sheet* later noted crossly that "there is room among some members of the Fellowship for a more enthusiastic development of their lives than has so far been attempted."

> The Society has set an example during recent years in the way it has courageously changed its life and work to meet the opportunities of the present moment. In these days of bold experiment in new ways of community living and prayer it would seem possible for some members of the Fellowship to learn about them.

By way of encouragement Slade began including "exercises in contemplative prayer" at the back of the *News Sheet*, with length of time, symbols to be included, and physical postures to be adopted; and his books *Meeting Schools*

---

30 NS 4/73.
31 NS 9/73.
32 NS 3/74.
33 See *Ascent to the Depth of the Heart: The Spiritual Diary (1948–1973) of Swami Abhishiktananda*, Delhi: ISPCK (1998).
34 NS 3/74.

of Oriental Meditation (1973),[35] *Exploration into Contemplative Prayer* (1975),[36] and *Contemplative Intimacy* (1977)[37] drew on his experience of the developing life at Haywards Heath. He regretted that "it has been surprising to find so few members of the Fellowship offering to share in this particular experiment";[38] but as David Campbell knew, "Fr Slade's way of thinking and writing are all his own, and not everyone can move on his 'wavelength'."[39] When Slade took three of the novices to Bossey, in the Haute-Savoie, for a conference on Spirituality and Ecumenism in 1976, the Cowley contingent caused consternation by doing Tai Chi in the grounds. "As this was averbal", Slade conceded, "it left the German theologians in a state of high perplexity, which we did little to resolve, beyond showing some slides of the Anchorhold."[40]

After members of the Society attended the third Conference for Religious at York in the summer of 1973, it was noted that "it was in worship that the greatest effort was made to face our present liturgical sickness [...] What was encouraging was that most were prepared to give the new forms a trial, to exchange organs for guitars, women's voices for men's, dancing for stillness."[41] In 1975 liturgical dance was introduced at the Anchorhold "as a joyful expression of our community life and commitment";[42] but at the end of the year the *News Sheet* earnestly reassured its readers that the celebrations for Alan Young and Francis Dalby's forthcoming golden jubilees of priesthood would be "High Mass at the high altar of our church at Oxford sung to a fully plainsong setting."[43]

Young in particular had not found "changes in church discipline and outlook, particularly the changes in liturgical practice, at all congenial",[44] and by 1978 Br Anselm was able to write of "the beautiful Solesmes rhythm [...] which it is our duty and privilege to preserve", and to note the concession that "in recent years we have revived the custom of singing the Gregorian chant at the Solemn Mass of great feasts which fall on a weekday."[45] A couple of years later Slade reported enthusiastically that at the Anchorhold "Miss Ogilvey has introduced us to Scottish dancing and Miss Harriet Geddes has taken us through a course of shiatsu massage. We have been able to share these new accomplishments by running courses for local people in massage, dance and meditation."[46]

In London other transformations had taken place. After a "purple tide from the Lambeth Conference lapped against our walls" in August 1968,

---

35 H. E. W. Slade SSJE, *Meeting Schools of Oriental Meditation*, London: Lutterworth (1973).

36 H. E. W. Slade SSJE, *Exploration into Contemplative Prayer*, London: Darton, Longman & Todd (1975).

37 H. E. W. Slade SSJE, *Contemplative Intimacy*, London: Darton, Longman & Todd (1977).

38 *NS* 12/73.

39 *NS* 5/77.

40 *NS* 8/76.

41 *NS* 10/74.

42 *NS* 4/75.

43 *NS* 11/75.

44 *NS* 2/87.

45 *NS* 2/78.

46 GenC 1980, SSJE/2/8 (loose).

during which time "bishops from near and far were constantly in and out", St Edward's House had been redecorated, and its rooms re-arranged. This was in addition to the opening of the chapel and lower floors to guests of both sexes, and the brethren in London, led by Campbell, did not feel "that retreatants have suffered by the fact that the house is more open than it used to be."

> We have already developed a real family spirit. In addition to the domestic staff and ourselves, we are fortunate to have half a dozen others living with us and sharing our life. These have included the chief cashier of a bank, a schoolmaster, a solicitor, a lecturer in the history of art, a post-graduate student researching in African history, and a Rumanian Orthodox priest.

"When people come to the house", he continued, "they find a community which is broader than the SSJE alone. This, we believe, is proving a benefit all round."[47] Although the *News Sheet* continued to refer to St Edward's House as an "outpost of the Society",[48] its work was burgeoning in major and previously unanticipated directions. After a group of Barbadians wrote to say how much they had enjoyed their visit in fulsome terms, it was clear that things were going well.

> Were Fr Campbell trying to be the most successful hotelier in London (which of course he is not) this letter would place him easily at the head of all forms of the accommodation services. One can imagine what use could be made of a reference like this not only in the catering world but in the world of retreat houses as well.[49]

By the start of 1971 the novitiate at Cowley had begun to grow, and there was "everywhere a feeling that the sap is beginning to rise".[50] The ceremony for the clothing of novices had also been overhauled.

> It is a happy thing to think that on these occasions in their new form so much of the 'take heeds' and 'bewares' have disappeared and replaced by a much more light-hearted approach to what is not in any way a funeral but the most worthwhile adventure in the world [...] Our clothing ceremony has now quite rightly taken the form of what it really is: the setting out of a pilgrim for his own state of *'en recherche'* with 'destiny heaven' clearly marked on his travelling papers.[51]

The *News Sheet* reported that the General Chapter in the summer of 1971 had been "a uniting experience when the gradual formation of a common mind in the community was very much in evidence"; while the style of retreat had been completely transformed. In 1969 Slade had thought that "retreats of thirty years ago were very different from what they are now".

---

47 *NS* 3/69.
48 *NS* 9/72.
49 *NS* 10/71.
50 *NS* 1/71.
51 *NS* 4/71.

In those days, when there were giants to give addresses of almost an hour, they were formidable long-distance experiences. Besides the long addresses, and there were two of them, there were three meditations; and for good measure at meals there were long readings from the Religious Vocation, in addition to a paragraph or two from Thomas à Kempis with the more than meagre breakfast. Work went on in between as usual.

The modern retreat consisted of one twenty-minute address each day, with "a lighter book for one meal and music for the other". Kempis was "silent during a much more adequate breakfast". Slade was more than aware that "superficially this comparison could evoke the comment that the old days of asceticism had been replaced by something much less severe and that the age of the giants had been succeeded by one of pygmies".

"But", he went on, "this would not be the full answer". He felt that the transformed way of keeping the Society's retreats was "to counteract the new form of danger to the spiritual life", which was strain: "the new form of response which the new ways of keeping retreat encourage is the practice of relaxation."[52] By 1971 the need for relaxation had entirely displaced rigour as the pattern for the Chapter retreats.

> Our community experiences during the past few years have revealed how nearly a well-spent holiday resembles a well-kept retreat. By siting the retreat in good walking country [in 1971 it was spent at Old Alresford, the Winchester diocesan retreat house] we have been able to combine country walks and other pursuits such as painting and bird-watching with the silence and other exercises of retreat. Music instead of endless reading at meals has introduced a welcome atmosphere of relaxation. Longer uninterrupted nights and the chance for a rest in the middle of the day have in no way interfered with those disciplines of prayer and meditation and a Sunday with practically nothing else but the duty of what the Buddhists would describe as 'doing nothing' is a rare experience of the greatest spiritual value.[53]

In 1973 members of the Society went to Clacton to help lead one of Bishop Mervyn Stockwood's retreats at Butlin's for the clergy of the Diocese of Southwark.[54] The developed thinking on best practice for retreats remained the same.

> There was the ideal cell: a working-sleeping room, and adjoining a simple bathroom with all that was needed. The small veranda outside gave a moderate contact with a world of friendly people and happy children, and there was a remarkable silence after 11 p.m. and the midday siesta. The Conference arrangements were as good as the meals, served by young people who seemed glad to be there; and there was a daily celebration of the Holy Communion. What more could a retreatant want? Yes, there was swimming as well, and the sea and walks.

---

52 *NS* 8/69.

53 *NS* 8/71.

54 Footage of the retreat of 1961 at Bognor Regis – in which the SSJE was not involved – remains popular in certain ecclesiastical circles, and is readily available on YouTube.

"Those three days," closed the piece, "were an experience of what can be done with God's people when they are treated in this way." Counterbalancing the argument in Chapter in 1966, the writer made a point of noting that in these circumstances "the habit was an immense help [which] made the wearer an immediate member of a large family all seeking relaxation."[55]

Inevitably, there were gains and losses: an announcement in the *News Sheet* early in 1972 proclaimed that "the vigorous novitiate is a line of communication between the members of the family who are further on and the newer generations who are coming over the hill";[56] telegrams were abandoned in April;[57] and by November the music of Andrew Lloyd Webber's *Jesus Christ Superstar* was being played at social gatherings at St Edward's House.[58] At Provincial Chapter at the end of the year, however, while the Novice Master, Edward Bishop, "felt it necessary to look at the whole situation past, present, and future, and not to concentrate on any one of these in isolation", he nonetheless lamented the fact that "since his last report to Chapter ten men had left."[59]

AUTHENTICITY, COMMUNITY & SIMPLICITY

At the start of the Greater Chapter of 1976 Gerald Triffitt announced his desire to retire as Superior General; and David Campbell was elected to succeed him, with a clear majority on the first ballot. Triffitt had served for four terms, during which Campbell's ascendancy through the offices of the SSJE had been combined with his near-constant drive to reform the Society along the lines of contemporary theological and liturgical developments. Not all the changes Campbell had guided through Chapter had been universally popular; and he had not had his way on every matter: when in General Chapter 1970 he had suggested that the confessionals in the community church should be removed, his confrères had simply declined to discuss the matter.[60] Nevertheless, a paean in his praise appeared in the *News Sheet* in 1972, probably written by Slade.

> One never ceases to marvel at the way he puts himself at everyone's disposal and never seems busy. He has mastered the art of listening, which some say lies at the heart of our Christian ministry. But he not only listens. He inserts into the conversation just the right amount of salt to make it live.

Conversational skills notwithstanding, Campbell had recently returned to Cowley as Assistant Superior General, with James Naters succeeding him at St Edward's House. He was a senior member of the community who had himself been the architect of most of the recent changes, and was an obvious choice to lead the Society in the direction to which it had by now committed itself.

---

55 *NS* 7/73.
56 *NS* 2/71.
57 *NS* 4/72.
58 *NS* 11/72.
59 PC 1972, SSJE/2/3.
60 GreC 1970, SSJE/2/8.

The new Superior General went as far as to describe his predecessor as "cautious and conservative by temperament"; but conceded that he had been "always open to listen to fresh ideas, and more than that, prepared to give them a try provided the unity and fundamental traditions of the Society were not in danger of being impaired". He also took the opportunity to lay out his own vision for the future of the SSJE.

> I believe that our Society is heir to a tradition of spirituality handed down from our Father Founder and the early members of the Society, which can be of great value to the religious life as a whole, indeed to the Church at large. But this spirituality has to be fostered in an environment which is very different from that of one hundred years ago.

Campbell felt that the Society's spirituality now needed to be "expressed in a way that speaks to the present day and generation".[61] Soon afterwards the members of the Society began sharing the Sign of Peace with each other at mass – Triffitt had been particularly impressed by the accretion when he went to Boston for Central Council in 1976 – extemporary intercessions were introduced; and the singing of the psalms at the early morning office was abandoned.

The autumn of 1977 was "a time of breaking down", as the now-empty buildings of the girls' school in the back garden came to be demolished: "the preliminary to building up a new and exciting community housing project on the site."[62] Most startling of all was the address Campbell gave in the house chapel at the beginning of the Christmas Chapter at the end of the year. It was, as he acknowledged, "not customary for the Superior to give an address at this Chapter"; but he wanted "after eighteen months as Superior to break with tradition and take an opportunity to-day to share with you a number of thoughts that have been going through my mind". He hoped that they might be "starting points for community thought and community action during the coming year".

> I do not, of course, expect everybody to agree with everything I say, yet at the same time I do think that I may have one or two things that should be heeded.
>
> The face of the Western Church is going through a process of radical transformation, and this certainly includes the face of the religious communities. It is a process which we cannot stop, but which we can, to some extent, direct. And I believe that the process can be in the right direction, if we are always seeking to do two things.
>
> The first is to be constantly seeking to know Christ revealed to us through the Holy Spirit in the Church, and this means in particular bathing ourselves in the New Testament; and the second is to be making every attempt to understand the rapid changes going on in the world, in society, and in man. It seems to me that the agenda of the Church's business, and therefore of a religious community's business comes from two sources which it is our task to relate to one another, namely The New Testament and the World of Today.

---

61 NS 8/76.
62 NS 10/77.

As might be expected from one who had spent so much time at the heart of the Society's affairs, in many ways Campbell's following analysis of the situation in which the SSJE now found itself was brutally accurate. There was a general "paucity of men and women of lively and balanced character offering themselves for the religious life"; and at the same time the Society itself was aging, which came with its own challenges.

"There is no use blinking the fact", thought the Superior General, "that those born and brought up in the years since the Second World War inevitably look at many things in an entirely different way from the majority of us who were born during or before the First World War." Campbell himself had been born in 1915, and he had been 61 at the time of his election. He recognised that "while each one of us would no doubt give a slightly different reason for responding to a vocation to come here, I think that the average young man today would give a very different kind of answer from that of most of us of the older generation."

> Most of us older ones entered the Society as priests and by doing so believed that we would be able to place ourselves more completely at the disposal of God, and that this would involve us in working either as missionaries in India or South Africa, or engaging in missionary, evangelistic or pastoral work here in England. The average young aspirant today comes to us as a layman – often with very little church training, and I think I am not wrong in saying that which he is looking for is a Christian life which is authentic, which is communal, and which is simple.

Under the three headings of "authenticity, community, [and] simplicity" Campbell proceeded to lay out his thoughts for what was to come. In the pursuit of authenticity prayer had to come first; but there needed to be "room for order and room for flexibility, room for tradition and room for new leadings of the Spirit. There must always be discipline – community discipline and individual self-discipline – but there must also be joy and scope for spontaneity."

On community, he was openly critical of the way the Society's common life had been ordered in the past – "as I have said more than once".

> [T]here has always been a strong element of restraint in our ethos which has tended to militate against the openness and frankness and sharing which is what young people are looking for when they talk of community. There is no question that over the last ten years or more we have developed a more relaxed community life than we used to have; and that is why I am confident that we can together tackle our problems, face our difficulties and make our decisions as a thinking, praying community.

He foresaw a more frequent use of the community conference as a means of discussing important matters – and particularly in the forthcoming months and years, when there would be much to consider: "I am sure that the time has come when we need to meet together as a community far more frequently than we have done in the recent past." Like many of his predecessors, Campbell also felt that another realignment of the SSJE's outside commitments might be called for.

12 years ago our so-called "fallow-year" helped to open us out as a community. Without necessarily using the term "fallow-year", I think we have now reached a point when we must once again pray and think through together our vocation as Christians, as religious, and as S.S.J.E. I therefore intend, if possible, to reduce our outside engagements, and I hope you will co-operate with me in this. I am sure that we all need – and the Superior needs most of all – to use more discernment about the value of some of the engagements we take on, and be more careful to conserve our energies and gifts so that they may be channelled in the best possible ways.

For Campbell this was all bound up in the quest for simplicity: "I believe the counsel of poverty is in most ways well-expressed as 'simplicity of lifestyle'." Under this last heading he reopened a seismic piece of business.

It is certainly more difficult to live a life of simplicity in a large place than a small one, for in large houses such as ours, so much energy as well as money has to be spent in keeping them going. It was nearly ten years ago that at a community conference the proposal was put forward that the time had come gradually to phase out the large mother house, and we had a lengthy discussion on it. The proposal met with very little support so that, rightly or wrongly, we committed ourselves afresh to the responsibility of continuing to maintain our large and ageing houses in Oxford and London.

As shocking as the suggestion of the SSJE leaving Cowley may have seemed – again, "lengthy discussion" was likely to have been a euphemistic understatement – Campbell now made no bones about his own thoughts on the matter: "I believe that we can more easily fulfil our function as religious and as missionaries in a simple homely environment than in one which smacks of the institution."

Martin Smith, who was professed into first vows in May 1976, thought that, in the context of the general decline in church attendance, the Society was "sitting in what is from a pastoral point of view a redundant church";[63] while Campbell had already told the Society's supporters that "religious communities such as our own have allowed themselves to be almost as saddled with such things as the church at large. Unless we are bold in our breaking down we may well be overwhelmed by suffocation."

The Superior General wanted to see the Society "untrammelled by a superfluity of dead wood";[64] and only a few years earlier the *News Sheet* had congratulated the Society of the Sacred Mission on its departure from Kelham, which, although it had been "the end of an era", had also been "the beginning of another going forth which lies at the heart of all spiritual vocations".

[L]ike other great discoveries in the spiritual life this one [the SSM] has had to move on to a resurrection dimension which involves the transformation of death. In the way Kelham has faced this test some can see her finest hour.

---

63 *NS* 11/76.
64 *NS* 10/77.

Nothing this great community has done in the past so became her as the way she handled this.

All this had involved careful planning, and "a new approach to the religious life, a parting with the large structures, a putting into practice what so many have been talking about and which so often have lacked the courage to do."[65]

Building on the SSM's example, Campbell thought that "God is working a mighty transformation in His Church today, involving no less than death and resurrection, to make it more truly an instrument for furthering the Gospel of God's love than it has been for many centuries past." Effectively, he now presented his brethren with an agenda for the future of the SSJE from which there could be no reasonable dissent.

I believe that this transformation, also involving death and resurrection, is going on in our Society. We must allow it to happen, we must not hinder it, nor must we do anything to force it. It is the work of God.[66]

Campbell brought his proposal to General Chapter in 1978: "Fr Superior proposed that preparations be taken in hand for the community to move out of 16, Marston Street, and for the transfer of the property into other hands." Bryant, meanwhile, had prepared the ground from the pulpit shortly before the meeting.

It is my strong conviction, and has been for some while, that the nature of our buildings in Oxford, including the church, together with the unbalanced age range and ever-increasing age of the community combine to make it well-nigh impossible in this place to recover a pioneering, exploring spirit to which young men can respond.[67]

The motion was carried, with 22 votes in favour, two against, and one abstention.[68] "We have resolved to prepare to move on", Campbell wrote in August 1978. "It is a great and momentous step forward." He realised that there might be those who would regard it "as a sign of retreat and defeat"; but thought that "nothing could be further from the truth."

The community is in very good heart. Many are getting on in years, and the average age of the community is high, but we have a handful of young men who are truly dedicated and for whom this resolution gives new hope for the future.

He was pleased that of the letters and comments he received after the news was announced "the great majority have been encouraging, and, I am glad to say, look upon it as a sign that we refuse to sink down into a static old age".[69]

---

65 *NS* 11/73.
66 PC 1977, SSJE/3/2.
67 *NS* 8/78.
68 GenC 1978, SSJE/2/8.
69 *NS* 11/78.

The sense of the Society's ongoing engagement with the Church and the world is borne out by Ronald Blythe, who spent time with the SSJE while preparing *The View in Winter: Reflections on Old Age*, which he brought out in 1979, ten years after his acclaimed *Akenfield: Portrait of an English Village*. He found a community that was clearly aging, but that while "bodies fail and time closes in, yet often as much as sixty years' observance of their religious rules has clearly separated their experience of decline from that of the majority". To grow old as a Cowley Father, thought Blythe, was to experience old age differently from others. "They are not an enclosed order, physically or intellectually", he noted. "Most of them have travelled extensively and many of them study incessantly, so that their Christian argument is lively in the extreme when compared with that of the many a parish priest."

Channelling George Congreve, Blythe thought that elderly religious were to be comforted "by constantly reminding themselves that the world to which they belong is not that of any one generation but the eternal world and they are to make a positive effort to concern themselves with it for as long as they are part of it." The time Blythe spent with the Society, interviewing some of its members and taking in the rhythm of its life, furnished an almost romantic depiction of its day-to-day existence.

> The Anglican Cowley Fathers' *régime* contains far less manual labour [than that at Caldey] and perhaps more study. Their house is warm, bright and roomy, and their Conventual Church a handsome achievement by Bodley and Comper [*sic*]. A beautiful walled town garden winds its way round refectory, library and common rooms. The community eats very simply, spends a lot of time in comfortable book-lined cells, gathers seven times a day to sing the office, walks to the centre of Oxford to visit colleges and bookshops, and keeps its Rule not so much by some obvious strictness as by a very English kind of duty expressed gently. Everybody works, everybody dreams, everybody sings, and nearly everybody seems to have travelled a lot.

It was this genteel community that was now "prepared once again to take the pilgrim way"; and by the time *The View in Winter* appeared, the Society was already committed to leaving its buildings at Cowley.

Campbell also noted that, inevitably, there had been those who had "expressed great sadness that we should be moving", and at the thought of "passing the care of our beautiful church into other hands".[70] Initially the main site and various houses in the surrounding streets were offered to the newly-amalgamated Ripon College Cuddesdon; but by September 1978 negotiations had broken down, and Chapter resolved to instruct an estate agent to act on the Society's behalf in the disposal of its Oxford property. At the end of December, the Superior General summoned a Special General Chapter to deal with the pressing questions of whether the Society should move into the Community of the Presentation's house at Hythe; and whether it should subdivide further and move into three houses (including St Edward's House and the Anchorhold) or four. Campbell had warned that the Chapter "must be

---

70 *NS* 11/78.

prepared to meet all day"; but the former matter was answered in the negative, and the latter was inconclusive.[71]

With the potential arrangement with Ripon College having come to nothing, the Society took the drastic step of putting the church up for sale.

> For those who have known and worshipped in our beautiful church it came as a distressing shock to read in cold print in the Oxford papers that the church is up for sale. It is still the hope of all of us that it may be able to continue as a place of Christian worship. It is only if this hope cannot be fulfilled that, rather than leaving the building closed and empty, a use might be found for it as a centre for music or some other suitable purpose.[72]

No buyer was forthcoming, and by 1979 things were moving on apace: it was decided that the Society should divide itself between the Anchorhold and St Edward's House, and acquire other properties as necessary. The Superior General would normally reside at Westminster, and the other brethren would be dispersed as he saw fit. Campbell had already arranged that Smith would be sent to Boston at the end of the year, to continue his journey in the SSJE as a member of the American congregation.[73] The guest-house accommodation would be reduced, and from September 1979 all community worship would take place in the Lady Chapel; with the exception of a morning mass on Sundays – "sung or a low mass with hymns" – and Wednesdays in the community church.

Triffitt died at the end of April, a few weeks after his very elderly mother, who had lived around the corner from Marston Street until her death at the age of 99 and to whom he had remained devoted. By the time he was buried in a grave near hers in the Rose Hill plot at the start of May,[74] St Stephen's House had decided to move to Marston Street. Campbell later noted with relief that as "it was an act of faith that we made last year in deciding to divest ourselves of this enormous property, [...] it is in the same spirit of faith that we face the future even when the Lord seems to leave it to the very last minute before he shows us the next step."[75] The Superior General was returned to office at Greater Chapter a few weeks later;[76] and by the end of the year a Special General Chapter authorised the purchase of 2 Woodland Avenue in Leicester, for another "Dagenham" attempt, and 228 Iffley Road so that the Society could retain a presence in Oxford[77] – as "to have no Cowley Fathers in Oxford seems to some almost as incongruous as having no Beefeaters at the Tower of London."[78]

The Chapter had met at the mother house for the last time; and Campbell cited four reasons behind the SSJE's decision to leave. The first issue had been

---

71 GenC 1978, SSJE/2/8.
72 NS 2/79.
73 GenC 1979, SSJE/2/8.
74 *Church Times*, 11 May 1979; NS 5/79.
75 NS 7/79.
76 GreC 1979, SSJE/2/8.
77 GenC 1979, SSJE/2/8.
78 *Church Times*, 1 Feb 1980.

obvious to Ronald Blythe, who noted at the time of his visits that "the members of the S.S.J.E. are aged from early twenties to mid-ninety": part of the problem facing the Society was lack of the middle-aged.[79] As Campbell himself realised, "we have almost skipped a whole generation, so that we have only a handful of men between thirty and sixty which is the prime of life".[80] Consequently, the younger brethren were now "having to expend more than a disproportionate part of their energies in just keeping the plant going".

Secondly, "the inevitable institutional atmosphere" of the Society's large Victorian and Edwardian buildings was felt to be "not at all helpful" to those considering testing their vocation with the Society; and thirdly, while the community church might have "had in former years a useful role to play in Oxford not only as a church of the parish but also as a centre of traditional worship and music which at one time drew many from the university", things were now different.

> Times have changed, and it is unrealistic to expect a revival of large congregations here when the young Christians of today quite rightly want to belong to a church in which the laity have full participation in an active corporate life of worship and service.

Above all – "a reason far more important than all this" – the Superior General thought that "the way we are living our life bears little resemblance to the ideals of our Founder".

> In the decree on the renewal of the religious life [Perfectæ Caritatis], the Second Vatican Council decreed that religious communities should renew their life according to gospel values and the spirit of the Founder. Although there is much that is monastic in the ideals and rule for the community given by the Founder, he did not found a monastic order of men which would be concentrated in large monasteries.

Campbell interpreted Richard Meux Benson's original intention as having been to found "a Society of mission priests and laymen living in small units" – he cited the original Mission House as an example of the intention to keep buildings modest – and of course made reference to the fact that when the Founder returned from the United States "he expressed great disapproval that we should have built so large a place". The end of the colonial work had exacerbated the matter: "since we withdrew, as we had to, from India and South Africa in the late 1960s, nearly the whole community has been concentrated in this one mother house, a situation which Fr Benson would surely deplore."[81]

This approach did not necessarily take into account the fact that the SSJE's historic triumphs and ongoing successes had in fact been those of the Society as restructured by Robert Page in the 1890s; or perhaps it did, but chose to reject them. Benson's floundering and moribund Society had been transfigured; and had the rate of professions in the 1890s and 1900s continued, then even the new

---

79 Blythe, *View in Winter*, 289ff.
80 *NS* 2/71.
81 *NS* 8/78.

large buildings would have become cramped soon enough. Had that trans-formation not taken place – as Congreve and others agreed at the time – then the SSJE might well have fizzled out, like many of its contemporaries.

Furthermore, in 1978 Campbell openly averred that he – the Superior General of the Cowley Fathers – had "never cared to ally myself too closely with any ecclesiastical party"; and in the same breath criticised the Catholic Renewal Movement for having the potential, as he saw it, to "degenerate into a backward escape to the excessive Anglo-Catholic dogmatism and triumphal-ism of fifty years ago".[82] A few years later, musing on his perceived misuse of "Catholic" in ecclesiastical circles as the Church of England began to discuss the matter of women's ordination, he regretted that "the way that this word is used in ecclesiastical talk has the overtones of narrowness, rigidity, and even, at times, intolerance."

> I wish that all Christians, whatever their confessional allegiance, would only use this glorious word according to its fundamental meaning, and cease altogether to use it in conversation and controversy on ecclesiastical party matters.[83]

The Society of St John the Evangelist lacked the centuries of bedrock pos-sessed by most of the religious orders to whom *Perfectæ Caritatis* was actu-ally addressed; and so the attempt by Campbell to return it to the genuinely original character of its first quarter-century, and at the same time distance it from a large part of its essential identity of the preceding decades, was some-thing of a risky business. "We are all very conscious of the wonderful support of you all, our friends", the Superior General wrote in the *News Sheet*. "Please go on praying for us as we adapt ourselves to a pretty radical change in the ordering of our Society."[84]

---

82 *NS* 10/78.
83 *NS* 11/85.
84 *NS* 8/79.

24

Beyond the Sunset

We do not know whether or not there will be many chapters to follow.

—Frederick David Gordon Campbell SSJE[1]

S t Stephen's House had outgrown its premises in Norham Gardens, on the other side of Oxford; and its Committee of Management had discussed enthusiastically the possibility of taking over the SSJE's buildings in April 1979.[2] The committee – chaired by Eric Kemp, who was by then Bishop of Chichester – soon elected the Superior General of the SSJE to its membership; and agreed that the new building on the site of the old girls' school should be called Moberly Close, in honour of Robert Moberly, its first Principal. The staff and students moved premises over the Long Vacation of 1980. It had been arranged that the college would take responsibility for the community church, and that the panelling carved with the names of the deceased members of the Society would remain in the Lady Chapel. The reredos of the college chapel, an eclectic depiction of the martyrdom of St Stephen, also came: Kemp felt that "ill-feeling might be generated if this was not transferred";[3] and it was later squeezed onto the west wall of the Founder's Chapel.

David Campbell thought the arrangement "a happy solution": the Society handed over the not inconsiderable sum of £100,000 to St Stephen's House as an endowment, as well as the patronage of the SSJE parishes of Worksop and Cowley St John.[4] The new site was inaugurated on 15 October 1980: the Principal, David Hope (a future Archbishop of York) noted that the whole summer had been taken up with the move.[5] The SSJE continued to provide the college with confessors, and the portrait of the Founder still hung over the fireplace in the old lower library. The names of the dead brethren would go on being carved into the panelling in the Lady Chapel for as long as St Stephen's House wished,[6] and Campbell identified "a very real sense of continuity".

It is indeed a cause of gratitude that the Society has been able to transfer buildings which no longer served its own purposes into the hands of a college which is bent upon giving the church priests who (to use words of Fr Benson applicable to priests as well as religious) are "men of the moment, men precisely

---

1 *NS* 1/80.
2 SSH Committee of Management, 9 April 1979.
3 SSH Committee of Management, 4 June 1980.
4 GenC 1980, SSJE/2/8.
5 SSH Committee of Management, 18 Nov 1980.
6 GenC 1984, SSJE/2/9.

up to the mark of the times, men who are far from being the traditional imitators of bygone days".[7]

By 1980 St Stephen's House had itself been overtaken by the contemporary pottery-and-polyester trend in church furnishings; but some students who took a longer view of the matter benefited from the dispersal of the remaining vestments in the sacristy drawers. Much of the old furniture was removed from the cells, the better to dispel the monastic atmosphere and replace it with that of a modern theological college; while the great choir lectern – which might well be regarded as one of the most significant items of ecclesiastical furnishing in the Church of England, but which by then had been banished to the Song School – was only very narrowly saved from a bonfire. When the pond in the garden was filled in, its displaced colony of frogs invaded the house.

Campbell later observed that "we live in an age very remote from that of the Victorians, and this is making much of the religious life as it has been lived until very recently both irrelevant and inappropriate".[8] A new expression of life saw the Cowley Fathers dispersed between the Priory at Oxford, St Edward's House at Westminster, the Anchorhold at Hayward's Heath, and the new house at Leicester. It would be, thought Campbell, "the beginning of an entirely new chapter in the history of SSJE".[9]

It is difficult to foretell what the religious life will look like by the end of the century, as indeed to foretell what the Church will look like. But of one thing I am convinced and that is that as more and more people are searching for a spirituality that can give direction to their lives, and more and more people are also searching for community, so there will be an increasing need and demand for more and more houses of spirituality which will provide "still centres" of community in a confused world.[10]

He was also quite clear that the new chapter might also be the SSJE's last; but he still thought that the venture was worth the gamble: "even if it proves to be the beginning of the final chapter, it is going to be a renewing and invigorating one for those of us who have a part in it."[11]

To his brethren he was more frank. "We cannot see far ahead," he said at General Chapter in 1980, "and, as I have constantly reiterated, we are learning how to live as those who are only shown one step at a time in our pilgrimage".

We do not know whether the Lord is going to send others to join our Society or not. Even if the answer is "no", we can now reasonably look forward to a few years of prayer and service in circumstances which, I believe, make it more possible to be open to God, open to one another, and open to the world at our doors.[12]

---

7 *NS* 8/80.
8 *NS* 3/83.
9 *NS* 11/79.
10 GenC 1980, SSJE/2/8 (loose).
11 *NS* 1/80.
12 GenC 1980, SSJE/2/8 (loose).

It might be, he thought later, "that in the revival of religious life in the Church of England, SSJE has been called to be – like John the Baptist – the Forerunner; and now we must decrease that they may increase".

> In the meantime we continue day by day to live together in mutual love, encouraging one another, bearing one another's burdens, and rejoicing in our privileged opportunities for prayer and praise and service.[13]

At Leicester Cyril Woolley and Alan Grainge had been "left in no doubt that people were glad to see us and anxious to do all they could to make us feel at home";[14] and Bishop Richard Rutt – an experienced missionary who had been Bishop of Daejeon in South Korea, besides being also a world authority on knitting – blessed St John's House at the end of February. By 1982 Rutt was writing in his diocesan newsletter that although the SSJE had been in Leicester for under two years, "their doorstep will shortly need renewing, so rapidly is it being worn away by the stream of visitors".[15]

In Oxford, the new Priory was blessed on Whitsunday 1980 by Bishop Patrick Rodger, who had been translated from Manchester in 1978: it had room for six members of the Society with a spare room for guests and "space for a good library and a small private chapel". The most significant books in the Society's "mammoth library" were dispersed between the Oxford Centre for Medieval Studies and St Deiniol's Library at Hawarden, with Mark Gibbard accompanying the latter part to take up permanent residence.[16] The new chapel was in the Priory's former garage, with the central piece of alabaster of the destroyed retable from the old community church serving as its altar: an ineffable new function in ignominious surroundings.[17] The marble mensa was a gift from the Benedictine nuns at Burford Priory – it had previously served as the cold slab in their pantry – and various items had been brought from Marston Street "[to] carry out the intention of the donors in their new position".[18] The tabernacle was that in which Leonard Strong had reserved the Blessed Sacrament in his church-tent at Salonica.[19]

Life at Haywards Heath, meanwhile, continued in its now-established vein. Ranulph Fiennes had a claim on the Society's prayers through his mother's longstanding and active membership of the Fellowship of St John – his own distinction notwithstanding, he was sometimes referred to simply as "Lady Fiennes' son"[20] – and while he was wintering in Antarctica during his vertical circumnavigation of the globe the Anchorhold community made him and his companions the focus of weekly meditation.

> On Mondays, using a globe as our meditation symbol, it is our custom to meditate on the members of the Transglobe Expedition [...] Our meditation becomes

13 GenC 1981, SSJE/2/9.
14 NS 1/80.
15 *News & Views*, Diocese of Leicester, Jan 1982.
16 GenC 1980, SSJE/2/8 (loose).
17 NS 11/80.
18 NS 5/81.
19 GenC 1980, SSJE/2/8 (loose).
20 cf NS 3/81.

an intercession in which his courage and vision are shared by us as we engage on a somewhat different expedition of our own.

William Slade quickly noted that the new guest house had room for six people, "who may also like to use it for purposes similar to the members of the Transglobe Expedition, that is to wait for light and kindly hope and make plans for future journeys". Its front door was that of the old Mission House on Marston Street, which had been removed during the renovations of 1961. Never one to miss an opportunity for metaphor, Slade noted that "normally this door will be shut, though it will open to the slightest touch. It will in this way constantly remind us of our work."[21] Returning to a former theme, he also mentioned that "we should especially like to have it used by members of the FSJ who may want to share in some of the new forms of the Society and its new voyages of discovery."[22]

Other new voyages were underway. On his return from Central Council in 1981 the Superior General noted that "each of the three communities within our Society [England, America, and Canada] was moving in a rather different direction to meet the needs within its own particular context".[23] Campbell also attended the first ecumenical "residential consultation" of superiors of Anglican and Roman Catholic communities, which he thought might prove to be "the beginning of increasing co-operation between the religious communities of our two churches";[24] and when Pope John Paul II visited the United Kingdom in 1982 he and other of the brethren attended the gathering of members of religious communities at Roehampton: "his words to us were an inspiration to renew our religious vows with eagerness and resolve".[25] Campbell was considerably less impressed by the Islamic Congress in the Royal Albert Hall, which he thought to have been "well nigh a fiasco".

> A considerable number of eminent Islamic leaders and scholars gave addresses in which they attempted to stress the unifying of the Moslem world which would eventually bring unity to the nations. We heard a lot about Allah and his compassion. We were also entertained by vociferous and angry protests from various corners of the vast hall which seemed to contradict completely the message that was being most boringly delivered from the platform.

James Naters attended the Anglican Charismatic Renewal Conference as "one of several representatives of Anglican Religious Communities"[26] – Campbell thought that the charismatic revival had "released a spirit of joy and freedom into many church congregations and gatherings such as was rare twenty years ago"[27] – while Alan Bean noted that when Robert Runcie arrived in the Abbey grounds at Walsingham to preach at the National Pilgrimage in his first year as Archbishop of Canterbury, "he was clapped in the new uninhibited style,

21 NS 12/80.
22 NS 8/80.
23 GenC 1981, SSJE/2/9.
24 NS 4/80.
25 NS 6/82.
26 NS 5/80.
27 NS 1/83.

(so suitable on such an occasion), and clapped even again after his sermon".[28] When the Alternative Service Book appeared, Campbell hoped "that the new rites for Holy Communion will take on in those churches (and surely nowadays they are the majority) where the Eucharist is the chief Sunday service". He thought that experimental forms of worship which had prepared the ground had "got people used to a Eucharistic service which has a meaningful shape and expresses traditional catholic doctrines of the Eucharist far more clearly than is expressed in the B.C.P.", and suggested that the readers of the *News Sheet* might give copies of the ASB to their friends.[29]

The Society's liturgy had been simplified still further at General Chapter in 1980, when all feasts save Christmas, Epiphany, Ascension, Pentecost, and All Saints were shorn of their First Evensongs – the Superior General had himself proposed from the chair that the Annunciation and Corpus Christi should lose theirs[30] – while at mass the community adopted the practice of forming a semi-circle around the altar and passing the chalice and paten from one to the next.[31] St Edward's House replaced the SSJE office book with the ASB almost immediately: the early mass continued to supply the Blessed Sacrament for the chaplaincy rounds at the nearby Westminster Hospital in the Horseferry Road; but the adoption of the ASB may well have been a conscious decision to ape parish worship. Whether it proved sufficient to nourish the prayer-life of a community whose spiritual life and insight went far deeper than those of most parish priests remains open to question; as does its appeal to clergy who appreciated the former SSJE offices for their depth and rigour.

The London brethren continued the Society's ministry at the heart of Westminster: at tea time the Common Room was frequently busy with officials from Church House, Lambeth Palace, and the Houses of Parliament.[32] The Speaker of the House of Commons, Bernard Weatherill, was a regular visitor and joined the FSJ in 1983. Entertainment for St Edward's House's Open Evenings was sometimes provided by Donald Swann;[33] spare rooms were occupied by students; and the conversion of the attic space with the introduction of large skylights made it "an ideal temporary studio for anyone wanting to paint",[34] which soon attracted a succession of artisans.

Alan Cotgrove, who was by then Prior, reported on developments immediately after the move from the old Mission House and made a point of referring to the members of the community by their Christian names – a practice that jars in the formal records, even two decades after Bishop Harry Carpenter first suggested it might be adopted.[35] Cotgrove, who combined a passion for the relationship between art and religion with a near-iconoclastic determination

---

28 *NS* 6/80.

29 *NS* 12/80.

30 GenC 1980, SSJE/2/8 (loose).

31 cf *NS* 8/81.

32 St Edward's House was also where A. N. Wilson's aristocratic and conflicted monk, Vivyan Chell – whose background and experience reflected that of a number of Cowley Fathers, at least publicly – took refuge in the closing pages of *My Name is Legion*. A. N. Wilson, *My Name is Legion*, London: Arrow Books (2005), 467ff.

33 cf *NS* 5/80.

34 *NS* 7/80.

35 GenC 1980, SSJE/2/8 (loose).

to streamline anything on which he could lay his hands,[36] soon started clearing out the old fittings from the cells in favour of "new look furniture", which he thought "much more convenient".[37]

Engagement with the situation in Northern Ireland also came to the fore. At the end of August 1979, the Superior General, himself the son of a highly-decorated admiral,[38] called the assassination of Earl Mountbatten and the murder of eighteen soldiers "dastardly". He thought that it "brought home to many of us in a most vivid way the diabolical nature of the IRA", and that it had obvious lessons for the spiritual life.

> Diabolical deeds of this kind are being blazenly perpetrated in many lands all over the world reminding us Christians that we are not called to dwell at ease in Zion but to fight the good fight against the world, the flesh and the devil in all their various disguises and forms.

A few months later David Bleakley, a Privy Counsellor who had been Minister for Community Relations at Stormont and was General Secretary of the Irish Council of Churches, addressed a conference for Priest Associates on the subject of "Peace and Reconciliation with special reference to Ulster".[39] Campbell was adamant the situation should claim a place in the Society's prayers.

> It is of great importance that all of us who live in England, and especially those of us who are Christians, should never forget that the people of Northern Ireland are just as much our own kith and kin as are Welshmen or Cornishmen or Yorkshiremen. Northern Ireland is part of the United Kingdom, and we must never forget it.[40]

When he returned from a visit to the Province in 1981 Campbell was optimistic that "in spite of the violence and the antagonisms, the forces of good are stronger than those of evil, and that there will eventually be a break-through towards a solution".[41] Although the Society committed itself publicly to prayer for peace and reconciliation,[42] particularly in its support of the Columbanus Community for Reconciliation in Belfast,[43] its wider role in the preparations for brokering peace in Northern Ireland must necessarily be alluded to only loosely until more time has passed. It has been suggested that some of the lay residents with jobs in Whitehall may not have operated under their real names; and perhaps it is not indiscreet to say that Bleakley himself – whom Cotgrove called one of the community's "residents extraordinary"[44] – retained the use of a meeting-room at St Edward's House for many years.[45]

---

36 cf NS 4/86.
37 NS 1/83.
38 Vice-Admiral Gordon Campbell, VC, DSO**.
39 NS 9/79.
40 NS 11/79.
41 NS 9/81.
42 cf NS 11/83.
43 cf NS 12/84; 12/85; 12/86.
44 NS 10/80.
45 Readers will understand the necessary omission of a citation in this instance.

A few years later, after the ceasefire, Bleakley paid tribute to the Society's part in the peace process on "Seeds of Faith" on BBC Radio 4.

> During my Province's twenty-five years of violence SSJE have held Ireland in their prayers and members of the Fellowship have made many personal visits to stand alongside us in our crisis. We in Northern Ireland owe the Society much.[46]

Campbell insisted that the various new directions of the Society's life were possible because "our small houses are more free to be adaptable to the leading of the Holy Spirit."

> All our Anglican religious communities are experiencing a time of crisis with dwindling numbers, and a sense of lack of direction. It is a time when each community is called to welcome joyfully and deeply the central motif of the Christian religion – the motif of death and resurrection. We cannot have the one without the other.[47]

Slade applied a similar metaphor from the successful digging up and replanting of the Anchorhold lawn in autumn 1980, against the advice of those who felt the work might be better held over until the next spring.

> Some of us share with the community the autumn of our days. We might well surrender to the geriatric solution and let things be. [This] example teaches us another way: to disintegrate certainly but also to re-plant in autumn and prepare "to sail beyond the sunset" and sow our best seed.[48]

DEATH & RESURRECTION?

Not all seed flourished. 8000 miles away in the Transkei, Gordon Shrive was becoming increasingly more reliant on Br Josiah's help in his work at Upper Mjika; and Campbell felt that it was time to reconsider the wisdom of attempting to found an African brotherhood.

> [I]t has for a long time been our hope and prayer that a brotherhood of Africans might coming into being named the Brotherhood of St Joseph. This has not yet come to pass. Fr Shrive, although in excellent physical and mental health, is now 84 years old, and it seems apparent that there is urgent need for a review of and action to be taken on the future.[49]

Shrive was recalled to England in March 1981, and took up permanent residence at St Edward's House. The Superior General realised that "the wrench of leaving Africa after fifty years must be hard for him to bear"; and Mark Woodruff has observed that "he pined for Africa and its people to his dying day".[50] Campbell hoped that Josiah might yet "bear much fruit for the

---

46 *NS* 7/95.
47 *NS* 9/80.
48 *NS* 10/80.
49 *NS* 11/80.
50 *NS* 4/81; Woodruff, *True Man a Long Season*.

Kingdom of Christ in Southern Africa";[51] but in the end he was integrated into the Diocese of St John's, and the Brotherhood of St Joseph came to nothing.[52] Many people, including Shrive – whose friend Oliver Tambo had served his masses in the Transkei[53] – had argued that fully integrated white, black, and coloured communities would be an important witness in the face of racial segregation;[54] but although it was an argument that had also found favour at Mirfield and Kelham, Alistair Mason notes that in the end "the three Anglican orders in South Africa, SSJE, CR and SSM, even when they compared notes, could not work out a good formula for training black religious".[55]

The Society continued to watch the situation in South Africa very closely indeed, and often with "deep sorrow":[56] not least through the prism of Shrive's "intense sadness at the violence and strife in that beloved land".[57] The old Mission House in Cape Town, renamed "Cowley House", became a guest-house for visitors to prisoners on Robben Island;[58] and by 1985 the Superior thought that "the President [P. W. Botha] and his government are now beginning to reap the harvest of a policy which has been ruthlessly pursued for forty years."

> [This] is both iniquitous and unworkable. That apartheid must be dismantled is agreed by all who have any beliefs in the rights of man, but how to do it without utter chaos is not an easy question to answer.[59]

He also observed that the Cowley Fathers who had gone out to India and South Africa a century earlier had "worked heroically according to their lights", but that now "a different approach is needed".

> [This] will both remedy mistakes caused by past blindness, and be more effective when promoting the church's mission which is not the extension of itself but the advancement of the kingdom of Christ among all the various peoples of the world.[60]

The SSJE, now "freed from institutional works and forms", was left to look for positive signs at home.[61] At General Chapter in 1981 – after which Campbell, like Gerald Triffitt before him, began to be referred to only as "Father Superior" – he noted "the undoubted spirit of loving community that pervades all four houses", and also spoke of the new emphasis of the Society's work.

---

51 GenC 1983, SSJE/2/9.
52 cf GenC 1986, SSJE/2/9.
53 NS 10/94.
54 *Minutes of Conference of Religious Communities*, 14 & 15 Feb 1966, Witwatersrand Historical Papers, AB1886/P.1.35.1(4).
55 Mason, *SSM*, 210.
56 cf NS 7/92.
57 NS 8/87.
58 cf NS 2/87.
59 NS 10/85.
60 NS 2/84.
61 NS 11/83.

While some members of the Society are much occupied in giving retreats, schools of prayer and other addresses, it is perhaps true to say that the primary work of mission is now carried on in our houses. The primacy of prayer, and the quality of loving community life are of greater importance than our outside works, and are, we hope, able to make some spiritual impact on the numerous guests who come.[62]

At the same time a couple of members of the Society continued to keep up far-flung ministries. Francis Dalby was for several years seconded to the Canadian congregation in cheerful old age – where "in spite of increasing deafness and lameness [he] plays a vital part in keeping the SSJE light burning"[63] – while the relative freedom given to Gibbard in his work at Hawarden enabled him to develop international influence, with engagements all over the world and talks on radio and television.[64] Naters was a regular visitor to South Africa, where he made a concerted effort to invigorate the branches of the Fellowship of St John at Cape Town and Umtata;[65] while at the end of the decade Cyril Woolley returned to Hamburg, where he had been stationed with the RAF after the end of the Second World War, to take part in ecumenical engagement. He particularly noted a change in "returning to Germany behind a German pilot".[66]

The international influence of the English congregation of the SSJE had not entirely receded; but the ongoing narrative of death and resurrection, within which the move from Cowley had been framed, continued. When the Canadian congregation folded in 1984 – the remaining brethren moved to Boston, taking Dalby with them – Campbell called it "undoubtedly the leading of the Holy Spirit";[67] and when in the early 1980s St Matthew's, Westminster, was being rebuilt on a much smaller footprint after having been gutted by fire – "a smaller and more labour-saving building" – he thought that it was "symbolic of what is going on in the church at large".

There is a great deal that still needs to die before the new shoots of spiritual life can really spring into flower. To preserve and conserve and restore in the interests of spiritual revival may sometimes be right, but the transformation of spiritual life implied by the word "renewal" involves taking the risk to leave the past in order to nurture the future.[68]

Shortly afterwards he conceded that "many of us have passed the allotted span of three score years and ten, and there is little sign of fresh aspirants".[69] He delighted in the relative sprightliness of two of the more senior brethren after their respective hip replacements, and announced mischievously that "we rejoice that by the skill of modern surgery the Society has two elderly

---

62 GenC 1981, SSJE/2/9.
63 GenC 1983, SSJE/2/9.
64 GenC 1982, SSJE/2/9.
65 cf GenC 1983, SSJE/2/9; NS 3/88.
66 NS 8/88.
67 NS 4/84.
68 NS 11/82.
69 GenC 1982, SSJE/2/9.

but rejuvenated hippies in its membership";[70] but time continued to take its toll. When Walter Fitch died in 1981 – he had been professed in SSJE in 1938 after service in the Indian Army and a period with the Cambridge Delhi Brotherhood – Bean called him "a gentleman, and a priest to the backbone; [who] never lost his soldier's carriage."

> There was about him a certain air of natural authority and good taste, upon which the good Lord had grafted many pleasant things in the course of his long dedicated life [...] About eight years ago he said he could no longer manage gardening. (He always volunteered for this, though it was *not* his line). He then went on to say: "But I shall walk in it: precious few of us seem to have time for that. It will give the place tone."[71]

The Superior thought him "an unforgettable character, and a model religious"; but he was old and his death had not been unexpected. Leonard Wilks was in the same category: he had spent almost his whole life linked to the Society, having attended Cowley St John School, been an altar boy in the community church, sung in the choir under Basil Bucknall, and served his curacy at Cowley St James. Campbell thought that this had influenced his tendency to present an appearance of "severity and reserve".

> Brought up from an early age to know some of the Cowley Fathers of sixty or seventy years ago he cultivated an austerity which a few of them undoubtedly had, and which unfortunately helped to give the society a reputation for *gravitas* rather than *hilaritas* which was never really true.[72]

Fitch and Wilks were very much relicts of the SSJE's days of summer, and others followed them soon enough. In 1985 Dalby and Alan Young celebrated their diamond jubilees of priesthood;[73] but both had gone to their reward by the end of the decade, as had Shrive, Lonsdale Wain, and Henry Bruce – a particularly tragic case who had spent the last 25 years of his life in specialist psychiatric care.[74] The loss of Christopher Bryant, however, was a particular blow: Campbell called him "one of the most outstanding members of the Society", who "had for many years played a leading role.

> There is no need for me to repeat the numerous tributes that have been paid to his memory as a man of God and widely influential as a Spiritual guide through

---

70 GenC 1983, SSJE/2/9.

71 NS 6/81.

72 NS 6/84.

73 NS 12/85. Fr Young's diamond-jubilee mass was celebrated by him in the chapel at St John's Home, where he was being cared for by the All Saints Sisters alongside others who had played their part in the SSJE's later history. Fr Bishop, who had a room next to Fr Young, led the intercessions; while Bishop Carpenter read the gospel from his wheelchair. Lord and Lady Ramsey of Canterbury were also residents by this point, and Fr Dalby would soon join them.

74 NS 12/86. Fr Bruce was among the patients at the Holloway Sanatorium at Virginia Water when the young Bill Bryson worked there in the early 1970s. *Notes from a Small Island*, London: Doubleday (1995), 8off.

his writings, *New Fire*, lectures, and individual counselling [...] We miss him greatly.[75]

The tributes to Bryant poured in much as they had done for Frederick Puller and Philip Waggett decades earlier; but *New Fire* – which Ronald Blythe thought "one of the best written of modern religious periodicals" and an important antidote to "the limitation and unexcitingness of some of the Christian press"[76] – scarcely outlived its editor.

The Superior had earlier emphasised that "our Society always had members with strong individual characteristics, and has wisely given considerable freedom to enable each to make use of his particular individual gifts".[77] By the 1980s Bean and Wain were such well-regarded lepidopterists that they served as Honorary Associate Curators of the University's Museum of Natural History, and often holidayed together in search of new specimens for their collections[78] – on one trip Bean was mugged and badly beaten by brigands while collecting butterflies near Poona[79] – but the demise of *New Fire* reflected the more troublesome side of such latitude. The issue had dogged some aspects of the Society's work for much of its life: that which had depended for its success on the genius of a single member of the Society could not necessarily continue without him. The same had been true of Yerendawana after the death of Edward Elwin in 1921; and, to at least some extent, of the work at Cape Town after that of David Gardner in 1964.

New work was now out of the question, and Campbell reminded his brethren "that any work outside our houses, however apparently insignificant and trivial, which an individual wishes to undertake should receive our permission".[80] He later observed that "demands are made on us to go here, there, and everywhere. Many of these invitations are temptations, rather than calls, and we need prayer and discernment to distinguish which."[81]

It was obvious anyone with eyes to see that the Society's decline had continued: by 1983 the English congregation's numbers had fallen to twenty-four.

> Seven are octogenarians, seven are septuagenarians, six are sexagenarians and the remaining four all quinquagenarians. We can thank God that in spite of such a venerable average age, and other limitations, the Society is able to bear witness to a quiet and ordered life of prayer in all our houses, and to carry on a considerable amount of useful work and ministry. It is, however, difficult to see how we can on our own initiate new undertakings, or take on fresh work, unless and until we are granted more vocations.

A trickle of men came to test their vocations as the 1980s passed, but none stayed the course. It must have been tempting for Campbell to envy the American congregation when he visited Boston at the end of 1984.

---

75 GenC 1986, SSJE/2/9.
76 Blythe, *View in Winter*, 282.
77 GenC 1983, SSJE/2/9.
78 cf GenC 1988, SSJE/2/9; NS 9/84.
79 *NS* 12/91.
80 GenC 1982, SSJE/2/9.
81 GenC 1985, SSJE/2/9.

Our community there is in a very different stage of its progress to our community in England. While here in England we are largely a membership of ripe years, very much alive, but getting rather limited in the amount of activity we can shoulder; in America the average age of the community is under forty-five, and one gets an impression of considerable vigour.

He thought, in fact, that "what is more important is that the American community, while rooted in the best of the SSJE tradition, is also, as Fr Benson would wish, a community of the present moment precisely up to the mark of the times".[82] Later he went as far to say that "to be in touch with SSJE in America today is to receive the same spiritual inspiration as that given by the Society a hundred years ago".

SSJE America is providing the same foundation for a renewal of religious and spiritual life in the Anglican communion as was provided by Fr Benson and his first companions in the Society [...] Far from being traditional imitators of by-gone days, they are men of the present moment and its life! They are indeed worthy to be the inheritors of all that is fundamental and lasting in the Cowley tradition.[83]

The installation of a "Prayerline" in 1985 demonstrated how the English congregation's engagement with its wider family had changed. "Up until recently", wrote Campbell a year later, "a considerable part of a Cowley Father's ministry was taken up in the confessional".

In these days the number of people who regularly use the sacrament of confession in a formal way in church has been decreasing, but at the same time those seeking spiritual direction or counselling are increasing.[84]

The "Prayerline" was a designated telephone service "offered in the belief that more things occur through the activity of prayer than we can imagine", and "open 24 hours a day through the use of an answerphone".[85] Godfrey Callaway would have utterly hated it; but different times seemed to call for different methods. Simultaneously, without vocations even the new expressions of the SSJE's life became difficult to keep up. Campbell realised that "the next few years of our life in community are likely to be fraught with difficulties owing to the gradually increasing limitations of our manpower resources".

We may have to be quite ruthless about this. Our witness as religious is not measured by the amount of active work we take on, but by the quality of our life of prayer and friendship and caring for one another. A community such as ours which consists mostly of elderly men must seek to generate an atmosphere of calm and never of strain.

---

82 NS 11/84.
83 NS 10/87.
84 NS 10/86.
85 NS 10/85.

He felt that the Society needed "to have some idea as to the expectations of the future of our houses" – a few years later Slade made an original and unsuccessful attempt to have the Anchorhold made the mother house[86] – and which would be the house that the SSJE would seek to keep open longest.[87] Soon enough, the Superior was of the opinion that "the English congregation of the Society is now in the final phase of its life as we have known it"; and that situation had led him to the conclusion that "I do not consider that the Society can now provide suitable conditions for the training of men in the religious life as we have interpreted it in the past".

This prompted another "frank Community discussion", but Campbell was adamant that "God is working his purpose out most of all when we have to face adversity and confusion."

> I have no reason to suppose that His purpose necessarily involves the survival or revival of the Society of St John the Evangelist. Nevertheless I believe that so long as the Society exists, however small it may become, it has its unique part to play in the furthering of the Kingdom of Christ.[88]

Admissions to the novitiate were suspended in 1987, and in the same year the Society entered into a brief collaboration with the Society of the Sacred Mission as a way of combining forces, particularly in the running of St Edward's House.[89] It withdrew from Leicester at the same time, seven years after its arrival: "it seems right that we should withdraw now rather than allow the life and work to 'run down', which is what would inevitably happen if we were to try to continue."[90] It retained St John's House in the hope that members of the Fellowship of St John might step up to "to carry on actively part of the function for which the Society has existed", and that the house "may continue to be lived in and used as a centre of Christian life and prayer".[91] Barry and Helen Morley, staunch members of the FSJ, took up residence shortly afterwards to run it as a retreat house on behalf of the Society.[92]

Campbell now thought that the English congregation had "now come to the brink of an even more radical stage in its transformation than the evacuation of the Mission House at Oxford".

> At that time there was some hope that moving out of a large institution into smaller houses might be more attractive to aspirants, with some necessary revision and adaptation of the SSJE life as it had been lived at Oxford. Yet it is becoming more and more evident to me that for the last 25 or 30 years God has been working in our Society a process of transformation which is now leading us beyond a mere revision and adaptation of our old life, but to a new thing – it may be a new birth.

---

86 GenC 1990, SSJE/2/9.
87 GenC 1985, SSJE/2/9.
88 GenC 1986, SSJE/2/9.
89 GenC 1987, SSJE/2/9.
90 NS 5/87.
91 NS 6/87.
92 GenC 1988, SSJE/2/9.

He was now determined to throw off at least part of the SSJE's former image once and for all: "for 100 years we served a church which had been paternalistic in attitude both at home and abroad, and people still delighted to call us 'the Cowley Fathers'. What could be more paternalistic than that?"

> Whether we like it or not, paternalism is dead and finished as a way of relationship towards adult groups of people today: whether nations, churches, or indeed religious communities. So, it seems to me, the Society is in a process of transformation into a new and somewhat different way of community life, glimpses of which we can see at the Anchorhold and St John's House.[93]

The Superior had earlier observed that the SSJE's "slow but apparent decline" in England had been mitigated to some extent by the "constant trickle of men and women of all kinds and ages" who continued to seek membership of the Fellowship of St John. Campbell thought that some of the members might well "feel called to a very close association with us in our life, without being called to make the commitment of full religious vows", and that this was "a possibility" to which the Society should be ready to respond.[94] His observation was bound up in a major piece of business that would, in the end, enable and direct the work of the SSJE's English congregation for the rest of its days: "a call to work together to explore different ways of developing".[95]

PLANNING AHEAD

The Fellowship of St John (U.K.) Trust Association was set up in 1984 as a Company Limited by Guarantee. Its object was "to engage in works missionary and educational for the advancement of the Kingdom of Christ"; and its purpose was to supersede the SSJE's former Trust Association and subsume the various funds for which the Society was also responsible. Oversight of the FSJTA – and therefore also the management of its assets – was to be shared between representatives of the SSJE and the members of the Fellowship of St John: the first three members of the new Company were Campbell, as Superior; Slade, as Bursar; and, representing the FSJ, Audrey, Lady Fiennes.[96] By 1986 – after not a little to-ing and fro-ing with the Charity Commission – it was "in full operation".[97]

"This is the age of the laity", thought Campbell, in which the religious communities would play "a less public role in the life and work of the church". He thought that that in such a context "religious orders, including our own, have a quiet contribution to make as leaven in the lump", and hoped that the establishment of the FSJTA might "bear fruit in some of the Society's financial resources being freed to help forward the Kingdom of Christ, and lay community projects of one kind or another".[98]

93 GenC 1989, SSJE/2/9.
94 GenC 1983, SSJE/2/9.
95 NS 2/90.
96 GenC 1984, SSJE/2/9.
97 GenC 1986, SSJE/2/9.
98 GenC 1985, SSJE/2/9.

The Superior felt that this sort of arrangement – he particularly approved of a similar scheme set in train by the Community of the Epiphany at Truro – was good preparation for the 21st century, when he thought "the Church will no longer be a clerically dominated body, but will truly be the *laos* – the laity – the people of God".

> Of course it will still have its bishops and priests, but they will no longer be on a pedestal, but exercising their proper function of ministry as part of the *laos* for they never cease to be laymen.[99]

Within this understanding, the building up of the SSJE's lay wing could be cast not as a necessity brought on by the Society's ongoing failure to attract lasting vocations to its vowed life; but as a prophetic preparation for success in the future. Members of the FSJ later started leading days of reflection, organised themselves into regional prayer-cells, occasionally visited the former mission-outposts in India and South Africa, and began to contribute to the *News Sheet*.[100] In 1988 Campbell wrote of "the drop in vocations to the priesthood and the religious life which has been continuing for more than twenty years". "For myself", he assured his readers, "I cannot help thinking that this is a blessing rather than a tragedy, and that we are already finding that the ordinary laity are coming into their own as men and women called to a ministry in the church."[101]

The Superior soon clarified his comments: "I was not of course implying that we should not continue to pray for more vocations to the ordained priesthood and the religious life."

> [But] in the present era of rapid change in church and society, the view of the ordained priest and of the consecrated monk and nun is changing rapidly, particularly as the conception of the priesthood of all believers and the call to holiness is more deeply accepted and understood.

"The whole manner of life of both priest and religious is to be a sign of the coming of Christ's Kingdom", he went on. "He and she need constantly to refuse the pedestal on which the church in the past has often placed them. We should be praying not necessarily for more clergy and religious, but for clergy and religious who manifest the humility and sacrificial love of Jesus in their lives."[102]

By the time Campbell ceased to be Superior in 1991 the FSJTA had disbursed from its income around a quarter of a million pounds in grants, often – but not always – in connection with the SSJE's former overseas work. Among the first recipients were the CMS; the USPG; and St John's Home, where many Cowley Fathers spent their last days, and which continued to be run by the All Saints Sisters as something of a genteel Anglo-Catholic departure lounge. Other grants paid for maintenance at the former Mission House at Cape Town;

---

99 *NS* 6/85.
100 cf *NS* 2,3/95.
101 *NS* 8/88.
102 *NS* 11/88.

for a new vehicle to enable Bishop Paul Richardson of Aipo-Rongo in Papua New Guinea to visit his flock more effectively; for a priest "to visit an embryonic sisterhood in Madagascar"; and for repairs to the church roof at Tsolo.[103]

The FSJTA swiftly became a means of distributing the SSJE's considerable funds, after the cessation of its colonial liabilities, by furthering the Kingdom in ways of which the Society might approve: large sums also went to the Centre for Black and White Christian Partnership, and to various non-SSJE projects in other parts of Africa. The grants made in the late 1980s were wide-ranging, and included individual initiatives as well as group efforts: an effective and relatively straightforward way in which the Society could continue to support old works, and engage with new ones, without the pressure of having to supply men on the ground.

This was important work, for Campbell also realised that the Church of England was "on the threshold of crisis", as "accepted ideas of its order and the truths it exists to proclaim are being called in question".[104] He particularly identified "ways of interpreting fundamental doctrines such as the Virgin Birth and Resurrection, marriage discipline, the ordination of women, church and state relationship, Synodical Government, the apparent collapse of the church in some inner cities and some rural areas" as "examples of vital subjects which are causing fierce controversy". Nevertheless, he was a staunch supporter of Robert Runcie, and thought that "the Church of England is extraordinarily blest in its Primate."[105]

The News Sheet had itself opened up for discussion some of the controversial issues of the day, not least those surrounding women's ordination and divorce. The phrase "a second marriage can also be a sacrament of healing" would have been anathema in the Cowley Evangelist even in its final days; but it appeared in 1986 in the course of a debate that included – perhaps inevitably – a priest-member of the FSJ's reasoning that "society itself is changing, and, pastorally, I have to respond to the changes."[106] Perhaps more startling was the view, expressed after the General Synod debated sexual morality in 1987, that "it is to be hoped that one outcome of the debate on sexuality will be an acknowledgment that sex is a gift from God, to be used to His glory, whatever the individual's sexual orientation."[107] A few years later, reviewing Anthony Harvey's Promise or Pretence, Campbell noted that the author dealt with "such subjects as divorce, sex before marriage, family life and homosexuality" before emphasising that he was nonetheless "happily married with four grown-up daughters".[108]

The Superior was present in St Paul's Cathedral when Bishop Graham Leonard ordained seventy deaconesses to the diaconate: he thought that "a fitting tribute was at last being made by the Church to the Ministry of women". He also declared that he was "not impressed by the theological reasons used

---

103 FSJTA Committee of Management Minutes, 1986–1991.
104 NS 11/86.
105 NS 8/89.
106 NS 4/86.
107 NS 12/87.
108 A. E. Harvey, Promise or Pretence? A Christian's Guide to Sexual Morals, London: SCM Press (1994); NS 8/94.

against the ordination of women to the priesthood";[109] and thought it "a matter of secondary importance, on which it is legitimate for churches to differ".[110] Campbell was nevertheless confident that the highly emotive question of the admission of women to the presbyterate could be resolved peaceably and for the good of the Church.

> [I]f approached in the spirit of prayer with an absence of prejudice and a readiness to listen to theological arguments on both sides, I have every hope that by the time a decision is finally called for, there will be a pretty clear consensus of opinion either in favour or against.[111]

In the event this proved hopelessly optimistic, and the Society was left to weather the storm as the Church of England began to tear itself apart. "Rightly or wrongly", said Campbell, "I am not one of those who are dismayed at the apparent turbulence of church affairs, particularly in the Church of England and the Anglican Communion."

> I believe that this is only the beginning of a huge upheaval which will affect profoundly the whole church involving a lot of breaking up. It seems to me to prelude the process of transformation which the Lord is requiring of the church in order that it may be a more fit instrument to present the Gospel of the Kingdom to a secularised world.

The Society of St John the Evangelist had already done its own breaking up, but within the wider turmoil Campbell thought that "we need to go on working at making our community one where love reigns". He had earlier described recently-deceased brethren as having "joined the greater part of our Society beyond the grave", and his final Superior's address to General Chapter in 1991 bore out a similar theme.

> During the past few years I have occasionally referred to two undoubted facts which some seem to have felt I should not have mentioned. The one is that we are a group exclusively of elderly men and the second is that we are living in the concluding part of our history.

"In other words", thought Campbell, "the Society in England in the form we have known it is dying and cannot revive. Neither of these things is in any way a cause for sadness or depression; but as I see it they are part and parcel of our pilgrimage back to God."[112]

---

109 *NS* 4/87.
110 *NS* 7/86.
111 *NS* 10/85.
112 GenC 1991, SSJE/2/9.

25

THE LONG DAY CLOSES

Brethren, do our years last? They slip away day by day.
Those which were, no longer are; those to come are not yet here.

—Augustine of Hippo, *Commentary on Psalm 122*

As the Society of St John the Evangelist had begun to consider its future at Cowley, Kingsley Amis had been working on his next book. Amis had, by his own admission, "not a shred" of faith;[1] but he was up at Oxford in the 1940s, and his cutting satirical novel of ecclesiastical intrigue and skulduggery, *The Alteration*, was published in 1976. Two major conceits present themselves in its opening pages: the Reformation has not taken place, so England remains in full and visible communion with the Holy See; and its metropolitical church – "the mother church of all England and of the English Empire overseas", the seat of the Cardinal Archbishop of Canterbury, and the royal mausoleum – is, for deep historical reasons, long-established at a place called Coverley.

The Cathedral Basilica of St George boasts the longest nave in Christendom, and has been adorned sumptuously by the finest craftsmen that England has produced. Its world-famous choir is trained at a monastic establishment nearby, which in addition to the choristers also provides educational opportunities for students from across the Empire. That Amis took as his inspiration the ecclesiastical establishments of Oxford seems certain: the "exquisitely varicoloured brick-built churches for which middle England was famous" may easily be taken to allude to Butterfield's soaring chapel of Keble College, just around the corner from St John's, Amis's own college. More specifically, when the Abbot of the monastery greets visitors and welcomes them to Coverley, his etymological idiosyncrasy locates it absolutely: "he pronounced it 'Cowley', after the old fashion".[2]

When Amis was a student the buildings of the SSJE in East Oxford formed the major ecclesiastical establishment on the other side of Magdalen Bridge; and the sonorous bell atop the tower of the community church was, and still is, easily audible in the centre of the town. In using St John's Church as the prototype for St George's, Amis built from his fertile imagination an extreme of the very type of institution from which the SSJE was at that point seeking to distance itself. Robert Page or Henry Bull might well have been minded, had they been able, to commission work from the likes of Wren, Turner, Gainsborough,

---

1 Kingsley Amis, "Godforsaken", *The Amis Collection*, London: Hutchinson (1990), 226.
2 Kingsley Amis, *The Alteration*, London: Jonathan Cape (1976), 16.

Blake, and Hockney; but by the mid-1960s their successor Gerald Triffitt had anticipated the Society's departure from Marston Street when he wondered whether the very buildings themselves were a burden: "it is hard for S.S.J.E. to divest itself of the weight of authority and perhaps solemnity which hangs like an aura about our Oxford House and St Edward's House."[3]

It had fallen to David Campbell to lead the exodus; and soon after Amis had let his own imagination run wild as to what might have been at Cowley in a different world, the Society finally abandoned its House Beautiful. Writing in the *Church Times*, John Madeley thought that "in future the Society will be seen to be even more closely in the thick of life to meet the demands which are placed upon it".

> [For] people searching for more meaningful ways of living, there could be, as Fr Campbell suggests, a fascinating resurgence of community life. The existence of a long-established community like the SSJE could be a tremendous support to such a movement of the Spirit. It is possible to see the move from Marston Street as a sign that God is equipping the Society to do a job of work in the 'eighties and 'nineties as demanding and challenging as anything that it has tackled before.[4]

It was surely a coincidence that Madeley's article appeared next to an advertisement for hearing-aids. Campbell's successor as Superior, James Naters, had to concede, after the Society hosted a day conference "for Anglicans aged between 18 and 40 who wish to understand more about the Religious Life" in conjunction with the Society of St Francis, the Wantage Sisters, and the Society of the Sacred Mission, that "not many people came". He took the opportunity of reminding the readers of the *News Sheet* of their "need to be concerned about the Religious Life, and to make it an object of prayer".

> Many communities, including SSJE, are much smaller today, and we are in need of new members if we are to continue our vital role in the life of the Church; this is why we ask you to pray, and to have a concern for us.[5]

One of Naters' first duties after his election in 1991 was to attend the enthronement of George Carey as Archbishop of Canterbury.[6] Shortly afterwards, he presided over the SSJE's 125th anniversary celebrations at St Stephen's House: the American brethren came from Cambridge for the occasion, and the chant was bolstered by the upper voices of members of the SLG and the ASSP.[7] A year later, the General Synod voted to proceed with the ordination of women to the priesthood.

Like his predecessor, Naters was not opposed to the ordination of women; while from retirement Campbell dismissed the suggestion "that the ordination of women to the priesthood may lead to a reduction of women going forward to join the religious communities": he thought that there was "room for priest

---

3 *CE* Sept 1966.
4 *Church Times*, 1 Feb 1980.
5 *NS* 10/93.
6 *NS* 5/91.
7 *NS* 9/91.

nuns as well as priest monks", and endorsed the establishment of Affirming Catholicism – as did Naters.[8] Campbell thought that "many of us rejoice that women today are ordained priests and preside at our altars".[9]

Naters felt that a majority of his brethren were in favour of the development; but at the same time knew that "as in any cross section of society members hold different views, and there are a few who will find it hard to adjust".[10] Alan Bean was among them: he called the vote "an act of daring, damaging to unity, when Synod claimed to extend the scope of the Apostolic Ministry"; and thought it "tragic" that we have given the matter of the ordination of women priority over unity and even charity [...] Up till then a way was opening towards greater unity in the Church of God."

> Our Synod, representing only the two Church of England provinces, has greatly presumed; no diocese or province can claim naked authority to pronounce on a matter involving the faith and well-being of the whole church. But for this rash act, in England and in several other Anglican provinces, dialogue might have pointed a better way towards a consensus, as near as possible, of all catholic Christians.[11]

It was a point on which the Society, like the Church of England, would remain divided. As David Hemming had observed from Canada over a decade earlier, "a Community of human beings can't be dragooned into a common mind".[12]

Away from ecclesiastical controversy, and in addition to its charitable disbursements, the Fellowship of St John Trust Association ensured that there was money available for repairs to the Society's houses, as well as provision for those members requiring advanced geriatric care at St John's Home or elsewhere. St Edward's House was totally overhauled in 1991, with the brethren dispersed far and wide to stay with friends, relatives, and other religious communities for a few months;[13] and another Visitation was conducted in 1995 by the Visitor, Ronald Gordon, assisted by Mother Anne SLG, and the Secretary of the Oxford Diocesan Board of Finance.

Gordon had been invited to become Visitor after the retirement of Patrick Rodger, and was the first Visitor of the SSJE not to have been Bishop of Oxford. His charge, like that of Harry Carpenter nearly 30 years earlier, recommended another period of self-examination. Naters summarised it in three questions.

1. How can the life of the community be maintained to promote the care and wellbeing of all its members?
2. How can the "missionary" and pastoral work, both inside and outside the community be sustained?
3. What is the role and purpose of each individual house?[14]

---

8 cf NS 4,5,6,9/94.
9 NS 1/96.
10 NS 12/92.
11 NS 2/93.
12 NS 6/79.
13 NS 4/91.
14 FSJTA Committee of Management, 22 March 1995.

Naters called the visitation "a happy and profitable time".[15] A working party was set up to review the way in which St Edward's House was run and what its future use might be – the new Superior wanted it to be a "centre for spirituality"[16] – and the administration of the Society in general. In 1989 the information leaflets that detailed the various SSJE houses and works began to be headed "Society and Fellowship of St John": at the time Campbell had explained that "the Society as we have known it is diminishing, and the time has come to discover how the Fellowship can be represented more fully in the work and administration".[17]

Although there had been a trickle of vocations as the 1990s went on, it was now obvious that the professed members of the SSJE needed help – notwith-standing Alan Cotgrove's determination at St Edward's House to do as much maintenance work as possible by himself.[18] A new Statute in 1996 erected formally new classes of membership within the Society: seekers and oblates. Seekers were to be "those who ask permission to seek a life of consecration to God under the direction of the Society for a fixed period"; while Oblates would be "those wishing so to live in this world that their life may be an oblation for the service and glory of God, and who promise to live faithfully according to the principles of Poverty, Chastity and Obedience, and to conform themselves to the mind and spirit of the Society".[19]

The further introduction of Internal Oblates, "men who are prepared to make a commitment of at least three years, living and working in one of our houses", was an attempt to "bring new strength to the Society";[20] but in antici-pation of the possibility of the Chapter reaching the stage where it was no longer able to manage the SSJE's affairs – nursing-home care for a number of the brethren had become a major expenditure[21] – a Statute was introduced whereby in consultation with the Visitor "the responsibility for the distribution of the houses of the Society and the maintenance of the remaining members of the Society" could be passed to the Management Committee of the FSJTA.[22]

A professional Bursar was appointed to take responsibility "for the general maintenance and oversight of all the properties of the Society, and for the overall accounting and financial management"; and as part of the new arrange-ments the SSJE also overhauled the Fellowship of St John: subsuming the pro-fessed members of the SSJE, the members of the former FSJ, and all others with a connection to the Society into one body. Two hand-drawn diagrams, one of a series of concentric circles and the other of a flower in bloom, appeared in a supplement to the *News Sheet* in March 1997. "The first", it observed, "shows SSJE and FSJ as we all experienced it in the past. At the centre were those living in community. The outer circles represented external oblates and FSJ

15 *NS* 9/95.
16 *NS* 4/92.
17 *NS* 3/89.
18 cf FSJTA CoM, 4 June 1998.
19 GenC 1996, SSJE/2/10.
20 *NS* 6/92.
21 FSJTA CoM, 7 Sept 1998.
22 FSJTA CoM, 18 Sept; 11 Nov 1996; GenC 1996, SSJE/2/10.

members. The second diagram shows the new thinking, the wider Society that is soon to be known just as The Fellowship of St John."

There is still a central core but now it is made up of several petals overlapping one other.

These petals represent:

1. The Professed under life vows.
2. Seekers living a consecrated life with the professed for a fixed period.
3. Those who see their calling as prayer support within the Fellowship.
4. Those residents sharing together in community life in a way that is combined with some external work or study.
5. Those living outside community life but wishing to maintain as close a link as possible with the Fellowship by study of its spirit, by local group member-ship and by undertaking to give assistance in whatever way is appropriate to one of the Fellowship's houses.
6. People, like those living apart, ordained or lay, who exercise a ministry ena-bling the Church to be the Church in the world. Some may be on the fringes of Church life.
7. Employees of the Fellowship.[23]

It was a final attempt to mould the SSJE along the lines of the less-clerically-focussed Society that Campbell had looked for a decade earlier. From 1997 the trustees of the FSJTA shadowed Chapter meetings in anticipation of the day when they might need to take up the reins. In the same year, it was decided that the work of St John's House, Leicester, should be wound up;[24] and the administration of the Society moved from Oxford to London, to be run from the same house in which the Superior was resident.[25] At the same time the SSJE's long-serving Secretary, Olive Norton, retired; and the *News Sheet* came to an end.[26]

Naters particularly regretted the closure of St John's House, with its "busy programme" of quiet days, retreats, and spiritual counselling; its interfaith work; and its outreach to those with AIDS; but "we could no longer retain responsibility for administering the house, and so the only alternative was closure".[27] By now much of the detail of the Statues and Rule had effectively fallen into abeyance through "the rapidly changing nature of the Society"; and as a comprehensive overhaul would be time-consuming "and possibly abor-tive", the brethren resolved "to live as far as possible in the spirit of the rules, as written, making adaptations where necessary".

Campbell remained hopeful that "if the Society were to pass through its present frail condition, it could be possible that what would emerge would be virtually a new society, requiring a completely new book of statutes and

---

23 *NS* 3/97.
24 FSJTA CoM, 5 July; 10 Sept 1997; GenC 1997, SSJE/2/10.
25 *NS* 10/97.
26 *NS* 12/97.
27 GenC 1998, SSJE/2/11/5.

rules".[28] That St Edward's House was a much-needed and valued resource was borne out by the numbers of visitors it received: in the first part of 1998 Naters made a tally of visitors, which he presented to Chapter in May.

> We have had 68 people coming for an overnight [stay], most of them for more than one night; five people coming for a private retreat; fifteen people coming for an individual Quiet Day; and 54 people coming to conducted Quiet Days. There have been thirty groups coming for the day, or part of the day, some of them parish groups, others such as the Franciscan Third Order, the Delhi Brotherhood, the Julian Group, the Guild of St Barnabas, etc. These groups do not include a weekly eucharist and a monthly study group, run by Fr Ivor Smith Cameron, a monthly group meeting to pray for Africa, and a small group of wives of MPs who meet for two hours each week to pray here.

He thought that the Society had an "ongoing ministry",[29] and by 1998 its seekers and oblates had been incorporated even more fully into its life: the Oblates received "the privileges and security otherwise given to members in First Vows", and a vote in Chapter after six months' probation; while the seekers were given the rights "formerly given to one who is a Novice".[30]

This further change to the Statutes, wrote Naters, was an attempt "to widen the involvement of non-professed members in the life and work of our Society.[31] The need had been underlined in February 1997 by the death at St John's Home of Mark Gibbard, the SSJE's last public theologian;[32] closely followed by that of Arthur Phalo, eight thousand miles away from his native Transkei.[33] He felt that the new arrangements of seekers and oblates meant that "we may well have a future";[34] and in a bold move in 1999 it was decided that time spent in either state could be counted towards what would formerly have been the period of the novitiate.

After discussion with representatives from the Advisory Council for Religious Communities and consultation with a new Visitor, the Bishop of Reading, Dominic Walker OGS, the novitiate was effectively reopened; and Br James Simon and Peter Huckle were duly professed. Both "helped to provide a new vision of a new SSJE, and a new vision of St Edward's House for a modern-day church":[35] they were the first men to be professed in the English congregation for a quarter of a century; but would also be the last.

James Naters was succeeded by Alan Cotgrove in 2000. Almost immediately the Anchorhold went the way of St John's House, and so did the Priory in Oxford. Cotgrove now consolidated the remaining members of the Society in London, with the exception of Bean, who remained in Oxford to serve as confessor to St Stephen's House – to whom the Society also looked to sell 228 Iffley Road. In the end the members of the Committee of Management were left to

---

28 GenC 1997, SSJE/2/10.
29 GenC 1998, SSJE/2/11/6.
30 FSJTA CoM, 4 June 1998; GenC 1998, SSJE/2/11/1.
31 *NS* 6/96.
32 *NS* 3/97.
33 *NS* 7/97.
34 GenC 1998, SSJE/2/11/5.
35 GenC 1999, SSJE/2/11/13.

regret "that their hoped-for transfer to theological use had fallen through".[36] Some of the contents were returned to the former mother house, and the rest were disposed of;[37] while the carved piece of alabaster that had served as an altar in the garage-chapel, and which had previously formed the centrepiece of the high altar in the community church, disappeared.

By April 2002 Cotgrove was terminally ill, and had summoned his brethren to his bedside at the Royal Marsden Hospital to announce his immediate resignation. He was succeeded by Huckle, who had made his life vows only a few weeks earlier: votes arrived from nursing homes by telephone and letter.[38] The outlook was particularly bleak; Cotgrove was soon in a nursing home near Cambridge, waiting to die; Campbell was going blind and waiting for a place to become available at St John's Home, where he was joined in short order by Bean and his butterflies; and Naters was already being cared for at the College of St Barnabas, Lingfield, where Peter Palmer would also soon retire. A stark report by the Bursar noted the considerable outlay owing to the number of members of the Society in residential nursing care; and that an earlier forecast "had anticipated a slower rise in these numbers but more funerals in the same period".[39]

The remaining brethren had sustained an ever-diminishing round of small-scale retreats; quiet days; chaplaincy duty at local hospitals; preaching engagements; cover in nearby parishes; assistance at St Margaret's Church and Westminster Abbey; ministry to schoolchildren; and, above all, the ongoing pastoral care of those who came to their door for confession and spiritual direction. By 2007, however, it was clear that there was no realistic option but to close the novitiate once more, this time permanently;[40] and at General Chapter in 2009 the Superior delivered his address to the only other active member of the Society.[41]

Although an urgent programme to improve the comfort of visitors had been instigated in 2002 – with a concomitant and immediate increase in the numbers of guests – the funerals inevitably came in the end. By 2011 there remained only three professed members, of whom only two were active. Plans had by then been put into place to prepare for the final withdrawal of the SSJE from public ministry; and at a Special General Chapter in November 2010 the Chapter – all three of them – voted unanimously in favour of the motion "that St Edward's House be declared superfluous to the present and future needs of the Society". They asked for it to be sold "in accordance with established custom",[42] and a buyer was soon found in Westminster School.

The Headmaster and other dignitaries attended mass on Ascension Day 2011, and stayed to luncheon with the Trustees of the FSJTA "to celebrate the past, present and future". In 2012 St Edward's House was transferred to the school to serve as its Chaplaincy and as a girls' boarding house. The two last

---

36 FSJTA CoM, 7 June 2000.
37 FSJTA CoM, 6 Dec 2001.
38 Special GenC 2002, SSJE/2/11/35.
39 FSJTA CoM, 7 March 2002.
40 GenC 2007, SSJE/2/11/86.
41 GenC 2009, SSJE/2/11/102.
42 Special GenC Nov 2011, SSJE/2/11.

resident members of the Society went into private retirement;[43] and the penultimate meeting of the Management Committee at the Society's final remaining house noted that even with the necessary expenditure on the care of the three surviving members of the English congregation the large injection of funds from the sale meant that "there would be a considerable amount of money available each year for projects great and small [...] Exciting times lay ahead, and, as there was no other business, the meeting ended on this very high note."[44]

So ended the active and public ministry of the English congregation of Richard Meux Benson's Society of St John the Evangelist, 146 years after he, Charles Chapman Grafton, and Simeon Wilberforce O'Neill took their vows in the little house on the Iffley Road which was briefly the SSJE's first home. In his final Superior's Address to the Chapter Huckle noted that "as we started with three people in 1866 it is fitting that we finish with three people in 2012". He ended, as Benson had begun, with prayer.

> We pray God's blessing on our retirement and on the Fellowship Trust with its new responsibilities. For all that God has achieved through us we thank Him; for our Founder and his vision and all those who have striven to follow their calling, for their labour all around the world and those who have suffered in far-off countries, we praise God. For our failings, for our timidity, for those who lost their vision we ask forgiveness. For our end, we ask peace. On us all we ask God's blessing. Amen.[45]

GREATER WORKS TO COME

It may be tempting to regard the English congregation of the SSJE as having ultimately failed to produce enough vocations for it to continue; and so also to see it as having been one of the victims of the decline in interest in matters ecclesiastical which characterised the period that followed Edward Norman's "religious age",[46] and of the ever-variable fortunes of the Catholic Movement within the Church of England of which it was a part. To some extent that is true; but it is a fate that it has shared with every contemporaneous community as time has passed. The work of the Sisterhood of the Holy Childhood is now accomplished; while the Community of St John the Baptist and the All Saints Sisters have also left their historic buildings, and gone into retirement. At the time of writing the Community of St Mary the Virgin, the Sisters of the Love of God, and the Community of the Resurrection remain in their mother houses; but in diminished and diminishing numbers.

The bare history of the SSJE is perhaps best divided into seven phases – although any urge to compare it with Jacques' soliloquy in *As You Like It* should be resisted. Despite the appearance of many Cowley Fathers "with spectacles on nose", it is difficult to pinpoint the Society's high-water mark,

---

43 FSJTA CoM, 2 June 2011.
44 FSJTA CoM, 15 Sept 2011.
45 GenC 2012, SSJE/2/11/123.
46 Norman, *Anti-Catholicism*, 19.

because the nuances of its own outlook shifted on a number of occasions – and often after the election of a new Superior General. In numerical terms the 1890s were its zenith; but it also played a prominent part in that of the Catholic Movement in general, which William Davage dates to the days of the Anglo-Catholic Congresses of the 1920s and 1930s. Later members would descry both periods as having been distractions from what they thought was the true identity of the Society, whose purest form they dated to the 1870s and 1880s. Nevertheless, in each phase the SSJE offered something distinctive both to the men who joined and to the Church at large.

The first phase saw the SSJE's foundation in the second- and third-generation Tractarianism of the mid-nineteenth century: after John Henry Newman had seceded to Rome; but while John Keble's memory remained strong, and while Edward Bouverie Pusey still lived. The community's earliest expression of life was informed by Benson's own theological and ecclesiological studies, and his membership and leadership of the Brotherhood of the Holy Trinity; his yearning for India, which he shared with O'Neill; but also by the prevailing prejudice in the popular mind towards religious communities in general, and men's communities in particular.

The Society's second phase involved growth in two directions: as a parochial community rooted in East Oxford, sustaining the life of a parish that epitomised Tractarian ideals; and internationally with the establishment of work in the United States and India, and later in South Africa. The last grew substantially; although all three mission fields were challenging, and difficulties in the early years of the American work were nearly disastrous. All flourished, from Philadelphia to Boston and beyond; from Bombay to Poona; and from Cape Town to the Transkei. Much of this growth took place after the resignation of Benson as Superior General in 1890 and the election of Robert Page.

Under Benson the severity of life at Cowley had threatened to destroy the entire venture; but Page's election effectively sealed the general direction of the SSJE for the next six decades: as a competent and effective provider of overseas mission work with – after the erection of an independent American congregation – an emphasis on India and South Africa. It was to this phase that Bernard Wilkins referred when he wrote in *With Wings as Eagles* that "Cowley Fathers have 'followed the eagles' [....] to all the countries, outside England, where we have been called to live and labour." The second phase also involved the raising of significant buildings to function as the Society's mother house: lasting monuments to the skill and art of their builders and the sensibilities and taste of those who commissioned them; and from where individual Cowley Fathers went out to their labour, near and far.

It may well be argued that the SSJE had by this stage become more a creation of its second Superior General than of its Founder – and particularly in its liturgical life – which became a position that would trouble some of their successors. "From the humble beginnings at Oxford", Wilkins wrote, "the Society has spread *per orbem terrarum*";[47] and although this was a rhetorical exaggeration, it was true that by the turn of the twentieth century the SSJE's most

---

47 Wilkins, *With Wings As Eagles*, 3.

evocative expression was its overseas work – as evinced by the enthusiastic support of the Cowley, Wantage, & All Saints Missionary Association and the Fellowship of St John.

Its position as a well-established and well-respected provider of mission-work, as well as its developing international character, led the SSJE into its third phase. Stability and purpose allowed the Society to take a successful stand against heterodoxy in India; to weather the sudden death of a serving Superior General, Gerald Maxwell; and to root deeply within an incarnational theology of the Cross the sacrifices of the First World War, in which lay and ordained members of the Society served and in which one lost his life. The same incarnational theology also underpinned the Society's developing approach towards its people in India and South Africa as time went on: major plant was raised in both provinces, which included churches, schools, hostels, clinics, and workshops.

Under the leadership of Henry Bull and William O'Brien, the SSJE's inter-war developments saw it oppose the attempted revision of the Book of Common Prayer and become a leading force in the Anglo-Catholic Congress Movement – and a champion of Anglo-Catholic principles in the wider Church of England. Members of the Society were the confessors of choice of many of the women's communities from its earliest days, and also exercised prodigious ministries to individuals as spiritual directors; while some contributed to the life of scholarship and the church with numerous publications on learned subjects. Although aesthetically the SSJE eschewed John Betjeman's "divine baroque [that] transformed our English altars and our ways",[48] it remained closely allied with the overt Ritualism of the Anglo-Catholic Congresses and the ecclesiological and theological causes that the Congress Movement espoused.

With this fighting spirit the Society entered the Second World War, with the loss of another member; and took up a position in the vanguard in the battle against the looming crisis surrounding the proposed establishment of the Church of South India. It could well be argued that this third phase was the English congregation's last period of buoyant self-confidence: a modest peak in vocations in the 1940s saw more men professed than had been in the 1920s and 1930s, but it was the last decade in which professions outnumbered deaths. In the event the English congregation failed to enact the threat made by O'Brien that it might secede from the Church of England if the South India Scheme went ahead; and was firmly chastised by its sister congregations for having threatened to do so at all.

It fell to Francis Dalby to lead the Society into its fourth phase of life: the post-war engagement with a changed world and a changed Church, during which the SSJE abandoned its implacable and corporate opposition to the Church of South India – effectively embracing a latitude in Catholic principles that earlier members would certainly have rejected – and a combination of polit-ical change and declining numbers obliged it to begin to curtail most of its former colonial work. Such a realignment left the SSJE a changed body in both identity and outlook. The American and Canadian congregations now exer-cised their right of a share in the international Society's governance through

---

48 John Betjeman, *Summoned by Bells*, London: John Murray (1960), 95.

the SSJE's Central Council; but the decline in vocations in the English congregation meant that even had Indian independence not been a consequence of the Second World War, it would have been nearly impossible to maintain the work there. The same applied to the South African province twenty years later.

In the SSJE's fifth stage of existence a rising mortality rate and an ongoing decline in vocations precipitated a good deal of soul-searching as the 1960s dawned; and a broad view of the contemporary religious life voluntarily took into account the various documents of the Second Vatican Council. Under their influence and the leadership of Gerald Triffitt the Society simplified its liturgy and reordered its churches, adopting a series of experimental changes in an earnest attempt to perfect its life and to make it more appealing to prospective postulants; but the decline in numbers continued.

Under David Campbell, who had been the architect of most of the Society's reforms of the 1960s, the SSJE eventually abandoned its mother house at Cowley, partly out of a desire to return to what he and others perceived to be the Society's first principles, and partly out of sheer paucity of members. The sixth and penultimate phase of the Society's active life saw it subdivided into smaller houses spread across the country, which offered spiritual succour in a number of different styles. Some of its ministry remained recognisably rooted in its former ways of life; while other aspects departed from it entirely, to the alienation of a number of the SSJE's traditional supporters. None of it brought the increase in vocations for which the Society had hoped.

The final phase of the SSJE's active life centred on St Edward's House, where a long and distinguished ministry of spiritual counsel at the heart of Westminster continued under James Naters, Alan Cotgrove, and Peter Huckle respectively. After the closure of all the branch houses, the SSJE's London home continued to host visitors from near and far; but once there were more members of the community in nursing care than active in the house, it was inevitable that closure would follow. Although Campbell had cast the rapid and terminal decline of the SSJE in terms of the leading of the Holy Spirit, he had nevertheless had the foresight to set up a means by which its work might go on; and the trustees of the Fellowship of St John Trust Association continue to distribute the Society's remaining funds.

At the end of the day, the Cowley Fathers disappeared almost as quickly as they had come. In terms of numbers, between 1866 and 2002 just over a hundred members who remained in vows until death were professed in the English congregation. Of those, thirty-two made their vows between 1890 and 1910, and another twenty-four between 1930 and 1950. The SSJE effectively consisted of no more than three generations of long-lived men, of whom forty-five died between 1930 and 1970.[49] To reduce its history to numerical statistics and an analysis of the ebb and flow of a series of delineated phases, however, is to miss the point.

"We must see things born in weakness", wrote Benson, "and perish in death, ere they can live to eternity".[50] The Society's main concern was the perfection and salvation of souls; so its relative success or failure in its primary object, as

---

49 See Appendix 1.
50 Longridge, *Further Letters of Richard Meux Benson*, 208.

was noted in the Introduction, is entirely impalpable. All this book has been able to do is to seek to trace the story of the SSJE through the playing out of its relationships: of the members of the Society with each other; with their people at home and abroad; and with their God. That story was underpinned at every moment by a constant round of prayer; and it is only with that underlying principle in mind that we can make some sense of the real breadth of the life of the Society in all its triumphs, disasters, and eccentricities.

Although there was a clear delineation in social background between the clerical and lay members of Society for most of its life, their individual talents were diverse. To name just a handful, theologians like George Congreve, Edward Trenholme, Mark Gibbard, and Christopher Bryant found their foil in the great builders that were Robert Page, Hugh Nicholson, Edward Elwin, and – literally – Br Maynard. Frederick Puller and Philip Waggett straddled both categories, and more beside. Lucius Cary was expert on the women's communities; while George Hollings founded his own. Marcel Conran and William Longridge were masters of the spiritual life; and John Biscoe and Godfrey Callaway were content to be experts on their respective mission fields. Lonsdale Wain and Alan Bean excelled in lepidoptery; Alfred Rose was an accomplished musician and composer;[51] and Br Anselm worked in the laundry and the kitchens, while at the same time being a sought-after expert on the practice of Solemnes-style plainsong. Others distinguished themselves as linguists on the foreign missions; or in the heat of war; or as schoolmasters.

Most of the Superiors General were relatively unknown until elected; because after Benson's retirement the Society invariably declined to elect any of its public figures to its highest office, preferring solid administrators who had proved themselves capable of dealing with the more mundane aspects of its day-to-day affairs. Nevertheless, through their work a number became very distinguished indeed, and regarded as *de facto* leaders of the Catholic Movement of the day. At the other end of the scale there were other members of the Society who simply said their prayers and kept the rule – whose lives were almost entirely hidden from view, and of whom little more exists than an obituary in the *Cowley Evangelist*, and a carved name in the Lady Chapel of St Stephen's House.

The SSJE came into being at the height of the Victorian age, and at a time when the world – and, indeed, the Church of England – was beginning to change more quickly than had been the case in any preceding era. It took its part in conflicts that changed forever first the old order of Europe, and secondly that of the entire globe. Against that backdrop, however, the tension that dogged the Society for the whole of its life was its inability to come to a firm conclusion about whether it was an active or contemplative community. In the end it had no choice but to be increasingly contemplative in the wake of the withdrawal from the overseas missions, and when the advancing age of the later members finally took its toll.

Successive Superiors General tried to trim the boat, but generally the work grew to meet the need on the ground; and away from Cowley, whether in India or South Africa, it was a case of fitting in as much as could be done between the

---

51 *NS* 2/70.

daily punctuations of prayer. Long periods of silent contemplation sustained the spiritual lives of a number of brethren; but as a personal, rather than a corporate, exercise. For others, there was enough room in the interpretation of the Statutes and Rule, despite their outward severity, to allow individual members to pursue their own strengths – although this could sometimes be a problem when it came to choosing successors to lead projects after the departure of their instigators.

Perhaps it is most helpful to regard the Cowley Fathers – whatever the intentions of the Founder may have been – as having fallen into a way of life best described Peter Anson as that of "clerks-regular"[52]: an existence, particularly for the priests, that was neither purely regular or secular, but concerned itself particularly with preaching, administering the sacraments, the teaching of children, and the exercise of the traditional works of mercy; while bound to regular prayer and life according to rule, and wearing a habit resembling ordinary clerical dress.[53] Such flexibility, including between the norms of life observed at the mother house and in the branch houses, enabled the members of the Society to adapt themselves to local conditions while retaining a sense of community identity – particularly through the SSJE office book, while it remained normative – with their brethren in other houses and provinces.

The Society's surviving buildings, meanwhile, serve as evocative reminders of the men whom they once housed. In Oxford, the former mother house remains the home of St Stephen's House, which continues to train Anglican clergy in the Catholic tradition; and whose secondary use of the former community church as a concert venue now brings large numbers of people into Bodley's architectural masterpiece. Apart from recent cosmetic improvements, the building is much as it stood when the SSJE left; although the windows in the formerly bare and draughty cloister have finally been glazed.

Other local memories also linger. The Gladiator Club on the Iffley Road still stands, although St John's Hall – the scene of so many of the social aspects of the Society's life in Oxford – has been demolished. When in 2005 the artist Liam Curtin installed a series of bronze ingots along the Cowley Road as part of a pavement-art project, the one outside the former Boys' School – which is now the East Oxford Community Centre – depicted a shovel hat inside an outline map of India, with "CF" and a pointer directed at Mumbai.[54] In London, St Edward's House has been renamed "Purcell's"; but the statue of its patron remains over its front door, and the main chapel remains in regular use for worship by Westminster School. The Chaplain's office occupies the front parlour, and the Superior's study – now used by the Housemistress – retains its brass plaque. Cowley Street, just around the corner, is a red herring; for it was there long before the foundation of the SSJE.

Cowley Street in Cape Town, however, together with Cowley House on Chapel Street, are named after the community that ministered for so long in the area; while St Philip's, District Six, St Cyprian's, Langa, and Holy Cross, Nyanga East, continue to house their respective congregations. In the

---

52 Anson, *Benedictines of Caldey*, xxviii.

53 cf John F. X. Murphy, "Clerks Regular", *The Catholic Encyclopaedia v.4*, New York: Robert Appleton & Co. (1912).

54 www.liamcurtin.co.uk/projects-archive/pavement-jewellery

Transkei, the buildings at Tsolo also survive, along with the numerous out-station churches that the Society raised in the vicinity. The same applies in India: at Pune the tower of the Church of the Holy Name still dominates the skyline; while at Erandwane, now a busy suburb, St Crispin's also survives. At Mumbai St Peter's, Mazagon, retains its close connection with St Peter's School, where a plaque in the Principal's study records the names of the members of the Society who were his predecessors.

Writing to O'Neill in 1879, Benson thought that "[God] has been pleased to call our little Society to varied works far beyond our strength." At that stage, for the SSJE to take on more work than it might reasonably hope to be able to accomplish was an act of faith.

> In so doing we may be sure that He desires to sanctify us and prepare us for greater works to come. Then, if we will yield ourselves up to Him, how wonderful is the future, as we see it stretching out with continual expanse to the fullness of the infinite love with which He is calling us.[55]

As the SSJE grew, burgeoning work – and particularly that which lay overseas – became a recognised part of its identity; but the Society's successes did not belong solely to the professed members.

The SSJE could hardly have worked as effectively as it did in India and South Africa without the symbiotic relationship that it enjoyed with the All Saints Sisters of the Poor and the Community of St Mary the Virgin; nor without its doctors, teachers, and assistant clergy; and certainly not without its valued local catechists and interpreters. At home the secretaries of the various branches of the Fellowship of St John worked to enable the Society to be able to call for much of its life on a wide network of supporters for prayer and alms-giving; and over several decades the Society invested vast sums into its work in India and South Africa, which it later passed into local hands.

As we have seen, the roll-call of those who supported the SSJE was as long as it was diverse; and ranged from peers to paupers. All contributed what they could to the life of the Society, from munificent donations to quiet and incalcul-able prayer; and a whole host of co-workers – men and women, rich and poor, Indians and Africans – worked for, through, and with the Society to enable its work to flourish in suburban East Oxford and well-heeled Westminster, in the steaming fleshpots of Cape Town and Bombay, and in the clearer air of Tsolo and Poona. To them, as various members of the Society admiringly and freely conceded in the pages of the *Cowley Evangelist*, belonged the credit for no small part of the SSJE's achievements in every sphere of its work.

Those achievements ranged far and wide; and in England, and India, and South Africa the legacy of the SSJE's English congregation continues. This work has been an attempt to sketch out the main areas of its members' activity, and their most significant contributions to theology, spirituality, philanthropy, and the wider Church on four continents over 150 years. There remains much other work still to be done, with more tales of derring-do to be told, and more academic themes to be analysed. Theologians, anthropologists, historians –

---

55 Longridge, *Further Letters of Richard Meux Benson*, 208.

ecclesiastical, architectural, and imperial – and even musicologists will all find rich material in the history of the English congregation of the Society of St John the Evangelist. Perhaps even then, however, because its deepest spiritual work remains forever hidden from view, we shall never really know all the books that should be written.

APPENDIX 1

Men of the English Congregation of SSJE who died as professed members of the Society;
those who died as novices; and the few exceptions noted below.

		Profession	Death
Richard Meux Benson ✠ (1866–90)	Priest	1866	1915
Simeon Wilberforce O'Neill	Priest	1866	1882
Robert Lay Page ✠ (1890–1907)	Priest	1872	1912
George Congreve	Priest	1875	1918
George Edmund Sheppard	Priest	1878	1888
Charles Neale Field #	Priest	1881	1929
Maynard (William Maynard Shaw)	Lay Brother	1883	1918
John Wooldridge Biscoe	Priest	1883	1918
William Hawks Longridge	Priest	1883	1930
Frederick William Puller	Priest	1883	1938
Charles Edwyn Gardner	Priest	1885	1908
Walter (Walter Stephen Cousins)	Lay Brother	1885	1887
Duncan Convers #	Priest	1886	1929
George Seymour Hollings	Priest	1892	1914
Thomas Ernest Bignold	Priest	1893	1945
William Relton	Priest	1894	1897
James (John James William Thurston)	Lay Brother	1894	1933
William (William Buckingham)	Lay Brother	1894	1933
Edmund Kershaw	Priest	1894	1901
Edward Fenton Elwin	Priest	1894	1921
Marcell William Townend Conran	Priest	1894	1945
Alfred Frederick Langmore	Priest	1895	1911
Albert Edward Tovey	Priest	1895	1935
Nalbro' Frazier Robinson	Priest	1896	1921
Philip Napier Waggett	Priest	1896	1939
Halhed Sydney Moore	Priest	1897	1940

		Profession	Death
Hugh Smith Nicholson	Priest	1898	1930
Herbert (Herbert George Rendall)	Lay Brother	1898	1933
Frederic Cecil Powell	Priest	1898	1938
Gerald Speirs Maxwell ✠ (1907–15)	Priest	1899	1915
Henry Power Bull ✠ (1916–31)	Priest	1899	1947
Arthur Pridham	Priest	1901	1964
Henry Lucius Moultrie Cary	Priest	1903	1950
Charles Hedgman Turner	Priest	1904	1930
Godfrey Callaway ◆	Priest	1904	1942
Henry George Augustine Chard	Priest	1904	1948
Robert (Robert Lightfoot)	Lay Brother	1904	1941
Arthur (Arthur Nickless)	Lay Brother	1904	1950
Edward Craig Trenholme	Priest	1905	1949
Frederic Augustus Douglas Noel	Priest	1906	1929
John (John Doe)	Lay Brother	1907	1921
Sydney James Wallis ◆	Priest	1907	1956
Leonard Thomas Strong	Priest	1908	1959
William Braithwaite O'Brien ✠ (1931–49)	Priest	1908	1960
Robert Gerald Ley ◆	Priest	1909	1946
John Hamilton Cowper Johnson #	Priest	1909	1961
Oswald Charles Barton	Priest	1911	1936
Spence Burton # ⁂	Bishop	1912	1966
Frederick Southerden Playne	Priest	1914	1966
Arthur Newton Taylor	Priest	1915	1948
Walter Frederick Adams	Priest	1916	1952
John Clifford Williams	Priest	1917	1951
Percy Solly Wigram	Priest	1918	1953
Francis James Rumsey	Priest	1918	1969
Charles Norton Joseph Savage	Priest	1919	1956
Harold Thomas Alexander Peacey	Priest	1920	1952
Henry Arthur Thomson	Priest	1923	1963
Edward Douglas Sedding	Priest	1925	1972
Gerrard Todd Pulley	Priest	1926	1976
Bernard Dashwood Wilkins	Priest	1927	1960
Alfred Leslie Rose	Priest	1928	1970
George Scott Dakers	Priest	1929	1958

		Profession	Death
Cyril Clinton Allen Whitworth	Priest	1931	1955
Francis <u>Gordon</u> Shrive	Priest	1931	1987
Reginald Thompson Podmore §	Priest	1933	1940
Frank <u>Lonsdale</u> Wain	Priest	1934	1990
Christopher Rex Bryant	Priest	1935	1985
Vivian <u>Alan</u> Young	Priest	1935	1987
Edward <u>Forbes</u> Bishop	Priest	1935	1991
George Huntley	Priest	1936	1966
Alfred Francis Joseph	Priest	1937	1951
Walter Ogle Fitch	Priest	1938	1981
Albert Rangaswamy	Priest	1940	1968
David Norman Wirgman Hemming ±	Priest	1940	1979
Henry Douglas Bruce	Priest	1940	1986
David Mapple Gardner	Priest	1941	1964
Arthur Percival Hill	Priest	1941	1969
Terence Leslie Manson	Priest	1941	1980
Francis Bruce Dalby ✠ (1949–64)	Priest	1942	1990
Herbert Edwin <u>William</u> Slade	Priest	1942	1999
Alfred <u>Leonard</u> Wilks	Priest	1943	1984
Alban (Harold William Waite)	Lay Brother	1943	1993
Sydney <u>Mark</u> Gibbard	Priest	1945	1997
Anselm (Robert Henry John Chiverton)	Lay Brother	1945	2000
James <u>Raymond</u> Molyneux	Priest	1946	1963
Alan Evison Bean	Priest	1947	2009
Gerald Carrington Triffitt ✠ (1964–76)	Priest	1951	1979
Arthur Moore Cooper	Priest	1952	1977
Edward <u>Stuart</u> Churchill Lennard	Priest	1957	2002
Frederick <u>David</u> Gordon Campbell ✠ (1976–91)	Priest	1957	2010
Aubrey <u>Claude</u> Beasley-Robinson	Priest	1958	1975
Alan Edward Cotgrove ✠ (2000–2002)	Priest	1958	2002
Charles <u>James</u> Reginald Naters ✠ (1991–2000)	Priest	1958	2009
Peter Parson Palmer ≠	Priest	1958	2018
Arthur Ramoabi Phalo	Priest	1960	1997
William <u>George</u> Herbert Gater	Priest	1962	1993

		Profession	Death
Cyril George Woolley	Priest	1964	1994
Gerald (Gerald Charles Perkins)	Lay Brother	1975	2006
Alan Herbert Grainge	Priest	1976	2000
James Simon (Morley James Stewart) ✳	Lay Brother	2001	—
Peter Huckle ✳ ✠ (2002–)	Priest	2002	—
Freeborn Coggeshall	Novice	—	1876
Edward Hill Beale	Novice	—	1893
Walter Frederick (Walter Frederick Pleasance) §	Lay Novice	—	1917
David Procter	Novice	—	1923

✠ Superior General
♦ Formerly of the Society of St Cuthbert
\# Transferred to America
± Transferred to Canada
≠ Transferred from Canada
§ Fell in war
⁂ Remained a member of the Society after consecration to the episcopate
✳ Still living at time of publication

Visitors of the English Congregation of the Society of St John the Evangelist

1866–1869	Samuel Wilberforce	Bishop of Oxford	Translated to Winchester
1869–1889	John Mackarness	Bishop of Oxford	Died in office
1889–1901	William Stubbs	Bishop of Oxford	Died in office
1901–1911	Francis Paget	Bishop of Oxford	Died in office
1911–1932	Charles Gore CR	Bishop of Oxford	Visitor until death
1932–1937	Thomas Strong	Bishop of Oxford	Retired
1937–1954	Kenneth Kirk	Bishop of Oxford	Died in office
1955–1971	Harry Carpenter	Bishop of Oxford	Retired
1971–1978	Kenneth Woollcombe	Bishop of Oxford	Retired
1978–1986	Patrick Rodger	Bishop of Oxford	Retired
1986–1997	Ronald Gordon	Bishop at Lambeth	Retired
1997–present	Dominic Walker OGS	Bishop of Reading	Translated to Monmouth

APPENDIX 2

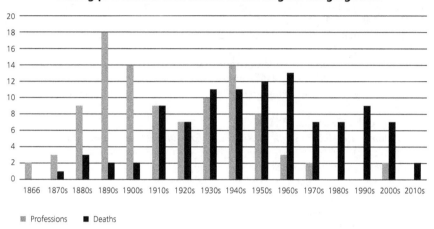

Lasting professions and deaths in the English congregation

■ Professions ■ Deaths

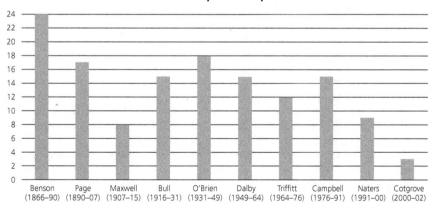

Years of service of departed Superiors General

Select Bibliography

"F.S.A.", *English Monasteries: From Saxon Days to their dissolution*, London: G. J. Palmer & Sons (1904).

Adams, Walter Frederick, SSJE, *Thoughts from the Note-books of a Priest Religious*, Westminster: Faith Press (1949).

Addison, James Thayer, *The Episcopal Church in the United States, 1789–1931*, New York: Scribner (1951).

Advisory Council on Religious Communities
— *A Directory of the Religious Life*, London: SPCK (1943).
— *Guide to the Religious Communities of the Anglican Communion*, London: Mowbray (1962).

Allchin, Arthur Macdonald [Donald]
— *The Silent Rebellion: Anglican Religious Communities 1845–1900*, London: SCM Press (1958).
— *The Spirit and the Word. Two studies in nineteenth century Anglican theology. With special reference to Richard Meux Benson and Thomas Hancock*, London: Faith Press (1963).
— *The World is a Wedding: Explorations in Christian Spirituality*, London: DLT (1978).
— *The Kingdom of Love and Knowledge: The Encounter between Orthodoxy and the West*, London: DLT (1979).
— *The Dynamic of Tradition*, London: Darton, Longman & Todd (1981).

Allen, Hugh, *New Llanthony Abbey: Father Ignatius's Monastery at Capel-y-ffin*, Peterscourt Press (2016).

Amis, Kingsley
— *The Alteration*, London: Jonathan Cape (1976).
— *The Amis Collection*, London: Hutchinson (1990).

Andrews, C. F., *Handbooks of English Church Expansion: North India*, London: Mowbray (1908).

Anglo-Catholic Congress Movement
— *Report of the First Anglo-Catholic Congress, London, 1920*, London: SPCK (1920).
— *The Anglo-Catholic Congress: An Illustrated Record of Work for the Three Years 1923–1926*, London: ACC (1927).
— *Report of the Anglo-Catholic Congress* [1927], London: Society of Ss Peter & Paul (1927).

Anson, Harold, *T. B. Strong: Bishop, Musician, Dean, Vice-Chancellor*, London: SPCK (1949).

Anson, Peter F.
— *Benedictines of Caldey*, Prinknash Abbey (1944).
— *The Call of the Cloister: Religious Communities and Kindred Bodies in the Anglican Communion*, London: SPCK (1955).

— *Abbot Extraordinary: A memoir of Aelred Carlyle, monk and missionary, 1874–1955*, London; Faith Press (1958).

— *Fashions in Church Furnishings, 1840–1940*, London: Faith Press (1960).

— *Building up the Waste Places: The Revival of the Monastic Life on Medieval Lines in the Post-Reformation Church of England*, London: Faith Press (1973).

Arnstein, Walter L., *Protestant versus Catholic in Mid-Victorian England: Mr Newdegate and the Nuns*, University of Missouri Press (1982).

Ashwell, Arthur Rawson & Wilberforce, Reginald Garton, *Life of the Right Reverend Samuel Wilberforce*, London: John Murray (1883).

Atterbury, Francis, *Maxims, Reflections and Observations, Divine, Moral and Political*, London (1723).

Attwater, Donald, *Father Ignatius of Llanthony: A Victorian*, London: Cassell & Co. (1931).

Austen, Jane, *Northanger Abbey*, London: John Murray (1818).

Babington Smith, Constance, *Rose Macaulay*, London: Collins (1972).

Bailey, Brian, *Almshouses*, London: Robert Hale (1988).

Baldwin, Monica, *I Leap over the Wall*, London: Hamish Hamilton (1949).

Baring-Gould, Sabine, *The Church Revival: Thoughts Thereon and Reminiscences*, London: Methuen & Co. (1914).

Barnes, Bertram Herbert, *Johnson of Nyasaland: A Study of the Life and Work of William Percival Johnson*, London: UMCA (1933).

Barnes, John E., *George Ratcliffe Woodward 1848–1934: Priest, Poet and Musician*, Norwich: Canterbury Press (1996).

Basham, A. L. (ed), *A Cultural History of India*, OUP (1975).

Batten, Helen, *Sisters of the East End*, London: Ebury Press (2013).

Bayliffe, Dorothy M. & Harding, Joan N., *Starling Benson of Swansea*, Cowbridge: D. Brown & Sons Ltd (1996).

Baynes, A. Hamilton, *Handbooks of English Church Expansion: South Africa*, London: Mowbray (1908).

Beaken, Robert, *The Church of England and the Home Front 1914–1918*, Woodbridge: The Boydell Press (2015).

Bellenoit, Hayden J. A., *Missionary Education and Empire in Late Colonial India, 1860–1920*, London: Pickering & Chatto (2007).

Benson, Arthur Christopher, *The Life of Edward White Benson, sometime Archbishop of Canterbury*, London: Macmillan & Co. (1899).

Benson, Richard Meux, SSJE

— *A Calendar, with some Words chiefly from the unpublished retreat addresses of R. M. Benson, compiled by G. T. Pulley*, Oxford: A. R. Mowbray & Co. (1932).

— *A Village Sermon upon the Divorce Bill*, London: Joseph Masters (1857).

— *An Exposition of the Epistle of St Paul to the Romans*, London: J. Masters & Co. (1892).

— *Benedictus Dominus: A course of meditations for most days of the year*, London: Hayes (1879).

— *Bible Teachings: The Discourse at Capernaum*, London: J. T. Hayes (1875).

— *Eight Sermons and Addresses delivered at a Parochial Retreat*, London: J. T. Hayes (1888).

— *Five Addresses and Sermons delivered at a Parochial Retreat*, Merthyr Tydfil: Farrant & Frost (1887).

— *Instructions on the Religious Life*. First Series, Oxford: SSJE (1927); Second Series, London: A. R. Mowbray & Co. (1935); Third Series, London: A. R. Mowbray & Co. (1951).

— *Lays of Memory, Sacred and Social*, London: Hurst & Blackett (1856).

— *Redemption: Some of the aspects of the work of Christ considered in a course of sermons*, London: J. T. Hayes (1861).

— *The Divine Rule of Prayer; or, Considerations upon the Lord's Prayer. With various forms of analysis and paraphrase*, London: Bell & Daldy (1866).

— *The Final Passover. A series of meditations upon the Passion of our Lord Jesus Christ*, London, Hayes (1884); Longmans (1893–95).

— *The Followers of the Lamb. A series of meditations especially intended for persons living under religious vows and for seasons of retreat*, London: Longmans & Co. (1900).

— *The Magnificat: A series of meditations upon the Song of the Blessed Virgin Mary*, London: Hayes (1889).

— *The Manual of Intercessory Prayer*, London: Bell & Daldy (1862).

— *The Name of Jesus. A sermon preached before the University of Oxford on the Fifth Sunday after Epiphany, 1865*, London: Rivingtons (1865).

— *The Religious Vocation*, Oxford: A. R. Mowbray & Co. (1939).

— *The War Songs of the Prince of Peace*, London: John Murray (1901).

— *The Way of Holiness*, London: Methuen & Co. (1901).

— *The Wisdom of the Son of David*, London: Bell & Daldy (1860).

Bentley, James, *Ritualism and Politics in Victorian Britain: The Attempt to Legislate for Belief*, OUP (1978).

de Bertouch, Beatrice, *The Life of Father Ignatius, O.S.B.: The Monk of Llanthony*, London: Methuen & Co. (1904).

Bethge, Eberhard, *Dietrich Bonhoeffer: Theologian, Christian, Contemporary*, London: Collins (1970).

Betjeman, John

— *Summoned by Bells*, London: John Murray (1960).

— *High and Low*, London: John Murray (1966).

Bill, E. G. W., *Anglican Initiatives in Christian Unity*, London: SPCK (1967).

The Earl of Birkenhead [F. W. F. Smith], *Halifax: The Life of Lord Halifax*, London: Hamilton (1965).

Blagden, Claude Martin, *Well Remembered*, London: Hodder & Stoughton (1953).

Blomberg, Paula Dorothea von, *Allerlei aus Süd-Afrika*, Gütersloh: Bertelsmann (1899).

Blythe, Ronald, *The View in Winter: Reflections on Old Age*, London: Allen Lane (1979).

Bompas, George C., *Life of Frank Buckland*, London: Nelson & Sons (1909).

Bonham, Valerie

— *A Joyous Service: The Clewer Sisters and their Work*, Clewer: CSJB (1989).

— *A Place in Life: The Clewer House of Mercy, 1849–83*, Clewer: CSJB (1992).

— *Sisters of the Raj: The Clewer Sisters in India*, Clewer: CSJB (1997).

Booty, John and Sykes, Stephen (eds), *The Study of Anglicanism*, London: SPCK (1988).

Boyd, Robin, *An Introduction to Indian Christian Theology*, Delhi: ISPCK (1969).

Brandreth, Henry Reynaud Turner, *Dr Lee of Lambeth: A Chapter in Parenthesis in the History of the Oxford Movement*, London: SPCK (1951).

Brendon, Piers, "Newman, Keble, and *Froude's Remains*", *The English Historical Review*, vol.87, no.345 (Oct 1972).

Brendon, Vyvyen, *Children of the Raj*, London: Weidenfeld & Nicholson (2005).

Brilioth, Yngve
— *Eucharistic Faith and Practice, Evangelical and Catholic*, London: SPCK (1930).
— *The Anglican Revival*, London: Longmans, Green & Co. (1933).

Briscoe, J. F. (ed), *V. S. S. Coles: Letters, Papers, Addresses, Hymns and Verses, with a Memoir*, London: Mowbray (1930).

Brombert, Victor H., *The Romantic Prison: The French Tradition*, Princeton: Princeton University Press (1978).

Brontë, Charlotte, *Villette*, London: Smith, Elder & Co (1853).

Brown, C. K. Francis, *A History of the English Clergy 1800–1900*, London: Faith Press (1953).

Brown, Stewart J., Nockles, Peter, & Pereiro, James (eds), *The Oxford Handbook of the Oxford Movement*, OUP (2017).

Browning, Elizabeth Barrett, *The Lay of the Brown Rosary* (1840).

Browning, W. R. F. (ed), *The Anglican Synthesis: Essays by Catholics and Evangelicals*, Derby: Peter Smith (1964).

Bryant, Christopher Rex, SSJE
— *Depth Psychology and Religious Belief*, Mirfield: House of the Resurrection (1972).
— *Jung and the Christian Way*, London: Darton, Longman & Todd (1983).
— *Sunday Meditations*, London: SPCK (1968).
— *The Heart in Pilgrimage: Christian Guidelines for the Human Journey*, London: Darton, Longman & Todd (1980).
— *The River Within: The Search for God in Depth*, London: Darton, Longman & Todd (1978).

Bucknall, Stephen and Symondson, Anthony, *Sir Ninian Comper: an Introduction to his Life and Work, with complete Gazetteer*, Reading: Spire Books (2006).

Buettner, Elizabeth, *Empire Families: Britons and Late Imperial India*, OUP (2004).

Bunting, Ian (ed), *Celebrating the Anglican Way*, London: Hodder & Stoughton (1996).

Burgess, G. H. O., *The Curious World of Frank Buckland*, London: John Baker (1967).

Burne, Kathleen E. (ed), *The Life and Letters of Father Andrew S.D.C.*, London: A. & R. Mowbray & Co. (1948).

Burnet, Gilbert, *History of his Own Time*, London (1734).

Butler, Arthur John (ed), *Life and Letters of William John Butler, late Dean of Lincoln and sometime Vicar of Wantage*, London: Macmillan & Co. (1897).

Butler, Cuthbert, OSB, *Ways of Christian Life*, London: Sheed & Ward (1932).

Butler, C. Violet, *Social Conditions in Oxford*, London: Sidgwick & Jackson (1912).

Butler, Perry (ed), *Pusey Rediscovered*, London: SPCK (1983).

Butler, Samuel, *Ernest Pontifex, or The Way of All Flesh*, London: Methuen & Co. (1965).

Calder-Marshall, Arthur, *The Enthusiast: An Enquiry into the Life, Beliefs and Character of the Rev Joseph Leycester Lyne, alias Fr Ignatius OSB, Abbot of Elm Hill, Norwich, & Llanthony, Wales*, London: Faber & Faber (1962).

Callaway, Godfrey, SSJE
— *A Shepherd of the Veld: Bransby Lewis Key, Bishop of St John's, Kaffraria*, London: Wells, Gardner, Darton & Co. (1911).
— *Building for God in Africa*, London: SPCK (1936).
— *Notes on the Ministry of Reconciliation, for Young Missionaries*, London: SPCK (1922).
— *Sketches of Kafir Life*, Oxford: Mowbray (1905).

— *The Fellowship of the Veld: Sketches of Native Life in South Africa*, London: SPCK (1926).

— *The Pilgrim Path: The Story of an African Childhood*, London: SPG (1933).

— *The Soul of an African Padre*, London: A. R. Mowbray (1932).

Cameron, Allan Thomas, *The Religious Communities of the Church of England*, London: Faith Press (1918).

Cannadine, David, *Victorious Century: The United Kingdom, 1800–1906*, London: Allen Lane (2017).

Carey, Hilary M., *God's Empire: Religion and Colonialism in the British World, c.1801–1908*, Cambridge University Press (2011).

Carleton, George, SSM, *The King's Highway*, London: Anglo-Catholic Congress Committee (1924).

Carpenter, Humphrey, *Robert Runcie: The Reluctant Archbishop*, London: Hodder & Stoughton (1996).

Carpenter, S. C., *Church and People, 1789–1889: A History of the Church of England from William Wilberforce to "Lux Mundi"*, London: SPCK (1937).

Carrington, Philip, *The Anglican Church in Canada*, Toronto: Collins (1963).

Carter, J. F. M., *Life and Work of the Rev T. T. Carter, Hon. Canon of Christ Church, Oxford, and Warden of the House of Mercy, Clewer*, London: Longmans, Green & Co. (1911).

Cary, Henry Lucius Moultrie, SSJE

— *Audi Filia: Notes of Addresses given in Retreat*, Oxford: A. R. Mowbray & Co. (1915).

— *Called of God: Notes on some Questions concerning the Religious Life; with an Introductory Essay on the Meaning of the Religious State*, London: A. R. Mowbray & Co. (1937).

— *Hortus Inclusus, etc. An essay on the contemplative life in a religious community*, London: Pax House (1944).

The Catholic Literature Association

— *Richard Meux Benson*, London (1933).

— *Heroes of the Catholic Revival*, London (1933).

Cell, John W., *British Colonial Administration in the Mid-Nineteenth Century: The Policy-Making Process*, Yale University Press (1970).

Chadwick, Owen

— *The Founding of Cuddesdon*, OUP (1954).

— *The Mind of the Oxford Movement*, London: A. & C. Black (1960).

— *Victorian Church*, London: A. & C. Black (1970).

— *The Spirit of the Oxford Movement: Tractarian Essays*, Cambridge University Press (1990).

Chandler, Michael

— *The Life and Work of John Mason Neale*, Gracewing (1995).

— *The Life and Work of Henry Parry Liddon*, Leominster: Gracewing (2000).

Chapman, Mark D.

— *Ambassadors of Christ: Commemorating 150 years of Theological Education in Cuddesdon 1854–2004*, Aldershot: Ashgate (2004).

— *The Fantasy of Reunion: Anglicans, Catholics, and Ecumenism, 1833–1882*, OUP (2014).

Chatterton, Eyre, *A History of the Church of England in India; since the early days of the East India Company*, London: SPCK (1924).

Cheney Smith, Robert, SSJE

— *The Shrine on Bowdoin Street*, Boston: SSJE (1958).

— *The Cowley Fathers in America: The Early Years* (n.d.).

Chesterton, G. K., *The Everlasting Man*, London: Hodder & Stoughton (1925).

Chorley, Edward Clowes, *Men and Movements in the American Episcopal Church*, Hamden, CT: Archon Books (1961).

Clarke, Adam, *Memoirs of the Wesley Family: Collected Principally from Original Documents*, London: J. & T. Clarke (1823).

Clarke, Basil F. L., *Church Builders of the Nineteenth Century: A Study of the Gothic Revival in England*, London: SPCK (1938).

Clarke, C. P. S., *The Oxford Movement and After*, London: Mowbray (1932).

Clements, Keith, *Bonhoeffer and Britain*, London: Churches Together in Britain (2006).

Clutterbuck, Ivan, *Marginal Catholics: Anglo-Catholicism, a further Chapter of Modern Church History*, Leominster: Gracewing (1993).

Coakley, J. F., *The Church of the East and the Church of England: A History of the Archbishop of Canterbury's Assyrian Mission*, Oxford: Clarendon Press (1992).

Collins, Timothy, "From Anatomy to Zoophagy: A Biographical Note on Frank Buckland", *Journal of the Galway Archaeological and Historical Society*, v.55 (2003), 94.

Congar, Yves, OP, *Lay People and The Church*, London: Geoffrey Chapman (1959).

Congreve, George, SSJE

— *Christian Life, a Response, with other retreat addresses and sermons*, London: Longmans, Green & Co. (1899).

— *Christian Progress, with other papers and addresses*, London: Longmans, Green & Co. (1910).

— *My Communion: Twenty-Six Short Addresses in Preparation for Holy Communion*, London: Longmans, Green & Co. (1905).

— *Of Advance in Lent*, London: A. R. Mowbray & Co. (1899).

— *Orient Leaves*, Oxford: A. R. Mowbray & Co. (1915).

— *Preparatio, or Notes of Preparation for Holy Communion, Founded on the Collect, Epistle and Gospel for Every Sunday in the Year*, London: Longmans, Green & Co. (1901).

— *Quiet Days*, London: A. R. Mowbray & Co. (1909).

— *Sisters: Their Vocation and Their Special Work*, London: SPCK (1908).

— *The Interior Life, and other addresses*, Oxford: A. R. Mowbray & Co. (1913).

— *The Sacrifice of Christ*, Oxford: A. R. Mowbray & Co. (1899).

— *The Spiritual Order*, London: Longmans, Green and Co. (1905).

— *Treasures of Hope for the Evening of Life*, London: Longmans (1918).

— & Longridge, William Hawks, SSJE, *Letters of Richard Meux Benson*, London: A. R. Mowbray (1916).

Conran, Marcell William Townend, SSJE

— *The National Mission: How it may be conducted on a Basis of 'Calling upon the Name of the Lord', With Notes on Fifteen Addresses on the Mysteries of Our Lord's Life, together with Instructions for use in the Mission*, London & Brighton: SPCK (1916).

— *Two Chaplets of Prayer*, London (1914).

Convers, Duncan, SSJE, *Marriage and Divorce in the United States: as they are and as they ought to be*, Philadelphia (1889).

Cox, Jeffrey, *The British Missionary Enterprise since 1700*, New York: Routledge (2008).

Cross, F. L.

— *Darwell Stone: Churchman and Counsellor*, London: Dacre Press (1943).

— & Livingstone, E. A. (eds), *The Oxford Dictionary of the Christian Church*, OUP (1998).

Cross, Gordon, *Charles Gore: A Biographical Sketch*, Milwaukee: Morehouse (1932).

Crowther, M. A., *Church Embattled: Religious Controversy in Mid-Victorian England*, Hamden, CT: Archon Books (1970).

Cuming, G. J.

— *A History of Anglican Liturgy*, London: Macmillan (1969).

— (ed), *Studies in Church History Volume 6: The Mission of the Church and the Propagation of the Faith*, Cambridge University Press (1970).

Dalmia, Vasudha, *The Nationalization of Hindu Traditions*, OUP (1997).

Dasgupta, Surendranath, *A History of Indian Philosophy*, Cambridge University Press (1922).

Davage, William (ed), *In This Sign Conquer*, London: Continuum (2006).

Davies, Edward, *Chepstow: A Poem in Six Cantos*, Bristol: (1786).

Davies, Horton, *Worship and Theology in England, Vol. IV: From Newman to Martineau 1850–1900*, OUP (1962); *Vol. V: The Ecumenical Century 1900–1965*, OUP (1965).

Dearing, Trevor, *Wesleyan and Tractarian worship: an ecumenical study*, London: Epworth Press (1966).

de Blank, Bartha, *Joost de Blank: A Personal Memoir*, Ipswich: Boydell Press (1977).

de Gruchy, John W., with de Gruchy, Steve, *The Church Struggle in South Africa*, London: SCM Press (2004).

De-la-Noy, Michael, *The Church of England: A Portrait*, London: Simon & Schuster (1993).

De Mille, George, *The Catholic Movement in the American Episcopal Church*, Philadelphia: Church Historical Society (1950).

Deshpande, Anirudh, *Hope and Despair: Mutiny, Rebellion and Death in India, 1946*, Delhi: Primus Books (2016).

Dessain, Charles S. (ed), *The Letters & Diaries of John Henry Newman*, OUP (2016).

Dewey, Clive, *Anglo-Indian Attitudes: The Mind of the Indian Civil Service*, London: Hambledon Press (1993).

Doll, Peter Michael (ed), *Anglicanism and Orthodoxy: 300 Years after the 'Greek College' in Oxford*, Oxford: Peter Lang (2006).

Donald, Gertrude, *Men who Left the Movement: John Henry Newman, Thomas W. Allies, Henry Edward Manning, Basil William Maturin*, London: Burns, Oates & Washbourne Ltd (1933).

Donovan, Marcus, *After the Tractarians*, Glasgow: Philip Allan (1933).

Douglas, Henry Alexander, *A Charge Delivered At his Primary Visitation*, Bombay: Education Society (1875).

Douglas, John Albert, *The Relations of the Anglican Churches with the Eastern-Orthodox, Especially in regard to Anglican Orders*, London: Faith Press (1921).

Douglas-Fairhurst, Robert, *Victorian Afterlives: The Shaping of Influence in Nineteenth-Century Literature*, OUP (2002).

Dowland, David A., *Nineteenth-Century Anglican Theological Training: The Redbrick Challenge*, Oxford: Clarendon Press (1997).

Duffy, Mark J (ed), *The Episcopal Diocese of Massachusetts, 1784–1984*: Boston, Diocese of Massachusetts (1984).

Dunstan, Petà

— *This Poor Sort: A History of the European Province of the Society of St Francis*, London: Darton, Longman & Todd (1997).

— "Bishops and Religious 1897–1914", *Anglican Religious Life Journal*, 1 (March 2004).

— *The Labour of Obedience: The Benedictines of Pershore, Nashdom and Elmore — A History*, Norwich: Canterbury Press (2009).

Edwards, David L., *Christian England, Vol. III: From the Eighteenth Century to the First World War*, London: Collins (1984).

Elliott-Binns, L. E., *Religion in the Victorian Era*, London: Lutterworth Press (1964).

Ellsworth, L. E., *Charles Lowder and the Ritualist Movement*, London: Darton, Longman & Todd (1982).

Elphick, Richard & Davenport, Rodney (eds), *Christianity in South Africa: A Political, Social & Cultural History*, Cape Town: David Philip (1997).

Elwin, Edward Fenton, SSJE

— *Forty-Five Years in Poona City*, London: Mowbray & Co. (1922).

— *India and the Indians*, London: John Murray (1913).

— *Indian Jottings from ten years' experience in and around Poona City*, London: John Murray (1907).

— *Stories of Indian Boys*, Oxford: A. R. Mowbray & Co. (1915).

— *Thirty-Four Years in Poona City: Being the History of the Panch Howds Poona City Mission, India*, London: A. R. Mowbray & Co. (1911).

— *Thirty-Nine Years in Bombay City: Being the History of the Mission Work of the Society of St John the Evangelist in that City*, London: Mowbray & Co. (1913).

— & Moore, Halhed Sydney, SSJE, *Forty-Eight Years in Bombay*, Oxford: A. R. Mowbray & Co. (1922).

— & Moore, Halhed Sydney, SSJE, *Forty-Five years in Poona City, being the history of the Panch Howds Poona City Mission, India*, Oxford: A. R. Mowbray (1922).

Embry, James, *The Catholic Movement and the Society of the Holy Cross*, London: Faith Press (1931).

Euan-Smith, Edith, *Twenty-Four Hymn-Tunes*, London: Laudy & Co. (1895).

Evans, G. R. (ed), *A History of Pastoral Care*, London: Cassell (2000).

Farrant, Jean, *Mashonaland Martyr: Bernard Mizeki and the pioneer Church*, OUP (1966).

Feiling, Keith, *In Christ Church Hall*, London: Macmillan & Co. (1960).

Ferguson, Niall, *Empire: How Britain Made the Modern World*, London: Penguin (2003).

Flaxman, Radegunde, *A Woman Styled Bold: The Life of Cornelia Connelly 1809–1879*, London: Darton, Longman & Todd (1991).

Flindall, R. P. (ed), *The Church of England 1815–1948: A Documentary History*, London; SPCK (1972).

Forrest, S. L., *Parson's Play-Pen*, London: A. R. Mowbray & Co. Ltd (1968).

Foss, Michael, *Out of India: A Raj Childhood*, London: Michael O'Mara (2001).

Fouyas, Methodios, *Orthodoxy, Roman Catholicism and Anglicanism*, OUP (1972).

Freeman, Andrew, *English Organ-Cases*, London: Geo. Aug. Mate & Son (1921).

Gardner, Charles Edwyn, SSJE

— *Life of Father Goreh*, London: Longmans, Green & Co. (1900).

— *A Catechism of Church History: from the day of Pentecost until the present day*, Milwaukee, WI: Young Churchman Co. (1903).

Gelpi, Barbara Charlesworth, "John Keble and Hurrell Froude in Pastoral Dialogue", *Victorian Poetry* 44:1 (2006).

Gibbard, Sydney Mark, SSJE
— *Dynamic of Love: an Exploration into Believing, Praying, Being Human*, Oxford: A. R. Mowbray & Co. (1982).
— *Guides to Hidden Springs: a History of Christian Spirituality through the Lives of some of its Witnesses*, London: SCM Press (1979).
— *Jesus, Liberation & Love: Meditative Reflections on our Believing & Praying, Maturity & Service*, Oxford: A. R. Mowbray & Co. (1987).
— *Love and Life's Journey: Venture in Prayer*, Oxford: A. R. Mowbray & Co. (1987).
— *Prayer and Contemplation: an Invitation to discover*, Oxford: A. R. Mowbray & Co. (1976).
— *Tomorrow's Church, a survey of the Church's work among children with special reference to Evangelism*, London: SPCK (1950).
— *Twentieth-Century Men of Prayer*, London: SCM Press (1974).
— *Unity is not Enough: Reflections after a visit to the Church of South India*, London: A. R. Mowbray & Co. (1965).
— *Why Pray?* London: SCM Press (1970).

Gilley, Sheridan
— *Newman and his Age*, London: Darton, Longman & Todd (2003).
— & Sheils, W. J. (eds), *A History of Religion in Britain: Practice and Belief from Pre-Roman Times to the Present*, Oxford: Blackwell (1994).

Gopal, Samuel
— "Some Reminiscences of the Late Father Goreh, S.S.J.E.", *Indian Church Quarterly Review*, 9 (1896).
— "Simeon Wilberforce O'Neill", *Nagpur Diocesan Quarterly*, July 1904.

Goreh, Nehemiah Nilakantha Sastri, [SSJE]
— *A Letter to the Brahmos from a Converted Brahman of Benares*, Allahabad: North India Tract Society (1868).
— *A Mirror of the Hindu Philosophical Systems*, London: Christian Literature Society for India (1911).
— *Christianity Explained to a Hindu, or Christianity and Hinduism Compared*, Madras: Christian Literature Society (1893).
— *Criticism on the Present Hindi Translation of the Holy Scriptures*, Allahabad: Mission Press (1882).
— *God's Foreknowledge does not Deprive Man of his Freedom*, Allahabad: Mission Press (1889).
— *Proofs of the Divinity of Our Lord*, Bombay: Anglo-Vernacular Press (1887).
— *The Existence of Brahmoism itself a Proof of the Divine Origin of Christianity*, Allahabad: North India Tract Society (1889).
— *Theism and Christianity*, Calcutta: Oxford Mission Press (1882).
— *The Supposed and Real Doctrines of Hinduism, as held by Educated Hindus: with the True Source of the Former*, Madras: Christian Literature Society (1892).

Gourgey, Percy S., *The Indian Naval Revolt of 1946*, Hyderabad: Orient Longman Ltd (1996).

Grafton, Charles Chapman, [SSJE]
— *A Journey Godward*, London: Mowbray & Co. (1912).
— *Christian and Catholic*, New York: Longmans & Co. (1905).
— *Letters & Addresses*, New York: Longmans, Green & Co. (1914).
— *The Church of the New Testament*, Oxford: A. R. Mowbray & Co. (1900).
— *The Lineage from Apostolic Times of the American Catholic Church, commonly called the Episcopal Church*, Milwaukee: WI, Young Churchman Co. (1911).

— *The Roman Question*, Milwaukee, WI, Young Churchman Co. (1909).

Graham, Malcolm, *On Foot in Oxford, no. 12: East Oxford*, Oxfordshire County Council, Department Of Leisure & Arts (1987).

Graham, Malcolm and Waters, Laurence, *Cowley & East Oxford: Past and Present*, Thrupp: Sutton Publishing (2002).

Gray, G. F. S., *The Anglican Communion: A Brief Sketch*, London: SPCK (1958).

Greene, Graham, *Collected Essays*, London: Vintage (2014).

Gresley, William, *Bernard Leslie: or, A Tale of the Last Ten Years*, London: James Burns (1842).

Griffin, Susan M., *Anti-Catholicism and Nineteenth-Century Fiction*, Cambridge University Press (2004).

Guerinot, J. V., "The Pleasures of Rose Macaulay", *Twentieth Century Literature*, 33:1 (Spring 1987).

Hale, Robert, *Canterbury and Rome, Sister Churches: A Roman Catholic Monk reflects upon reunion in diversity*, London: Darton, Longman & Todd (1982).

Viscount Halifax [Charles Lindley Wood], *Reservation of the Blessed Sacrament*, London: English Church Union (1917).

Hall, Arthur Crashaw Alliston, [SSJE]

— *Catholic, not Protestant nor Roman: Two Lectures*, New York: James Pott & Co. (1887).

— *Christ's Temptation and Ours*, London: Longmans, Green & Co. (1897).

— *Considerations on the Sacrament of Our Lord's Body and Blood*, New York: Longmans, Green & Co. (1917).

— *Hints for Meditations on the Litany of the Name of Jesus*, London: Skeffington & Son (1890).

— *Holy Orders: Training of Candidates*, London: SPCK (1908).

— *Marriage with Relatives: Prohibited Degrees of Kindred and Affinity*, New York: Longmans & Co. (1901).

— *Preaching and Pastoral Care*, London: Longmans & Co. (1913).

— *The Christian Doctrine of Prayer*, London: Longmans & Co. (1904).

— *The Church's Discipline concerning Marriage and Divorce*, New York: Longmans & Co. (1896).

— *The Relations of Faith and Life*, New York: Longmans & Co. (1906).

— *The Sevenfold Unity of the Christian Church*, New York: Longmans, Green and Co. (1911).

Hall, Michael, *George Frederick Bodley and the Later Gothic Revival in Britain and America*, New Haven, CT: Yale University Press (2014).

Hammond, Peter, *Liturgy and Architecture*, London: Barrie & Rockliff (1960).

Hanbury-Tracy, A. F. A., *Faith and Progress: The Witness of the English Church during the last fifty years*, London: Longmans & Co. (1900).

Hannah, Walton, *The Anglican Crisis: The Church of South India*, London: Catholic Truth Society (1957).

Hardiman, David, *Missionaries and their medicine: A Christian modernity for tribal India*, Manchester University Press (2008).

Harris, Charles and Williams, N. P., *Northern Catholicism: Centenary studies in the Oxford and parallel Movements*, London: SPCK (1933).

Harvey, G. L. H. (ed), *The Church and the Twentieth Century*, London: Macmillan & Co. (1936).

Hastings, Adrian
— *One and Apostolic*, London: Darton, Longman & Todd (1963).
— *A History of English Christianity, 1920–1990*, Philadelphia, PA: Trinity Press (1991).
— *The Church in Africa: 1450–1950*, OUP (1994).
Hayes, Paul, *The Nineteenth Century 1814–1880*, New York: St Martin's Press (1975).
Heeney, Brian
— *A Different Kind of Gentleman: Parish Clergy as Professional Men in Early and Mid-Victorian England*, Hamden, CT: Archon Books (1976).
— *The Women's Movement in the Church of England 1850–1930*, Oxford: Clarendon Press (1988).
Heffer, Simon, *The Age of Decadence: Britain 1880–1914*, London: Random House (2017).
Hemming, David Norman Wirgman, SSJE, *Church, Nation and Youth: Dangers and Opportunities for the Church in the Government's Direction of Youth Work*, London: Church Literature Association (1942).
Herklots, H. G. G., *Frontiers of the Church: The Making of the Anglican Communion*, London: Ernest Benn (1961).
Herring, George
— *What was the Oxford Movement?* London: Continuum (2002).
— *The Oxford Movement in Practice: The Tractarian Parochial World from the 1830s to the 1870s*, OUP (2016).
Hewitt, Gordon, *The Problems of Success: A History of the Church Missionary Society 1910–1942, Vol. II: Asia, Overseas Partners*, London: SCM Press (1977).
Hill, Michael, *The Religious Order: A Study of Virtuoso Religion and its Legitimation in the Nineteenth Century Church of England*, London: Heinemann (1973).
Hilliard, David, "Unenglish and Unmanly: Anglo-Catholicism and Homosexuality", *Victorian Studies*, vol. 25, no. 2 (Winter 1982).
Hinchliff, Peter, *The Anglican Church in South Africa*, London: Darton, Longman & Todd (1963).
Holland, Henry Scott, *A Bundle of Memories*, London: Wells Gardner, Darton & Co. (1915).
Hollings, George Seymour, SSJE
— (ed), *A Golden Treatise of Mental Prayer*, London: A. R. Mowbray & Co. (1905),
— *In Via: Verses written on the way*, London: Longmans, Green & Co. (1906).
— *Jesus in the Midst; or, Penitent Thoughts and Prayers on the Passion of the Divine Redeemer*, London: Longmans & Co. (1898).
— *Paradoxes of the Love of God*, London: Masters & Co. (1887).
— *Porta Regalis; or, Considerations on Prayer*, London: J. Masters & Co. (1894).
— *The Divine Lover, or, The Day-Star Arising in the Heart, and other poems*, London: Longmans, Green & Co. (1908).
— *The Heavenly Stair; or, a ladder of the love of God for sinners*, London: Longmans & Co. (1897).
Hooper, Walter (ed), *C. S. Lewis Collected Letters*, London: HarperCollins (2000–2006).
Houghton, Walter E., *The Victorian Frame of Mind*, OUP (1957).
Houtin, Albert, *Une Vie de Prêtre 1867–1912*, Paris: Rieder (1928).
Hughes, Anselm, OSB, *The Rivers of the Flood*, London: Faith Press (1961).
Hughes, Michael, *Archbishop Randall Davidson*, Abingdon: Routledge (2018).
Hutton, William Holden, *Letters of William Stubbs, Bishop of Oxford, 1825–1901*, London: Archibald Constable & Co. (1904).

Hylson-Smith, Kenneth
— *High Churchmanship in the Church of England: From the Sixteenth Century to the late Twentieth Century*, Edinburgh: T. & T. Clark (1993).
— *The Churches in England from Elizabeth I to Elizabeth II, Vol III: 1833–1998*, London: SCM Press (1998).

Janes, Dominic, *Victorian Reformation: The Fight over Idolatry in the Church of England, 1840–1860*, OUP (2009).
Johnson, Howard A., *Global Odyssey: Visiting the Anglican Churches*, London: Geoffrey Bles (1963).
Johnston, Anna, *Missionary Writing and Empire, 1800–1860*, Cambridge University Press (2003).
Johnston, John Octavius, *Life and Letters of Henry Parry Liddon*, London: Longmans, Green & Co. (1904).

Keble, John, *Women Labouring in the Lord*, Oxford & London: John Henry & James Parker (1863).
Kelly, Herbert, SSM, *The National Mission and the Church*, London: Longmans, Green & Co. (1916).
Kemp, Eric Waldram, *The Life and Letters of Kenneth Escott Kirk: Bishop of Oxford 1937–1954*, London: Hodder & Stoughton (1959).
Kennedy, Deborah, "Wordsworth, Turner, and the Power of Tintern Abbey", *The Wordsworth Circle*, vol. 33, no. 2 (Spring 2002).
Kent, John, *Holding the Fort: Studies in Victorian Revivalism*, London: Epworth Press (1978).
Ker, Ian Turnbull
— *John Henry Newman*, OUP (2009).
— *G. K. Chesterton: A Biography*, OUP (2012).
Kingsley, Francis (ed), *Charles Kingsley: His Letters and Memories of his Life*, London: Kegan Paul (1881).
Kirk, Kenneth Escott
— *Some Principles of Moral Theology and their application*, London: Longmans, Green & Co. (1948).
— *Beauty and Bands*, London: Hodder & Stoughton (1955).
Knight, Frances, *The Nineteenth-Century Church and English Society*, Cambridge University Press (1995).
Knight-Bruce, G. W. H., *Memories of Mashonaland*, London & New York: Edward Arnold (1895).
Knowles, David, *Christian Monasticism*, London: Weidenfeld & Nicolson (1969).
Knox, Ronald
— *Enthusiasm: A Chapter in the History of Religion*, Oxford: Clarendon Press (1950).
— *A Spiritual Aeneid*, London: Burns Oates (1950).
Kollar, Rene, OSB
— "Lord Halifax and Monasticism in the Church of England", *Church History*, Vol. 53, no.2 (June 1984).
— *A Foreign and Wicked Institution? The Campaign against Convents in Victorian England*, Cambridge: James Clarke & Co. (2011).

Lacey, T. A., *A Roman Diary*, London: Longmans, Green & Co. (1910).

Lake, Crystal B., "The Life of Things at Tintern Abbey", *Review of English Studies* (2012), vol. 63, no. 260.

LeFanu, Sarah, *Rose Macaulay*, London: Virago (2003).

Leigh Fermor, Patrick, *A Time To Keep Silence*, London: John Murray (1957).

Lewis, C. S.
— *The Screwtape Letters*, London: Geoffrey Bles (1942).
— *Perelandra: a novel*, London: Bodley Head (1943).

Lewis, Cecil, & Edwards, G. E., *South Africa: The Growth of the Church of the Province*, London: SPCK (1935).

Lewis, Matthew, *The Monk*, Waterford: J. Saunders (1796).

Liddon, Henry Parry, *Life of E. B. Pusey*, London: Longmans, Green & Co. (1893–97).

Lloyd, Roger Bradshaigh
— *The Church of England in the Twentieth Century*, London: Longmans, Green & Co. (1946–50).
— *The Church of England 1900–1965*, London: SCM Press (1966).

Loades, Judith (ed), *Monastic Studies: The Continuity of Tradition*, Bangor: Copycat (1990).

Lochhead, Marion, *Episcopal Scotland in the 19th Century*, London: John Murray (1966).

Lockhart, John Gilbert, *Charles Lindley, Viscount Halifax*, London: Geoffrey Bles (1935).

Longridge, George, *A History of the Oxford Mission to Calcutta*, London: Mowbray (1910).

Longridge, William Hawks, SSJE
— *Spiritual Letters of Richard Meux Benson*, London: A. R. Mowbray & Co. (1924).
— *Ignatian Retreats*, Oxford: A. R. Mowbray & Co. (1926).
— *Retreats for Laymen*, London: A. R. Mowbray & Co. (1962).
— *Retreats for Priests, according to the method and plan of the Spiritual Exercises of S. Ignatius*, London: A. R. Mowbray & Co. (1930).
— (ed) *Spiritual Letters of Father Congreve*, Oxford: A. R. Mowbray & Co. (1928).
— *The Spiritual Exercises of Saint Ignatius of Loyola*, London: Robert Scott (1922).

Lovat, Alice Mary Fraser, *A Short Cut to Happiness*, London: Sands & Co. (1904).

Lowther Clarke, William Kemp (ed), *Liturgy and Worship: a companion to the Prayer Books of the Anglican Communion*, London: SPCK (1933).

Macaulay, Rose
— *The Towers of Trebizond*, London: Collins (1956)
— *Letters to a Friend, 1950–1952*, London: Collins (1961).
— *Last Letters to a Friend, 1952–58*, London: Collins (1962).

Machin, George Ian Thom, *Politics and the Churches in Great Britain, 1869 to 1921*, Oxford: Clarendon Press (1987).

Mackarness, Charles Coleridge, *Memorials of the Episcopate of John Fielder Mackarness, DD, Bishop of Oxford from 1870 to 1888*, Oxford: J. Parker & Co. (1892).

Mackay, Henry Falconar Barclay, *Saints and Leaders*, London: P. Allan & Co. (1928).

Mackenzie, Kenneth D., *Anglo-Catholic Ideals*, London: SCM Press (1931).

Macnutt, H. B. (ed), *The Church in the Furnace: Essays by Seventeen Temporary Church of England Chaplains on Active Service in France and Flanders*, London: Macmillan & Co. (1917).

Madigan, Edward
—*Faith under Fire: Anglican Army Chaplains and the First World War*, Basingstoke: Palgrave Macmillan (2011).
—& Snape, Michael (eds), *The Clergy in Khaki: New Perspectives on British Army Chaplaincy in the First World War*, Farnham: Ashgate (2013).
Maison, Margaret, *The Victorian Vision: Studies in the Religious Novel*, New York: Sheed & Ward (1961).
Mangion, Carmen, *Contested Identities: Catholic women religious in nineteenth-century England and Wales*, Manchester University Press (2008).
Manktelow, Emily J., *Missionary Families: race, gender and generation on the spiritual frontier*, Manchester University Press (2013).
Marrin, Albert, *The Last Crusade: The Church of England in the First World War*, Durham, NC: Duke University Press (1974).
Marsh, Charles, *Strange Glory: A life of Dietrich Bonhoeffer*, London: SPCK (2014).
Marsh, P. T., *The Victorian Church in Decline*, London: Routledge & Kegan Paul (1969).
Mascall, E. L.
—*Pi in the High*, London: Faith Press (1959).
—*Saraband*, Leominster: Gracewing (1992).
Mason, Alistair, *SSM: History of the Society of the Sacred Mission*, Norwich: Canterbury Press (1993).
Mason, Arthur James, *Memoir of George Howard Wilkinson*, London: Longmans & Co. (1909).
Mason, Philip, *The Men Who Ruled India*, London: Pan Books (1987).
Maturin, Basil William, [SSJE]
—*Confession and Absolution*, Oxford: A. R. Mowbray & Co. (1891).
—*Laws of the Spiritual Life*, London: Longmans & Co. (1907).
—*Letters of the Late Father B. W. Maturin to Lady Euan-Smith*, London: Hutchinson & Co. (1928).
—*Old Testament Meditations*, London: Sheed & Ward (1926).
—*Practical Studies on the Parables of Our Lord*, London: Longmans, Green & Co. (1897).
—*Self-Knowledge and Self-Discipline*, London: Longmans & Co. (1905).
—*Some Principles and Practices of the Spiritual Life*, London: Longmans & Co. (1896).
—*The Fruits of the Life of Common Prayer*, London: Longmans & Co. (1916).
—*The Incarnation*, Oxford: A. R. Mowbray & Co. (1892).
—*The Price of Unity*, London: Longmans & Co. (1912).
Maughan, Steven S., *Mighty England Do Good: Culture, Faith, Empire, and World in the Foreign Missions of the Church of England, 1850–1915*, Grand Rapids, MI: Eerdmans (2014).
Maycock, A. L., *Nicholas Ferrar of Little Gidding*, London: SPCK (1968).
Mayhew, Peter, *All Saints: Birth and Growth of a Community*, Oxford: ASSP (1987).
McCulloch, David G., *The Johnstown Flood*, London: Hutchinson (1968).
McGrandle, Piers, *Trevor Huddleston: Turbulent Priest*, London: Continuum (2004).
McGrath, Alister E., *The Intellectual World of C. S. Lewis*, Chichester: Wiley-Blackwell (2014).
Merricks, Patrick T., *Should Such a Faith Offend? Bishop Barnes and the British Eugenics Movement, c.1924–1953*, PhD Thesis: Oxford Brookes University (2014).
Meyrick, Frederick, *Memories of Life at Oxford and Elsewhere*, London: John Murray (1905).

Misra, Maria, *Vishnu's Crowded Temple: India since the Great Rebellion*, London: Allen Lane (2007).

Monk, Maria, *Awful disclosures of Maria Monk, a narrative of her sufferings in the Hotel Dieu nunnery at Montreal*, London (1836).

Moorman, J. R. H., *A History of the Church in England*, London: A. & C. Black (1953).

Moran, Maureen, *Catholic Sensationalism and Victorian Literature*, Liverpool University Press (2007).

Morgan, William, *The Almighty Wall: The Architecture of Henry Vaughan*, London: Architectural History Foundation (1983).

Morse-Boycott, Desmond, *They Shine like Stars*, London: Skeffington & Son (1947).

Mosley, Nicholas, *The Life of Raymond Raynes*, London: Faith Press (1961).

Moss, C. Beaufort, *The Body is One: an Introduction to the Problem of Christian Unity*, London: SPCK (1920).

Moxley, Cyril, *Apostles of Love*, Oxford: Amate Press (1992).

Müller, Max (trans & ed), *The Sacred Books of the East, Vol. I: The Upanishads*, Oxford: Clarendon Press (1879).

Mumm, Susan
— *Stolen Daughters, Virgin Mothers: Anglican Sisterhoods in Victorian Britain*, Leicester University Press (1999).
— (ed), *All Saints Sisters of the Poor: An Anglican Sisterhood in the Nineteenth Century*, Woodbridge: Boydell (2001).

Murdoch, Iris, *The Bell*, London: Chatto & Windus (1958).

Mursell, Gordon, *English Spirituality from 1700 to the Present Day*, London: SPCK (2001).

Neale, John Mason, *Ayton Priory: or, The Restored Monastery*, Cambridge (1843).

Newman, John Henry
— *Apologia Pro Vita Sua*, London: Collins (1959).
— "Indulgence in Religious Privileges", *Sermons Bearing on Subjects of the Day*, London: Longmans Green (1902).
— *Verses for Various Occasions*, London: Burns, Oates & Co (1880).
— & Keble, John (eds), *Remains of the late Reverend Richard Hurrell Froude*, London: J. G. and F. Rivington (1838–39).

Newsome, David
— *Godliness and Good Learning*, London: John Murray (1961).
— "The Churchmanship of Samuel Wilberforce", *Studies in Church History III* (1966).
— *The Parting of Friends: A study of the Wilberforces and Henry Manning*, London: John Murray (1966).
— *The Victorian World Picture: Perceptions and Introspections in an Age of Change*, London: John Murray (1997).

Newton, John A., *Search for a Saint: Edward King*, London: Epworth Press (1977).

Nias, John, *Flame from an Oxford Cloister: The Life and Writings of Philip Napier Waggett SSJE*, London: Faith Press (1961).

Nockles, Peter Benedict, *The Oxford Movement in Context: Anglican High Churchmanship, 1760–1857*, Cambridge University Press (1994).

Norman, E. R., *Anti-Catholicism in Victorian England*, London: Allen & Unwin (1968).

O'Brien, William Braithwaite, SSJE
— et al., *The Unity of the Faith: An Open Letter to His Grace the Lord Archbishop of Canterbury from the Superiors of Certain Religious Communities*, London: Dacre Press (1943).

— *Vital Issues*, Pax House (1944).

— *A Cowley Father's Letters*, London: Darton, Longman & Todd (1962).

— & Pridham, Arthur, SSJE, *A Novena of Prayer for the War*, Oxford: A. R. Mowbray & Co. (1915).

O'Connell, Marvin J., *The Oxford Conspirators: A History of the Oxford Movement 1833–45*, London: Macmillan (1969).

O'Connor, Daniel (ed), *Three Centuries of Mission: The United Society for the Propagation of the Gospel 1701–2000*, London: Continuum (2000).

Oddie, Geoffrey (ed), *Religious Conversion Movements in South Asia: Continuities and Change, 1800–1990*, London: Routledge (1997).

Ollard, Sidney Leslie

— *The Anglo-Catholic revival: some persons and principles*, London: A. R. Mowbray & Co. (1925).

— *A Short History of the Oxford Movement*, London: A. R. Mowbray & Co. (1932).

O'Neill, Simeon Wilberforce, SSJE, *A Contribution to the Cause of Christian Unity, or, The Thoughts of an Indian Missionary on the Controversies of the Day*, London: J. T. Hayes (1879).

Örsy, Ladislas M., *Open to the Spirit: Religious Life after Vatican II*, London: Geoffrey Chapman (1971).

Osborne, Edward William, [SSJE]

— *Boys and Girls I have Known*, London: SPCK (1915).

— *Church Fasts and Festivals. Short Papers for Young Children*, London: SPCK (1901).

— *Our Wonderful Faith. Papers for Children on the Apostles' Creed*, London: SPCK (1913).

— *Pictorial Church Teaching. Short Papers for Young Children*, London: SPCK (1902).

— *Self-Examination for Children*, Oxford: A. R. Mowbray & Co. (1898).

— *Some Wonderful Things in the Catechism*, London: SPCK (1912).

— *The Children's Saviour: Instructions to Children on the Life of Our Lord*, London: Rivingtons (1882).

— *The Saviour King: Instructions to Children on Old Testament Types and Illustrations of the Life of Our Lord Jesus Christ*, London: Rivingtons (1888).

Overton, J. H., *The Anglican Revival*, London: Blackie & Son (1897).

Oxford Mission to Calcutta, *India and Oxford. Fifty Years of the Oxford Mission to Calcutta*, London: SPCK (1933).

Packard, Kenneth, *Brother Edward: Priest & Evangelist*, London: Geoffrey Bles (1955).

Page, B. T., *The Harvest of Good Hope: An Account of the Expansion of the Church of the Province of South Africa*, London: SPCK (1947).

Paget, Stephen and Crum, J. M. C., *Francis Paget: Bishop of Oxford, Chancellor of the Order of the Garter, Honorary Student and sometime Dean of Christ Church*, London: Macmillan & Co. (1913).

Pahls, John Bernard, *An Anglican Understanding of the Theology and Practice of Sanctification in the Thought of Charles Chapman Grafton, Second Bishop of Fond du Lac*, STM Thesis, Nashotah House (2005).

Paradkar, Balwant A. M., *The Theology of Nehemiah Goreh*, Bangalore: CISRS (1969).

Parfitt, Jessie, *The Health of a City: Oxford, 1770–1974*, Oxford: Amate Press (1987).

Parker, Stephen G. & Lawson, Tom (eds), *God and War: The Church of England and Armed Conflict in the Twentieth Century*, Burlington: Ashgate (2012).

Parsons, Gerald & Moore, James R. (eds), *Religion in Victorian Britain*, Manchester University Press (1988).

Paton, Alan, *Apartheid and the Archbishop: The Life and Times of Geoffrey Clayton*, London: Jonathan Cape Ltd (1973).

Pawley, Bernard and Pawley, Margaret, *Rome and Canterbury through Four Centuries*, London: Mowbrays (1974).

Paz, Denis, *Popular Anti-Catholicism in Mid-Victorian England*, Stanford University Press (1992).

Peart-Binns, John S.

— *Archbishop Joost de Blank: Scourge of Apartheid*, London: Muller, Blond & White (1987).

— *Herbert Hensley Henson: A Biography*, Cambridge: Lutterworth Press (2013).

Perkin, Joan, *Women and Marriage in Nineteenth-Century England*, London: Routledge (1988).

Pendleton, Eldridge Honaker, SSJE

— "The Early Missionary Work of the Society in Africa", *Cowley* (Summer 2009).

— "Building Hope: Constructing the Monastery during the Great Depression", *Cowley* (Spring 2009).

— *Press On, The Kingdom: The Life of Charles Chapman Grafton*, Cambridge, MA: Society of St John the Evangelist (2014).

Peters, Greg

— *Reforming the Monastery: Protestant Theologies of the Religious Life*, Eugene, OR: Cascade Books (2014).

— *The Story of Monasticism: Retrieving an Ancient Tradition for Contemporary Spirituality*, Grand Rapids, MI: Baker (2015).

Phipps, Simon, *God on Monday*, London: Hodder & Stoughton (1966).

Pickering, W. S. F., *Anglo-Catholicism: A Study in Religious Ambiguity*, London: Routledge (1989).

Platten, Stephen (ed), *Oneness: The Dynamics of Monasticism*, London: SCM Press (2017).

Plumptre, Edward H., *Life of Thomas Ken D.D.*, London: William Ibister (1889).

Ponting, Clive, *The Crimean War*, London: Chatto & Windus (2004).

Ponting, Lucie, *Public Health in Oxfordshire: The Past*, Oxfordshire Health Authority (1998).

Poor Clares of Reparation and Adoration, *Religious Communities in the American Episcopal Church and in the Anglican Church of Canada*, West Park, NY: Holy Cross Press (1956).

Porter, Andrew

— (ed) *The Imperial Horizons of British Protestant Missions, 1880–1914*, Grand Rapids, MI: Eerdmans (2003),

— *Religion versus Empire?: British Protestant Missionaries and Overseas Expansion, 1700–1914*, Manchester University Press (2004).

Porter, Bernard, *Critics of Empire: British Radicals and the Imperial Challenge*, London: I. B. Tauris (2008).

Prestige, George Leonard

— *Pusey*, London; Philip Allan (1933).

— *The Life of Charles Gore: A Great Englishman*, London: Heinemann (1935).

Pugh, R. K.

— *The Episcopate of Samuel Wilberforce, Bishop of Oxford*, Bodleian Library, MS.D.Phil.d.1912.

— & J. F. A. Mason (eds), *The Letter-Books of Samuel Wilberforce, 1843–1868*, Oxfordshire Record Society (1970).

Puller, Frederick William, SSJE
— *The Anointing of the Sick in Scripture and Tradition*, London: SPCK (1904).
— *Concerning the Fast before Communion*, London: Masters (1891).
— *The Duties and Rights of Parish Priests and the Limits of Obedience due from them to their Bishops*, London: Rivingtons (1877).
— *Essays and Letters on Orders and Jurisdiction*, London: Longmans (1926).
— *Marriage with a deceased wife's sister: forbidden by the laws of God and of the Church*, London: Longmans, Green & Co. (1912).
— *The Primitive Saints and The See of Rome*, London: Longmans, Green & Co. (1893).
Pulley, Gerrard Todd, SSJE
— (ed) *Colloquies and Prayers for Holy Communion, from the writings of R. M. Benson*, Oxford: A. R. Mowbray & Co. (1934).
— (ed) *Cowley* Calendar, Oxford: A. R. Mowbray & Co. (1931).

Ramsey, Arthur Michael
— *The Resurrection of Christ: an essay in biblical theology*, London: Geoffrey Bles (1946).
— *From Gore to Temple: The Revival of Anglican Theology between Lux Mundi and the Second World War, 1889–1939*, London: Longmans (1960).
— *Canterbury Pilgrim*, London: SPCK (1974).
Reed, John Shelton, *Glorious Battle: The Cultural Politics of Victorian Anglo-Catholicism*, Nashville: Vanderbilt University Press (1996).
Reed, Rebecca, *Narrative of Six Months' Residence in a Convent*, London (1835).
Richardson, George Lynde, *Arthur C. A. Hall, Third Bishop of Vermont*, New York: Houghton Mifflin Co. (1932).
Robb, Graham, *Strangers: Homosexual Love in the Nineteenth Century*, London: Picador (2003).
Robert, Dana L., *Christian Mission: How Christianity became a World Religion*, Chichester: Wiley-Blackwell (2009).
Roberts, Stephen, *Sir Benjamin Stone 1838–1914: photographer, traveller and politician*, Charleston, SC: Create Space (2014).
Robinson, John A. T., *The New Reformation?* London: SCM Press (1965).
Robinson, Nalbro' Frazier, SSJE, *Monasticism in the Orthodox Churches*, London: Cope & Fenwick (1916).
Robson, Robert, *Ideas and Institutions of Victorian Britain: Essays in Honour of George Kitson Clark*, London: Bell (1967).
Rouse, Ruth and Neill, Stephen Charles (eds), *A History of the Ecumenical Movement 1517–1948*, London: SPCK (1954).
Routley, Eric
— *The English Carol*, London: Herbert Jenkins (1958).
— *Twentieth Century Church Music*, London: Herbert Jenkins (1964).
Rowell, Geoffrey, *The Vision Glorious: Themes and Personalities of the Catholic Revival in Anglicanism*, Oxford: Clarendon Press (1983).
Rowell, Geoffrey, Stevenson, Kenneth and Williams, Rowan (compilers), *Love's Redeeming Work: An Anglican Quest for Holiness*, OUP (2001).
Russell, George W. E.
— (ed), *Leaders of the Church 1800–1900: Dr Liddon*, London: A. R. Mowbray & Co. (1905).
— *Edward King, Sixtieth Bishop of Lincoln*, London: Smith, Elder & Co. (1912).

Sachs, William L., *The Transformation of Anglicanism: From state Church to global communion*, Cambridge University Press (1993).

Santayana, George, *My Host the World*, London: Cresset Press (1953).

Schlingensiepen, Ferdinand, *Dietrich Bonhoeffer 1906–1945*, London: T. & T. Clark (2010).

Scott, Paul, *Staying On*, London: Heinemann (1977).

Scott, Walter, *Marmion*, London: John Murray (1808).

Seaver, George, *David Livingstone: his life and letters*, London: Lutterworth Press (1957).

Sedding, Edward Douglas, SSJE
— (ed) *Glory to God on High: Instructions on the Holy Eucharist for Teachers & Children of the Church*, London: SPCK (1943).
— *God be in my Head*, Oxford: A. R. Mowbray & Co. (1941).
— *Godfrey Callaway: Missionary in Kaffraria 1892–1942*, London: SPCK (1945).
— *In the Voice of Praise, an anthology*, Oxford: A. R. Mowbray & Co. (1936).
— *The Flame of Prayer: A study of the life of prayer in the English Church*, Oxford: A. R. Mowbray & Co. (1934).
— *The Hidden Garden of Prayer: of Friendship with God in Ways of Prayer*, London: SPCK (1931).

Shand-Tucci, Douglass, *Church Building in Boston 1720–1970*, Concord: Rumford Press (1974).

Shatford, Susanne and Williams, Trevor, *The Changing Faces of St Clement's and East Oxford, Book One*, Witney: Robert Boyd Publications (1997).

Sherwood, Jennifer & Pevsner, Nikolaus, *The Buildings of England: Oxfordshire*, London: Penguin Books (1974).

Simkhovitch, Mary Kingsbury, "Father Field – friend of Coloured Children", *Journal of Negro Life* (Jan 1930).

Sinclair, Catherine, *Hill and Valley, or Hours in England and Wales*, New York: Robert Carter (1838).

Skinner, Annie, "Unearthing the Past: An exploration into the people behind the development of a Victorian suburb", *Family & Community History*, v.12:2 (Nov 2009).

Slade, Herbert Edward William, SSJE
— *A Work Begun: The Story of the Cowley Fathers in India 1874–1967*, London: SPCK (1970).
— *Meeting Schools of Oriental Meditation*, London: Lutterworth (1973).
— *Exploration into Contemplative Prayer*, London: Darton, Longman & Todd (1975).
— *Contemplative Intimacy*, London: Darton, Longman & Todd (1977).

Smith, H. Maynard, *Frank, Bishop of Zanzibar: Life of Frank Weston, DD, 1871–1924*, London: SPCK (1926).

Smith, Martin Lee, [SSJE]
— (ed) *Benson of Cowley*, OUP (1980).
— *Reconciliation: Preparing for Confession in the Episcopal Church*, Cambridge, MA: Cowley Publications (1985).
— *The Word is very near you: A Guide to Praying with Scripture*, London: Darton, Longman & Todd (1989).

Smith, Sydney, "Indian Missions", *Edinburgh Review* 12 (April 1808).

Smith, William, *Dwij: The Conversion of a Brahman to the Faith of Christ*, London: James Nisbet & Co. (1850).

Sparrow-Simpson, William John, *The History of the Anglo-Catholic Revival from 1845*, London: G. Allen & Unwin (1932).

Spencer, Stephen, *SCM Studyguide to Anglicanism*, London: SCM Press (2010).

Spinks, G. Stephens, *Religion in Britain since 1900*, London: Andrew Dakers (1952).

Spurr, Barry, *Anglo-Catholic in Religion: T. S. Eliot and Christianity*, Cambridge: Lutterworth Press (2010).

Stephenson, Alan M. G.

— *Anglicanism and the Lambeth Conferences*, London: SPCK (1978).

— *The First Lambeth Conference 1867*, London: SPCK (1967).

Stephenson, Colin

— *Walsingham Way*, London: Darton, Longman & Todd (1970).

— *Merrily on High: An Anglo-Catholic Memoir*, London: Darton, Longman & Todd (1972).

Stewart, *Empire Lost: Britain, The Dominions, and the Second World War*, London: Continuum (2008).

Stock, Eugene, *The History of the Church Missionary Society: Its Environment, its Men and its Work, Vol. III*, London: Church Missionary Society (1899).

Stone, Darwell, *The English Church Union and the Lambeth Conference: The Report of the Committee of the Council*, London: ECU (1931).

Strong, Rowan

— *Alexander Forbes of Brechin: The First Tractarian Bishop*, Oxford: Clarendon Press (1995).

— "Origins of Anglo-Catholic Missions: Fr Richard Benson and the Initial Missions of the Society of St John the Evangelist, 1869–1882", *Journal of Ecclesiastical History*, no.66 v. 1 (Jan 2015).

Sundkler, Bengt & Steed, Christopher, *A History of the Church in Africa*, Cambridge University Press (2000).

Surman, Phyl, *An Oxford Childhood: Pride of the Morning*, Stroud: The History Press (2009).

Sweet, Matthew, *Inventing the Victorians*, London: Faber & Faber (2001).

Symondson, Anthony, SJ

— "'An Ass or a Devil'? Sir Ninian Comper and Charles Eamer Kempe", *Journal of Stained Glass*, 34 (2010).

— & Bucknall, Stephen, *Sir Ninian Comper: An Introduction to his life and work*, London: The Ecclesiological Society (2006).

Talbot, Edward and Stone, Darwell, *Henry Parry Liddon, 1829–1929: A Centenary Memoir*, London: A.R.M. & Co. (1929).

Taylor, Brian

— *Brother Michael*, Gloucester: The British Publishing Co. (1964).

— "The Cowley Fathers and the First World War" in *The Church and War, Studies in Church History*, 20, Oxford: Blackwell (1983).

Temple, Frederick, & Maclagan, William

— *The Archbishops on the Lawfulness of the Liturgical Use of Incense and the Carrying of Lights in Procession*, London: Macmillan & Co. (1899).

— *Sæpius Officio: The Reply of the English Archbishops to the Bull Apostolicæ Curæ*, London: Longmans, Green & Co. (1897).

Thompson, H. P., *Into all Lands: The History of the Society for the Propagation of the Gospel in Foreign Parts 1701–1950*, London: SPCK (1951).

Thornton, L. H., & Fraser, Pamela, *The Congreves*, London: John Murray (1930).
Tournier, Wilton, *The Cross of Iron: with a sketch of the Life and Work of Father Field*, Philadelphia: Wm Fell (1891).
Trenholme, Edward Craig, SSJE
— *Anglican Low Mass*, London: Faith Press (1931).
— *The Story of Iona*, Edinburgh: David Douglas (1909).
— *Rescue Work*, London: SPCK (1927).
— *The Hours of Prayer, from Lauds to Compline inclusive. Compiled from the Sarum Breviary and other rites*, London: A. R. Mowbray & Co. (1910).
Trollope, Anthony
— *The Warden*, London: Longman, Brown, Green & Longmans (1855).
— *South Africa*, London: Chapman & Hall (1878).

Underhill, Evelyn, *Worship*, London: Nisbet & Co. (1936).

Victor, Osmund, *The Salient of South Africa*, London: SPG (1931).
Villain, Maurice, *Unity: A History and some Reflections*, London: Harvill Press (1963).
Vaiss, Paul (ed), *From Oxford to the People: Reconsidering Newman and the Oxford Movement*, Leominster: Gracewing (1996).
Voll, Dieter, *Catholic Evangelicalism*, London: Faith Press (1963).

Wadham, Juliana, *The Case of Cornelia Connelly*, London: Collins (1956).
Waggett, Philip Napier, SSJE
— "Church Affairs in South Africa", *Journal of Theological Studies*, v.1, Jan 1900.
— *Hope and Strength: addresses*, London: Longmans & Co. (1907).
— *"Is There a Religion of Nature?" Lectures given in St Paul's Cathedral, January 1902*, London: SPCK (1902).
— *Knowledge and Virtue: The Hulsean Lectures for 1920–1*, Oxford: Clarendon Press (1924).
— *Our Profession: a Penitent's Desire of Christian Loyalty*, London: Longmans (1912).
— *Religion and Science: some suggestions for the study of the relations between them*, London: Longmans, Green & Co. (1904)
— *The Heart of Jesus. Being addresses upon the present reality of the Passion*, London: SPCK (1902).
— *The Industry of Faith*, London: A. R. Mowbray & Co. (1925).
Wakefield, Gordon (ed), *The Westminster Dictionary of Spirituality*, Philadelphia: Westminster Press (1983).
Wallace, Ethel M., *A Scrapbook of Transkei Memories*, Bognor Regis: New Horizon (1978).
Walpole, Horace, *The Castle of Otranto*, London: Thomas Lownds (1764).
Walsh, Walter
— *The Secret History of the Oxford Movement*, London: Church Association (1897).
— *The History of the Romeward Movement in the Church of England 1833–1864*, London: James Nisbet & Co. (1900).
Wand, J. W. C.
— *Anglicanism in History and Today*, London: Weidenfeld & Nicholson (1961).
— (ed) *The Anglican Communion: a survey*, OUP (1948).
— *What the Church of England stands for*, London: A. & R. Mowbray & Co. (1951).
Ward, Kevin, *A History of Global Anglicanism*, Cambridge University Press (2006).

Ward, Maisie, *Father Maturin: A Memoir*, London: Longmans, Green and Co. (1920).

Ward, Wilfrid, *W. G. Ward and the Oxford Movement*, London: Macmillan & Co. (1889).

Warner, R. T., *Marion Rebecca Hughes*, OUP (1933).

Waugh, Evelyn, *Life of Rt Revd Ronald Knox*, London: Penguin Classics (2011).

Webster, John C. B., *A Social History of Christianity: North-west India since 1800*, OUP (2007).

Welch, Pamela, *Church and Settler in Colonial Zimbabwe: A Study in the History of the Anglican Diocese of Mashonaland/Southern Rhodesia, 1890–1925*, Boston: Brill (2008).

Weller, Reginald Heber, *Religious Orders in the Anglican Communion*, Milwaukee: Young Churchman Co. (1909).

Wheeler, Michael, *St John and the Victorians*, Cambridge University Press (2012).

Whitham, A. R., *Holy Orders*, London: Longmans, Green & Co. (1903).

Whyte, William, *Unlocking the Church: The lost secrets of Victorian sacred space*, OUP (2017).

The Earl of Wicklow [W. C. J. P. J. P. Howard], "The Monastic Revival in the Anglican Communion", *Studies: An Irish Quarterly Review*, 42:168 (Winter, 1953).

Wilkins, Bernard Dashwood, SSJE, *With Wings As Eagles*, London: Cowley, Wantage & All Saints Missionary Association (1953).

Wilkinson, Alan

— *The Church of England and the First World War*, London: SPCK (1978) & Cambridge: Lutterworth Press (2014).

— *The Community of the Resurrection: A Centenary History*, London: SCM Press (1992).

Willan, B. P., "The South African Native Labour Contingent, 1916–1918", *Journal of African History*, v.19 no.1 (1978).

Williams, Isaac, *On Reserve in Communicating Religious Knowledge (continued)* [Tract 87], Oxford: Parker (1840).

Williams, Granville Mercer, SSJE

— *Look to the Glory: an anthology taken from the writings and from notes made at retreats of the Reverend Richard Meux Benson*, Bracebridge, ON: SSJE (1966).

— *The Touch of Christ: Lectures on the Christian Sacraments*, New York: Edwin S. Gorham (1928).

Williams, Thomas J.

— "The beginnings of Anglican Sisterhoods", *Historical Magazine of the Protestant Episcopal Church*, 16 (Dec 1947).

— & Campbell, Allan Walter, *The Park Village Sisterhood*, London: SPCK (1965).

Wilson, A. N.,

— *C. S. Lewis: A Biography*, London: Collins (1990).

— *My Name is Legion*, London: Arrow Books (2005).

Wolff, Robert Lee, *Gains and Losses: Novels of Faith and Doubt in Victorian England*, London: John Murray (1977).

Wood, Michael H. M., *A Father in God: The Episcopate of William West Jones, DD*, London: Macmillan & Co. (1913).

Woodgate, Mildred Violet

— *Father Benson, Founder of the Cowley Fathers*, London: Geoffrey Bles (1953).

— *Father Congreve of Cowley*, London: SPCK (1956).

Woodruff, Mark (ed), *True Man a Long Season: Poems of Gordon Shrive SSJE*, London: FSJ (2016).

Woodward, George Ratcliffe
— *Songs of Syon: A Collection of Psalms, Hymns, & Spiritual Songs*, London: Schott (1908).
— & Wood, Charles, *The Cowley Carol Book for Christmas, Easter and Ascensiontide. Second Series*, London: A. R. Mowbray & Co. (1919).
Woolf, Robert Lee, *Gains And Losses: Novels of Faith and Doubt in Victorian England*, London: John Murray (1977).
Worsnip, Michael E., *Between the Two Fires: The Anglican Church and Apartheid, 1948–1957*, Pietermaritzburg: University of Natal Press (1991).
Wyon, Olive, *Living Springs: New Religious Movements in Western Europe*, London: SCM Press (1963).

Yates, Nigel, *Anglican Ritualism in Victorian Britain 1830–1910*, OUP (1999).
Yelton, Michael
— *The South India Controversy and the Converts of 1955–56: An Episode in Recent Anglo-Catholic History*, Anglo-Catholic History Society, Occasional Papers no.11 (2010).
— & Warrener, Rodney, *Martin Travers 1886–1948: An Appreciation*, London: Unicorn Press (2002).
Young, Richard Fox
— *Resistant Hinduism: Sanskrit Sources on Anti-Christian Apologetics in Early Nineteenth-century India*, Leiden: Brill (1981).
— "Enabling Encounters: The Case of Nilakanth-Nehemiah Goreh, Brahmin Convert", *International Bulletin of Missionary Research*, 29:1 (2005).
— "Holy Orders: Nehemiah Goreh's Ordination Ordeal and the Problem of 'Social Distance' in Nineteenth-Century North Indian Anglicanism", *Church History and Religious Culture*, 90:1 (2010).
— & Seitz, Jonathan A. (eds), *Asia in the Making of Christianity: Conversion, Agency, and Indigeneity, 1600s to the Present*, Leiden: Brill (2013).
Young, Ronald B., *The Viscount Halifax and the Transformation of Lay Authority in the Church of England (1865–1910)*, STM thesis: General Theological Seminary, NY (2003).

Zimmerman, Jervis S., *An Embattled Priest: The Life of Father Oliver Sherman Prescott, 1824–1903*, AuthorHouse: Bloomfield, CT (2012).

Index of Names and Subjects

CPSIA information can be obtained
at www.ICGtesting.com
Printed in the USA
LVHW081457180919
631479LV00006B/164/P